WORDS
ON
WAR

★ ★ ★ ★ ★ ★ ★ ★ ★ ★ ★ ★

MILITARY QUOTATIONS
FROM ANCIENT TIMES
TO THE PRESENT

★ ★ ★ ★ ★ ★ ★ ★ ★ ★ ★ ★

JAY M. SHAFRITZ

Prentice Hall

New York   London   Toronto   Sydney   Tokyo   Singapore

First Edition

 Prentice Hall

Simon & Schuster, Inc.
15 Columbus Circle
New York, New York 10023

Colophons are registered trademarks
of Simon & Schuster, Inc.

DISTRIBUTED BY PRENTICE HALL TRADE SALES

Manufactured in the United States of America

1 2 3 4 5 6 7 8 9 10

Library of Congress Cataloging-in-Publication Data

LC no. 90-39309

Dedicated
to the officers and men of the
USS Quick,
the World War II destroyer
on which my father,
Philip Shafritz,
served from 1942 to 1945

Preface

This is a collection of quotations on military and naval affairs from ancient times to the present. Included are significant remarks by illustrious commanders (such as Napoleon, MacArthur, and Patton); essential points of analysis by classic theorists of war (such as von Clausewitz, Mahan, and Brodie); bits of dialogue from great playwrights (such as Shakespeare and Shaw); fragments from major war novels (such as those of Tolstoy, Mailer, and Heller); conclusions from the works of military historians (such as Carlyle, Taylor, and Tuchman); portions from the diaries, letters, and memoirs of soldiers, sailors, and diplomats (such as Nelson, Montgomery, and Eisenhower); official statements of wartime leaders (such as Roosevelt, Churchill, and Hitler); and even memorable lines from war films (such as *Gone With the Wind*, *Dr. Strangelove*, and *Apocalypse Now*).

I started this compilation by first "round[ing] up the usual suspects" (Claude Rains in the 1941 film *Casablanca*). Thus, you will find "Don't give up the ship," "Damn the torpedoes," "Nuts!" and all their equally famous friends. Every effort was made to include everything that modern readers would expect to find in a comprehensive book of military quotations. But these expected entries account for only a small part of the total. The majority of entries have never before appeared in any volume of quotations. Indeed, many of the quotations really are short anecdotes. Consequently, this is far more than a book of familiar military quotations; it is also one man's collection of the most quotable parts from the world's literature on the art, science, history, and practice of military affairs.

Many of the sources are well known to those with an interest in military matters; others are known only to military specialists; still others are virtually unknown outside the stacks of research libraries. For almost forty years, starting with war comics when I was seven years old, I have been reading military news, fiction, history, and commentary. As a full-time professor for the past twenty years I have had both a professional excuse and the time to delve into all aspects of military affairs. The present collection consists of the things I have found that have given me pleasure in reading—because they were witty, poignant, or interesting—augmented by what I felt was expected or important.

There are two basic kinds of quotations: (1) those that constitute news because they were uttered by a public or newsworthy figure, and (2) those that were written as part of a larger work. The sentences and paragraphs quoted from this second category are, in effect, reviews of the works of hundreds of authors. You are encouraged, if a particular writer attracts you, to find and read the original source. Citations appear at the bottom of a quotation. The major exceptions are statements by presidents of the United States, statements by members of the United States Congress on the floors of the Senate or House of Representatives, and statements by members of the British Parliament—mainly the House of Commons. However, the exact dates of these statements are always given. This makes it possible for the complete statement to be readily found in the *Public Papers of the Presidents*, in the *Congressional Record*, in comparable British publications, or in leading newspapers of record such as *The New York Times* or *The Times* (London). All citations to books will have the earliest date of publication, as opposed to dates of subsequent reprintings or translations.

Quotations are organized alphabetically by themes, from action, ambush, and attrition to weapons, West Point, and wounded. The complete list of themes makes up the Table of Contents. Comments *about* famous soldiers, sailors, or commentators on war generally are under their names. Comments *by* such people generally are integrated with the various themes. All of the comments about and by these characters can be located by looking up their names in the index. Because many quotations could logically fit under a variety of headings, an extensive index is provided.

Within each heading quotations are in rough chronological order—rough because the exact date on which something was said (as opposed to when someone else wrote about it) might not be known and because comments by current writers may be placed at earlier periods. For example, a comment on the American Civil War by a mid-twentieth-century writer might be placed as if it were written in 1865, because it deals with that period. This rough chronological placement is designed to give the reader a sense of the evolutionary development of thinking within a heading.

Authors are often identified by their military rank, whether active or retired, at the time they wrote or said something quotable. Generals or admirals of whatever grade are usually identified simply as general or admiral. However, when individuals who have attained the rank of a general officer are quoted from the time they held a lower rank (such as Lt. Col. Eisenhower), they are identified by that lower rank. Once a man becomes President of the United States, he is always referred to as President even if his quotation is that of an ex-President. A biographical appendix identifies all public figures and provides the birth and (if appropriate) death years.

As the acknowledgments indicate, I had considerable assistance in producing this book. Nevertheless all mistakes, omissions, or other flaws are solely my responsibility. Yet I hope that as the years go by, this work will warrant a subsequent edition, and I encourage those readers who might have useful suggestions for improvement to write to me.

Jay M. Shafritz
Graduate School of Public and International Affairs
University of Pittsburgh
Pittsburgh, PA 15260

Acknowledgments

When I started this project I contacted a variety of military officers and scholars and asked them to recommend quotations for inclusion. I am pleased to thank the following for their many helpful suggestions:

From the U.S. Navy: Commander Mark Baker; Captain M. E. Cherry; Rear Admiral Jimmie Finkelstein; Jan K. Herman; Admiral D. E. Jeremiah; Commander Thomas J. Jurkowsky; Admiral Frank B. Kelso II; Ernest Milner; Henry I. Shaw, Jr., of the Marine Corps Historical Center; Rear Admiral F. Neale Smith; Admiral Carlisle A. H. Trost; Vice Admiral Jerry O. Tuttle; and Vice Admiral James A. Zimble.

From the U.S. Army: Brigadier General Pat Brady; Colonel James N. Hawthorne; Major General Frederick M. Franks, Jr.; Colonel John McAllister; Colonel Charles W. McClain, Jr.; Lt. General Dave R. Palmer; Lt. General Donald S. Pihl; General Carl E. Vuono; and Major General Albin G. Wheeler.

From the U.S. Air Force: General Michael J. Dugan;Major General Richard B. Boetze, Jr.; Lt. Colonel Darrel A. Massey; Lt. General George L. Monahan, Jr.; and Vice Admiral William D. Smith.

From the academic world: Harry A. Bailey, Jr., of Temple University; Ronald S. Calinger of the Catholic University of America; Peter Foote of the Royal Naval College; Arthur I. Marsh of St. Edmund Hall, Oxford University; Daniel Oran of Foresight Corporation; J. Steven Ott of the University of Maine; David B. Robertson of St. Hugh's College, Oxford University; David H. Rosenbloom of Syracuse University; Sam N. J. Shafritz of Ingomar Middle School; Todd J. A. Shafritz of Cornell University; and Earl Gibbons, Donald Goldstein, Albert C. Hyde, Sheila Kelly, Andrea Lewis, Gregory Scott, Frederick C. Thayer, and Phil Williams, all from the University of Pittsburgh.

Thanks are also due my agent, Mitchell Rose, who deserves much credit for helping me to conceptualize this project; and to my editors at Simon and Schuster, who made many valuable suggestions for inclusions (and exclusions): Toni Kamins, Kate Kelly, Susan Lauzau, Charles Levine, and Ken Wright.

Before this was a book, it was a database in need of much manipulation. Thus, my greatest debt is to my database consultant and wife, Luise Alexander Shafritz.

Contents

action

When people are entering upon a war they do things the wrong way round. Action comes first, and it is only when they have already suffered that they begin to think.
Thucydides, *History of the Peloponnesian War* (5th century B.C.).

What moved [14th-century] knights to war was desire to do deeds of valor ... not the gaining of a political end by force of arms. They were concerned with action, not the goal—which was why the goal was so rarely attained.
Barbara W. Tuchman, *A Distant Mirror* (1978).

Action in war is movement in a resistant medium. Just as a man immersed in water is unable to perform with ease and regularity even the most natural and simplest of movements, that of walking, so in war, with ordinary powers one cannot keep even the line of mediocrity. This is the reason why the correct theorist is like a swimming master, who teaches on dry land movements which are required in the water, which must appear ludicrous ... to those who forget about the water.
Karl von Clausewitz, *On War* (1832).

Maneuvers are the movements of troops in the theater of action, and they are the swift and ordered movement on the scene of action of tactical units of all sizes. They do not constitute action. Actions follow them.
Ardant du Picq, *Battle Studies* (1868).

For us is the life of action, of strenuous performance of duty; let us live in the harness, striving mightily; let us rather run the risk of wearing out than rusting out.
Theodore Roosevelt, speech in New York City, October 5, 1898, "The Duties of a Great Nation," *The Works of Theodore Roosevelt*, 14 (1926).

In tactics, action is the governing rule of war.
Marshal Ferdinand Foch, *Precepts and Judgments* (1920).

The relief which normally follows upon action after a long period of tension—that vast human sigh of relief—is one of the most recurrent phenomena of history, marking the outset of every great conflict. That urge to gain release from tension by action is a precipitating cause of war.
B. H. Liddell Hart, *Thoughts on War* (1944).

admirals

In this country [Britain] it is a good thing to kill an admiral from time to time to encourage the others.
Voltaire, *Candide* (1759). In the novel, Voltaire refers to the death of Admiral John Byng. According to Barbara W. Tuchman, *The First Salute* (1988), Byng "was duly shot [in 1757] by a firing squad of brother officers for no discernible purpose except to 'encourage the others,' as remarked by a mean-minded Frenchman. Voltaire's comment would immortalize the act, whose peculiar excess was another aberration of the enlightened century."

There is in the naval profession a specialized, technical mentality which blocked all my plans. No sooner had I proposed a new idea than I had [Admiral] Ganteaume and the whole navy on my neck: "Sire, this is impossible."—"Why?"—"Sire, the winds don't allow it, and then the doldrums, the currents"—and with that they stopped me short. How can a man argue with people who speak a different language?
Napoleon I, speaking in 1816, quoted in J. C. Herold, *The Mind of Napoleon* (1955).

No profession in England has done its duty until it has furnished a victim; even our boasted Navy never achieved a great victory until we shot an admiral.
Benjamin Disraeli, *Tancred* (1847).

The First Sea Lord [63-year-old Admiral Sir Dudley Pound] fell down first one flight of steps and then ... another, ending in a heap on the ground where a sentry threatened him with a bayonet.... Winston's [Prime Minister Churchill] comment was, "Try and remember you are an Admiral of the Fleet and not a Midshipman!"
John Colville, *The Fringes of Power* (1985), diary entry for August 9, 1940.

"An army," it is said, "is as brave as its privates and as good as its generals." But in a navy the admirals determine the bravery as well as the merit of the whole force.
Bernard Brodie, *A Guide to Naval Strategy* (1944).

It is dangerous to meddle with Admirals when they say they can't do things. They have always got the weather or fuel or something to argue about.
Winston Churchill, *The Second World War: Their Finest Hour* (1949).

We've long been aware that much of the Navy equipment is old and obsolete. I'm asking the Defense Department to inquire whether this might also be true of the Navy top command.
Representative Clarence D. Long, testimony before a House of Representatives Appropriations Subcommittee (June 4, 1969).

If there's one thing I can't stand it's an intellectual admiral!
Henry Kissinger quoted in Elmo R. Zumwalt, Jr., *On Watch* (1976).

Halsey, Admiral William F., Jr. (1882–1959)

Halsey, the public's favorite in the Navy, will always remain a controversial figure, but none can deny that he was a great leader; one with the true "Nelson touch." His appointment as Commander [of the] South Pacific Force at the darkest moment of the Guadalcanal campaign lifted the hearts of every officer and bluejacket. He hated the enemy with an unholy wrath, and turned that feeling into a grim determination by all hands to hit hard, again and again, and win.... Unfortunately, in his efforts to build public morale in America and Australia, Halsey ... built up an image of himself as an exponent of Danton's famous principle, "Audacity, more audacity, always audacity."
Samuel Eliot Morison, *The Two-Ocean War* (1963).

From 1927, like Yamamoto in Japan, Halsey worked for the cause of the Navy's air arm, eating, drinking and breathing aviation, as he himself put it. He tried to take a course in flying, was turned down for inadequate eyesight, then paradoxically was appointed commander of a carrier on condition he took a flying course as an observer. Somehow this was converted into a pilot's course, with Captain Halsey wearing special goggles. At the age of fifty-one he earned his golden wings.
Richard Hough, *The Great Admirals* (1977).

[Admiral Halsey] was of the same aggressive type as John Paul Jones, David Farragut, and George Dewey. His one thought was to close with the enemy and fight him to the death. The bugaboo of many sailors, the fear of losing ships, was completely alien to his conception of sea action.
General Douglas MacArthur, *Reminiscences* (1964).

A true story then going the rounds.... Two South Pacific enlisted men were ambling down a passageway talking about Halsey. "I'd go to hell for that old son of a bitch," said one of them.

Just then he felt a stiff finger in his back. It was Halsey. "Young man," said the admiral in mock indignation, "I'm not so old."
E. B. Potter, *Bull Halsey* (1985).

If one wonders at Halsey's good fortune in arriving on the scene [Guadalcanal] at a pivotal moment, wonder no more; his presence, his combative brand of leadership, as much as anything, affected the outcome of those battles. For at both Santa Cruz and off Savo it was Halsey's orders that caused his fleets to stand and fight. Halsey's place in history was not a fluke brought on by his arrival at a lucky moment but upon the aggressive acts of will he imposed upon events occurring at the critical moment that coincided with his arrival.
Eric Hammel, *Guadalcanal: Decision at Sea* (1988).

Jellicoe, Admiral John R. (1859–1935)

[Admiral] Jellicoe was the only man on either side who could lose the war in an afternoon.
Winston Churchill, *The World Crisis* (1923).

Criticism of Jellicoe's personal rigidity and caution is unfair; the failure was not on the afternoon of May 31, 1916, but in the preceding fifty years, and the responsibility was that of the British people and its politicians as well as the sailors.
Given the Grand Fleet as it was, it is difficult to fault Jellicoe's general handling of it. His prudent tactical sense enabled it to fight the High Seas Fleet twice at a great advantage and where its weaknesses of organization and officer quality would not tell. Contrasting his low-keyed realism with Beatty's initial dash and its results, it is difficult not to conclude that more risky and aggressive tactics might have resulted in a disaster.
Correlli Barnett, *The Swordbearers* (1963).

King, Admiral Ernest J. (1878–1956)

King was a sailor's sailor. He believed that what was good for the Navy was good for the United States, and indeed the world. In that sense and that alone he was narrow.
Samuel Eliot Morison, *The Two-Ocean War* (1963).

[Admiral King] sometimes seemed as willing to fight the Army as he was to fight the Japanese. And he was so eager to fight the Japanese that he sometimes seemed unable to understand or accept the Allied grand strategy . . . to hold off the Japanese while concentrating on the defeat of Germany. . . .
King was a battleship admiral who had only lately come to acknowledge the importance of air. Though he had earned his wings at the age of forty-nine, he was hardly an aviator. Sometimes he seemed to blame [General] Arnold personally for the fact that airplanes were now threatening to make his battleships obsolete.
Thomas M. Coffey, *Hap* (1982).

Eisenhower thought King "the antithesis of cooperation, a deliberately rude person, which means he's a mental bully," and commented, "One thing that might help win this war is to get someone to shoot King."
Stephen E. Ambrose, *Eisenhower*, I (1983).

[King] was also a gifted administrator and a passionate and determined fighter for the Navy. Highly respected but unloved in the service, King found affection with an unending series of women and relied on copious supplies of alcohol to help him unwind, despite the US Navy's "dry" tradition. Among his other less than endearing foibles was a monumental obstinacy and a fearsome temper, as well as a sometimes stupendous rudeness. All three of these qualities were easily evoked simultaneously by

what he saw as British (specifically English) affectations of manner, accent and class-superiority among the admirals with whom he now had to deal. This prejudice made it difficult (if not always impossible) for him to recognize that the Royal Navy might have something to teach the Americans at sea.
Dan van der Vat, *The Atlantic Campaign* (1988).

Mahan, Admiral Alfred Thayer (1840–1914)

During the last two days I have spent half my time, busy as I am, in reading your book [*The Influence of Sea Power upon History*]; and that I found it interesting is shown by the fact that having taken it up, I have gone straight through and finished it. . . . It is a very good book—admirable; and I am greatly in error if it does not become a naval classic.
Theodore Roosevelt, letter of May 12, 1890 to Alfred Thayer Mahan, quoted in W. D. Puleston, *Mahan* (1939).

[Mahan was] practically the naval Mohammed of England.
Arthur J. Marder, *Anatomy of British Sea Power* (1940).

Unfortunately for Mahan's memory, he is much more often criticized than read.
Bernard Brodie, *A Guide to Naval Strategy* (1944).

The name of Mahan immediately evokes images of gray ships and blue water.
Stephen B. Jones, "Global Strategic Views," *Geographical Review*, 45 (1955).

[Mahan was] the maritime Clausewitz, the Schlieffen of the sea.
Barbara W. Tuchman, *The Guns of August* (1962).

[Mahan was the] American who would explain the Royal Navy to the world.
Robert L. O'Connell, *Of Arms and Men* (1989).

Mountbatten of Burma, Admiral of the Fleet Louis (1900–1979)

Mountbatten was by all odds the most colorful on the British Chiefs of Staff level. He was charming, tactful, a conscious gallant knight in shining armor, handsome, bemedaled, with a tremendous amount of self-assurance. Because of his youthfulness which was emphasized by his appearance, it was obvious that the older officers did not defer readily to his views. They were careful, however, to give him a semblance of courteous attention. After all, he was a cousin of the King and, no doubt about it, a great favorite of the Prime Minister.
General Albert Wedemeyer, *Wedemeyer Reports* (1958).

A very gallant sailor. Had three ships sunk under him. Three ships sunk under him. [Pause] Doesn't know how to fight a battle.
Field Marshal Montgomery quoted in Nigel Hamilton, *Monty* (1981).

Mountbatten turned up at a Joint Chiefs of Staff meeting, somewhat damp and dishevelled. . . . Churchill looked at him in dismay. He had never before seen Mountbatten improperly turned out. "What have you been up to, Dickie?" he asked.
"I have been trying out a new one-man submarine," Mountbatten replied.
"What on earth for?"
"Well, I think it might be useful for Commando raids, or fixing limpet mines and that sort of thing."
Churchill glanced up and down at the figure again. "How did you get so wet?"
"I tried it."
Churchill, aghast, demanded, "You don't mean to say you went down by yourself?"
"It's a one-man submarine, so only one man can go down in it."

Churchill bellowed at him like a sergeant-major on the parade ground. "This is the most irresponsible thing I've ever heard! I give you an important job in the conduct of the war and you go and try to kill yourself. If you do it again, I shall fire you."
Richard Hough, *Mountbatten* (1981).

Mountbatten was a likely lad,
A nimble brain Mountbatten had,
And this most amiable trait:
Of each new plan which came his way
He'd always claim in accents pat
"Why, I myself invented that!"
Adding when he remembered it,
For any scoffer's benefit,
Roughly the point in this career
When he'd conceived the bright idea,
As "August 1934"
Or "Some time during the Boer War."
A poem written by a staff officer when Mountbatten was Chief of Combined Operations. According to Philip Ziegler in *Mountbatten* (1985), Mountbatten "cherished and frequently quoted" it.

The Glamor Boy is just that. He doesn't wear well and I begin to wonder if he knows his stuff. Enormous staff, endless walla-walla, but damned little fighting.
Dean Rusk, diary entry for January 1944, quoted in Thomas J. Schoenbaum, *Waging Peace and War* (1988).

Nelson, Admiral Horatio (1758–1805)
The death of Nelson was felt in England as something more than a public calamity; men started at the intelligence, and turned pale, as if they had heard of the loss of a dear friend.
Robert Southey, *The Life of Nelson* (1813).

Calling [Captain] Hardy back, he [Admiral Nelson] said to him, in a low voice, "Don't throw me overboard"; and he desired that he might be buried by his parents, unless it would please the king to order otherwise. Then, reverting to private feelings: "Take care of my dear Lady Hamilton, Hardy; take care of poor Lady Hamilton.— Kiss me, Hardy," said he. Hardy knelt down, and kissed his cheek: and Nelson said, "Now I am satisfied. Thank God, I have done my duty. . . . "
Death was, indeed, rapidly approaching. He said to the chaplain: "Doctor, I have *not* been a *great* sinner"; and, after a short pause, "Remember that I leave Lady Hamilton, and my daughter Horatia, as a legacy to my country." His articulation now became difficult; but he was distinctly heard to say, "Thank God, I have done my duty!" These words he had repeatedly pronounced; and they were the last words he uttered.
Robert Southey, describing Nelson's death at Trafalgar, *Life of Nelson* (1813).

Rarely has a man been more favored in the hour of his appearing; never one so fortunate in the moment of his death.
Alfred Thayer Mahan, *Life of Nelson* (1897).

He gave his country more than the century of unchallenged maritime supremacy when the British Empire was expanded and consolidated; he gave the nation in general and the Royal Navy in particular the implacable self-confidence that remained a decisive factor when, in 1940, invasion was again threatened. He set new standards for a new class of naval officer: before Nelson officers had often been recruited from the social extremes of British society; he had established the breed of middle-class, professional naval officers, from whom exceptional standards of courage and initiative would now be expected.

Tom Pocock, *Horatio Nelson* (1988).

Nimitz, Admiral Chester W. (1885–1966)

It would be difficult to imagine a less propitious moment [right after the Pearl Harbor attack] to take over command of the U.S. Pacific Fleet. "I'm the new Commander in Chief." Thus baldly did Rear Admiral Chester W. Nimitz break the news to his wife, Catherine. He was in such obvious distress that she reminded him, "You've wanted this all your life."

"But sweetheart," protested the admiral, "all the ships are at the bottom." Under the circumstances, this was an understandable bit of exaggeration.

Gordon W. Prange, Donald M. Goldstein, and Katherine V. Dillon, *Miracle at Midway* (1982).

[Admiral] Nimitz proposed by-passing the outer islands altogether, assaulting Kwajalein straight away, leaving the American communications vulnerable. At a conference called to discuss the operation, the advice of every single officer was "outer islands first." After a pause, Nimitz quietly announced, "Well, gentlemen, our next target will be Kwajalein."

Later, [Admirals] Spruance, Turner and Major-General Holland M. Smith of the Marines called on Nimitz to ask him to reverse his decision. Nimitz heard them out patiently and then said: "Sitting behind desks in the United States are able officers who would give their right arms to be out here fighting the war. If you gentlemen can't bring yourselves to carry out my orders, I can arrange an exchange of duty . . . make up your minds. You have five minutes."

Oliver Warner, *Command at Sea* (1976).

Nimitz was soft-spoken and relaxed, a team player, a leader by example rather than exhortation. "The admiral was frequently the despair of his public relations men," wrote correspondent Robert Sherrod; "it simply was not in him to make sweeping statements or to give out colorful interviews."

Ronald H. Spector, *Eagle Against the Sun* (1985).

Rickover, Admiral Hyman G. (1900–1986)

Once, while he was meeting with Paul [Nitze], [Admiral] Rickover began bragging about how strongly he encouraged dissent and debate in his shop, how he ran it on the basis of an adversary process, in fact. When Paul expressed polite skepticism, Rick offered to send over some officers . . . to give their account of how his personnel system operated. Sure enough, a few days later two such officers did call on the Secretary. They told Paul essentially the same story Rick had. On their way out, one of them took me aside and said, "Bud, I have now carried out my orders from Admiral Rickover to say exactly what we have just said to the Secretary. However Admiral Rickover did not tell me what to say to *you*. Be sure to tell the Secretary that we said to him what we were told to say to him, and that the Rickover system doesn't work that way at all." Crude, you say? Well, Rick is not subtle, just devious.

Elmo R. Zumwalt, Jr., *On Watch* (1976).

Rickover would strive toward a goal single-mindedly, without care about whom he insulted, cajoled, hurt, or helped. . . . Rickover survived his critics in Congress and in the Navy and elsewhere because he did achieve his goal. When the Nautilus got underway on January 17, 1955, his methods were vindicated. He had earned the title of

"father of the atomic submarine," a term that journalists began to use a short time later.
Norman Polmar and Thomas B. Allen, *Rickover* (1982).

The president [Reagan] began by telling Admiral Rickover how much he personally had admired his accomplishments over the years and what a debt the country owed him. . . . He could not have been more cordial.
After about three minutes of this, Admiral Rickover broke in and said, "Well, if all that is so, then why are you firing me?"
The president, somewhat jolted, paused a moment and then said, "Well, I'm certainly not firing you, it's just that the Pentagon has recommended that it is time for a transition."
John F. Lehman, Jr., *Command of the Seas* (1988).

Yamamoto, Admiral Isoroku (1884–1943)
For all his personal qualities, his fine tactical leadership and his percipience, energy and thoroughness, Yamamoto was a disaster as a strategist. But for his powerful persuasion, his navy would never have been allowed to attack Pearl Harbor. The earlier and long-agreed strategy was to carry out the southern conquests while the battle fleet and the carriers lurked in home waters awaiting the arrival of the Americans, already savaged by submarine and air attack on the long and hazardous voyage, threading between the outer Japanese bases. Yamamoto alone was responsible for the reversal of this sound strategy.
Richard Hough, *The Great Admirals* (1977).

The Americans believed, correctly, that Admiral Yamamoto was a passenger in one of the downed bombers. When the usually sobersided Admiral Turner displayed unwonted enthusiasm at the recitation of this achievement, Halsey remarked, "Hold on, Kelly! What's so good about it? I'd hoped to lead that bastard up Pennsylvania Avenue, with the rest of you kicking him where it would do the most good."
E. B. Potter, *Bull Halsey* (1985).

Pop goes the weasel.
This was the prearranged signal indicating that Admiral Yamamoto's plane had been shot down by U.S. fighters; quoted in Elmer B. Potter, *Nimitz* (1976).

Not quite the visionary extolled by his countrymen nor quite worthy of the almost unseemly posthumous praise heaped on him by the men he defeated . . . Yamamoto was a bright, forceful leader, but he was no innovator. The surprise-attack strategy he forced upon his service and nation was cribbed from his hero and mentor, VAdm Heihachiro Togo, who launched surprise war upon the Russians at Port Arthur in 1904. . . .
Yamamoto drew the wrong lessons from his youthful experience at Port Arthur, and he drew the wrong lessons from Midway, a defeat he, as much as anyone, brought upon his nation. As had Togo at Port Arthur, Yamamoto spurned the concept of the second—killing—strike. He had tacitly withheld permission for a death-dealing second strike at Pearl Harbor, a strike that certainly would have destroyed the bulk of American reserve fuel stocks in the Pacific and undoubtedly would have prevented American warships, particularly American carriers, from carrying out spoiling raids and the strategic actions at the Coral Sea and Midway.
Eric Hammel, Guadalcanal: *The Carrier Battles* (1987).

advance

The duty of an advance guard does not consist in advancing or retreating, but in maneuvering.
Napoleon I, *Military Maxims* (1827).

When one moves at night, without a light, in one's own house, what does one do? Does one not (though it is a ground one knows well) extend one's arm in front of one so as to avoid knocking one's head against the wall? The extended arm is nothing but an advance guard.
Marshal Ferdinand Foch, *Precepts and Judgments* (1920).

Go forward, always go forward. You must not fail. Go until the last shots are fired and the last drop of gasoline is gone. Then go forward on foot.
General George S. Patton, Jr., quoted in *The New York Times Magazine* (April 4, 1943).

If I advance, follow me; if I retreat, kill me; if I die, avenge me.
Benito Mussolini, *Time* (August 2, 1943).

The object of all advance guards is not merely to ward off an enemy blow but to preserve the freedom of action of the commander of the whole force (or unit).
B. H. Liddell Hart, *Thoughts on War* (1944).

Afghanistan

When you're wounded and left on Afghanistan's plains,
And the women come out to cut up what remains,
Jest roll to your rifle and blow out your brains
   An' go to your Gawd like a soldier.
Rudyard Kipling, "The Young British Soldiers," *Rudyard Kipling's Verse* (1927).

If all that [Soviet] military prowess can't succeed in a country of goats and mountains, then where can it succeed?
Richard Falk, *The Christian Science Monitor* (February 4, 1982).

It's a defeat, no question about it. We had your experience in Vietnam right before our eyes, and we still went in like fools.
An anonymous aide to the Soviet Union's Communist Party's Central Committee quoted in *The New York Times* (January 27, 1989).

Has the Afghan war driven the Russians to behave like Marx, the Groucho variety? Consider the departure ceremony . . . according to . . . *Pravda:* "On February 15th at 10 o'clock local time General Gromov [Soviet Commander-in-chief in Afghanistan] will be the last to cross the bridge [from Afghanistan to the Soviet Union]. He will pass without looking back. Then he will stop and 'deliver a speech', but just to himself. It will last one minute, seven seconds. It will not be written down or listened to."
"A Bridge Surreal," *The Economist* (February 11, 1989).

We are sending the very best to Afghanistan, those in top condition. Strange as it may sound, the children of leading officials are very often unfit for service in the army.
An article in *Pravda* that sarcastically explains why the sons of the Soviet elite avoided military service in Afghanistan, quoted in Zbigniew Brzezinski, *The Grand Failure* (1989).

Before we hit and run. Now we hit and sit. It's conventional war. It's not guerrilla war.
Haji Din Mohammed, rebel commander besieging Jalalabad, quoted in *The New York Times* (May 5, 1989).

We violated the norms of proper behavior. We went against general human values. I am talking, of course, about the dispatch of troops to Afghanistan. We committed the most serious violations of our own legislation, our party and civilian norms.
Eduard A. Shevardnadze, Foreign Minister of the Soviet Union, *The New York Times*, October 24, 1989.

after-action reports

With the jaw of an ass have I [Samson] slain a thousand men.
The Bible, Judges 15:16.

Captain Hardy, . . . returned; and again taking the hand of his dying friend [Admiral Horatio Nelson] and commander, congratulated him on having gained a complete victory [at Trafalgar]. How many of the enemy were taken he did not know, as it was impossible to perceive them distinctly—but fourteen or fifteen at least. "That's well," cried Nelson; "but I bargained for twenty."
Robert Southey, *Life of Nelson* (1813).

We have met the enemy and they are ours—two ships, two brigs, one schooner and one sloop.
Oliver Hazard Perry, dispatch to General William Henry Harrison, announcing his victory at the Battle of Lake Erie on September 10, 1813, quoted in Glenn Tucker, *Poltroons and Patriots*, I (1959).

The army report confined itself to a single sentence: All quiet on the Western Front.
Erich Maria Remarque, *All Quiet on the Western Front* (1929).

In a battle nothing is ever as good or as bad as the first reports of excited men would have it.
Sir William Slim, *Unofficial History* (1959).

Integrity—which includes full and accurate disclosure—is the keystone of military service. . . . In any crisis, decisions and risks taken by the highest national authorities depend, in large part, on reported military capabilities and achievements. In the same way, every commander depends on accurate reporting from his forces. . . .
Therefore, we may not compromise our integrity—our truthfulness. . . . False reporting is a clear example of a failure of integrity. Any order to compromise integrity is not a lawful order.
Integrity is the most important responsibility of command. Commanders are dependent on the integrity of those reporting to them in every decision they make. Integrity can be ordered but it can only be achieved by encouragement and example.
General John D. Ryan, Air Force Chief of Staff, policy letter of November 1, 1972, reprinted in M. M. Wakin, *War, Morality, and the Military Profession* (1979).

Agent Orange

Only You Can Prevent Forests.
Sign used by U.S. airmen spraying defoliants in Vietnam, quoted in General Westmoreland, *A Soldier Reports* (1976).

We checked with the Army and Air Force about the possible injurious effects on humans of Agent Orange. . . . We were told there were none. You trust those things.
Admiral Elmo Zumwalt, Jr., and Elmo Zumwalt III, *My Father, My Son* (1986). Admiral Zumwalt, as Chief of Naval Operations, ordered the spraying of Agent Orange in Vietnam. His son, who served in Vietnam, later developed cancer, and his grandson was born with a severe learning disability. Nevertheless, Admiral Zumwalt maintains, "Knowing what I now

know, I still would have ordered the defoliation to achieve the objectives it did, of reducing casualties."

The fetuses, many of them stillborn after eight or nine months in utero, continue to be collected from women suffering the effects of Agent Orange. The tiny, surreal figures stare out of glass jars displayed on three walls of a fairly large room, bearing witness to the wonders of modern military science. I saw a child with three faces superimposed on a single head, another with a large eye instead of a nose, still others with webbed feet or hands and ears protruding from their chests.
Lewis A. Lapham, "Vietnam Diary," *Harper's* (May 1989).

aggression

Men rise from one ambition to another: First, they seek to secure themselves against attack, and then they attack others.
Niccolò Machiavelli, *The Discourses* (1517).

To a good many Southerners the events of 1861–65 have been known as "The War of Northern Aggression." Never mind that the South took the initiative by seceding in defiance of an election of a president by a constitutional majority. Never mind that the Confederacy started the war by firing on the American flag. These were seen as preemptive acts of defense against northern aggression.
James M. McPherson, "The War of Southern Aggression," *New York Review of Books* (January 19, 1989).

The nineteen thirties taught us a clear lesson. Aggressive conduct, if allowed to go unchallenged, ultimately leads to war.
President John F. Kennedy, speech during Cuba Missile Crisis, October 22, 1962.

The world remembers—the world must never forget—that aggression unchallenged is aggression unleashed.
President Lyndon B. Johnson, speech in Syracuse, New York, August 5, 1964.

The central lesson of our time is that the appetite of aggression is never satisfied. To withdraw from one battlefield means only to prepare for the next.
President Lyndon B. Johnson, speech at Johns Hopkins University, April 7, 1965.

An unprejudiced observer from another planet, looking down on man as he is today, in his hand the atom bomb, the product of his intelligence, in his heart the aggressive drive inherited from his anthropoid ancestors, which this same intelligence cannot control, would not prophecy long life for the species.
Konrad Lorenz, *On Aggression* (1966).

Aggression unopposed becomes a contagious disease.
President Jimmy Carter, speech on Soviet Invasion of Afghanistan, January 4, 1980.

The defense policy of the United States is based on a simple premise: the United States does not start fights. We will never be an aggressor. We maintain our strength in order to deter and defend against aggression—to preserve freedom and peace.
President Ronald Reagan, speech in Washington, D.C., March 3, 1983.

air bases

In aircraft organization the main tactical limitation is not to be sought in the air, but on the ground. There lies its "rear," which can be struck at from the air or from the

ground, and of these two attacks the second is likely to prove so deadly that aero-dromes and aircraft depots, etc., will be kept as far back as possible.
J. F. C. Fuller, *Armoured Warfare* (1943).

The large ground organization of a modern air force is its Achilles' heel.
B. H. Liddell Hart, *Thoughts on War* (1944).

Air power is a thunderbolt launched from an egg-shell invisibly tethered to a base.
Hoffman Nickerson, *Arms and Policy* (1945).

We're rather comfortable on our bases. It's been that way for 50 years. To an extent, we don't understand how really vulnerable we are. . . . We're trying to get the rest of the Air Force to think of the air base as a weapon system—part of the plane itself.
Colonel George Freshholtz, Pentagon Deputy Chief of Air Base Operability, *Insight* (February 6, 1989).

aircraft carriers

America's first true aircraft carrier, a converted collier, was recommissioned Langley on March 20, 1922, and designated CV-1 ("C" for carrier and "V" for heavier-than-air, a common designator for nongas-filled flying machines).
Eric Hammel, Guadalcanal: *The Carrier Battles* (1987).

Scratch one flat-top.
Lieutenant Commander Robert E. Dixon, radio message to his aircraft carrier [the York-town] after sinking a Japanese carrier during the battle of the Coral Sea, May 7, 1942. Quoted in Stanley Johnston, *Queen of the Flat-Tops: The U.S.S. Lexington and the Coral Sea Battle* (1942).

Who said a Wasp couldn't sting twice?
Winston Churchill, message to *USS. Wasp* thanking the aircraft carrier for delivering a second shipment of fighter planes to Malta, May 9, 1942.

One of the carrier opponents in the Senate remarked privately to another, "Don't ever go aboard one of those things and watch air operations at sea—you'll get so charged up, you'll vote for every nuclear carrier they try to slide into the pipeline."
John Wicklein, "The Navy Prepares for World War II," *Washington Monthly* (February, 1970).

To control the oceans of the world, you have to cover them with air power. To do that, you've got to have aircraft carriers. Because we haven't been challenged on the seas for so many years, people have forgotten why we built aircraft carriers in the first place. We build them to sink other ships.
Admiral Gerald E. Mille, *The New York Times* (August 22, 1970).

Any aircraft carrier . . . is a floating gasoline station. All you have to do is start a fire on board and that carrier is out of commission. That is what one missile or one tor-pedo will do.
Senator Gary Hart, *The New York Times* (July 7, 1982).

Aircraft carriers are splendid for little wars; they are just not very good against Russia.
Robert W. Komer, *The New York Times* (May 6, 1986).

The critics argue that "if you buy a carrier, you've got to buy all these frigates and cruisers to protect it." Actually, the truth is what the Falklands War illustrated—that it is genuinely the reverse: You buy the carriers to protect everything else.
John F. Lehman, Jr., *U.S. News and World Report* (June 15, 1987).

Nothing beats the show an aircraft carrier provides. Unable to sleep (jets slamming onto the deck a few floors above my head may have something to do with it), I tiptoe into the officer's lounge and commandeer the XO—the executive officer—who is happy to escort me to the flag deck to watch flight ops in the moonlight.... "I never get tired of this," my XO murmurs, echoing a refrain I've heard from officers and enlisted men alike on every ship we've visited. "It's just too much fun."
Joan M. Stapleton, "Dame at Sea," *The New Republic* (May 22, 1989).

air power

They shall mount up with wings as eagles.
The Bible, Isaiah 40:31.

One sprightly morning in the early summer of 1916 ten or twenty small German bombers appeared over London, looking like gnats.... They dropped a few bombs, killed some horses in Billingsgate and turned Cloth Fair, Cheapside, and Aldersgate into rivers of broken glass.... On this morning Great Britain ceased to be an island.
V. S. Pritchett, *London Perceived* (1962).

I have mathematical certainty that the future will confirm my assertion that aerial warfare will be the most important element in future wars, and that in consequence not only will the importance of the Independent Air Force rapidly increase, but the importance of the army and the navy will decrease in proportion.
Giulio Douhet, *The Command of the Air* (1921).

It is highly unlikely that an airplane, or fleet of them, could ever sink a fleet of Navy vessels under battle conditions.
Franklin D. Roosevelt, former Assistant Secretary of the Navy, speaking in 1922, quoted in Burke Davis, *The Billy Mitchell Affair* (1967).

Just stay out of them [wars] as long as you can, and the best way to stay out of them for quite a while, instead of teaching a boy to run an automobile, teach him to fly, because the nation in the next war that ain't up in the air, is just going to get something dropped on its bean.
Will Rogers, writing in 1922, *The Autobiography of Will Rogers*, ed. D. Day (1949).

It is probable that future wars again will be conducted by a special class, the air force, as it was by the armored knights of the Middle Ages.
William Mitchell, *Winged Defense* (1925).

In our victory over Japan, airpower was unquestionably decisive. That the planned invasion of the Japanese home islands was unnecessary is clear evidence that airpower has evolved into a force in war co-equal with land and sea power, decisive in its own right and worthy of the faith of its prophets.
General Carl A. Spaatz, "Evolution of Air Power," *Military Review* (June 1947).

If the Almighty were to rebuild the world and asked me for advice, I would have English Channels round every country. And the atmosphere would be such that anything which attempted to fly would be set on fire.
Winston Churchill quoted in Lord Moran, *Churchill* (1966).

alliances

Close alliances with despots are never safe for free states.
Demosthenes, *Second Philippic* (4th century B.C.).

A wise prince sees to it that never, in order to attack someone, does he become the ally of a prince more powerful than himself, except when necessity forces him.
Niccolò Machiavelli, *The Prince* (1513).

I think that a young state, like a young virgin, should modestly stay at home, and wait the application of suitors for an alliance with her; and not run about offering her amity to all the world; and hazarding their refusal.
Benjamin Franklin, letter to Charles W. F. Dumas, September 22, 1778, reprinted in *The Papers of Benjamin Franklin*, 27, ed. C. A. Lopez (1988).

Tis our true policy to steer clear of permanent alliances, with any portion of the foreign world . . . we may safely trust to temporary alliances for extraordinary emergencies.
President George Washington, Farewell Address, September 7, 1796.

Peace, commerce, and honest friendship with all nations, entangling alliances with none.
President Thomas Jefferson, first Inaugural Address, March 4, 1801.

The moment we engage in confederations, or alliances with any nation, we may from that time date the downfall of our republic.
Senator Andrew Jackson, criticizing President John Quincy Adams on March 3, 1826, quoted in Robert V. Remini, *Andrew Jackson and the Course of American Freedom* (1981).

The proverbial weakness of alliances is due to inferior power of concentration.
Alfred Thayer Mahan, *Naval Strategy* (1911).

In international politics, [an alliance is] the union of two thieves who have their hands so deeply inserted in each other's pocket that they cannot separately plunder a third.
Ambrose Bierce, *The Devil's Dictionary* (1911).

A steadfast concert for peace can never be maintained except by a partnership of democratic nations.
President Woodrow Wilson, war message to Congress, April 2, 1917.

Alliances are held together by fear, not by love.
Harold Macmillan, speaking in 1959, quoted in Richard M. Nixon, *The Real War* (1980).

No lover ever studied every whim of his mistress as I did those of President Roosevelt.
Winston Churchill on Anglo-American relations during World War II, quoted in John Colville, *The Fringes of Power* (1985).

Pray enter—the Prime Minister of Great Britain has nothing to hide from the President of the United States.
Winston Churchill, as he rose naked from his bath, to President Roosevelt during a 1942 visit to the White House, according to Robert E. Sherwood, *Roosevelt and Hopkins* (1948). But according to Merle Miller in *Ike the Soldier* (1987), Churchill claimed that he had never greeted Roosevelt without wearing at least a towel.

An alliance is like a chain. It is not made stronger by adding weak links to it.
Walter Lippmann, *New York Herald Tribune* (August 5, 1952).

Only when a menaced country has the whole-hearted support of its people and the will to resist to the limit of its resources should we consider an appeal for help.
J. Lawton Collins, *War in Peacetime* (1969).

The existing structure of the Western Alliance is based on a premise that, once clearly and explicitly stated, is both unconvincing to Europeans and unacceptable to Americans: that the United States will automatically use its nuclear weapons to defend Europe if the latter is attacked, even though such use would lead to the destruction of the U.S. itself.
Christopher Layne, "Continental Divide," *National Interest* (Fall 1988).

allies

Love for the same thing never makes allies. It's always hate for the same thing.
Howard Spring, *My Son, My Son* (1938).

Personally I feel happier that we have no Allies to be polite to and pamper.
King George VI, after the defeat of France in 1940, quoted in Len Deighton, *Battle of Britain* (1980).

With the approval of the Allies, their co-belligerent, Italy, this week declared war against her ex-Axis ally, Japan. Said Alberto Tarchiani, Italian ambassador to Washington: "We hope soon to become Allies ourselves."
Time (July 23, 1945).

There is only one thing worse than fighting with allies—and that is fighting without them.
Winston Churchill quoted in David Irving, *The War Between the Generals* (1981).

Extremists on both sides of the water can indulge in all the backbiting and name-calling that they please—they can never get away from the historical truth that the United States and the British Empire, working together, did a job that looked almost impossible at the time it was undertaken.
General Dwight D. Eisenhower, letter to Lord Ismay, July 13, 1946, quoted in Stephen E. Ambrose, Eisenhower I (1983).

In war it is not always possible to have everything go exactly as one likes. In working with Allies it sometimes happens that they develop opinions of their own.
Winston Churchill, *The Second World War: The Hinge of Fate* (1950).

Geography has made us neighbors. History has made us friends. Economics has made us partners, and necessity has made us allies. Those whom God has so joined together, let no man put asunder.
President John F. Kennedy, speech to the Canadian Parliament, May 17, 1961.

Unhappily, amity is not the inevitable result of close relations between either people or peoples. Marriage and war lock both into close embrace. Sometimes the parties live happily ever after; sometimes they don't. So it is with allies.
Dean Acheson, "Withdrawal from Europe? 'An Illusion,'" *The New York Times Magazine* (December 15, 1963).

A people "saved" by us through our free use of nuclear weapons over their territories would probably be the last that would ever ask us to help them.
Bernard Brodie, *Strategy in the Missile Age* (1965).

Let me be quite blunt. Our fighting men are not going to be worn down. Our mediators are not going to be talked down. And our allies are not going to be let down.
President Richard Nixon, speech to the nation on Vietnam, May 14, 1969.

collective security

On the basis of their grudging, minimal contribution to the fighting in Vietnam, it would appear that our Asian and Pacific allies do not take the ostensible threat to their own security very seriously, or they are content to have the United States do the fighting for them.
Senator J. William Fulbright, *U.S. News and World Report* (January 12, 1970).

America is not the policeman of the world, But we continue to be the backbone of Free World collective security.
President Gerald R. Ford, speech in Chicago, August 19, 1974.

[Dean Rusk said to President Lyndon B. Johnson] We have taken 600,000 casualties in dead and wounded since the end of World War II in support of collective security. We put up 90 percent of the non-Korean forces in Korea, 80 percent of the non-Vietnamese forces in Vietnam. And that's not very collective. So if my Cherokee County cousins were to say to me, "Look, if collective security means 50,000 dead Americans every ten years, and it is not even collective, maybe it's not a very good idea."
Thomas J. Schoenbaum, *Waging Peace and War* (1988).

ambush

When the enemy pursue a retreating foe, the following snare is usually laid. A small body of cavalry is ordered to pursue them on the direct road. At the same time a strong detachment is secretly sent another way to conceal itself on their route. When the cavalry have overtaken the enemy, they made feint attacks and retire. The enemy, imagining the danger past, and that they have escaped the snare, neglect their order and march without regularity. Then the detachment sent to intercept them, seizing the opportunity, falls upon them unexpectedly and destroys them with ease.
Vegetius, *De Re Militari* (378 A.D.).

War between savage tribes . . . even today, is a war of ambush by small groups of men of which each one, at the moment of surprise, chooses, not his adversary, but his victim, and is an assassin.
Ardant du Picq, *Battle Studies* (1868).

The whole idea [of the defoliation program] was to prevent ambushes, to clear the area. Some idiot somewhere sold somebody the idea that if the gooks couldn't hide, then they couldn't ambush you. . . . The trouble with the whole thing is that the VC and NCA use guns in their ambushes instead of bows and arrows. . . . They don't have to be sitting on top of you to pull off an ambush. . . . So the gooks will start shooting at you from 300 meters away instead of five, only now you're the one that ain't got no place to hide.
Anonymous Vietnam soldier quoted in Ronald J. Glasser, *365 Days* (1971).

American Revolution

Waiving all considerations of right and wrong, I ask is it common sense to use force toward the Americans? Not 20,000 troops, not treble that number, fighting 3,000

miles away from home and supplies could hope to conquer a nation fighting for liberty.
John Wesley, June 14, 1775 letter to Lord Dartmouth, reprinted in Luke Tyerman, *Wesley*, III (1872).

The ardor of the [British] nation in this cause has not arisen to the pitch one could wish.
Lord North quoted in John Brooke, *King George III* (1972).

Stand your ground! Don't fire unless fired upon! But if they want to have a war, let it begin here!
Captain Jonas Parker's orders to his "minute men" at Lexington just before the British opened fire on April 19, 1775, quoted in Christopher Ward, *The War of the Revolution*, I (1953). According to Richard Shenkman, *Legends, Lies, and Cherished Myths of American History* (1988): "As with many other famous quotes, this one has a dubious pedigree. It did not surface until 1858. The person who brought it to the attention of the world was Parker's grandson."

Don't fire until you see the whites of their eyes.
Colonel William Prescott, orders to his men as they defended Breed's Hill (near Bunker Hill) against advancing British redcoats, June 16, 1775, quoted in George Bancroft, *The American Revolution*, I (1852). Other sources, such as Richard Frothingham, *History of the Siege of Boston* (1849), often credit this phrase to Israel Putnam or claim that Putnam was relaying Prescott's order. According to Gwynne Dyer, *War* (1985), this order "was not bravado, but the standard tactical doctrine of the time."

These are the times that try men's soul's. The summer soldier and the sunshine patriot will, in this crisis, shrink from the service of their country; but he that stands it now deserves the love and thanks of man and woman.
Thomas Paine, *The American Crisis* (1776).

The time is now near at hand which must probably determine, whether Americans are to be freemen or slaves; whether they are to have any property they can call their own; whether their houses and farms are to be pillaged and destroyed, and they consigned to a state of wretchedness from which no human efforts will probably deliver them. The fate of unborn millions will now depend, under God, on the courage and conduct of this army—our cruel and unrelenting enemy leaves us no choice but a brave resistance, or the most abject submission; that is all we can expect—we have therefore to resolve to conquer or die.
General George Washington, general orders of July 2, 1776, *The Writings of George Washington* ed., John C. Fitzpatrick, 5 (1932).

We will gain the victory, or Molly Stark shall be a widow to-night.
American General John Stark, motivating his men at the 1777 Battle of Bennington in New Hampshire, quoted in Edward Everett, *Life of John Stark* (1834).

If I were an American, as I am an Englishman, while a foreign troop was landed in my country, I never would lay down my arms—never—never—never.
William Pitt, Earl of Chatham, speech in the House of Lords, November 18, 1777.

When the news of [the 1777 Battle of] Saratoga reached Paris . . . the time seemed to have arrived for the house of Bourbon to take a full revenge for all its humiliations and losses in previous wars. In December a treaty was arranged, and formally signed in the February following, by which France acknowledged *The Independent United States of America*. This was, of course, tantamount to a declaration of war with England.
E. S. Creasy, *The Fifteen Decisive Battles of the World* (1851).

What do we mean by the revolution? The war? That was no part of the revolution; it was only an effect and consequence of it. The revolution was in the minds of the people, and this was effected from 1760 to 1775, in the course of fifteen years, before a drop of blood was shed at Lexington.
John Adams, August 24, 1815 letter to Thomas Jefferson, *The Works of John Adams*, ed. Charles Francis Adams (1856).

By the rude bridge that arched the flood,
Their flag to April's breeze unfurled,
Here once the embattled farmers stood,
And fired the shot heard round the world.
Ralph Waldo Emerson, *Concord Hymn* (1837).

Listen, my children, and you shall hear,
Of the midnight ride of Paul Revere,
On the eighteenth of April, in Seventy-five;
Hardly a man is now alive
Who remembers that famous day and year.
Henry Wadsworth Longfellow, "Paul Revere's Ride," *Tales of a Wayside Inn* (1863).

ammunition

Put your trust in God, my boys, and keep your powder dry.
Attributed to Oliver Cromwell at the Battle of Marston Moor, July 2, 1644.

You can always tell an old soldier by the inside of his holsters and cartridge boxes. The young ones carry pistols and cartridges: the old ones, grub.
George Bernard Shaw, *Arms and the Man,* Act I (1894).

Praise the Lord and pass the ammunition!
Navy Chaplain Howell Forgy, speaking to the men of the cruiser *New Orleans* during the December 7, 1941 Pearl Harbor attack. According to Gordon W. Prange, Donald M. Goldstein, and K. V. Dillon, *December 7, 1941* (1988); "As a 'sky pilot' he could not man a gun or even handle the missiles and powder, but he could offer encouragement. . . . The fine swing of the words stuck in men's minds and inspired one of the war's best remembered songs [by Frank Loesser]."

Perhaps the crowning example of military stupidity is in the revelation that [during the Pearl Harbor attack] while our army's mobile anti-aircraft artillery was in a state of instant readiness, it had no ammunition. The ammunition was in a crater a mile away. General Short and Ordnance had rejected pleas for artillery shells several days earlier on the ground that "they didn't want to issue any of the clean ammunition, let it get out and get dirty, and have to take it back in later on and renovate it." The slogan of the Pearl Harbor high command seems to have been, "Praise the Lord, but don't muss the ammunition."
I. F. Stone, "Brass Hats Undaunted," *The Nation* (September 8, 1945).

amphibious operations

As I said when I went to Morocco, the only way I can repay you is to promise that when I get my feet on the next historic beach, I shall not leave it except as a conqueror or a corpse.
General George S. Patton, Jr., letter to General George C. Marshall, May 8, 1943, quoted in Forrest C. Pogue, *George C. Marshall: Organizer of Victory* (1973).

Offensive military operations are rarely easy, and amphibious attacks have special hazards of their own. "There are no foxholes in the surf," as one reporter has trenchantly put it.

Bernard Brodie, *A Guide to Naval Strategy* (1944).

I had hoped that we were hurling a wildcat onto the shore, but all we had got was a stranded whale.

Winston Churchill, on the January 22, 1944 landing at Anzio, Italy, *The Second World War: Closing the Ring* (1951).

Successful penetration of a defended beach is the most difficult operation in warfare.

General Dwight D. Eisenhower, *At Ease* (1967).

Annapolis

Not so many years ago, a lad who asked a Congressman for a West Point appointment found that he had received an appointment and had passed the examination for Annapolis. He wrote in protest to his Congressman, who replied, "Son, go on to Annapolis and be happy; that school down there in Maryland is only the Southern branch of West Point."

Leland P. Lovette, *School of the Sea* (1941).

Flag Lieutenant Magaw of the Home Squadron expressed the misgivings of some officers to Midshipman Mahan in 1858; Magraw thought it was a mistake not to permit midshipmen to learn to drink liquor at the Academy, for when they went to sea and visited a foreign ship they would not be able to hold their own with foreigners.

Captain W. D. Puleston, *Annapolis* (1942).

[A] favorite indulgence of upperclassmen was to send erring plebes off to service Bill the Goat—a large bronzed statue which . . . depicted a raging goat in an attack mode down to every last detail—including his testicles. Though the Academy officially frowned on it, upperclassmen persisted in frying plebes by sending them sprinting out on a moment's notice to brasspolish Bill the Goat's privates. With the regular polishing that the balls received, they were far shinier than any other part of his anatomy.

Ben Bradlee, Jr., *Guts and Glory* (1988).

antiaircraft fire

I always knew the British fliers were tough babies. But I never fully realized quite how tough they were until the other afternoon when I was out on a British airdrome. . . . A plane broke through the clouds. The British antiaircraft artillery went after it hammer and tongs. It was clear to me that it was a British Spitfire, but it was not clear to them. They shot at it with machine guns until it was on the ground, and continued shooting as it taxied up. The plane taxied up to the line and a 19-year-old kid got out of the cockpit, walked over to the artillery commander, and said: "I say, my good fellow, if this sort of thing continues, I shall have to report you."

General Henry H. "Hap" Arnold, *Time*, (December 2, 1940).

The influence of anti-aircraft armament may be even more moral than material. And it is none the less important in consequence. The moral effect of anti-aircraft guns works two ways: first, by the nerve-strain and disturbance it causes to the enemy pilots; second, by the comfort it brings to one's own people in the area which is threatened by air attack. The feeling of being able to hit back is an invaluable relief from tension.

B. H. Liddell Hart, *Thoughts on War* (1944).

The AA fire from scattered [Japanese] ships and the wide area in which forces were involved made it comparable to watching a ten-ring circus with a sniper shooting at you from behind the lion's cage.
Commander James M. Peters, on the June 20, 1944 Battle of the Philippine Sea, quoted in James H. Belote and William M. Belote, *Titans of the Sea* (1975).

appeasement

We must always be wary of those who with sounding brass and a tinkling cymbal preach the "ism" of appeasement.
We must especially beware of that small group of selfish men who would clip the wings of the American eagle in order to feather their own nests.
President Franklin D. Roosevelt, message to Congress, January 6, 1941.

In international politics, . . . you must either be ready to practise appeasement indefinitely, or at some point you must be ready to fight.
George Orwell, *New Leader* (March 29, 1947).

Realizing that common sense and common decency alike dictate the futility of appeasement, we shall never try to placate an aggressor by the false and wicked bargain of trading honor for security. Americans, indeed all free men, remember that in the final choice a soldier's pack is not so heavy a burden as a prisoner's chains.
President Dwight D. Eisenhower, first Inaugural Address, January 20, 1953.

If you let a bully come in your front yard, he'll be on your porch the next day and the day after that he'll rape your wife in your own bed.
President Lyndon B. Johnson quoted in Walter Isaacson and Evan Thomas, *The Wise Men* (1986).

Europeans who remember history understand better than most that there is no security, no safety, in the appeasement of evil.
President Ronald Reagan, speech in Washington, D.C., April 14, 1986.

Armageddon

Doomsday is near; die all, die merrily.
William Shakespeare, *Henry IV*, Part I, Act III (1598).

This is the way the world ends.
Not with a bang but a whimper.
T. S. Eliot, *The Hollow Men* (1924).

Military alliances, balances of power, leagues of nations, all in turn failed, leaving the only path to be by way of the crucible of war. The utter destructiveness of war now blocks out this alternative. We have had our last chance. If we will not devise some greater and more equitable system, Armageddon will be at our door.
General Douglas MacArthur, speech after accepting the surrender of Japan, September 2, 1945, reprinted in his *Reminiscences* (1964).

I turn back to your ancient prophets in the Old Testament and the signs foretelling Armageddon, and I find myself wondering if—if we're the generation that's going to see that come about. . . . There have been times in the past when we thought the world was coming to an end, but never anything like this.
President Ronald Reagan quoted in Gwynne Dyer, *War* (1985).

armor

Major General Julian C. Smith, who was at Tarawa as the Second Division Commander, once put the picture in sharp perspective during a turbulent session. . . . "Even though you Navy officers do come in to about one thousand yards," he said, "I remind you that you have a little more armor. I want you to know that Marines are crossing the beach with bayonets, and the only armor they'll have is a khaki shirt."
Bill D. Ross, *Iwo Jima* (1985).

There was only one neurosis common to aircrews throughout the war. Rather sheepishly, some met it by installing a piece of armour plate under their seat; others by putting a steel helmet beneath themselves as they approached the target. There is no evidence that this ever saved life or even manhood, but it made them feel better.
Max Hastings, *Bomber Command* (1979).

arms control

What would you think about a meeting of a town council which is concerned because an increasing number of people are knifed to death each night in drunken brawls, and which proceeds to discuss just how long and how sharp shall be the knife that the inhabitants of the city may be permitted to carry?
Albert Einstein, when asked his opinion of the 1926 Geneva disarmament conference, quoted in David P. Barash, *The Arms Race and Nuclear War* (1987).

It never has made and never will make any sense trying to abolish any particular weapon of war. What we have to abolish is war.
Sir John Slessor, *Strategy for the West* (1954).

The trouble is not that the Soviets and Americans do not have the same positions; the trouble is that they do not have them at the same time.
Lawrence D. Weiler quoted in Chalmers M. Roberts, *The Nuclear Years* (1970).

I wish it were not too late to start a boycott against the use of "arms control" as an overall term. It is nothing but a euphemism, serving regrettably to lead thinking and action towards the acceptance as "arms control measures" of compromises with scant or nil disarmament effect.
Alva Myrdal, *The Game of Disarmament* (1977).

One hopes to achieve the zero option, but in the absence of that we must achieve balanced numbers.
Margaret Thatcher quoted in *The New York Times* (January 20, 1983).

Arms control has to have a future, or none of us does.
Stanley Hoffmann, *Newsweek* (October 1, 1984).

We must be prepared to stay at the negotiating table one day longer than the Soviets.
Max M. Kampelman, *Time* (March 11, 1985).

Wishful thinking is equally as effective for arms control as it is for birth control.
Caspar W. Weinberger, Secretary of Defense, *USA Today* (October 6, 1986).

The history of arms control is a history of great vision eventually mugged by reality.
Kenneth Adelman, Director, U.S. Arms Control and Disarmament Agency, *Newsweek* (December 1, 1986).

A joke was told a few years ago by one of the Soviet [arms-control] negotiators. . . . The story goes this way: A man visits the city of Leningrad and goes to the zoo, where

he sees a marvelous sight. There in the lion's cage is the lion sitting side-by-side with a lamb. Well, this fellow is just astonished, and he hurries on his way, feeling happy and uplifted. The next day he sees the same thing, so he decides to ask the zookeeper: "You know, that display in the lion's cage is the most marvelous thing I have ever seen. How do you ever train the lion to do it?" The zookeeper answers, "We don't train him—we just give him a different lamb every day." Now, that's a peculiar story, but it's not a bad way of approaching ... arms control and human freedom. The moral of this story is clear: When it comes to assessing what is really going on in the Soviet system, things are not often exactly what they seem.
> Kenneth I. Adelman, Director, U.S. Arms Control and Disarmament Agency, speech in Chicago, quoted in *The Wall Street Journal* (February 23, 1987).

The Soviets approach arms control much the same way Andy Warhol approached art: anything you can get away with.
> Representative Jack Kemp, *Newsweek* (March 16, 1987).

arms race
I do not hold that we should rearm in order to fight. I hold that we should rearm in order to parley.
> Prime Minister Winston Churchill, BBC broadcast, October 8, 1951, quoted in *Winston S. Churchill: His Complete Speeches,* ed. R. R. James, 8 (1974).

The worst to be feared and the best to be expected can be simply stated. The worst is atomic war. The best would be this: a life of perpetual fear and tension; a burden of arms draining the wealth and labor of all peoples. Every gun that is made, every warship launched, every rocket fired, signifies, in the final sense, a theft from those who are cold and are not clothed. The world in arms is not spending money alone. It is spending the sweat of its laborers, the genius of its scientists, the hopes of its children.
> President Dwight D. Eisenhower, speech to the American Society of Newspaper Editors, Washington, D.C., April 16, 1953.

If the great powers continue to look for solutions in the area of science and technology the only result will be to worsen the situation. . . . The clearly predictable course of the arms race is a steady open spiral downward into oblivion.
> Herbert York and Jerome Wiesner, "National Security and the Nuclear Test Ban," *Scientific American* (October 1964).

We are not engaged in an arms race, but rather in a race of technology.
> Edward Teller, "Technology," *The United States in the 1980s,* P. Duignan and A. Rabushka, eds. (1980).

The arms race between the U.S. and Russia is like two kids standing up to their knees in a room full of gasoline. One has 10 matches, the other eight. Neither kid says he will feel safe unless he has more matches; yet each has many more than he needs to blow up the place. That's why people don't feel more secure with more missiles.
> David Brunell, *U.S. News & World Report* (March 22, 1982.)

Those who speak so often about the so-called arms race ignore a central fact. In the decade before 1981, the Soviets were the only ones racing.
> President Ronald Reagan, speech to the nation, February 26, 1986.

The arms race, just like nuclear war, is unwinnable. Continuing such a race on the Earth, and extending it into space, would accelerate the accumulation and modernization of nuclear weapons, the rate of which is already feverish. The world situation can

become such that it would no longer depend on politicians but would become captive to chance.
    Mikhail Gorbachev, *Perestroika* (1987).

Nations are now lined up like people before the ovens of Auschwitz, while we are trying to make the ovens more efficient.
    Isidor Rabi quoted in Gregg Herken, *Counsels of War* (1987).

Modern history offers no example of the cultivation by rival powers of armed force on a huge scale that did not in the end lead to an outbreak of hostilities. And there is no reason to believe that we are greater, or wiser, than our ancestors.
    George F. Kennan quoted in Seyom Brown, *The Causes and Prevention of War* (1987).

action-reaction
What is essential to understand here is that the Soviet Union and the United States mutually influence one another's strategic plans. Whatever their intentions or our intentions, actions—or even realistically potential actions—on either side relating to the build-up of nuclear forces necessarily trigger reactions on the other side. It is precisely this action-reaction phenomenon that fuels an arms race.
    Robert S. McNamara, "The Dynamics of Nuclear Strategy," *Department of State Bulletin* (October 9, 1967).

Once the counter to a new weapon system has been invented and put into use, then, of course, the cycle repeats itself. And new offensive or defensive systems must be developed. You may call this an arms race, but it is the same kind of arms race mankind has been running since the dawn of time.
    General Curtis E. LeMay, *America Is In Danger* (1968).

The United States must realize that in both physics and politics each action causes a corresponding counteraction.
    Soviet Premier Alexei Kosygin quoted in Chalmers M. Roberts, *The Nuclear Years* (1970).

The notion of an "action-reaction" sequence in the development of new war equipment and newer countermeasures . . . is deceptively familiar . . . slightly less obvious is the relationship (inevitably paradoxical) between the very success of new devices and the likelihood of their eventual failure [since] any sensible enemy will focus his most urgent efforts on countermeasures meant to neutralize whatever opposing device seems most dangerous at the time.
    Edward N. Luttwak, *Strategy* (1987).

SALT (Strategic Arms Limitation Talks)
A SALT treaty is not a reward for Soviet good behavior. It's a way in which we advance our own interests.
    Paul C. Warnke, Director, U.S. Arms Control and Disarmament Agency, *The Washington Post* (March 2, 1978).

We consider SALT II to be dead. We have so informed the Soviet Union, and they . . . understand it, even if they may not like it. The worst thing we could do now would be to attempt to resurrect an agreement that could only generate massive controversy, confuse our allies, confuse the Soviets and confuse public opinion.
    Alexander M. Haig, Jr., U.S. Secretary of State, testimony before the Foreign Relations committee of the U.S. Senate, May 11, 1982.

The Soviet regime, for seven years, has been violating the restraints of the treaty . . . the treaty was really nothing but the legitimizing of an arms race. It didn't do anything

to reduce nuclear weapons or the nuclear threat. All it did was regulate how fast and how much we could continue increasing the number of weapons.
President Ronald Reagan, news conference, June 11, 1986.

army

Didn't I tell you, Don Quixote, sir, to turn back, for they were not armies you were going to attack, but flocks of sheep?
Miguel de Cervantes, *Don Quixote* (1605).

And we are here as on a darking plain
Swept with confused alarms of struggle and flight,
Where ignorant armies clash by night.
Matthew Arnold, *Dover Beach* (1867).

There is a soul to an army as well as to the individual man, and no general can accomplish the full work of his army unless he commands the soul of his men as well as their bodies and legs.
General William T. Sherman, *Personal Memoirs, II* (1875).

The real object of having an army is to provide for war.
Elihu Root, Secretary of War, *Annual Report of the Secretary of War* (1899).

An army is still a crowd, though a highly organized one. It is governed by the same laws . . . and under the stress of war is ever tending to revert to its crowd form. Our object in peace is so to train it that this reversion will become extremely slow.
J. F. C. Fuller, *Training Soldiers for War* (1914).

The army ages men sooner than the law and philosophy; it exposes them more freely to germs, which undermine and destroy, and it shelters them more completely from thought, which stimulates and preserves.
H. G. Wells, *Bealby* (1915).

No nation ever had an army large enough to guarantee it against attack in time of peace or insure it victory in time of war.
President Calvin Coolidge, speech of October 6, 1925.

The Army, for all its good points, is a cramping place for a thinking man. As I have seen too often, such a man chafes and goes—or else decays.
B. H. Liddell Hart, *Thoughts on War* (1944).

The Army is always the same. The sun and the moon change, but the Army knows no seasons.
John Wayne in *She Wore A Yellow Ribbon* (1949), directed by John Ford; screenplay by Frank S. Nugent and Laurence Stallings.

Now an army is a team. It lives, eats, sleeps, fights as a team. This individuality stuff is a bunch of crap. The bilious bastards who wrote that stuff about individuality for the Saturday Evening Post don't know any more about real battle than they do about fornicating.
George C. Scott in *Patton* (1970), directed by Franklin Schaffner; screenplay by Francis Ford Coppola and Edmund J. North.

all-volunteer army
I think the only way to get an all-volunteer Army is to draft it.
Representative F. Edward Hebert, Chairman of the House Armed Services Committee, *The New York Times* (February 24, 1971).

Let us not fool ourselves. . . . An all-volunteer Army will be a poor boys' Army. . . . Congress has a rather immaculate record of not deeply concerning itself with the pleas of the poor.
Senator Thomas F. Eagleton, *The Wall Street Journal* (June 11, 1971).

The fundamental argument for the volunteer Army is that it's just, it's fair. People are in the Army now because they want to be there. They're not in the Army because they're forced to be there. And in a society which is at peace, that's the way it ought to be.
Senator William Proxmire, *U.S. News & World Report* (February 14, 1977).

We must address the question of who will serve and who will not serve in the armed forces. I do not believe the American people want to be protected by a praetorian guard or an army of Gurkhas. Our entire history and tradition support the concept of citizen-soldiers serving the nation—not soldier-mercenaries served by the nation.
Senator Sam Nunn, speech in the Senate, May 8, 1981.

To be accurate, we do not have a "volunteer" armed force anyway. We have a "recruited" armed force, an important distinction.
Arthur T. Hadly, "Back to the Front," *The New Republic* (November 16, 1987).

British Army

The conscription calls out a share of every class—no matter whether your son or my son—all must march; but our friends—I may say it in this room—are the very scum of the earth. . . . [Wellington then went on to analyze the volunteer material] People talk of their enlisting from their fine military feeling—all stuff—no such thing. Some of our men enlist from having got bastard children—some for minor offences—many more for drink; but you can hardly conceive such a set brought together, and it really is wonderful that we should have made them the fine fellows they are.
Duke of Wellington quoted in Elizabeth Longford, *Wellington: The Years of the Sword* (1969).

War against savages could not really test an army. The colonial triumphs created a dangerous impression at home that wars were distant and exotic adventure stories, cheaply won by the parade-ground discipline of the British line, that to win a modern war you called for a hero.
C. Barnett, *Britain and Her Army* (1971).

I myself had served for many years with soldiers, but had never heard the words or expressions that Rudyard Kipling's soldiers used. Many a time did I ask my brother Officers whether they had heard them. No, never. But sure enough, a few years later, the soldiers thought, and talked, and expressed themselves exactly like Rudyard Kipling had taught them in his stories. . . . Rudyard Kipling made the modern soldier.
Sir George Younghusband, *A Soldier's Memories in Peace and War* (1917).

Although privates were the lowest on the army's social scale . . . Tommy felt himself superior to all foreigners and . . . . Once at Secunderabad, when a private was giving evidence before a military court, he referred to three coolies. An officer reminded him that one of the three was the Nizam of Hyderabad, one of the richest men in the world and ruler of the largest independent state in India. The private amended his statement to "the Nizam of Hyderabad and two other coolies."
Byron Farwell, *Mr. Kipling's Army* (1981).

But it's "Thin red line of 'eroes" when
the drums begin to roll . . .
Rudyard Kipling, *Tommy* (1892).

[The British Army should be] a projectile to be fired by the Navy.
Sir Edward Grey quoted in Keith Robbins, *Sir Edward Grey* (1971).

I have not been in the army very long but quite long enough to see that nine officers out of every ten, I might say ninety-nine out of every hundred, know no more of military affairs than the man in the moon and do not intend or want to know more. . . . It is no more a profession than shooting pheasant or hunting foxes. . . . That we ultimately will win in this war is highly probable, but unless the tactics of our generals change it will be simply through sheer force of numbers.
J. F. C. Fuller, a February 1900 letter home during the Boer War, quoted in A. J. Trythall, *"Boney Fuller"* (1977).

The [British] army, with its detailed administrative ability, was able to organize brothels in a surprisingly short time and a pavement in Tripoli held a long queue of men, four deep, standing in orderly patience to pay their money and break the monotony of desert celibacy. The queue was four deep because there were only four women in the brothel. The soldiers stood like units in a conveyor belt waiting for servicing. . . . Brothels for officers were opened in another part of town, where a few strolling pickets of military police ensured that the honored ladies were not importuned by those who did not have the King's Commission.
N. McCallum, recalling duty in North Africa with the Eighth Army during World War II, *Journey with a Pistol* (1959).

Yet it is peculiarly true of the British Army that it only gives of its best on a well-filled stomach. This is as true of training as of fighting. There is profundity, not merely a surface satire, in the old rhyme— "Battles may be fought and won, but the British Army dines at one."
B. H. Liddell Hart, *Thoughts on War* (1944).

Confederate Army
However long you live and whatever you accomplish, you will find that the time you spent in the Confederate army was the most profitably spent portion of your life. Never again speak of having lost time in the army!
General Robert E. Lee quoted in Douglas Southall Freeman, *R. E. Lee,* IV (1935).

After four years of arduous service, marked by unsurpassed courage and fortitude, the Army of Northern Virginia has been compelled to yield to overwhelming numbers and resources. I need not tell the survivors of so many hard-fought battles, who have remained steadfast to the last, that I have consented to this result from no distrust of them; but, feeling that valor and devotion could accomplish nothing that could compensate for the loss that would have attended the continuation of the contest, I have determined to avoid the useless sacrifice of those whose past services have endeared them to their countrymen.
With an increasing admiration of your constancy and devotion to your country, and a grateful remembrance of your kind and generous consideration of myself, I bid you an affectionate farewell.
General Robert E. Lee, Farewell Message to the Army of Northern Virginia, April 10, 1865. Reprinted in *Memoirs of Robert E. Lee,* ed. A. L. Long (1886).

I am a good old rebel—
Yes; that's just what I am—
And for this land of freedom
I do not give a damn.
I'm glad I fit agin'em,
An I only wish we'd won;

And I don't ax no pardon
For anything I've done.
Innes Randolph, "A Good Old Rebel," *Poems* (1898).

Mark Twain, like the nation itself, was divided by the Civil War. He was opposed to slavery, but he was Missourian too, and Missouri was on the Confederate side. Mark Twain served in the Confederate Army for two weeks, but his heart was never in it, and he decided to retire. "There was but one honorable course for me to pursue and I pursued it," he said. "I withdrew to private life and gave the Union cause a chance."
Alex Ayres, *The Wit and Wisdom of Mark Twain* (1987).

The Confederate soldier was probably the finest individual fighter the world has ever seen.
J. F. C. Fuller, *Grant and Lee* (1957).

"Never depreciate the adversary. What honor was there for a Confederate, if he was supposed to be fighting a coward. They were not cowards, those men of the North. Indeed"—and he drew himself up with all his Confederate discipline of spirit— "Indeed, there never was a greater army in the world than the Army of the Potomac, save one, which modesty forbids me to mention."
Douglas Southall Freeman, quoting his father in *A Civil War Treasury,* ed. G. A. Botkin (1960).

German Army
Most states have an army; the Prussian army is the only one that has a state.
Compte de Mirabeau (1749–1791) quoted in John U. Nef, *War and Human Progress* (1950).

Germany is already well on her way to become, and must become, incomparably the most heavily-armed nation in the world and the nation most completely ready for war.... We cannot have any anxieties comparable to the anxiety caused by German rearmament.
Winston Churchill, speech in the House of Commons, October 21, 1933.

Major General Raymond O. Barton of the American 4th Infantry Division visited one of his battalions to spur them on with assurances that the German formation in front of them [in 1944 France] was only second rate and not much of an opponent. A young S-2 (Intelligence) lieutenant remarked: "General, I think you'd better put the Germans on the distribution list. They don't seem to realize that."
Russell F. Weigley, *Eisenhower's Lieutenants* (1981).

Every German who did not spend the entire Nazi era in prison camps must feel responsible and must atone for the sins committed by the murderers in German uniforms and in the name of Germany.
Heinrich Albertz, acting mayor of West Berlin, *The New York Times* (April 19, 1963).

standing army
To keep watchdogs, who from want of discipline or hunger, or from some evil habit or other, would turn upon the sheep and worry them, would be a foul and monstrous thing in a shepherd ... and therefore every care must be taken that our auxiliaries, being stronger than our citizens, may not grow too much for them and become savage beasts.
Plato, *The Republic* (370 B.C.).

A standing army may be likened to a standing member—an excellent assurance of domestic tranquility, but a dangerous temptation to foreign adventure.
Attributed to Elbridge Gerry during the Constitutional Convention of 1787.

The Greeks and Romans had no standing armies, yet they defended themselves. The Greeks by their laws, and the Romans, by the spirit of their people, took care to put into the hands of their rulers no such engine of oppression as a standing army. Their system was to make every man a soldier, and oblige him to repair to the standard of his country whenever that was reared. This made them invincible, and the same will make us so.

Thomas Jefferson, in a letter to Dr. Thomas Cooper, September 10, 1814. Reprinted in *The Writings of Thomas Jefferson*, XIV, ed. A. E. Bergh (1853).

It is against sound policy for a free people to keep up large military establishments and standing armies in time of peace, both from the enormous expenses with which they are attended, and the facile means which they afford to ambitious and unprincipled rulers to subvert the government, or trample upon the rights of the people.

Joseph Story, *Commentaries on the Constitution of the United States* (1833).

The objections which have been brought against a standing army, and they are many and weighty, and deserve to prevail, may also at last be brought against a standing government.

Henry David Thoreau, *On the Duty of Civil Disobedience* (1849).

Standing armies are always used to exercise tyranny over people, and are one of the prime causes of a rupture in a country.

Samuel Gompers, writing in 1899, quoted in Leonard D. White, *The Republican Era* (1958).

I am not one of those who believe that a great standing army is the means of maintaining peace, because if you build up a great profession those who form parts of it want to exercise their profession.

President Woodrow Wilson, speech in Pittsburgh, Pennsylvania, January 29, 1916.

U.S. Army

The American Army is a beautiful little army. Some day, when all the Indians are happily dead or drunk, it ought to make the finest scientific and survey corps that the world has ever seen.

Rudyard Kipling, *American Notes* (1891).

They looked larger than ordinary men; their tall, straight figures were in vivid contrast to the under-sized armies of pale recruits to which we had grown accustomed. At first I thought their spruce, clear uniforms were those of officers, yet obviously they could not be officers, for there were too many of them; they seemed, as it were, Tommies in heaven. . . .

Then I heard an excited exclamation from a group of Sisters behind me. "Look! Look! Here are the Americans!"

I pressed forward with the others to watch the United States physically entering the War, so god-like, so magnificent, so splendidly unimpaired in comparison with the tired, nerve-racked men of the British Army.

Vera Brittain, writing of World War I, *Testament of Youth* (1933).

Among the armies of the world, the American ranks 16th in strength, although this nation ranks fourth in population and first in wealth. Further reductions would bring us to prostration—a condition not conductive to the promotion of a feeling of security at home nor to enhancing the respect with which our pacific counsels are received abroad.

General Douglas MacArthur, letter of May 9, 1932 to representative Bertrand D. Snell, reprinted in D. Clayton James, *The Years of MacArthur*, I (1970).

Among the armies of the major powers, America's is not only the smallest but the worst equipped; most of its arms are outmoded World War [I] leftovers; some of its post-War weapons are already, in the military sense, obsolete; it has developed up-to-date weapons, but has far too few of them for modern war; if America should be attacked, it would be eight months before the nation's peacetime industry could be converted to production of the war supplies which the Army would need; whether there would be any Army left to supply at the end of the those months is disputable.
   Life magazine's analysis of the state of American military preparedness at the end of 1938, quoted in Loudon Wainwright, *The Great American Magazine* (1986).

Although most history books glorify our military accomplishments, a closer examination reveals a disconcerting pattern: unpreparedness at the start of a war; initial failures; reorganizing while fighting; cranking up our industrial base; and ultimately prevailing by wearing down the enemy—by being bigger, not smarter.
   General David C. Jones, quoted in Archie D. Barrett, *Reappraising Defense Organization* (1983).

I didn't become Secretary of the Army to go around hangdog and half-ashamed, apologizing for the United States Army in Vietnam, because it needed no apologies.
   John O. Marsh, Jr., Secretary of the Army, *The New York Times* (January 3, 1989).

arsenal of democracy

We must be the great arsenal of democracy.
   President Franklin D. Roosevelt, speech to the nation, December 29, 1940. According to Walter Isaacson and Evan Thomas, *The Wise Men* (1986), "[John] McCloy was instrumental in the fight for Lend-Lease and even helped contribute its key slogan. In a conversation with [Felix] Frankfurter, he used the phrase 'arsenal of democracy,' which he had picked up from Jean Monnet. 'Don't use those words for a few weeks,' said Frankfurter, who then went to the White House and told Robert Sherwood to use the phrase in an address he was writing for Roosevelt."

The Axis powers knew that they must win the war in 1942—or eventually lose everything. ... As each day goes by, Japanese strength in ships and planes is going down and down, and American strength in ships and planes is going up and up. The eventual outcome can be put on a mathematical basis.
   I can report to you with genuine pride on what has been accomplished in 1942. We produced 48,000 military planes—more than the airplane production of Germany, Italy and Japan put together. We produced 56,000 combat vehicles. We produced 670,000 machine guns. I think the arsenal of democracy is making good.
   President Franklin D. Roosevelt, State of the Union Message to Congress, January 7, 1943.

I have long felt that the United States should not become the weapons arsenal for the so-called free world. It is bad enough when the recipient can afford our new and shiny weapons. It is even worse when the recipient cannot.
   Representative Silvio O. Conte, speech in the House, December 9, 1969.

There has been a lot of talk about the "military-industrial complex" and a lot of criticism of it. I think we ought to remind ourselves that it wasn't too long ago that this industry was considered the "arsenal of democracy."
   David Packard, Deputy Secretary of Defense, *U.S. News & World Report* (August 3, 1970).

This profligate policy of selling arms to all comers, no matter how repressive or tyrannical the government, has had a terrible impact on our world position and repu-

tation. America was once proud to call itself the arsenal of democracy. But recent
Administrations have tried to turn us into just an arsenal.
  Senator Walter F. Mondale, *World Issues* (December 1976).

art and science of war

War in its ensemble is not a science, but an art.
  General Antoine Henri Jomini, *Summary of the Art of War* (1838).

In popular language, however, it is usual to speak of the military art when we refer
to the general subject of war, and of the military sciences when we wish to call attention more particularly to the scientific principles upon which the art is founded.
  H. Wagner Halleck, *Elements of Military Art and Science* (1846).

I am now reading Clausewitz, *On War*. A strange way of philosophizing but very
good on the subject. To the question whether war should be called an art or a science,
the answer given is that war is most like a trade. Fighting is to war what cash payment
is to trade, for however rarely it may be necessary for it actually to occur, everything is
directed towards it, and eventually it must take place all the same and must be decisive.
  Friedrich Engels, letter to Karl Marx of September 25, 1857, quoted in Edward Mead Earle,
  ed., *Makers of Modern Strategy* (1945).

There is no "science" of war, and there never will be any. There are many sciences
war is concerned with. But war itself is not a science; war is practical art and skill.
  Leon Trotsky quoted in D. F. White, "Soviet Philosophy of War," *Political Science Quarterly*,
  5 (1936).

art of war

The art of war is divided between force and stratagem. What cannot be done by
force, must be done by stratagem.
  Frederick the Great, *Instructions for His Generals* (1747).

The art of war is an immense study, which comprises all others.
  Napoleon I quoted in J. Holland, *The Personality of Napoleon* (1912).

The art of war is a simple art; everything is in the performance. There is nothing
vague in it; everything in it is common sense; ideology does not enter in.
  Napoleon I quoted in J. C. Herold, *The Mind of Napoleon* (1955).

The art of war is the art of making use of the given means in combat.
  Karl von Clausewitz, *On War* (1832).

The art of war is simple enough. Find out where your enemy is. Get at him as soon
as you can. Strike at him as hard as you can, and keep moving on.
  General Ulysses S. Grant quoted in T. Harry Williams, "Military Leadership North and
  South," *Why the North Won the War*, ed., D. H. Donald (1960).

There are only two sorts of soldiers: old ones and young ones. I've served fourteen
years: half of your fellows never smelt powder before. Why, how is it that you've just
beaten us? Sheer ignorance of the art of war, nothing else. [Indignantly] I never saw
anything so unprofessional.
  George Bernard Shaw, *Arms and the Man*, Act I (1894).

[Colonel Mosby captured a] young German lieutenant who ... was on his way to
join his regiment in Sheridan's army. ... He was dressed in a fine beavercloth over-
coat; high boots, and a new hat with gilt cord and tassel. After we were pretty well

acquainted, I said to him, "We have done you no harm. Why did you come over here to fight us?" "Oh," he said, "I only come to learn de art of war." I then left him and rode to the head of the column, as the enemy were about, and there was a prospect of a fight. It was not long before the German came trotting up to join me. There had been such a metamorphosis that I scarcely recognized him. One of my men had exchanged his old clothes with him for his new ones, and he complained about it. I asked him if he had not told me that he came to Virginia to learn the art of war. "Yes," he replied. "Very well," I said, "this is your first lesson."
John S. Mosby, *Memoirs* (1917).

They forget that the whole art of war is to gain your objective with as little loss as possible.
Field Marshal B. L. Montgomery, letter to his mother, November 8, 1917, quoted in Nigel Hamilton, *Monty* (1981).

The art of war is the art of preserving one's freedom of action.
General Ferdinand Foch, *The Principles of War* (1918).

The art of war should be enunciated in the form of maxims, such as those of Napoleon, and doctrines, such as those of von Bernhardi, and should constitute an ensemble capable of informing with precision the mind of the student upon the various questions it embraces; so that having the formula the student merely applies it and gets the results prescribed.
William K. Naylor, *Principles of Strategy* (1921).

The conduct of war, like the practice of medicine, is an art, and because the aim of the physician and surgeon is to prevent, cure, or alleviate the diseases of the human body, so should the aim of the statesman and soldier be to prevent, cure, or alleviate the wars which inflict the international body.
J. F. C. Fuller, *The Conduct of War* (1961).

War is manifestly an art and not a science, an art by which, as is true of all arts, the sublime cannot be taught.
Field Marshal Graf Radetzky quoted in Cyril Falls, *The Art of War* (1961).

artillery

And he made in Jerusalem engines invented by cunning men, to be on the towers and upon the bulwarks, to shoot arrows and great stones withal.
The Bible, 2 Kings 26:15.

Every gunner ought to know that it is a wholesome thing for him to eat and drink a little meat before he doth discharge any piece of artillery because the fumes of the saltpeter and brimstone will otherwise be harmful to his brain.
Niccolò Fontana Tartaglia, *Nova Scientia* (1537).

And but for these vile guns,
He would himself have been a soldier.
William Shakespeare, *Henry IV, Part I*, Act I (1597).

Blessed be those happy ages that were strangers to the dreadful fury of these devilish instruments of artillery, whose inventor I am satisfied is now in hell, receiving the reward of his cursed invention, which is the cause that very often a cowardly base hand takes away the life of the bravest gentleman.
Miguel de Cervantes, *Don Quixote* (1615).

Where a goat can go a man can go, and where a man can go he can drag a gun.
British General William Phillips, speaking of mountains near Ticonderoga, New York, during July 1777, quoted in H. Nickerson, *The Turning-Point of the Revolution* (1928).

Cannon fired salutes when princes were born, decorated their palaces while they reigned, and increasingly figured in their funerals when they died. Louis XIV even caused his guns to be emblazoned with the words *ultima ratio regis* [final argument of kings], which was an accurate if cynical description of their function.
Martin van Creveld, *Technology and War* (1989).

A whiff of grapeshot.
Thomas Carlyle, describing the technique Napoleon used to disperse a Paris mob on October 5, 1795, in his *The French Revolution* (1837).

Elevate them guns a little lower.
Attributed to General Andrew Jackson during the January 8, 1815, Battle of New Orleans.

In siege warfare, as in the open field, it is the gun which plays the chief part; it has effected a complete revolution ... it is with artillery that war is made.
Napoleon I quoted in J. F. C. Fuller, *A Military History of the Western World*, II (1955).

As the Mexicans bore down upon the guns, [General] Zachary Taylor had one final discussion with the artilleryman:
"What are you using, Captain [Bragg], grape or canister?"
"Canister, General."
"Single or double?"
"Single."
"Well, double-shot your guns and give 'em hell."
K. Jack Bauer, *The Mexican War* (1974). Taylor's orders during this, the Battle of Buena Vista, on February 23, 1847, have also been quoted as "A little more grape, Captain Bragg." However, this latter remark, while much attributed, has never been authenticated.

Cannon to right of them,
Cannon to left of them,
Cannon in front of them
Volleyed and thundered;
Stormed at with shot and shell,
Boldly they rode and well,
Into the jaws of Death,
Into the mouth of Hell
Rode the six hundred.
Alfred, Lord Tennyson, *The Charge of the Light Brigade* (1854).

Artillery was the great leveller. Nobody could stand more than three hours of sustained shelling before they start[ed] falling sleepy and numb. You're hammered after three hours and you're there for the picking when he comes over. It's a bit like being under an anaesthetic; you can't put a lot of resistance up. The first to be affected were the young ones who'd just come out. They would go to one of the older ones—older in service that is —and maybe even cuddle up to him and start crying.
Martin Middlebrook, *The Kaiser's Battle* (1978).

What a dignified old autocrat a gun was! What a suite of servants and attendants he required to wait on him. He could go nowhere and do nothing without a whole retinue of attendants. We were all his servants—we were there for no other purpose than to wait on him. That is all we had been trained for, that is all we had come to France for. A battery of four 6-inch Howitzers demanded the services of a Major, a Captain and at least four Subalterns and about 120 other ranks to wait on them, also four F.W.D.s [four-wheel drives] to draw them and a column of about 15 three ton lorries with the necessary A.S.C. [Army Service Corps] drivers and officers. All of these just to wait on four guns. You would see a battery on the road,—the four guns in front, looking very solemn and dignified, with all this following in attendance.

Lieutenant E. C. Allfree, on World War I guns, quoted in Trevor Wilson, *The Myriad Faces of War* (1986).

I do not have to tell you who won the war. You know our artillery did.

General George S. Patton, Jr., quoted in R. Ernest Dupuy and Trevor N. Dupuy, *Military Heritage of America* (1956).

They say you never hear the one that hits you. That's true of bullets, because, if you hear them, they are already past.

Ernest Hemingway, "Hemingway Reports Spain," *The New Republic* (January 12, 1938).

Our army seems less reluctant than the German army to expend shells instead of men. If one of our artillery observers in an infantry position sees a few Germans, he's very likely to get excited and throw a concentration of shells at them.

The battered krauts, who come from a land where shells are costly, lives are cheap, and logic governs action, can't understand why we didn't send an infantry patrol instead.

Bill Mauldin, *Up Front* (1945).

If there is one thing a dogface loves, it is artillery—his own.

Audie Murphy, *To Hell and Back* (1949).

"Well, Padre," said Sergeant Jack Spratt, "they're throwing everything at us but the kitchen stove." He had barely said the words when the building suffered another direct hit. "The ceiling fell in, showering us with dirt and plaster. When we picked ourselves up, there right in front of us was a kitchen stove." Spratt looked at it and shook his head. "I knew the bastards were close," he said, "but I didn't believe they could hear us talking."

Cornelius Ryan, *A Bridge Too Far* (1974).

In the Ninth Army men knew [General William H.] Simpson had a rule which he stuck to in every battle and drilled into his subordinate officers: "Never send an infantryman in to do a job that an artillery shell can do for him."

Leonard Mosley, *Marshall* (1982).

Artillerymen with their cold-blooded mathematics seemed subversive of all that made a soldier's life heroic, admirable, worthy.

William H. McNeill, *The Pursuit of Power* (1982).

assassination

War is the statesman's game, the priest's delight.
The lawyer's jest, hired assassin's trade.

Percy Bysshe Shelley, *Queen Mab* (1813).

Assassination has never changed the history of the world.

Benjamin Disraeli, on the death of Abraham Lincoln, speech in the House of Commons, May 1, 1865.

He [Winston Churchill] is very cross with Archie Sinclair . . . [Secretary of State for Air, who] gave an interview . . . saying that dictators were military objectives. The

P. M. thinks this may cause unpleasant reactions on himself and says such a statement almost amounts to incitement to assassination. But, if you are allowed to bomb Heads of States, surely you may shoot them?
John Colville, *The Fringes of Power* (1985), diary entry for November 11, 1940.

We never assassinated anyone.
William E. Colby, Director of the CIA, testimony before the Senate Government Operations Committee, January 23, 1976.

No person employed by or acting on behalf of the United States Government shall engage in, or conspire to engage in, assassination.
President Ronald Reagan, Executive Order 12333, December 4, 1981.

In 1984, Edgar Chamorro, a disillusioned member of the Directorate of the FDN, leaked a CIA contra training manual to the American press. The manual, *Psychological Operations in Guerrilla Warfare*, clearly advocated a strategy of terror as the means to victory over the hearts and minds of Nicaraguans.... The contra pupils whom it was intended to instruct were told of the most effective use of assassinations, preferably in the form of public executions, to impress Nicaraguan villagers. "Neutralize" was the actual euphemism employed, but its meaning left nothing to the imagination. The little booklet thus violated President Reagan's own Presidential Directive 12333, signed in December 1981, which prohibited any U.S. government employee—including the CIA—from having anything to do with assassinations.
Leslie Cockburn, *Out of Control* (1987).

A special program to capture or kill the cadres of the clandestine Viet Cong government, the so-called VCI, for Viet Cong Infrastructure . . . was [created and] given the English name Phoenix, a compromise translation for the Vietnamese name Phung Hoang, a mythical bird that could fly anywhere. The rival intelligence and police agencies on the Saigon side were forced to pool their information so that dossiers and blacklists could be drawn up and cadres targeted. The CIA's assassination squads, the former Counter Terror Teams that were now known as Provincial Reconnaissance Units (PRUs), constituted the action arm.... Technically, no cadres were marked for assassination, only for arrest, because a prisoner led to others when he or she talked. In practice, the PRUs anticipated resistance in disputed areas and shot first.... [Robert] Komer set a quota for all of South Vietnam. He wanted 3,000 VCI "neutralized" every month.
Neil Sheehan, *A Bright Shining Lie* (1988). According to Frances FitzGerald, *Fire in the Lake*, (1972), the Phoenix "program in effect eliminated the cumbersome category of "civilian"; it gave ... license and justification for the arrest, torture, or killing of anyone in the country, whether or not the person was carrying a gun. And many officials took advantage of that license."

assault

Once more into the breach, dear friends, once more;
Or close the wall up with our English dead!
William Shakespeare, *Henry V*, Act III (1598).

In battle, contrary to popular impression, actual shock is the rarest episode. When an assault takes place, the weaker side—weaker either in numbers, morale, or momentum—have almost invariably surrendered or fled before the clash actually comes.
B. H. Liddell Hart, *Thoughts on War* (1944).

The days of the frontal attack should be over. Modern infantry weapons are too deadly, and frontal assault is only for mediocre commanders. Good commanders do not turn in heavy losses.

General Douglas MacArthur, speaking to President Franklin D. Roosevelt during World War II, recounted in his *Reminiscences* (1964).

A key part in Red Army attacks was played by NKVD units armed with automatic weapons, who went in behind the first wave, with the result that, as Stalin observed, "In the Red Army it takes more courage to retreat than to advance." There was also a standing order that any soldier should shoot his neighbor if he appeared to be holding back during an assault—the Soviet version of the honor system.

Alex de Jonge, *Stalin* (1986).

attack

Decline the attack altogether unless you can make it with advantage.
Marshal Maurice de Saxe, *Reveries Upon the Art of War* (1757).

Never to attack in front a position which admits of being turned.
Napoleon I, *Military Maxims* (1827).

The attack should be like a soap bubble, which distends itself until it bursts.
Karl von Clausewitz, *On War* (1832).

A swift and vigorous transition to attack—the flashing sword of vengeance—is the most brilliant point of the defensive.
Karl von Clausewitz, *On War* (1832).

There is only one form of war—to wit, the attack of the enemy.
Karl von Clausewitz, *On War* (1832).

Napoleon once said: "I attack to be attacked." What he meant was that he threw forward a small fraction of his forces for the enemy to bite on, and when his adversary's jaws were fixed he moved up his large reserves—the capital of his tactical bank—and struck his real blow. Here is another saying of his: "Victory is to him who has the last reserve."
J. F. C. Fuller, "Co-Ordination of the Attack," *Infantry Journal* (January 1931).

My center is giving way, my right is in retreat; situation excellent. I shall attack.
Marshal Ferdinand Foch, during the Second Battle of the Marne in 1918, quoted in George Grey Aston, *The Biography of the Late Field Marshal Foch* (1929).

Every attack, once undertaken, must be fought to a finish; every defense, once begun, must be carried on with the utmost energy.
Marshal Ferdinand Foch, *Precepts and Judgments* (1920).

Attack, attack, and attack again, even when you are on the defensive.
General Sir Harold R. L. Alexander, *Newsweek* (August 31, 1942).

The frontal threat and the frontal holding attack are quite different operations. The object of the first is to compel an enemy to assume the defensive, and of the second to force him to maintain it; in other words, to pin him to a locality. Once this is accomplished the true attack takes the form of a flank or rear maneuver.
J. F. C. Fuller, *Armoured Warfare*, II (1943).

A tramp once went to a house and asked for some boiling water to make rock soup. The lady was interested and gave him the water, in which he placed two polished white stones. He then asked if he might have some potatoes and carrots to put in the

soup to flavor it a little, and finally ended up with some meat. In other words, in order to attack, we had first to pretend to reconnoiter, then reinforce the reconnaissance, and finally put on an attack.
General George S. Patton, Jr., *War As I Knew It* (1947).

attrition

Attrition becomes the essence of war. To kill, if possible, more of the enemy troops than your own side loses, is the sum total of this military creed. . . .
The absurdity and wrong-headedness of this doctrine should have been apparent to any mind which attempted to think logically instead of blankly accepting inherited traditions.
B. H. Liddell Hart, *Thoughts on War* (1944).

We all know what attrition is. It is war in the administrative manner . . . in which the really important command decisions are in fact logistic decisions. The enemy is treated as a mere inventory of targets, and warfare is a matter of mustering superior resources to destroy his forces by sheer firepower and weight of material.
Edward N. Luttwak, "The American Style of Warfare," *Survival* (March/April 1979).

Drawing distinctions between "attrition theory" and "maneuver theory" simply obfuscates the real nature of war. Maneuver is of value, maybe decisive value, because it increases the rate of attrition.
Chris Bellamy, *The Future of Land Warfare* (1987).

battalions

The number of wise men will always be small. It is true that it has increased, but that is nothing compared with the fools, and unfortunately it is said that God is always on the side of the big battalions.
Voltaire, letter of February 6, 1770 to François le Riche, reprinted in *Voltaire's Correspondence*, LXXIV, ed. T. Besterman (1962).

When you have it in contemplation to give battle it is a general rule to collect all your strength and to leave none unemployed. One battalion sometimes decides the issue of the day.
Napoleon I, *Military Maxims* (1827).

If sixty determined men can rout a battalion, these sixty must be found.
Ardant du Picq, *Battle Studies* (1868).

[Victory would go] to that one of the two adversaries who had kept the last reserve battalion to throw into the furnace when his opponent had none.
Marshal Ferdinand Foch, *Precepts and Judgments* (1920).

When the World War came in 1914, the fallacy of the "big battalions" was exposed by the mechanical progress embodied in the machine-gun, which enabled one man to cancel out many "bayonets."
B. H. Liddell Hart, *Thoughts on War*, (1944).

It was as simple as this: three men and a machine gun can stop a battalion of heroes.
G. Blond, *Verdun* (1967).

The only place you can get the real smell of battle in your nostrils and know what is going on is at the battalion command posts.
General Brian Horrocks quoted in John M. Gavin, *On To Berlin* (1978).

When General Abrams was Chief of Staff of the Army in the early seventies, he used to be asked how the tank battalions in Vietnam and in NATO compared with his World War II battalion. He always replied that as a lieutenant colonel he really commanded two tank battalions: the superb unit he took into action in Normandy, and what that same battalion became later, after it had been filled up with the mediocre personnel provided by the Army to replace his casualties.
Arthur T. Hadley, *The Straw Giant* (1986).

battle cry

The war cry should not be begun till both armies have joined, for it is a mark of ignorance or cowardice to give it at a distance. The effect is much greater on the enemy when they find themselves struck at the same instant with the intimidating din of the noise and the points of the weapons.
Vegetius, *De Re Militari* (378 A.D.).

I see you stand like greyhounds in the slips,
Straining upon the start. The game's afoot:
Follow your spirit, and upon this charge
Cry "God for Harry, England, and Saint George!"
William Shakespeare, *Henry V*, Act II (1599).

Westminster Abbey, or victory!
Admiral Horatio Nelson's personal battle cry quoted in Robert Southey, *Life of Nelson* (1813). Because Westminster Abbey was the place where the English traditionally bury their most famous dead, Nelson was really saying "death or victory." But he liked to dwell on Westminster Abbey. Before the 1798 Battle of the Nile he said, "Before this time to-morrow I shall have gained a peerage, or Westminster Abbey."

The Rebel yell was a variation on traditional Celtic animal calls, especially those used to call cattle and hogs and hunting dogs. "Woh-who-ey! who-ey! who-ey!" is the way one man remembered it with the first syllable "woh" short and low, and the second "who" with a very high and prolonged note deflecting upon the third syllable "ey." One thing is clear: it was totally different from the Yankee "cheer" that repeated the word "hurrah" but pronounced it "hoo-ray," with emphasis upon the second syllable.
Grady McWhiney and Perry D. Jamieson, *Attack and Die* (1982).

At Chateau-Thierry [in World War I], when Allied lines were collapsing, the story goes that one of our officers yelled: "Retreat, Hell! We just got here!" Maybe you've seen that expression in the history books along with some of our other battle cries.
Leon M. Uris, *Battle Cry* (1953).

The enemy's positions beyond the hill's crest were close enough so we could hear them shouting orders. They were a talkative bunch, hollering in our direction, "Fuck the Americans," "Roosevelt eats crap," or worse, "Fuck Eleanor." Several men not overly fond of the president yelled back agreeing with the Germans' comments. Our responses must have dumbfounded our adversaries—the dialogue quickly ended.
Harold P. Leinbaugh and John D. Campbell, *The Men of Company K* (1985).

battlefield

There is in every battlefield a decisive point, the possession of which, more than of any other, helps to secure the victory, by enabling its holder to make a proper application of the principles of war. . . .

The decisive point of a battlefield is determined . . . by the character of the position, the bearing of different localities upon the strategic object in view, and, finally, by the arrangement of the contending forces.
General Antoine Henri Jomini, *Summary of the Art of War* (1838).

It was a war between two races of ants, the red always pitted against the black, and frequently two red ones to one black. The legions of these Myrmidons covered all the hills and vales in my wood-yard, and the ground was already strewn with the dead and dying, both red and black. It was the only battle which I have ever witnessed, the only battlefield I ever trod while the battle was raging; internecine war; the red republicans on the one hand, and the black imperialists on the other. On every side they were engaged in deadly combat, yet without any noise that I could hear, and human soldiers never fought so resolutely. I watched a couple that were fast locked in each other's embraces, in a little sunny valley amid the chips, now at noonday prepared to fight till the sun went down, or life went out. The smaller red champion had fastened himself like a vise to his adversary's front, and through all the tumblings on that field never for an instant ceased to gnaw at one of his feelers. . . . They fought with more pertinacity than bulldogs. Neither manifested the least disposition to retreat. It was evident that their battle-cry was "Conquer or die." I should not have wondered by this time to find that they had their respective musical bands stationed on some eminent chip, and playing their national airs the while, to excite the slow and cheer the dying combatants. . . . I have no doubt that it was a principle they fought for.
Henry Thoreau, *Walden* (1854).

I have always regarded the forward edge of the battlefield as the most exclusive club in the world.
General Sir Brian Horrocks, *A Full Life* (1960).

The weakest must come to the conference table with the same confidence as do we. . . . That table, though scarred by many past frustrations, cannot be abandoned for the certain agony of the battlefield.
President Dwight D. Eisenhower, Farewell Address, January 17, 1961.

There is never a convenient place to fight a war when the other man starts it.
Admiral Arleigh Burke quoted in David Rees, *Korea* (1964).

The most important single outcome of technological progress during the decades since World War II has been that, on the modern battlefield, a blizzard of electromagnetic blips is increasingly being superimposed on—and to some extent substituted for—the storm of steel in which war used to take place.
Martin van Creveld, *Technology and War* (1989).

battles

Good officers never engage in general actions unless induced by opportunity or obliged by necessity.
Vegetius, *De Re Militari* (378 A.D.).

I do not favor pitched battles, especially at the beginning of a war, and I am convinced that a skillful general could make war all his life without being forced into one.
Marshal Maurice de Saxe, *Reveries Upon The Art of War* (1757).

It is a bad thing always to be fighting. While in the thick of it I am too much occupied to feel anything; but it is wretched just after. It is quite impossible to think of glory. Both mind and feelings are exhausted. I am wretched even at the moment of

victory, and I always say that, next to a battle lost, the greatest misery is a battle gained.
Duke of Wellington quoted in *The Diary of Lady Frances Shelley, 1787–1817* (1912).

In giving battle a general should regard it as his first duty to maintain the honor and glory of his arms. To spare his troops should be but a secondary consideration. But the same determination and perseverance which promote the former object are the best means of securing the latter.
Napoleon I, *Military Maxims* (1827).

Battles are the actual conflicts of armies contending about great questions of national policy and of strategy. Strategy directs armies to the decisive points of a zone of operations, and influences, in advance, the results of battles; but tactics, aided by courage, by genius and fortune, gains victories.
General Antoine Henri Jomini, *Summary of the Art of War* (1838).

[Battles] are buffooneries, and none the less buffooneries because they are made terrible by the spilling of blood. The actors, heroes in the eyes of the crowd, are only poor folk torn between fear, discipline and pride. They play some hours at a game of advance and retreat, without ever meeting, closing with, even seeing closely, the other poor folks, the enemy, who are as fearful as they but who are caught in the same web of circumstance.
Ardant du Picq, *Battle Studies* (1868).

War loses a great deal of its romance after a soldier has seen his first battle. I have a more vivid recollection of the first than the last one I was in. It is a classical maxim that it is sweet and becoming to die for one's country; but whoever has seen the horrors of a battlefield feels that it is far sweeter to live for it.
John S. Mosby, *War Reminiscences* (1887).

A certain readiness to perish is not so very rare, but it is seldom that you meet men whose souls, steeled in the impenetrable armor of resolution, are ready to fight a losing battle to the last.
Joseph Conrad, *Lord Jim* (1900).

Battle [is] a method of untying with the teeth a political knot that would not yield to the tongue.
Ambrose Bierce, *The Devil's Dictionary* (1911).

Joseph de Maistre wrote: "A battle lost is a battle one thinks one has lost; for," he added, "a battle cannot be lost physically." Therefore, it can only be lost morally. But then, it is also morally that a battle is won, and we may extend the aphorism by saying: A battle won, is a battle in which one will not confess oneself beaten.
Marshal Ferdinand Foch, *Precepts and Judgments* (1920).

The risks of maternity are equal to the risks of battle. There is no more credit to a man for risking death in the one than to a woman for risking death in the other.
René Quinton, *Soldier's Testament* (1930).

Nearly all the battles which are regarded as masterpieces of the military, from which have been derived the foundation of states and the fame of commanders, have been battles of maneuver.
Winston Churchill, *The World Crisis*, II (1923).

The late [Eleutherios] Venizelos [a Greek statesman] observed that in all her wars England—he should have said Britain, of course—always wins one battle—the last.
Winston Churchill, speech in London, November 10, 1942. Churchill often expressed this attitude during the war. Thomas M. Coffey in *Hap* (1982) quotes Churchill telling General Henry H. "Hap" Arnold in 1941 that "England may not always win battles, but always wins wars." Karl von Clausewitz, in *On War* (1832), said something similar: "There is only one decisive victory: the last. All that precede it, however great they may be, amount to nothing but an expenditure of energy which imperils the chances of winning the decisive final battle."

Every man in the army must have the light of battle in his eye.
General B. L. Montgomery quoted in *Time* (November 16, 1942).

When things are going badly in battle the best tonic is to take one's mind off one's own troubles by considering what a rotten time one's opponent must be having.
Sir Archibald P. Wavell, *Other Men's Flowers* (1944).

The art of battle consists in maintaining and strengthening the psychological cohesion of one's own troops while at the same time disrupting that of the enemy's.
Andre Beaufre, *An Introduction to Strategy* (1965).

Many veterans who are honest with themselves will admit, I believe, that the experience of communal effort in battle, even under altered conditions of modern war, has been a high point in their lives.
J. Glenn Gray, *The Warriors* (1970).

battleships

A fully equipped duke costs as much to keep up as two Dreadnoughts; and they are just as great a terror and they last longer.
David Lloyd George, replying to a Duke's complaint that taxes might be too high, *The Times* (London) (October 11, 1909).

The Admiralty had demanded six ships; the economists offered four; and we finally compromised on eight.
Winston Churchill, on the 1909 British decision to build more battleships, *The World Crisis*, I (1923).

The offensive power of modern battleships is out of all proportions to their defensive power. Never was the disproportion so marked. If you want to make a true picture in your mind of a battle between great modern ironclad ships you must not think of it as if it were two men in armour striking at each other with heavy swords. It is more like a battle between two egg-shells striking each other with hammers.
Winston Churchill, speech in the House of Commons, March 17, 1914.

That idea is so damned nonsensical and impossible that I'm willing to stand on the bridge of a battleship while that nitwit tries to hit it from the air.
Newton D. Baker, Secretary of War, responding in 1921 to Billy Mitchell's offer to sink a battleship using bombs dropped from airplanes, quoted in Emile Gauvreau and Lester Cohen, *Billy Mitchell* (1942).

The visual impact of a United States battleship on the horizon springs from its ability to put Soviet ships on the bottom of the sea and to put devastating firepower ashore.
John F. Lehman, Jr., Secretary of the Navy, *U.S. News & World Report* (May 4, 1981).

I would not give the battleship a chance of survivability of more that 20 or 30 minutes in hostilities . . . the Soviet Navy is not sailing around in old battleships that fought in World War II. They are sailing around in new modern cruisers, new modern fast ships that can out-maneuver that big ship any day of the week. So, Mr. President, I am going to vote against this battleship [the *New Jersey*]. Even though I love to watch them sail through the water, I do not like to see them go down, and that is where this one would go in a big, fat hurry.

Senator Barry M. Goldwater, *Los Angeles Times* (July 26, 1981).

At a late-afternoon meeting at the White House ... , President Reagan, who had just returned from horseback riding at Quantico, turned to me in jest, but with a touch of nostalgia, and asked, "Isn't there some way we can bring back the horse cavalry?" My reply was: "Just wait, Mr. President. We are starting by resurrecting battleships."

General David C. Jones, writing in 1982, quoted in C. W. Kegley, Jr., and E. R. Wittkopf, *The Domestic Sources of American Foreign Policy* (1988).

If any of the sixteen successful attacks against British ships [in the Falklands] had instead hit the battleship *New Jersey*, it could not have done sufficient damage to prevent continuing operations of the ship. The Exocet missile that sank the *Sheffield* would not have been able to penetrate the armor anywhere on a battleship.

John F. Lehman, Jr., *Command of the Seas* (1988).

bayonets

The bristling points and the glitter of the bayonets were fearful to look upon as they were levelled in front of a charging line; but they were rarely reddened with blood. The day of the bayonet is passed.

General John B. Gordon, *Reminiscences of the Civil War* (1904).

The bayonet is essentially an offensive weapon. In a bayonet assault all ranks go forward to kill or be killed, and only those who have developed skill and strength by constant training will be able to kill. The spirit of the bayonet must be inculcated into all ranks, so that they go forward with that aggressive determination and confidence of superiority born of continual practice, without which a bayonet assault will not be effective.

The Manual of Bayonet Training (British Army, World War I) quoted in *Siegfried Sassoon's Long Journey*, Paul Fussell, ed. (1983).

The attack will be pressed with the ruthless vigor that has routed every enemy formation opposing the 3rd Div. All men will be brought to the highest possible state of offensive spirit prior to the jump-off. *Bayonets will be sharpened.*

General John W. O'Daniel's March 1945 field order to his 3rd Infantry Division as they advanced into Germany, quoted in Russell F. Weigley, *Eisenhower's Lieutenants* (1981).

"How do you get a bayonet out of a Jap, once you've got it in?" I asked. . . .

"Shoot it out," he told me. And that's what the Marines did at Saipan and Guadalcanal on the rare occasions that they used bayonets.

General Holland M. Smith and Percy Finch, *Coral and Brass* (1948).

Corporal Robert E. Lee ran around the base of one of the ack-ack guns, and a Japanese soldier, thought to be dead, jumped up to face him. They each sprang forward, lunging with their bayonets. They missed and stared at each other for a fraction of a second, then lunged again. This time neither one missed, and they both fell dead.

Duane Schultz, *Wake Island* (1978).

Once I watched the French make a bayonet charge. They dug two series of holes, one row behind the other. When things got touchy, they'd get out of the forward holes and drop back to the second line of holes. Once the Chinese attacked and got into the

front holes, the French knew where they were and would finish them off. Ingenious, those French.
Richard Turner quoted in Donald Knox, *The Korean War: Uncertain Victory* (1988).

We are told that, like karate, proper bayoneting requires a lusty shout to convince your adversary that you are marching to a different drummer and not about to be logically persuaded to drop your spear in favor of a panel discussion of the issues. "You've got to let him know that you're a mad-assed mother-fucker," shouts Drill Sergeant Brown. "He's got to think that you're dangerously crazy." The short, lusty word "kill" is recommended, and would indeed frighten any English-speaking foe into respect. As for non-English-speaking combatants, any visceral grunt is acceptable. I choose "Sorry!"
Peter Tauber, *The Sunshine Soldiers* (1971).

Communist leaders believe in Lenin's precept: Probe with bayonets. If you encounter mush, proceed; if you encounter steel, withdraw.
President Richard M. Nixon, *RN: Memoirs* (1978).

The fixing of bayonets is more than a fixing of steel to the rifle since it puts iron into the soul of the soldier doing the fixing. . . . [The bayonet is] an emotive rather than a seriously practical weapon.
R. G. Lee, *Introduction to Battlefield Weapons Systems and Technology* (1981).

Regimes planted by bayonets do not take root.
President Ronald Reagan, speech to the British Parliament, June 8, 1982.

Berlin

The Battle of Berlin will continue until the heart of Nazi Germany ceases to beat.
Air Marshal Sir Arthur Harris, *Time* (December 6, 1943).

Methods of blackmail and reckless threats of force will be least of all appropriate in solving such a problem as the Berlin question. Such methods will not help solve a single question, but can only bring the situation to the danger point. But only madmen can go to the length of unleashing another world war over the preservation of privileges of occupiers in West Berlin. If such madmen should really appear, there is no doubt that strait jackets could be found for them.
Nikita Khrushchev, writing on November 27, 1958, quoted in *Department of State Bulletin* (January 19, 1959).

For if Khrushchev could split the western alliance over Berlin and force the Allies ignominiously to withdraw, abandoning the 2,500,000 citizens of West Berlin whom we had sworn to defend, Germany and all Europe would know that Khrushchev was master of Europe. And we Americans would have shown that we, too, knew that Khrushchev was master.
Dean Acheson, "Wishing Won't Hold Berlin," *Saturday Evening Post* (March 7, 1959).

Your generals talk of maintaining your position in Berlin with force. That is bluff. If you send in tanks, they will burn and make no mistake about it. If you want war, you can have it, but remember it will be your war. Our rockets will fly automatically.
Nikita Khrushchev quoted in Averell Harriman, "My Alarming Interview with Khrushchev," *Life* (July 13, 1959).

Berlin is a cancerous sore in the throat that has to be cut out.
Nikita Khrushchev to President John F. Kennedy in Vienna, *Newsweek* (June 19, 1961). This has also been translated as "Berlin is a bone that must come out of the Soviet throat."

All free men, wherever they may live, are citizens of Berlin. And therefore, as a free man, I take pride in the words, *"Ich bin ein Berliner!"*
President John F. Kennedy, speech at West Berlin City Hall, June 26, 1963.

Isn't it strange that . . . people build walls to keep an enemy out, and there's only one part of the world and one philosophy where they have to build walls to keep their people in?
President Ronald Reagan, press conference, August 12, 1986.

The wall was raised in a concrete situation and was not dictated only by evil intentions. . . . The wall can disappear when those conditions that created it fall away.
Mikhail S. Gorbachev, *The New York Times* (June 16, 1989).

[In 1989] Voyager 2 discovered 1,500-mph winds on Neptune, but even more impressive winds blew down the Berlin wall.
George F. Will, *Newsweek* (January 1, 1990).

big stick

The only safe rule is to promise little, and faithfully to keep every promise; to "speak softly and carry a big stick."
President Theodore Roosevelt, *Autobiography* (1913).

Pacifists? Hell, I'm a pacifist, but I always have a club behind my back.
General Smedley Butler, USMC, *The New York Times* (August 21, 1931).

Teddy Roosevelt . . . once said "Speak softly and carry a big stick." Jimmy Carter wants to speak loudly and carry a fly swatter.
President Gerald Ford, campaign speech, October 16, 1976.

We've tended to forget Teddy Roosevelt's advice. Speak softly and carry a big stick. We've tended to speak too threateningly while we carried a feather.
Alexander M. Haig, Jr., *USA Today* (December 2, 1986).

bombers

"Bombers!" [General] Eaker exclaimed [in World War II]. "But I've been in fighters all my life!" "That's why I'm giving you this job." [General] Arnold said. "I want you to put some fight into the bombers."
Thomas M. Coffey, *Hap* (1982).

Once you've launched a missile, there's no calling it back. . . . bombers can be used short of going to war. When we sent the B-52s into the air during the 1962 Cuban missile crisis, the Soviets knew we meant business.
General Glenn A. Kent, *The Christian Science Monitor* (April 4, 1972).

The age of the manned strategic penetrating bomber is over. Flying missions into the heart of the U.S.S.R. with gravity bombs is virtually a suicide flight. But just as the Navy could not give up its battleships, the Air Force refuses to recognize the end of the World War II bomber mission. If the Air Force had a ground-force mission, we would still be breeding cavalry horses.
Senator William Proxmire, speech in the Senate, May 19, 1976.

The only purpose of the B-1 bomber is as a clean-up weapon, and there won't be much to clean up if a war comes. You could use an ox-cart.
Representative George H. Mahon, speech in the House of Representatives, October 20, 1977.

The B-1 bomber is a waste of money.
President Jimmy Carter, *Time* (October 11, 1982).

A friend of mine who wears wings told me: "I would never fly it [the B-2 stealth bomber]. You'd never jump out of a plane that cost $600 million."
Robert Costello, *Newsweek* (May 22, 1989).

bombing

Would a declaration of war between Russia and Japan be made, if within an hour thereafter, a swiftly gliding aeroplane might take its flight from St. Petersburg and drop half a ton of dynamite above the [Japanese] war offices? Could any nation afford to war upon any other with such hazards in view?
John Brisben Walker, *Cosmopolitan* (March 1904).

The third peculiarity of aerial warfare was that it was at once enormously destructive and entirely indecisive.
H. G. Wells, *The War in the Air* (1908).

A people who are bombed today as they were bombed yesterday, and who know that they will be bombed again tomorrow and see no end to their martyrdom, are bound to call for peace at length.
Giulio Douhet, *Command of the Air* (1922).

Any town which is within reach of an aerodrome can be bombed within the first five minutes of war from the air, to an extent that was inconceivable in the last war, and the question will be whose morale will be shattered quickest by the preliminary bombing? I think it is well for the man in the street to realize that there is no power on earth that can protect him from being bombed. Whatever people may tell him, the bomber will always get through.
Stanley Baldwin, speech in House of Commons, November 10, 1932.

Total war from the air against an undeveloped country or region is well nigh futile; it is one of the curious features of the most modern weapon that it is especially effective against the most modern types of civilization.
Alexander Seversky, *Victory Through Air Power* (1942).

Carelessly aimed or wildly dropped bombs are now "incontinent ordnance."
Paul Fussell, *The Great War in Modern Memory* (1975).

bombing—Vietnam

My solution to the problem would be to tell them frankly that they've got to draw in their horns and stop their aggression, or we're going to bomb them back into the Stone Age.
General Curtis E. LeMay, *Mission With LeMay*, written with MacKinlay Kantor (1965). However, Thomas M. Coffey, in *Iron Eagle* (1986), states that LeMay's most famous statement was entirely written by Kantor.

It became necessary for us to increase our response and to make attacks by air. And we do this to convince the leaders of North Viet-Nam—and all who seek to share their conquest—of a very simple fact: We will not be defeated. We will not grow tired. We will not withdraw, either openly or under the cloak of a meaningless agreement.
President Lyndon B. Johnson, speech at Johns Hopkins University, Baltimore, Maryland, April 7, 1965.

The Air Force comes in every morning and says, "Bomb, bomb, bomb".... And then the State Department comes in and says, "Not now, or not there, or too much, or not at all."
President Lyndon B. Johnson on Vietnam quoted in Philip L. Geyelin, *Lyndon B. Johnson and the World* (1966).

We have no reason to believe that it would break the will of the North Vietnamese people or sway the purpose of their leaders . . . or provide any confidence that they can be bombed to the negotiating table.
Robert S. McNamara, Secretary of Defense, August 1967, testimony before the Senate Armed Services Committee, quoted in Barbara W. Tuchman, *The March of Folly* (1984).

The American people do not seem to realize that their air power is carrying out one of the most terrible mass exterminations in history, not only in the North but in the South Vietnam that it is supposed to be defending.
Tom Wicker, *The New York Times* (September 12, 1972).

The bastards have never been bombed like they're going to be bombed this time.
President Richard M. Nixon, on the 1972 bombing of North Vietnam, quoted in Dave Richard Palmer, *Summons of the Trumpet* (1978).

I would like to ask a question: Would this sort of war or savage bombing which has taken place in Vietnam have been tolerated for so long had the people [in Vietnam] been European?
Indira Gandhi, Prime Minister of India, *Newsweek* (February 19, 1973).

You always write it's bombing, bombing, bombing. It's not bombing. It's air support.
U.S. Air Force Colonel David H. E. Opfer quoted in *The New York Times* (November 28, 1974).

The deeper tragedy of . . . the loss of . . . thousands of . . . airmen in the war was that they were used so foolishly by the bureaucrats in the uniformed chain of command and in Washington. In every year of the war except 1972 the targets they flew against were by and large meaningless and stupidly selected: suspected truck parks, ferry landings, and others with absolutely no military utility, picked by faraway staff officers pursuing the academic game theory approach of "sending messages" with "surgical strikes" and "measured responses."
John F. Lehman, Jr., *Command of the Seas* (1988).

bombing—World War II

There are a lot of people who say that bombing can never win a war. Well, my answer to that is that it has never been tried yet, and we shall see.
Air Marshal Sir Arthur Harris, head of RAF Bomber Command in World War II, quoted in Gwynne Dyer, *War* (1985).

Investigation seems to show that having one's house demolished is most damaging to morale. People seem to mind it more than having their friends or even relatives killed.
Lord Cherwell, writing in 1942, quoted in Max Hastings, *Bomber Command* (1979).

It is apparent that an extraordinary lack of sense of proportion affects outside appreciation of the meaning, extent and results of Bomber Command's operations. What shouts of victory would arise if a Commando wrecked the entire Renault factory in a night, with a loss of seven men! What credible assumptions of an early end to the

war would follow upon the destruction of a third of Cologne in an hour and a half by some swift moving mechanized force which, with but 200 casualties, withdrew and was ready to repeat the operation 24 hours later! What acclaim would greet the virtual destruction of Rostock and the Heinkel main and subsidiary factories by a Naval bombardment! All this, and far more, has been achieved by Bomber Command; yet there are many who still avert their gaze, pass by on the other side, and question whether the 30 squadrons of night bombers make any worth-while contribution to the war.
Air Marshal Sir Arthur Harris, memorandum for the Prime Minister and War Cabinet, June 28, 1942, reprinted in Anthony Verrier, *The Bomber Offensive* (1968).

Sixty percent of the bombs dropped are not accounted for, less than one percent have hit the aiming point and about three percent [land] within 500 feet.
Colonel Curtis LeMay, in a January 12, 1943 letter concerning the bombing of Germany, quoted in Thomas M. Coffey, *Iron Eagle: The Turbulent Life of General Curtis LeMay* (1986).

We have as much right to bomb Rome as the Italians had to bomb London, and we should not hesitate to do so to the best of our ability and as heavily as possible if the course of the war should render such action convenient and helpful.
Anthony Eden, British Foreign Secretary, speech in the House of Commons, January 20, 1943. John Colville, *The Fringes of Power* (1985), writes in his diary entry for November 2, 1940 that Winston Churchill said in regard to bombing Rome: "We must be careful not to bomb the Pope; he has a lot of influential friends!"

In the burning and devastated cities we daily experienced the direct impact of war. It spurred us to do our utmost.
Neither did the bombings and the hardships that resulted from them weaken the morale of the populace. On the contrary, from my visits to armament plants and my contacts with the man in the street, I carried away the impression of growing toughness. It may well be that the estimated loss of 9 per cent of our production capacity was amply balanced out by increased effort.
Albert Speer, *Inside the Third Reich* (1970).

Accounts of the bombing that I have so far seen . . . [put] emphasis on the destruction that air raids inflicted on German industrial potential and thus upon armaments. In reality the losses were not quite so serious. . . . The real importance of the air war consisted in the fact that it opened a second front long before the invasion of Europe. That front was the skies over Germany. . . . Defense against air attacks required the production of thousands of anti-aircraft guns, the stockpiling of tremendous quantities of ammunition all over the country, and holding in readiness hundreds of thousands of soldiers. . . . As far as I can judge from the accounts I have read, no one has yet seen that this was the greatest lost battle on the German side.
Albert Speer, *Spandau: The Secret Diaries* (1976).

[Over Germany] Missions frequently lost a third of their planes, sometimes half of them or more. . . . These were not what a military man would call "acceptable" losses. Again and again the bombing had to be halted or slowed in order to build up the backlog of planes. To fly in the Eighth Air Force in those days was to hold a ticket to a funeral. Your own.
Harrison E. Salisbury, *A Journey for Our Time* (1983).

As a young Air Corps officer in World War II, [Robert] McNamara had been in awe of [General Curtis] LeMay. McNamara observed how LeMay inspired airmen to fly nearly suicidal bombing raids over Germany by flying the lead plane. Later in the

Pacific, McNamara listened as LeMay conducted a 20th Air Force debriefing after the first low altitude bombing attack on Tokyo.

"Who was the son-of-a-bitch who sent us in at seven thousand feet when the B-29s are supposed to be flying at twenty-five thousand?" asked a young pilot who had lost his wingman in the raid.

"I did," replied LeMay. "We lost fewer men and got better results that way."
Nick Kotz, *Wild Blue Yonder* (1988).

Referring to his military service in the South Pacific, Richard Nixon quipped: "I was there when the bombs were dropping. But I didn't get hit and I didn't hit anyone. All I got was a good case of fungus."
Senator Richard M. Nixon, speaking in Washington, D.C. on July 26, 1952, quoted in Bill Adler, ed., *The Wit and Humor of Richard Nixon* (1969).

It can be seen that where the preinvasion attacks really paid off was not nearly so much in the damage they did, but rather in the effect they had on causing the Germans to put a very significant part of their total war effort into air defense.
Burton H. Klein, *Germany's Economic Preparations for War* (1959).

bravery

Few men are born brave; many become so through training and force of discipline.
Vegetius, *De Re Militari* (378 A.D.).

None but the brave deserves the fair.
John Dryden, *Alexander's Feast* (1697).

To believe yourself brave is to *be* brave; it is the one only essential thing.
Mark Twain, *Joan of Arc* (1896).

Even experience cannot cure a man of bravery.
René Quinton, *Soldier's Testament* (1930).

War is an unmitigated evil. But it certainly does one good thing. It drives away fear and brings bravery to the surface.
Mohandas K. Gandhi, *Non-Violence in Peace and War* (1948).

bullets

I heard the bullets whistle; and believe me, there is something charming in the sound.
Lieutenant Colonel George Washington, letter to his brother written after his encounter with the French at Great Meadows, May 3, 1754. James T. Flexner noted in *George Washington: The Forge of Experience* (1965) that "after this letter had been published in the *London Magazine* [XIII 1754], George II commented that the Colonial officer would not consider the sound of bullets charming 'if he had been used to hear many.' "

The tough old Duke of Danzig, Lefebvre, twice wounded ... assuredly said it all when an old friend was enviously admiring his fine Paris mansion. "So you're jealous of me," exclaimed the veteran. "Very well; come out into the courtyard and I'll have twenty shots at you at thirty paces. If I don't hit you, the whole house and everything is yours." The friend hastily declined to take the chance, whereupon Lefebvre remarked drily, "I had a thousand bullets fired at me from much closer range before I got all this."
David Chandler, *Napoleon's Marshals* (1987).

The bullet that is to kill me has not yet been moulded.
Attributed to Napoleon I. He was right if he said it, because he died in bed.

To give the victory to the right, not bloody bullets, but peaceful ballots only, are necessary.
President Abraham Lincoln, 1858 speech reprinted in *Collected Works of Abraham Lincoln*, 2, ed. R. P. Basler, (1953). In a July 4, 1861 message to Congress, Lincoln said that "ballots are the rightful, and peaceful, successors of bullets; and that when ballots have fairly, and constitutionally, decided, there can be no successful appeal, back to bullets."

There is no great sport in having bullets flying about one in every direction, but I find they have less horror when among them than when in anticipation.
President Ulysses S. Grant, in a letter to his wife during the Mexican War, quoted in William S. McFeely, *Grant* (1981).

Nothing in life is so exhilarating as to be shot at without result.
Winston Churchill, *The Story of the Malakand Field Force* (1898).

Officers were expected to remain cool under fire and not to "bob"—that is, not to duck when bullets whistled close or shells exploded near them.
Byron Farwell, *Mr. Kipling's Army* (1981).

[On December 7, 1941 Commander Maurice] Curts was standing beside [Admiral Husband] Kimmel at the window when a spent bullet crashed through the glass. It struck the admiral on the chest, left a dark splotch on his white uniform, then dropped to the floor. Kimmel picked it up. It was a .50 caliber machine-gun bullet. Somehow the slug seemed symbolic. Much as Kimmel craved the chance to avenge this terrible day, in his heart he knew that the debacle [at Pearl Harbor] spelled the end of his career. . . . Kimmel was not given to dramatics. But such was the depth of his sorrow and despair that he murmured, more to himself than to Curts, "It would have been merciful had it killed me."
Gordon W. Prange, Donald M. Goldstein, and Katherine V. Dillon, *At Dawn We Slept* (1981).

Out here, due process is a bullet.
John Wayne in *The Green Berets* (1968), directed by John Wayne and Ray Kellogg; screenplay by James Lee Barrett, from the novel by Robin Moore.

Cambodia

There is one area, however, immediately above Parrot's Beak, where I have concluded that a combined American and South Vietnamese operation is necessary.

Tonight, American and South Vietnamese units will attack the headquarters for the entire communist military operation in South Vietnam. This key control center has been occupied by the North Vietnamese and Vietcong for five years in blatant violation of Cambodia's neutrality

This is not an invasion of Cambodia. The areas in which these attacks will be launched are completely occupied and controlled by North Vietnamese forces. Our purpose is not to occupy the areas. Once enemy forces are driven out of these sanctuaries and once their military supplies are destroyed, we will withdraw.
President Richard M. Nixon, speech to the nation on the incursion into Cambodia, April 30, 1970.

The President's action in sending troops into Cambodia amounts to a declaration of war against the Senate.
Senator Vance O. Hartke, *Newsweek* (May 11, 1970).

Vietnam is like a bunch of mosquito bites on your arm. And when Nixon went into Cambodia, he scratched them and spread the misery.
Hubert H. Humphrey, *Los Angeles Times* (August 18, 1970).

As we see it there are two possibilities. Either, one, the President didn't understand when he went into Cambodia that he was invading another country; or, two, he did understand. We just don't know which one is scarier.
Thomas Schelling, speaking to Henry Kissinger, quoted in William Shawcross, *Sideshow* (1979).

Next to his rifle, his spoon was his favorite possession. It was U.S.-military issue, made of stainless steel that would last forever without rusting. Khmer Rouge soldiers, who never used forks or knives for eating, always valued the U.S. spoons highly, which was strange considering how much they hated the United States.
Haing Ngor, *A Cambodian Odyssey* (1987).

camouflage

Let every soldier hew him down a bough
And bear't before him: thereby shall we
    shadow
The numbers of our host, and make
    discovery
Err in report of us.
William Shakespeare, *Macbeth*, Act V (1606).

All moved under a cloak of invisibility. Only after the most numerous and severe tests at all distances, with all materials and combinations of colors that give forth no color, could this grey have been discovered. That it was selected to clothe and disguise the German when he fights is typical of the German staff in striving for efficiency to leave nothing to chance, to neglect no detail. . . .
It is a grey green, not the blue grey of our Confederates. It is the grey of the hour just before daybreak, the grey of unpolished steel, of mist among green trees.
Later, as the army passed below my window, under the trees of the Botanical Park, it merged and was lost against the green leaves. It is no exaggeration to say that at a hundred yards you can see the horses on which the Uhlans ride, but you cannot see the men who ride them.
Richard Harding Davis, *News Chronicle* (August 23, 1914).

Remember, God provides the best camouflage several hours out of every 24.
General David M. Shoup quoted in *The New York Herald Tribune* (January 5, 1961).

cannibalism

Between twenty and thirty million persons will die of hunger in Russia. Perhaps it is well that it should be so, for certain nations must be decimated. . . . In the camps for Russian prisoners they have begun to eat each other.
Herman Goering quoted in William L. Shirer, *The Rise and Fall of the Third Reich* (1959).

Naked bodies with gaping wounds in their backs and chests showed where those who still had the strength to use a knife had cut out the kidneys, livers and hearts of their fellow men and eaten them that they themselves might live. Perhaps it can all be summed up in the few croaking words that came from a pitiful pile of rags and bones that lay at my feet: "Look, Englishman, this is German culture."
George Rodger describing the Belsen concentration camp in Germany, *Time* (April 30, 1945).

At the other end of the [German concentration] camp [at Maidanek, Poland] there were enormous mounds of white ashes; but as you looked closer, you found that they were not perfect ashes: for they had among them masses of small human bones: collar bones, finger bones, and bits of skulls. . . . And, beyond these mounds there was a sloping plain on which there grew acres and acres of cabbages. They were large luxuriant cabbages, covered with a layer of white dust. As I heard somebody explaining: "Layer of manure, then layer of ashes, that's the way it was done. . . . These cabbages are all grown on human ashes. . . . The SS-men used to cart most of the ashes to their model farm, some distance away. A well-run farm; the SS-men like to eat these overgrown cabbages, and the prisoners ate these cabbages, too, although they knew that they would almost certainly be turned into cabbages themselves before long . . . ."
Alexander Werth, *Russia at War* (1964).

I believe in compulsory cannibalism. If people were forced to eat what they killed there would be no more war.
Abbie Hoffman, *Revolution for the Hell of It* (1968).

MacArthur's intelligence staff had a file, No. 384, which dealt with Allied war crimes, and which included cases of American and Australian cannibalism. One of his officers told me that whereas Japaneses cases of cannibalism were frequently the result of necessity, at least one of those cases of Allied cannibalism which he had investigated was the result of a dare or a bet.
Phillip Knightley, *The First Casualty* (1975).

They can kill us, but they can't eat us. It's against the law.
Audie Murphy, *To Hell and Back* (1949).

careerism

[Winston] Churchill spotted me from the far end of the table. I had heard before that he was an ardent moviegoer, but I was unprepared for what was to come. He marched the whole length of the dining room and shook me by the hand.
"Young man," he growled, "you did a very fine thing to give up a most promising career to fight for your country."
I was conscious that the great and the near-great in the room had remained standing and were listening with interest.
I stammered some inane reply and Churchill continued with a twinkle, "Mark you, had you not done so, it would have been despicable!"
David Niven, on first meeting Churchill during World War II, *The Moon's a Balloon* (1972).

As a young officer I had cherished a deep respect for the Higher Command, but I was sadly disillusioned about many of them when I came to see them more closely from the angle of a military correspondent. It was saddening to discover how many apparently honorable men would stoop to almost anything to help advance their careers.
B. H. Liddell Hart, *Why Don't We Learn From History?* (1971).

Six months in a combat command was the norm. The idea was to get your "ticket punched" for promotion purposes. As soon as an officer learned something about the 'Nam, it was time to go home. The troops paid the price for green leadership.
Harry Maver, *Strange Ground* (1989).

Throughout the military there are too many officers chasing too few commands. What results is an artificially and unrealistically old group of commanders who shuffle in and out of command billets too rapidly. Command is supposed to be what the career is all about, but it has become a mere adjunct to career advancement—and therefore a place of passage, a place to play safe and make no mistakes. The current system militates towards homogenized mediocrity. That we have any excellent commanders at all—and we do have quite a few—is testimony to the quality of the people who choose this way of life, not to the system that is supposed to support them.

Tom Clancy, "We Need to Restore the Warrior Ethic to Our Navy," *The Washington Post National Weekly* (January 2–8, 1989).

casualties

How are the mighty fallen in the midst of battle.
The Bible, 2 Samuel 1:25.

A man like me cares little about losing the lives of a million men.
Napoleon I quoted in Desmond Seward, *Napoleon and Hitler* (1989).

One Paris night will replace them.
Attributed to Napoleon I, after the Battle of Borodino, September 7, 1812.

Well, thank God, I don't know what it is to lose a battle; but certainly nothing can be more painful than to gain one with the loss of so many of one's friends.
Duke of Wellington, on the Battle of Waterloo, quoted in Elizabeth Longford, *Wellington: The Years of the Sword* (1969).

I begin to regard the death and mangling of a couple thousand men as a small affair, a kind of morning dash—and it may be well that we become so hardened.
General William T. Sherman, June 30, 1864 letter to his wife, Ellen, reprinted in *Home Letters of General Sherman*, ed. M. A. DeWolfe Howe (1909).

The first casualty when war comes is truth.
Senator Hiram Warren Johnson, 1917 speech in the U.S. Senate, quoted in Phillip Knightley, *The First Casualty* (1975).

I proposed to capture the Cote-de-Chatillon by concentrating troops on it, instead of continuing to spread the troops. . . .
The night of October 11th [1918] was wet and black, and I had just completed plans for the attack when Major General Charles P. Summerall, the V Corps commander entered. . . .
"Give me Chatillon, MacArthur," he suddenly said, his voice strained and harsh. "Give me Chatillon, or a list of five thousand casualties." His abruptness startled me.
"All right, General," I assured him, "we'll take it, or my name will head the list."
General Douglas MacArthur, *Reminiscences* (1964). Chatillon was taken with heavy casualties; General MacArthur was in his words "wounded, but not incapacitated."

There are casualties in war who are neither killed nor wounded. A shell kills four men and intimidates a thousand.
René Quinton, *Soldier's Testament* (1930).

The [French] Deuxieme Bureau had a curious mathematical formula for computing enemy losses [in World War I], based on some marvellous racial equation whereby it was assumed that if two Frenchmen had fallen then three casualties had been suffered by the Germans. It was, alas, nearly always the other way about.
Alistair Horne, *The Price of Glory* (1962).

[War] is terrible. But we cannot help its happening. We must take a practical view. It is like the London traffic. We know that so many children will be run over and killed every week. But we cannot stop the traffic because of that. Motor traffic is a part of

civilized life. . . . War is a part of civilized life. We cannot give it up because of its
shocking casualties.
George Bernard Shaw, *Geneva*, Act IV (1938).

World War II probably "saved" over 50,000 American lives because the rationing
of gasoline and the drafting of so many dangerous drivers led to a reduction in traffic
casualties to levels significantly below pre- and postwar ones.
John Mueller, *Retreat from Doomsday* (1989).

At that very moment the survivors of the Italian Eighth Army [in Russia] on the Don
were scurrying for their lives, and when one member of [Italian Foreign Minister]
Ciano's party asked an OKW [German] officer whether the Italians had suffered heavy
losses he was told, "No losses at all: they are running."
William L. Shirer, *The Rise and Fall of the Third Reich* (1959).

One man's life seems mighty important if you're standing next to him. But in a war
of this size whether one man dies, or a hundred, or a thousand, doesn't really make
any difference except to the man who dies and maybe to three or four relatives for a
little while. And they collect his insurance and forget.
William Bradford Huie, *The Americanization of Emily* (1959).

It is a terribly sad business to total up the casualties each day—even in an air war—
and to realize how many youngsters are gone forever. A man must develop a veneer of
callousness that lets him consider such things dispassionately; but he can never escape
a recognition of the fact that back home the news brings anguish and suffering to
families all over the country.
General Dwight D. Eisenhower, letter to his wife, Mamie, April 16, 1944, quoted in *Letters
to Mamie* (1978).

If the Marines had received better cooperation from the Navy our casualties would
have been lower. More naval gunfire would have saved many lives. I had to beg for
gunfire, and I rarely received what the situation called for.
Marine General Holland M. Smith quoted in Bill D. Ross, *Iwo Jima* (1985).

It is, for example, a military maxim, repeated down the ages, that casualties of 30
percent are usually the most a fighting unit can endure without losing combative spirit.
Tarawa, where over 40 percent fell, proved that wasn't true of the Marine Corps.
William Manchester, *Goodbye, Darkness* (1980).

Dear Mrs, Mr, Miss or Mr and Mrs Daneeka:
Words cannot express the deep personal grief I experienced when your husband,
son, father or brother was killed, wounded, or reported missing in action.
Joseph Heller, *Catch-22* (1961). The recipient of this "novel" letter is instructed to strike out
"what does not apply."

cavalry

A horse! a horse! my kingdom for a horse!
William Shakespeare, *Richard III*, Act V (1593).

It is a function of the cavalry to follow up the victory and prevent the beaten army
from rallying.
Napoleon I, *Military Maxims* (1827).

I have just read your dispatches about sore-tongued and fatigued horses. Will you pardon me for asking what the horses of your army have done since the battle of Antietam that fatigues anything?
President Abraham Lincoln, telegram of October 24, 1862 to General George McClellan, quoted in J. G. Nicolay and J. Hay, *Complete Works of Abraham Lincoln*, VIII (1905).

The utility of cavalry has always been doubted.
Ardant du Picq, *Battle Studies* (1868).

The rifle, effective as it is, cannot replace the effect produced by the speed of the horse, the magnetism of the charge, and the terror of cold steel.
Cavalry Training Manual [of Great Britain] (1907) quoted in Geoffrey Blainey, *The Causes of War* (1973).

Cavalry will die a lingering though natural death, but the cavalry idea will certainly not die. It will live on in the form of the motorized trooper, and the mechanized one as well.
J. F. C. Fuller, *Armoured Warfare* (1943).

I've discovered a gap—the cavalry gap. The Russian Army has 3,000 horses and our Army has only 29 and never uses them except for military funerals. We should be on our guard. What if it turns out the Russians are coming by horse?
Senator Eugene McCarthy, *The New York Times* (September 4, 1976).

cavalry charge

The old-fashioned cavalry charge against infantry, already obsolescent, became obsolete in the face of rifles that could knock down horses long before their riders got within saber or pistol range. The Civil War hastened the evolution of dismounted cavalry tactics in which the horse was mainly a means of transportation rather than a weapon in its own right.
James M. McPherson, *Battle Cry of Freedom* (1988).

My idea is that the best model of fighting is to reserve your fire till the enemy get—or you get them—to close quarters. Then deliver one deadly, deliberate fire—and charge!
General Thomas J. "Stonewall" Jackson quoted in G. F. R. Henderson, *Stonewall Jackson and the American Civil War*, I (1926).

Celtic warfare may best be described as a continuum. Not only have people of Celtic culture exhibited an abiding love of combat; they have fought much the same way for more than two thousand years. Consider, for example, the similarities of three climactic battles in Celtic history: Telamon, Culloden, and Gettysburg. In each of these battles Celtic forces used the same tactics with the same results. Boldly they attacked a strongly positioned enemy, who knew what to expect and was prepared to meet the charges. The enemy always had better weapons; in each encounter, superior military technology and defensive tactics overcame Celtic dash and courage. The Celts risked everything on the outcome of their charges and every time they lost not just a battle but a war.
Grady McWhiney and Perry D. Jamieson, *Attack and Die* (1982).

THE MAN: You never saw a cavalry charge, did you?
RAINA: How could I?

THE MAN: Ah, perhaps not. No: of course not! Well, it's a funny sight. It's like slinging a handful of peas against a window pane: first one comes; then two or three close behind him; and then all the rest in a lump.
George Bernard Shaw, *Arms and the Man*, Act I (1894).

I had got amongst the first of them, and was shooting (with a pistol, of course, for only an expert rider can use a rifle at the gallop), when suddenly my camel tripped and went down emptily on its face. I was torn completely from the saddle, and went sailing grandly through the air for a considerable distance, landing with a crash that seemed to beat all the life and feeling out of me. I just lay there passively, waiting for the Turks to kill me. . . . However . . . no Turks came to me. . . . So I sat up and saw the battle over, and our men driving together and cutting down the last broken remnants of the enemy. Behind me was my camel's body . . . and in the back of its skull was the heavy bullet of the fifth shot I had fired!
Colonel Thomas E. Lawrence, "A Camel Charge. . .," *The World's Work* (September 1921).

In one respect a cavalry charge is very like ordinary life. So long as you are all right, firmly in your saddle, your horse in hand, and well armed, lots of enemies will give you a wide berth. But as soon as you have lost a stirrup, have a rein cut, have dropped your weapon, are wounded, or your horse is wounded, then is the moment when from all quarters enemies rush upon you.
Winston Churchill, *My Early Life* (1930).

censorship

The official censors pretty well succeeded in putting over the legend that the war was won without a single mistake by a command consisting exclusively of geniuses.
Fletcher Pratt, "How the Censors Rigged the News," *Harper's* (February 1946).

General Ike has had a standing rule that censors must strike any quotations of Patton. The correspondents with the Third Army and elsewhere understand this rule and co-operate. They are permitted to write about Patton, but he is protected from his own flamboyant and sometimes hasty words.
Captain Harry C. Butcher, writing on September 7, 1944, *My Three Years With Eisenhower* (1946).

[During World War II] mail from the U. K. to America passed through Bermuda where it was censored by masses of WRENS, the women's division of the Royal Navy. . . . Niv [David Niven] wrote me an *eight*-page letter—all crowded in a small but clear hand. The missive described in hilarious detail a surprisingly uninhibited amorous adventure he had recently experienced in a car, at night, in blacked-out London, during a heavy bombing raid, with a mutual female acquaintance of ours. Niv left nothing out. Every detail of every moment of their mutual lechery was carefully noted. But the primary and naughty fun of the letter was in contemplating the reactions of all those giggling blue-jacketed WRENS in Bermuda gathering around to read along a letter from Major David Niven in England to his friend Doug Fairbanks, in Hollywood, and splitting their sides with laughter—or *shock*!
I read on. After omitting absolutely nothing, Niv ended his report by writing, ". . . and at that precise moment a large bomb dropped in . . ." and some dear, sweet WREN, anxious to deny the enemy any knowledge of the Luftwaffe's accuracy, had carefully cut out where the bomb had dropped!
Douglas Fairbanks, Jr., *The Salad Days* (1988).

[War] correspondents had no quarrel with censors. They had a tough job. They didn't know what might be brought up against them. No one could discipline them for

eliminating, and so in self-preservation they eliminated pretty deeply. Navy censors were particularly sensitive to names of places, whether they had any military importance or not. It was the safest way. Once when I felt a little bruised by censorship I sent through Herodotus' account of the battle of Salamis fought between the Greeks and Persians in 480 B.C., and since there were place names involved, albeit classical ones, the Navy censors killed the whole story.
John Steinbeck, *Once There Was a War* (1958).

A recent letter of mine . . . was cut to pieces by the censor. Sometimes I think all staff officers are without brains. I've never written a personal letter that could possibly violate some censorship. . . . I lean over backward to avoid violations in that regard. The d——fool censor should know that (if I so chose) I could send all my letters to the W.D. [War Department] for transmission, because I, not the censors, carry the responsibility for the safety of this command.
General Dwight D. Eisenhower, letter to his wife, Mamie, April 6, 1943, quoted in *Letters to Mamie* (1978).

I am convinced that without censorship—and with unlimited television—we would have lost World War II. There is nothing that looks quite like blood on color television. You can't have scenes of American bodies, thrown into trucks like so much cordwood, served up with dinner night after night after night and expect the American people to support the situation.
George Jacobson, *Newsweek* (April 15, 1985).

In the evenings junior officers took turns doing the dreariest of squadron jobs—censoring the letters that the enlisted men wrote. Most of the men were not very literate, and their letters home were composed of clumsy expressions of affection and preposterous lies about their military exploits. . . .
Sometimes their amorous feelings for their wives and sweethearts were expressed with a forthrightness that seemed pornographic to middle-class young men like us. We'd be sitting in the tent, each with a pile of letters to be censored, and someone would begin to laugh: "Hey, listen to this guy," and he'd read out some mechanic's fancy, addressed to his wife, of what he'd do to and with her when he got home. It was funny, and it was astonishing, that there were marriages in the world in which a man said *cunt* to his wife, and in which sexual relations were apparently conducted with such violent and inventive enthusiasm. Men like that mechanic made censoring an endurable and sometimes an educational activity.
Samuel Hynes, *Flights of Passage: Reflections of a World War II Aviator* (1988).

Vietnam was the first war ever fought without any censorship. Without censorship, things can get terribly confused in the public mind.
General William C. Westmoreland, *Time* (April 5, 1982).

chaplains

Ike is worrying about the weather for D-Day [in North Africa]. He wrote to Patton today, "I am searching the Army to find the most capable chaplain to assure a fairly decent break in the weather when the big day comes."
Captain Harry C. Butcher, *My Three Years With Eisenhower* (1946).

[General Montgomery insisted that] *everyone* must be imbued with the burning desire to "kill Germans". "Even the padres—one per weekday and two on Sundays!"
General F. de Guingand, *Operation Victory* (1947).

A chaplain visits our company. In a tired voice, he prays for the strength of our arms and for the souls of the men who are to die. We do not consider his denomination. Helmets come off. Catholics, Jews, and Protestants bow their heads and finger their weapons. It is front-line religion: God and the Garand.
Audie Murphy, *To Hell and Back* (1949).

It's a small war, God but it's the only one we've got.
An anonymous sign over a chaplain's bunker in Vietnam, 1967, quoted in Charles Anderson, *The Grunts* (1976).

Their task is to reassure the military flock that since God is on their side, the Sixth Commandment can be waived for the duration. How they reconcile this with the knowledge that enemy soldiers are in all probability receiving identical advice from their chaplains remains one of the mysteries of the ecclesiastical mind.
Norman F. Dixon, *The Psychology of Military Incompetence* (1976).

chemical warfare

The mines [tunnels] were met by countermines, in which the besieged opposed the enemy with arms or other means, one of which was to fill barrels with feathers, which they placed in the mines and set fire to them, so that the stench and smoke might impede the entrance of the enemy.
Niccolò Machiavelli, *The Discourse* (1517).

The smoke shell appeared in 1681, but was never extensively used. Similarly, a form of gas projectile, called a "stink shell," was invented by a Confederate officer during the Civil War. Because of its "inhumanity," and probably because it was not thought valuable enough to offset its propaganda value to the enemy, it was not popular. These were the beginnings of the modern chemical shells.
Albert Manucy, *Artillery Through the Ages* (1949).

The effects of the successful gas attack were horrible. I am not pleased with the idea of poisoning men. Of course the entire world will rage about it first, then imitate us [the Germans].
Rudolph Binding, *A Fatalist at War* (1915).

Lenin was sent into Russia by the Germans in the same way that you might send a phial containing a culture of typhoid or of cholera to be poured into the water supply of a great city, and it worked with amazing accuracy.
Winston Churchill, speech in the House of Commons, November 5, 1919. He was referring to the fact that the Germans allowed V. I. Lenin during the midst of World War I to travel to Russia from Switzerland in a sealed train.

A man in a gas mask is only half a soldier, if that. In a vesicant-proof suit of clothing he is worse off still, for he is three-quarters a diver and, consequently, no soldier at all.
J. F. C. Fuller, *Armoured Warfare* (1943).

At this stage of the war, any German invasion [of Britain]—seaborne or airborne—would have been cut to pieces. British experiments with setting the sea ablaze were fearsome, and Bomber Command were secretly training their squadrons in the use of poison gas. A cover story about spraying beaches to destroy vermin had been prepared for release should the Germans object to this form of warfare.
Len Deighton, *Fighter* (1978). According to William L. Shirer, *The Rise and Fall of the Third Reich* (1959), "The British had decided . . . as a last resort and if all other conventional methods of defense failed, to attack the German beachheads with mustard gas, sprayed from low-flying airplanes."

It may be several weeks or even months before I shall ask you to drench Germany with poison gas, and if we do it, let us do it one hundred percent. In the meanwhile, I want the matter studied in cold blood by sensible people and not by that particular set of psalm-singing uniformed defeatists which one runs across now here and there.
Winston Churchill, World War II memorandum, July 6, 1944, quoted in Joel Kovel, *Against the State of Nuclear Terror* (1983).

I do not think it is worse to be killed by a chemical agent than it is to be killed by a bit of shrapnel or by a bomb.
Representative Samuel S. Stratton, speech in the House of Representatives, October 3, 1969.

Soviet interest in chemical weapons is steeped in an assumption in Soviet military doctrine that, in a "decisive" clash between socialist and capitalist systems, the "logic of war" may inveigh against any restraints on the use of available weapons.
John Erickson, *Los Angeles Times* (August 2, 1981).

Chemical weapons (mustard gas and nerve gases) are low-tech, cheap to make and created by some of the same sorts of factories that turn common chemicals into pesticides, pharmaceuticals and fertilizers. To over-simplify only slightly, production can shift from one to the other almost like a soft drink fountain dispenser switches from cherry to orange soda.
John G. Kester, "Chemical Weapons, Cloudy Thinking," *The New York Times* (January 13, 1989).

If Iraq or Iran or any other state is suddenly in a position to produce chemical weapons, the raw materials and facilities were obtained from industrial countries. Europe is the main source. For Europe to be outraged and shed crocodile tears is pure hypocrisy.
Tariq Aziz, Foreign Minister of Iraq, quoted in *U.S. News & World Report* (January 16, 1989).

Churchill, Sir Winston (1874–1965)

Winston is back.
September 3, 1939 signal from the Admiralty to all ships and stations announcing that Winston Churchill, who was First Lord of the Admiralty at the beginning of World War I, had returned to that position.

The Prime Minister wins debate after debate and loses battle after battle. The country is beginning to say that he fights debates like a war and a war like a debate.
Aneurin Bevan, criticism of Winston Churchill in the House of Commons, July 2, 1942.

At the time of the Dunkirk evacuation, when Churchill made his often-quoted fighting speech, it was rumored that what he actually said, when recording the speech for broadcasting, was: "We will fight on the beaches, we will fight in the streets. . . . We'll throw bottles at the b——s [bastards], it's about all we've got left"—but, of course the BBC's switch-censor pressed his thumb on the key at the right moment. One may assume that this story is untrue, but at the time it was felt that it ought to be true.
George Orwell, *New Leader* (May 14, 1949).

He [Winston Churchill] asked me what I would drink at dinner and I replied—water. This astonished him. I added that I neither drank nor smoked and was 100 percent fit; he replied in a flash that he both drank and smoked and was 200 percent fit.
Field Marshal B. L. Montgomery, *Memoirs* (1958).

In the dark days and darker nights when England stood alone—and most men save Englishmen despaired of England's life—he mobilized the English language and sent it into battle. The incandescent quality of his words illuminated the courage of his countrymen.
President John F. Kennedy, speech conferring honorary citizenship on Winston Churchill, April 9, 1963.

He is not a man for whom I ever had esteem. Always in the wrong, always surrounded by crooks, a most unsuccessful father—simply a "Radio Personality" who outlived his prime. "Rallied the nation" indeed! I was a serving soldier in 1940. How we despised his oration.
Evelyn Waugh, letter to Ann Fleming, January 27, 1965, quoted in Nat Shapiro, *Whatever It Is, I'm Against It* (1984).

Churchill wrote his own speeches. When a leader does that, he becomes emotionally invested with his utterances. . . . If Churchill had had a speech writer in 1940, Britain would be speaking German today.
James C. Humes, *The New York Times* (June 15, 1986).

England was at war . . . and millions whose knowledge of Churchillian speeches had been confined to published versions heard his rich voice, resonant with urgency, dramatically heightened by his tempo, pauses, and crashing consonants, which, one listener wrote, actually made his radio vibrate. Churchill had been a name in the newspapers, but even his own columns lacked the power of his delivery. He found precisely the right words for convictions his audiences shared but had been unable to express. He spoke of "thoughtless dilettanti of purblind wordings who sometimes ask us: 'What is it that Britain and France are fighting for?' To this I answer: 'If we left off fighting you would soon find out.' " His elaborate metaphors, simplistic but effective, fortified his argument, and were often witty: "A baboon in a forest is a matter of legitimate speculation; a baboon in a zoo is an object of public curiosity; but a baboon in your wife's bed is a cause of the gravest concern."
William Manchester, *The Last Lion*, II (1988).

civil defense

In the paint shop at the London Zoo there was a sign ready to be nailed to a tree. The sign was both a directive and a wry commentary on the Europe of 1939. It bore a large black arrow, and the caption read: "To Air Raid Shelter In Monkey House."
Edward W. Beattie, Jr., *Freely to Pass* (1942).

They [the Soviets] believe their civil-defense system would allow them to get away with "only" about 13 million casualties [in a nuclear war]—5 per cent of their population—fewer than they suffered in World War II.
General Edward L. Rowny, *Time* (August 31, 1981).

What kind of civil-defense program is going to protect you against 6,000 nuclear warheads? It depends upon whether you want to die in the field or die in a hole. Would you rather be roasted or boiled? It doesn't make any real difference. There *is* no civil defense against the number of warheads that we and the Soviet Union have deployed against one another.
Paul C. Warnke, *Los Angeles Times* (September 29, 1981).

Dig a hole, cover it with a couple of doors and then throw three feet of dirt on top ... it's the dirt that does it ... you know, dirt is just great stuff ... if there are enough shovels to go around, everybody's going to make it.
Thomas K. Jones as a Deputy Undersecretary of Defense in the Reagan Administration advised the above measures in the event of nuclear war according to Robert Scheer in his *With Enough Shovels: Reagan, Bush, and Nuclear War* (1982).

civilian control

The subordination of the political point of view to the military would be contrary to common sense, for policy has declared the war; it is the intelligent faculty. War is only the instrument, and not the reverse. The subordination of the military point of view to the political is, therefore, the only thing which is possible.
Karl von Clausewitz, *On War* (1832).

From Caesar to Cromwell, and from Cromwell to Napoleon ... history presents the same solemn warning—beware of elevating to the highest civil trust the commander of your victorious armies.
President James Buchanan, speech at Greensburg, Pennsylvania, October 7, 1852.

It is my conviction that the necessary and wise subordination of the military to civil power will be best sustained, and our people will have greater confidence that it is so sustained, when lifelong professional soldiers, in the absence of some obvious and overriding reasons, abstain from seeking high political office.
General Dwight D. Eisenhower, 1948 letter, quoted in Harry S. Truman, *Memoirs*, II (1956).

I find in existence a new and heretofore unknown and dangerous concept that the members of the Armed Forces owe their primary allegiance and loyalty to those who temporarily exercise the authority of the executive branch of the government, rather than to the country and its Constitution they are sworn to defend.
No proposition could be more dangerous. None could cast greater doubt on the integrity of the Armed Forces.
General Douglas MacArthur, speech to the Massachusetts state legislature in Boston, July 25, 1951, quoted in D. Clayton James, *The Years of MacArthur*, III (1985). James called this statement an "affront to the officer's code" and observed that MacArthur lost considerable political support after this questioning of civilian supremacy over the U.S. armed forces.

I was at the White House that night to hear [President Nixon's] resignation speech, and what impressed me more than anything else was that while one leader of our country was resigning and another was taking his place, I did not see one tank or one helmeted soldier in the street and the only uniforms I saw that night were two motor-cycle policemen who were directing traffic on Pennsylvania Avenue.
Art Buchwald, delivering the commencement address at Vassar College, *The New York Times* (June 8, 1975).

In a news conference, Defense Secretary Weinberger defended the news blackout [during the invasion of Grenada] as necessary for the safety of newsmen, saying they might have been harmed in the action. The same tactic applied to World War II would have seen Ernie Pyle writing the story of GI Joe from the E ring [of the Pentagon] briefing room. Weinberger also said the censorship was the decision of the military commander of the invasion, whose authority Weinberger said he would never think of countermanding. So much for the constitutional dictate that the civilian chief executive control the American military.
James Coates and Michael Kilian, *Heavy Losses* (1985).

civil war

There is nothing unhappier than a civil war, for the conquered are destroyed by, and the conquerors destroy, their friends.
Dionysius of Halicarnassus, *Roman Antiquities* (1st century B.C.).

A foreign war is a scratch on the arm; a civil war is an ulcer which devours the vitals of a nation.
Victor Hugo, *Ninety-Three* (1879).

"I gather it's between the Reds and the Blacks."
"Yes, but it's not quite as easy as that. You see, they are all Negroes. And the Fascists won't be called black because of their racial pride so they are called White after the White Russians. And the Bolshevists *want* to be called black because of their racial pride. So when you *say* black you mean red, and when you *mean* red you say white and when the party who call themselves blacks say traitors they mean what *we* call blacks, but what *we* mean when *we* say traitors I really couldn't tell.... But, of course, it's really a war between Russia and Germany and Italy and Japan who are all against one another on the patriotic side. I hope I make myself plain?"
Evelyn Waugh, *Scoop* (1938).

In a civil war, a general must know—and I'm afraid it's a thing rather of instinct than of practice—he must know exactly when to move over to the other side.
Henry Reed, *Not a Drum Was Heard: The War Memoirs of General Gland*, BBC radio play (1959).

English Civil War

The people in general were so ignorant of their duty, as that not one perhaps of ten thousand knew what right any man had to command him, or what necessity there was of King or Commonwealth, for which he was to part with his money against his will; but thought himself to be so much master of whatsoever he possessed, that it could not be taken from him upon any pretence of common safety without his own consent.
Thomas Hobbes, *Behemoth: The History of the Causes of the Civil Wars of England* (1662).

If we beat the King 99 times, he would be King still and his posterity, and we subjects still but if he beat us but once we should be hanged and our posterity undone.
Edward M. (2nd Earl of) Manchester quoted by John Bruce in the preface to *The Quarrel between the Earl of Manchester and Oliver Cromwell* (1875).

There was certainly no difference in the clothing of the various commanders, and the pictorially traditional lacy splendor of the Cavalier as opposed to the puritan severity of the Roundhead Commander has no basis in historical fact. On both sides, officers could be distinguished simply by the ornate nature of their dress, having no particular badge of rank to mark them out.
Antonia Fraser, *Cromwell* (1973).

Spanish Civil War

"People of democratic Spain, people who are fighting for the liberty and rights of man!"—thundered the voice of Pasionaria, "the whole Spanish people—socialists, communists, anarchists alike—have taken up arms against the fascist revolt. Fascism shall not pass!
"Better to die standing, than live kneeling!"
Dolores Ibarruri, speech in Paris, September 3, 1936. Reprinted in her *Speeches and Articles* (1938).

When the war in Spain is over, I shall have to find something else: the Italian character has to be formed through fighting.
Benito Mussolini quoted in Paolo Monelli, *Mussolini: An Intimate Life* (1953).

Fire—without hatred.
Antonio Rivera, ordering his forces to fire on fellow Spaniards, quoted in Cecil D. Eby, *The Siege of the Alcazar* (1965).

Who could have foreseen that Franco's victory in the Civil War, deplored by most English and French writers, would result in his denying Hitler control of the Mediterranean and thus assuring an Allied victory?
Robert Graves quoted in C. Woolf and J. Bagguley, *Authors Take Sides on Vietnam* (1967).

U.S. Civil War

There they are cutting each other's throats, because one half of them prefer hiring their servants for life, and the other by the hour.
Attributed to Thomas Carlyle, nineteenth-century British historian.

A house divided against itself cannot stand. I believe this government cannot endure, permanently half slave and half free. I do not expect the Union to be dissolved—I do not expect the house to fall—but I do expect it will cease to be divided. It will become all one thing, or all the other.
Abraham Lincoln, speech in Springfield, Illinois, June 16, 1858, *The Collected Works of Abraham Lincoln*, ed. P. Basler, 2 (1953).

In *your* hands, my dissatisfied fellow countrymen, and not in *mine*, is the momentous issue of civil war. The government will not assail *you*. You can have no conflict, without being yourselves the aggressors. *You* have no oath registered in heaven to destroy the government, while I shall have the most solemn one to "preserve, protect, and defend" it.
I am loath to close. We are not enemies, but friends. We must not be enemies. Though passion may have strained, it must not break, our bonds of affection. The mystic chords of memory, stretching from every battlefield, and patriot grave, to every living heart and hearthstone, all over this broad land, will yet swell the chorus of the Union, when again touched, as surely they will be, by the better angels of our nature.
President Abraham Lincoln, first Inaugural Address, March 4, 1861.

I must say that I am one of those dull creatures that cannot see the good of secession.
Colonel Robert E. Lee, speaking on April 19, 1861, quoted in John S. Mosby, *War Reminiscences* (1887); Burke Davis, *Gray Fox* (1956).

Let us determine to die here, and we will conquer. There is [General Thomas J.] Jackson standing like a stone wall. Rally behind the Virginians.
Confederate General Bernard E. Bee at the first Battle of Bull Run, July 21, 1861. Thereafter General Jackson was known as "Stonewall." However, some historians contend that Bee (who was killed in the battle) was being sarcastic and critical when he said Jackson was "standing like a stone wall," meaning that he was not advancing and maneuvering. See Douglas Southall Freeman, *Lee's Lieutenants: A Study in Command*, I (1943).

"I am informed," said Major Carey, "that three Negroes belonging to Colonel Mallory have escaped within your lines. I am Colonel Mallory's agent and have charge of his property. What do you mean to do with those Negroes?"
"I intend to hold them," said I.
"Do you mean, then, to set aside your constitutional obligation to return them?"

"I mean to take Virginia at her word, as declared in the ordinance of secession passed yesterday. I am under no constitutional obligations to a foreign country, which Virginia now claims to be."

"But you say we cannot secede," he answered, "and so you cannot consistently detain the Negroes."

"But you say you have seceded, so you cannot consistently claim them. I shall hold these Negroes as contraband of the war, since they are engaged in the construction of your battery and are claimed as your property."

General Benjamin F. Butler, *Butler's Book: Autobiography* (1892). This 1861 incident is the origin of the use of the phrase "contraband of war" to mean former slaves now free within the union lines.

My paramount object in this struggle is to save the Union, and is not either to save or destroy slavery. If I could save the Union without freeing any slave, I would do it; and if I could do it by freeing all the slaves, I would do it; and if I could save it by freeing some and leaving others alone, I would also do that.

President Abraham Lincoln, August 22, 1862 letter to Horace Greeley, editor of the New York *Tribune*, reprinted in *Complete Works*, VIII, eds. J. Nicolay and J. Hay (1894).

So you're the little woman who wrote the book that made this great war!

President Abraham Lincoln, upon meeting Harriet Beecher Stowe, the author of *Uncle Tom's Cabin* (1852), during the Civil War, quoted in Carl Sandberg, *Abraham Lincoln: The War Years* (1939).

That on the 1st day of January, in the year of our Lord 1863, all persons held as slaves within any state or designated part of a state, the people whereof shall then be in rebellion against the United States, shall be then, thenceforward, and forever free; and the executive government of the United States, including the military and naval authority thereof, will recognize and maintain the freedom of such persons and will do no act or acts to repress such persons, or any of them, in any efforts they may make for their actual freedom.

President Abraham Lincoln, The Emancipation Proclamation, September 22, 1862.

If the people raise a howl against my barbarity and cruelty, I will answer that war is war, and not popularity-seeking. If they want peace they and their relatives must stop the war.

General William T. Sherman, letter of September 4, 1864 to General Henry Halleck, quoted in *Personal Memoirs* (1875).

With malice toward none; with charity for all; with firmness in the right, as God gives us to see the right, let us strive on to finish the work we are in; to bind up the nation's wounds; to care for him who shall have borne the battle, and for his widow, and his orphan—to do all which may achieve and cherish a just, and a lasting peace, among ourselves, and with all nations.

President Abraham Lincoln, second Inaugural Address, March 4, 1865.

To the Fifty-fourth Regiment of Massachusetts Infantry:

The white officers, taking life and honor in their hands, cast in their lot with men of a despised race unproved in war, and risked death as inciters of servile insurrection if taken prisoners, besides encountering all the common perils of camp, march and battle.

The black rank and file volunteered when disaster clouded the Union cause, served without pay for eighteen months till given that of white troops, faced threatened enslavement if captured, were brave in action, patient under heavy and dangerous labors, and cheerful amid hardships and privations.

Together they gave to the nation and the world undying proof that Americans of African descent possess the pride, courage, and devotion of the patriot soldier. One hundred and eighty thousand such Americans enlisted under the Union flag in 1863–1865.
Charles William Eliot, inscription on Robert Gould Shaw Memorial, Boston Common (1897).

There must be more historians of the Civil War than there were generals fighting in it. . . . Of the two groups, the historians are the more belligerent.
David Donald, *Lincoln Reconsidered* (1961).

Before 1861 the two words "United States" were generally rendered as a plural noun: the United States *are* a republic." The war marked a transition of the United States to a singular noun.
James M. McPherson, *Battle Cry of Freedom* (1988).

classified information

"Secret" and "confidential" are the most abused words in the official vocabulary, the refuge of the clerkly-minded staff officer whose sense of discrimination has long since been submerged by his sense of regulations, and this very abuse of the words defeats its own end, for when minutes relating to a change of soldiers' underwear are labelled "secret" it is little wonder that the word becomes meaningless in use.
B. H. Liddell Hart, *Thoughts on War* (1944).

I believe we have classified too much. Secrecy is a measure that hurts our opponents a little and us a great deal. . . . In nuclear weapons, where we had the greatest of secrecy, the Soviets are now ahead of us. In electronics, where we had very little government secrecy, we are way ahead of others, particularly the Soviets. It looks like an absurdity, but who is ahead depends not only on what they learn from us but on the speed of our own development.
Edward Teller, *Los Angeles Times* (April 10, 1985).

The ultimate in U.S. military security absurdity occurred in 1987, when the U.S. Air Force asked its civilian employees with security clearances to sign an agreement calling on them not to discuss or publish classified information *and information that could be classified in the future.* Thus to the concept of "classified" information was added the bizarre idea of "classifiable" information—ordinary data that someday might undergo a transformation into secret data.
Thomas B. Allen and Norman Polmar, *Merchants of Treason* (1988).

code names

Operations in which large numbers of men may lose their lives ought not to be described by code-words which imply a boastful and overconfident sentiment, such as "Triumphant," or conversely, which are calculated to invest the plan with an air of despondency, such as "Woebetide", "Massacre", "Jumble", "Trouble", "Fidget", "Flimsy", "Pathetic", "Jaundice". . . .
After all, the world is wide, and intelligent thought will readily supply an unlimited number of well-sounding names which do not suggest the character of the operation or disparage it in any way and do not enable some widow or mother to say that her son was killed in an operation called "Bunnyhug" or "Ballyhoo."
Winston Churchill, August 8, 1943 note to General Ismay, reprinted in *The Second World War: Closing the Ring* (1951).

Since recently assuming command of ISBELL this Commanding Officer has been concerned over the anemic connotation of the present voice radio call. When in company with such stalwarts as "FIREBALL," "VIPER," and others, it is somewhat embarrassing and completely out of keeping with the quality of the sailormen aboard to be identified by the relatively ignominious title "SAPWORTH."

In order that ISBELL may carry on in the "31 knot Burke" tradition and proudly identify herself to all and sundry consorts, it is requested that our voice call be changed to "HELLCAT," which call is currently unassigned. . . .

Elmo R. Zumwalt, as Captain of the destroyer *Arnold J. Isbell*, writing to the chief of Naval Operations on October 26, 1955, quoted in Elmo R. Zumwalt, Jr., *On Watch* (1976).

The much vaunted German Intelligence Service regularly called England Golfplatz, and the United States Samland or sometimes Farmland. Even the High Command could not have been more helpful than to use Sealion for the invasion of England. . . . Sometimes the code-names were more obscure, but even then the Germans remained helpful. A code-name used on one service. . . . would occur in a signal . . . to another service. The latter would send a signal saying that they could not understand. "What does so-and-so mean?" And they (and we!) would get the reply, "It means such and such." We regretted that we could not send them our thanks!

Ewen Montagu, *Beyond Top Secret Ultra* (1977).

combat

Each [Roman] soldier daily throws all his energy into his drill, as though he were in action. . . . Indeed it would not be wrong to describe their maneuvers as bloodless combats and their combats as sanguinary maneuvers.

Flavius Josephus, *History of the Jewish War* (1st century B.C.).

Combat is the only effective force in war; its aim is to destroy the enemy's forces as a means to a further end. That holds good even if no actual fighting occurs, because the outcome rests on the assumption that if it came to fighting, the enemy would be destroyed.

Karl von Clausewitz, *On War* (1832).

A force engaged is out of the hand of its commander.

Ardant du Picq, *Battle Studies* (1868).

The psychic isolation of major commanders on both sides [in World War I] from the realities of combat became proverbial. The emotional breakdown of the British Expeditionary Forces' chief of staff [General Sir Launcelot Kiggell], on his first visit to the swampy charnel-house of the Passchendaele front in late 1917, is often quoted: "My God, did we really send men to fight in that?" as is the reply of his escort: "Oh sir, it's much worse further up."

Roger Beaumont, *The Nerves of War* (1986); also told in Paul Fussell, *The Great War in Modern Memory* (1975).

He had more combat with his superiors than he did with the enemy.

Isadore Feldman, speaking of Norman Mailer as an enlisted man in World War II, quoted in Peter Manso, *Mailer* (1985).

There is no such thing as "getting used to combat." . . . Each moment of combat imposes a strain so great that men will break down in direct relation to the intensity and duration of their exposure.

J. W. Appel and G. W. Beebe, "Preventative Psychiatry," *Journal of the American Medical Association*, 131 (1946).

Combat is not John Wayne.
Lieutenant William L. Calley, Jr., *The Washington Post* (January 9, 1971).

In soldiers who have been in battle over a sustained period it is the jaws that one notices first of all: they have been clenched for hours, and when they eventually relax mouths droop open, giving men an almost idiot appearance.
Tim Carew, *The Longest Retreat* (1972).

Our defenses today are good . . . . The Air Force, for instance, has very few people in any responsible position who haven't been in combat. This is a tremendous asset.
General George S. Brown, U.S. Air Force Chief of Staff, *U.S. News and World Report* (February 25, 1974).

What overcomes instinct to make combat possible are just those intangible qualities that armies seek to cultivate by parade-ground drills . . . by speeches, songs, and flags (to inspire pride), by uniforms and daily routines, by punishments and rewards: individual morale, group discipline, and unit cohesion. Of these decisively important but unmeasurable attributes, small-unit cohesion is usually the most important, because the willingness of men to fight for the sake of one another survives the terrible impact of battle far better than any other individual source of morale.
Edward N. Luttwak, *Strategy* (1987).

We have a military force to *deter* war. When we're successful, we aren't going to have any combat leaders.
Admiral Frank B. Kelso, II, *All Hands* [magazine] (August 1987).

No one talked about anything to do with combat. You just did your job. You went back to the rear—drank a little whiskey, partied and went back to the front. Any time you got back you just tried to forget about everything. . . . If someone got killed, you didn't talk about it. You didn't even mention the name anymore. If you did, maybe you wouldn't make it. . . . You had to wipe things out of your mind to keep your sanity.
Randy Herrod quoted in Ben Bradlee, Jr., *Guts and Glory* (1988).

Something starts to build up as you experience success in close-in fighting. You see you're achieving success, and you realize you can't stop—you're out in the open, you have to keep going. If there's such a thing as what people call a lust for blood, this momentum is perhaps as close as I can come to describing it.
Colonel Wesley B. Taylor, Jr., quoted in Ivan Prashker, *Duty, Honor, Vietnam* (1988).

combat efficiency

A proper measure of democracy should be put into effect in the army, chiefly by abolishing the feudal practice of bullying and beating and by having officers and men share weal and woe. Once this is done, unity will be achieved between officers and men, the combat effectiveness of the army will be greatly increased.
Mao Tse-tung, *On a Prolonged War* (1938).

We're not doing too badly. We've only lost about a quarter of the Empire.
General Alan Brooke's assessment of the British war effort at the end of 1941, quoted in David Fraser, *Alanbrooke* (1982). A different assessment was provided by Ian Morrison in *This War Against Japan* (1943). He argued, "If the British ran the rest of their Empire as they had run things recently in Singapore, then they did not deserve to have an empire at all."

Casualties many; percentage dead not known; combat efficiency: We are winning.
Colonel David M. Shoup, situation report from Betio Island, November 21, 1943, quoted in James R. Stockman, *The Battle for Tarawa* (1947).

As a perceptive admiral once put it: "There is nothing more useless than doing something with great efficiency that should not be done at all."
Senator Walter F. Mondale, speech in the Senate, September 12, 1969.

The proportion of service to combat formations ... is frequently cited as a rough indicator of an army's efficiency—a low proportion representing a high efficiency.... To work out this ratio with its thousands of component parts in theory, however, is an almost impossible task, involving as it does a model of tremendous complexity, worthy of a battery of computers presided over by a mathematical prodigy. Moreover, when all the calculations have been done, and the preparations made on the basis of them completed, there is always a strong possibility that a fresh strategic or political requirement will render them worthless.
Martin Van Creveld, *Supplying War* (1977).

When one assesses the actual record of war, not from official accounts but rather from those who were there, it becomes quite clear that battles are won not by perfection but rather by the supremacy of forces that are 5 percent effective over forces that are 2 percent effective.
Edward N. Luttwak, *The Pentagon and the Art of War* (1985).

combined operations

Of the three arms—cavalry, infantry, and artillery—none must be despised. All three are equally important.
Napoleon I quoted in J. C. Herold, *The Mind of Napoleon* (1955).

It is not so much the mode of formation as the proper combined use of the different arms which will insure victory.
General Antoine Henri Jomini, *Summary of the Art of War* (1838).

When circumstances made it worthwhile, there could be combined operations. An old cannoneer recalled one stratagem: "Artillerymen, who had tender consciences (and no muskets), seldom if ever shot stray pigs, but they did sometimes, as an act of friendship, wholly disinterested, point out to the infantry a pig which seemed to need shooting, and by way of dividing the danger and responsibility of the act, accept privately a choice part of the deceased."
Robert G. Tanner, *Stonewall in the Valley* (1976).

Ground, air, and sea operations were thoroughly coordinated. It was a new type of campaign—three-dimensional warfare—the triphibious concept.
General Douglas MacArthur speaking of his World War II tactics in the Pacific in his *Reminiscences* (1964).

The Russians are real believers in this combined-arms stuff. When they come at you, they come with the whole inventory.
Tom Clancy, *Red Storm Rising* (1986).

command

The man who commands efficiently must have obeyed others in the past, and the man who obeys dutifully is worthy of being some day a commander.
Marcus Tullius Cicero, *De Legibus* (52 B.C.).

A prince should therefore have no other aim or thought, nor take up any other thing for his study, but war and its organization and discipline, for that is the only art that is necessary to one who commands, and it is of such virtue that it not only maintains

those who are born princes, but often enables men of private fortune to attain to that rank.
Niccolò Machiavelli, *The Prince* (1513).

Those he commands move only in command,
Nothing in love: now does he feel his title
Hang loose about him, like a giant's robe
Upon a dwarfish thief.
William Shakespeare, *Macbeth*, Act V (1606).

If you command wisely, you'll be obeyed cheerfully.
Thomas Fuller, *Gnomologia* (1732).

Be easy and condescending in your deportment to your officers, but not too familiar, lest you subject yourself to a want of that respect, which is necessary to support a proper command.
General George Washington, letter of November 10, 1775 to Colonel William Woodford, reprinted in J. C. Fitzpatrick, ed., *The Writings of George Washington*, IV (1931–44).

To be at the head of a strong column of troops, in the execution of some task that requires brain, is the highest pleasure of war.
General William T. Sherman, *Personal Memoirs*, II (1875).

The only prize much cared for by the powerful is power. The prize of the general is not a bigger tent, but command.
Oliver Wendell Holmes, Jr., February 15, 1913 speech at Harvard Law School, reprinted in J. D. Howe, ed., *The Occasional Speeches of Justice Oliver Wendell Holmes* (1962).

Whenever a General was offered an inferior command and refused it, he did very wrong. You should always accept the command offered to you when it is an active one. I would have taken over any command, however small, without hesitation. And I would have commanded it in such a way that I should soon have been given a more important one.
Marshal Ferdinand Foch quoted in Raymond Recouly, *Marshal Foch* (1929).

It happens too often in war that those who command cannot see and that those who can see do not command.
René Quinton, *Soldier's Testament* (1930).

Bob, I'm putting you in command at Buna. Relieve Harding ... [and] all officers who won't fight. . . . If necessary put sergeants in charge of battalions and corporals in charge of companies—anyone who will fight. Time is of the essence. . . . I want you to take Buna, or not come back alive.
General Douglas MacArthur's oral orders to General Robert L. Eichelberger, November 29, 1942, recalled by Eichelberger in Jay Luvaas, editor, *Dear Miss Em: General Eichelberger's War in the Pacific* (1972).

In my youthful days I used to read about commanders of armies and envied them what I supposed to be a great freedom in action and decision. What a notion!! The demands upon me that must be met make me a slave rather than a master. Even my daily life is circumscribed with guards, aides, etc., etc., until sometimes I want nothing so much as complete seclusion.
General Dwight D. Eisenhower, letter to his wife, Mamie, May 27, 1943, quoted in *Letters to Mamie* (1978).

One word of command from me is obeyed by millions but I cannot get my three daughters, Pamela, Felicity and Joan, to come down to breakfast on time.
Field Marshal Archibald Wavell, speaking as the new Viceroy of India, quoted in *Time* (June 28, 1943).

The true military objective is a mental rather than a physical objective—the paralysis of the opposing command, not the bodies of the actual soldiers.
B. H. Liddell Hart, *Thoughts on War* (1944).

The art of command is the art of dealing with human nature. The soldier is governed through his heart and not through his head.
Lord Moran, *The Anatomy of Courage* (1945).

It is sad to remember that, when anyone has fairly mastered the art of command, the necessity for that art usually expires—either through the termination of the war of through the advanced age of the commander.
General George S. Patton, Jr., *War as I Knew It* (1947).

Naval command is the greatest strain that can be brought to bear on a person. The captain is a god—in theory. Some lapse more, some less, from that ideal.
Herman Wouk, *The Caine Mutiny* (1951).

Command doth make actors of us all.
John Masters, *The Road Past Mandalay* (1961).

These were crazy moments [during the D-Day airborne assault] for everyone—particularly the generals [who parachuted into France]. They were men without staffs, without communications, and without men to command. Major General Maxwell Taylor found himself with several officers but only two or three enlisted men. "Never," he told them, "have so few been commanded by so many."
Cornelius Ryan, *The Longest Day* (1967).

The strain that a commander must bear is inevitably severe. . . . In most situations his position may be likened to that of a surgeon who, after performing minor operations for twenty years, is suddenly expected to operate on the chest or abdomen; and probably in an ill-lit theatre and under shell fire.
Hugh L'Etang, *The Pathology of Leadership* (1970).

command and control

A beaten army is no longer in the hands of its general.
Archduke Charles of Austria quoted in Cyril Falls, *The Art of War* (1961).

[The "Modern Alexander" would direct the battle] from a house with roomy offices where telegraph, telephone and wireless signaling apparatus are at hand, while a fleet of autos and motorcycles ready to depart, wait for orders. Here in a comfortable chair by a large table the modern commander overlooks the whole battlefield on a map. From here he telephones inspiring words and here he receives the reports from army and corps commanders and from balloons and dirigibles which observe the enemy's movements.
Field Marshal Alfred von Schlieffen, *Cannae* (1936).

There is always some so-and-so who doesn't get the word.
President John F. Kennedy, commenting on unauthorized acts by subordinates during the Cuban Missile Crisis of 1962, quoted in Roger Hilsman, *To Move a Nation* (1967).

In Vietnam, overcontrol led to disasters large and small. On the last day of the American involvement there, the White House was requesting the tail numbers of the helicopters being used to lift the Americans off the embassy roof in Saigon. Mired in such gnat-sized details, those at the command summit had lost control over the strategic direction of American policy, while those at the bottom were robbed of initiative and lost flexibility and confidence in themselves.
Arthur T. Hadley, *The Straw Giant* (1986).

Improvements in the accuracy, yield, and versatility of nuclear weapons are prejudicial to presidential calm and deliberation in a crisis. So, too, are some of the newer radars and other detection and tracking systems. These disgorge information by the yard and at a speed that adds heavily to the pressure on commanders in tense or critical moments. The commander of NORAD (North American Air Defence Command) would in some presumed crises have only three minutes in which to authenticate reports of a Soviet missile attack. In that event, the President would have no more than four minutes in which to make his fateful decision. That was the amount of time available to the captain of the USS *Vincennes*, which mistakenly shot down an Iranian Airbus over the Persian Gulf in the summer of 1988.
John Newhouse, *War and Peace in the Nuclear Age* (1988).

commander-in-chief

The President shall be Commander in Chief of the Army and Navy of the United States, and of the militia of the several States, when called into the actual Service of the United States.
Constitution of the United States, Article II, Section 2 (1789).

The character of the man is above all other requisites in a commander-in-chief.
General Antoine Henri Jomini, *Summary of the Art of War* (1838).

Though the President is commander-in-chief, Congress is his commander; and, God willing, he shall obey.
Thaddeus Stevens, speech in the House of Representatives, January 3, 1867.

I want to say that I wish all of you the greatest success. While I say that, I am not unmindful of the fact that two graduates of this Academy have reached the White House and neither was a member of my party. Until I'm more certain that this trend will be broken, I wish that all of you may be generals and not commanders-in-chief.
President John F. Kennedy, West Point Commencement Address, June 7, 1962.

William Watts was chosen to coordinate the NSC [National Security Council] staff work on the invasion [of Cambodia], but he went to Kissinger's office to tell him he objected to the policy and could not work on it. Kissinger replied, "Your views represent the cowardice of the Eastern Establishment." This, on top of the strain of recent weeks, was too much for Watts. He . . . stalked out to write a letter of resignation. In the White House Situation Room he was confronted by Alexander Haig, who, by contrast, was delighted by Nixon's decision. Haig barked at Watts that he could not resign: "You've just had an order from your commander in chief." "Fuck you, Al," Watts said, "I just did."
William Shawcross, *Sideshow* (1979).

commanders

Commanders should be counselled . . . by those who have made the art of war their particular study, and whose knowledge is derived from experience; from those who

are present at the scene of action . . . and who, like people embarked in the same ship, are sharers of the danger. If, therefore, any one thinks himself qualified to give advice respecting the war which I am to conduct, which may prove advantageous to the public, let him not refuse his assistance to the state, but let him come with me into Macedonia. He shall be furnished with a ship, a horse, a tent; even his travelling charges shall be defrayed. But if he thinks this too much trouble, and prefers the repose of a city life to the toils of war, let him not, on land, assume the office of pilot.
Attributed to Lucius Aemilius Paulus, Roman General of the 2nd century B.C., quoted in Titus Livy, *Annals of the Roman People* (1st century A.D.). President Franklin D. Roosevelt used this quotation to attack armchair critics of his war policies in a March 17, 1942 news conference. John Gunther, in *The Riddle of MacArthur* (1951), reports that MacArthur had this quotation framed on the wall of his office.

As the forces in one individual after another become prostrated, and can no longer be excited and supported by an effort of his own will, the whole inertia of the mass gradually rests its weight on the will of the commander: by the spark in his breast, by the light of his spirit, the spark of purpose, the light of hope, must be kindled afresh in others.
Karl von Clausewitz, *On War* (1832).

Great results in war are due to the commander. History is therefore right in making generals responsible for victories—in which case they are glorified; and for defeats—in which case they are disgraced.
Marshal Ferdinand Foch, *Precepts and Judgments* (1920).

All very successful commanders are prima donnas, and must be so treated.
General George S. Patton, Jr., *War as I Knew It* (1947).

Subordinate commanders exist because discretion and judgment in the enemy's presence are essential. If an officer is not capable of the necessary decisions, no outside direction can substitute; if he is capable, none is needed.
Robert G. Tanner, *Stonewall in the Valley* (1976).

command of the air

To conquer the command of the air means victory; to be beaten in the air means defeat.
Giulio Douhet, *The Command of the Air* (1921).

To have command of the air means to be in a position to prevent the enemy from flying while retaining the ability to fly oneself.
Giulio Douhet, *The Command of the Air* (1921).

For good or for ill, air mastery is today the supreme expression of military power, and fleets and armies, however vital and important, must accept subordinate rank.
Winston Churchill, speaking in 1949, quoted in Fred Kaplan, *The Wizards of Armageddon* (1983).

Command of the air is . . . not just a matter of tactical or technological superiority or advantages, such as the ability to destroy interceptors or beat radar or ignore anti-aircraft fire. The pith of this command is to be able to say: "We will do such and such *within a predetermined time scale*. If we fail it will be due to our errors."
Anthony Verrier, *The Bomber Offensive* (1968).

command of the sea

For we [the Athenians] are masters of the sea, and you who are islanders, and insignificant islanders too, must not be allowed to escape us.
Thucydides, *The Peloponnesian Wars* (5th century B.C.).

Whosoever commands the sea commands the trade; whosoever commands the trade of the world commands the riches of the world, and consequently the world itself.
Sir Walter Raleigh, *History of the World* (1614); *The Works of Sir Walter Ralegh* [sic], 8 (1829).

[At the 1805 battle of Trafalgar] the British had lost no ships, but nearly seventeen hundred men had been killed or wounded. The combined French and Spanish fleets had, however, lost eighteen ships captured or destroyed in action, nearly six thousand men killed or wounded and twenty thousand taken prisoner, including Admiral Villeneuve. Although it had not been the total annihilation that Nelson had planned, it was a total victory: any danger of invasion to Britain was averted; the Royal Navy had taken command of the seas.
Tom Pocock, *Horatio Nelson* (1988).

It is not the taking of individual ships or convoys, be they few or many, that strikes down the money power of a nation; it is the possession of that overbearing power on the sea which drives the enemy's flag from it, or allows it to appear only as the fugitive; and by controlling the great common, closes the highways by which commerce moves to and from the enemy's shores. This overbearing power can only be exercised by great navies.
Alfred Thayer Mahan, *The Influence of Sea Power Upon History* (1890).

When we speak of command of the seas, it does not mean command of every part of the sea at the same moment, or at every moment. It only means that we can make our will prevail ultimately in any part of seas which may be selected for operations, and thus indirectly make our will prevail in every part of the seas.
Winston Churchill, speech in the House of Commons, October 11, 1940.

So long as one bears in mind that "command" is always relative and means simply a marked ascendancy in the contest for control, one might as well continue to use a phrase which has so ancient and honorable a tradition.
Bernard Brodie, *A Guide to Naval Strategy* (1944).

"Command of the sea" has become like constitutional monarchy—subject to important limitations.
B. H. Liddell Hart, *Thoughts on War* (1944).

No matter what the atomic age brings, America will always need sailors and ships and shipborne aircraft to preserve her liberty, her communications with the free world, even her existence. If the deadly missiles with their apocalyptic warheads are ever launched at America, the Navy will still be out on blue water fighting for her, and the nation or alliance that survives will be the one that retains command of the oceans.
Samuel Eliot Morison, *The Two-Ocean War* (1963).

The conventional surface ship is now a marginalised instrument of military force, while the submarine and the aircraft carrier directly challenge each other for command of the sea.
John Keegan, *The Price of Admiralty* (1988).

communism

A spectre is haunting Europe—the spectre of communism.
Karl Marx and Friedrich Engels, *The Communist Manifesto* (1848).

Now Lenin [was] gripping the edge of the reading stand, letting his little winking eyes travel over the crowd as he stood there waiting, apparently oblivious to the long-rolling ovation, which lasted several minutes. When it finished he said simply, "We shall now proceed to construct the Socialist order!"
V. Lenin, speaking as he assumed power in Petrograd in 1917, quoted in John Reed, *Ten Days that Shook the World* (1926).

All animals are equal, but some animals are more equal than others.
George Orwell, *Animal Farm* (1945).

Communism is not love. Communism is a hammer which we use to crush the enemy.
Mao Tse-tung quoted in *Time* (December 18, 1950).

Trying to maintain good relations with a Communist is like wooing a crocodile. You do not know whether to tickle it under the chin or beat it over the head. When it opens its mouth, you cannot tell whether it is trying to smile or preparing to eat you up.
Winston Churchill, *The Second World War: Triumph and Tragedy* (1953).

Whether you like it or not, history is on our side. We will bury you.
Soviet Premier Nikita Khrushchev, speaking in Moscow, *The Washington Post* (November 19, 1956). Three years later Khrushchev extended his remarks at the National Press Club in Washington, on September 16, 1959: "The expression I used was distorted, and on purpose, because what was meant was not the physical burial of any people but the question of the historical force of development. . . . Looking at the matter from the historical point of view, socialism, communism, would take the place of capitalism and capitalism thereby would be, so to speak, buried." The *New York Times* (September 17, 1959).

I can no longer sit back and allow Communist infiltration, Communist indoctrination, Communist subversion and the international Communist conspiracy to sap and impurify all of our precious bodily fluids.
Sterling Hayden (as General Jack D. Ripper) in *Dr. Strangelove* (1964), directed by Stanley Kubrick; screenplay by Stanley Kubrick and others from the novel *Red Alert* by Peter George.

In dealing with the Communists, remember that in their mind what is secret is serious, and what is public is merely propaganda.
Charles E. Bohlen quoted in *The New York Times* (January 2, 1966).

The free nations of the world must say again to the militant disciples of Asian communism: This far and no further. The time is now, and the place is Vietnam.
President Lyndon B. Johnson, speech in Manila, Philippines, October 27, 1966.

You [Americans] say that you cannot allow Communism to take over Indochina, but you decide to be friends with China and the Soviet Union, the two most powerful Communist countries in history. Why do you accept friendship with Chinese and Soviet Communism and consider Indochinese Communism as dangerous?
Norodom Sihanouk, former Chief of State of Cambodia, *Time* (May 21, 1973).

[One] of the simple, but overwhelming facts of our time is this: of all the millions of refugees we have seen in the modern world, their flight is always away from, not toward, the communist world.
President Ronald Reagan, speech to the British Parliament, June 8, 1982.

[Communists are] like burglars in a hotel corridor, looking for open doors, and they're going to exploit doors that aren't locked. So we've got to make sure the doors are locked.
Representative Jack Kemp, *Los Angeles Times* (May 16, 1985).

What we see is the death of an ideology, in that it is now universally repudiated by those who live under it and increasingly rejected in practice by those who allegedly subscribe to it and have been forcing it down people's throats.
Zbigniew Brzezinski, *The Grand Failure* (1989).

conquest

Hence to fight and conquer in all our battles is not supreme excellence; supreme excellence consists in breaking the enemy's resistance without fighting.
Sun Tzu, *The Art of War* (4th century B.C.).

I came, I saw, I conquered [*veni, vidi, vici*].
Julius Caesar, quoted in Suetonius, *Lives of the Caesars* (A.D. 116). A variant of this is: "I came, I saw, God conquered," attributed to Charles V after the Battle of Muhlberg in 1547.

The right of conquest has no foundation other than the right of the strongest.
Jean Jacques Rousseau, *The Social Contract* (1762).

If there be one principle more deeply rooted than any other in the mind of every American, it is that we should have nothing to do with conquest.
Thomas Jefferson, July 28, 1791 letter to William Short, reprinted in *The Writings of Thomas Jefferson*, VIII, ed. A. E. Bergh (1853).

There is no state, the chief of which does not desire to secure to himself a constant state of peace by the conquest of the whole universe, if it were possible.
Immanuel Kant, *Perpetual Peace* (1795).

A conqueror is always a lover of peace.
Karl von Clausewitz, *On War* (1832).

The conquered always console themselves with their bravery and conquerors never contradict.
Ardant du Picq, *Battle Studies* (1868).

We [the English] seem, as it were, to have conquered and peopled half the world in a fit of absence of mind.
John Seeley, *The Expansion of England* (1883). William H. McNeil, *The Pursuit of Power* (1982), writes that "from the 1840s onward, far more drastically than in any earlier age, Europe's near monopoly of strategic communication and transportation, together with a rapidly evolving weaponry that remained always far in advance of anything local fighting men could lay hands on, made imperial expansion cheap—so cheap that the famous phrase to the effect that Britain acquired its empire in a fit of absence of mind is a caricature rather than a falsehood."

We want no wars of conquest. We must avoid the temptation of territorial aggression.
President William McKinley, first Inaugural Address, March 4, 1897.

Pothinus: Is it possible that Caesar, the conqueror of the world, has time to occupy himself with such a trifle as our taxes?

Caesar: My friend: taxes are the chief business of a conqueror of the world.

George Bernard Shaw, *Caesar and Cleopatra* (1901).

The conquest of the earth, which mostly means the taking it away from those who have a different complexion or slightly flatter noses than ourselves, is not a pretty thing when you look into it too much.

Joseph Conrad, *The Heart of Darkness* (1902).

The rare case where the conquered is very satisfied with the conqueror.

Conrad Adenauer, Chancellor of West Germany, on the occupation of West Berlin by the United States, Great Britain, and France, quoted in *The New York Times* (March 21, 1960).

conscientious objectors

There are only two classes who, as categories, show courage in war—the front-line soldier and the conscientious objector.

B. H. Liddell Hart, *Thoughts on War* (1944).

Conscientious objection must be reserved for only the greatest moral issues, Vietnam is not of this magnitude.

Henry A. Kissinger quoted in *Look* (August 12, 1969).

The ones I have unending admiration for are the guys who say, "I simply will not serve in the Army of the United States in Vietnam, and I am willing to take the consequences for it . . . ." These are the guys who are heroic.

John V. Lindsay, Mayor of New York, *Newsweek* (May 11, 1970).

I discovered that the opponents to the war are not simply those who are deserting or burning their draft cards or filing for conscientious objector. The military is filled with men who are against the war!

Jane Fonda, *The New York Times* (March 2, 1971).

conscription

From this moment and until all enemies are driven from the territory of the Republic all French persons are placed in permanent requisition for the service of the armies. The young men will go to battle; married men will forge arms and transport provisions; women will make tents and clothing and serve in the hospitals; children will shred old linen; old men will have themselves carried to public places to arouse the courage of warriors. . . .

The order for the *Levée en Masse*, decreed by the French National Convention on August 23, 1793, quoted in Jean-Paul Bertaud, *The Army of the French Revolution* (1988).

In 1803 . . . Napoleon issued a new law of conscription: all males between twenty and twenty-five years of age were made subject to the draft. Many were exempted: young married men, seminarians, widowers or divorcés with children, anyone who had a brother already taken, and the eldest of three orphans. Moreover, a draftee could pay a substitute to take his place. At first this seemed to Napoleon to be unjust; then he allowed it, chiefly on the ground that advanced students should be left to continue their studies to fit themselves for administrative posts.

Will and Ariel Durant, *The Age of Napoleon* (1975).

A rich man's war and a poor man's fight.
Joseph Kirkland, *The Captain of Company K* (1891). This was the slogan of the 1863 Civil War draft rioters in New York City, because anyone could buy exemptions from the draft for three hundred dollars.

A new phase has been reached in the conscription controversy, and the burning question appears to be whether the necessary men are to be compelled to volunteer or persuaded to be compulsorily enrolled.
Punch (October 1915).

They talk about conscription as being a democratic institution. Yes, so is a cemetery.
Representative Meyer London, speech in the House of Representatives, April 25, 1917.

I am violently against a professional Army, and violently for the draft. Unless the wealthiest people's children, or the smartest people's children or the politicians' children are drafted along with the poorest people's children, we are sowing the seeds of our own destruction.
Carl A. Gerstacker, Chairman, Dow Chemical, *Nation's Business* (July 1971).

Because the military has to meet its manpower needs solely by attracting volunteers, it has to offer beginning pay of around $600 a month. If a draft were instituted, the pay could be cut in half. The other half represents the bribe that persuades the poor to enlist and permits the affluent to avoid doing their part. The waste and the immorality are so blatant that one wonders how anyone can justify not having a draft that takes both rich and poor.
Charles Peters, *Tilting at Windmills* (1988).

conscription—Vietnam War

I ain't got no quarrel with them Viet Cong.
Muhammad Ali, Heavyweight boxing champion, explaining why he is refusing to be drafted, *The New York Times* (January 11, 1967).

If drafted, we will not accept a combat role in Indochina.
Pledge by one-third of Colgate University's new graduates, reported in *The New York Times* (May 31, 1971).

The draft has an evil name because it would have dragged young people into an evil war. Yet it remains the only way, if administered justly, to preserve the principle of the nation in arms. The college deferrals made it a mockery. The deferral system was as anti-democratic and elitist (to use the favorite word of those who consider themselves equalizers) as anything that has ever happened in the United States. I may be happy that it kept my kin and the sons of some of my friends out of Vietnam, but I am nonetheless ashamed of it.
Barbara W. Tuchman, June 1972 Commencement address at Williams College, reprinted in her *Practicing History* (1981).

A citizen of a free country should not be forced to fight in a war that neither he nor his elected representatives chose to initiate or declare.
Chesterfield Smith, President of the American Bar Association, *The Washington Post* (August 13, 1974).

Service to one's country became a matter of bad luck.
James Reston, Jr., on the Vietnam draft lottery, *Sherman's March and Vietnam* (1984).

So pervasive was this practice of college deferment [during Vietnam] that the chief of Selective Service, General Lewis B. Hershey, bitterly remarked: "In the Civil War it

required $300 to escape service. In this war it requires sufficient funds to attend college."
Arthur T. Hadley, *The Straw Giant* (1986).

contact

In war, as in love, we must achieve contact ere we triumph.
Napoleon I, *Political Aphorisms* (1848).

[Contact is] a word which perhaps better than any other indicates the dividing line between tactics and strategy.
Alfred Thayer Mahan, *The Influence of Sea Power Upon History* (1890).

Contact is information of the most tangible kind, an enemy met with is an enemy at grips, and, as in a wrestling match, contact is likely to be followed by much foot-play. Time still remains the decisive factor, time wherein to modify a plan according to the information contact gains.
J. F. C. Fuller, *Armoured Warfare* (1943).

containment

Soviet pressure against the free institutions of the Western World is something that can be contained by the adroit and vigilant application of counterforce at a series of constantly shifting geographical and political points, corresponding to the shifts and maneuvers of Soviet policies.
"X" [George F. Kennan], "The Sources of Soviet Conduct," *Foreign Affairs* (June 1947).

In its foreign policy the United States is somewhat hampered by the US system of education in which ideology is strong and geography weak. A policy of containing communism everywhere may be theologically admirable but it is geographic nonsense.
C. Northcote Parkinson quoted in C. Woolf and J. Bagguley, *Authors Take Sides on Vietnam* (1967).

Wise men . . . crafted the strategy of containment. They believed that the Soviet Union, denied the easy course of expansion, would turn inward and address the contradictions of its inefficient, repressive and inhumane system. And they were right. The Soviet Union is now publicly facing this hard reality. Containment worked.
President George Bush, speech at Texas A & M University, May 12, 1989.

councils of war

The effect of discussions, making a show of talent, and calling councils of war will be what the effect of these things has been in every age: they will end in the adoption of the most pusillanimous or (if the expression be preferred) the most prudent measures, which in war are almost uniformly the worst that can be adopted. True wisdom, so far as a general is concerned, consists in energetic determination.
Napoleon I, *Military Maxims* (1827).

Councils of war are a deplorable resource and can be useful only when concurring in opinion with the commander, in which case they may give him more confidence in his own judgment, and, in addition, may assure him that his lieutenants, being of his opinion, will use every means to insure the success of the movement.
General Antoine Henri Jomini, *Summary of the Art of War* (1838).

Call no council of war. It is proverbial that councils of war never fight.
Major General H. W. Halleck, telegram to General George Meade after Gettysburg, July 13, 1863, quoted in Shelby Foote, *The Civil War: Fredricksburg to Meridian* (1963).

Councils of war are invariably fraught with danger in military operations. In most cases they merely lead to nothing decisive being accomplished; successful war is not waged by a congress but by one single military leader.
John Donaldson, *Military History Applied to Modern Warfare* (1907).

A council of war never fights, and in a crisis the duty of the leader is to lead and not to take refuge behind the generally timid wisdom of a multitude of councilors.
Theodore Roosevelt, *Autobiography* (1913).

coup d'oeil

The coup d'oeil is a gift of God and cannot be acquired. . . . To look over a battle-field, to take in at the first instance the advantages and disadvantages is the great quality of a general.
Chevalier Folard, *Nouvelles Decouvertes sur la Guerre* (1724).

Within a single square mile a hundred different orders of battle can be formed. The clever general perceives the advantages of the terrain instantly; he gains advantage from the slightest hillock, from a tiny marsh; he advances or withdraws a wing to gain superiority; he strengthens either his right or his left, moves ahead or to the rear, and profits from the merest bagatelles.
This also is required of the general when the enemy is found in position and must be attacked. Whoever has the best coup d'oeil will perceive at first glance the weak spot of the enemy and attack him there.
Frederick the Great, *Instructions for His Generals* (1747).

In . . . battles, theory becomes an uncertain guide; for it is then unequal to the emergency, and can never compare in value with a natural talent for war, nor be a sufficient substitute for the intuitive coup d'oeil imparted by experience in battles to a general of tried bravery and coolness.
General Antoine Henri Jomini, *Summary of the Art of War* (1838).

Success in war depends on coup d'oeil, and on sensing the psychological moment in battle. At Austerlitz, had I attacked six hours earlier, I should have been lost.
Napoleon I quoted in J. F. C. Fuller, *The Conduct of War* (1961).

A vital faculty of generalship is the power of grasping instantly the picture of the ground and the situation, of relating the one to the other, and the local to the general. It is that flair which makes the great executant.
B. H. Liddell Hart, *Thoughts on War* (1944).

courage

Investigation reveals that there are actually fewer deaths in battle among the Spartans than in armies which give way to fear and prefer to leave the field; so that in reality courage turns out to be a more effective survival-factor than cowardice.
Xenophon (4th century B.C.) quoted in Arnold J. Toynbee, *War and Civilization* (1950).

But screw your courage to the sticking-place,
And we'll not fail.
William Shakespeare, *Macbeth*, Act I (1606).

The courage of the troops must be reborn daily . . . nothing is so variable . . . the true skill of the general consists in knowing how to guarantee it.
Marshal Maurice de Saxe, *Reveries Upon the Art of War* (1757).

Napoleon said, he had rarely encountered the "courage of 2 A.M."—that is, the extemporaneous courage which, even in the most sudden emergencies, leaves one's freedom of mind, judgment, and decision completely unaffected. He asserted unequivocally that he had known himself to possess that 2 A.M. courage to a higher degree than any other man.
Emmanuel de Las Casas, *Memoirs of the Emperor Napoleon* (1883). Henry David Thoreau, *Walden* (1854), writes of "the three-o'clock in the morning courage which Bonaparte thought was the rarest."

The pitifulest thing out is a mob; that's what an army is—a mob; they don't fight with courage that's born in them, but with courage that's borrowed from their mass, and from their officers.
Mark Twain, *The Adventures of Huckleberry Finn* (1884).

I would define true courage to be a perfect sensibility of the measure of danger, and a mental willingness to incur it.
General William T. Sherman, *Personal Memoirs*, II (1875).

Courage is resistance to fear, mastery of fear, not absence of fear.
Mark Twain, *Pudd'nhead Wilson* (1894).

The Red Badge of Courage.
Stephen Crane, title of his best-known novel (1895). The "badge" was a bleeding wound.

Courage is almost a contradiction in terms. It means a strong desire to live taking the form of a readiness to die.
G. K. Chesterton, *Orthodoxy* (1909).

Fighting is like champagne. It goes to the heads of cowards as quickly as of heroes. Any fool can be brave on a battle field when it's be brave or else be killed.
Margaret Mitchell, *Gone With the Wind* (1936).

There is a certain blend of courage, integrity, character and principle which has no satisfactory dictionary name but has been called different things at different times in different countries. Our American name for it is "guts."
Louis Adamic, *A Study in Courage* (1944).

Courage is a moral quality; it is not a chance gift of nature like an aptitude for games. It is a cold choice between two alternatives, the fixed resolve not to quit; an act of renunciation which must be made not once but many times by the power of the will. Courage is will power.
Lord Moran, *The Anatomy of Courage* (1945).

Stories of past courage can . . . teach, they can offer hope, they can provide inspiration. But they cannot supply courage itself. For this each man must look into his own soul.
Senator John F. Kennedy, *Profiles in Courage* (1956).

There is nothing like seeing the other fellow run to bring back your courage.
General William Slim, *Unofficial History* (1959).

Colonel Cathcart had courage and never hesitated to volunteer his men for any target available.
Joseph Heller, *Catch-22* (1961).

Until the day of his death, no man can be sure of his courage.
Jean Anouilh, *Becket* (1962).

Courage is doing what you're afraid to do. There can be no courage unless you're scared.
Edward V. "Eddie" Rickenbacker quoted in Peggy Streit, "What Is Courage," *The New York Times Magazine* (November 24, 1963).

There is a type of soldier who considers death very real for others but without power over him. These soldiers cherish the conviction that they are mysteriously impervious to spattering bullets and exploding shells. . . . It is a conviction that is responsible for much rashness in battle, misnamed courage. . . .
Fortunate is the unit that can count one or more of these soldiers in its ranks; and in fact most units do appear to contain them. They are a perennial phenomenon in war, a cause of wonder and admiration. . . . If such soldiers command men, as frequently happens, they have the capacity to inspire their troops to deeds of recklessness and self-sacrifice.
In most of these soldiers, the source of their relationship toward death—as a reality for others only—is not too difficult to discover. They have simply preserved their childish illusion that they are the center of the world and are therefore immortal.
J. Glenn Gray, *The Warriors* (1967).

The test before us as a people is not whether our commitments match our will and our courage; but whether we have the will and the courage to match our commitments.
President Lyndon B. Johnson, message to Congress, August 3, 1967.

court martial

Too many courts-martial in any command are evidence of poor discipline and inefficient officers.
General William T. Sherman, *Personal Memoirs*, II (1875).

After the formal reading of the [1894 court martial] sentence I exclaimed to the troops: "Soldiers, an innocent man is degraded. Soldiers, an innocent man is dishonored! *Vive la France! Vive l'armée!*" An adjutant of the Republican Guard came up to me and rapidly tore the buttons from my coat, the stripes from my trousers, and the marks of rank from my cap and coat-sleeves, and then broke my sword across his knee.
Alfred Dreyfus, *Five Years of My Life* (1901). Dreyfus would later be pardoned and restored to ranks. He was entirely innocent of the treason with which he was charged.

These accidents are the direct result of the incompetency, criminal negligence and almost treasonable administration of the national defense by the Navy and War Departments. The lives of the airmen are being used merely as pawns in their hands.
Colonel William "Billy" Mitchell, statement to the press that led to his court martial, *Time* (May 4, 1925).

One of the great defects in our military establishment is the giving of weak sentences for military offenses. . . . In justice to other men, soldiers who go to sleep on post, who go absent for an unreasonable time during combat, who shirk battle, should be executed.
General George S. Patton, Jr., *War as I Knew It* (1947).

When I came back to Dublin, I was courtmartialled in my absence and sentenced to death in my absence, so I said they could shoot me in my absence.
Brendan Behan, *The Hostage*, Act I (1958).

The popular conception of a court martial is half a dozen bloodthirsty old Colonel Blimps, who take it for granted that anyone brought before them is guilty . . . and who at intervals chant in unison, "Maximum penalty—death!" In reality courts martial are almost invariably composed of nervous officers, feverishly consulting their manuals; so anxious to avoid a miscarriage of justice that they are, at times, ready to allow the accused any loophole of escape. Even if they do steel themselves to passing a sentence, they are quite prepared to find it quashed because they have forgotten to mark something "A" and attach it to the proceedings.
General William Slim, *Unofficial History* (1959).

covert action

I strongly believe in covert operations. I have no hesitancy to say so. I don't know how a President could conduct foreign policy without a degree of covert operations.
President Gerald R. Ford, *Time* (January 26, 1976).

When the Soviets use armed forces outside their own borders or when they use proxy troops outside their own borders, covert action can raise the cost for them and may discourage them from expanding. And where Russia mounts a major propaganda campaign to shape the attitudes of other countries, covert action to counter them can be useful. At that point, I've run the gamut of where I believe covert action can be truly useful to the United States.
Admiral Bobby R. Inman, former Deputy Director of the CIA, *U.S. News & World Report* (December 20, 1982).

We have to get over the idea that "covert" is a dirty word.
George P. Shultz, Secretary of State, *The Washington Post* (May 16, 1986).

My own feeling is we must simplify—deregulate, if you will—the conduct of foreign policy generally and covert actions particularly.
Vice President George Bush, *The Washington Post* (January 31, 1987).

cowardice

Cowards die many times before their deaths;
The valiant never taste of death but once.
William Shakespeare, *Julius Caesar*, Act II (1599).

It is thus that mutual cowardice keeps us in peace. Were one half of mankind brave and one half cowards, the brave would be always beating the cowards. Were all brave, they would lead a very uneasy life; all would be be continually fighting; but being all cowards, we go on very well.
Samuel Johnson quoted in James Boswell, *Life of Samuel Johnson* (1791).

It were better to be a soldier's widow than a coward's wife.
Thomas Bailey Aldrich, *Mercedes*, Act II (1884).

Except a creature be part coward, it is not a compliment to say he is brave.
Mark Twain, *Pudd'nhead Wilson* (1894).

Man loves to think of himself as bold and bad. He is neither one nor the other: he is only a coward. Call him tyrant, murderer, pirate, bully; and he will adore you, and swagger about with the consciousness of having the blood of the old sea kings in his veins. Call him liar and thief; and he will only take an action against you for libel. But call him coward; and he will go mad with rage: he will face death to outface that stinging truth.
George Bernard Shaw, *Don Juan in Hell* in *Man and Superman*, Act III (1903).

[A coward is] one who in a perilous emergency thinks with his legs.
Ambrose Bierce, *The Devil's Dictionary* (1911).

It has come to my attention that a very small number of soldiers are going to the hospital on the pretext that they are nervously incapable of combat. Such men are cowards, and bring discredit on the Army and disgrace to their comrades who they heartlessly leave to endure the danger of a battle which they themselves use the hospital as a means of escaping....
Those who are not willing to fight will be tried by Court-Martial for cowardice in the face of the enemy.
General George S. Patton, *The Patton Papers*, M. Blumenson, ed. (1982).

Cowardice, as distinguished from panic, is almost always simply a lack of ability to suspend the functioning of the imagination. Learning to suspend your imagination and live completely in the very second of the present with no before and no after is the greatest gift a soldier can acquire.
Ernest Hemingway, introduction to *Men at War* (1942).

Fear even when morbid is not cowardice. That is the label we reserve for something that a man does. What passes through his mind is his own affair.
Lord Moran, *The Anatomy of Courage* (1945).

Try to remember that, though ignorance becomes a Southern gentleman, cowardice does not.
Fredric March, *Another Part of the Forest* (1948), directed by Michael Gordon; screenplay by Vladimir Pozner, from the play by Lillian Hellman.

No man who rises to command of a United States naval ship can possibly be a coward. And that therefore if he commits questionable acts under fire, the explanation must lie elsewhere.
Herman Wouk, *The Caine Mutiny* (1951).

This republic [the United States] was not established by cowards; and cowards will not preserve it.
Elmer Davis, *But We Were Born Free* (1954).

Some of you boys, I know, are wondering whether or not you'll chicken out under fire. Don't worry about it. I can assure you that you will all do your duty. The Nazis are the enemy. Wade into them. Spill their blood. Shoot them in the belly. When you put your hand into a bunch of goo that a moment before was your best friend's face, you'll know what to do.
George C. Scott in *Patton* (1970), directed by Franklin Schaffner; screenplay by Francis Ford Coppola and Edmund H. North, based on Ladislas Farago's *Patton* and General Omar Bradley's *A Soldier's Story*.

Crimean War

When Lord Lucan received the order from Captain Nolan and had read it, he asked, we are told, "Where are we [the Light Brigade] to advance to?"
Captain Nolan pointed with his finger to the line of the Russians, and said, "There are the enemy, and there are the guns, sir, before them. It is your duty to take them," or words to that effect, according to the statements made since his death.
Lord Lucan with reluctance gave the order to Lord Cardigan to advance upon the guns, conceiving that his orders compelled him to do so. The noble Earl, though he did not shrink, also saw the fearful odds against him. Don Quixote in his tilt against the

windmill was not near so rash and reckless as the gallant fellows who prepared without a thought to rush on almost certain death.
William Howard Russell, *The Times* (London) (November 14, 1854).

Are we to be the Don Quixotes of Europe, to go about fighting for every cause where we find that someone has been wronged?
Richard Cobden, speech in the House of Commons in opposition to the Crimean War, December 22, 1854.

We are not of those who regard the expedition to the Crimea as a mistake. We urged it early in the day.... As it is, however, we must admit that it has turned out unfortunately. From some cause or other our losses have been frightful and our profit has been microscopic. We have displayed marvellous valor in fight; marvellous patience in suffering—but we have made no way. We have lost 20,000 men, and we have not gained land enough to make them 20,000 graves.
Editorial, *The Economist* (April 14, 1855).

The Crimean War is one of the bad jokes of history.
Philip Guedalla, *The Two Marshals* (1943).

Charge of the Light Brigade

Half a league, half a league,
Half a league onward,
All in the valley of Death
Rode the six hundred.
'Forward, the Light Brigade!
Charge for the guns!' he said:
Into the valley of Death
Rode the six hundred

'Forward, the Light Brigade!
Was there a man dismayed?
Not though the soldier knew
Some one had blundered:
Their's not to make reply,
Their's not to reason why,
Their's but to do and die:
Into the valley of Death
Rode the six hundred.
Alfred, Lord Tennyson, *The Charge of the Light Brigade* (1854).

It is magnificent, but it is not war. [*C'est magnifique, mais ce n'est pas la guerre.*]
Attributed to French General Pierre Bosquet, on viewing the charge of the Light Brigade, October 25, 1854.

cruelty

Man's inhumanity to man
Makes countless thousands mourn!
Robert Burns, *Man Was Made to Mourn* (1786).

You cannot qualify war in harsher terms than I will. War is cruelty and you cannot refine it. . . . When peace does come, you may call on me for anything. Then will I share with you the last cracker.
William T. Sherman, *Memoirs* (1875). This remark was made on September 12, 1864, in response to complaints by the municipal officials of Atlanta over his occupation policies.

It is not merely cruelty that leads men to love war, it is excitement.
Henry Ward Beecher, *Proverbs from Plymouth Pulpit* (1887).

War, which used to be cruel and magnificent, has now become cruel and squalid. It is all the fault of democracy. . . . Instead of a small number of well-trained professionals championing their country's cause with ancient weapons . . . , we now have entire populations, including even women and children, pitted against each other in brutish mutual extermination, and only a set of blear-eyed clerks left to add up the butcher's bill. From the moment when democracy was admitted to, or rather forced itself upon, the battlefield, war ceased to be a gentleman's pursuit.
Winston Churchill, *My Early Life* (1930).

This is a story of the Battle of the Atlantic, a story of an ocean, two ships and a handful of men. The men are the heroes. The heroines are the ships. The only villain is the sea—the cruel sea—that man has made more cruel.
Jack Hawkins, in *The Cruel Sea* (1953), directed by Charles Frend; screenplay by Eric Ambler from the novel by Nicholas Monsarrat.

Cuba

I would say that if it hadn't been for Cuba [the Bay of Pigs experience], we probably would have sent large numbers of troops into Laos and Vietnam. That would have been very damaging.
Robert Kennedy quoted in Edwin O. Guthman and Jeffrey Shulman, eds., *Robert Kennedy in His Own Words* (1988).

But you Americans must understand what Cuba means to us old Bolsheviks. We have been waiting all our lives for a country to go communist without the Red Army, and it happened in Cuba. It makes us feel like boys again.
Deputy Premier Anastas Mikoyan of the Soviet Union quoted in Thomas J. Schoenbaum, *Waging Peace and War* (1988).

The Soviet Union does not intend to have nuclear missiles deployed here, or any other means of mass extermination.
Mikhail Gorbachev, speaking in Havana, *The New York Times* (April 5, 1989).

Bay of Pigs

Unless you are prepared to use our planes to knock out Cuban planes, then you shouldn't have started the thing in the first place.
General Maxwell Taylor quoted in Ralph G. Martin, *A Hero for Our Times* (1983).

All my life I've known better than to depend on the experts. How could I have been so stupid, to let them go ahead?
President John F. Kennedy, assessing his judgment on the Bay of Pigs, quoted in Theodore C. Sorensen, *Kennedy* (1965).

When some in Washington argued that the Cuban [Bay of Pigs] plan had been devised during the previous administration, John Eisenhower urged his father to issue a statement saying, "I don't run no bad invasions," but the father thought it "smallminded."
Michael R. Beschloss, *Mayday* (1986).

They said afterward it was because President Kennedy was such an amateur that he went ahead. Well, if he hadn't gone ahead with it, everybody would have said it showed that he had no courage.
Robert F. Kennedy quoted in Edwin O. Guthman and Jeffrey Shulman, eds., *Robert Kennedy in His Own Words* (1988).

Cuban Missile Crisis

It shall be the policy of this nation to regard any nuclear missile launched from Cuba against any nation in the Western Hemisphere as an attack by the Soviet Union on the United States, requiring a full retaliatory response on the Soviet Union.
President John F. Kennedy, speech to the nation (October 22, 1962).

They talk about who won and who lost. Human reason won. Mankind won.
Nikita Khrushchev, *The Observer* (November 11, 1962).

We were eyeball-to-eyeball and the other fellow just blinked.
Dean Rusk, U.S. Secretary of State, quoted in *The Saturday Evening Post* (December 8, 1962).

The Cuban crisis raised the prospect of a very different species of "limited war." More than just raising the prospect, probably it should be construed as an actual instance of the new species, one in which no shots were actually fired. This new species is the competition in risk-taking, a military-diplomatic maneuver with or without military engagement but with the outcome determined more by manipulation of risk than by an actual contest of force.
Thomas C. Schelling, *Arms and Influence* (1966).

General Curtis LeMay argued strongly with the president that a military attack was essential. When the president questioned what the response of the Russians might be, General LeMay assured him there would be no reaction. President Kennedy was skeptical. "They, no more than we, can't let these things go by without doing something. They can't, after all their statements, permit us to take out their missiles, kill a lot of Russians, and then do nothing. If they don't take action in Cuba, they certainly will in Berlin."
Robert F. Kennedy, *Thirteen Days* (1969).

When [Dean] Acheson got to Paris [during the Cuban Missile Crisis] he was smuggled into de Gaulle's office by an underground tunnel from across the street. Acheson went in alone except for the Elysee interpreter. . . . De Gaulle greeted him. . . . Acheson explained everything, and added he had brought along pictures to confirm what he was saying. De Gaulle said: "It is not necessary to show me the pictures because obviously a great government like yours would not risk war for nothing."
C. L. Sulzberger, *The Last of the Giants* (1970).

I now know how Tojo felt when he was planning Pearl Harbor.
Robert F. Kennedy, in a note passed to President John F. Kennedy in a meeting considering a surprise air attack on Cuba, in *Thirteen Days* (1969).

The Soviet force of 42 medium-range missiles in Cuba represented two-thirds of the Kremlin's nuclear strike capability against the United States at the time of the crisis. Soviet officials said that only 20 or so intercontinental missiles were deployed in the Soviet Union in 1962, meaning that the United States at the time had a significant strategic superiority.
Michael Dobbs, "How Close We Really Come to Armageddon," *Washington Post National Weekly* (February 6–12, 1988).

On Saturday, Oct. 27, 1962, at the height of the Cuban missile crisis, Nikita Khrushchev's personal assistant and a Central Committee colleague moved their families out of Moscow, expecting an American nuclear strike on their capital. At the same time in Washington, on a beautiful fall evening, as I left President Kennedy's office to return to the Pentagon, I thought I might never live to see another Saturday night. As melodramatic as it sounds, this is what we were thinking on both sides at that critical moment.
Robert S. McNamara, "The Lessons of October," *Newsweek* (February 13, 1989).

When the crisis had passed, a Kennedy insider told the following story: When the President and his inner circle were briefed on the plans to hurry to the South Lawn for the helicopter lift, one aide was deeply troubled. This fellow went to the President and told Kennedy that he did not plan to leave the White House and his family, attack or not. Kennedy reportedly looked up with that wry smile on his face and said, "That's O.K. Neither do I. I'm staying right here."
Hugh Sidey, "The Presidency," *Time* (February 13, 1989).

danger

Danger is part of the friction of war. Without an accurate conception of danger we cannot understand war.
Karl von Clausewitz, *On War* (1832).

Some men approach danger as a virgin approaches love. They think there are no consequences.
René Quinton, *Soldier's Testament* (1930).

There was only one catch and that was Catch-22, which specified that a concern for one's own safety in the face of dangers that were real and immediate was the process of a rational mind. Orr was crazy and could be grounded. All he had to do was ask; and as soon as he did, he would no longer be crazy and would have to fly more missions. Orr would be crazy to fly more missions and sane if he didn't, but if he was sane he had to fly them. If he flew them he was crazy and didn't have to; but if he didn't want to he was sane and had to.
Joseph Heller, *Catch-22* (1961).

dead, the

Your son, my lord, has paid a soldier's debt.
William Shakespeare, *Macbeth*, Act V (1606).

Remember, gentlemen, what a Roman emperor said: "The corpse of an enemy always smells sweet."
Napoleon I, speaking in 1812, quoted in J. C. Herold, *The Mind of Napoleon* (1955).

He who has once gazed into the glazed eye of a dying warrior on the field of battle will think twice before beginning a war.
Otto von Bismarck quoted in Charles Lowe, *Bismarck's Table Talk* (1895).

Pile the bodies high at Austerlitz and
    Waterloo,
Shovel them under and let me work—
I am the grass; I cover all.
Carl Sandburg, "Grass," *Cornhuskers* (1918).

The dead men looked wonderfully beautiful. The night was shining gently down, softening them into new ivory. . . . The corpses seemed flung so pitifully on the ground, huddled anyhow in low heaps. Surely if straightened they would be comfortable at last. So I put them all in order, one by one, very wearied myself, and longing to be of these quiet ones, not of the restless, noisy, aching mob up the valley, quarrelling over the plunder.
T. E. Lawrence, *Seven Pillars of Wisdom* (1935).

Near Efogi [in New Guinea], on a slimy section of the track that reeks with the stench of death, the remains of an enemy soldier lie on a crude stretcher, abandoned by the Japanese retreat. The flesh has gone from his bones, and a white bony claw sticks out of a ragged uniform sleeve, stretching across the track. Every Australian who passes, plodding up the muddy rise that leads to the pass, grasps the skeleton's grisly hand, shakes it fervently and says, "Good on you, sport!" before wearily moving on.
George H. Johnson, *The Toughest Fights in the World* (1943).

Marine humor, no matter what the situation, never failed to amaze me. The first North Korean I saw was a dead one. Left so we newcomers would see him, he was propped up in a sitting position in a bend on one of the trails on Hill 749. He held in one hand a dead man's poker hand of aces and eights.
Joe Havens quoted in Donald Knox, *The Korean War: Uncertain Victory* (1988).

death

It is sweet and fitting to die for one's country. (*Dulce et decorum est pro patria mori.*)
Horace, *Odes* (1st century B.C.).

Hail Caesar, we who are about to die salute you. (*Ave Caesar, morituri te salutant.*)
The gladiators' salute, quoted in Suetonius, *Lives of the Twelve Caesars* (2nd century A.D.).

What pity is it
That we can die but once to serve our country!
Joseph Addison, *Cato* (1713).

Death is nothing; but to live defeated and without glory is to die every day.
Napoleon I, 1804 letter to General Lauriston, quoted in J. C. Herold, *The Mind of Napoleon* (1955).

Then out spake brave Horatius,
The Captain of the Gate:
"To every man upon this earth
Death cometh soon or late.
And how can man die better
Than facing fearful odds,
For the ashes of his fathers,
And the temples of his God?"
Thomas Babington Macaulay, *Lays of Ancient Rome* (1842).

But I've a rendezvous with Death
At midnight in some flaming town,
When spring trips north again this year,
And I to my pledged word am true,
I shall not fail that rendezvous.
Alan Seeger, "I Have a Rendezvous With Death," *Poems* (1917).

That man has only to be told that he will die in a certain place to go straightaway and die there, is the greatest achievement of war.
René Quinton, *Soldier's Testament* (1930).

I found that reading books about other people fighting wars is adventurous, but when you are doing the fighting, it's a helluva lot different. . . . All that time while you are putting yourself into the hero's place you still have the knowledge that after the hero dies you still will be around to feel sad about it. When at any second you may die, there is no adventure; all you want is to get the fighting over with. You don't spend any time consoling yourself that if you die, you will be dying for your country and Liberty and Democracy and Freedom, because after you are dead, there is no such thing as Liberty or Democracy or Freedom.
James Jones, letter to Jeff Jones from Guadalcanal, January 28, 1943, reprinted in *The New York Times Magazine* (March 8, 1989).

To save your world you asked this man to die:
Would this man, could he see you now, ask why?
W. H. Auden, "Epitaph for an Unknown Soldier" (1945).

One thing he [General Patton] said always stuck with me, for it was contrary to what I had believed up to that moment, but when I had been in combat only a short while, I knew he was right. Speaking to all of us late one afternoon as we assembled in the North African sunset, he said, "Now, I want you to remember that no sonuvabitch ever won a war by dying for his country. He won it by making the other poor dumb sonuvabitch die for his country."
General James M. Gavin, *On To Berlin* (1978).

A lot of guys make mistakes, I guess, but every one we make, a whole stack of chips goes with it. We make a mistake, and some guy don't walk away —forevermore, he don't walk away.
John Wayne in *Sands of Iwo Jima* (1949), directed by Allan Dwan; screenplay by Harry Brown and James Edward Grant.

For us, the Battle of the Atlantic was becoming a private war. If you were in it, you knew all about it. You knew how to keep watch on filthy nights, and how to go without sleep; and how to bury the dead and how to die without wasting anyone's time.
Jack Hawkins in *The Cruel Sea* (1953), directed by Charles Frend; screenplay by Eric Ambler from the novel by Nicholas Monsarrat.

Men on hazardous missions joke about death. Joking is better than thinking; obscenity is better than prayer.
William Bradford Huie, *The Americanization of Emily* (1959).

"Crash" is not a word pilots ever use. I don't really know why, but the word is avoided in describing what happens when several tons of metal plows itself and its pilot into the ground. Instead, we might say, "He augered in," or, "He bought the farm."
General Chuck Yeager and Leo Janos, *Yeager* (1985).

deception

All warfare is based on deception.
Sun Tzu, *The Art of War* (4th century B.C.).

Who asks whether bravery or cunning beat the enemy?
Virgil, *Aeneid* (19 B.C.).

Although deceit is detestable in all other things, yet in the conduct of war it is laudable and honorable; and a commander who vanquishes an enemy by stratagem is equally praised with one who gains victory by force.
Niccolò Machiavelli, *The Discourses* (1517).

And still more generous was the answer of the great Alexander to Polypercon, who was persuading him to take advantage of the darkness of night to attack Darius; "By no means, he said; it is not for me to steal a victory; I had rather complain of fortune than steal a victory."
Michel de Montaigne, writing in 1580, quoted in Bernard Brodie, *War and Politics* (1973).

Force, and fraud, are in war the two cardinal virtues.
Thomas Hobbes, *Leviathan* (1651).

Do you at all realize, sir, that we have nothing standing between us and destruction but our own bluff.
General Burgoyne in George Bernard Shaw's *The Devil's Disciple* (1901).

To achieve victory we must as far as possible make the enemy blind and deaf by sealing his eyes and ears, and drive his commanders to distraction by creating confusion in their minds.
Mao Tse-tung, *On a Prolonged War* (1938).

"In wartime" I said, "truth is so precious that she should always be attended by a bodyguard of lies." Stalin and his comrades greatly appreciated this remark when it was translated, and upon this note our formal conference ended gaily.
Winston Churchill, speaking of the 1943 Teheran Conference discussion of the forthcoming invasion of France, in his *The Second World War: Closing the Ring* (1951).

Unnecessary firing gives your position away, and when you give your position away here, you pay for it. . . . I have observed the Japs often get short of ammunition. They cut bamboo and crack it together to simulate rifle fire to draw our fire. They ain't supermen; they're just tricky bastards.
Corporal Joseph S. Stankus quoted in K. Ayling, *Semper Fidelis* (1943).

declaration of war

Cry "Havoc!" and let slip the dogs of war.
William Shakespeare, *Julius Caesar*, Act III (1599).

They may ring their bells now; before long they will be wringing their hands.
Sir Robert Walpole, on the declaration of war with Spain, speech in the House of Commons, October 19, 1739.

The civil constitution of every state shall be republican, and war shall not be declared except by a plebescite of all the citizens.
Immanuel Kant, *Perpetual Peace* (1795).

The Royal Serbian Government not having answered in a satisfactory manner the note of July 23, 1914, presented by the Austro-Hungarian Minister at Belgrade, the Imperial and Royal Government are themselves compelled to see to the safeguarding of their right and interests, and, with this object, to have recourse to force of arms.

Austria-Hungary consequently considers herself henceforward in state of war with Serbia.

The Austro-Hungarian Declaration of War on Serbia, July 28, 1914, reprinted in Great Britain, *Collected Documents Relating to the Outbreak of the European War* (1915). This is what formally started World War I.

With a profound sense of the solemn and even tragic character of the step I am taking and of the grave responsibilities which it involves, but in unhesitating obedience to what I deem my constitutional duty, I advise that the Congress declare the recent course of the Imperial German Government to be in fact nothing less than war against the government and people of the United States; that it formally accept the status of belligerent which has thus been thrust upon it.

President Woodrow Wilson, War Message to Congress, April 2, 1917.

Yesterday, December 7, 1941—a date which will live in infamy—the United States of America was suddenly and deliberately attacked by naval and air forces of the empire of Japan.

. . . the distance of Hawaii from Japan makes it obvious that the attack was deliberately planned many days or even weeks ago. During the intervening time the Japanese government has deliberately sought to deceive the United States by false statements and expressions of hope for continued peace.

The attack yesterday on the Hawaiian Islands has caused severe damage to American naval and military forces. I regret to tell you that very many American lives have been lost. In addition, American ships have been reported torpedoed on the high seas between San Francisco and Honolulu.

Yesterday the Japanese government also launched an attack against Malaya.

Last night Japanese forces attacked Hong Kong.

Last night Japanese forces attacked Guam.

Last night Japanese forces attacked the Philippine Islands.

Last night the Japanese attacked Wake Island.

And this morning the Japanese attacked Midway Island.

Japan has therefore undertaken a surprise offensive extending throughout the Pacific. . . .

As Commander-in-Chief of the Army and Navy, I have directed that all measures be taken for our defense.

Always will we remember the character of the onslaught against us.

No matter how long it may take us to overcome this premeditated invasion, the American people, in their righteous might, will win through to absolute victory.

I believe that I interpret the will of the Congress and of the people when I assert that we will not only defend ourselves to the uttermost, but will make it very certain that this form of treachery shall never again endanger us.

Hostilities exist. There is no blinking at the fact that our people, our territory, and our interests are in grave danger.

With confidence in our armed forces, with the unbounding determination of our people, we will gain the inevitable triumph. So help us God.

I ask that the Congress declare that since the unprovoked and dastardly attack by Japan on Sunday, December 7, 1941, a state of war has existed between the United States and the Japanese Empire.

President Franklin D. Roosevelt, Message to Congress, December 8, 1941.

As a woman I can't go to war, and I refuse to send anyone else.
Jeannette Rankin, Congresswoman from Montana, on casting the single vote in Congress against a declaration of war on Japan, December 8, 1941; quoted in Hanna Josephson, *Jeannette Rankin* (1974).

Older men declare war. But it is youth that must fight and die. And it is youth who must inherit the tribulation, the sorrow, and the triumphs that are the aftermath of war.
President Herbert Hoover, speech at the Republican Party National Convention, Chicago, June 27, 1944.

When you have to kill a man it costs nothing to be polite.
Winston Churchill, in justifying why the declaration of war against Japan was made in diplomatic language, December 8, 1941, *The Second World War: The Grand Alliance* (1950).

defeat

He defeated the Americans with great slaughter.
Ironic inscription on the tomb of Lord Cornwallis at Westminster Abbey. It was his surrender to George Washington at Yorktown, Virginia, on October 17, 1781, that effectively ended the American Revolutionary War.

Monarchs reared on the old traditions of limited commitments in war had no stomach for the heavy outlays required to redress defeats when the enterprise seemed to promise so little profit. They were solidly enough established and sufficiently undisturbed by nationalist fever to be able to cede a little territory here and there. . . . As late as 1859 a European monarch could still say, as the young Emperor Francis Joseph did in terminating the brief Franco-Austrian War with the cession of Lombardy: "I have lost a battle; I pay with a province."
Bernard Brodie, *Strategy in the Missile Age* (1959).

Please understand that there is no depression in *this* house; we are not interested in the possibilities of defeat; they do not exist.
Queen Victoria, speaking of the Boer War in December 1899, quoted in Elizabeth Longford, *Queen Victoria: Born to Succeed* (1964).

Too much success is not wholly desirable; an occasional beating is good for men—and nations.
Alfred Thayer Mahan, *Life of Nelson* (1897).

Moreover, though it is criminal for a nation not to prepare for war, so that it may escape the dreadful consequences of being defeated in war, yet it must always be remembered that even to be defeated in war may be far better than not to have fought at all.
President Theodore Roosevelt, Message to Congress, December 4, 1906.

A beaten general is disgraced forever.
Marshal Ferdinand Foch, *Precepts and Judgments* (1920).

We have sustained a defeat without a war.
Winston Churchill, speech on the Munich Agreement, in the House of Commons, October 5, 1938.

The defeats and victories of the fellows at the top aren't always defeats and victories for the fellows at the bottom.
Bertolt Brecht, *Mother Courage*, Act III (1939).

A chief is a man who assumes responsibility. He says, "I was beaten." He does not say, "My men were beaten." Thus speaks a real man.
Antoine de Saint-Exupéry, *Flight to Arras* (1942).

I claim we got a hell of a beating. We got run out of Burma and it is humiliating as hell. I think we ought to find out what caused it, go back and retake it.
General Joseph W. Stilwell, *The New York Times* (May 26, 1942).

A man can be destroyed but not defeated.
Ernest Hemingway, *The Old Man and the Sea* (1952).

Victory has a thousand fathers but defeat is an orphan.
President John F. Kennedy, on the defeat of the Bay of Pigs invasion in April 1961, quoted in Arthur M. Schlesinger, Jr., *A Thousand Days* (1965). At an April 21, 1961 news conference he said, "There's an old saying that victory has 100 fathers and defeat is an orphan." It seems that victory lost 900 fathers.

defeat in detail
Generals unskilled in war think a victory incomplete unless the enemy are so straightened in their ground or so entirely surrounded by numbers as to have no possibility of escape. But in such a situation, where no hopes remain, fear itself will arm an enemy and despair inspires courage. When men find they must inevitably perish, they willingly resolve to die with their comrades and with their arms in their hands.

The maxim of Scipio, that a golden bridge should be made for a flying enemy, has much been commended. For when they have free room to escape they think of nothing but how to save themselves by flight, and the confusion becoming general, great numbers are cut to pieces.
Vegetius, *De Re Militari* (378 A.D.).

What difference does it make if you have two tanks to my one, when you spread them out and let me smash them in detail?
Field Marshal Erwin Rommel to a captured British officer in 1941, quoted in W. G. F. Jackson, *The Battle for North Africa* (1975).

When we have concentrated an absolutely superior force and encircled one of the enemy columns . . . our attacking formations (or units) should not attempt to wipe out all the encircled enemy simultaneously. . . . Instead, we should concentrate an absolutely superior force, that is to say, a force six, five, four or at least three times that of the enemy, concentrate the whole or the bulk of our artillery, select one (not two) of the weaker spots in the enemy's positions, attack it fiercely and be sure to win. This accomplished, swiftly exploit the victory and destroy the enemy forces one by one.
Mao Tse-tung, *Selected Military Writings* (1963).

We must arrange all our operations so that no significant part of our forces can be isolated and defeated in detail. There must exist either the definite capacity of both forces to combine tactically, or the probability that each force can operate independently without danger of defeat.
General Eisenhower in Alfred D. Chandler, Jr., ed., *The Papers of Dwight David Eisenhower: The War Years*, III (1970).

defense

The true strength of a prince does not consist so much in his ability to conquer his neighbors, as in the difficulty they find in attacking him.
Charles de Montesquieu, *The Spirit of the Laws* (1748).

If a madman were to come into this room with a stick in his hand, no doubt we should pity the state of his mind; but our primary consideration would be to take care of ourselves. We should knock him down first, and pity him afterwards.
Samuel Johnson quoted in James Boswell, *Life of Johnson* (1791).

It is axiomatic in the art of war that the side which remains behind its fortified line is always defeated.
Napoleon I, writing in 1793, quoted in J. C. Herold, *The Mind of Napoleon* (1955).

Defense without an active purpose is self-contradictory both in strategy and in tactics.
Karl von Clausewitz, *On War* (1832).

The defensive is the stronger form of making war.
Karl von Clausewitz, *On War* (1832).

Every army which maintains a strictly defensive attitude must, if attacked, be at last driven from its position; whilst by profiting by all the advantages of the defensive system, and holding itself ready to take the offensive when occasion offers, it may hope for the greatest success. A general who stands motionless to receive his enemy, keeping strictly on the defensive, may fight ever so bravely, but he must give way when properly attacked. It is not so, however, with a general who indeed waits to receive his enemy, but with the determination to fall upon him offensively at the proper moment, to wrest from him and transfer to his own troops the moral effect always produced by an onward movement.
General Antoine Henri Jomini, *Summary of the Art of War* (1838).

He who stays on the defensive does not make war, he endures it.
Colmar von der Goltz, *The Nation in Arms* (1883).

It is the fashion to call our [British] navy our first line of defence; but this refers only to material means. Our first line of defence should be the respect of Europe.
Edward B. Hamley, speaking in 1885, quoted in Jay Luvaas, *The Education of an Army* (1964).

Truth telling is not compatible with the defense of the realm.
George Bernard Shaw, *Heartbreak House* (1920).

Do not let us be hair-splitters. Let us not ask ourselves whether the Americas should begin to defend themselves after the first attack, or the fifth attack, or the tenth attack, or the twentieth attack. The time for active defense is now.
President Franklin D. Roosevelt, speech to the nation on the sinking of USS *Greer* by Germany (on September 5, 1941), September 11, 1941.

A true posture of defense is composed of three factors—spiritual, military and economic.
President Dwight D. Eisenhower, press conference, April 30, 1953.

Defensive weapons do not spring like the hydrogen bomb from the brains of brilliant professors of physics. . . . Defense is not technically sweet.
Freeman Dyson, *Disturbing the Universe* (1979).

The tactical predominance of the defense helps explain why the Civil War was so long and bloody. The rifle and trench ruled Civil War battlefields as thoroughly as the machine-gun and trench ruled those of World War I.
James M. McPherson, *Battle Cry of Freedom* (1988).

defense contractors

I'd like to see the government get out of war altogether and leave the whole feud to private industry.
Joseph Heller, *Catch-22* (1961).

The problem with government weapons procurement is that the system protects the suppliers instead of the taxpayers. After a weapons manufacturer wins a contract from the military—sometimes by "underbidding" with unrealistically low amounts—the manufacturer can become the sole source for 20 years, at which time costs are typically doubled and tripled in the absence of competition.
Grace Commission (chaired by J. Peter Grace) report of August 30, 1983. This was formally the *President's Private Sector Survey on Cost Control.*

You've got to realize that there are welfare queens in the Pentagon, too. They're the big contractors.
Senator Charles Grassley, to President Ronald Reagan, quoted in A. Ernest Fitzgerald, *The Pentagonists* (1989).

President Bush is starting to get tough. Last week he said he wouldn't tolerate cost overruns from defense contractors. So from now on if the Pentagon wants to get sophisticated weapons, they're going to have to go down and buy 'em at the gun shop like everybody else.
Jay Leno quoted in Peter Tauber, "Not Just Another Funny Face," *The New York Times Magazine* (February 26, 1989).

defense financing

The sinews of war are infinite money [*Nervos belli, pecuniam infinitam*].
Marcus Tullius Cicero, *Orationes Philippicae*, V, (60 B.C.). Niccolò Machiavelli, in *The Discourses* (1517), disagreed. He wrote that the "sinews of war are not gold, but good soldiers; for gold alone will not procure good soldiers, but good soldiers will always procure gold."

Those who try to be tightfisted while waging war always end by spending more. For nothing requires a more boundless effusion of money than war. The greater the provisions, the quicker the undertaking will be ended. Failure to make such provisions, just to save money, will make the enterprise take longer and, what is more, will result in incomparably greater cost. Accordingly, nothing is more pernicious than waging a war by disbursing monies desultorily and without large amounts of cash at hand. For that is not the way to finish a war but to nourish it.
Francesio Guicciardini, *Ricordi* (1530).

Nowadays the whole art of war is reduced to money: and nowadays, that prince who can best find money to feed, clothe and pay his army, not he that has the most valiant troops, is surest of success and conquest.
Charles Davenant, *Essay Upon Ways and Means of Supplying the War* (1695), quoted in Michael Howard, *War in European History* (1976).

Millions for defense, but not one cent for tribute.
Usually attributed to Charles C. Pinckney, speaking in 1797 of French efforts to extort a "loan" from the United States, quoted in Edward Channing, *A History of the United States*, IV (1917). Other sources hold that all Pinckney said was "No, no; not a sixpence," or "not a penny." The "millions for defense . . ." line is then attributed to Robert Goodloe Harper of South Carolina.

I am a thorough believer in a policy of adequate military preparation. The real question is whether spending more money to make a better military force would really make a better country. I would be the last to disparage the military art. . . . But I can

see no merit in any unnecessary expenditures of money to hire men to build fleets and carry muskets when international relations and agreements permit the turning of such resources into the making of good roads, the building of better homes, the promotion of education, and all the other arts of peace which minister to the advancement of human welfare.
President Calvin Coolidge, speech to the American Legion, quoted in *Time* (October 19, 1925).

Only poets make strategy without budgets.
Giulio Douhet, writing in the 1920s, quoted in B. Bruce-Briggs, *The Shield of Faith* (1988).

Paralyzing nausea began to creep over me. In my emotional exhaustion I spoke recklessly [to President Franklin D. Roosevelt in 1933] and said something to the general effect that when we lost the next war, and an American boy, lying in the mud with an enemy bayonet through his belly and an enemy foot on his dying throat, spat out his last curse, I wanted the name not to be MacArthur, but Roosevelt. The President grew livid. "You must not talk that way to the President!" he roared. He was, of course, right, and I knew it almost before the words had left my mouth. I said that I was sorry and apologized. But I felt my Army career was at an end. I told him he had my resignation as Chief of Staff. As I reached the door his voice came with that cool detachment which so reflected his extraordinary self-control, "Don't be foolish, Douglas; you and the budget must get together on this."
[George] Dern [the Secretary of War] had shortly reached my side and I could hear his gleeful tones, "You've saved the Army." But I just vomited on the steps of the White House.
General Douglas MacArthur, *Reminiscences* (1964).

Some day there is going to be a man sitting in my present chair who has not been raised in the military services and who will have little understanding of where slashes in their estimates can be made with little or no damage. If that should happen while we still have the state of tension that now exists in the world, I shudder to think of what could happen in this country . . . .
President Dwight D. Eisenhower, August 20, 1956 letter to Everett E. Hazlett, quoted in William Bragg Ewald, Jr., *Eisenhower the President* (1981).

The determination of United States strategy has become a more or less incidental byproduct of the administrative process of the defense budget.
General Maxwell D. Taylor, *The Uncertain Trumpet* (1960).

The nation should be told why the military budget is going up while the Vietnam war is being wound down. The cruel fact is that there is no peace dividend. It is the only time in American history that we will spend more for the military at the end of a war than while the war was still going strong.
Senator William Proxmire, speech in the Senate, February 3, 1971.

How many billions would we have gladly paid to avoid Pearl Harbor! Ten billion! Twenty billion! Thirty-five billion dollars! Who's going to step forward and say, "My children's lives are not worth that much"?
Vice President George Bush, *The New York Times* (August 18, 1981).

The Republicans are now giving the impression that the only way of solving national-security problems is throwing money at it. The Democrats have given the impression that the way of dealing with social problems is throwing money at it. Neither works.
Senator Dan Quayle, *The New York Times* (April 19, 1982).

The public doesn't connect military spending with strength—it connects it with waste.
Senator Carl Levin, *The Washington Post* (December 2, 1982).

For there is one rule in strategy that is truly universal: nothing worthwhile comes cheaply. There are *no* cheap weapons that cannot be defeated by equally cheap countermeasures.
Edward N. Luttwak, *Strategy and History*, II (1985).

Before we give you billions more, we want to know what you've done with the trillion you've got.
Congressman Les Aspin, Chair of the House Armed Services Committee, letter to Secretary of Defense Caspar Weinberger, quoted in *The New York Times* (February 5, 1985).

Getting a fix on just how much money the Pentagon really needs is like trying to nail Jell-O to a wall.
Senator Carl Levin, *U.S. News & World Report* (May 27, 1985).

The defense budget has to be determined by the size of the threat. And the size of the threat is going up.
Caspar W. Weinberger, Secretary of Defense, *Time* (October 14, 1985).

There's only one continuing, never-changing factor about [defense budget] outlay estimates: They are always wrong.
Caspar W. Weinberger, Secretary of Defense, testimony before the Senate Budget Committee, February 6, 1986.

This is a defense budget with no priorities and no discipline. It's a Twinkie defense. It's like a child loose in a pastry shop. Even if one swallows hook, line and Trident the Reagan–Weinberger sermon on the national-security need for increased defense spending to meet the Soviet threat, the Administration still ought to be able to reform, terminate or cut those Department of Defense activities least useful to defending America in order to provide more money for those programs most useful to defending America.
Representative Patricia Schroeder, *The New York Times* (February 17, 1986).

[Congressman] Carl Vinson once said the most expensive thing in the world is a cheap Army and Navy. Weakness invites attack.
Admiral James A. Lyons, *Los Angeles Times* (August 10, 1986).

I think [the Defense Department] is awash in extra money. The Pentagon is like a squirrel's lair—there's lots of little acorns hidden away.
Representative Charles E. Schumer, *The Washington Post* (October 5, 1987).

Soviet leaders set out to present the Soviet Union to its own citizens and to those of the non-aligned countries as a peace-seeking nation, reluctantly obliged to arm itself in response to the aggressive armaments expansion of the capitalist nations. Such claims are unlikely to impress if the "correct" figures were to reveal a level of spending in excess of that of any other country in the world.
R. T. Maddock, *The Political Economy of Soviet Defence Spending* (1988).

In a budget hearing in Congress, a senator asked a general why the army needed money for enlisted men to do household chores for the officers.
"Sir," came the reply, "would you like to see a general in the United States Army out pushing his own lawn mower?"
"Well, I am a senator of the United States and I push my own lawn mower."
David Brinkley, *Washington Goes to War* (1988).

defense versus offense

The passage from the defensive to the offensive is one of the most delicate operations of war.
Napoleon I, *Military Maxims* (1827).

What Wellington comprehended was that the firepower of infantry, when infantry was disposed in careful conformity to the topography of a defensive position, would ... defeat any attack thrown against it; and by defeating it create the circumstances in which counter-attack would deliver victory. He had grasped, in short, that the *defensive* was the stronger form of war between gunpowder armies and devised a "system"—his word—to capitalize on that perception. Nelson had perceived an opposite truth: that the *offensive* was the stronger form of warfare between gunpowder navies.... Both indeed had "systems," but with this difference: Wellington's system, ... did not expose him continuously to the fire of the enemy at close range; Nelson's, by contrast, did exactly that. As a result, while Wellington survived sixteen battles as a commander at the cost of some near misses, Nelson succumbed in his first command of a general engagement at sea.
John Keegan, *The Price of Admiralty* (1988).

The best thing for an army on the defensive is to know how to take the offensive at the proper time, and to take it.
General Antoine Henri Jomini, *Summary of the Art of War* (1838).

In war, the defensive exists mainly that the offensive may act more freely.
Alfred Thayer Mahan, *Naval Strategy* (1911).

The only defense is in offense, which means that you have to kill more women and children more quickly than the enemy if you want to save yourselves.
Stanley Baldwin, 1932 speech quoted in G. M. Young, *Stanley Baldwin* (1952).

We are defending Mother Russia—that's moral. You are increasing your offensive forces—that's immoral.
Soviet President Alexei Kosygin, to President Lyndon B. Johnson during their 1967 meeting in Glassboro, New Jersey, quoted in Gregg Herken, *Counsels of War* (1987).

Department of Defense

If we look forward, there will be a ministry of defense, combining army, navy, and air force under one direction.
General Billy Mitchell, speaking in 1919, quoted in Roger Burlingame, *General Billy Mitchell* (1952).

When I became Secretary of Defense in 1961, I felt that either of two broad philosophies of management could be followed by the man at the head of this great establishment. He could play an essentially passive role—a judicial role. In this role the Secretary would make the decisions required of him by law by approving recommendations made to him. On the other hand, the Secretary of Defense could play an active role providing aggressive leadership—questioning, suggesting alternatives, proposing objectives and stimulating progress. This active role represents my own philosophy of management.
Robert S. McNamara, "McNamara Defines His Job," *The New York Times Magazine* (April 26, 1964).

I consider the Department of Defense to be a department of peace.
President Richard M. Nixon, news conference, February 6, 1969.

The Defense Department, on the military side—they change jobs every two years—the top people. On the civilian side, they generally come in without experience. So you have sort of two groups constantly rotating, and nobody ever gets time to find out what's really going on.

Admiral Hyman G. Rickover, testimony before the Congressional Joint Economic Committee, January 28, 1982.

The Office of the Secretary of Defense, originally 50 people, is now 2,000 people. The Joint Staff, originally to be not more than 100 people, is now 2,000 people. The Office of the Secretary of the Navy, the Chief of Naval Operations and the Commandant of the Marine Corps, originally to be 300 people, is now 2,000 people. The Defense Logistics Agency, originally to be the "coordinator" of commodities, is now 50,000 people. . . . These are the results, every one of them, of reform. . . . What has been created over the last 40 years is an incredible, and unwieldy, "monster."

John F. Lehman, Jr., Secretary of the Navy, *The New York Times* (April 6, 1985).

forward defense

The harsh experience in 1941 provided further arguments for a forward defense. Once again, space had turned out to be vitally important. Axis forces had advanced six hundred miles in four months on their whole front and were only held at the outskirts of Moscow. . . . Leningrad would certainly have fallen to the Germans if they had not had to cover four hundred miles (the Baltic states) before launching their assault. Distance was itself a defense and if war did come and the Soviets should be forced to retreat, the five hundred miles of Eastern Europe could be critical in providing time to mobilize the full defense effort.

Forward defense also meant the battle would not be fought on Russian soil.

Michael MccGwire, *Military Objectives in Soviet Foreign Policy* (1987).

We can't pull out of Germany and still declare a forward defense strategy. If an airplane is back [out of the immediate danger area] it doesn't serve as a proper deterrent. If deterrence works then you don't worry about the fact that you have expensive things at risk. So the point is, you have to have capable aircraft forward-deployed.

General Larry D. Welch, USAF Chief of Staff, *Insight* (February 6, 1989).

Secretary of Defense

The nomination of [Charles E.] Wilson as Defense Secretary [in 1953] ran into a hornet's nest of opposition in the closely divided Senate Armed Services Committee when the sixty-three-year-old industrialist balked at selling his stock in General Motors, a major defense contractor. Wilson argued at a closed hearing that "what was good for our country was good for General Motors, and vice versa." His critics quoted him as saying "what is good for General Motors is good for the country," and in the ensuing political fury President Eisenhower nearly lost his Defense Secretary even before he was confirmed.

Clark R. Mollenhoff, *The Pentagon* (1967).

I felt in my heart that my appointment as Secretary of Defense was wrong. I told President-elect Kennedy this, and we worked out a deal. It was based on the following propositions: (a) I would accept the job. It was a tremendous opportunity to serve the country. (b) I wasn't qualified for the job. And, therefore, (c) if I took the job, I could appoint all of my senior people—my advisors—myself, and these choices would be made solely on the basis of ability and experience. Of course, the President would have to endorse my own choices formally. But the emphasis was to be on talent, not politics.

Robert S. McNamara quoted in James G. Blight and David A. Welch, *On the Brink* (1989).

Asked why he gave Reagan's claims about Grenada such credence after the administration had first misled him about the impending invasion and later refused to allow him or other reporters the chance to independently verify those claims, [John] McWethy asked rhetorically, "Do you report nothing? What you do is say, 'Administration officials say.' You report that Weinberger *says* the fighting was heaviest here, or Weinberger *says* the barracks are under siege. Well, shit, he's the fucking Secretary of Defense. What are you going to do? You report what he says."
Mark Hertsgaard, *On Bended Knee* (1988).

defiance

My lord, my country is indeed in danger, but there is one way to never see it lost, and that is to die in the last ditch.
William III, Prince of Orange and [later] King of England, speaking to the Duke of Buckingham, who wanted him not to fight the French, July 5, 1672, quoted in Mary C. Trevelyan, *William the Third and the Defence of Holland* (1930).

The poorest man may in his cottage bid defiance to all the forces of the Crown. It may be frail—its roof may shake—the wind may blow through it—the storm may enter—the rain may enter—but the King of England cannot enter!—all his force dares not cross the threshold of the ruined tenement!
William Pitt, the elder, Earl of Chatham, 1763 speech in the House of Lords, reprinted in H. P. Brougham, *Historical Sketches of Statesmen Who Flourished in the Time of George III*, 1 (1939).

I have not yet begun to fight!
John Paul Jones, on being asked by British Captain Pearson of the HMS *Serapis* if he had struck the colors of USS *Bonhomme Richard* during the Battle off Flamborough Head, September 23, 1779. According to Samuel Eliot Morison in *John Paul Jones* (1959), this famous phrase first appeared in print in an 1825 account of the battle by Lieutenant Richard Dale published in John Henry Sherburne, *Life and Character of the Chevalier John Paul Jones*.

After the train had been captured by 150 Boers, the last four men, though completely surrounded, and with no cover, continued to fire until three were killed, the fourth wounded. On the Boers asking the survivor the reason why they had not surrendered, he replied, "Why, man, we are the Gordon Highlanders."
Lord Kitchener, telegram from Pretoria, to Edward VII (August 10, 1901), quoted in Thomas Gilby, *Britain at Arms* (1953).

They shall not pass [*Ils ne passeront pas*].
French General Robert Nivelle, speaking of the Germans at Verdun on January 23, 1916. According to Alistair Horne, *The Price of Glory* (1962), "Nivelle's . . . irradiating self-confidence . . . really swept people away. His square shoulders gave a potent impression of strength and audacity. His face burned with ruthless determination, and when he expressed an intent his audience was somehow made to feel that it was already a fait accompli. It was he, not Petain as is sometimes thought, who gave birth to the immortalised challenge at Verdun: 'Ils ne passeront pas!' "

We . . . would rather die on our feet than live on our knees.
President Franklin D. Roosevelt, third Inaugural Address, January 20, 1941.

Send us more Japs!
Attributed to Lt. Col. James P. S. Devereux, USMC, Commander of the U.S. Marine contingent on Wake Island [in December 1941] as they were being overrun by Japanese forces. Devereux was taken prisoner; after the war he said; "I did not send any such message. As far as I know, it wasn't sent at all. None of us was that much of a damn fool. We already had

more Japs than we could handle." See his: "This Is How It Was," *The Saturday Evening Post* (February 23, 1946).

democracy

Remember, democracy never lasts long. It soon wastes, exhausts, and murders itself. There never was a democracy yet that did not commit suicide.
John Adams, April 15, 1814 letter to John Taylor, *The Works of John Adams*, 6, ed. Charles Francis Adams, (1851).

There is no military spirit in a democratic society, where there is no aristocracy, no military nobility. A democratic society is antagonistic to the military spirit.
Ardant du Picq, *Battle Studies* (1868).

The world must be made safe for democracy. Its peace must be planted upon the tested foundations of political liberty. We have no selfish ends to serve. We desire no conquest, no domination. We seek no indemnities for ourselves, no material compensation for the sacrifices we shall freely make. We are but one of the champions of the rights of mankind. . . .
It is a fearful thing to lead this great peaceful people into war, into the most terrible and disastrous of all wars, civilization itself seeming to be in the balance. But the right is more precious than peace.
President Woodrow Wilson, speech before a Joint Session of Congress requesting a Declaration of War against Germany, April 2, 1917. According to William Safire in *Safire's Political Dictionary* (1978): "Had it not been for one man . . . Wilson's phrase might never have caught on. Senator John Sharp Williams of Mississippi . . . was leaning forward, concentrating intently on the speech. When Wilson said, 'The world must be made safe for democracy,' he began slowly—and alone—to clap, continuing until others joined him. This underlined for the reporters in the press gallery that a phrase had been turned."

The cure for the evils of democracy is more democracy!
H. L. Mencken, *Notes on Democracy* (1926).

My job is to teach these natives the meaning of democracy, and they're going to learn democracy if I have to shoot every one of them.
Paul Ford in *The Teahouse of the August Moon* (1956), directed by Daniel Mann; screenplay by John Patrick from the book by Vern J. Sneider.

According to one [British] regimental history, 56 men of a particular company voted, 37 of them for the Conservatives and 19 for Labor. When the votes were being dispatched back to England the company commander found his clerk in a state of great distress. At first he was unable to explain his agitation and then asked for a private interview. After beating about the bush for some minutes he finally managed to spit it out. "I am sorry to tell you, sir, that nineteen of your Company have voted Socialist. Shall I burn their votes, sir?"
John Ellis, *The Sharp End: The Fighting Man in World War II* (1980).

desertion

To seduce the enemy's soldiers from their allegiance and encourage them to surrender is of especial service, for an adversary is more hurt by desertion than by slaughter.
Vegetius, *De Re Militari* (378 A.D.).

To be secure against surprise by numbers of light troops in which the enemy is ordinarily superior to us, we have adopted the usage of the Romans of making light entrenchments all around our camp. . . . This also prevents desertion.
Frederick the Great, *Instructions for His Generals* (1747).

The general and faithful attachment of the Soldiers of this Army to the cause of the King, gives no apprehension of the Crime of Desertion spreading, nevertheless, to prevent the Straggling from the Camp for the purpose of marauding, drunkenness, or other Disorders, leading to Desertion, it is positively ordered that a Report of absent men be sent to Head Quarters within one hour after each roll-calling, in order that parties of Savages may be immediately sent in pursuit, who have orders to scalp all Deserters.
Orderly Book of Lieut.-Gen. John Burgoyne, August 6, 1777, quoted in Thomas Gilby, *Britain at Arms* (1953).

Not upon a man from the colonel to the private in a regiment—both inclusive. We may pick up a marshal or two perhaps; but not worth a damn.
Duke of Wellington, before the Battle of Waterloo, when asked if he anticipated any desertions from the French, quoted in Thomas Creevy, *The Creevy Papers* (1934).

Come, come, let us fight another battle to-day: if I am beaten, we will desert together to-morrow.
Frederick the Great, to a captured deserter who left because "things are going very badly with us," quoted in Thomas Campbell, *Frederick the Great* (1843).

For the man who considered desertion, the likelihood of making a complete escape was favorable. The army only caught one of every five deserters.... The small reward of thirty dollars for capturing a deserter, even when it was doubled in 1891, was not sufficient to endanger most deserters. Rather then report such men, the tendency of civilians was to shield them. As one letter writer said in the *Army and Navy Journal*, "The average citizen regards desertion as but little worse than enlistment."
Edward M. Coffman, *The Old Army* (1986).

There might be a tendency to say now—to those few hundreds who went to Canada or Sweden or someplace else and chose to desert their country because they had a higher morality—we should now give them amnesty. Now, amnesty means forgiveness. We cannot provide forgiveness for them. Those who served paid their price. Those who deserted must pay their price; and the price is not a junket in the Peace Corps or something like that, as some have suggested. The price is a criminal penalty for disobeying the laws of the United States.
President Richard M. Nixon, news conference, January 31, 1973.

deterrence

Men are not hanged for stealing horses, but that horses may not be stolen.
Sir George Savile, Marquis of Halifax, *Political Moral and Miscellaneous Thoughts and Reflections* (1685).

Perhaps my [dynamite] factories will put an end to war even sooner than your congresses. On the day when two army camps may mutually annihilate each other in a second, all civilized nations will probably recoil with horror and disband their troops.
Alfred Nobel, 1892 letter to Bertha von Suttner, quoted in Nichola Halasz, *Nobel* (1959).

Where air equality existed between rival nations, and each was as industrially and politically vulnerable, it is possible that either would hesitate to employ the air attack for fear of instant retaliation.
B. H. Liddell Hart, *Paris, or the Future of War* (1925).

The fact remains that when all is said and done as regards defensive methods, pending some new discovery the only direct measure of defense upon a great scale is the certainty of being able to inflict simultaneously upon the enemy as great damage as he

can inflict upon ourselves. Do not let us undervalue the efficacy of this procedure. It may well prove in practice— I admit I cannot prove it in theory—capable of giving complete immunity. If two Powers show themselves equally capable of inflicting damage upon each other by some particular process of war, so that neither gains an advantage from its adoption and both suffer the most hideous reciprocal injuries, it is not only possible but it seems probable that neither will employ that means.
Winston Churchill, speech of November 1934, quoted in Thomas C. Schelling, *Arms and Influence* (1966).

The first and most vital step in any American security program in the age of atomic bombs is to take measures to guarantee to ourselves in case of attack the possibility of retaliation in kind. The writer in making that statement is not for the moment concerned about who will win the next war in which atomic bombs are used. Thus far the chief purpose of our military establishment has been to win wars. From now on its chief purpose must be to avert them.
Bernard Brodie, *The Absolute Weapon* (1946).

A deterrent force is an effective nuclear offensive force which is secure from destruction by the enemy regardless of what offensive and defensive action he takes against it.
General Curtis E. LeMay, testimony before a U.S. Senate subcommittee, April 30, 1956.

The major deterrent [to war] is in a man's mind. The major deterrent in the future is going to be not only what we have, but what we do, what we are willing to do, what they think we will do. Stamina, guts, standing up for the things that we say—those are deterrents.
Admiral Arleigh Burke, *U.S. News & World Report* (October 3, 1960).

Only when our arms are sufficient beyond doubt can we be certain beyond doubt that they will never be employed.
President John F. Kennedy, Inaugural Address, January 20, 1961.

For Honorable Members opposite the [nuclear missile] deterrent is a phallic symbol. It convinces them that they are men.
George Wigg, speaking in the House of Commons, quoted in *The Observer* (March 8, 1964).

Military strategy can no longer be thought of, as it could be for some countries in some areas, as the science of military victory. It is now equally, if not more, the art of coercion, of intimidation and deterrence.
Thomas C. Schelling, *Arms and Influence* (1966).

My sole object is peace. . . . If you rub it in both at home and abroad that you are ready for instant war with every unit of your strength in the first line, and intend to be first in and hit your enemy in the belly and kick him when he is down, and boil your prisoners in oil (if you take any!), and torture his women and children, then people will keep clear of you.
Admiral Sir John Fisher quoted in Ruddock F. Mackay, *Fisher at Kilverstone* (1973).

The jargon of American strategic analysis works like a narcotic. It dulls our sense of moral outrage about the tragic confrontation of nuclear arsenals, primed and constantly perfected to unleash wide-spread genocide. It fosters the current smug complacency regarding the soundness and stability of mutual deterrence. It blinds us to the fact that our methods for preventing nuclear war rest on a form of warfare universally condemned since the Dark Ages—the mass killing of hostages.
Fred Ikle, "Can Nuclear Deterrence Last Out the Century," *Foreign Affairs* (January 1973).

Deterrence is a psychological phenomenon. It depends above all on what a potential aggressor considers an unacceptable risk. In the nuclear age a bluff taken seriously is useful; a serious threat taken as a bluff may prove disastrous. The longer deterrence succeeds, the more difficult it is to demonstrate what made it work. Was peace maintained by the risk of war, or because the adversary never intended aggression in the first place?
Henry Kissinger, *White House Years* (1979).

If the adversary feels that you are unpredictable, even rash, he will be deterred from pressing you too far.
President Richard M. Nixon, *The Real War* (1980).

Deterrence is in part a bluff.
Zbigniew Brzezinski, *The New York Times* (January 18, 1981).

The Chinese philosopher, Sun Tzu, 2,500 years ago said winning a hundred victories in a hundred battles is not the acme of skill; to subdue the enemy without fighting is the acme of skill. A truly successful army is one that, because of its strength and ability and dedication, will not be called upon to fight because no one will dare to provoke it.
President Ronald Reagan, speech at West Point, May 27, 1981.

Our strategy is one of preventing war by making it self-evident to our enemies that they're going to get their clocks cleaned if they start one.
General John W. Vessey, Jr., Chairman, Joint Chiefs of Staff, quoted in *The New York Times* (July 15, 1984).

Both our countries know from bitter experience that conventional weapons do not deter war in Europe whereas nuclear weapons have done so for over 40 years.
Prime Minister Margaret Thatcher, speaking to Mikhail Gorbachev, quoted in *The New York Times* (April 27, 1989).

dictators

I have heard, in such a way as to believe it, of your recently saying that both the army and the government needed a dictator. Of course it was not for this, but in spite of it, that I have given you the command. Only those generals who gain successes can set up dictators. What I now ask of you is a military success, and I will risk the dictatorship.
President Abraham Lincoln, letter of January 26, 1863 to General Joseph Hooker, quoted in J. G. Nicolay and J. Hay, *Complete Works of Abraham Lincoln*, VIII (1905).

A dictatorship can last forever, if properly managed. Parliament is there. I use it whenever necessary. Socialism works on the principle that all are equal, but Fascism knows that we are far from equal. The masses like rule by the few.
Benito Mussolini, *Time* (November 12, 1923).

So long as men worship the Caesars and Napoleons, Caesars and Napoleons will arise to make them miserable.
Aldous Huxley, *Ends and Means* (1937).

Of course, the Saigon militarist regime headed by Thieu and Ky will strenuously object to any extension of the cease-fire or to any change in our policy. . . . The fact is that these tinhorn dictators could not remain in power for more than three days without the support of our armed forces. They are well aware of the fact that, once there is

peace in Vietnam, they will be forced to flee and to join their unlisted bank accounts in Hong Kong and Switzerland.
Senator Stephen M. Young, speech in the Senate, September 9, 1969.

I oppose military and supporting assistance to dictatorships in various less-developed countries. While we are fighting in Vietnam, ostensibly to defend the South Vietnamese right of free elections and self-determinations, it seems anomalous to donate American treasure to the aid of governments systematically oppressing their citizens.
Representative William J. Randall, speech in the House, December 9, 1969.

In man's heart, if not in fact, the day of the dictator is over.
President George Bush, Inaugural Address, January 20, 1989.

diplomacy

In statesmanship get the formalities right, never mind about the moralities.
Mark Twain, *Following the Equator* (1897).

Diplomacy [is] the patriotic art of lying for one's country.
Ambrose Bierce, *The Devil's Dictionary* (1911).

The diplomacy of the present administration has sought to respond to modern ideas of commercial intercourse. This policy has been characterized as substituting dollars for bullets.
President William Howard Taft, annual message to Congress, December 3, 1912.

Open covenants of peace, openly arrived at, after which there shall be no private international understandings of any kind but diplomacy shall proceed always frankly and in the public view.
President Woodrow Wilson, address to Congress (this was the first of "Fourteen Points"), January 8, 1918.

Diplomacy is always equal. It's like good bookkeeping. He don't believe you and you don't believe him, so it always balances.
Will Rogers, writing in 1927, *The Autobiography of Will Rogers*, ed. D. Day (1949).

Diplomacy is to do and say the nastiest thing in the nicest way.
Isaac Goldberg, *The Reflex* (1930).

[American diplomacy is] easy on the brain but hell on the feet.
Charles G. Dawes, American Ambassador to Great Britain, *The New York Times* (June 3, 1931).

The greater part of what passes for diplomatic history is little more than the record of what one clerk said to another clerk.
George Malcolm Young, *Victorian England* (1936).

"We have found you a very tough man to deal with," said [Soviet Foreign Minister] Molotov when the new ambassador paid his formal courtesy call in October of 1943.
"I have come as a friend," [Averell] Harriman responded.
"Oh, I know that," Molotov said. "I intended my remarks to be complimentary."
Walter Isaacson and Evan Thomas, *The Wise Men* (1986).

Diplomacy is the lowest form of politeness because it misquotes the greatest number of people. A nation, like an individual, if it has anything to say, should simply say it.
E. B. White, *One Man's Meat* (1944).

Ought we to recognize them or not? Recognizing a person is not necessarily an act of approval. I will not be personal, or give instances. One has to recognize lots of things and people in this world of sin and woe that one does not like. The reason for having diplomatic relations is not to confer a compliment, but to secure a convenience.
Winston Churchill, speech in the House of Commons on recognizing Communist China, November 17, 1949.

All diplomacy is a continuation of war by other means.
Chou En-Lai quoted by Edgar Snow, *The Saturday Evening Post* (March 27, 1954).

To jaw-jaw is always better than to war-war.
Winston Churchill, speaking at a White House luncheon, *The New York Times* (June 27, 1954).

A Foreign Secretary . . . is always faced with this cruel dilemma. Nothing he can say can do very much good, and almost anything he may say may do a great deal of harm. Anything he says that is not obvious is dangerous; whatever is not trite is risky. He is forever poised between the cliché and the indiscretion.
Harold Macmillan, speech in the House of Commons, July 27, 1955.

What could the guy do? He had a war on his hands and plenty of weapons left to fight it with. I'd say it was the same in all the countries, after the statesmen got killed. It makes a war very difficult to stop.
Nevil Shute, *On The Beach* (1957).

Diplomacy and defense are not substitutes for one another. Either alone would fail.
President John F. Kennedy, speech at the University of Washington, Seattle, November 16, 1961.

Successful diplomacy, like successful marriage, is not much publicized.
John Paton Davies, *The New York Times Magazine* (May 23, 1965).

There are few ironclad rules of diplomacy but to one there is no exception. When an official reports that talks were useful, it can safely be concluded that nothing was accomplished.
John Kenneth Galbraith, "The American Ambassador," *Foreign Service Journal* (June 1969).

You cannot in today's world have successful diplomacy without secrecy. It is impossible. I used to say that I believe in the Wilsonian doctrine of open covenants openly arrived at. But that was Wilson at his idealistic best and his pragmatic worst.
President Richard M. Nixon, *Los Angeles Times* (May 17, 1974).

In relations between nations, the progress of civilization may be seen as movement from force to diplomacy, from diplomacy to law.
Lewis Henkin, *How Nations Behave* (1979).

It was Stalin who once said that to speak of honest diplomacy is "like speaking of dry water."
Abba Eban, *The New Diplomacy* (1983).

Running the Latin American bureau in the State Department is like being given 1,000 pounds of canaries and a box that will only hold 500 pounds. Right away, you begin banging on the sides of the box, trying to keep enough canaries in the air so that the box won't burst open. After a while, your arms get tired.
Langhorne A. Motley, Former Assistant Secretary of State for Inter-American Affairs, *The New York Times* (May 10, 1985).

The essence of diplomacy is how you manage the day-to-day business, the confidence you build, the atmosphere you create, so that when the tough times come you can do business.
Lawrence S. Eagleburger, *The New York Times* (June 23, 1986).

brinkmanship
The ability to get to the verge without getting into the war is the necessary art. If you cannot master it, you inevitably get into war. If you try to run away from it, if you are scared to go to the brink, you are lost.
John Foster Dulles, U.S. Secretary of State, *Life* (January 16, 1956). *Time* reported on January 23, 1956 that Democratic Presidential Candidate Adlai Stevenson responded to this by saying "I am shocked that the Secretary of State is willing to play Russian roulette with the life of our nation."

[John Foster Dulles] spent most of his time on aeroplanes and invented Brinkmanship, the most popular game since Monopoly.
Richard Armour, *It All Started With Columbus* (1961).

We will not act prematurely or unnecessarily risk the costs of world-wide nuclear war in which even the fruits of victory would be ashes in our mouth. But neither will we shrink from that risk at any time it must be faced.
President John F. Kennedy, speech to the nation during the Cuban Missile Crisis, October 22, 1962.

[Brinkmanship is the] deliberate creation of a recognizable risk of war, a risk that one does not completely control. It is the tactic of deliberately letting the situation get somewhat out of hand, just because its being out of hand may be intolerable to the other party and force his accommodation.
Thomas C. Schelling, *The Strategy of Conflict* (1963).

detente
Detente is a velvet glove—a mailed fist in a velvet glove. Should we be discussing the beauty and texture of the glove, or the import of the mailed fist?
James R. Schlesinger, U.S. Secretary of Defense, *The Christian Science Monitor* (September 1, 1973).

Detente is appeasement—nothing else, pure and simple, but appeasement.
George Meany, President of the AFL-CIO, *The New York Times* (June 5, 1974). Meany had earlier said: "I pray every night that [U.S. Secretary of State] Henry Kissinger won't give the Russians the Washington Monument—he's given them every God damn thing else." *The New York Times* (April 2, 1974).

Detente is a process, not a permanent achievement.
Henry Kissinger, testimony before the Foreign Relations Committee of the U.S. Senate, September 19, 1974.

I believe in detente. But while I'm detenting, as they say, I wouldn't turn my back on them.
George C. Wallace, Governor of Alabama, *Los Angeles Times* (May 8, 1975).

[Under detente] the Soviets see the United States right now as a great placid bovine chewing its cud in the sun, with two huge udders extending over them—one labelled "grain" and the other labelled "technology." It stands there letting itself be milked dry, twitching its tail contentedly, too lazy and too placid to notice.
Admiral Elmo R. Zumwalt, Jr., *The Washington Post* (February 15, 1976).

I don't use the word "detente" any more. I think that we ought to say that the United States will meet with the superpowers—the Soviet Union, China, and others— and seek to relax tensions so that we can continue a policy of peace through strength.
President Gerald R. Ford, *Los Angeles Times* (March 2, 1976).

Detente, which started out worthily and with a good purpose, has become a one-way street.
Ronald Reagan, *The Christian Science Monitor* (June 3, 1976).

Genuine detente also includes restraint in the use of military power and an end to the pursuit of unilateral advantage.
President Jimmy Carter, speech in Bonn, West Germany, July 14, 1978.

diplomacy and war

Does the cessation of diplomatic notes stop the political relations between different nations and governments? Is not war merely another kind of writing and language for their thought? It has, to be sure, its own grammar, but not its own logic.
Karl von Clausewitz, *On War* (1832).

If foreign ministers had always followed their sovereigns to the front history would have fewer wars to tell of.
Otto von Bismarck quoted in Edward Crankshaw, *Bismarck* (1981).

No man can qualify for the duties of statesman until he has made a thorough study of the science of war in its broadest sense. He need not go to military school, much less serve in the army or in the militia. But unless he makes himself thoroughly acquainted with the methods and conditions requisite to success in war he is liable to do almost infinite damage to his country.
John MacAllister Schofield, *Forty-Six Years in the Army* (1897).

The statesman has nothing in his gift but disaster so soon as he leaves his own business of creating or obviating wars, and endeavors to conduct them.
Sir Ian Hamilton, *A Staff Officer's Scrapbook* (1905).

Diplomats are just as essential to starting a war as soldiers are for finishing it. You take diplomacy out of war and the thing would fall flat in a week.
Will Rogers, writing in 1927, *The Autobiography of Will Rogers*, ed. D. Day (1949).

diplomats

It is better for aged diplomats to be bored than for young men to die.
Attributed to Warren Austin (1877–1962), U.S. diplomat.

Diplomatists have no right to complain of mere lies; it is their own fault, if, educated as they are, the lies deceive them.
Henry Adams, *The Education of Henry Adams* (1907).

It is good to be on your guard against an Englishman who speaks French perfectly; he is very likely to be a card-sharper or an attaché in the diplomatic service.
W. Somerset Maugham, *The Summing Up* (1938).

While I cannot take the time to name all of the men in the State Department who have been named as members of the Communist Party and members of a spy ring, I have here in my hand a list of 205 that were known to the Secretary of State as being members of the Communist Party and who nevertheless are still working and shaping the policy of the State Department.

Joseph R. McCarthy, speech at Wheeling, West Virginia, making unfounded accusations that heralded the era of McCarthyism, quoted in Richard H. Rovere, *Senator Joe McCarthy* (1959).

A diplomat's life is made up of three ingredients: protocol, Geritol and alcohol.

Adlai E. Stevenson quoted in *The New York Times Magazine* (February 7, 1965).

Diplomats never ask. They make representations.

John Kenneth Galbraith, *Economics, Peace and Laughter* (1971).

Internationally, they [The Carter Administration] don't seem to know the difference between being a diplomat and a doormat.

Ronald Reagan, *The Christian Science Monitor* (December 12, 1977).

There's something about the Foreign Service that takes the guts out of people. The tendency is to avoid confronting an issue.

Evan G. Galbraith, United States Ambassador to France, *The New York Times* (February 13, 1985).

Oh, you know, I am Secretary of State. My trips aren't successful. I just talk to people.

George P. Schultz quoted in *The New York Times* (May 17, 1985).

What's the difference between the diplomat and the military man? The answer is . . . they both do nothing, but the military get up very early in the morning to do it with great discipline, while the diplomats do it late in the afternoon, in utter confusion.

Vernon A. Walter, Ambassador to the United Nations, *Newsweek* (March 3, 1986).

gunboat diplomacy

A man-of-war is the best ambassador.

Attributed to Oliver Cromwell (1599–1658).

A fleet of British ships of war are the best negotiators in Europe.

Admiral Horatio Nelson quoted in Alfred Thayer Mahan, *Life of Nelson* (1897).

This Government wants Perdicaris alive or Raisuli dead.

Secretary of State John Hay, June 22 [1904] telegram to the Sultan of Morocco concerning the kidnapping of Ion H. Perdicaris by Raisuli, a Moroccan outlaw. While U.S. warships were sent to Morocco, this telegram, according to Barbara W. Tuchman, "Perdicaris Alive or Raisuli Dead," *American Heritage* (August 1959), "was not an ultimatum, because Hay deliberately deprived it of meaningfulness by adding, 'Do not land marines or seize customs without Department's specific instructions.' But this sentence was not allowed to spoil the effect: It was withheld from the press." In the end Perdicaris was released and Raisuli became a local governor. Ironically, this whole incident over the protection of an American citizen was misguided, because Pedicaris was *not* an American citizen; but people thought he was at the time.

In time of peace the economic and military might of a country can be demonstrated outside of its own frontiers; therefore the capacity of the navy to suddenly appear near the beaches of other countries and immediately commence the operations it is ordered to conduct, has long been regarded as an important weapon of diplomacy in time of peace. Thus in many cases it becomes possible to achieve political goals without starting a war, but with a threat to start it.

Admiral S. G. Gorshkov, *The Sea Power of The State* (1976).

summits

The old-world diplomacy of Europe was largely carried on in drawing-rooms, and, to a great extent, of necessity still is so. Nations touch at their summits.
Walter Bagehot, *The English Constitution* (1867).

The only summit meeting that can succeed is the one that does not take place.
Senator Barry M. Goldwater, *Why Not Victory?* (1962).

What really happens at even the most serious . . . summit conference where there are significant issues to be discussed? Though little serious conversation takes place at the banquet table, the time consumed in eating and drinking is appalling. . . .

Thus, in trying to measure the period permitted for a substantive exchange of views during ten hours of top-level propinquity, one should deduct at least four hours for eating and drinking. Another hour or two for small talk . . . then divide the remainder by two and one half for the translation. What is left is about two or three hours.
George Ball, *Diplomacy for a Crowded World* (1976).

Gorbachev's three predecessors, Leonid Brezhnev, Yuri Andropov, and Konstantin Chernenko, had all died during Reagan's first four years in office. Whenever Reagan was asked why he waited so long for a summit with the Soviets, his answer was, "They kept dying on me."
Larry Speakes, *Speaking Out* (1988).

disarmament

They shall beat their swords into plowshares, and their spears into pruning hooks; nation shall not lift up sword against nation, neither shall they learn war any more.
The Bible, Isaiah II:4.

Rebuke the company of spearmen. . . scatter thou the people that delight in war.
The Bible, Psalms 68:30.

Among other evils which being unarmed brings you, it causes you to be despised.
Niccolò Machiavelli, *The Prince* (1513).

When the necessity for arms ceases, armaments will disappear. The basic causes of war are not armaments, but in human minds.
Alfred Thayer Mahan, *Armaments and Arbitration* (1912).

Once upon a time all the animals in the zoo decided that they would disarm, and they arranged to have a conference to arrange the matter. So the Rhinoceros said when he opened the proceedings that the use of teeth was barbarous and horrible and ought to be strictly prohibited by general consent. Horns, which were mainly defensive weapons, would, of course, have to be allowed. The Buffalo, the Stag, the Porcupine, and even the little Hedgehog all said they would vote with the Rhino, but the Lion and the Tiger took a different view. They defended teeth and even claws, which they described as honorable weapons of immemorial antiquity. . . . Then the Bear spoke. He proposed that both teeth and horns should be banned and never used again for fighting by any animal. It would be quite enough if animals were allowed to give each other a good hug when they quarreled.
Winston Churchill, speech of October 24, 1928, reprinted in *Winston S. Churchill: His Complete Speeches*, ed. R. R. James, 5 (1974).

It is the greatest possible mistake to mix up disarmament with peace. When you have peace you will have disarmament.
Winston Churchill, speech in the House of Commons, July 13, 1934.

If you carry this resolution and follow out all its implications and do not run away from it you will send a Foreign Minister, whoever he may be, naked into the conference chamber.
Aneurin Bevan, arguing against a proposal for unilateral nuclear disarmament at a British Labour Party meeting, October 3, 1957, quoted in Michael Foot, *Aneurin Bevan*, II (1973).

If the history of the past fifty years teaches us anything, it is that peace does not follow disarmament—disarmament follows peace.
Bernard M. Baruch quoted by Arthur Krock, "In the Nation," *The New York Times* (December 26, 1963).

I listened to Oppy for an hour and a half, and I didn't understand a thing he was saying. How can you expect a paranoid adversary to disarm by example?
Dean Acheson, on J. Robert Oppenheimer's opposition to building the H-bomb, quoted in John Newhouse, *War and Peace in the Nuclear Age* (1988).

What you have to remember is that when I faced the problem of disarmament, we lagged significantly behind the US in both warheads and missiles, and the US was out of range for our bombers. . . . That's why I was convinced that as long as the US held a big advantage over us, we couldn't submit to international disarmament controls.
Nikita Khrushchev, *Khrushchev Remembers: The Last Testament* (1974).

disinformation

The rulers of the state are the only ones who should have the privilege of lying, either at home or abroad; they may be allowed to lie for the good of the state.
Plato, *The Republic* (370 B.C.).

It is necessary to be . . . a great feigner and dissembler; and men are so simple and so ready to obey present necessities, that one who deceives will always find those who allow themselves to be deceived.
Niccolò Machiavelli, *The Prince* (1513).

The greater the lie, the greater the chance that it will be believed.
Adolf Hitler, *Mein Kampf* (1924).

divisions

[In 1935] Stalin and Molotov were, of course, anxious to know above all else what was to be the strength of the French Army on the Western Front; how many divisions? What period of service? After this field had been explored, [French Premier Pierre] Laval said: "Can't you do something to encourage religion and the Catholics in Russia? It would help me so much with the Pope." "Oho!" said Stalin. "The Pope! How many divisions has he got?"
Winston Churchill, *The Second World War: The Gathering Storm* (1948). According to John Colville, *The Fringes of Power* (1985), Churchill responded to Stalin by "replying that the fact they could not be measured in military terms did not mean they did not exist." This seems to have been a favored phrase of Stalin's. At the Potsdam Conference of July 1945 Admiral William D. Leahy [in his 1950 memoir, *I Was There*], an advisor to President Harry Truman, remarked that Stalin's response to pleas from Winston Churchill to consider the rights of Polish Catholics was "How many divisions has the Pope?" President Dwight D. Eisenhower is quoted in *The New York Times*, May 10, 1965, as saying, "Communists only respect force. You remember the remark attributed to Stalin at the Yalta Conference when he was told of the importance of the views of Pope Pius XII. 'How many divisions does Pope Pius command?' Stalin asked at the time. That shows us the Communist mentality clearly."

[A division is] the smallest formation that is a complete orchestra of war and the largest in which every man can know you.
Field Marshal William Slim, *Defeat Into Victory* (1956).

A division is, by tradition, the smallest unit in which infantry, artillery, and cavalry (later tanks) combined with supporting services under one commander and were capable of fighting independently. Such a division was called a "general command" and the commander came to be called a "general."
Len Deighton, *Blitzkrieg* (1980).

dogfights

Like the other combatant forces, they [the Air Service] were a destructive arm in the great battle on land. This, indeed, became their main object, and the aerial combat was only a means of attaining it.
German General Erich von Ludendorff, *Ludendorff's Own Story* (1919).

Though we were out to shoot down planes . . . I would have been delighted to learn that . . . any pilot I had shot down had escaped with his life.
Edward V. Rickenbacker, expressing World War I attitudes, *Rickenbacker* (1979).

I stalked him through the cloud, and when he emerged into a patch of clear sky, I saw that it was a Ju 87. I was in an ideal position to attack, and opened fire and put the remainder of my ammunition—about 2,000 rounds— into him at very close range. Even in the heat of the moment I well remember my amazement at the shattering effect of my fire. Pieces flew off his fuselage and cockpit covering, a stream of smoke appeared from the engine, and a moment later a great sheet of flame licked out from the engine cowling and he dived down vertically. The flames enveloped the whole machine and he went straight down, apparently quite slowly, until he was just a shapeless burning mass of wreckage. Absolutely fascinated by the sight, I followed him down and saw him hit the sea with a great burst of white foam. He disappeared immediately, and apart from a green patch in the water there was no sign that anything had happened. . . . I had often wondered what would be my feelings when killing somebody like this, and especially when seeing them go down in flame. . . . I was rather surprised to reflect afterwards that my only feeling had been one of considerable elation, and a sort of bewildered surprise that it had been so easy.
D. M. Crook, RAF pilot, writing on July 9, 1940, quoted in Len Deighton, *Battle of Britain* (1980).

One of the items on the Chiefs of Staff's agenda is the situation caused by the insistence of innumerable spectators on crowding the pier at Dover to watch the aerial battles [during the Battle of Britain]. It is encouraging that the passion for sightseeing should still be greater than that for self-preservation.
John Colville, *The Fringes of Power* (1985), diary entry for July 30, 1940.

When I am chasing a Hun, I bounce up and down on the seat and bay like a beagle until I can get him in my sights. Then I squirt. If he catches fire or explodes, I cheer and yell, "Sieg heil!" All this time I am scared to death. I must say that I get a certain thrill out of terror. But the real thrill comes when you get home safely. It is a wonderful feeling. I guess the process is something like beating yourself on the head with a club, so that you can appreciate the contrast when you quit.
RAF Squadron Leader Kendrick H. Salusbury-Hughes quoted in Jack Alexander, "Lone Wolves of the RAF," *The Saturday Evening Post* (July 12, 1943).

Never since the Middle Ages and the invention of the long-bow had the battlefields of Europe seen this kind of single combat. When the champions of either side met to fight spectacular duels in and out of the clouds, the rest of the war seemed forgotten; even the man in the trenches paused to watch, as the hosts of Greece and Troy stood by when Hector and Achilles fought.
Alistair Horne, *The Price of Glory* (1962).

I changed course, dropping down and to the left, then fired as I flew down diagonally across them. Some of my bullets pierced the windshield and struck the pilot's body. His head lolled back, he looked as if he had been clubbed. I went into an Immelmann to the left before side-slipping across the front of the Grumman. My adversary went down in a tail spin. . . . At that instant, I was seized by a nameless terror. It is a horrifying moment when you bring down an enemy. You cannot help imagining yourself in the same situation!"
Ryuji Nagatsuka, *I Was a Kamikaze* (1972).

When he blew up, it was a pleasing, beautiful sight. There was no joy in killing someone, but real satisfaction when you outflew a guy and destroyed his machine. That was the contest: human skill and machine performance.
General Chuck Yeager and Leo Jenos, *Yeager* (1985).

dog tags

Veterans of North Africa and Italy during World War II can tell you dog-tag stories about the British Gurkhas and the French "Goumiers." These fierce colonial troops, fabulous patrol experts, learned to feel for the shape of dog tags when they came on sleeping soldiers of whose identity they were not sure. Many a startled American awoke with a knife at his throat and lay paralyzed with terror while the Gurkha or Goumier felt for his dog tag to see whether he would slit his throat for a German or whisper "nice American" and disappear back into the night.
Major Mark M. Boatner, III, *Military Customs and Traditions* (1956).

I came into the [B-17] crew as a last-minute replacement. My predecessor had been competent, I am told, but worried because he was operating under what he conceived to be double jeopardy. If he had to parachute into enemy territory and was captured, he thought, he would be singled out for particularly nasty treatment not only as a member of a crew that had dropped bombs but also as a Jew. (Insistent that every soldier have the comfort of the particular last rites enjoined by his upbringing, the Army had stamped every dogtag with an initial indicating the soldier's presumed faith. And every American soldier was expected to have one of the standard religious affiliations. I suppose that if one wanted to fight the battle for agnostics and atheists one could have demanded an "A," but few Jews would try to dodge the "H" lest it be thought they were running to cover.)
I do not know why I never shared this nightmare of my predecessor. Perhaps it was because it seemed a bit obsessive to fasten on one conceivable disaster when the future had such an abundance of alarming possibilities. . . . In any case . . . my predecessor delightedly moved up to . . . an older and more seasoned crew. In the irony that frequently accompanies such gambling my predecessor went down over Schweinfurt.
Elmer Bendiner, *The Fall of Fortresses* (1980).

domino theory

You have the broader considerations that might follow what you would call the "falling domino" principle. You have a row of dominos set up, you knock over the

first one, and what will happen to the last one is the certainty that it will go over very quickly.
  President Dwight D. Eisenhower, on the strategic importance of Indochina, press conference (April 7, 1954).

The inference we have drawn from this is that we must fight in one country in order to avoid having to fight in another, although we could with equal logic have inferred that it is useless to fight in one country when the same conditions of conflict are present in another.
  J. William Fulbright, *The Arrogance of Power* (1966).

The President [Kennedy] felt that he had a strong, overwhelming reason for being in Vietnam and that we should win the war in Vietnam. [There would be] the loss of all of Southeast Asia if you lost Vietnam. I think everybody was quite clear that the rest of Southeast Asia would fall.
  Robert F. Kennedy quoted in Edwin O. Guthman and Jeffrey Shulman, eds., *Robert Kennedy In His Own Words* (1988).

It is my duty today to announce the discovery of a new "domino theory" that says in essence: If you disregard the advice of General Douglas MacArthur and go into the quicksand of an Asian country, like a domino you will fall into the quicksand of another Asian country.
  Representative Andrew Jacobs, Jr., speech in the House of Representatives, May 14, 1970.

Now I know there are those that say, "Well, the domino theory is obsolete." They haven't talked to the dominoes.
  President Richard M. Nixon, *The New York Times* (July 3, 1970).

I knew that if the aggression succeeded in South Vietnam, then the aggressors would simply keep on going until all of Southeast Asia fell into their hands, slowly or quickly.
  President Lyndon B. Johnson quoted in Doris Kearns, *Lyndon Johnson and the American Dream* (1976).

The battle against Communism must be joined in Southeast Asia with strength and determination . . . or the United States, inevitably, must surrender the Pacific and take up our defenses on our own shores.
  Vice President Lyndon B. Johnson quoted in Stanley Karnow, *Vietnam: A History* (1983).

The Soviet Union underlies all the unrest that is going on. If they weren't engaged in this game of dominoes, there wouldn't be any hot spots in the world.
  President Ronald Reagan quoted in Robert Dallek, *Ronald Reagan* (1984).

doomsday machine

With mock sincerity [Herman] Kahn proposed what he called a "Doomsday Machine." It would be a vast computer wired up to a huge stockpile of H-bombs. When the computer sensed that the Soviet Union had committed an act defined as intolerable, the machine would automatically set off the Doomsday bombs, covering the earth with sufficient radioactive fallout to kill billions of people.
  As Kahn half expected, not a single military officer liked the idea. Yet the Doomsday Machine was only a slightly absurd extension of existing American and NATO policy: the Soviets do something provocative, and we blow up most of their citizens, which provokes them to blow up most of ours.
  Fred Kaplan, *The Wizards of Armageddon* (1983).

We have, by slow and imperceptible steps, been constructing a Doomsday Machine. Until recently—and then, only by accident—no one ever noticed. And we have distributed its triggers all over the Northern Hemisphere. Every American and Soviet leader since 1945 has made critical decisions regarding nuclear war in total ignorance of the climatic catastrophe.
Carl Sagan, "Nuclear War and Climatic Catastrophe," *Foreign Affairs* (Winter 1983–84).

The statesmen of the world who boast and threaten that they have Doomsday weapons are far more dangerous, and far more estranged from "reality," than many of the people on whom the label "psychotic" is affixed.
R. D. Laing, *The Divided Self* (1960).

[Herman] Kahn's own impishness about such a grave subject as nuclear war invited misunderstanding. One such case concerned the book's [*On Thermonuclear War*] discussion of the "doomsday machine"—a fanciful device meant to ensure peace by blowing up the world as the penalty for aggression. He had actually borrowed the idea from physicist Leo Szilard in order to burlesque the concept of deterrence. Critics, however, mistook Kahn's subtle satire for advocacy.
Gregg Herken, *Counsels of War*, expanded edition (1987).

double agents

When [double] agents were working voluntarily, it was found advisable to let them share on a percentage basis in the money received from the Germans, especially when large sums were involved. . . . The agent who is not treated generously is apt to become disgruntled, especially when he observes large sums coming to us through his instrumentality. But it should not be forgotten that the agent could receive no money at all unless we [the British] were running the case, and he should therefore be taught from the beginning that all incomings belong in right and and in fact to us, but that to reward him for his collaboration we are prepared to give him his percentage. Fortunately in this war the Germans paid highly enough to make a double-cross system practically self-supporting, besides providing us, according to the sum offered, with a rough and ready but generally reliable criterion of the trust which they reposed in any particular agent.
J. C. Masterman, *The Double-Cross System in the War of 1939 to 1945* (1972).

When the post-mortem was made in Overlord . . . the Chiefs of Staff had no hesitation in deciding that the work of double agents had been an invaluable success. Indeed in December 1944 Garbo was awarded the M.B.E. for the services that he had rendered to this country. It is fascinating that the Germans were equally satisfied with his work in sending the completely bogus reports about Overlord and had, in June 1944, awarded him the Iron Cross—a most exceptional award as they had to give him, a Spaniard, special naturalization as a German in order to do it. I doubt whether anyone else has ever been decorated by both sides for the same messages!
Ewen Montagu, *Beyond Top Secret Ultra* (1977).

drill

The basic forms of military drill are among the most pervasive and unchanging elements of human civilization. The Twelfth Dynasty Egyptian armies of 1900 B.C. stepped off "by the left," and so has every army down to the present day.
Gwynne Dyer, *War* (1985).

Reason will convince us that what is necessary to be performed in the heat of action should constantly be practiced in the leisure of peace.
Vegetius, *De Re Militari* (378 A.D.).

I remember [Abraham Lincoln] narrating his first experience in drilling his company [in the 1832 Blackhawk War]. He was marching with a front of over twenty men across a field, when he desired to pass through a gateway into the next inclosure.

"I could not for the life of me," said he, "remember the proper word of command for getting my company endwise so that I could get through the gate, so as we came near the gate I shouted, "This company is dismissed for two minutes, when it will fall in again at the other side of the gate!"
Allen T. Rice, *Reminiscences of Lincoln* (1886).

The incident [at Sandhurst between the World Wars] derived from the presence at the College as a cadet of Prince Henry... third son of King George V. One morning on parade, the Prince was singled out for special reproof by the meticulous drill-sergeant—though what precise aspect of drill the Prince had got wrong is not recorded. The sergeant exploded—an event which, with him, was wont to happen every five minutes. "Mr. Prince 'Enry," he boomed, "if I was your father I'd—" he paused, realising just in time that he could hardly conclude in the traditional manner by bellowing "shoot m'self". The King, after all, was the King. The whole parade, meantime, was agog, fascinated, riveted by what was to follow. At last, with infinite logic, the sergeant-major shouted, at the top of his lungs, triumphantly, and with complete confidence: "I'd *habdicate*, sir!"
Hugh Thomas, *The Story of Sandhurst* (1961).

The common notion that discipline is produced by drill is a case of putting the cart before the horse. A well-drilled battalion has often proved a bad one in the field. By contrast, a *good* battalion is often good at drill—because if the spirit is right, it likes to do all things well. Here is the real sequence of causation.
B. H. Liddell Hart, *Thoughts on War* (1944).

No one who has participated in it or seen it well done should doubt the inspiration of ceremonial drill.
Field Marshal Archibald P. Wavell, *Soldiers and Soldiering* (1953).

He paraded before the new platoon. . . . "My name is Whitlock . . . you address me as sir. You sonofabitches aren't human beings any more. I don't want any of you lily-livered bastards getting the idea you are Marines either. You're boots! Crapheads! The lowest, stinking, scummiest form of animal life in the universe. I'm supposed to attempt to make Marines out of you in the next three months. I doubt it. You goddamyankees are the most putrid-looking specimens of slime I have ever laid eyes on. . . . Remember this, you sonofabitches—your soul may belong to Jesus, but your ass belongs to me."
Leon M. Uris, *Battle Cry* (1953).

Drill sergeants often take a very paternalistic orientation toward trainees, particularly when dealing with them on an individual basis. . . . Not infrequently the drill sergeant uses "son" instead of "you," "trainee," "shithead," and other appellations common in other situations. Trainees often come to view their drill sergeant as a substitute father and almost invariably prefer the older, experienced drill sergeant to his younger assistant (who is often virtually the same age as the trainees).
John H. Faris, "The Impact of Basic Combat Training," in *International War*, 2nd ed., ed. M. Small and J. D. Singer (1989).

drums

See, the conquering hero comes!
Sound the trumpets, beat the drums!
Thomas Morell, *Joshua*, Part III (1748).

The sound of the drum drives out thought; for that very reason it is the most military of instruments.
Joseph Joubert, *Pensées* (1842).

If a man does not keep pace with his companions, perhaps it is because he hears a different drummer. Let him step to the music which he hears, however measured or far away.
Henry David Thoreau, *Walden* (1854).

As soon as war is declared it will be impossible to hold the poets back. Rhyme is still the most effective drum.
Jean Giraudoux, *Tiger at the Gates*, Act I (1935).

The most persistent sound which reverberates through men's history is the beating of war drums.
Arthur Koestler, *Janus: A Summing Up* (1978).

Military historians beat their drums with the bones of the dead.
Attributed to Georges Clemenceau in Richard Holmes, *Acts of War* (1985).

duels

On receiving his antagonist's shot, which took effect in his [Colonel Harvey Aston's] body, he staggered a few paces; then, recovering himself, he presented his pistol deliberately at his opponent, and said, "I could kill him" (for he was a capital shot); "but the last act of my life shall not be an act of revenge."
John Blakiston, *Twelve Years' Military Adventures* (1829).

War is nothing but a duel on an extensive scale.
Karl von Clausewitz, *On War* (1832).

Much as the modern French duel is ridiculed by certain smart people, it is in reality one of the most dangerous institutions of our day. Since it is always fought in the open air the combatants are nearly sure to catch cold.
Mark Twain, *A Tramp Abroad* (1880).

Once or twice private duels were fought [at Gallipoli in 1914]. While the rest of the soldiers on both sides held their fire an Australian and a Turk would stand up on the parapets and blaze away at one another until one or the other was wounded or killed, and something seemed to be proved—their skill, their wish "to dare," perhaps most of all their pride. Then in a moment all would dissolve into the horror and frenzy of a raid or a setpiece battle.
Alan Moorehead, *Gallipoli* (1956).

A purely defensive battle is like a duel in which one of the men does nothing but parry. He can never defeat his opponent, but on the contrary, and in spite of the greatest possible skill, he is bound to be hit sooner or later.
General Ferdinand Foch, *The Principles of War* (1918).

While the medieval customs by which princes had sometimes actually settled international controversies by a personal duel, and usually instituted war by sending a defiance by herald in the manner of a challenge, had fallen into abeyance in the

Renaissance, these practices showed that modern war and the duel were one and same in origin, though the two institutions had diverged.
Quincy Wright, *A Study of War* (1942).

duty

Every subject's duty is the king's; but every subject's soul is his own.
William Shakespeare, *Henry V*, Act IV (1599).

Do your duty and leave the rest to the Gods.
Pierre Corneille, *Horace*, Act II (1640).

Three things prompt men to regular discharge of their duty in time of action: natural bravery, hope of reward, and fear of punishment. The first two are common to the untutor'd, and the disciplin'd Soldiers; but the latter, most obviously distinguishes the one from the other. A coward, when taught to believe, that if he breaks his ranks, and abandons his colors, he will be punished by death by his own party, will take his chance against the enemy.
George Washington, letter to the President of Congress, February 9, 1776, reprinted in J. C. Fitzpatrick, *The Writings of George Washington*, IV (1931–44).

We all did our duty, which, in the patriot's, soldier's, and gentleman's language, is a very comprehensive word, of great honor, meaning, and import.
Rudolf Erich Raspe, *Travels of Baron Munchausen* (1785).

[Just before the 1805 Battle of Trafalgar, Admiral] Nelson joined Pasco on deck and ordered him to make a signal. "I wish to say . . . 'England confides that every man will do his duty'," he told him. "You must be quick for I have one more to make, which is for close action." Pasco asked if he could substitute the word "expects," which was a single flag in the signal book, for "confides," which would involve a complicated hoist of alphabetical flags. "That will do," answered Nelson.
Tom Pocock, *Horatio Nelson* (1988).

The brave man inattentive to his duty, is worth little more to his country, than the coward who deserts her in the hour of danger.
President Andrew Jackson, address to soldiers during the Battle of New Orleans, January 8, 1815, quoted in J. S. Bassett, ed., *Correspondence of Andrew Jackson*, II (1927).

Duty, then is the sublimest word in the English language. Do your duty in all things
. . . You can never do more, you should never wish to do less.
Attributed to Robert E. Lee, in a April 5, 1852 letter to his son. Charles Alfred Graves, *The Forged Letter of General Robert E. Lee* (1914), calls the letter spurious.

Duty, duty must be done:
The rule applies to everyone.
William S. Gilbert, *Rudigore* (1887).

When a stupid man is doing something he is ashamed of, he always declares that it is his duty.
George Bernard Shaw, *Caesar and Cleopatra*, Act III (1899).

I should indeed consider myself a despicable person if, now that I have achieved fame and wear many decorations, I should consent to exist as a pensioner of my dignity and to preserve my life for the nation, while every poor fellow in the trenches—who is doing his duty equally as much as I—has to stick it out.
Baron Manfred von Richthofen, 1917 memorandum to German General Staff, quoted in William E. Burrows, *Richthofen* (1969).

These men don't ask for comfort. They don't ask for safety. If they could speak to you, they'd say, "Let us choose to do our duty willingly, not the choice of a slave but the choice of free Englishmen." They ask only the freedom that England expects for every man. If one man among you believed that—one man!—he could command the fleets of England. He could sweep the seas for England if he called his men to duty, not by flaying their backs but by lifting their hearts—their hearts, that's all.
Franchot Tone in *Mutiny on the Bounty* (1935), directed by Frank Lloyd; screenplay by Talbot Jennings and others from the novel by Charles Nordhoff and James Norman Hall.

Any commander who fails to attain his objective, and who is not dead or severely wounded, has not done his full duty.
General George S. Patton, Jr., *War as I Knew It* (1947).

I'm just a Kansas farmer boy who did his duty.
General Dwight D. Eisenhower, *The New York Times* (June 20, 1945).

I am closing my fifty-two years of military service. When I joined the army, even before the turn of the century, it was the fulfillment of all of my boyish hopes and dreams.
The world has turned over many times since I took the oath on the plain at West Point, and the hopes and dreams have long since vanished, but I still remember the refrain of one of the most popular barracks ballads of that day which proclaimed most proudly that old soldiers never die; they just fade away.
And like the old soldier of that ballad, I now close my military career and just fade away, an old soldier who tried to do his duty as God gave him the light to see that duty. Good-by.
General Douglas A. MacArthur, address to Joint Session of Congress, April 19, 1951.

Duty largely consists of pretending that the trivial is critical.
John Fowles, *The Magus* (1965).

The West Point formula may no longer suffice. Country is clear enough, but what is Duty in a wrong war? What is Honor when fighting is reduced to "wasting" the living space—not to mention the lives—of a people that never did us any harm? The simple West Point answer is that Duty and Honor consist in carrying out the orders of the government. That is what the Nazis said in their defense, and we tried them for war crimes nevertheless.
Barbara W. Tuchman, "Generalship," *Parameters* (Spring 1972).

Military life ... is unique in that it clearly levels upon the officer, or any other member for that matter, responsibilities which transcend his career or material self-interest. The problem has been, however, a failure to realize this and to regard the military life as the same as working at any other occupation. This equation is false, misleading, and ultimately dangerous, for it does not recognize that at some point an officer may be called upon to do his duty and "be faithful unto death."
Richard A. Gabriel and Paul L. Savage, *Crisis in Command* (1978).

elephants and the military

Elephants by their vast size, and their trumpeting and their novelty are at first very terrible both to men and horses. . . . Among the ancients, the velites usually engaged them. They were young soldiers, lightly armed, active and very expert in throwing their missile weapons on horseback. These troops kept hovering round the elephants continually and killed them with large lances and javelins. Afterwards, the soldiers, as their apprehensions decreased, attacked them in a body and, throwing their javelins together, destroyed them by a multitude of wounds.

Slingers with round stones . . . killed both the men who guided the elephants and the soldiers who fought in the towers on their backs. This was found by experience to be the best and safest expedient. At other times on the approach of these beasts, the soldiers opened their ranks and let them pass through. When they got into the midst of the troops, who surrounded them on all sides, they were captured with their guards unhurt.
Vegetius, *De Re Militari* (378 A.D.).

In 1943, a young Navy pilot named George Bush was "unofficially grounded" while training at Chincoteague Naval Air Base, on the Maryland-Virginia border. . . . Bush, it seems, had met an attractive young lady. . . . [and] buzzed her house one afternoon. The house was near the fairgrounds where a traveling circus was put up for a few days. Bush's buzzing frightened one of the circus elephants, who promptly took off, in turn frightening some of the residents of Crisfield, Md. One woman complained to the mayor. The mayor complained to the base commander and, as George Bush recalled in mock hyperbole years later, "I was grounded for causing an elephant stampede."
Walter Scott, "Personality Parade," *Parade* (April 23, 1989).

One pilot spotted a disturbance in the jungle. . . . Down swooped the Americans to investigate. There was a fantastic sight below. Fifty huge elephants were battering their way through the tangled jungle, uprooting trees and trampling vegetation. Behind them marched a column of Japanese jungle infantry in shorts and sun helmets, and armed with light machine guns. Behind the troops came a line of light tanks and scout cars. The Japanese were using the elephants to open a path through the jungle to bring up the armored units for the big push on Moulmein [Burma].

The Tigers circled and then peeled off to strafe. Their bullets ripped into the elephants, killing some and stinging others into a blind fury. There was a gap in the infantry column where 6 machine guns cut a swath. The stampeding elephants turned on the armored column, upsetting the tiny tanks and the cars. The Tigers swooped down on the panic-stricken column with their guns. The advance on Moulmein went into reverse.
Robert B. Hotz, *With General Chennault: The Story of the Flying Tigers* (1943).

Suddenly I realized that I should have to shoot the elephant after all. The people expected it of me and I had got to do it; I could feel their two thousand wills pressing me forward, irresistibly. And it was at this moment, as I stood there with the rifle in my hands, that I first grasped the hollowness, the futility of the white man's dominion in the East. Here was I, the white man with his gun, standing in front of the unarmed native crowd—seemingly the leading actor of the piece; but in reality I was only an absurd puppet pushed to and fro by the will of those yellow faces behind.
George Orwell, *Shooting an Elephant* (1950).

encirclement

To a surrounded enemy you must leave a way of escape.
Sun Tzu, *The Art of War* (4th century B.C.).

When you occupy a position which the enemy threatens to surround, you should collect your forces quickly and menace him with an offensive movement. By this manoeuvre you prevent him from detaching a part of his troops and annoying your flanks, in case you should deem a retreat indispensable.
Napoleon I, *Military Maxims* (1827).

So they got us surrounded again, the poor bastards!
Ladislas Farago in *Patton* (1964) credits this statement made during the Battle of the Bulge to an anonymous GI. However, Nat Frankel and Larry Smith in *Patton's Best* identify him as "Constant Klinga, a noncom, a joker, a swaggerer, a fucker if not a lover, a great Dodgers fan, an occasional drinker, a man that no writer . . . could invent." Klinga was later killed in action.

In every battle, concentrate an absolutely superior force (two, three, four and sometimes even five or six times the enemy's strength), encircle the enemy forces completely, strive to wipe them out thoroughly and do not let any escape from the net.
Mao Tse-tung, *Selected Military Writings* (1963).

enemies

The practical measures that we take are always based on the assumption that our enemies are not unintelligent.
King Archidamus of Sparta, quoted in Thucydides, *The Peloponnesian War* (5th century B.C.).

His enemies shall lick the dust.
The Bible, Psalms 72:9.

I do not have to forgive my enemies, I have had them all shot.
Ramón Maria Narváez, nineteenth-century Spanish general, quoted in B. Conrad, *Famous Last Words* (1961).

You shall judge of a man by his foes as well as by his friends.
Joseph Conrad, *Lord Jim* (1900).

When you jumped in here, you were my enemy—and I was afraid of you. But you're just a man like me, and I killed you. Forgive me, comrade. Say that for me. Say you forgive me! Oh, no, you're dead! You're better off than I am—you're through—they can't do any more to you now. Oh, God! why did they do this to us? We only wanted to live, you and I. Why should they send us out to fight each other? If we threw away these rifles and these uniforms, you could be my brother, just like Kate and Albert. You'll have to forgive me, comrade.
Lew Ayres in *All Quiet on the Western Front* (1930), directed by Lewis Milestone; screenplay by Dell Andrews and others from the novel by Erich Maria Remarque.

I do not approve the extermination of the enemy; the policy of exterminating or, as it is barbarously said, liquidating enemies, is one of the most alarming developments of modern war and peace, from the point of view of those who desire the survival of culture. One needs the enemy.
T.S. Eliot, *Notes Toward the Definition of Culture* (1940).

Despise the enemy strategically, but take him seriously tactically.
Mao Tse-tung quoted in *Time* (March 22, 1963).

There is nothing ignoble in loving one's enemies; but much that is dangerous.
Bernard Levin, *The Pendulum Years* (1976).

We certainly do not need an "enemy image" of America, neither for domestic nor for foreign-policy interests. An imaginary or real enemy is needed only if one is bent on maintaining tension, on confrontation with far-reaching and, I might add, unpredictable consequences. . . .
Yet some people in the United States, it turns out, "need" the Soviet Union as an enemy image. Otherwise it is hard to understand some films, the inflammatory Ameri-

can broadcasts from Munich, the spate of articles and programs full of insults and hatred toward the Soviet people. All this dates back to the forties, if not earlier.
Mikhail Gorbachev, *Perestroika* (1987).

We have been ready for war in Europe for 40 years. Are we ready for what passes for peace? The leading Soviet academician, Georgi Arbatov, put his finger on the emerging dilemma for the East when he remarked: "We are going to do something terrible to you. We are going to deprive you of an enemy." Fear, not love, is the cement of alliances. It has bound NATO together against Stalin, Khrushchev and Brezhnev, from the Berlin blockade to Moscow's massive arms buildup. Now, Mikhail Gorbachev has weakened the cement by convincing Europe that he wants to return the Soviet Union to the family of nations.
Mortimer B. Zuckerman, "The Key to the Alliance," *U.S. News & World Report* (January 30, 1989).

England

If I should die, think only this of me:
That there's some corner of a foreign field
That is for ever England.
Rupert Brooke, *The Soldier* (1915).

When you think about the defense of England, you no longer think of the chalk cliffs of Dover. You think of the Rhine. That is where our frontier lies today.
Stanley Baldwin, speech in the House of Commons, July 30, 1934.

When I warned [the French] that Britain would fight on alone whatever they did, their generals told their Prime Minister and his divided Cabinet, "In three weeks England will have her neck wrung like a chicken." Some chicken; some neck.
Winston Churchill, speech to the Canadian Parliament, December 30, 1941.

Mr. Attlee described my speeches in the war as expressing the will not only of Parliament but of the whole nation. It fell to me to express it, and if I found the right words you must remember that I have always earned my living by my pen and by my tongue. It was a nation and race dwelling all around the globe that had the lion's heart. I had the luck to be called upon to give the roar. I also hope that I sometimes suggested to the lion the right place to use his claws.
Winston Churchill, speech to both houses of Parliament in honor of his 80th birthday, November 30, 1954.

Europe has always been for us [the British], in a sense, a nuisance; somewhere we get dragged into wars that are of no concern to us because of the mistakes that Europeans have made. We liberate them over and over again, and then they aren't grateful.
A. J. P. Taylor, *The New York Times* (June 16, 1976).

Great Britain—it's pathetic now. It just makes you want to cry. They're no longer a world power. All they've got are Generals and Admirals and bands. They do things in great style, grand style. God, they do it well. On the protocol side. But it makes you sick to see their forces.
General George S. Brown, Chairman, Joint Chiefs of Staff, *U.S. News & World Report* (November 1, 1976).

envelopment

The Roman maniples followed with spirit, and easily cut their way through the enemy's line; since the Celts had been drawn up in a thin line, while the Romans had closed up from the wings towards the center and the point of danger. For the two wings did not come into action at the same time as the center: but the center was first engaged, because the Gauls, having been stationed on the arc of the crescent, had come into contact with the enemy long before the wings, the convex of the crescent being towards the enemy. The Romans, however, going in pursuit of these troops, and hastily closing in towards the center and the part of the enemy which was giving ground, advanced so far, that the Libyan heavy-armed troops on either wing got on their flanks. Those on the right, facing to the left, charged from the right upon the Roman flank; while those who were on the left wing raced to the right, and dressing by the left, charged their right flank, the exigency of the moment suggesting to them what they ought to do. Thus it came about, as Hannibal had planned, that the Romans were caught between two hostile lines of Libyans.
Polybius, description of the 216 B.C. Battle of Cannae, *Histories* (2nd century B.C.).

Ancient examples . . . show that almost all excellent generals, when they knew the enemy had made one part of his line of battle strong, did not oppose that part with their strongest portion but with their weakest, and opposed their strongest to the enemy's weakest. Then on joining battle, they commanded their most powerful part merely to resist the enemy and not to push him, and their weakest part they ordered to let itself be overcome and to draw back as far as the rearmost section of the army. This causes an enemy great confusion in two ways: first, he finds his strongest part surrounded; second, since he supposes he has gained the victory quickly, he seldom escapes being thrown into confusion; the result is his speedy defeat.
Niccolò Machiavelli, *The Art of War* (1520).

The enemy's front is not the objective. The essential thing is to crush the enemy's flanks . . . and complete the extermination by attack upon his rear.
Field Marshal Alfred von Schlieffen, *Cannae* (1936).

The system was popularly called "leapfrogging," and hailed as something new in warfare. But it was actually the adaptation of modern instrumentalities of war to a concept as ancient as war itself. Derived from the classic strategy of envelopment, it was given a new name, imposed by modern conditions. Never before had a field of battle embraced land and water in such relative proportions. Earlier campaigns had been decided on either land or sea. However, the process of transferring troops by sea as well as by land appeared to conceal the fact that the system was merely that of envelopment applied to a new type of battle area. It has always proved the ideal method for success by inferior but faster-moving forces.
General Douglas MacArthur, speaking of his World War II strategy in the Pacific in his *Reminiscences* (1964).

Flank envelopments have been basic techniques of war for thousands of years, but some soldiers have more success in carrying them out than others. When they could, the North Koreans followed the model of the greatest of all armies at envelopment, the Mongols of the thirteenth century under Genghis Khan and his successors. The Mongol methods of attack were based upon their methods of hunting, and Genghis Khan trained his armies by means of a great hunt each winter in peacetime. An army would begin by pressing the game backward, then the flanks of the army would advance ahead of the center, around the game and to the rear encircling the increas-

ingly terrified animals, then pressing them together from all points of the compass. . . .
For soldiers adept in corralling animals in a great hunt, hunting men became easy.
   Bevin Alexander, *Korea: The First War We Lost* (1986).

escalation

Against naked force the only possible defense is naked force. The aggressor makes
the rules for such a war; the defenders have no alternative but matching destruction
with more destruction, slaughter with greater slaughter.
   President Franklin D. Roosevelt, speech in Louisville, Kentucky, August 21, 1941.

I have devised a ladder—a metaphorical ladder—that provides a convenient list of
some of the more important options facing the strategist. This ladder indicates that
there are many continuous paths between a low-level crisis and an all-out war, none of
which are necessarily or inexorably to be followed. My ladder provides a useful framework for the systematic study of a crisis. There is no attempt here to recommend any
courses of action. What is attempted is to describe the way stations of ascending conflict so that the elements can be recognized, and the distance from all-out war estimated.
   Herman Kahn, "Escalation as a Strategy," *Problems of National Strategy*, ed. Henry A. Kissinger (1965).

Lyndon Johnson told the Nation
Have no fear of escalation,
I am trying everyone to please.
And though it isn't really war,
We're sending 50,000 more
To help save Vietnam from Vietnamese.
   Tom Paxton, "Lyndon Johnson Told the Nation" (1965).

Our numbers have increased in Vietnam because the aggression of others has
increased in Vietnam. There is not, and there will not be, a mindless escalation.
   President Lyndon B. Johnson, *Time* (March 4, 1966).

The civilian policy-makers at the Pentagon do not appear to have grasped the fact
that their notions about surgical strikes and controlled escalation have been rendered
irrelevant by the military's commitment to traditions that predate the nuclear age by a
few millennia. The Air Force is simply not prepared to abandon its offensive plans or
to exchange the bludgeon for the scalpel; the Navy is not prepared to do anything but
respond to a Soviet attack with biblical fury.
   Daniel Ford, *The Button* (1985).

Our ships are built to fight . . . on every rung in the ladder of escalatory violence.
   Admiral Carlisle A. H. Trost, Chief of Naval Operations, *The New York Times* (October
8,1988).

esprit de corps

That silly, sanguine notion, which is firmly entertained here, that one Englishman
can beat three Frenchmen, encourages, and has sometimes enabled, one Englishman,
in reality, to beat two.
   Philip D. Stanhope, 4th Earl of Chesterfield, letter to his son of February 7, 1749, reprinted in
Chesterfield: Letters and Other Pieces, ed. R. P. Bond (1935).

All that can be done with the soldier is to give him *esprit de corps*, i.e., a higher
opinion of his own regiment than of all the other troops of the country, and since the

officers have sometimes to lead him into the greatest danger (and he cannot be influenced by a sense of honor) he must be more afraid of his officers than of the dangers to which he is exposed.
Frederick the Great quoted in E. M. Lloyd, *A Review of the History of the Infantry* (1908).

Force (the volume of motion) is the product of the mass into the velocity. In warfare the force of armies is the product of the mass multiplied by something else, an unknown X.

Military science, seeing in history an immense number of examples in which the mass of an army does not correspond with its force, and in which small numbers conquer large ones, vaguely recognize the existence of this unknown factor. . . .

X is the spirit of the army, the greater or less desire to fight and to face dangers on the part of all the men composing the army, which is quite apart from the question whether they are fighting under leaders of genius or not, with cudgels or with guns that fire thirty times a minute. . . . The spirit of the army is the factor which multiplied by the mass gives the product of the force. To define and express the significance of this unknown factor, the spirit of the army, is the problem of science.
Leo Tolstoy, *War and Peace* (1865–69).

Esprit de corps is secured in war. But war becomes shorter and shorter and more and more violent. Consequently, secure esprit de corps in advance.
Ardant du Picq, *Battle Studies* (1868).

The men thought that victory was chained to my standard. Men who go into a fight under the influence of such feelings are next to invincible, and are generally victors before it begins.
John S. Mosby, *War Reminiscences* (1887).

The importance of patriotic instruction, or, as we first called it, the "work of enlightenment among the troops," was summed up in the following sentences: "The German Army, owing to the spirit which animates it, is superior to its enemies and a powerful support to its allies . . . ."
German General Erich von Ludendorff, *Ludendorff's Own Story* (1919).

The spirit in the trenches was largely defensive; the idea being not to stir the Germans into more than their usual hostility.
Robert Graves, *Goodbye to All That* (1929).

In war, the quality and quantity of arms are important; without them, one cannot win. Even with them, one can lose. The most important attribute of a victorious army is the military spirit. In every conceivable way, thought of possible defeat must be eliminated from the army and replaced with an iron will to win.
Mao Tse-tung quoted in Kenmin Ho, "Mao's 10 Principles of War," *Military Review* (July 1967).

estimate of the situation

The wise general in his deliberations must consider both favorable and unfavorable factors. By taking into account the favorable factors, he makes his plan feasible; by taking into account the unfavorable, he may resolve the difficulties.
Sun Tzu, *The Art of War* (4th century B.C.).

A good general not only sees the way to victory; he also knows when victory is impossible.
Polybius, *Histories* (125 B.C.).

'Tis best to weigh
The enemy more mighty than he seems.
William Shakespeare, *Henry V*, Act II (1598).

If . . . we reflect how much more we are inclined . . . to estimate the strength of our opponent too high rather than too low, because it lies in human nature to do so, we must also admit that imperfect knowledge of the situation must in general greatly contribute to putting a stop to military action and modifying the principles on which it is conducted.
Karl von Clausewitz, *On War* (1832).

A general should say to himself many times a day: If the hostile army were to make its appearance in front, on my right, or on my left, what should I do? And if he is embarrassed, his arrangements are bad; there is something wrong; he must rectify his mistake.
Napoleon I, *Military Maxims* (1827).

First reckon, then risk.
Field Marshal Helmuth von Moltke's maxim quoted in J. F. C. Fuller, *A Military History of the Western World*, III (1956).

Calculating risks does not mean taking a gamble. It is more than figuring the odds. It is not reducible to a formula. It is the analysis of all factors which collectively indicate whether or not the consequences to ourselves will be more than compensated for by the damage to the enemy or interference with his plans.
Admiral Ernest J. King quoted in Bernard Brodie, *A Guide to Naval Strategy* (1944).

When [General Hans] Guderian protested that the Russians [in 1944] were about to attack in overwhelming strength and cited figures of the Soviet build-up, Hitler shouted, "It's the greatest bluff since Genghis Khan! Who's responsible for producing all this rubbish?"
William L. Shirer, *The Rise and Fall of the Third Reich* (1959).

The graveyard of history is dotted with the tombstones of nations whose leaders "knew" their enemy's intentions in war and, neglecting his capabilities, built their defense on sand.
General Matthew B. Ridgway, *Soldier* (1956).

Although a great commander must have an almost feminine sensitivity and intuition about the enemy and his intentions, he must also be able to screen all the impressions crowding on his consciousness, so that their emotional reality is blocked and only neutral factors of calculation are allowed into the mind.
Correlli Barnett, *The Swordbearers* (1963).

execution

I went out to Charing Cross, to see Major-General Harrison hanged, drawn and quartered; which was done there, he looking as cheerful as any man could do in that condition.
Samuel Pepys, diary entry for October 13, 1660, *The Diary of Samuel Pepys* (1825–99).

In mid-April [1945], Ferdinand [Marcos] learned that his father Mariano Marcos, after months as a prisoner of Major [George] Barnett, had been tried for war crimes and executed. It was not a simple execution. Barnett's guerrillas . . . after interrogating Mariano and confirming that he had worked for the Japanese throughout the war, executed him by tying him to four carabao water buffaloes, which tore him limb from limb. They hung the pieces in a tree.

[Ferdinand] . . . always told people that his father had been executed by the Japanese.
Sterling Seagrave, *The Marcos Dynasty* (1988).

How can one expect any sort of respect for normal international agreements from a regime that in the thirty-seven years since the Revolution has shot as spies and traitors, amongst others, all the members of their first Inner Cabinet and all members of the party Politburo as constituted after Lenin's death except Stalin, forty-three out of fifty-three Secretaries of the Central Organization of the Party, seventy out of the eighty members of the Soviet War Council, three out of every five marshals and about 60 percent of the generals of the Soviet Army?
Sir John Slessor, *Strategy for the West* (1954).

executive officers

Such an executive officer the sun never shone on. I have but to show him [General "Stonewall" Jackson] my design, and I know that if it can be done it will be done. No need for me to send or watch him. Straight as the needle to the pole he advances to the execution of my purpose.
General Robert E. Lee quoted in G. F. R. Henderson, *Stonewall Jackson and the American Civil War* (1898).

The captain was the father. The executive officer, everyone would readily agree, was the mother.
Tom Clancy, *The Hunt for Red October* (1984).

The XO [executive officer] is the man who translates the command goals into reality. I come up with the goals, the ideas. The XO makes them happen. In the final analysis, the man who makes the hard decisions is the captain. You don't get to be a captain by making the easy decisions. I am the man who must punish at mast. The XO may be perceived as being the bad guy because he has got to make things happen. He has to keep the pressure on.
Captain Gary F. Wheatley, commanding officer of the aircraft carrier USS *John F. Kennedy*, quoted in George C. Wilson, *Super Carrier* (1986).

exhortations

Scoundrels, would ye live forever?
Frederick the Great, on forcing some soldiers back onto the line during a 1757 battle, quoted in Thomas Carlyle, *The French Revolution* (1837). World War I Marine Corps Sergeant Daniel Daly is often credited with an updated version: "Come on you sons of bitches! Do you want to live forever?"

Soldiers . . . forty centuries have their eyes upon you.
Napoleon I, speaking to his Army of the Nile in Egypt within sight of the pyramids, July 21, 1798, quoted in Will and Ariel Durant, *The Age of Napoleon* (1975).

A shot through the mainmast knocked the splinters about; and he [Admiral Horatio Nelson] observed to one of his officers, with a smile: "It is warm work; and this day may be the last to any of us at a moment. But mark you! I would not be elsewhere for thousands."
Robert Southey, on the April 2, 1801 Battle of Copenhagen, *Life of Nelson* (1813).

At the very commencement [of the Battle of Albuera, May 16, 1811] Colonel Inglis had his horse shot under him, but went on dressing the line unmoved. When a little later he was himself severely wounded he refused to be taken to the rear, and lay where he had fallen in front of the colors encouraging and exhorting his men: "Die Hard, 57th! Die hard!" They gave him a splendid answer. Where they fought they fell, with their faces to the foe and their wounds all in front.
C. L. Kingsford, *The Story of the Middlesex Regiment*, quoted in Thomas Gilby, *Britain at Arms* (1953).

It is not by harangues at the moment of engaging that soldiers are rendered brave. Veterans hardly listen to them and recruits forget them at the first discharge of a cannon. If speeches and arguments are at any time useful it is during the course of the campaign by counteracting false reports and causes of discontent, maintaining a proper spirit in the camp and furnishing subjects of conversation in the bivouacs.
Napoleon I, *Military Maxims* (1827).

Give them the cold steel, boys!
Attributed to Confederate General Lewis Addison Armistead during the U.S. Civil War (1861).

Up, men, and to your posts! Don't forget today that you are from Old Virginia!
Confederate General George Pickett's reminder to his troops as they began their charge at Gettysburg on July 3, 1863, quoted in Douglas S. Freeman, *Lee's Lieutenants*, III (1951).

The high sentiments always win in the end, the leaders who offer blood, toil, tears and sweat always get more out of their followers than those who offer safety and a good time. When it comes to the pinch, human beings are heroic.
George Orwell, "The Art of Donald McGill," *Dickens, Dali and Others* (1946).

The defense of Egypt lies here at Alamein. . . . if we lose this position we lose Egypt; all the fighting troops now in the Delta must come here at once, and will. Here we will stand and fight; there will be no further withdrawal. I have ordered that all plans and instructions dealing with further withdrawal are to be burnt, and at once. We will stand and fight here.
If we can't stay here alive, then let us stay here dead.
General B. L. Montgomery, to his officers on taking command of the British Eighth Army, August 13, 1942, quoted in Nigel Hamilton, *Monty* (1981).

Ranging up and down [on D-Day] . . . , oblivious to the artillery and machine gun fire that raked the sands, was . . . Colonel George A. Taylor. "Two kinds of people are staying on this beach," he yelled, "the dead and those who are going to die. Now let's get the hell out of here."
Cornelius Ryan, *The Longest Day* (1959).

We will attack the Japanese home islands, destroy what is left of her navy and air force, destroy factories and communications. Our planes will strike inland. My only regret is that our ships don't have wheels, so that when we drive the Japs from the coast we can chase them inland.
Admiral William F. Halsey quoted in Richard Hough, *The Great Admirals* (1977).

The 101st was earmarked to go to the Pacific. . . . So upon my return to Europe at the end of June [1945], I made the rounds of all the units telling them all that I could about our probable future. Anticipating their probable lack of enthusiasm for going around the world to another war, I pulled out all the stops in appealing to their pride of unit and trying to stir up enthusiasm for new worlds to conquer. Speaking before one regiment, I ended with the peroration, "We've licked the best that Hitler had in France and Holland and Germany. Now where do we want to go?" Instead of "Japan," as I hoped, they bellowed back as one man, "Home," and then laughed at their discomfited commander who should have known better than to ask such a question.

General Maxwell D. Taylor, *Swords and Plowshares* (1972).

morale-building exhortations

Soldiers! Your country is entitled to expect great things of you. Will you justify her expectations? Your greatest obstacles are already overcome, but you have yet many battles to fight, many towns to capture, many rivers to pass over. Is there one among you whose courage fails him? Is there one, I say, who would rather retreat to the summits of Apennines and Alps, and patiently endure the insults of that slavish rabble? No, no one among the victors of Montenotte, Millesimo, Dego, and Mondovi! All burn with the ambition to spread the fame of the French nation throughout the world; the desire of every one of you is to humble those proud rulers who would fetter us in chains. All long for the dictation of a glorious peace, which shall compensate our country for the tremendous sacrifices she has made. All, when they return to their homes, would wish to be able to say proudly, "I was with the victorious Army of Italy."

General Napoleon Bonaparte, address to his army in Italy, April 26, 1796, reprinted in Houston Peterson, ed., *A Treasury of the World's Great Speeches (1965).*

Drawing his sword he [Pizarro] traced a line with it on the sand from East to West. Then, turning towards the South, "Friends and comrades!" he said, "on that side are toil, hunger, nakedness, the drenching storm, desertion, and death; on this side ease and pleasure. There lies Peru with its riches; here, Panama and its poverty. Choose, each man, what best becomes a brave Castilian. For my part, I go to the South." So saying, he stepped across the line.

William H. Prescott, *The Conquest of Peru* (1847).

This is what I have to offer those who follow me: Hunger, cold, the heat of the sun; no wages, no barracks, no ammunition; but continual skirmishes, forced marches and bayonet-fights. Those of you who love your country and love glory, follow me.

General Guiseppe Garibaldi, address to his besieged troops in St. Peter's Square, Rome, July 2, 1849, quoted in Jaspar Ridley, *Garibaldi* (1974).

I have, myself, full confidence that if all do their duty, if nothing is neglected, and if the best arrangements are made, as they are being made, we shall prove ourselves once again able to defend our island home, to ride out the storm of war, and to outlive the menace of tyranny, if necessary for years, if necessary alone. . . . Even though large tracts of Europe and many old and famous states have fallen or may fall into the grip of the Gestapo and all the odious apparatus of Nazi rule, we shall not flag or fail. We shall go on to the end, we shall fight in France, we shall fight on the seas and oceans, we shall fight with growing confidence and growing strength in the air, we shall defend our island, whatever the cost may be, we shall fight on the beaches, we shall fight on the landing grounds, we shall fight in the fields and in the streets, we shall fight in the hills; we shall never surrender, and even if, which I do not for a moment believe, this island or a large part of it were subjugated and starving, then our Empire beyond the seas, armed and guarded by the British fleet, would carry on the struggle, until, in God's good time, the New World, with all its power and might, steps forth to the rescue and the liberation of the old.

Winston Churchill, speech to the House of Commons after the Dunkirk evacuation, June 4, 1940.

exploitation

He who rashly pursues a flying enemy with troops in disorder, seems bent upon throwing away that victory which he had before obtained.
Vegetius, *De Re Militari* (378 A.D.).

When we have incurred the risk of a battle, we should know how to profit by the victory, and not merely content ourselves, according to custom, with possession of the field.
Marshal Maurice de Saxe, *Reveries Upon the Art of War* (1757).

A pursuit should generally be as boldly and actively executed as possible, especially when it is subsequent to a battle gained; because the demoralized army may be wholly dispersed if vigorously followed up.
There are very few cases where it is wise to make a bridge of gold for the enemy, no matter what the old Roman proverb may say; for it can scarcely ever be desirable to pay an enemy to leave a country, unless in the case when an unexpected success shall have been gained over him by an army much inferior to his in numbers.
General Antoine Henri Jomini, *Summary of the Art of War* (1838).

Always mystify, mislead, and surprise the enemy, if possible; and when you strike and overcome him, never give up the pursuit as long as your men have strength to follow; for an army routed, if hotly pursued, becomes panic-stricken, and can then be destroyed by half their number.
General Thomas J. "Stonewall" Jackson quoted in G. F. R. Henderson, *Stonewall Jackson and the American Civil War*, I (1926).

Falklands War

It does not matter what we want or what the Argentinians want, but what the islanders want. It is their rights that have been taken away by naked aggression and it is their rights that shall be restored.
John Nott, Minister of Defense of the United Kingdom, speech in the House of Commons, April 7, 1982.

Why are you telling me this? The British won't fight.
General Leopoldo Galtieri, President of Argentina, speaking on April 10, 1982 to Vernon Walters, U.S. Ambassador-at-Large, quoted in Alexander M. Haig, Jr., *Caveat* (1984).

The eyes of the world are now focused on the Falkland Islands; others are watching anxiously to see whether brute force or the rule of law will triumph. Wherever naked aggression occurs it must be overcome. The cost now, however high, must be set against the cost we would one day have to pay if this principle went by default. And that is why, through diplomatic, economic and if necessary through military means, we shall persevere until freedom and democracy are restored to the people of the Falkland Islands.
Prime Minister Margaret Thatcher, speech in the House of Commons, April 14, 1982.

This is an absolutely pointless war. It's a silly war between countries which have great connections with each other, which have a great deal in common. What you really have here is a problem of two machismos, and the machismo of women is even more sensitive than the machismo of men. Without attributing fault to either side, I am just stating a fact.
General Vernon A. Walters, *Los Angeles Times* (May 11, 1982).

Since the first use of force did not come from outside the hemisphere, this is not a case of extra-continental aggression against which we are all committed to rally.
Alexander M. Haig, Jr., U.S. Secretary of State, speaking to the Latin American foreign ministers at a meeting of the Organization of American States, *Los Angeles Times* (May 28, 1982).

Early this morning in Port Stanley, 74 days after the Falkland Islands were invaded, General Moore accepted from General Menendez the surrender of all the Argentine forces in East and West Falkland together with their arms and equipment. In a message to the Commander-in-Chief Fleet, General Moore reported: "The Falkland Islands are once more under the Government desired by their inhabitants. God Save the Queen."
Margaret Thatcher, speech in the House of Commons, June 15, 1982.

What has occurred in no way alters Argentine sovereignty over the Malvinas [the Falklands] and does not affect the decision to continue our struggle on all fronts, opportunities and forms to gain full recognition of Argentine sovereignty over these islands.
Nicanor Costa Mendez, Foreign Minister of Argentina, on British victory, *Los Angeles Times* (June 16, 1982).

I think it very uncivilized to invade British territory. You are here illegally.
Rex Hunt, British Governor of Falkland Islands, to an Argentine officer, quoted in *Life* (January 1983).

It was Mrs. Thatcher's war. She held us to it. She never seemed to flinch from her conviction about its course. She took the risks on her shoulders and she won.
Max Hastings and Simon Jenkins, *The Battle for the Falklands* (1983).

The Argentinians have been claiming for 200 years that they own those islands. If they own those islands, then moving troops into them is not armed aggression.
Jeane Kirkpatrick, U.S. Ambassador to the United Nations, quoted in Alexander M. Haig, Jr., *Caveat* (1984).

The Pentagon had been backing Britain from the start, and its aid increased dramatically once America came off the fence. Directed by Caspar Weinberger, the Anglophile defense secretary, the United States provided Britain's ill-equipped and overextended forces with crucial help at a speed rarely achieved by the Pentagon's cumbersome bureaucracy. Weinberger set up a central clearinghouse, with direct access to his office. Fifteen stages were eliminated from the supply-authorization process and material was transferred from inventories in twenty-four hours instead of the normal two weeks. . . . Most useful of all, Britain was given vital military intelligence from intercepted signals and from one of America's surveillance satellites, which, it was alleged, had been specially moved away from its orbit over Russia for the purpose.
David Dimbleby and David Reynolds, *An Ocean Apart* (1988).

An Argentinian military analyst . . . wrote . . . that "the British intercepted all our radio transmissions, and almost certainly broke our codes," and noted that the reason the Argentine headquarters on the Falklands was never bombed was that "its destruction would have deprived the British of its source."
Jeffrey T. Richelson, *Foreign Intelligence Organizations* (1988).

fear

Considius, a very old man, took occasion one day to tell Caesar that the senators did not meet because they were afraid of his soldiers. Caesar asked, "Why don't you, then,

out of the same fear, keep at home?" To which Considius replied, that age was his guard against fear, and that the small remains of his life were not worth much caution.
Plutarch, *The Lives* (A.D. 106).

From this arises the question whether it is better to be loved more than feared, or feared more than loved. The reply is, that one ought to be both feared and loved, but as it is difficult for the two to go together, it is much safer to be feared than loved, if one of the two has to be wanting.
Niccolò Machiavelli, *The Prince* (1513).

An utterly fearless man is a far more dangerous comrade than a coward.
Herman Melville, *Moby-Dick* (1851).

Nothing is so much to be feared as fear.
Henry David Thoreau, *The Writings* (1906); journal entry for September 7, 1851.

My die is cast, they [the French] may overwhelm me, but I don't think they will outmaneuver me. First, because I am not afraid of them, as everybody else seems to be; and secondly, because if what I hear of their system of maneuver, is true, I think it a false one as against steady troops. I suspect all the continental armies were more than half beaten before the battle was begun—I, at least, will not be frightened beforehand.
Duke of Wellington quoted in John Wilson Croker, *The Croker Papers, 1808–1857* (1884).

There is only one universal passion: fear. . . . It is fear that makes men fight: it is indifference that makes them run away: fear is the mainspring of war.
George Bernard Shaw, *The Man of Destiny* (1897).

How does one kill fear, I wonder? How do you shoot a specter through the heart, slash off its spectral head, take it by its spectral throat?
Joseph Conrad, *Lord Jim* (1900).

The real enemy was Terror, and all this heel-clicking, saluting, bright brass and polish were our charms and incantations for keeping him at bay.
Alan Hanbury-Sparrow, *The Land-Locked Lake* (1932).

The only thing we have to fear is fear itself—nameless, unreasoning, unjustified terror which paralyzes needed efforts to convert retreat into advance.
President Franklin D. Roosevelt, first Inaugural Address, March 4, 1933.

This terrifying power which nobody and nothing can check is mostly explained as fear of the neighboring nation, which is supposed to be possessed by a malevolent fiend. Since nobody is capable of recognizing just where and how much he is himself possessed . . ., he simply projects his own condition upon his neighbor, and thus it becomes a sacred duty to have the biggest guns and the most poisonous gas. The worst of it is that he is quite right. All one's neighbors are in the grip of some uncontrollable fear, just like oneself. In lunatic asylums it is a well-known fact that patients are far more dangerous when suffering from fear than when moved by rage or hatred.
Carl G. Jung, *Psychology and Religion* (1937).

Only those are fit to live who are not afraid to die.
General Douglas MacArthur, speaking in 1941, quoted in Robert Considine, *MacArthur the Magnificent* (1942).

To make an Army work you have to have every man in it fitted into a fear ladder. Men in prison camps, deserters, or men in replacement camps are in the backwaters of the Army and the discipline has to be proportionately more powerful. The Army func-

tions best when you're frightened of the man above you, and contemptuous of your subordinates.
Norman Mailer, *The Naked and the Dead* (1948).

Never take counsel of your fears.
General Thomas J. "Stonewall" Jackson; quoted in Douglas S. Freeman, *Lee's Lieutenants*, I (1942).

Those who threaten to unleash the forces of war on a dispute over West Berlin should recall the words of the ancient philosopher: "A man who causes fear cannot be free from fear."
President John F. Kennedy, speech during the Berlin crisis, July 25, 1961.

Any man who claims never to have known fear is either lying or else he is stupid. But by an act of will, he refuses to think of the reasons for fear and so concentrates entirely on winning.
Richard M. Nixon, *Six Crises* (1962).

I went where I was told to go, and I did what I was told to do, but no more. I was scared shitless just about all the time.
James Jones, *WWII* (1977).

fifth column

As you see, around me here I have four columns. In Madrid I have a fifth column; men now in hiding will rise and support us the moment we march.
General Emilio Mola, speaking in 1936 during the Spanish Civil War, quoted in Peter Wyden, *The Passionate War* (1983). Wyden notes: "Mola made the phrase famous but did not coin it. . . . It was first applied to Russian sympathizers within the besieged fortress of Ismail in 1790."

Parliament has given us the powers to put down fifth-column activities with a strong hand, and we shall use those powers, subject to the supervision and correction of the House, without the slightest hesitation until we are satisfied, and more than satisfied, that this malignancy in our midst has been effectively stamped out.
Winston Churchill, speech in the House of Commons, June 4, 1940.

Most Americans recognize the [Vietnam] Moratorium mob as the enemy's fifth column. Without these "dear American friends," Hanoi would have jumped at peace offers two years ago.
Representative John R. Rarick, speech in the House of Representatives, November 13, 1969.

Girls were passed from dead pilots to their successors with the fatalism that became part of the harsh legend of Bomber Command. They always seemed to know the targets, and at this time when Fifth Column mania was rife, more than one pilot began to study the blonde beside him at the bar with the most extravagant suspicions.
Max Hastings, *Bomber Command* (1979).

fighting

Hard pounding, this, gentlemen; try who can pound the longest.
Duke of Wellington, at the 1815 Battle of Waterloo, to his officers, quoted in Elizabeth Longford, *Wellington: The Years of the Sword* (1969).

Every military activity ... necessarily relates to the engagement, either directly or indirectly. The soldier is levied, clothed, armed, trained, sleeps, eats, drinks, and marches merely to fight at the right place and the right time.
Karl von Clausewitz, *On War* (1832).

'Tis better to have fought and lost,
Than never to have fought at all.
Arthur Hugh Clough, *Peschiera* (1862).

I'm a professional soldier! I fight when I have to, and am very glad to get out of it when I haven't to.
George Bernard Shaw, *Arms and the Man* (1894).

The example of America must be the example not merely of peace because it will not fight, but of peace because peace is the healing and elevating influence of the world, and strife is not. There is such a thing as a man being too proud to fight. There is such a thing as a nation being so right that it does not need to convince others by force that it is right.
President Woodrow Wilson, speech in Philadelphia, May 10, 1915.

Fighting is like champagne. It goes to the heads of cowards as quickly as of heroes. Any fool can be brave on a battlefield when it's be brave or else be killed.
Margaret Mitchell, *Gone With the Wind* (1936).

The world is a fine place and worth fighting for.
Ernest Hemingway, *For Whom the Bell Tolls* (1940).

What counts is not necessarily the size of the dog in the fight—it's the size of the fight in the dog.
General Dwight D. Eisenhower quoted in Stephen E. Ambrose, *Eisenhower*, I (1983).

"Jesus had guts! He wasn't afraid of the whole Roman army. Think that quarterback's hot stuff? Well, let me tell you, Jesus would have made the best little All-American quarterback in the history of football. Jesus was a real fighter—the best little scrapper, pound for pound, that you ever saw. And why, gentlemen? Love! Jesus had love in both fists!"
Burt Lancaster in *Elmer Gantry* (1960), directed by Richard Brooks; screenplay by Richard Brooks, from the novel by Sinclair Lewis.

Men do not fight because they have arms. They have arms because they deem it necessary to fight. Take away their arms, and they will either fight with their bare fists or get themselves new arms with which to fight.
Hans J. Morgenthau, *Politics Among Nations*, 4th ed. (1967).

Now, I want you to remember that no bastard ever won a war by dying for his country. He won it by making the other poor dumb bastard die for his country. Men, all this stuff you heard about America not wanting to fight, wanting to stay out of the war, is a lot of horse dung. Americans, traditionally, love to fight. All real Americans love the sting of battle. When you were kids, you all admired the champion marble shooter, the fastest runner, the big-league ballplayer, the toughest boxer. Americans love a winner and will not tolerate a loser. Americans play to win all the time. I wouldn't give a hoot in hell for a man who lost and laughed. That's why Americans

have never lost—and will never lose—a war, because the very thought of losing is hateful to Americans.
George C. Scott in *Patton* (1970), directed by Franklin Schaffner; screenplay by Francis Ford Coppola and Edmund H. North based on Ladislas Farago's *Patton* and General Omar Bradley's *A Soldier's Story*.

ERNIE: Where did you spend your war years?
ERIC: Everywhere. I fought with Mountbatten in Burma, with Alexander in Tunis, with Monty at Alamein . . . I couldn't get on with anyone.
Eric Morecambe and Ernie Wise, *The Morecambe and Wise Joke Book* (1979).

If you go into their [the British] pubs, don't get into any fights with them. But if you do, make sure you win.
Colonel Curtis E. LeMay, to his bomber crews upon arrival in England in 1942, quoted in Thomas M. Coffey, *Iron Eagle* (1986).

fire

Gentlemen of the French Guard, fire first!
Attributed to Lord Charles Hay, the British Commander at the 1745 French versus English Battle of Fontenoy. This kind of bravado was possible only before the modern era of accurate fire.

Battles are won by superiority of fire.
Frederick the Great, *Military Testament* (1768).

In a battle, like in a siege, skill consists in converging a mass of fire on a single point: once the combat is opened, the commander who is adroit will suddenly and unexpectedly open fire with a surprising mass of artillery on one of these points, and is sure to seize it.
Napoleon I, *Military Maxims* (1827).

You may fire when you are ready, Gridley.
Commodore George Dewey, to Captain Charles V. Gridley, commander of Dewey's flagship, *Olympia*, during the battle of Manila Bay, May 1, 1898.

Emotion never allows them [soldiers] to sight, or to more than approximately adjust their fire. Often they fire into the air. [Oliver] Cromwell knew this very well, dependable as his troops were, when he said, "Put your trust in God and aim at their shoe laces."
Ardant du Picq, *Battle Studies* (1868).

There is but one means to extenuate the effects of enemy fire: it is to develop a more violent fire oneself.
Marshal Ferdinand Foch, *The Principles of War* (1918).

Out of an average one hundred men along the line of fire during the period of an encounter, only fifteen men on average would take any part with the weapons. . . . In the most aggressive infantry companies, under the most intense local pressure, the figure rarely rose above 25% of total strength from the opening to the close of an action.
S. L. A. Marshall, *Men Against Fire* (1947). Marshall's analysis, long accepted as classic, has recently been discredited, since according to Roger Spiller, "S. L. A. Marshall and the Ratio of Fire," *Journal of the Royal United Services Institute* (December 1988), "the systematic collection of data that made Marshall's ratio of fire so authoritative appears to have been invented."

I have found again and again that in encounter actions, the day goes to the side that is the first to plaster its opponent with fire. The man who lies low and awaits developments usually comes off second best. Motorcyclists at the head of the column must keep their machine guns at the ready and open fire the instant an enemy shot is heard. This applies even when the exact position of the enemy is unknown, in which case the fire must simply be sprayed over enemy-held territory.
Field Marshal Erwin Rommel, *The Rommel Papers*, ed. B. H. Liddell Hart (1953).

American soldiers love to fire on full automatic; there is something soul-satisfying about "switching your iron to rock and roll" and sending a torrent of lead out at an enemy. Whether or not you hit him is sometimes irrelevant.
J.D. Coleman, *Pleiku* (1988).

friendly fire

A certain loss of life is inseparable from war, and it makes little difference whether a man is shot by his own side or cut down by the other. But even the rawest recruit in the moment of extreme agitation has a distinct preference for shooting his enemies rather than his friends.
Winston Churchill, *The River War* (1899).

Some of our sailors were shooting five-inch guns at the Japanese planes [during the Pearl Harbor attack]. You just cannot down a plane with a five-inch shell. They were landing in Honolulu. . . . They hurt and killed a lot of people in the city.
When I came back . . . they told me that a shell had hit the house of my girl. We had been going together for, oh, about three years. Her house was a few blocks from my place. At the time, they said it was a Japanese bomb. Later we learned it was an American shell. She was killed.
John Garcia quoted in Studs Terkel, *The Good War* (1985).

"We're going to talk about this message," Peg [Mullen] said. "I want you to explain it to me. This word, what do you mean by 'friendly'?"
"It merely means that it wasn't enemy artillery," the sergeant said. "Your son was killed by friendly fire."
"Friendly fire? *Friendly fire?*" Peg repeated incredulously.
Sergeant Fitzgerald shrugged lamely. "It means any artillery from forces not the enemy."
"*Not* the enemy! *Goddamn you!*" Peg cried, beating the chairback with her fists in frustration. "You couldn't even give him the . . . the decency of being killed by the enemy."
C. D. B. Bryan, *Friendly Fire* (1976).

It was at once accepted and resented among the boys of Charlie Company that they were as much in peril from America's own instruments of war as from the other side's. The possibility of death or injury by what the statisticians of war chose to call "friendly fire" was the surreal flip side of the vast technological edge America brought to Vietnam.
Peter Goldman and Tony Fuller, *Charlie Company* (1983).

flags

The soldiers should make it an article of faith never to abandon their standard. It should be sacred to them; it should be respected; and every type of ceremony should be used to make it respected and precious.
Marshal Maurice de Saxe, *Reveries Upon the Art of War* (1757).

Even then dishonour's peace he spurn'd,
The sullied olive-branch return'd,
Stood for his country's glory fast,
and nail'd her colours to the mast!
Walter Scott, *Marmion* (1808).

And the rockets' red glare, the bombs bursting in air,
Gave proof thro' the night that our flag was still there.
Francis Scott Key, *The Star Spangled Banner* (1814).

Have not I myself known five hundred living soldiers sabred into crows' meat for a piece of glazed cotton which they called their flag; which, had you sold it in any market-cross, would not have brought above three groschen?
Thomas Carlyle, *Sartor Resartus* (1836).

Yes, we'll rally round the flag, boys, we'll rally once again,
Shouting the battle-cry of Freedom,
We will rally from the hill-side, we'll gather from the plain,
Shouting the battle-cry of Freedom.
George F. Root, *The Battle-Cry of Freedom* (1861).

Quick, as it fell, from the broken staff
Dame Barbara snatched the silken scarf.
She leaned far out on the window sill,
And shook it forth with a royal will.
"Shoot, if you must, this old gray head,
But spare your country's flag," she said.
A shade of sadness, a blush of shame,
Over the face of the leader came;
The nobler nature within him stirred
To life at that woman's deed and word;
"Who touches a hair of yon gray head
Dies like a dog! March on!" he said.
All day long through Frederick street
Sounded the tread of marching feet:
All day long that free flag tossed
Over the heads of the rebel host.
John Greenleaf Whittier, *Barbara Frietchie* (1863). This poem tells what Whittier thought was the true story of 90-year-old Barbara Frietchie, who defiantly waved the American flag as "Stonewall" Jackson's troops invaded her hometown of Frederick, Maryland. The only uncontested truth is that a very old Barbara Frietchie did live in Frederick at the time; the rest is most likely fiction.

I have loved but one flag and I can not share that devotion and give affection to the mongrel banner invented for a league.
Senator Henry Cabot Lodge, speaking in the Senate on the League of Nations, August 12, 1919.

One of the purest fallacies is that trade follows the flag. Trade follows the lowest price current. If a dealer in any [British] colony wished to buy Union Jacks he would order them from Britain's worst foe if he could save a sixpence. Trade knows no flag.
Andrew Carnegie quoted in Frederick H. Hartman, *The Relations of Nations*, 6th ed. (1983).

I would not voluntarily march under this country's flag, or any other, when it was my private judgment that the country was in the wrong.
Mark Twain, *Mark Twain's Autobiography*, II, A. B. Paine, ed. (1924).

In the early spring of 1941, relations between Germany and the United States seemed to be deteriorating every day. When the German consulate in San Francisco unfurled a huge four-by-eight-foot swastika flag from its ninth-story offices,... a crowd of two thousand people gathered in the avenue below to jeer at the Nazi symbol.... Then a pair of irate sailors climbed up ... to the tenth floor and entered the empty office above the German flag; one of the sailors then let himself down from a window, sat astride the flagpole, and started slashing at the halyard with a penknife.... "I couldn't let that flag stay up there," the sailor explained to reporters. "It was up to someone to get it down, so I just went up there." Since the diplomatic offices were, by international law, sovereign German territory, Washington was forced to issue a formal apology.... But the knife-wielding sailor became a popular American hero overnight, despite the revelation that he and his partner had just been released from the psychopathic ward of a West Coast naval hospital.
William K. Klingaman, *1941* (1988).

Take every other normal precaution for the protection of the headquarters, but let's keep the flag flying.
General Douglas MacArthur's response to an officer who suggested that the American flag over the headquarters in the Philippines should be taken down because it might function as a beacon for Japanese planes, quoted in *The New York Times* (December 16, 1941).

The trouble with America is that the dollar gets restless when it earns only 6 percent over here. It goes overseas to get 100 percent. The flag follows the money—and the soldiers follow the flag.
General Smedley Butler, USMC, quoted in Bernard Brodie, *War and Politics* (1973).

We can imagine no more appropriate response to burning a flag than waving one's own, no better way to counter a flag-burner's message than by saluting the flag that burns, no surer means of preserving the dignity even of the flag that burned than by— as one witness here did—according its remains a respectful burial. We do not consecrate the flag by punishing its desecration, for in doing so we dilute the freedom that this cherished emblem represents.
Justice William J. Brennan writing the majority opinion of the U.S. Supreme Court in *Texas v. Johnson* (1989), which holds that the public desecration of the American flag is a protected form of free speech under the U.S. Constitution.

flanks

When a general finds his army larger than his enemy's and wishes to surround him unforeseen, he can arrange his army with a front equal to that of his adversary; then when the battle is joined he can have the front retire little by little and the flanks extend themselves. It will happen every time that the enemy will find themselves surrounded before they realize it.
Niccolò Machiavelli, *The Art of War* (1520).

It is an invariable axiom of war to secure your own flanks and rear and endeavor to turn those of your enemy.
Frederick the Great, *Instructions for His Generals* (1747).

Nothing is more rash or more opposed to the principles of war than a flank march in presence of an army in position, especially when that army occupies heights at the foot of which you must defile.
Napoleon I, *Military Maxims* (1827).

Little success can be expected from mere frontal attack, but very likely a great deal of loss. We must therefore turn towards the flanks of the enemy's position.
Field Marshal Helmuth von Moltke's 1869 instructions, quoted in Rudolf von Caemmerer, *The Development of Strategical Thought in the 19th Century* (1905).

Unless very urgent reasons to the contrary exist, strike at one end rather than at the middle, because both ends can come up to help the middle against you quicker than one end can get to help the other; and as between the two ends, strike at the one upon which the enemy most depends for reinforcements and supplies to maintain his strength.
Alfred Thayer Mahan, *Sea Power in its Relations with the War of 1812* (1905).

In small operations, as in large, speed is the essential element of success. If the difference between two possible flanks is so small that it requires thought, the time wasted in thought is not well used.
General George S. Patton, Jr., *War as I Knew It* (1947).

There is never any point in attempting an outflanking movement round an enemy force unless it has first been tied down frontally.
Field Marshal Erwin Rommel, *The Rommel Papers*, B. H. Liddell Hart, ed. (1953).

Though Patton habitually decried generalship that worried about the security of flanks—the enemy should be forced to worry about *his* flanks—he just as habitually attended with care to the safety of his own. It was the usual Patton disjuncture between reckless words and sound tactical practice.
Russell F. Weigley, *Eisenhower's Lieutenants* (1981).

flexible response

Flexible response should contain at the outset an unqualified renunciation of reliance on the strategy of massive retaliation. It should be made clear that the United States will prepare itself to respond anywhere, any time, with weapons and forces appropriate to the situation. Thus, we would restore to warfare its historic justification as a means to create a better world upon the successful conclusion of hostilities.
General Maxwell D. Taylor, *The Uncertain Trumpet* (1960).

We intend to have a wider choice than humiliation or all-out war.
President John F. Kennedy, Inaugural Address, January 20, 1961.

Morton Halperin, when he was US Deputy Assistant Secretary of Defense, described NATO's policy of flexible response and mutual assured destruction very aptly. "The NATO doctrine is," he said, "that we will fight with conventional forces until we are losing, then we will fight with tactical nuclear weapons until we are losing, and then we will blow up the world."
Frank Barnaby, *The Automated Battlefield* (1986).

fog of war

The *coup d'oeuil* is a gift of God and cannot be acquired; but if professional knowledge does not perfect it, one only sees things imperfectly and in a fog.
Chevalier Folard, *Nouvelles Decouvertes sur la Guerre* (1724).

In the event of signals being invisible through the smoke, he [Admiral Horatio Nelson] told his captains in the written instructions he sent them: "No captain can do very wrong if he places his ship alongside that of an enemy."
Tom Pocock, *Horatio Nelson* (1988).

War is the province of uncertainty; three-fourths of the things on which action in war is based lie hidden in the fog of a greater or lesser certainty.
Karl von Clausewitz, *On War* (1832).

He who wars walks in a mist through which the keenest eye cannot always discern the right path.
Sir William Napier, *History of the War in the Peninsula* (1840).

The unknown is the governing condition of war.
Marshal Ferdinand Foch, *Precepts and Judgments* (1920).

Errors of judgment there must be in war, and few would cavil at them, especially those due to the fog of war. But it is different when the fog is self-created by confused thought and limited study.
B. H. Liddell Hart, *Thoughts on War* (1944).

As soon as *movement* begins, so does the fog of war.
Edward N. Luttwak, *Strategy* (1987).

Ambiguity and uncertainty are fundamental phenomena in all military strategy. The "fog of deterrence" is as dense as the "fog of war."
Fred Charles Ikle, "Discriminate Deterrence: A Reply to Critics," *National Interest* (Fall 1988).

force

If you calmly reflect ... you are not fighting against equals to whom you cannot yield without disgrace, but you are taking counsel whether or not you shall resist an overwhelming force. The question is not one of honor but of prudence.
The Athenians trying to convince the Melians to surrender without a fight, quoted in Thucydides, *The Peloponnesian Wars* (5th century B.C.).

Who overcomes by force,
hath overcome but half his foe.
John Milton, *Paradise Lost* (1667).

The use of force alone is but temporary. It may subdue for a moment; but it does not remove the necessity of subduing again; and a nation is not governed, which is perpetually to be conquered.
Edmund Burke, speech "On Conciliation with the American Colonies," in the House of Commons, March 22, 1775.

It is far more convenient to commit an act of violence, and afterwards excuse it, than laboriously to consider convincing arguments, and lose time listening to objections. This very boldness itself indicates a sort of conviction of the legitimacy of the action, and the God of success is afterwards the best advocate.
Immanuel Kant, *Perpetual Peace* (1795).

Germany has once more said that force, and force alone, shall decide whether peace and justice shall reign in the affairs of men, whether right as America conceives it, or dominion as she conceives it, shall determine the destinies of mankind. There is, therefore, but one response possible from us: force, force to the uttermost, force without

stint or limit, the righteous and triumphant force which shall make right of the law of the world and cast every selfish dominion down in the dust.
President Woodrow Wilson, speech at Baltimore, Maryland, April 6, 1918.

Other nations use "force"; we Britons alone use "Might."
Evelyn Waugh, *Scoop* (1938).

Once you decide to use force, you had better make sure you have plenty of it. If you need a battalion to do a job, it's much better to have the strength of a division. You probably won't suffer any casualties at all in that way.
President Dwight D. Eisenhower, *The New York Times* (May 10, 1965).

Much of the analysis of military opinion has confirmed the conclusion of other students of American foreign policy, that once a decision is made to use force, the generals want to use it more quickly and decisively than do their civilian counterparts ... the navy and air force are likely to advocate more hawkish courses than the army.
Rosemary Foot, *The Wrong War* (1985).

For the first time we have talked to each other using the force of arguments, and not arguments of force.
Lech Walesa, on talks between Solidarity and the Polish communist regime, quoted in *The New York Times* (April 6, 1989).

force ratios

A poor prince who is weak in cavalry, and whose whole infantry does not exceed a single man, had best quit the field.
Laurence Sterne, *A Sentimental Journey* (1768).

Elbridge Gerry tried to have written into the Constitution a specific limitation of the national army to 2000 or at most 3000 men. On this occasion, [George] Washington is said to have departed from the impartiality of his chairmanship of the Constitutional Convention to offer a stage-whispered amendment making it unconstitutional for any enemy to attack with a larger force.
Russell F. Weigley, *History of the United States Army*, enlarged ed. (1984).

A French soldier would not be equal to more than one English soldier, but he would not be afraid to meet two Dutchmen, Prussians, or soldiers of the Confederation.
Napoleon I, speaking before the 1815 Battle of Waterloo, quoted in E. S. Creasy, *The Fifteen Decisive Battles of the World* (1851).

What good is an army of two hundred thousand men of whom only one-half really fight, while the other one hundred thousand disappear in a hundred ways? Better to have one hundred thousand who can be counted upon.
Ardant du Picq, *Battle Studies* (1868).

A regiment of 3,000 rifles properly handled means, after a few days of campaigning, 2,800 rifles; with a smaller amount of care it may mean only 2,000 rifles. Variations in morale are at least equivalent. How can we then compare two regiments? They represent under a same name two bodies absolutely different. Sickness, fatigue, strain of every kind influence different units in different ways. Some of them soon cease to have any fighting value and become mere groups of starving, sick, worn-out men.
General Ferdinand Foch, *The Principles of War* (1918).

Due to the substitution of machine power for muscle power ... fighting man-power will decline, until mechanized forces will more and more revert to the numerical level

of armies in the Middle Ages. Then 500 knights in armour were a large and powerful army, so will 500 tanks be in the future.
J. F. C. Fuller, *Armoured Warfare* (1943).

When I was Secretary of State I was being pressed constantly ... to give the Russians hell. ... At that time [1947], my facilities for giving them hell—and I am a soldier and know something about the ability to give hell—was 1 1/3 divisions over the entire United States. That is quite a proposition when you deal with somebody with over 260 and you have 1 1/3.
General George C. Marshall quoted in Stephen E. Ambrose, *Rise to Globalism*, 2nd rev. ed. (1980).

The efficient commander does not seek to use just enough means, but an excess of means. A military force that is just strong enough to take a position will suffer heavy casualties in doing so; a force vastly superior to the enemy's will do the job without serious loss of men.
Mark S. Watson, *Chief of Staff* (1950).

Military power is not simply the sum total of all the soldiers, tanks, ships, aircraft and missiles in the national inventory. If it were, the United States probably would be permanently relegated to a position of military inferiority vis-à-vis the Soviet Union. ... The key to our true military capacity has always been the maintenance of technological supremacy over our potential adversaries, a supremacy which traditionally has offset our quantitative inferiority.
Senator Sam Nunn, *The Washington Post* (April 8, 1976).

You can no longer calculate the alignment of forces on the basis of who has the most men. Back in the days when a dispute was settled with fists or bayonets, it made a difference who had the most men and the most bayonets on each side. Then when the machine gun appeared, the side with more troops no longer necessarily had the advantage. And now with the atomic bomb, the number of troops on each side makes practically no difference to the alignment of real power and the outcome of a war. The more troops on a side, the more bomb fodder.
Nikita Khrushchev, *Khrushchev Remembers*, I (1971).

If they've been put there to fight, there are far too few. If they've been put there to be killed, there are far too many.
Senator Ernest F. Hollings, on U.S. Marines sent to Lebanon by President Ronald Reagan, *Time* (December 26, 1983).

Foreign Legion, French

Honneur et Fidelité [Honor and Fidelity]
Motto of the French Foreign Legion.

When they arrived in Haiphong [Vietnam] in November 1883, General [François] de Negrier greeted them with a classic military welcome. "You legionnaires," he barked, "are soldiers in order to die, and I am sending you where you can die."
Hugh McLeave, *The Damned Die Hard* (1973).

Every man who joins the Legion does so in ignorance of what awaits him. If the real conditions of Legion life were known, the Legion as such would soon cease to exist, for it would not get a single recruit. Men become beasts before they have worn the uniform for a year.
Three months after I joined, I found myself laughing at the expressions on the face of a prisoner who had been stripped naked and tied by his thumbs to a wall with his

toes barely touching the ground . . . I have seen other prisoners go mad when serving the same sentence.
Michael Donovan, *March or Die!* (1932).

At the 1st Foreign Legion Cavalry [in Indochina in 1953], one crew which must have contained an ex-Nazi electronic engineer, actually succeeded in mounting a regular air-conditioner into an armored car. The story came to light when the vehicle got caught in an ambush and its crew went to unusual lengths to defend it, and, when it was disabled, to retrieve it. The men were duly decorated for their bravery and then in true Foreign Legion tradition, were sent to the stockade for "taking liberties with Government property."
Bernard B. Fall, *Street Without Joy* (1961).

Every man marched or was driven along by the sergeants; or, if he could not get to his feet, he was dragged behind the mule cart which followed the column. The justification for this form of torture was the Legion slogan, *March or Die*, a precept originating from the early campaigns in the Sahara where a man could not hope to survive unless he kept his place in the column.
James Wellard, *The French Foreign Legion* (1974).

The Legion is demanding; the work is tough and its punishments are hard. The old stories about men buried up to the neck in sand are not the inventions of some Hollywood hack.
Len Deighton, Introduction to John Robert Young, *The French Foreign Legion* (1984).

foreign policy

Much of what Mr. [Henry A.] Wallace calls his global thinking is, no matter how you slice it, still Globaloney.
Clare Boothe Luce, in a speech in the House of Representatives, February 9, 1943.

My [foreign] policy is to be able to take a ticket at Victoria Station and go anywhere I damn well please.
Ernest Bevin, *The Spectator* (April 20, 1951).

When I was in Paris last week, I said that . . . the United States would have to undertake an agonizing reappraisal of basic foreign policy in relation to Europe. This statement, I thought, represented a self-evident truth.
John Foster Dulles, Secretary of State, address to the National Press Club, Washington, D.C., December 22, 1953.

We cannot be any stronger in our foreign policy—for all the bombs and guns we may heap up in our arsenals—than we are in the spirit which rules inside the country. Foreign policy, like a river, cannot rise above its source.
Adlai E. Stevenson, *What I Think* (1956).

Foreign policy is really domestic policy with its hat on.
Vice President Hubert H. Humphrey, speech to the United States Junior Chamber of Commerce in Detroit, June 29, 1966.

Domestic policy can only defeat us; foreign policy can kill us.
President John F. Kennedy quoted in Arthur M. Schlesinger, Jr., *The Imperial Presidency* (1973).

No foreign policy—no matter how ingenious—has any chance of success if it is born in the minds of a few and carried in the hearts of none.
Henry Kissinger, *The Washington Post* (August 4, 1973).

The objectives of foreign policy must be defined in terms of national interest and must be supported with adequate power.
Hans J. Morgenthau, *Politics Among Nations*, 5th ed. (1978).

We must make it perfectly clear that we are revolted by torture and can never feel spiritual kinship with a government that engages in torture. But the central goal of our foreign policy should be not the moral elevation of other nations, but the preservation of a civilized conception of our own national self-interest.
Jeane J. Kirkpatrick, United States Ambassador to the United Nations, *U.S. News & World Report* (March 2, 1981).

We hear very often, with the advent of the new Soviet General Secretary, calls for a meeting between our President and the General Secretary of the Soviet Union. This reflects a profound American temptation to believe that foreign policy is a subdivision of psychiatry and that relations among nations are like relations among people.
Henry A. Kissinger, *Time* (June 17, 1985).

I don't believe I'll ever get credit for anything I do in foreign affairs, no matter how successful it is, because I didn't go to Harvard.
President Lyndon B. Johnson quoted in Walter Isaacson and Evan Thomas, *The Wise Men* (1986).

When the Congress tries to limit the Executive's power in foreign policy, it has to do it clearly. Any ambiguity will be determined in favor of the President.
John Norton Moore, *The Washington Post* (May 18, 1987).

Foreign affairs is not always a zero-sum game. We do not necessarily advance our own vital interests at another nation's cost.
George Shultz, U.S. Secretary of State, *USA Today* (June 15, 1987).

They [the Bush Administration] are criticizing Gorbachev for conducting foreign policy in precisely the same way the Bush people conducted their election campaign, which was to manipulate the media with public-relations gimmicks and subordinate the substantive policy debate. Now they are suddenly the wounded ones. No wonder they are angry. They are being beaten at their own game.
Michael J. Sandel, *The New York Times* (May 18, 1989).

adventurism
Because of its importance, the Caribbean Basin is a magnet for adventurism.
President Ronald Reagan, speech before Congress, April 27, 1983.

Our Army . . . is the ultimate symbol of American will. It is an indispensable component of a flexible response strategy and essential to deterring or defeating an adversary's adventurism.
General Carl E. Vuono, Chief of Staff of the Army, "The United States Army is a Strategic Force," *Armed Forces Journal* (February 1989).

The Soviets hope that the world will view their withdrawal [from Afghanistan] as a sign that they've turned away from adventurism, that they mean it when they say that force no longer drives their foreign policy.
Marshall D. Shulman, *The New York Times* (February 5, 1989).

coexistence
For a long, long time, everybody in the United States had urged that we attempt to reach a proper basis for peaceful coexistence. We had found, though, an aggressive attitude on the part of the other side that had made such an accomplishment or consummation not easy to reach. In other words, there had to be good faith on both sides.

Moreover, we had to make certain that peaceful coexistence did not mean appeasement.
President Dwight D. Eisenhower, press conference, June 30, 1954.

The only alternative to coexistence is codestruction.
Jawaharial Nehru, *The Observer* (August 29, 1954).

Pravda wrote the truth when it declared in Brezhnev's time, "the Marxist-Lenninist concept of peaceful coexistence does in no way contain the pacifist-like promotion of peace."
Paul Seabury and Angelo Codevilla, *War* (1989).

imperialism

We came here to serve God and also to get rich.
Bernal Diaz del Castillo, 16th-century Spanish soldier, quoted in Samuel Eliot Morison, *The European Discovery of America: The Southern Voyages* (1974).

To found a great empire for the sole purpose of raising up a people of customers, may at first sight appear a project fit only for a nation of shopkeepers. It is, however, a project altogether unfit for a nation of shopkeepers; but extremely fit for a nation whose government is influenced by shopkeepers.
Adam Smith, *The Wealth of Nations* (1776).

His Majesty's dominions, on which the sun never sets.
Christopher North, *Noctes Ambrosianae* (1829). This is often phrased as: "The sun never sets on the British Empire." However, in 1598 Friedrich von Schiller has Philip II of Spain say in his play *Don Carlos*: "The sun does not set in my dominions."

All the territorial possessions of all the political establishments in the earth—including America, of course—consist of pilferings from other people's wash.
Mark Twain, *Following the Equator* (1897).

Take up the White Man's Burden—
        Send forth the best ye breed—
Go bind your sons to exile
        To serve your captives' need;
To wait in heavy harness
        On fluttered folk and wide—
Your new-caught, sullen people,
        Half-devil and half-child.
Rudyard Kipling, *The White Man's Burden* (1899).

We assert that no nation can long endure half republic and half empire, and we warn the American people that imperialism abroad will lead quickly and inevitably to despotism at home.
Democratic Party national platform, 1900.

The more of the world we [the British] inhabit the better it is for the human race.
Cecil Rhodes quoted in Robert Rotberg, *The Founder* (1989).

I have not become the King's First Minister in order to preside over the liquidation of the British Empire.
Winston Churchill, speech in London, November 10, 1942, quoted in *Time* (November 23, 1942).

As far as I'm concerned, it's an imperialist tossup. Either we louse up Asia or Japan does. And I imagine our methods will be a little less drastic.
Norman Mailer, *The Naked and the Dead* (1948).

But the great danger of communism does not lie in its false promises. It lies in the fact that it is an instrument of an armed imperialism which seeks to extend its influence by force.
President Harry S. Truman, speech in Alexandria, Virginia, February 22, 1950.

In the end it may well be that Britain will be honored by the historians more for the way she disposed of an empire than for the way in which she acquired it.
Sir David Ormsby Gore, British Ambassador to United States, *The New York Times* (October 28, 1962).

One of the strange things of life in the modern world ... is that there are some people who like to be colonies of Great Britain.
Alec Douglas-Home, British Foreign Secretary, speaking of Gibraltar, *The New York Times* (March 1, 1972).

No one should get into the habit of thinking that the Russians don't know how to be imperialists. Theirs is the only 19th century empire to have survived the 20th century—not only to have survived it but to have expanded. They got back parts they had lost. They had lost Lithuania and Estonia and Latvia. The got them back; they got chunks of Poland back.
Daniel P. Moynihan, *Newsweek* (January 19, 1976).

isolationism

Why quit our own to stand upon foreign ground? Why, by interweaving our destiny with that of any part of Europe, entangle our peace and prosperity in the toils of European ambition, rivalship, interest, humor or caprice?
President George Washington, Farewell Address, September 17, 1796.

I have no confidence in the system of isolement [isolation]. It does not answer in social life for individuals, nor in politics for nations. Man is a social animal.
Duke of Wellington, letter to Thomas Raikes, March 1, 1841, *Private Correspondence of Thomas Raikes*, ed. Harriet Raikes (1861).

We have stood alone in that which is called isolation—our splendid isolation, as one of our colonial friends was good enough to call it.
George J. Goschen, First Lord of the Admiralty, *The Times* (London) (February 27, 1896).

Our whole duty for the present, at any rate, is summed up in the motto "American First: Let us think of America before we think of Europe."
President Woodrow Wilson, speech in New York, April 20, 1915.

Let us not delude ourselves. If we enter the quarrels of Europe during war, we must stay in them in time of peace as well. It is madness to send our soldiers to be killed as we did in the last war if we turn the course of peace over to the greed, the fear and the intrigue of European nations.
Charles Lindbergh, *Time* (September 25, 1939).

Isolationism is the road to war. Worse than that, isolationism is the road to defeat in war.
President Harry S. Truman, speech in St. Louis, Missouri, June 10, 1950.

There can be no such thing as Fortress America. If ever we were reduced to the isolationism implied by that term we would occupy a prison, not a fortress.
President Dwight D. Eisenhower, State of the Union Address, January 9, 1959.

fortunes of war

We know that the fortune of war is sometimes impartial, and not always on the side of numbers. If we yield now, all is over; but if we fight, there is yet a hope that we may stand upright.
Thucydides, *The Peloponnesian Wars* (5th century B.C.).

Fortune favors the brave.
Terence, *Phormio* (161 B.C.).

It is very unwise for a captain to go into battle unless he is moved by necessity or by the knowledge that he has a great advantage. A battle is very subject to Fortune; and defeat is too important a matter ever to risk.
Francesco Guicciardini, *Ricordi* (1530).

There is nothing so subject to the inconstancy of fortune as war.
Miguel de Cervantes, *Don Quixote* (1605).

The more helpless the position in which an officer finds his men, the more it is his bounden duty to stay and share their fortune, whether for good or ill.
Sir Garnet Wolseley quoted in Donald R. Morris, *The Washing of the Spears* (1968).

The fortunes of war flow this way and that, and no prudent fighter holds his enemy in contempt.
Johann Wolfgang von Goethe, *Iphigenie and Tauris*, Act V (1787).

There is always inequity in life. Some men are killed in a war, and some men are wounded, and some men are stationed in the Antarctic and some are stationed in San Francisco. It's very hard in military or personal life to assure complete equality. Life is unfair.
President John F. Kennedy, press conference, March 21, 1962.

foxholes

There are no atheists in the foxholes.
William T. Cummings, a chaplain with the U.S. Army in Bataan, quoted in Carlos P. Romulo, *I Saw the Fall of the Philippines* (1942).

You and your Hollywood sycophants have been jamming that chaplain sequence into every war picture. The sequence is a lie. The old no-atheists-in-fox-holes lie. Foxholes multiply atheists. War doesn't draw men closer to God. War causes men to curse God.
William Bradford Huie, *The Americanization of Emily* (1959).

One particularly supercilious cliché that was bandied around the American rear areas and home front was that "There are no atheists in the fox-holes". Those who believed this might have been in for a rude shock had they tried to put it to the test. For many men nothing so utterly and completely dissipated their residual religious beliefs as the randomness and pervasiveness of violent death.
John Ellis, *The Sharp End: The Fighting Man in World War II* (1980).

Do you know what it's like? Of course you don't. You have never slept in a hole in the ground which you have dug while someone tried to kill you . . . a hole dug as deep as you can as quick as you can . . . . It is an open grave, and yet graves don't fill up with water. . . .

At night the infantryman gets some boards, or tin, or an old door and puts it over one end of his slit trench; then he shovels on top of it as much dirt as he can scrape up near by. He sleeps with his head under this, not to keep out the rain, but to protect his head and chest from airbursts. Did I say sleeps? Let us say, collapses. You see, the infantryman must be awake for one-half the night. The reason is that one half of the troops are on watch and the other half are resting, washing, shaving, writing letters, eating, or cleaning weapons; that is if he is not being shot at, shelled, mortared, or counter-attacked. . . .
Captain Athol Steward, a World War II Canadian infantry officer, quoted in D. Hawkins, *War Report* (1946).

Outside Seoul we were all scared. I didn't even know how to dig a foxhole. Hadn't any idea. A gunnery sergeant told me how. "Make it like a grave," he said.
Merwin Perkins quoted in Donald Knox, *The Korean War: Pusan to Chosin* (1985).

fragging

Many fraggings were the culmination of a long, gradual process of disgruntlement; only the most inattentive of officers could fail to grasp that something was amiss. There were often enough warnings to "hard chargers" before an actual fragging took place and, even then, some of the fraggings were intended to warn rather than kill. Sometimes the warnings took on ominous forms as when one group of soldiers actually took up a collection to raise a "bounty" and then openly offered it to anyone who was willing to "waste" a particularly disliked officer.
Richard A. Gabriel and Paul L. Savage, *Crisis in Command* (1978).

One of the remarkable findings of the Vietnam years was that the incompetence of the officer corps was readily perceived by the common soldier. In the U.S. Army alone, over one thousand officers and NCOs were killed or wounded by their own men. In peacetime, of course, things rarely go so far.
Richard A. Gabriel, *Military Incompetence* (1985).

Officers, NCOs or even private soldiers who were identified as being too eager for action risked "fragging." The term was derived from the use of a fragmentation grenade, conveniently rolled into the victim's hooch at night, although assassination with small-arms fire in the confusion of a firefight was not unknown. The incidence of fragging peaked in 1971, with no less than 333 confirmed incidents and another 158 possible ones.
Richard Holmes, *Acts of War* (1985).

France

Every French soldier carries a marshal's baton in his knapsack.
Attributed to both Louis XVIII and Napoleon I of France.

About 1850 every educated person knew the French were the belligerent, martial fighting nation *par excellence* and Germany was a nation of watchmakers, porcelain makers, poets, and musicians.
Edward Luttwak, "The Strategy of Survival," *American Heritage* (July/August 1988).

Perhaps symbolic of the whole spirit of [France in] 1916 was the divine Sarah Bernhardt, one leg amputated, but still stumping the boards with a wooden leg. Here was France herself, mutilated but undaunted.
Alistair Horne, *The Price of Glory* (1962).

The P. M. [Winston Churchill] made a gaffe. He is speaking on the wireless in French tonight [October 21, 1940], and just before dinner he came into the room, where the French B.B.C. expert and translator, M. Duchesne, was standing, and exclaimed: "Where is my frog speech?" M. Duchesne looked pained.
John Colville, *The Fringes of Power* (1985).

France has lost a battle. But France has not lost the war.
General Charles de Gaulle, radio broadcast from London to France after the German conquest, June 18, 1940, quoted in *Life* (July 28, 1941).

The French leaders desire to cut loose from all that France has represented during the past two generations, that their physical and moral defeat has been so absolute that they have accepted completely for France the fate of becoming a province of Nazi Germany. Moreover, in order that they may have as many companions in misery as possible they hope that England will be rapidly and completely defeated by Germany.
William C. Bullitt, writing of 1940 France, quoted in Will Brownell and Richard N. Billings, *So Close to Greatness: A Biography of William C. Bullitt* (1989).

I was France.
General Charles de Gaulle, on his role as leader of the French resistance during World War II, from his *War Memoirs* (1955).

The Almighty in His infinite wisdom did not see fit to create Frenchmen in the image of Englishmen.
Winston Churchill, speech in the House of Commons, December 10, 1942.

From Paris last week came a new definition of a collaborationist: "Anybody who collaborated more than you did."
Time (January 29, 1945).

[In September 1958] the head of the French government asked the American general [Lauris Norstad] for a precise account of the deployment of nuclear weapons in France and of the targets assigned to them. Norstad: "Sir, I can answer only if we are alone." "So be it," said de Gaulle. The two staffs withdrew. "So then?" "Then, sir, I cannot reply to your questions, to my very great regret ..." and de Gaulle in conclusion: "General, that is the last time, and make yourself understand it, that a responsible French leader will allow such an answer to be made."
Jean Lacouture, *De Gaulle*, III (1986).

[During the Indochina War] one French convoy after another passing on the road had been either shelled or ambushed by the black-clad infantry of Viet-Minh Regiment 95, a battle-hardened regular Communist unit infiltrated behind French lines. This inspired the French soldiers with that kind of black humor proper to all soldiers, to christen that stretch of Road 1 *"la rue sans joie"* or in English, "Street Without Joy."
Bernard B. Fall, *Street Without Joy* (1961).

The British radio, more than anything else, helped to establish de Gaulle's name. The B.B.C. literally made de Gaulle. . . . Distance gave him an aura of mystery, and yet he was in daily communication with us; that was what gave him such prestige.
Georges Bidault, *Resistance* (1967).

We [France] must provide ourselves, over the next few years, with a force capable of acting on our own behalf, with what is commonly known as a "strike force" [*force de frappe*], capable of being deployed at any moment and in any place. The basis of this force must obviously be atomic weapons.
Charles de Gaulle, *Memoirs of Hope: Renewal and Endeavor* (1971).

fraternization

[On October 1, 1916] a queue of 150 men waiting outside the door of a Calais brothel, each to have his short turn with one of the three women of the house .... Each woman served nearly a battalion of men each week for as long as she lasted. According to the assistant provost-marshal, three weeks was the usual limit: "after which she retired on her earnings, pale but proud."
John Ellis quoted in Peter Vansittart, *Voices From the Great War* (1984).

Patton's eagerness kept puzzling Bradley, so now he asked, "Why does everyone in the Third Army want to liberate the Czechs?"
Patton said nothing about the Russians. "Oh, Brad," he answered, "can't you see? The Czechs are our allies and consequently their women aren't off limits. On to Czechoslovakia and fraternization!" he yelled into the telephone. "How in hell can you stop an army with a battle cry like that?"
Ladislas Farago, *Patton* (1964).

The brothels [in French North Africa] proved to be a particularly sensitive political question. The French feared that the Americans with all their money and chocolates and everything else would monopolize the girls' attention and squeeze the French out completely. A command-level agreement was made. The Americans instituted a ten o'clock curfew for the brothels; the rest of the evening belonged to the French. . . . [I] returned . . . to the three brothels to make sure that the ten o'clock curfew was being observed. This required a room-by-room inspection. Sometimes I would kick a door open only to have it kicked shut. I would then point out to a somewhat aroused American soldier that professional international relations ended at ten o'clock. I cannot remember ever being thanked for this information!
General Vernon Walters, while a lieutenant during World War II, *Silent Missions* (1978).

freedom

Those who expect to reap the blessings of freedom, must, like men, undergo the fatigues of supporting it.
Thomas Paine, *The American Crisis* (September 11, 1777).

No people in the world ever did achieve their freedom by goody-goody talk and moral suasion: it being immutable law that all revolutions that will succeed, must begin in blood, whatever may answer afterward. If history teaches anything, it teaches that.
Mark Twain, *A Connecticut Yankee in King Arthur's Court* (1889).

No man who is not willing to bear arms and to fight for his rights can give a good reason why he should be entitled to the privilege of living in a free community.
Theodore Roosevelt, *Thomas Hart Benton* (1897).

In the long history of the world, only a few generations have been granted the role of defending freedom in its hour of maximum danger. I do not shrink from this responsibility—I welcome it.
President John F. Kennedy, Inaugural Address, January 20, 1961.

friction of war

Everything is very simple in war, but the simplest thing is difficult. These difficulties accumulate and produce a friction which no man can imagine exactly who has not seen war.
Karl von Clausewitz, *On War* (1832).

War is a gamble first of all because it depends to so large an extent upon the human element, and the human element is in itself uncertain. Another element which makes war a gamble is friction, the difference between theory and practice.
Cyril Falls, *The Nature of Modern Warfare* (1941).

The chief advantage which the regular soldier has over the temporary wartime soldier is that he becomes so habituated to military processes that he can perform them instinctively in the heat of action, so that his functional efficiency is apt to be less affected by the "friction" of war.
B. H. Liddell Hart, *Thoughts on War* (1944).

Friction is the basic medium in which strategic action unfolds, and war's most constant companion.
Edward N. Luttwak, *Strategy* (1987).

fuck

Always there was the word. Always there was that four-letter ugly sound that men in uniform have expanded into the single substance of the linguistic world. It was a handle, a hyphen, a hyperbole; verb, noun, modifier.... It described food, fatigue, metaphysics. It stood for everything and meant nothing; an insulting word, it was never used to insult; crudely descriptive of the sexual act, it was never used to describe it.
Robert Leckie, *Helmet For My Pillow* (1957).

I was invited to speak on a Chicago TV program.... At the last minute a retired brigadier general turned up to participate in the discussion. For ten minutes, he talked in a calm, cool, nice way about nuclear war and the possibility of the world being blown up.... As the arc lights were turned off at the end, he turned to me and aggressively said, "You should go to Russia." I thought for several seconds and decided to let him see the true fear in my soul, and I said to him, "I fucking want my kids to grow up." Well, he could talk about nuclear war with absolutely no emotion, the deaths of hundreds of millions of human beings, but when a lady said "fuck" to him, he was undone. He went wild and almost physically attacked me. The producer came running out to separate us, and there was nearly a brawl on the floor of the TV studio.
Helen Caldicott, *Missile Envy* (1984).

Once and for all this has to be cleared up forever: I never used the word "fuck" in *The Naked and the Dead*. It was "fug" from the beginning.... Nobody could print "fuck" at that point, and I never considered it. I used to rationalize it to myself, right from the word go, saying to myself, "They didn't really say 'fuck' in the army, they say 'fug.' Even if I could use "fuck," I wouldn't. "Fug" works better. It's closer to the deadness of the word the way we used to use it, "Pass the fuggin' bread." So "fug" was it from the beginning. If I had used "fuck," it would've been hopeless. The story that's been around forever is that they broke my balls on it. It's not true. My balls, if you will, were broken before I began the book. So were everyone else's in the publishing world.
Norman Mailer quoted in Peter Manso, *Mailer* (1985).

The ugly truth is that war is thin gruel. It is repetitive. Again and again the same thing—death and destruction. Only the geography changes, the terrible process of man's self-degradation which Ernie Pyle [during World War II] once put into three words. Sitting on the edge of a bed, a mosquito-netting enfolding a colleague who was suffering from dysentery in the Aletti hotel in Algiers, Pyle, just back from America and facing another combat tour, said he could hardly bear it, could hardly bear going back to the GIs. I just can't take it any more, he said, I can't take them. I can't take war, I can't listen to them. Every other word is fuck or shit. The other day one of them said, over and over: "Fuck my shit. Fuck my shit." That's the bottom.

Harrison Salisbury, *A Time of Change* (1988).

Gatling gun

It occurred to me that if I could invent a machine—a gun—that would by its rapidity of fire enable one man to do as much battle duty as a hundred, that it would to a great extent, supersede the necessity of large armies, and consequently exposure to battle and disease would be greatly diminished.

Richard J. Gatling quoted in P. Wahl and D. R. Toppel, *The Gatling Gun* (1966).

General George Armstrong Custer was guilty of monumental folly in this respect. In 1876, when he led his entire troop to be massacred at the Battle of the Little Big Horn, there were four Gatlings available with his headquarters. But Custer declined to take any of them with him. One can only explain this oversight as a typical piece of arrogant bravado. He said that it would be too difficult to haul them over the terrain, but in fact they were of a model specially designed to be dismantled and carried on pack mules.

John Ellis, *The Social History of the Machine Gun* (1975).

generals

The Creator has not thought proper to mark those in the forehead who are of stuff to make good generals. We are first, therefore, to seek them blindfold, and then let them learn the trade at the expense of great losses.

President Thomas Jefferson, letter to General Theodorus Bailey, February 6, 1813, reprinted in *The Writings of Thomas Jefferson*, 13, ed. A. E. Bergh (1907).

The first qualification of a general-in-chief is to possess a cool head, so that things may appear to him in their true proportions and as they really are. He should not suffer himself to be unduly affected by good or bad news.

Napoleon I, *Military Maxims* (1827).

To conduct a whole War, or its great acts, which we call campaigns, to a successful termination, there must be an intimate knowledge of State policy in its higher relations. The conduct of a War and the policy of the State here coincide, and the General becomes at the same time the Statesman . . . but he must not cease to be the General. He takes into view all the relations of the State on the one hand; on the other, he must know exactly what he can do with the means at his disposal. . . . In this sense, Bonaparte was right when he said that many of the questions which come before a General for decision would make problems for a mathematical calculation not unworthy of the powers of Newton or Euler.

Karl von Clausewitz, *On War* (1832).

Let us not hear of generals who conquer without bloodshed. If bloody slaughter is a horrible sight, then that is a reason for paying more respect to war; but not for making the sword we bear blunter and blunter by degrees from feelings of humanity, until once again someone steps in with a sword that is sharp and hews away the arms from our body.

Karl von Clausewitz, *On War* (1832).

Russia has two generals whom she can trust—Generals Janvier [January] and Fevrier [February].

Czar Nicholas I quoted in *Punch* (March 10, 1853).

I am the very model of a modern Major-General,
I've information vegetable, animal and mineral;
I know the kings of England, and I quote the fights historical,
From Marathon to Waterloo, in order categorical,
I'm very good at integral and differential calculus,
I know the scientific names of beings animalculous;
In short, in matters vegetable, animal and mineral, I am the very model of a modern
Major-General.
William S. Gilbert, *The Pirates of Penzance* (1879).

NAPOLEON: What shall we do with this officer, Giuseppe? Everything he says is wrong.
GIUSEPPE: Make him a general, excellency; and then everything he says will be right.
George Bernard Shaw, *The Man of Destiny* (1897).

Battles are lost or won by generals, not by the rank and fiie.
General Ferdinand Foch, *The Principles of War* (1918).

The war the Generals always get ready for is the previous one.
Henry M. Tomlinson, *All Our Yesterdays* (1930).

Efficiency in a general, his soldiers have a right to expect; geniality they are usually right to suspect.
Sir Archibald Wavell, *Generals and Generalship* (1939).

If they lose Egypt, blood will flow. I will have firing parties to shoot the Generals.
Winston Churchill, expressing restrained confidence in the British generals in North Africa in 1941, quoted in W. G. F. Jackson, *The Battle for North Africa* (1975).

Ambitious officers when they came in sight of promotion to the generals' list, would decide that they would bottle up their thoughts and ideas, as a safety precaution, until they reached the top and could put these ideas into practice. Unfortunately the usual result, after years of such self-repression for the sake of their ambition, was that when the bottle was eventually uncorked the contents had evaporated.
B. H. Liddell Hart, *Why Don't We Learn From History?* (1943).

When I got home from a long trip I found awaiting me a notification that I'd been appointed a reg. Major General by the President. That practically floored me. . . . Seems odd to try to think of myself as a permanent Major General. Have always considered my present rank as just a happenstance of war—and myself as a creature of war! Subconsciously, I think, I've always expected to come back to you as a Colonel.
General Dwight D. Eisenhower, letter to his wife, Mamie, September 1, 1943, quoted in *Letters to Mamie* (1978).

The drinking at Stalin's table was perfectly awful. [Marshal] Timoshenko got dead drunk. Stalin was a little ashamed. "Do your generals drink as much?" he asked Winston [Churchill]. "No, but then it may be because they are not such good generals." Stalin was delighted by this.
Harold Nicolson, diary entry of July 5, 1944, *Diaries and Letters of Harold Nicolson*, II (1967).

An important difference between a military operation and a surgical operation is that the patient is not tied down. But it is a common fault of generalship to assume that he is.
B. H. Liddell Hart, *Thoughts on War* (1944).

Sometimes a general has to go to the front and let the troops see him. . . . That's the only way he can make them realize there's nothing ahead of them.
General Holland M. Smith and Percy Smith, *Coral and Brass* (1948).

I prefer our military past. The harm's done and there it is. As for being a General, well at the age of four with paper hats and wooden swords we're all Generals. Only some of us never grow out of it.
Peter Ustinov, *Romanoff and Juliet*, Act I (1956).

I am convinced that the best service a retired general can perform is to turn in his tongue with his suit, and to mothball his opinions.
General Omar Bradley, *The New York Times*, May 17, 1959.

Let me give you some advice, Lieutenant. Don't become a general. Don't ever become a general. If you become a general you just plain have too much to worry about.
President Dwight D. Eisenhower, speaking to Lieutenant Andrew Wnukowski, *The New York Times* (May 10, 1965).

There is an anecdote of a general, on the defensive, being taunted by the opposing general, "If you are a great general, come down and fight it out." His reply was, "And if you are a great general, make me fight it out against my will."
Thomas C. Schelling, *Arms and Influence* (1966). It was Sun Tzu who wrote in *The Art of War* (4th century B.C.): "Those skilled in war bring the enemy to the field of battle and are not brought there by him."

Generals can be divided broadly into two classes. To make the distinction I will use two very expressive French definitions. *Le bon general ordinaire* is the general who is good so long as his superior will tell him in detail what to do, will stand by him and help him, and will see that he does what he is told. *Le grand chef* requires only a general directive covering the operations which are envisaged; he requires no detailed instructions, he knows what to do and can safely be left alone to do it; he is a very rare bird.
Field Marshal Viscount Montgomery of Alamein, *A History of Warfare* (1968).

Really when I reflect upon the characters and attainments of some of the General officers of this army . . . on whom I am to rely . . . against the French Generals . . . I tremble: and, as Lord Chesterfield said of the Generals of his day, "I only hope that when the enemy reads the list of their names he trembles as I do."
Duke of Wellington, letter to Colonel Torrens, August 29, 1810, quoted in Elizabeth Longford, *Wellington: The Years of the Sword* (1969).

The brass must get off their ass. In 1945, as World War II ended, we had more than 12 million men and women on active duty. Of those, about 17,000 had the rank of O-6 and above. These included 101 three-star generals and admirals. A few years ago, we had somewhat more than 2 million service personnel—about 10 million less than at the end of World War II. Yet we have nearly the same number of high-ranking officers today—almost 15,500 men and women. There were nearly 120 three-star generals and admirals—more than in 1945! As Sam Nunn put it, "Apparently, it takes more admirals and generals to wage peace than run a war."
Barry Goldwater, *Goldwater* (1988).

Alexander the Great (356–323 B.C.)

Do you think I have not just cause to weep, when I consider that Alexander at my age had conquered so many nations, and I have all this time done nothing that is memorable.
Julius Caesar quoted in Plutarch, *The Lives* (A.D. 106).

Alexander's career was piracy pure and simple, nothing but an orgy of power and plunder, made romantic by the character of the hero.
William James, "The Moral Equivalent of War," *McClure's* (August 1910).

He is known as Alexander the Great because he killed more people of more different kinds than any other man of this time. He did this in order to impress Greek culture upon them.
Will Cuppy, *The Decline and Fall of Practically Everybody* (1950).

The natural watershed between his boyhood and adolescence is the famous episode of his taming [the seemingly untamable] Bucephalas. The popular notion is still of high-spirited youngsters meeting; the more interesting truth is that Bucephalas was twelve years old.
Mary Renault, *The Nature of Alexander* (1975).

After making his dispositions and issuing his orders, he [Alexander] had exercised no general control over the battle, nor could he have done so, being thrust so deep into the action that he had no time or thought for anything but a fight for life; "heroic" leadership had nevertheless done its work. The knowledge that their king was taking the supreme risk drove capable and well-briefed subordinates, at the head of drilled and self-confident troops, to fight as hard and skillfully as if he had been at the elbow of each one of them.
John Keegan, *The Mask of Command* (1987).

Bradley, General of the Army Omar N. (1893–1981)

Ernie Pyle had called on Ike some time ago: Ike had told him that when he went up front again he should "go and discover Bradley." Pyle had written almost exclusively of GIs and junior officers, not caring much for the brass hats. He really discovered Bradley, though, and when the lid was off, five or six of his columns were devoted to him.
Captain Harry C. Butcher, writing about May 8, 1943, *My Three Years With Eisenhower* (1946).

Of all the ground commanders I have known, and even of those of whom I've read, I would put General Omar Bradley in the highest classification. In every aspect of military command, from the planning of an operation to the cleanup after its success, Brad was outstanding. I have yet to meet his equal as an offensive leader and a defensive bulwark, as wielder of every arm that can be practically employed against an enemy. In the aftermath of war, I'm surprised that he seems at times to be ignored or undervalued by those who write of the Mediterranean and European campaigns. Patton, for instance, was a master of fast and overwhelming pursuit. Headstrong by nature, and fearlessly aggressive, Patton was the more colorful figure of the two, compelling attention by his mannerisms as much as by his deeds. Bradley, however, was master of every military maneuver, lacking only in the capacity—possibly the willingness—to dramatize himself. This, I think, is to his credit.
President Dwight D. Eisenhower, *At Ease* (1967).

General of the Army Omar Bradley once told some civilians that he had been in the Army for over forty-seven years but that he had never observed anything that might be

called "the military mind." This remarkable statement bears out what anthropologists have long known, that to observe a culture or subculture in all its dimensions one must have not only the opportunity to observe it closely over a long period of time but also the detachment of being an outsider.
Bernard Brodie, *War and Politics* (1973).

Clausewitz, General Karl von (1780–1831)

[Clausewitz] unfortunately died while his own thought was still fermenting—leaving his papers in sealed packets, with this significant note: "Should the work be interrupted by my death, then what is found can only be called a mass of formless conceptions . . . open to endless misconceptions." So they proved.
B. H. Liddell Hart, *Thoughts on War* (1944).

[Clausewitz is] the most important influence on Soviet military doctrine to this day.
Raymond L. Garthoff, *Soviet Military Doctrine* (1953).

But of all Clausewitz's blind spots, the blindest was that he never grasped that the true aim of war is peace and not victory; therefore that peace should be the ruling idea of policy, and victory only the means toward its achievement. Nowhere does he consider the influence of violence on eventual peace; actually the word "peace" barely occurs half a dozen times in *On War*.
J. F. C. Fuller, *The Conduct of War* (1961).

It has long been a practice for writers on military strategy to quote Clausewitz, and his writings are so probing and inquiring and perceptive that he has mused on nearly all aspects of politico-military policy and relationships. And, in a fashion that would do credit to any scholar, he has looked at all sides of his problem. . . .
The result is that one can support nearly any side of any argument by citing Clausewitz.
Rear Admiral J. C. Wylie, *Military Strategy* (1967).

Clausewitz's military disciples only saw in *On War* those sections they wanted to see. . . . Clausewitz had been careful with his forecasts of the future, and had written in the context of his own age; but the generals seemed to believe that he had written in a vacuum, and that his words were valid for all time. They overlooked Clausewitz's belief, so often repeated, that the defensive was the strongest form of strategy. They overlooked the fact that *On War* was unfinished; they believed that *On War* contained a blueprint for victory, even though Clausewitz had many times reiterated that his work could not be regarded as a military manual.
Roger Parkinson, *Clausewitz* (1970).

The unfortunate thing about "On War" is that nine-tenths of it are now obsolete, and the one-tenth, which is pure gold, gets lost in the rubble.
J. F. C. Fuller, 1961 letter, quoted in A. J. Trythall, '*Boney Fuller*,' II (1977).

His is not simply the greatest, but the only great book about war.
Bernard Brodie quoted in Michael Howard, *Clausewitz* (1983).

When a cadet would try to answer one of Rommel's questions with a quote from Clausewitz, Rommel would invariably interrupt and bark: "Never mind what Clausewitz thought, what do *you* think?" Rommel never did admire Clausewitz very much.
Samuel W. Mitcham, Sr., *Triumphant Fox* (1984).

If there can be such a thing as a joke in military history, surely a small one is the belief that with the posthumous publication of Clausewitz in the 1830s, *On War* became the bible of the Prussian army, the source of their great victories of 1866 and

1870, and soon thereafter the chief military theory of the Western world. The truth is that most German students of war found Clausewitz no less difficult, obscure, and of doubtful utility than did non-Germans, most of whom read Clausewitz in poor translations.
John Shy, "Jomini," *Makers of Modern Strategy,* ed. Peter Paret (1986).

Clausewitz . . . belongs in context, though he is rarely put there. His famous "principles of war"—written originally as a school text for the Prussian Crown Prince—are, in a sense, words to the unwise. It is inconceivable that Alexander or Caesar or Frederick the Great or even Wellington should have needed to be reminded that a general should husband his resources and expend them only for good purpose—which is what the principles of "decision," "concentration" and "offensive action" counsel. It is even less conceivable that any should have needed reminding, from Clausewitz's later work, that "war is the continuation of policy by other means."
John Keegan, *The Mask of Command* (1987).

A way of thinking and a way of acting, based on the use of force in world politics, have formed over centuries, even millennia. It seems they have taken root as something unshakable. Today, they have lost all reasonable grounds. Clausewitz's dictum that war is the continuation of policy only by different means, which was classical in his time, has grown hopelessly out of date. It now belongs to the libraries.
Mikhail Gorbachev, *Perestroika* (1987).

The German language, like the French, uses the same word to refer to both policy and politics. Clausewitz clearly meant that war was a continuation of *policy* by other means.
Albert Wohlstetter, "Swords Without Shield," *National Interest* (Summer 1987).

Custer, General George Armstrong (1839–1876)
Cut off from aid, abandoned in the midst of incredible odds, waving aloft the sabre which had won him victory so often; the pride and glory of his comrades, the noble Custer fell; bequeathing to the nation his sword, to his comrades an example, to his friends a memory; and to his beloved one a hero's name.
Lawrence Barrett quoted in Frederick Whittaker, *A Complete Life of General George A. Custer* (1876).

The North was given new hope when Custer's cavalry victories made the headlines, for up to that time Union cavalry victories were a rarity. It was natural that he became the beau ideal of cavalry. Generals who led men were rare; generals who won battles were rarer. It is no wonder that he was idolized from President Lincoln down. All the world loves a winner.
Lawrence A. Frost, *The Custer Album* (1964).

The most brilliant master of tactics cannot win a battle if he has the soul of a subaltern. Neither can the most magnetic and dashing soldier carry the day if, like General Custer, he is a nincompoop in deployment.
Barbara W. Tuchman, "Generalship," *Parameters* (Spring 1972).

Custer . . . was the embodiment of the romantic cavalryman, a stereotype he sought and nurtured. Graduated from West Point as the goat of the class of 1861, Custer had, through good fortune and hard work, won a brigadier's star at the age of twenty-three in 1863. The press labeled him "the Boy General with his flowing yellow curls," and they reported his wild charges from Gettysburg to Appomattox. . . . Sheridan purchased the table on which the surrender terms were written and presented it to Elizabeth Custer, declaring that "there is scarcely an individual in our service who has

contributed more to bring about this desirable result than your very gallant husband." In the army reorganization following the war Custer was awarded the lieutenant-colonelcy of the new Seventh Cavalry. Custer was Sheridan's protegé. . . . But Sheridan also recognized the volatile side of Custer's character, for he "was as boyish as he was brave" and "always needed someone to restrain him."
Paul Andrew Hutton, *Phil Sheridan and His Army* (1973).

He gives the impression of a man on stage performing as he has been instructed to perform, delivering lines composed by somebody else. Throughout the Civil War his smashing victories were plotted by other men. . . . In a tight situation his response was instantaneous and predictable: he charged. This response to challenge was not something he learned; he reacted as instinctively as a Miura fighting bull. When he was a schoolboy he once drove his fist through a window at a classmate outside who was making faces at him. Such uncontrolled violence quite often will carry the day, although not necessarily.
Evan S. Connell, *Son of the Morning Star* (1984).

Douhet, General Giulio (1869–1930)
Douhet's book [*Command of the Air*] might have provided some help to [General Billy] Mitchell, but it was not translated until 1933, and then it was produced only in manuscript form without publicity . . . . this manuscript was studied in a somewhat clandestine way at the Air Corps Tactical School. The first public translation . . . did not appear before 1941, too late to have an effect on the strategy of the second World War.
Dale O. Smith, *U.S. Military Doctrine* (1955).

Brigadier General Giulio Douhet possessed the largest and most original mind that has thus far addressed itself to the theory of air power. The few basic ideas which he elaborated were not altogether his own creations—the general merits of strategic bombing were being advanced in British and American official circles more than a year before World War I ended—but he was the first to weave them into a coherent and relatively comprehensive philosophy. That philosophy is fairly completely presented in his first book-length publication, *The Command of the Air,* published originally in 1921.
Bernard Brodie, *Strategy in the Missile Age* (1959). According to Brodie, "When American Air Force officers have talked about 'understanding air power' they have usually meant what is actually the Douhet thesis on air power, practically *in toto.*"

Douhet was looked upon as a futurist; but actually he was a tactical reactionary, because he harked back to the great artillery bombardments of World War I, which were purely destructive operations, and tilted them from a horizontal into a vertical position. He compared the aeroplane "to a special gun capable of firing shells a distance equal to its flying range"; therefore an air force was no more than "a large battery of guns."
J. F. C. Fuller, *The Conduct of War* (1961).

Eisenhower, President Dwight David (1890–1969)
MacArthur said of Eisenhower in a fitness report in the 1930's, "This is the best officer in the Army. When the next war comes, he should go right to the top."
Stephen E. Ambrose, *Eisenhower,* I (1983).

The best clerk I ever fired.
General Douglas MacArthur on General Eisenhower, quoted in Marquis Childs, *Eisenhower, Captive Hero* (1958).

I said some nice things about Ike. But I put on record our entire correspondence on the Normandy campaign. I told Ike if he didn't pull back Patton on the right and hit the Germans a smashing blow in 1944, the war would last until spring. But Ike didn't follow my advice. He lost a lot of lives. Eighty thousand American boys in the Ardennes alone. Damned fool Ike.

I don't know why Ike was angry. He wrote the first book after the war, *Crusade in Europe*. And he said some bad things about Alanbrooke and me.
Field Marshal B. L. Montgomery, speaking of his memoirs on March 22, 1963, quoted in C. L. Sulzberger, *The Last of the Giants* (1970).

I read a very interesting quote by Senator Kerr of Oklahoma. In summing up Ike, he said "Eisenhower is the only living unknown soldier." Even this is giving him all the best of it.
Groucho Marx, *The Groucho Letters* (1967).

Eisenhower was a subtle man, and no fool, though in pursuit of his objectives he did not like to be thought of as brilliant; people of brilliance, he thought, were distrusted.
David Halberstam, *The Best and the Brightest* (1972).

There was considerable gossip about Kay Summersby. It must have been troublesome to General Eisenhower—if he was aware of it. I once asked John "Beaver" Thompson of the *Chicago Tribune* if it wasn't just gossip. "Well," he replied, "I have never before seen a chauffeur get out of a car and kiss the General good morning when he comes from his office."
General James M. Gavin, *On To Berlin* (1978).

Eisenhower treated the press the way he treated enlisted men, with respect, though he preferred reporters remain at a distance. He knew, too, that reporters, like enlisted men, could instantly spot a pretentious phony, and he took the trouble not to be one.
Merle Miller, *Ike The Soldier* (1987).

It is a tragedy that the Old Guard has succeeded in doing what Hitler's best general never could do: they have captured Eisenhower.
Adlai Stevenson, *Time* (November 3, 1952). "Old Guard" here refers to conservative Republicans.

Foch, Marshal Ferdinand (1851–1929)

Here is the commander who, as he watched the seventh charge of the theretofore invincible Prussian Guard, remarked cheerfully, and with unerring instinct, to his staff: "Well, gentlemen, they must be in great straits somewhere or other if they are in such a desperate hurry here!"
George Wharton Pepper, introducing Marshal Foch in Philadelphia, November 15, 1921, quoted in G.R. Lyle and K. Guinagh, *I Am Happy to Present* (1968).

They argued the same ground for a time, Foch continuing to press for American units in the French II Army, Pershing looking for ways to consolidate. Both men got madder as they talked.... At one last demand Pershing lost his temper.
"Marshal Foch, you have no authority as Allied Commander-in-Chief to call upon me to yield up my command of the American Army and have it scattered among the Allied forces where it will not be an American army at all."
Eyebrows up in the surprise, Foch fumed "I must insist upon the arrangement," and rose brusquely from the table. Pershing, too, stood, and answered coldly:

"Marshal Foch, you may insist all you please, but I decline absolutely to agree to your plan. While our army will fight wherever you may decide, it will not fight except as an independent American army."
Frank E. Vandiver, *Black Jack,* II (1977).

Fuller, Major General John Frederick Charles (1878–1966)

To General Swinton and Mr. Winston Churchill must be attributed the credit for the fact that the new weapon, the Tank, ever came into existence . . . but the brains behind it all were [J. F. C.] Fuller's. A flash of inspiration combined with faith may be responsible for initiating an invention, skilled hands may forge it into a weapon, gallant-hearted men be ready to use it, careful arrangements may bring the man and weapon to the scene of action—all this is useless without the brains that direct the weapon's use and that was Fuller's contribution.

For their success Tanks require tactics no less than petrol; Fuller devised them. Before an attack can be launched there must be a plan; Fuller made it. After an attack, lessons must be learnt both from success and failure; Fuller absorbed them.
Stephen Foot, *Three Lives* (1934).

A little man, with a bald head, and sharp face and a nose of a Napoleonic cast, his general appearance, stature, and feature earning him the title of Boney. He stood out at once as a totally unconventional soldier, prolific in ideas, fluent in expression, at daggers drawn with received opinion, authority, and tradition. In the mess his attacks on the red-tabbed hierarchy were viewed in the spirit of a rat hunt; a spirit he responded to with much vivacity, and no little wit.
B. H. Liddell Hart, *The Tanks* (1959).

If fascism on the Continent had assumed "temporary" attitudes that were undesirable, Fuller believed that British Fascism would develop along constitutional lines. He supported Sir Oswald Mosely, the leader of the English Fascist movement, and attacked the so-called international conspiracy of the Jews; he talked with Hitler and Mussolini and was struck by the contrast between the virile spirit in their countries and the decadent materialism dominating England and France.
Jay Luvaas, *The Education of an Army* (1964). It was Fuller's fascist views that made it impossible for him to play any military role in World War II.

In 1919, much to the discomfort of his superiors, he [J. F. C. Fuller] won the Gold Medal Prize essay awarded by the Royal United Service Institution; and in 1921 he violated custom by competing for a similar prize for the best essay on "Future Naval Tactics." Uncertain whether to refer to a ship as "it" or "she," he nonetheless managed to conceal the fact that his entry did not come from the pen of a sailor. The naval authorities were astounded when the winner was identified as an army colonel and outraged when they learned that Fuller had actually written his article over a weekend and submitted it as a leg-pull.
Jay Luvaas, *The Education of an Army* (1964).

Grant, President Ulysses S. (1822–1885)

I can't spare this man; he fights.
President Abraham Lincoln's response to a friend's suggestion that he remove General Grant from command because of his performance at the 1862 Battle of Shiloh, quoted in Alexander K. McClure, *Abraham Lincoln and Men of War-Times* (1892).

When Grant once gets possession of a place, he holds on to it as if he had inherited it.
President Abraham Lincoln quoted in Horace Porter, *Campaigning With Grant* (1897).

Grant stood by me when I was crazy, and I stood by him when he was drunk, and now we stand by each other.
Attributed to General William Tecumseh Sherman.

That, two thousand years after Alexander the Great and Julius Caesar, a man like Grant should be called—and should actually and truly be—the highest product of the most advanced evolution, made evolution ludicrous. One must be as commonplace as Grant's own commonplaces to maintain such an absurdity. The progress of evolution from President Washington to President Grant, was alone evidence enough to upset Darwin.
Henry Adams, *The Education of Henry Adams* (1907).

[Colonel T. Lyle] Dickey remarked [to President Lincoln], "I hear that some one has been trying to poison you against Grant by reporting that he gets drunk.
"I wish to assure you, Mr. President, that there is not a scintilla of truth in the report."
"Oh, Colonel," replied the President, "we get all sorts of reports here, but I'll say this to you: that if those accusing General Grant of getting drunk will tell me where he gets his whiskey, I will get a lot of it and send it around to some of the other generals, who are badly in need of something of the kind."
Francis Browne, *The Every-day Life of Abraham Lincoln* (1915). According to Albert B. Chandler, *Abraham Lincoln* (1895), this story is not true. When someone asked Lincoln about it he "said that he had heard the story before, and that it would have been very good if he had said it, but that he didn't. He supposed it was 'charged to him, to give it currency.' He then said the original of the story was in King George's time. Bitter complaints were made to the King against his General Wolfe, in which it was charged that he was mad. The King replied angrily: 'I wish he would bite some of my other generals then.' "

The greatest general of the North was U.S. Grant, who is not to be confused with U.S. Mail or U.S. Steel. In a picture of the Northern generals, all of whom have identical untidy black whiskers, he is usually the one in the center with his coat unbuttoned.
Richard Armour, *It All Started With Columbus* (1961).

As early as April 1863, . . . he was writing that the war must achieve "the total subjugation of the south" and that the army's duty was "therefore to use every means to weaken the enemy" by destroying not only their armies in the field but their economy at home. Grant's title as "first of the moderns" among generals derives from that gospel of frightfulness. Christian though he was, he had persuaded himself that the Just War doctrine of "proportionality"—restraint of violence within the bounds necessary to make an enemy desist from it—did not apply in a war of principle.
John Keegan, *The Mask of Command* (1987).

Guderian, Field Marshal Heinz W. (1888–1954)
Guderian had a tremendous impact on the course of events in our time. Without him, it is probable that Hitler would have met early frustration in his offensive efforts when he embarked on war. For in 1939–40 Germany's forces in general were not sufficient to overcome any major Power. Her opening run of victory in the Second World War was only made possible by the panzer forces that Guderian had created and trained, and by his audacious leading of those forces in disregard of his superiors' caution as well as Hitler's fears.
B. H. Liddell Hart, foreword to General Heinz Guderian, *Panzer Leader* (1952).

Guderian began his book, *Achtung—Panzer!* [1937], by examining the causes underlying the success and failure of Allied tank operations . . . during the First War. He listed the following fundamental errors: the Allies did not attack in sufficient depth, and were never backed up by sufficiently powerful mobile reserves, so that they broke *into* the enemy front, but never *through*—where they would have been able "to knock out his batteries, his reserves, his staffs, all at the same time"; the full potential of the tanks was sacrificed by their being yoked to two such slow-moving components as foot infantry and horse-drawn artillery; they were thrown in by "penny packets" instead of powerful concentrations; and they were the wrong kind of tanks.

Guderian saw the remedy to all this in the fully mechanized panzer divisions, the components of which would collaborate closely, and which had to be capable of moving at equal speeds.

Alistair Horne, *To Lose a Battle; France 1940* (1969).

Without once being in major and independent command of a campaign (but then with Hitler no German general ever had such autonomy, except perhaps Rommel with his relatively tiny *Panzerarmee*), Guderian was the great architect of victory for a war lord who did not know what to do with victory.

John Strawson, "General Heinz Guderian," *The War Lords*, ed. Sir Michael Carver (1976).

More than any other man, Guderian had opposed the idea of tying tanks to infantry (as the French had largely done) or creating all-tank units for specialized use (as in prevailing British theories). He had insisted that the armored divisions must be versatile and equipped in hardware, training, and mental attitude to tackle almost any kind of fighting. While other armies calculated the speed of any combined units as that of the slowest element, Guderian measured by that of the fastest and insisted that his divisions move as fast as possible.

Len Deighton, *Blitzkrieg* (1980).

Hannibal (247–183 B.C.)

Among the noteworthy actions of Hannibal is numbered this, that although he had an enormous army, composed of men of all nations and fighting in foreign countries, there never arose any dissension either among them or against the prince, either in good fortune or in bad. This could not be due to anything but his inhuman cruelty, which together with his infinite other virtues, made him always venerated and terrible in the sight of his soldiers, and without it his other virtues would not have sufficed to produce that effect.

Niccolò Machiavelli, *The Prince* (1513).

Hannibal was the greatest general of antiquity by reason of his admirable comprehension of the morale of combat, of the morale of the soldier, whether his own or the enemy's. . . . His men were not better than the Roman soldiers. They were not as well armed, one-half less in number. Yet he was always the conqueror. . . . He had the art, in commanding an army, of always securing the advantage of morale.

Ardant de Picq, *Battle Studies* (1868).

Hannibal appears to have been weaker as a linguist than as a strategist. Plutarch tells us that while in Southern Italy Hannibal commanded his guides to take him to the plain of Casinum. (This was Cassino of World War II fame.) "They, mistaking his words . . . because his Italian tongue was but mean, took one thing for another and so brought him and his army . . . near the City of Casilinum." The terrain was such that Hannibal was nearly trapped, but he took time out to dispose of those who had misled him. "Knowing then the fault his guides had made and the danger wherein they had brought him, he roundly trussed them up and hung them by the necks." This story is often told today in intelligence schools to impress upon junior officers the need for accuracy.

Allen Dulles, *The Craft of Intelligence* (1965).

Jackson, General Thomas J. "Stonewall" (1824–1863)

[Jackson is] profoundly and, some say, fanatically religious, with a precise regard for discipline and army regulations. A man he is of contrasts so complete that he appears one day a Presbyterian deacon who delights in theological discussion and, the next, a reincarnated Joshua. He lives by the New Testament and fights by the Old.
Douglas Southall Freeman, *Lee's Lieutenants*, I (1942).

Give Jackson my affectionate regards, and tell him to make haste and get well, and come back to me as soon as he can. He has lost his left arm, but I have lost my right.
General Robert E. Lee, on learning that General Thomas J. "Stonewall" Jackson had lost his left arm after being accidentally shot by his own troops, quoted in Burke Davis, *Gray Fox* (1956).

He became one of the Great Captains, famed not only in his own embattled Confederacy, but also in the land of his enemies and beyond foreign seas. He came to epitomize the good and the virtue of what was finally a lost cause, and people would say that had he lived the cause might have fared differently. But death struck him down at the height of a military fame enjoyed by no other Civil War figure, struck him down at the high point of Confederate success.
Frank E. Vandiver, *Mighty Stonewall* (1957).

Henderson's dramatic portrayal of the colorful Jackson together with the sentimentalism of the dying Victorian era did much to produce that legendary atmosphere which in England was beginning to surround both Jackson and Lee. The former came to be regarded with an awe and admiration quite out of proportion to his genius.
Jay Luvaas, *The Military Legacy of the Civil War* (1959). The reference is to G. F. R. Henderson's *Stonewall Jackson and The American Civil War* (1906).

His speech was as ungainly as his movements. The only notable thing about him was the lemon he sucked incessantly; his expressionless look struck some as "wooden," some as "sleepy," and no one as inspiring. After meeting Jackson one group of officers despaired: ". . .there must be some mistake about him; if he was an able man he showed it less than any of us had ever seen."
Robert G. Tanner, *Stonewall in the Valley* (1976).

"Stonewall" Jackson had been an instructor there [the Virginia Military Institute] and had left his teaching on the outbreak of war for a brief but brilliant career in battle. On the day of Chancellorsville, where he was mortally wounded, he had seen so many former cadets in the line that he boasted "the Institute will be heard from today."
Forrest C. Pogue, *George C. Marshall: Education of a General* (1963).

Jomini, General Antoine Henri (1779–1869)

Jomini's analysis and classification of operations, in spite of its artificial terminology, was correct and useful. It was the first scientific exposition of strategy as a system of principles, and it has been used by all the subsequent strategical thinkers.
Spencer Wilkinson, *The French Army Before Napoleon* (1915).

When he first read a volume of Jomini's works Napoleon nearly had an apoplectic stroke.
"How did Fouché ever let this book be published?" he demanded. "It will give away all my secrets."
Then upon second thought he said:

"After all, it doesn't matter. The young men who read it will never command against me—and the old ones will never read it."
Arcades Ambo, "All God's Chillun Ain't Got Wings," *Infantry Journal Reader*, ed. J. I. Greene (1943).

It has been said with good reason that many a Civil War general went into battle with a sword in one hand and Jomini's *Summary of the Art of War* in the other.
J. D. Hittle, *Jomini and His Summary of the Art of War* (1947).

During the Civil War, the legend grew that a copy of the Holy Bible and a copy of Jomini's *Art of War* were carried in the knapsack of every successful general.
When the war ended, however, reassessment of Jomini seemed necessary. War had changed dramatically, at least in a technological sense. . . . During the American Civil War, however, Jominian ideas about war in general and about the principles of war in particular dominated both books on war and events on battlefields.
John I. Alger, *The Quest for Victory* (1982).

"Principles of War" continued to be part of the official statements of military doctrine in virtually every modern armed force, including those in the Soviet bloc. Although a question naturally arises as to the actual influence and function of the ritualistic assertion of doctrine. . ., there is no doubt that these principles, although varying slightly from one armed force to another, derive directly from Jomini.
John Shy, "Jomini," *Makers of Modern Strategy*, ed. Peter Paret (1986).

Many Jominian "principles" were common-sense ideas hardly original with Jomini: concentrate the mass of your own force against fractions of the enemy's; menace the enemy's communications while protecting your own; attack the enemy's weak point with your own strength; and so on. There is little evidence that Jomini's writings influenced Civil War strategy in a direct or tangible way; the most successful strategist of the war, Grant, confessed to having never read Jomini.
James M. McPherson, *Battle Cry of Freedom* (1988).

Lee, General Robert E. (1807–1870)

General [Winfield] Scott (seeing evidently that Lee showed no disposition to declare himself loyal, or even in doubt): "I suppose you will go with the rest. If you propose to resign, it is proper you should do so at once; your present attitude is an equivocal one."
Colonel [Robert E.] Lee: "General, the property belonging to my children, all they possess, lies in Virginia. They will be ruined if they do not go with their State. I can not raise my hand against my children."
The general then signified that he had nothing further to say, and Colonel Lee withdrew. The next day, April 20, 1861, he tendered his resignation.
E. D. Townsend, *Anecdotes of the Civil War* (1883).

I am heartily tired of hearing what Lee is going to do. Some of you always seem to think he is suddenly going to turn a double somersault, and land on our rear and on both our flanks at the same time. Go back to your command, and try to think what we are going to do ourselves, instead of what Lee is going to do.
An exasperated General U. S. Grant to one of his officers, quoted in Horace Porter, *Campaigning with Grant* (1897).

General Lee was returning to his camp [from Appomattox Court House on April 9, 1865] and was close to it when he met a cavalcade in blue and was greeted with a cheery "good morning, General" from a bearded man, who removed his cap as he spoke. For the moment Lee did not recognize the speaker, but the latter recalled himself as none other than George Gordon Meade, commanding the Army of the Potomac, and an old friend of kindly days.

"But what are you doing with all that gray in your beard?" Lee asked.

"You have to answer for most of it!" Meade magnanimously replied.

Douglas Southall Freeman, *R. E. Lee*, IV (1935).

Whatever General Lee's feelings [about his surrender on April 9, 1865] were I do not know. As he was a man of much dignity, with an impassable face, it was impossible to say whether he felt inwardly glad that the end had finally come, or felt sad over the result and was too manly to show it. . . . The much talked of surrendering of Lee's sword and my handing it back, this and much more that has been said about it is the purest romance.

President Ulysses S. Grant, *Personal Memoirs* (1885).

He was a foe without hate, a friend without treachery, a soldier without cruelty, and a victim without murmuring. . . . He was Caesar without his ambition, Frederick without his tyranny, Napoleon without his selfishness, and Washington without his reward.

Benjamin H. Hill quoted in Thomas N. Page, *Robert E. Lee* (1911).

It would not be accurate to say that Lee's general staff were glorified clerks, but the statement would not be too wide of the mark. Certainly his staff was not, in the modern sense, a planning staff, which was why Lee was often a tired general.

T. Harry Williams, *Lincoln and His Generals* (1952).

If I were on my death bed, and the President should tell me that a great battle was to be fought for the liberty or slavery of the country, and asked my judgment as to the ability of a commander, I would say with my dying breath, let it be Robert E. Lee.

General Winfield Scott quoted in Burke Davis, *They Called Him Stonewall* (1954).

The transcending facts of the American Civil War are the military genius of Robert E. Lee and the naval superiority of the North. Behind all the blood and sacrifice, behind the movements of armies and the pronouncements of political leaders, the war was essentially a contest between these two strategic forces. Lee's tactical opponent was the Army of the Potomac, but his strategic rival was the Union Navy.

Admiral John D. Hayes, *Sea Power in the Civil War* (1961).

Zebulon Vance, former Confederate governor of North Carolina . . . went to Massachusetts [after the war] to deliver a lecture. The Bay Staters, knowing his droll manner and practical jokes, baited him by hanging Robert E. Lee's picture in the men's outhouse. When Vance returned from it, he disappointed them by remaining silent. Finally, they were compelled to query him.

"Senator, did you see General Lee's picture hanging in the privy?" someone asked.

"Yes," Vance replied indifferently.

"Well, what did you think of it?" they prodded.

"I thought it was very appropriate," he responded. "That is a good place for General Lee's picture. If ever a man lived who could scare the dung out of the Yankees, that man was Robert E. Lee!"

Glenn Tucker, *Zeb Vance* (1965).

MacArthur, General of the Army Douglas (1880–1964)

MacArthur is the type of man who thinks that when he gets to heaven, God will step down from the great white throne and bow him into His vacated seat.

Harold Ickes, entry for Thursday July 27, 1933, *The Secret Diary of Harold L. Ickes* (1953).

MacArthur is the greatest general since Sergeant York.
Charles Bray, *Time* (March 2, 1942).

He does not look at all fierce or commanding until he puts his famous embroidered cap on. As we went out together to face the photographers, and he pulled his cap on, his whole manner changed. His jaw stuck out, he looked aggressive and tough, but as soon as the photographers had finished, he relaxed completely, took off his hat, and was his old charming self.
Admiral Lord Louis Mountbatten, describing General Douglas MacArthur in his diary, July 13 and 14, 1945, quoted in Philip Ziegler, *Mountbatten* (1985).

I studied dramatics under him [MacArthur] for twelve years.
General Dwight D. Eisenhower quoted in Quentin Reynolds, *By Quentin Reynolds* (1963).

[MacArthur] had no humility and hence no saving grace of a sense of humor. He could never laugh at himself—never admit mistakes or defeats. When these occurred they were never admitted, and he resorted to tricks—sometimes sly, childlike attempts—to cover up.
This petty but understandable trait of wanting to be perfect, to ignore his obvious warts—warts that were insignificant against his towering intellect, superb courage, and inflexible will—became important only because they were denied. That denial convinced his detractors that they could prove the whole structure itself to be only a facade. How mistaken they were!
Philip LaFollette, *Adventure in Politics* (1970).

[General Douglas MacArthur] could be called the father of modern Japan. It was MacArthur the statesman, MacArthur the humanitarian, MacArthur the educator—not MacArthur the conqueror—who transformed a feudalistic military state, ravaged by war, into what is now a true democracy and the third-ranking industrial nation in the world today.
General Bruce Palmer, *The Washington Post* (April 19, 1970). According to Bernard Brodie, *War and Politics* (1973), MacArthur's "role as the head of the occupation of Japan has been unconscionably inflated. He had at no time been indispensable."

With deep regret I have concluded that General of the Army Douglas MacArthur is unable to give his wholehearted support to the policies of the United States Government and of the United Nations in matters pertaining to his official duties. In view of the specific responsibilities imposed upon me by the Constitution of the United States and the added responsibility which has been entrusted to me by the United Nations, I have decided that I must make a change of command in the Far East. I have, therefore, relieved General MacArthur of his commands and have designated Lt. Gen. Matthew B. Ridgway as his successor.
Full and vigorous debate on matters of national policy is a vital element in the constitutional system of our free democracy. It is fundamental, however, that military commanders must be governed by the policies and directives issued to them in the manner provided by our laws and Constitution.
President Harry S. Truman, Statement of the President Relative to the Relief of General MacArthur, April 10, 1951.

I fired him because he wouldn't respect the authority of the President. That's the answer to that. I didn't fire him because he was a dumb son of a bitch, although he

was, but that's not against the law for generals. If it was half to three quarters of them would be in jail.
President Harry S. Truman, explaining why he removed MacArthur from command of U.S. and U.N. Troops in Korea, in Merle Miller, *Plain Speaking: An Oral Biography of Harry S. Truman* (1973).

An accomplished actor, he could play many parts, and no one has yet finally determined which reflected the real MacArthur. He probably preferred the role of the gentleman-warrior, the aristocrat at arms. . . .The general was deeply conscious of his position on the stage of one of the greatest dramas in history. Like the foremost actors of the theater, he thoroughly enjoyed being dramatic. . . .At times he would startle listeners by nonchalantly referring to himself in the third person. He once said "Marshall proposed this, but MacArthur suggested . . . ." On other occasions, as in his controversial communiqués, he would consider a decision or action as a projection of his own ego, for example, "I drove the enemy out. . . . My bombers and my ships. . . ." Some dismissed such language as that of an arrogant egotist, but others saw in his personal performances the supreme actor.
D. Clayton James, *The Years of MacArthur* (1975).

He was a great thundering paradox of a man, noble and ignoble, inspiring and outrageous, arrogant and sly, the best of men and the worst of men, the most protean, most ridiculous, and most sublime. No more baffling, exasperating soldier ever wore a uniform. Flamboyant, imperious, and apocalyptic, he . . . could not acknowledge errors, and tried to cover up his mistakes with sly childish tricks. . . .Unquestionably he was the most gifted man-at-arms this nation has produced. He was also extraordinarily brave. His twenty-two medals—thirteen of them for heroism—probably exceeded those of any other figure in American history. He seemed to seek death on battlefields. Repeatedly he deliberately exposed himself to enemy snipers. . . . Nevertheless, his troops scorned him as "Dugout Doug."
William Manchester, *American Caesar* (1978).

Throughout his life he acted on the assumption that the rules made for lesser men had no relevance to himself. Few commanders of any nationality could have borne so large a responsibility for the United States military debacle in the Philippines in 1941–42 yet escaped any share of it. Fewer still could have abandoned his doomed command on Bataan and escaped to safety with his own court, complete even unto personal servants, and made good the claim that his own value to his country surpassed that of a symbolic sacrifice alongside his men. Even less so could they have escaped public censure for accepting a vast personal financial gift from the Philippines President at the very hour when the battle for his country was being lost.
Max Hastings, *The Korean War* (1987).

As the great soldier [General MacArthur] had dramatically confessed to Congress several weeks earlier, he had simply "tried to do his duty as God gave him the light to see that duty."
The problem, evidently, was that God and President Truman did not see eye to eye.
John E. Shephard, Jr., "Where A Soldier's Loyalty Lies," *The Wall Street Journal* (March 26, 1987).

If they were in the Army they were called Doggies, which was short for Dog-faces, and Marines despised them, along with their commanders. Marines taught Okinawan children to stand by the road when Army units passed shouting "General MacArthur eats shit!" They thought it meant "Give me a cigarette."
Samuel Hynes, *Flights of Passage* (1988).

[MacArthur's] wartime accomplishments were as much a testament to this public relations abilities as to his military skill.
Michael Schaller, *Douglas MacArthur* (1989).

Marlborough, Duke of (1650–1722)

He had, to a degree above all other generals of his time, that calm courage in the midst of tumult, that serenity of soul in danger, which the English call a cool head [*que les Anglais appellent cold head, tête froide*], and it was, perhaps, this quality, the greatest gift of nature for command, which formerly gave the English so many advantages over the French.
Voltaire, *Le Siècle de Louis XIV* (1753).

With respect to the Duke of Marlborough, it goes against our feelings to admire the man who owed his first advancement in life to the court favor which he and his family acquired through his sister becoming one of the mistresses of the Duke of York. It is repulsive to know that Marlborough laid the foundation of his wealth by being the paid lover of one of the fair and frail favorites of Charles II. His treachery, and his ingratitude to his patron and benefactor, James II, stand out in dark relief even in that age of thankless perfidy.
E. S. Creasy, *The Fifteen Decisive Battles of the World* (1851).

He never rode off any field except as a victor. He quitted war invincible; and no sooner was his guiding hand withdrawn than disaster overtook the armies he had led.
Winston Churchill, *Marlborough*, I (1933).

Marlborough stands high above his contemporaries. Courteous and patient, he possessed what so few men of genius are endowed with—ability to tolerate fools gladly. Though his courage was of the highest, his imagination vivid, and his common sense profound, his master characteristic was his self-control. Nothing unbalanced him, whether it was the stupidity of his allies, the duplicity of the politicians, or the ability of his enemies.
J. F. C. Fuller, *A Military History of the Western World*, II (1955).

[Winston Churchill had] never the slightest doubt that he had inherited all the military genius of his great ancestor Marlborough.
Arthur Bryant, *The Turn of the Tide* (1957).

Marlborough . . . was the greatest British general of the 18th century. A master of maneuver, he combined tactical astuteness with administrative efficiency in achieving some of the most remarkable victories in military history. The brilliant manner in which he utilized maneuver and deception has tended to overshadow the emphasis he placed on administrative matters, which in the final analysis made his victories possible.
J. D. Hittle, *The Military Staff*, 3rd ed. (1961).

Marshall, General of the Army George Catlett Jr. (1880–1959)

We are engaged in a global war of which the end is still far distant and for the wise and strategical guidance of which we need our most accomplished officer as Chief of Staff. I voice the consensus of informed military opinion in saying that officer is General Marshall. To transfer him to a tactical command in a limited area, no matter how seemingly important, is to deprive ourselves of the benefit of his outstanding strategical ability and experience. I know of no one at all comparable to replace him as Chief of Staff.
General John J. Pershing, letter to President Franklin D. Roosevelt, September 16, 1943, quoted in Mrs. Katherine T. Marshall, *Together* (1946).

Ike, you and I know who was Chief of Staff during the last years of the Civil War but practically no one else knows, although the names of the field generals—Grant, of course, and Lee, and Jackson, Sherman, Sheridan and the others—every schoolboy knows them. I hate to think that 50 years from now practically nobody will know who George Marshall was. That is one of the reasons I want George to have the big command—he is entitled to establish his place in history as a great General.
President Franklin D. Roosevelt to General Dwight D. Eisenhower, explaining why General George Marshall should command the coming invasion of France, quoted in Robert E. Sherwood, *Roosevelt and Hopkins* (1948).

I wanted him to feel free to act in whatever way he felt was to the best interest of the country and to his satisfaction and not in any way to consider my feelings. I would cheerfully go whatever way he wanted me to go and I didn't express any desire one way or the other.... Then he evidently assumed that concluded the affair and that I would not command in Europe. Because he said, "Well I didn't feel I could sleep at ease if you were out of Washington."
George C. Marshall, explaining how President Franklin D. Roosevelt came to the decision that Marshall would remain as Chief of Staff and not command the invasion of France in World War II, quoted in Forrest C. Pogue, *George C. Marshall: Organizer of Victory* (1973).

In a war unparalleled in magnitude and horror, millions of Americans gave their country outstanding service. General of the Army George C. Marshall became commander of the United States Army on the day that Germany attacked Poland. His was the vision that brought into being the strongest military force in history. Because he was able to make the Allies understand the true potentiality of American greatness in personnel and material, he was able to exercise greater influence than any other man on the strategy of victory.
President Harry S. Truman, speech at the Pentagon, November 26, 1945.

What a joy it must be to him to see how the armies he called into being by his own genius have won immortal renown. He is the true "organizer of victory."
Winston Churchill, writing of General Marshall in a letter of March 30, 1945, quoted in Forrest C. Pogue, *George C. Marshall: Organizer of Victory* (1973).

I had referred to the idea [European Recovery Program] as the "Marshall Plan" when it was discussed in staff meetings, because I wanted General Marshall to get full credit for his brilliant contributions to the measure which he helped formulate. And it was Marshall who had envisioned the full scope of this approach. He had perceived the inspirational as well as the economic value of the proposal. History, rightly, will always associate his name with this program, which helped save Europe from economic disaster and lifted it from the shadow of enslavement by Russian Communism.
Harry S. Truman, *Memoirs*, II (1956).

If George Marshall ever took a position contrary to mine, I would know I was wrong.
General Henry H. "Hap" Arnold quoted in Thomas M. Coffey, *Hap* (1982).

[George C. Marshall, Jr.] collected a remarkable file of fitness reports, including Lieutenant Colonel (later Major General) Johnson Hagood's reply in 1916 to the question whether he would like to have Marshall under his command: "Yes, but I would prefer to serve under his command."
Russell F. Weigley, *History of the United States Army*, enlarged edition (1984).

McClellan, General George B. (1826–1885)

The President, waving his hand towards the scene before us [on November 5, 1862], and leaning towards me, said in almost whispering voice: "Hatch—Hatch, what is all this?"

"Why, Mr. Lincoln," said I, "this is the Army of the Potomac."

He hesitated a moment, and then, straightening up, said in a louder tone: "No, Hatch, no. This is General McClellan's bodyguard."
Francis F. Browne, *The Every-Day Life of Abraham Lincoln* (1915).

I said I would remove him if he let Lee's army get away from him, and I must do so. He has got the "slows."
President Abraham Lincoln, speaking to Frank Blair in late 1862, quoted in William E. Smith, *The Francis Blair Family in Politics*, II (1933).

If something was not soon done, the bottom would be out of the whole affair; and if General McClellan did not want to use the army, he would like to *borrow* it, provided he could see how it could be made to do something.
President Abraham Lincoln quoted in William Swinton, *Campaigns of the Army of the Potomac* (1866).

He is an admirable engineer but he seems to have a special talent for a stationary engine.
President Abraham Lincoln quoted in Isaac N. Arnold, *The Life of Abraham Lincoln* (1885).

[McClellan] wrote to his wife that he was sickened when he saw the battlefield, with its "mangled corpses" and suffering wounded. "Victory has no charms for me when purchased at such cost," he said. . . .McClellan was revealing another of his weaknesses as a soldier. He loved his men too much. He loved them so much that he did not want to hurt them. . . .They sensed that he wanted to care for them, and they idolized him as they did no other commander of the Army of the Potomac. But McClellan's affection for his soldiers was a dangerous emotion. It made him forget the hard fact that soldiers exist to fight and possibly to die. He had no business wandering around a battlefield crying over the dead. It was his business to win victories, and if men died in the process, that was war. The trouble with McClellan was that he liked to think of war as bloodless strategy, as moves on a gigantic chessboard.
T. Harry Williams, *Lincoln and His Generals* (1952).

McClellan was *par excellence* an "image" general.
Charles Fair, *From the Jaws of Victory* (1971).

McClellan was a man possessed by demons and delusions. He believed beyond any doubt that his Confederate enemies faced him with forces substantially greater than his own. He believed with equal conviction that enemies at the head of his own government conspired to see him and his army defeated so as to carry out their traitorous purposes.
Stephen W. Sears, *George B. McClellan: The Young Napoleon* (1988).

Mitchell, General William "Billy" (1879–1936)

Good God! This man [Billy Mitchell] should be writing dime novels.
Josephus Daniels, Secretary of the U.S. Navy, speaking in 1921, quoted in Emile Gauvreau and Lester Cohen, *Billy Mitchell* (1942).

The Court, upon secret written ballot, two-thirds of the members present at the time the vote was taken concurring in each finding of guilty, finds the accused guilty of all specifications and of the charge. Upon secret written ballot the Court sentences the accused to be suspended from rank, command and duty, with forfeiture of all pay and

allowances, for five years. The Court is thus lenient because of the military record of the accused during the World War.
Verdict in the Court Martial of Colonel William "Billy" Mitchell read by Major General Robert L. Howze, President of the Court, quoted in *Time*, December 28, 1925.

In February 1938, after being relieved as chief of staff, G. H. Q. Air Force, [Colonel Hugh] Knerr had been demoted to lieutenant colonel and sent to Fort Sam Houston in San Antonio as air officer for the Eighth Army Corps Area. He was assigned to the same "remote" office that Billy Mitchell had occupied during his "exile," and as soon as he settled into it he was "mortified to see an open-top latrine in the opposite corner." He was soon further mortified to find the outer office clerks walking in and out to use this latrine. The Army was teaching him a lesson.
Thomas M. Coffey, *Hap* (1982).

[Mitchell's] fame rests more on his qualities and conduct as a man and officer than on his stature as military philosopher. . . . He was full of ideas, some of them brilliant and original, but they were largely dedicated to the proposition that the airplane is a much better missile carrier than any other vehicle, especially the battleship. He developed as early as 1918 the idea of creating an airborne parachute division. . . . He also inspired the development of very large bombs. But his thinking was almost entirely tactical.
Bernard Brodie, *Strategy in the Missile Age* (1959).

Billy Mitchell propagandized for the doctrines of air power and the independent air force with increasing vehemence through the early 1920's—and with increasing insubordination as well, until he charged the War Department and the general staff with criminal negligence and "almost treasonable" conduct, and thus obliged them to bring him before a court-martial. The court convicted him of charges of insubordination, suspended him for two and a half years, and provoked his resignation from the service. . . . Mitchell has enjoyed a latter-day reputation as a prophet, having predicted so many things about the future of the airplane that advancing technology was bound to make some of the predictions come true. But World War II did not vindicate his prophecies about the decisiveness of air power in the next war, and in the 1920's his theories were utterly disproportionate to the military aircraft available.
Russell F. Weigley, *History of the United States Army*, enlarged edition (1984).

Moltke, Field Marshal Helmuth Karl von (1800–1891)

[Moltke] was an example of the gulf that separates theory from practice. He believed in mathematics rather than in maneuver, and in number rather than in moral force.
Marshal Ferdinand Foch, *Precepts and Judgments* (1920).

Moltke may be described as a general on rails, for his system of war was both direct and rigid. He was a supremely great war organizer, who relied on logic rather than on opportunity. For success his art depended on adherence to a somewhat static doctrine set in motion by *directives* rather than by orders. To him a war of masses was a war of accidents in which genius was subordinate to the offensive spirit. Whereas Napoleon I led and controlled throughout, Moltke brought his armies to their starting points and then abdicated his command and unleashed them. . . . Moltke is not a general to copy but to study.
J. F. C. Fuller, *A Military History of the Western World*, III (1956).

Moltke's own writings echo Clausewitz to the point of plagiarism.
Michael Howard, *Clausewitz* (1983).

Montgomery of Alamein, Field Marshal Bernard Law (1887–1976)

He is clever, energetic, ambitious, and a very gifted instructor. He has character, knowledge, and a quick grasp of military problems. But if he is to do himself full justice in the higher positions to which his gifts should entitle him he must cultivate tact, tolerance, and discretion. This is a friendly hint as I have a high opinion of his ability.
General Sir John Burnett-Stuart, 1932 "Personal Report" on Lt. Colonel B. L. Montgomery, quoted in Nigel Hamilton, *Monty* (1981).

But nowhere did the slight erect figure of Montgomery in his baggy and unpressed corduroys excite greater assurance than among the British soldiers themselves. Even Eisenhower with all his engaging ease could never stir American troops to the rapture with which Monty was welcomed by his. Among those men the legend of Montgomery had become an imperishable fact.
General Omar N. Bradley, *A Soldier's Story* (1951).

Monty has become a mellow, lovable exhibitionist; tamed but lonely and pathetic. He is not afraid of saying anything to anybody. But Maria de Casa Valdes scored (to Monty's great delight) when she asked him: "But you tell me you don't drink, and you don't smoke: what *do* you do that is wrong? Bite your nails?"
John Colville, *The Fringes of Power* (1985), diary entry for May 18, 1952.

[Montgomery] requires a lot of educating to make him see the whole situation and the war as a whole outside the Eighth Army orbit. A difficult mixture to handle, brilliant commander in action and trainer of men, but liable to commit untold errors, due to lack of tact, lack of appreciation of other people's outlook. It is most distressing that the Americans do not like him, and it will always be a difficult matter to have him fighting in close proximity to them.
Field Marshal Alan F. Brooke quoted in Sir Arthur Bryant, *The Turn of the Tide* (1957).

A report described him as a "troublesome and erratic figure, far too self-opinionated and grievously lacking in the polished manner one would like to see in a Sandhurst graduate." One officer said to him: "You are quite useless. You will never get anywhere in the Army."
Hugh Thomas, *The Story of Sandhurst* (1961).

Montgomery when he got into the fight was, I think, excellent, but on the other hand if we had about three commanders like Montgomery, we would have never made any fights because they never should have settled who was to get everything to do it.
General George C. Marshall quoted in Forrest C. Pogue, *George C. Marshall: Organizer of Victory* (1973).

He got so damn personal to make sure that the Americans and me, in particular, had no credit, had nothing to do with the war, that I eventually just stopped communicating with him. . . . I was just not interested in keeping up communications with a man that just can't tell the truth.
President Dwight D. Eisenhower quoted in Cornelius Ryan, *A Bridge Too Far* (1974).

He's just a little man, he's just as little inside as he is outside.
General Dwight D. Eisenhower on Field Marshall Montgomery quoted in Peter Lyon, *Eisenhower* (1974).

General Montgomery, who commanded the 8th Army in the desert at that time, was clearly a great leader who really inspired confidence in his troops, but we could not help feeling, as we watched action following "intelligence", that it was somewhat eas-

ier to defeat your opponent if you knew in advance just where his troops, tanks and other defences were, how many in each place, how short he was of petrol or ammunition and exactly what his plans were, both if he (the opponent) was successful but also if he wasn't. Montgomery had this advantage in North Africa, and incidentally, he and Eisenhower had it to nearly the same extent in Normandy.
Ewen Montagu, *Beyond Top Secret Ultra* (1977).

In our minds he was an overbearing martinet—a proper bastard. He demanded that we undergo hardships. To toughen us, he broke many in the process. We thought his methods were madness. But his system of training prevailed, and when we eventually went into action we knew he was right. . . . When we ended our five weeks of warfare in Sicily successfully, we realized it was because we had been moulded into a hard disciplined force by the hand of Montgomery, the *bête noire* of our days in Southern England.
Colonel Strome Galloway, *The General Who Never Was* (1981).

Monty is a tired little fart. War requires the taking of risks and he won't take them.
General George S. Patton, Jr. quoted in David Irving, *The War Between the Generals* (1981).

You [Montgomery] may be great to serve under, difficult to serve alongside, but you sure are hell to serve over!
General Walter Bedell Smith quoted in Nigel Hamilton, *Master of the Battlefield* (1983).

Patton, General George S., Jr. (1885–1945)
It's not only that, like yourself, I like to work with soldiers, but I'm weary of doing desk duty. I suppose it's too much to hope that I could have a regiment in your division, because I'm still almost three years away from my colonelcy, but I think I could do a damn good job.
Lieutenant Colonel Dwight D. Eisenhower, letter to Colonel George S. Patton, September 1940, quoted in Merle Miller, *Ike the Soldier* (1987).

While [General Troy] Middleton was in an inner office . . . his driver slumped in a chair outside to catch a few minutes sleep. No sooner had he dropped off than someone stepped heavily on his feet.
The driver woke angry. "Why, you son of a bitch," he cried, "Don't you know I'm trying to sleep?" Then he saw he was looking up at [General] George Patton.
Patton leaned back and laughed. "Son," he said, "you're the first son of a bitch I've met today who knows what he's trying to do."
John Toland, *Battle: The Story of the Bulge* (1959).

General [George] Patton knew of the comment going around amongst his GIs. Quent Reynolds had reported that 50,000 of them would shoot Patton on sight. So when "Georgie" was introduced, he merely stepped to the front of the platform, saying: "I just thought I'd stand up here and let you soldiers see if I'm as big a s.o.b. as you think I am."
The GIs practically raised the roof with their cheers.
Captain Harry C. Butcher, writing on September 14, 1943, *My Three Years With Eisenhower* (1946).

If anyone had told General Patton that he was as fiery as Murat, as brave as Ney and as wily as Davout, he would have been furious: he thought of himself as another Napoleon.
Gilles Perrault, *The Secret of D-Day* (1965).

When we had settled it all [the issue of air support for Patton's forces] and the three of us [Generals Coningham, Tedder, and Patton] were arm in arm over the odd drink,

there was the sudden noise of rifle, machine-gun, and anti-aircraft fire, and three F. W. 190s scooted across about two hundred feet up. I nodded to George Patton, and said, "I always knew you were a good stage manager, but this takes the cake." Bradley reports that Patton's summing up was: "If I could find the sonsabitches who flew those planes I'd mail them each a medal."
Sir Arthur Tedder, *With Prejudice* (1966).

If this thing ever gets out they'll be howling for Patton's scalp, and that will be the end of Georgie's service in this war. I simply cannot let that happen. Patton is *indispensable* to the war effort—one of the guarantors of our victory.
General Dwight D. Eisenhower on Patton's slapping of an enlisted man in Sicily, quoted in Stephen E. Ambrose, *Supreme Commander* (1970).

There is always the possibility that this war, possibly even this theater, might yet develop a situation where this admittedly unbalanced but nevertheless aggressive fighting man should be rushed into the breach.
General Dwight D. Eisenhower, in a letter to General George C. Marshall concerning General George S. Patton, Jr., April 30, 1944, quoted in Forrest C. Pogue, *George C. Marshall: Organizer of Victory* (1973).

This Nazi thing. It's just like a Democratic-Republican election fight.
General George S. Patton's remarks, made while U.S. Military Governor of Bavaria, upon being questioned by reporters on the denazification program, *Time* (October 1, 1945). The uproar over this was a major factor in his being removed from active command shortly thereafter.

[General] Patton's mouth does not always carry out the functions of his brain. George acts on the theory that it is better to be damned than say nothing—that some publicity is better than none.
General Walter Bedell Smith, *Time* (October 8, 1945).

Patton's weekly press conferences were always newsworthy, but especially memorable for the General's off-the-record remarks, which, because of his colorful vocabulary, could never have been printed anyway. The first week of September, as a war correspondent for the London *Daily Telegraph*, I was present when, in typical fashion, he expounded on his plans for the Germans. In his high-pitched voice and pounding the map, Patton declared that, "Maybe there are five thousand, maybe ten thousand, Nazi bastards in their concrete foxholes before the Third Army. Now, if Ike stops holding Monty's hand and gives me the supplies, I'll go through the Siegfried Line like shit through a goose."
Cornelius Ryan, *A Bridge Too Far* (1974).

There was an expression floating around the Third Army whenever Patton's nickname, Old Blood and Guts, was mentioned. We'd say, "Yeah, our blood and his guts."
Nat Frankel and Larry Smith, *Patton's Best* (1978).

Patton was probably a prototypical anti-Semite.
Who, then, was the enemy, and why? Hitler was not merely the enemy of my country, but a personal enemy of both my forebears and my children. It was not, of course, difficult for me to rationalize shooting either him or his enforcers. But the agonizing paradox was that I was being led to do so by a man who probably shared some of his opinions.... Of course there's nothing historically new about a soldier like Patton having something in common with the enemy. Sherman, for example, believed in slav-

ery. But how would I have felt being a freed slave in Sherman's army? Well, I know how I would have felt: the same way I felt being Jewish under Patton.

Nat Frankel and Larry Smith, *Patton's Best* (1978).

Early in April [1970] he [President Nixon] had a private viewing of the film *Patton*, in which George C. Scott gives a compelling performance as the gifted, demagogic, lonely and naive World War II general who defied conventional restraints and risked everything to achieve a success in the Battle of the Bulge. The film appealed to Nixon's self-image, and he had a second showing as the Cambodian crisis deepened. William Rogers was dismayed to hear the President repeatedly citing Patton in this context.

William Shawcross, *Sideshow* (1979).

[Secretary of War] Stimson often dispatched [John] McCloy to handle troublesome commanders, among them George Patton, who was publicly grumbling on the eve of D-Day about what he considered his insufficient role. McCloy told him to keep quiet. Drawing himself to his full height and wearing his ivory-handled pistols, Patton declared: "You're taking a good deal of responsibility to come here on eve of battle and destroy a man's confidence." Replied McCloy: "Listen George, if I thought I could destroy your confidence by anything I might say, I would ask General Eisenhower to remove you." Patton unpuffed and relented.

Walter Isaacson and Evan Thomas, *The Wise Men* (1986).

Patton ... was physically a large man and anxious to keep his weight down. I was traveling next to him in a car and he asked me if I had had any lunch yet and I told him I had had a couple of sandwiches just before he arrived. He said, "I have pills for lunch; if you have only had a couple of sandwiches you had better have a bit more— here is some meat and two veg" and he handed me three pills. Not to appear uncooperative I swallowed them at once.

Major-General Pip Roberts, *From the Desert to the Battle* (1987).

In 1927 it was written in the efficiency report of George Patton, Jr., then a captain, that "this man would be invaluable in time of war, but is a disturbing element in time of peace." It was an assessment that could not have been more astute, and time would prove the absolute necessity for the Pattons of the Army. Yet Patton never would have survived that ER in the New Look Army, or in the sixties Army, where clerks like Alexander Haig pushed for the goal of the Army education system not to be the production of leaders of men, but rather the development of political scientists, "because these are the officers who will ultimately influence the application of our power in the future." The dancers and prancers would have used Patton's ER to see him passed over and out of the service before the ink was dry on the page. And worst of all, so wrapped up in their self-importance, they would not even recognize the terrible error they had made.

David H. Hackworth, *About Face* (1989).

Ridgway, General Matthew B. (b. 1895)

Monty [Field Marshal B. L. Montgomery] told me he had got Ridgway sacked from S. H. A. P. E. He had gone off to America specifically to tell Ike [President Eisenhower] that this was necessary and had found Ike alive to the fact. But Ridgway, who had been made American Chief of Staff, still thought he had been promoted and not sacked!

John Colville, *The Fringes of Power* (1985), diary entry for August 6–9, 1953. At first glance this seems like Montgomery's notorious ego exercising itself; but General Omar N. Bradley confirms in his autobiography, *A General's Life* (1983), that Ridgway "was not proving to be the ideal choice for NATO." Bradley calls Ridgway "a field commander without peer but not a diplomat" and agrees that Ridgway was given this new assignment by President Eisenhower, at least in part, to remove him from NATO.

He possessed almost all the military virtues—courage, brains, ruthlessness, decision. He made the grenade and field dressing on his shoulder straps familiar symbols, as much as his own trademark as Montgomery's beret or Patton's pistols. It has been cruelly but appositely remarked that Walton Walker's death, making possible the coming of Ridgway, was the salvation of the Eighth Army.
Max Hastings, *The Korean War* (1987).

Rommel, Field Marshal Erwin (1891–1944)

If I say now that he [Rommel] is gone, that I salute him as a soldier and a man and deplore the shameful manner of his death, I may be accused of belonging to what Mr. Bevin has called the "trade union of generals." So far as I know, should such a fellowship exist, membership in it implies no more than recognition in an enemy of the qualities one would wish to possess oneself, respect for a brave, able and scrupulous opponent and a desire to see him treated, when beaten, in the way one would have wished to be treated had he been the winner and oneself the loser. This used to be called chivalry: many will now call it nonsense.
Field Marshal Sir Claude Auchinleck, Foreword to *Rommel* by Desmond Young (1950).

Rommel's men considered him to be invulnerable. "No bullet has ever been forged for the Old Man," they used to say in amazement, or with a shake of the head, when he had once more sensed the danger and moved off in his armored car, just before a shell had burst. They lay in the desert under a hail of enemy machinegun fire—could not even put their noses out of their slit trenches without the risk of having their heads blown off. The attack was halted, Rommel came rushing up and stood upright in the trench, shielding his eyes with his hands against the sun. "What the hell's the matter with you fellows? When things get a bit hot over there you don't have to belly-flop every time!" Hardly had he gone than there were casualties once more.
Paul Carell, *Scorched Earth* (1971).

There is a real danger that our friend Rommel will become a "bogy man" for our troops in view of the fact that he is so much discussed. However energetic and capable he may be he is no superhuman. Even were he a superman it would be undesirable that our troops should endow him with supernatural attributes. I must beg you to make every effort to destroy the concept that Rommel is anything more than an ordinary German general. First, we must stop speaking of Rommel when referring to the enemy in Libya. We must speak of the Germans, the Axis troops or the enemy, but never, in this particular context, of Rommel. I must ask you to see that this order is carried out and that all our junior commanders be instructed that the matter is of great psychological significance.
General Sir Claude Auchinleck, 1942 order to all senior British officers in North Africa, quoted in Desmond Young, *Rommel* (1950); David Irving, *The Trail of the Fox* (1977); Samuel W. Mitcham, Jr., *Triumphant Fox* (1984).

[On May 10, 1944] Rommel had planned to go to Cherborg, but the previous evening he had been told that the B.B.C.'s German service had just announced that he would be inspecting the troops at Cherborg the next day. So the schedule had been changed, with Morsalines being substituted for Cherborg. The B.B.C.'s German service had many listeners among the troops, and here was a chance to demonstrate its inaccuracy. But the trick had not come off. Rommel had listened to the enemy broad-

cast to find out how the war was going in Russia and the Pacific, and had learned that the enemy knew he had been in Morsalines three hours earlier. It was humiliating.
Gilles Perrault, *The Secret of D-Day* (1965).

He restored to generalship the idea of leadership in battle from the front, regardless of the increased mechanization or scale of operations. He may thus have epitomized the triumph of the tactician over the strategist, but he none the less brought to the art of the battle a luminous clarity and a tactical imagination that had the quality of genius, even without the strategic judgment to go with it.
Charles Douglas-Home, "Field-Marshal Erwin Rommel," *The War Lords*, ed. Sir Michael Carver (1976).

I heard my father come upstairs and go into my mother's room. Anxious to know what was afoot, I got up and followed him. . . . "Come outside with me," he said in a tight voice. . . . .I have just had to tell your mother," he began slowly, "that I shall be dead in a quarter of an hour. . . . I am to have the chance of dying by poison. The two generals have brought it with them. It's fatal in three seconds. If I accept, none of the usual steps will be taken against my family, that is against you. They will also leave my staff alone."
"Do you believe it?" I interrupted.
"Yes," he replied. "I believe it. It is very much in their interest to see that the affair does not come out into the open."
Manfred Rommel quoted in *The Rommel Papers*, ed. B. H. Liddell Hart (1953).

His heart belonged to the Fuehrer.
Field Marshal Gerd von Rundstedt, speech at Rommel's funeral, quoted in William L. Shirer, *The Rise and Fall of the Third Reich* (1959). Shirer notes that "it is only fair to add that Rundstedt probably did not know of the circumstances of Rommel's death."

The myth of Rommel as a "good" German hostile to Nazism prevailed in the west for many years after the war. In reality, the C-in-C of Army Group B remained passionately devoted to Hitler until he became convinced that the war was militarily unwinnable.
Max Hastings, *Overlord* (1984).

Sheridan, General Philip Henry (1831–1888)
[In 1867] Tosawi brought in the first band of Comanches to surrender. When he was presented to Sheridan, Tosawi's eyes brightened. He spoke his own name and added two words of broken English, "Tosawi, good Indian," he said.
It was then that General Sheridan uttered the immortal words: "The only good Indians I ever saw were dead."
Dee Brown, *Bury My Heart at Wounded Knee* (1970). Sheridan would later deny he ever said this. However, this was a pervasive attitude at the time. Hermann Hagedorn in *Roosevelt in the Badlands* (1921) quotes Theodore Roosevelt saying: "I don't go so far as to think that the only good Indians are the dead Indians, but I believe nine out of every ten are, and I shouldn't inquire too closely into the case of the tenth."

General Sheridan, when this peculiar war began I thought a cavalry man should be at least six feet four high; but I have changed my mind—five feet four will do in a pinch.
President Abraham Lincoln, statement to General Sheridan quoted in P. H. Sheridan, *Personal Memoirs*, I (1888). Sheridan was actually 5 feet, 5 inches tall.

[Sheridan] was, usually, a quiet man; when he was not in action he preferred a placid and easy-going company; Sheridan, then, was unimpressive. In battle he was totally different; combat had the effect of creating in him, as though he were a lamp, a

strong light. He was, at once, capable of a passionate cursing and a low-voiced impressive tranquility of confidence. "Damn you, sir," he said to an officer who came galloping up, crying out some bad news above the roar of battle, "don't yell at me!" In such moments of intensity he often leaned forward over his horse's neck and spoke with the utmost softness.
Joseph Hergesheimer, *Sheridan* (1931).

Although often described as the embodiment of the reckless cavalryman, Sheridan rarely exposed his men to needless danger. Unlike many other officers, he respected the intelligence of the common soldier and understood that "none realized more quickly than they the blundering that often takes place on the field of battle." If soldiers were to be called on to die, they must have "some tangible indemnity for the loss of life." He never sought glory at the expense of his men. At Richmond in May 1864 he turned aside, although the city was practically undefended and a raid into it would have made him "the hero of the hour," because his men "would have known as well as I that the sacrifice was for not permanent advantage."
Paul Andrew Hutton, *Phil Sheridan and His Army* (1973).

Sherman, General William Tecumseh (1820–1891)
The Attila of the American continent.
Jefferson Davis, *The Rise and Fall of the Confederate Government*, II (1881).

To a West Point classmate who accused him of "double-talk" and demanded a Sherman-like statement, Eisenhower responded furiously, "Did you ever look up the circumstances under which Sherman said it? For 20 years many people hounded Sherman to take a part in politics and he steadfastly refused. Finally in 1884 a political convention was actually in session. It deadlocked. The bosses communicated with him and asked him to step in as the one person around whom all might unite. Of course, under those circumstances, it was appropriate and proper for him to say exactly what he did."
Stephen E. Ambrose, *Eisenhower* (1983). Sherman's famous statement—"I will not accept if nominated and will not serve if elected"—was made on June 5, 1884, when he declined to allow his name to be entered for the Republican presidential nomination.

[General William T.] Sherman was a master strategist because he was a born quartermaster.
B. H. Liddell Hart, *Thoughts on War* (1944).

[Sherman] was the epitome of all the virtues and vices of the professional officer. A man of simple truths rather than of brilliant concepts, he glorified in the unadorned title of "soldier" and wished to be nothing more or nothing less. Disclaiming other interests, causes, motives, his constantly reiterated motto was: "It is enough for the world to know that I am a soldier." Loyal to the Union, but opposed to abolition and an admirer of the South, he did his duty during the Civil War in the manner of the professional.
Samuel P. Huntington, *The Soldier and the State* (1957).

Often I utilized illustrations from Sherman to drive home my points—particularly the value of unexpectedness as the best guarantee of security as well as of rapid progress; the value of flexibility in plan and dispositions, above all by operating on a line which offers and threatens alternative objectives (thus, in Sherman's phrase, putting the opponent on the "horns of a dilemma"); the value of what I termed the "baited gambit," to trap the opponent, by combining offensive strategy with defensive tactics,

or elastic defense with well-timed riposte; the need to cut down the load of equipment and other impedimenta—as Sherman did—in order to develop mobility and flexibility.
B. H. Liddell Hart, *Memoirs* (1965).

Most serious historians are now agreed that Sherman's Atlanta campaign was not only the greatest feat of arms of the Civil War, but the greatest military masterpiece of the whole age. . . . But his contemporaries completely overlooked the wholly novel ideas such as the oblique approach on which his strategy was based and the tactical skill with which he applied them. In essence the strategy of the indirect approach was a reversion to the pre-Napoleonic era: to the wars of maneuver of the seventeenth and eighteenth centuries.
William McElwee, *The Art of War: Waterloo to Mons* (1974).

[Sherman] expressly set out to make Georgia howl. But neither states nor soldiers howl; civilians do, particularly women. It took someone who knew the South and Southern pieties well to understand just how effective making war on women could be. The problem with historical writing about the end of the Civil War is that its language is grandiosely and deliberately imprecise. Sherman would break "the will of the South" to fight, but his technique was to demoralize the women back home, and let that have its effect on the soldiers at the front.
James Reston, Jr., *Sherman's March and Vietnam* (1984).

Stilwell, General Joseph W. (1883–1946)
Stilwell was totally lacking in the art of diplomatic finesse. A man with a compulsion to speak and damn the consequences, he sounded off against colleagues and superiors with a zest that caused momentary amusement but ultimate dislike. The nickname "Vinegar Joe," applied in affection, became a damaging trademark.
Forrest C. Pogue, *George C. Marshall: Ordeal and Hope 1939–1942* (1966).

[Dean Rusk] was with [General] Stilwell visiting the Chinese forces in Burma when they heard a grenade explosion. A Chinese soldier was "fishing" in the river. Stilwell was furious; he fumed at the idea that the grenade had "been brought over 12,000 miles to kill carp." In response the senior Chinese officer said a few words to his aides, and the soldier was brought in and summarily shot.
Thomas J. Schoenbaum, *Waging Peace and War* (1988).

Heading the Tactical Section at Benning in 1930 was an "old China hand," Lieutenant Colonel Stilwell. . . . The tall, lean, profane man who later became known as "Vinegar Joe" was at least as difficult then as when during World War II . . . . Intense, intolerant, energetic—many lunch hours he spent racing the clock over long distances—he spared neither himself nor those who worked for him. He was a rebel by instinct, chafed against any and all authority, mocked at those in command, continually burned to remake the situation in which he found himself, and throughout his Army career walked the razor's edge of insubordination. But he was nevertheless a brilliant soldier.
Forrest C. Pogue, *George C. Marshall: Education of a General* (1963).

In the China theater, Marshall had been forced to sack his commanding officer, General Joseph W. Stilwell, not because he lacked brilliance as a soldier but because he was a xenophobic Yankee who despised foreigners and could not keep his mouth shut about them. He called his overall commander, Chiang Kai-shek, who was president of China, "a lily-livered Chink" and a "slant-eyed snake." The fact that the descriptions were not wholly inaccurate did not lessen the nature of his offense. Moreover, he quarreled with the British in Southeast Asia, too, referring to Lord Louis Mountbatten

as "a limey mountebank" and "sometimes as dumb as that thick-headed cousin of his, the King."
Leonard Mosley, *Marshall* (1982).

Stuart, General James Ewell Brown ("Jeb") (1833–1864)
His horse furniture and equipment were polished leather and bright metal, and he liked to wear a red rose in his jacket when the roses bloomed, and a love knot of red ribbon when flowers were out of season. His soft, fawn-colored hat was looped up on the right with a gold star, and adorned with a curling ostrich feather. His boots sported little knightly spurs of gold—admiring ladies, even those who never saw him in their lives, sent him such things. He went conspicuous all gold and glitter, in the front of great battles and in a hundred little cavalry fights, which killed men just as dead as Gettysburg ... for Jeb Stuart was the first cavalier of the South.
John W. Thomason, Jr., *Jeb Stuart* (1930).

Brilliant and penetrating blue eyes ... made one forget the homeliness of his other features and his "loud" apparel. The Army boasted nothing to excel that conspicuous uniform—a short gray jacket covered with buttons and braid, a gray cavalry cape over his shoulder, a broad hat looped with a gold star and adorned with a plume, high jack boots and gold spurs, an ornate and tasselled yellow sash, gauntlets that climbed almost to his elbows. His weapons were a light French saber and a pistol, which he carried in a black holster.
Douglas Southall Freeman, *Lee's Lieutenants*, I (1942).

Among the gallant soldiers who have fallen in this war, General Stuart was second to none in valor, in zeal, and in unflinching devotion to his country. His achievements form a conspicuous part of the history of this army, with which his name and services will be forever associated. To military capacity of a high order and to the nobler virtues of the soldier he added the brighter graces of a pure life, guided and sustained by the Christian's faith and hope. ... To his comrades in arms he has left the proud recollections of his deeds and the inspiring influence of his example.
General Robert E. Lee quoted in Burke Davis, *Gray Fox* (1956).

Trenchard, Marshal of the RAF Hugh M. (1873–1956)
His life's work became ... the preservation of the Royal Air Force through thick and thin. His case turned upon the theory of a strategic air offensive, for without it there was no convincing case for the preservation of a separate air service, just as without it there would have been no case for its creation.
Noble Frankland, *The Bombing Offensive Against Germany* (1965).

Perhaps nobody should be called "the father of the Royal Air Force," but the fact remains that only one man has been so called. Marshal of the Royal Air Force Lord Trenchard loathed the phrase, though he learnt to live with it.
Gavin Lyall, "Marshal of the Royal Air Force: The Viscount Trenchard," *The War Lords*, ed. Sir Michael Carver (1976).

Washington, President George (1732–1799)
Suddenly every heart missed a beat. Something was the matter with His Excellency. He seemed unable to read the paper. He paused in bewilderment. He fumbled in his waistcoat pocket. And then he pulled out something that only his intimates had seen him wear. A pair of glasses. "Gentlemen, you will permit me to put on my spectacles, for I have not only grown gray but almost blind in the service of my country."
This simple statement achieved what all Washington's rhetoric and all his arguments had been unable to achieve. The officers were instantly in tears, and from behind the

shining drops, their eyes looked with love at the commander who had led them all so far and long.
  James T. Flexner, describing Washington's effect on his officers at Newburgh, New York, March 15, 1783, *George Washington: In the American Revolution* (1967).

And as to you, Sir, treacherous in private friendship (for so you have been to me, and that in the day of danger) and a hypocrite in public life, the world will be puzzled to decide whether you are an apostate or an imposter: whether you have abandoned good principles, or whether you ever had any.
  Thomas Paine, letter to George Washington, July 30, 1796, *The Writings of Thomas Paine*, 3, ed. D. Conway (1895).

His mind was great and powerful, without being of the very first order. . .and as far as he saw, no judgment was ever sounder. It was slow in operation, being little aided by invention or imagination, but sure in conclusion. Hence the common remark of his officers, of the advantage he derived from councils of war, where hearing all suggestions, he selected whatever was best. . . . He was incapable of fear, meeting personal dangers with the calmest unconcern. Perhaps the strongest feature in his character was prudence, never acting until every circumstance, every consideration, was maturely weighed; refraining if he saw a doubt, but, when once decided, going through with his purpose, whatever obstacles opposed. His integrity was most pure, his justice the most inflexible I have ever known, no motives of interest or consanguinity, or friendship or hatred, being able to bias his decision. He was, indeed, in every sense of the word, a wise, a good, and a great man.
  Thomas Jefferson, January 2, 1814 letter to Dr. Walter Jones, reprinted in *The Writings of Thomas Jefferson XIV*, ed. A. E. Bergh (1853).

Gentlemen, the character of Washington is among the most cherished contemplations of my life. It is a fixed star in the firmament of great names, shining without twinkling or obscuration, with clear, steady, beneficent light.
  Daniel Webster, Secretary of State, February 20, 1851 letter to the New York Committee for the Celebration of the Birthday of Washington, *The Writings and Speeches of Daniel Webster*, 12 (1903).

Above all, among the men of character who as individuals made a historic difference, there was Washington. When on his white horse he plunged into the midst of panicked men and with the "terrific eloquence of unprintable scorn" stopped the retreat from Monmouth, he evoked from Lafayette the tribute, "Never have I seen so superb a man."
  Is he needed in the new army of today whose most desired postgraduate course, . . . it has been said, is a term at the Harvard Business School?
  Barbara W. Tuchman, "Generalship," *Parameters* (Spring 1972).

A citizen, first in war, first in peace, and first in the hearts of his countrymen.
  Resolution adopted by the House of Representatives upon the death of President George Washington, December 19, 1799. While the resolution was introduced by John Marshall, it was written by Henry "Light-Horse Harry" Lee.

[On December 23, 1783, General George Washington] spoke what he took to be his last words on the public stage: "Having now finished the work assigned me, I retire from the great theater of Action. . . . I here offer my commission, and take my leave of all the employments of public life." At that moment the ancient legend of Cincinnatus—the Roman called from his plow to rescue Rome, and returning to this plow when danger had passed—was resurrected as a fact of modern political life.
  Gary Willis, *Cincinnatus: George Washington and the Enlightenment* (1984).

Wellington, Duke of (1769–1852)

An officer of the artillery came up to the Duke [of Wellington], and stated that he had a distinct view of Napoleon, attended by his staff; that he had the guns of his battery well pointed in that direction, and was prepared to fire. His Grace instantly and emphatically exclaimed, "No! no! I'll not allow it. It is not the business of commanders to be firing upon each other."

William Siborne, *History of the War in France and Belgium*, II (1844).

The French advanced to about fifty yards from where the British Guards were lying down, when the voice of one of the British officers was heard calling, as if to the ground before him, "Up, Guards, and at them!" It was the duke [of Wellington] who gave the order; and at the words, as if by magic, up started before them a line of the British Guards four deep, and in the most compact and perfect order. They poured an instantaneous volley upon the head of the French column, by which no less than three hundred of those chosen veterans are said to have fallen.

E. S. Creasy, *The Fifteen Decisive Battles of the World* (1851). According to Paul F. Boller, Jr., and John Beorge, *They Never Said It* (1989), the Duke later denied that he said, "Up, Guards, and at 'em!" They say he said, "Stand up, guards."

[Wellington] took over his army as an instrument . . . just as an engineer might take over a gang of laborers to dig a canal, having no love for the gang itself, but determined to make the best of it as a matter of duty. . . . When his purpose was fulfilled, he threw the instrument aside without compunction, having no further use for it and little or no sentiment about it.

Sir John W. Fortescue, *A History of the British Army*, X (1920).

geopolitics

Who rules East Europe commands the Heartland: Who rules the Heartland commands the World-Island: Who rules the World-Island commands the World.

Halford J. Mackinder, *Democratic Ideals and Reality* (1919). According to Michael Howard, "The Influence of Geopolitics . . .," *Parameters* (September 1988), this "is self-evident nonsense. There are few areas of less importance to the hegemony of the world than East Europe, however defined. I am reminded of the splendid rejoinder made by Marshal Blucher during the Allied invasion of France in 1814, when a pedantic member of his staff advised him to establish his army on the plateau of Langres since that was 'the key to the country.' Blucher examined the map and grunted, 'I can see that if I stand on the plateau and piss to the north it will drain into the Atlantic, while if I piss to the south it will drain into the Mediterranean. But I don't see how that will help me to win the war.'"

Who controls the Rimland rules Eurasia; who rules Eurasia controls the destinies of the world.

Nicholas Spykman, *America's Strategy and World Politics* (1942).

When 95 per cent of some of our brightest college students cannot locate Vietnam on a world map, we must sound the alarm. We cannot expect to be a world leader if our populace doesn't even know who the rest of the world is!

Senator Bill Bradley, *The Washington Post* (April 21, 1987).

Germany

Germans have no taste for peace; renown is easier won among perils, and you cannot maintain a large body of companions except by violence and war. . . . You will find it harder to persuade a German to plough the land and to await its annual produce with patience than to challenge a foe and earn the prize of wounds. . . . When not engaged in warfare, they spend some little time in hunting, but more in idling, abandoned to sleep and gluttony. All the heroes and grim warriors dawdle their time away, while the care of the house, hearth, and fields is left to the women, old men and weaklings of the family. The warriors themselves lose their edge. They are so strangely inconsistent. They love indolence but they hate peace.

Tacitus, *Agricola/Germania* (1st century A.D.).

The great questions of the day will be decided not by speeches and majority votes, that was the mistake of 1848 and 1849, but by iron and blood.

Otto von Bismarck, Premier of Prussia, September 30, 1862 speech in Berlin, quoted in Edward Crankshaw, *Bismarck* (1981).

We have won our position through the sharpness of our sword, not through the sharpness of our mind.

Field Marshal Colmar von der Goltz, *The Nation in Arms* (1887).

Our navy should be further strengthened, so that we may be sure that no one can dispute with us our place in the sun that is our due.

Kaiser William II, speech in Hamburg, August 27, 1911, quoted in *The New York Times* (August 28, 1911).

Events in Europe in the nineteenth century had encouraged many Germans to think of creating a single state in which all Germans could be combined. This was the meaning of their national hymn, *Deutschland, Deutschland über alles* [written by Heinrich Hoffman von Fallersleben in 1841]. The words seem threatening when translated into English as "Germany, Germany over all," but to those who heard it in the nineteenth century it meant they should put aside their parochial feelings as Bavarians or Saxons or Prussians and think of themselves as Germans above all.

David W. Ziegler, *War, Peace and International Politics*, 4th ed. (1987).

Germany has reduced savagery to a science, and this great war for the victorious peace of justice must go on until the German cancer is cut clean out of the world body.

President Theodore Roosevelt, speech in Johnstown, Pennsylvania, September 30, 1917.

Germany will be either a world power or will not be at all.

Adolf Hitler, *Mein Kampf* (1924).

In dealing with Germany, you should never lose sight of the abominable manner in which she declared and waged the late War.

Her conduct during the War was not accidental and unpremeditated. . . . For many years her professors, philosophers and so-called thinkers, inculcated the theory that she was superior to all other countries and, therefore, had the right to do with them whatever she would. The rules of morality, apparently, did not apply to Germany.

Marshal Ferdinand Foch quoted in Raymond Recouly, *Marshal Foch* (1929).

Won't you Germans ever be civilized? Won't you ever learn to keep your word? Or to regard other peoples as men, women and children of flesh and blood and not as inferiors to be treated as you see fit—all in the name of your discredited German Kultur and race superiority?

Alexander Knox as President Wilson in *Wilson*, screenplay by Lamar Trotti (1944).

We want a German nation that has lost the art of starting wars. Anything that keeps Germany divided is to be welcomed.

Richard Crossman, *U.S. News and World Report* (May 3, 1971).

I had no idea why the German people were stuck with Hitler and the Nazis and could care less. History was not one of my strong subjects. But when the time came, I

would hammer those Germans any chance I got. Them or me. Even a "D" history student from Hamlin High knew that it was better to be the hammer than the nail.
General Chuck Yeager and Leo Janos, *Yeager* (1985).

I love Germany so. Every day I thank God that there are two of them.
François Mauriac quoted in Gwynne Dyer, *War* (1985).

I can send the flower of German youth into the hell of war without the slightest pity.
Adolf Hitler quoted in Desmond Seward, *Napoleon and Hitler* (1989).

glory

The sacrifice which they collectively made was individually repaid to them; for they received again each one for himself a praise which grows not old, and the noblest of all sepulchres—I speak not of that in which their remains are laid, but of that in which their glory survives, and is proclaimed always and on every fitting occasion both in word and deed. For the whole earth is the sepulchre of famous men; not only are they commemorated by columns and inscriptions in their own country, but in foreign lands there dwells also an unwritten memorial of them, graven not on stone but in the hearts of men.
Pericles' funeral oration, quoted in Thucydides, *The Peloponnesian War* (5th century B.C.).

Seeking the bubble reputation
Even in the cannon's mouth.
William Shakespeare, *As You Like It*, Act II (1599).

We triumph without glory when we conquer without danger.
Pierre Corneille, *El Cid*, Act II (1637).

The boast of heraldry, the pomp of pow'r,
  And all that beauty, all that wealth, e'er gave
Awaits alike th' inevitable hour.
  The paths of glory lead but to the grave.
Thomas Gray, *Elegy Written in a Country Churchyard* (1751). Francis Parkman, in *Montcalm and Wolfe* (1906), quotes British General James Wolfe saying on the night before the battle for Quebec of Gray's poem: "I would rather have written those lines than taken Quebec." The next day, September 12, 1759, Wolfe took Quebec but died in the effort.

You do not get peace by shouting "Peace!" ... Peace is a meaningless word; what we need is a glorious peace.
Napoleon I, speaking in 1805, quoted in J. C. Herold, *The Mind of Napoleon* (1955).

There may they dig each other's graves,
And call the sad work glory.
Percy Bysshe Shelley, *Queen Mab* (1813).

For the notion of glory as the common man comprehended it, the Duke reserved one of the most cutting dismissals from his famously caustic repertoire. Asked if he were pleased to have been mobbed by the ecstatic population of Brussels on his return from Waterloo, he rejoined, "Not in the least; if I had failed, they would have shot me."
John Keegan, *The Mask of Command* (1987).

We carved not a line, and we raised not a stone—
But we left him alone with his glory.
Charles Wolfe, *The Burial of Sir John Moore at Corunna* (1817).

Our generation, though not indifferent to glory, prefers it when it is safe and cheap.
Lord Salisbury, *Quarterly Review* (July 1864).

The love of glory, the ardent desire for honorable distinction by honorable deeds, is among the most potent and elevating of military motives.
Alfred Thayer Mahan, *Life of Nelson* (1897).

Far better it is to dare mighty things, to win glorious triumphs, even though checkered by failure, than to rank with those poor spirits who neither enjoy much nor suffer much, because they live in the gray twilight that knows not victory or defeat.
President Theodore Roosevelt quoted in Allan R. Millett, *Semper Fidelis* (1980).

What Price Glory?
Title of a 1924 play by Maxwell Anderson.

Here rests in honored glory an American soldier known but to God.
Inscription on tomb of the Unknown Soldier, Arlington National Cemetery.

Who would prefer peace to the glory of hunger and thirst, of wading through mud, and dying in the service of one's country?
Jean Giraudoux, *Amphitryon 38*, Act I (1929).

In the England of 1932, glory has become a discredited word. After "the glorious dead" of 1914–1918, the word "glory" now soils the air.
William Manchester, *The Last Lion*, II (1988).

War still remains "glorious" in the secret imaginations of most people who have not fought.
George Orwell, *New Statesman and Nation* (August 28, 1937).

The object of government in peace and in war is not the glory of rulers or of races, but the happiness of the common man.
Lord Beveridge, *Social Insurance and Allied Services* (1942).

Glory is largely a theatrical concept. There is no striving for glory without a vivid awareness of an audience.
Eric Hoffer, *The True Believer* (1951).

Through bitter experience the machine taught that man himself was no longer master of the battlefield. The individual counted for nothing, all that mattered now was the machinery of war. If a machine gun could wipe out a whole battalion of men in three minutes, where was the relevance of the old concepts of heroism, glory and fair play between gentlemen?
John Ellis, *The Social History of the Machine Gun* (1975).

Grenada

[President Reagan once starred] in the kind of movies that recent incidents in Grenada cannot help but remind one of. Think about it for a moment—a small Caribbean island, a band of bearded local militia, a lot of beautiful and confused residents, and throw in a few angry tourists for comic relief. Unfortunately, this is not a grade B movie, it is not even a very good script—two American marines have already lost their lives.

But if that is the way Mr. Reagan persists in looking at these issues, maybe he will listen to a little advice from Mr. [George] Gershwin. If Gershwin were alive today, perhaps he would consider this rewrite:

You like po-ta-to, I like po-tah-to,
You say Gre-na-da, I say Gre-nah-da,
Po-ta-to, po-tah-to, Gre-na-da, Gre-nah-da,
Let's call the whole thing off.
Representative James M. Shannon, speech in the House of Representatives, October 26, 1983.

Grenada, we were told, was a friendly island paradise for tourism. Well it wasn't. It was a Soviet-Cuban colony being readied as a major military bastion to export terror and undermine democracy.
President Ronald Reagan, speech to the nation on Lebanon and Grenada, October 27, 1983.

All nations love "glorious little wars." Even World War II with its sequential victories was immensely popular in Germany—until 1942. The intelligentsia will no doubt have misgivings. . . . But popular support is hardly weakened by such quibbles. Thus, it is useful to have a Grenada to trump a loser like Beirut.
James R. Schlesinger, testimony before U.S. Senate Committee on Foreign Relations, February 6, 1985.

All four services continue to purchase independent, incompatible communications equipment.
The first Army assault waves were unable to speak with Navy ships offshore to request and coordinate naval gunfire. One Army officer reportedly was so frustrated in trying to communicate with the offshore ships that he went to a civilian phone on the island and used his AT&T credit card to call buddies at Fort Bragg so they could get to the navy and coordinate fire support. The JCS pooh-poohed the story, but some troops privately insist it's true.
Barry Goldwater, *Goldwater* (1988).

From Reagan's standpoint, the timing of the Grenada invasion could hardly have been more fortuitous. . . . The news media immediately made the invasion the nation's top story while relegating Lebanon [where 216 marines were killed by one bomb the previous week] to secondary status. And the invasion itself not only encouraged people to forget about the Beirut tragedy; it provided a release for the emotions of anger and grief it had triggered, emotions that might otherwise have been vented on Reagan.
Mark Hertsgaad, *On Bended Knee* (1988).

The Grenada affair did teach me one valuable lesson about dealing with people like [Admiral John] Poindexter: In the future, if I asked a question like, "Are you invading Grenada today?" and the answer came back, "Preposterous!" I would have to follow up with, "Then are you invading Grenada tomorrow?"
Larry Speakes, White House Press Spokesman during the Grenada invasion, *Speaking Out* (1988).

ground crews

"I wish Jim had joined the RAF," said Mrs. Leonard. "I'm sure it could have been managed. You know where you are with them. You just settle down at an RAF station as though it was business with regular hours and a nice crowd. Of course I shouldn't let Jim fly, but there's plenty of jobs like my brother's got."
"Ground staff is all right in war-time," said Sarum-Smith. "It won't sound so good afterwards. One's got to think of peace. . . ."
Evelyn Waugh, *Men At Arms* (1952).

The Battle of Britain ... was fought on the older system of servicing in which each pilot had his own aircraft, and that aircraft was serviced by a devoted ground crew, so that they regarded themselves as part of a team with the pilot, and felt that they shared in any victories that he achieved. ... One of the early results of Operational Research was to show that substantial economies could be effected by changing over to a kind of central garage system into which aircraft were sent for servicing after each operation and from which each pilot could draw a serviced aircraft, probably a different one from that which he last flew, for each new operation.

The scheme succeeded ... where the main criterion was the number of flying hours achieved per aircraft and per unit of ground crew. ... But it achieved flying hours at the expense of the esprit de corps that formerly existed between air crew and ground crew.

R. V. Jones, *The Wizard War* (1978).

guerrilla warfare

Guerrilla warfare opens a field of activity for every local capacity, forces the enemy into an unaccustomed method of battle, avoids the evil consequences of a great defeat, secures the national war from the risk of treason, and has the advantage of not confining it within any defined and determinate basis of operations. It is invincible, indestructible.

Giuseppe Mazzini, *General Instructions for Members of Young Italy* (1831).

According to our idea of a people's War, it should, like a kind of nebulous vapory essence, never condense into a solid body; otherwise the enemy sends an adequate force against this core [and] crushes it.

Karl von Clausewitz, *On War* (1832).

Our tactics were always hit and run, not pushes, but strokes. We never tried to maintain or improve an advantage, but to move off and strike again somewhere else. We used the smallest force, in the quickest time, at the farthest place. If the action had continued till the enemy had changed his dispositions to resist it, we would have been breaking the spirit of our fundamental rule of denying him targets.

T. E. Lawrence, "Evolution of a Revolt," *Army Quarterly* (October 1920), reprinted in *Evolution of a Revolt* (1968).

I began revolution with 82 men. If I had [to] do it again, I'd do it with 10 or 15 men and absolute faith. It does not matter how small you are if you have faith and plan of action.

Fidel Castro, Premier of Cuba, *The New York Times* (April 22, 1959).

The guerrilla fights the war of the flea, and his military enemy suffers the dog's disadvantages; too much to defend; too small, ubiquitous, and agile an enemy to come to grips with.

Robert Taber, *The War of the Flea* (1965).

The conventional army loses if it does not win. The guerrilla wins if he does not lose.

Henry Kissinger, "The Vietnam Negotiations," *Foreign Affairs* (January 1969).

Guerrilla warfare defies the possessor of superweapons by operating among the people. It thus challenges the strong to use weapons against an uncertain target, doing damage to the very people the strong do not wish to alienate.

Charles M. Simpson III, *Inside the Green Berets* (1983).

The enemy approaches, we retreat.
The enemy halts, we move in.
The enemy tires, we attack.
The enemy retreats, we pursue.
Mao Tse-tung quoted in Harrison E. Salisbury, *The Long March* (1985).

In the wake of South Vietnam's total defeat less than a year later, the Army and its Special Forces fell in such disfavor that the country's unconventional warfare capability nearly disappeared during the late 1970s. However, less than a decade after the 1st Special Forces Group was stricken from the Army's rolls, a renewed emphasis was placed on rebuilding the Special Forces as a viable military instrument to counter terrorism and insurgency where the use of conventional forces was considered premature, inappropriate, or unfeasible.
Shelby L. Stanton, *Green Berets At War* (1985).

One time I heard a general coming back from an aggressive campaign say, "Goddammit, they won't come out and fight." And I thought at that moment that some British general during the Revolutionary War, when the American squirrel rifles were knocking the red stripes off the chests of those Hessians from behind the rocks and trees, must also have said when he got to his tent at the end of a day, "Goddamn 'em, they won't come out and fight." There was a lot of that in Vietnam and we were not prepared for it.
Clark Clifford quoted in Kim Willenson, *The Bad War* (1987).

guns and butter

We can get along, if it is essential, without butter, but never without cannon. If we were to be attacked we could not defend ourselves with butter but only with cannon and rifles.
Paul Joseph Goebbels, German Minister of Propaganda, *The New York Times* (January 18, 1936).

You must choose between butter or guns. Germany must arm to assert herself.
Hermann Goering quoted in H. W. Blood-Ryan, *Göring* (1938).

It goes without saying that this happens in the Fascist countries, but "guns before butter" also rules in the democracies.
George Orwell, *New English Weekly* (May 26, 1938).

Time may require further sacrifices. If so, we will make them. But we will not heed those who will wring it from the hopes of the unfortunate in a land of plenty. I believe we can continue the Great Society while we fight in Vietnam.
President Lyndon B. Johnson, State of the Union Message, January 1966.

Not too long ago it was commonplace to hear that this nation could afford both guns and butter—that we could provide for our defense, meet our world commitments and take care of pressing national problems. Now it has become fashionable to take the opposite view—we can have either guns or butter, but not both.
Senator William Proxmire, speech in the Senate, September 3, 1969.

The Russians put guns before butter. We [Britain] put just about everything before guns.
Margaret Thatcher, *The Christian Science Monitor* (January 21, 1976).

Seeking both guns and butter is a policy that works only in the very short term. I think that Johnson belatedly came to understand this, because through the four years of my first term I cannot recall an instance when he urged me to go forward with any of his Great Society programs.
President Richard M. Nixon, *RN: Memoirs* (1978).

As a nation, we cannot afford to accept the "guns and butter" economics of Reagan. Imagine what would happen if we had asked for a 37 percent increase in expenditures for social programs and then said we'd figure out later how we wanted to spend it. Well, that is exactly what the Reagan Administration is doing with its proposed defense expenditures. We must stop giving our blank checks to the military.
Albert Shanker, *Los Angeles Times* (February 16, 1982).

hangings

Only on August 2 [1776] was the Declaration of Independence formally signed. John Hancock, the president, signed first, in large letters, it is said, so that George III could read his name without putting on spectacles. Legend asserts that he warned: "We must be unanimous; there must be no pulling different ways; we must all hang together," and that [Benjamin] Franklin replied: "Yes, we must, indeed, all hang together, or most assuredly we shall all hang separately." No contemporary record substantiates the story, which first surfaced in 1840.
Ronald W. Clark, *Benjamin Franklin* (1983).

I only regret that I have but one life to lose for my country.
Captain Nathan Hale, last words before being hanged by the British as a spy on September 22, 1776, quoted in George Dudley Seymour, *Captain Nathan Hale* (1933). According to Tom Burham, *The Dictionary of Misinformation* (1975), this "is not what he said. Recently discovered is the diary of Capt. Frederick Mackenzie, a British officer who was there. He praises Hale for his courage but records his last words as, 'It is the duty of every good officer to obey any orders given him by his commander-in-chief.' "

Depend upon it, Sir, when a man knows he is to be hanged in a fortnight, it concentrates his mind wonderfully.
Samuel Johnson quoted in James Boswell, *Life of Samuel Johnson* (1791).

For they're hangin' Danny Deever, you can hear the Dead March play,
The Regiment's in 'ollow square—they're hangin' him to-day;
They've taken of his buttons off an' cut his stripes away,
An' they're hangin' Danny Deever in the mornin'.
Rudyard Kipling, *Danny Deever* (1899).

RICHARD: I think you might have the decency to treat me as a prisoner of war, and shoot me like a man instead of hanging me like a dog.
BURGOYNE: [sympathetically] Now there, Mr. Anderson, you talk like a civilian, if you will excuse my saying so. Have you any idea of the average marksmanship of the army of His Majesty King George the Third? If we make you up a firing party, what will happen? Half of them will miss you: the rest will make a mess of the business and leave you to the provo-marshal's pistol. Whereas we can hang you in a perfectly workmanlike and agreeable way. [Kindly] Let me persuade you to be hanged, Mr. Anderson?
George Bernard Shaw, *The Devil's Disciple*, Act III (1900).

Field Marshal Keitel, who was immediately behind von Ribbentrop in the order of executions, was the first military leader to be executed under the new concept of international law—the principle that professional soldiers cannot escape punishment for waging aggressive wars and permitting crimes against humanity with the claim they were dutifully carrying out orders of superiors.

Keitel entered the chamber two minutes after the trap had dropped beneath von Ribbentrop, while the latter still was at the end of his rope. . . .

After his black-booted, uniformed body plunged through the trap, witnesses agreed Keitel has showed more courage on the scaffold than in the courtroom, where he had tried to shift his guilt upon the ghost of Hitler, claiming that all was the Fuhrer's fault and that he merely carried out orders and had no responsibility.
Kingsbury Smith, on the October 16, 1946 hanging of Nazi war criminals, *It Happened in 1946*, ed. Clark Kinnaird (1947).

Here, richly, with ridiculous display,
　The Politician's corpse was laid away.
While all of his acquaintance sneered and slanged
　I wept: for I had longed to see him hanged.
Hilaire Belloc, *Collected Verse* (1954).

Lenin is supposed to have said 60 years ago that the day would come when the capitalists would fight with each other for the privilege of selling the rope with which to hang them [the capitalists]. What he didn't know is that they would also offer credits to buy the rope.
Henry A. Kissinger, *The Christian Science Monitor* (October 13, 1982). According to Paul F. Boller, Jr., and John George, *They Never Said It* (1989), there is "no evidence" that Lenin ever said this.

hawks and doves

The hawks favoured an air strike to eliminate the Cuban missile bases. . . . The doves opposed the air strike and favoured a blockade.
Charles Bartlett, on the Cuban Missile Crisis, *The Saturday Evening Post*, (December 8, 1962).

Our "doves" must learn that there are times when power must be used. They must learn that there is no substitute for force in the face of a determined enemy who resorts to terror, subversion and aggression, whether concealed or open. Our "hawks" must learn that military power is not enough. They must learn, indeed, that it can be wholly unavailing if not accompanied by political effort and by the credible promise to ordinary people of a better life.
Vice President Hubert H. Humphrey, speech at West Point, June 8, 1966.

Past experience provides little basis for confidence that reason can prevail in an atmosphere of mounting war fever. In a contest between a hawk and a dove the hawk has a great advantage, not because it is a better bird, but because it is a bigger bird with lethal talons and a highly developed will to use them.
J. William Fulbright, speech in the U.S. Senate, April 21, 1966.

I am not conscious of falling under any of those ornithological divisions.
Clark M. Clifford, U.S. Secretary of Defense, on being asked if he thought of himself as a hawk or as a dove, *The New York Times* (January 2, 1968).

I'm not a hawk or a dove. I just don't want my country to be a pigeon.
Senator Henry M. Jackson, *Time* (March 22, 1971).

For the mass public, it is easier to understand problems if they are reduced to black/white dichotomies. It is easier to understand policies if they are attached to individuals

who are simplistically labeled as hawks or doves. Yet in today's world any attempt to reduce its complexities to a single set of ideological propositions, to a single personality, or to a single issue is in itself a distortion. Such a distortion also raises the danger that public emotions could become so strong as to make the management of a genuinely complex foreign policy well-nigh impossible.
Zbigniew Brzezinski, *Power and Principle* (1983).

Hawks emphasize calculated deterrence based on rationality and argue that the best way to avoid nuclear war is to strengthen our deterrent posture, that is, to maintain the survivability of our retaliatory forces.... Doves point out that in circumstances of extreme threat constrained rationality may suggest preventive or preemptive attack, and reassurance of one's adversary by reducing armaments would be a more appropriate way to reduce risks.
Joseph S. Nye, Jr., *Nuclear Ethics* (1986).

headquarters

[General John Pope on assuming command of the Army of the Potomac in June 1862] was reported as having said that his headquarters would be in the saddle. When this boast reached the humor-loving Confederates ..., they made indelicate jokes about the general who had his headquarters where his hindquarters should be.
Kenneth Williams, *Lincoln Finds a General*, I (1949). According to Burke Davis, *Gray Fox* (1956), General "Stonewall" Jackson was supposed to have said: "I can whip any man who doesn't know his headquarters from his hindquarters." President Lincoln is also thought to have commented that it [the saddle] was "a better place for his hindquarters."

When a general is no longer needed at his battle headquarters his honor requires him in the firing line.
René Quinton, *Soldier's Testament* (1930).

General [Wade] Haislip, one of my oldest friends, was commanding the XV Corps and I determined to visit him [shortly after D-Day]. As I reached his headquarters about noon, he came out in a Jeep to meet me. His greeting was almost surly:
"General, I think you should turn around and go back right away."
"What's the trouble?" I asked.
"We've got Nazi artillery firing on our flank and we think there's a counterattack building up that just might overrun the area."
"Well, Ham," I said, "I'd like to see the development of their attack and I'm really confident you can handle it. Besides, I don't see you running."
"Of course we'll handle it!" he said. "But in the meantime we could get some nasty artillery fire and you might get into it."
I reiterated, annoyingly, "After all, you might, too."
"This is my place!" he insisted. "But I don't want you here. Don't think I'm worrying about your possible demise. I just don't want it said that I allowed the Supreme Commander to get killed in my corps area. Now if you want to get killed, go into some other area."
President Dwight D. Eisenhower, *At Ease* (1967).

When one of the forward formations had to go on half rations, as throughout the campaign they often did, I used to put my headquarters on half rations too. It had little practical effect, but as a gesture it was rather valuable, and did remind the young staff

officers with healthy appetites that it was urgent to get the forward formations back to full rations as soon as possible.
Field Marshal William Slim, writing of World War II, quoted in Richard Holmes, *Acts of War* (1985).

helicopters

The new kind of land warfare—the airmobile battle—is unique in that it takes place not just on the surface of the earth but also in the first thousand feet or so above the ground, where air vehicles carry troops and supplies, provide supporting firepower, and allow commanders to move quickly from place to place to direct the fighting. The use of this third dimension frees the foot soldier from the restrictions of the terrain and makes possible a whole new range of tactical maneuver, where there is always an open flank—over the top.
John R. Galvin, *Air Assault* (1969).

In the final analysis, the helicopter's most pernicious contribution to the fighting in Vietnam may have been its undermining of the influence and initiative of small unit commanders. By providing a fast, efficient airborne command post, the helicopter all too often turned supervisors into over-supervisors.
General Dave R. Palmer, *Summons of the Trumpet* (1978).

The ubiquitous role of the helicopter in Vietnam doubtless has led many to believe that airmobility was the product of the war, rather than the war being the crucible in which were tested concepts and theories that had evolved since World War II.
J. D. Coleman, *Pleiku* (1988).

[Airland Battle is] a dopey strategy because it's not going to happen. National Training Center exercises show the helicopter cannot survive against today's defenses, and the strategy assumes the commander has tens of thousands of smart weapons on call that he won't have.
Colonel John B. Keeley quoted in *The Washington Post National Weekly* (January 9–15, 1989).

There has never been an example of conventional forces employing helicopters against unconventional forces and winning. Flying out from safe havens to drop upon the vulnerable population only distances you from your objective, which is to win over those people.
George Talbot quoted in *Newsweek* (February 20, 1989).

Hell

There is many a boy here to-day who looks on war as all glory, but, boys, it is all hell. You can bear this warning voice to generations yet to come. I look upon war with horror.
General William T. Sherman, speech to the Grand Army of the Republic Convention in Columbus, Ohio, August 11, 1880. Paul F. Boller, Jr., and John George, *They Never Said It* (1989), state that when Sherman was asked about his "war is hell" comment, he "confessed he couldn't remember having said it." Nevertheless, it was widely reported in the newspapers of the time.

The humanizing of war! You might just as well talk of humanizing Hell!
Admiral Sir John Fisher quoted in W. T. Stead, "Character Sketch: Lord Fisher," *Review of Reviews* (February 1910).

Before we're through with 'em, the Japanese language will be spoken only in hell!
Admiral Halsey, on first viewing the damage caused by the Japanese attack on Pearl Harbor, quoted in William F. Halsey and J. Bryan III, *Admiral Halsey's Story* (1947).

heroes

Every hero becomes a bore at last.
Ralph Waldo Emerson, *Representative Men* (1850).

What is our task? To make Britain a fit country for heroes to live in.
Prime Minister David Lloyd George, *The Times* (London) (November 25, 1918).

We prefer to be widows of heroes rather than wives of cowards.
Dolores Ibarruri, October 14, 1936 speech in Madrid during the Spanish Civil War, reprinted in her *Speeches and Articles* (1938).

Heroes are created by popular demand, sometimes out of the scantiest materials, or none at all.
Gerald W. Johnson, *American Heroes and Hero-Worship* (1943).

We call Japanese soldiers fanatics when they die rather than surrender, whereas American soldiers who do the same thing are heroes.
Robert Maynard Hutchins, Commencement Address at the University of Chicago, June 15, 1945, reprinted in *Vital Speeches* (July 15, 1945).

The hero was distinguished by his achievement; the celebrity by his image or trademark. The hero created himself; the celebrity is created by the media. The hero was a big man; the celebrity is a big name.
Daniel J. Boorstin, *The Image* (1962).

On a trip to the West Coast, President Kennedy was asked by a little boy, "Mr. President, how did you become a war hero?"
"It was absolutely involuntary. They sank my boat."
Bill Adler, ed., *The Kennedy Wit* (1964).

An American reporter, experienced in Vietnam, once said to me, "I finally realized we'd never win this war when I noticed that all of the streets in Saigon were named after Vietnamese heroes who fought against foreign invaders."
Frances FitzGerald, *Fire in the Lake* (1972).

One reason that even many heroes of the past no longer seem quite so heroic is that the art of biography has changed for the better.
George F. Will, *Newsweek* (August 6, 1979).

It is in disaster, not success, that the heroes and the bums really get sorted out.
James Bond Stockdale, "In War, In Prison, In Antiquity," *Parameters* (December 1987).

heroism

Had the women of the Confederacy lived in a more heroic age, in which their sex put on armor and went forth to battle with dignity, it is possible that they would have produced real Amazons and Joans of Arc. Such conditions, however, did not exist in the middle of the nineteenth century, and the Southern women had to express the most of their heroism in less spectacular forms.
F. B. Simkins and J. W. Patton, *The Women of the Confederacy* (1936).

Probably the most famous incident of black heroism in the Indian Wars took place in 1879, when Company D, Ninth Cavalry, made a forced march of seventy miles to

reinforce a beleaguered column. During the rest of the siege at Milk Creek, Colorado, Henry Johnson attracted particular attention for his courage in carrying out his duties as a sergeant of the guard under fire and in helping to get water. He received the Medal of Honor, but his company won the highest accolade a white in the Victorian Age could bestow when one of the captains in the siege called them "the whitest men" he had ever seen.
Edward M. Coffman, *The Old Army* (1986).

The hero is rarely appreciated by anyone else. Courage is the hardest thing to forgive in wartime: heroism carries a stern rebuke for the unheroic.
René Quinton, *Soldier's Testament* (1930).

To go against the dominant thinking of your friends, of most of the people you see every day, is perhaps the most difficult act of heroism you can have.
Theodore H. White, *Columbia Journalism Review* (Winter 1969–70).

Nip determination, their refusal to say die, was commonly attributed to "fanaticism." In retrospect it is indistinguishable from heroism. To call it anything less cheapens the victory, for American valor was necessary to defeat it.
William Manchester, *Goodbye, Darkness* (1980).

Hitler, Adolf (1899–1945)

Papers all state Hitler is trying to copy Mussolini. Looks to me like it's the Ku Klux [Klan] that he is copying. He don't want to be emperor, he wants to be Kleagle.
Will Rogers, writing in 1933, *The Autobiography of Will Rogers*, ed. D. Day (1949).

The German dictator, instead of snatching the victuals from the table, has been content to have them served to him course by course.
Winston Churchill, speech on the Munich Agreement in the House of Commons, October 5, 1938.

Probably, in Hitler's own mind, the Russo-German Pact represents no more than an alteration of time-table. The plan laid down in *Mein Kampf* was to smash Russia first, with the implied intention of smashing England afterwards. Now, as it has turned out, England has got to be dealt with first, because Russia was the more easily bribed of the two. But Russia's turn will come when England is out of the picture—that, no doubt, is how Hitler sees it. Whether it will turn out that way is of course a different question.
George Orwell, *New English Weekly* (March 21, 1940).

I'm proud to be here to fight beside you. Now let's cut the guts out of those krauts and get the hell on to Berlin. And when we get to Berlin, I am going to personally shoot that paper-hanging goddammed son-of-a-bitch [Hitler] just like I would a snake.
General George S. Patton, Jr., speaking on July 6, 1944 upon his arrival in Normandy, France, quoted in Anthony Cave Brown, *Bodyguard of Lies* (1975).

When Herr Hitler escaped his bomb on 20 July he described his survival as providential; I think that from a purely military point of view we can all agree with him, for certainly it would be most unfortunate if the Allies were to be deprived in the closing phases of the struggle, of that form of warlike genius by which Corporal Schicklgruber has so notably contributed to our victory.
Winston Churchill, speech in the House of Commons, September 28, 1944.

Hitler was a profoundly *uneducated* man of genius; there could be nothing more dangerous, with such a criminal mentality in a position of power.
A. L. Rowse, *The Uses of History* (1948).

I have only one purpose, the destruction of Hitler, and my life is much simplified thereby. If Hitler invaded Hell I would make at least a favorable reference to the Devil in the House of Commons.
Winston Churchill, *The Second World War: The Grand Alliance* (1950).

The people Hitler never understood, and whose actions continued to exasperate him to the end of his life, were the British.
Alan Bullock, *Hitler* (1952).

A racing tipster who only reached Hitler's level of accuracy would not do well for his clients.
A. J. P. Taylor, *The Origins of the Second World War* (1961).

Hitler was the living personification of Dr. Jekyll and Mr. Hyde. As the one he raised Germany from out of the slough of degradation into which the Treaty of Versailles and the inflation which followed the French occupation of the Ruhr had engulfed her, and restored her national dignity and economy. As the other, he brutalized vast numbers of her people and made her name stink in the nostrils of the world.
J. F. C. Fuller, *The Conduct of War* (1961).

During my reunion with the Pope [in 1944], His Holiness took a few minutes to reminisce about the events in Germany when Hitler failed to seize power during the so-called beer hall putsch. All the foreign representatives at Munich, including Nuncio Pacelli [later to be Pope Pius XII], were convinced that Hitler's political career had ended ignominiously in 1924. When I ventured to remind His Holiness of this bit of history, he laughed and said, "I know what you mean—Papal infallibility. Don't forget I was only a monsignor then!"
Robert Murphy, *Diplomat Among Warriors* (1964).

Colonel General Vasili Sokolovskii ordered a dental check to be made of each body [thought to be Hitler]. Fritz Echtmann ... the dental technician who had worked in the offices of Hitler's dentist ... was asked to draw a sketch of Hitler's teeth. When he had finished, his interrogators disappeared into another room with the sketch. A short while later they were back. "It fits," Echtmann was told. Then the Russians showed the technician Hitler's entire lower jaw and dental bridges.
Cornelius Ryan, *The Last Battle* (1966).

Unpopular though this view may now be, I must state that I have no doubt that Hitler's decision to invade the Soviet Union was correct, because it was inevitable. While Moscow had no firm plans to attack us before the Polish campaign of 1939 ... by the time we attacked Russia in June 1941 the picture was very different: it was clear that Stalin had resolved to postpone his attack on his former ally only so long as was necessary to see us bleeding to death and exhausted after a conflict with the Western Allies.
General Reinhard Gehlen, *The Service* (1971).

At Victoria Station [they] gave me a travel warrant, a white feather and a picture of Hitler marked "This is your enemy." I searched every compartment but he wasn't on the train.
Spike Milligan, *Adolf Hitler: My Part in His Downfall* (1971).

While many of Hitler's decisions were militarily disastrous, his underlying ego-weakness and fear of criticism eventuated in several other traits which are undesirable, to say the least, in a senior military commander. He promoted his aides and advisors for their sycophancy rather than their ability—Jodl and Keitel were two such. He

refused to accept, believe or even listen to unpalatable intelligence. And when things went really wrong he was the first to find scapegoats.
Norman F. Dixon, *On the Psychology of Military Incompetence* (1976).

The Fuehrer is a man totally attuned to antiquity. He hates Christianity, because it has crippled all that is noble in humanity.... What a difference between the benevolent, smiling Zeus and the pain-wracked, crucified Christ. The ancient people's view of God was also much nobler and more humane than the Christians'. What a difference between a gloomy cathedral and a light airy ancient temple....
Joseph Goebbels, *The Goebbels Diaries: 1939–1941* (1983).

Clausewitz would have approved the efforts of Hitler in the early years to use his armed forces as instruments of his policy, but would have noted how the unlimited nature of his objectives made the war a total one far beyond his capacity to wage.
Michael Howard, *Clausewitz* (1983).

One's imagination boggled at what the German army might have done to us without Hitler working so effectively for our side.
General Elwood R. Quesada, U.S. Army Air Corps, commenting to Max Hastings on Hitler's interference with military decisions after the 1944 invasion of Normandy, *Overlord* (1984).

The Fuehrer, in one part of his wild-and-crafty mind, was a believer in wonder weapons, but most of the time he trusted only what he had learned to trust as a corporal in World War I: tanks, U-boats, and within limits the aircraft that Goering pushed for.... He was also profoundly wary of experts of all sorts and still more mistrustful of academic people. His view of nuclear physics, in particular, was hopelessly confused by his pathological and murderous anti-Semitism; Jewish physics, he called it.
McGeorge Bundy, *Danger and Survival* (1988).

holding action

[Confederate General] Hood, on October 5 [1864] attacked a fortified Union post at Allatoona Pass. [General William T.] Sherman pulled part of his force out of Atlanta to go after Hood. From this move rose the legend about Sherman sending a dispatch by signal to [General] John M. Corse, defending Allatoona, "Hold the fort for I am coming."
Allan Nevins, *The War for the Union*, VII (1971). According to Shelby Foote in *The Civil War*, III (1974), what Sherman actually signaled was "hold fast; we are coming." Journalists then created the now legendary "Hold the fort for I am coming."

[During World War I, Marshal French of Britain] was without hope. His last reserves had melted away in the furnace of the battle, his divisions were quite worn out, decimated and shaken. They were no longer capable of any prolonged resistance, there was nothing left but to die.
[General] Foch [of France] replied, "No, Monsieur le Marechal. The first thing of all to do is to hold out at all costs. Dying can come afterwards. Hold out till this evening. I will come to your aid.... If Wellington's infantry will no longer hold, today, entrenched, my lads will have to go." Marshal French replied that it would hold.
Major A. Grasset, introduction to Marshal Ferdinand Foch, *Precepts and Judgments* (1920).

Suppose you're a sergeant machine-gunner, and your army is retreating and the enemy advancing. The captain takes you to a machine gun covering the road. "You're to stay here and hold this position," he tells you. "For how long?" you ask. "Never mind," he answers, "just hold it." Then you know you're expendable—money or gas-

oline or equipment or most usually men. They are expending you and that machine gun to get time.
  William Lindsay White, *They Were Expendable* (1942).

Now, there's another thing I want you to remember: I don't want to get any messages saying that we're holding our position. We're not holding anything. We'll let the Hun do that. We are advancing constantly, and we're not interested in holding onto anything—except the enemy. We're going to kick him in the ass. We're going to kick the hell out of him all the time, and we're going to go through him like crap through a goose.
  George C. Scott in *Patton* (1970), directed by Franklin Schaffner; screenplay by Francis Ford Coppola and Edmund H. North based on Ladislas Farago's *Patton* and General Omar Bradley's *A Soldier's Story*.

Hollywood

RHETT: I think it's hard winning a war with words, gentlemen.
CHARLES: What do you mean, sir?
RHETT: I mean, Mr. Hamilton, there's not a cannon factory in the whole South.
MAN: What difference does that mean, sir, to a gentleman?
RHETT: I'm afraid it's going to make a great deal of difference to a great many gentlemen, sir.
CHARLES: Are you hintin', Mr. Butler, that the Yankees can lick us?
RHETT: No, I'm not hinting. I'm saying very plainly that the Yankees are better equipped than we. They've got factories, shipyards, coal mines and a fleet to bottle up our harbors and starve us to death. All we've got is cotton and slaves and arrogance.
CHARLES: Just listen to that renegade talk.
RHETT: I'm sorry if the truth offends you.
Gone With the Wind (1939), directed by Victor Fleming; screenplay by Sidney Howard from the novel by Margaret Mitchell.

Work on any picture will be suspended while any invasion attempt is being made so that David Niven may return to his regiment. Work will be resumed immediately the invasion attempt has failed.
  Movie contract clause for Captain David Niven of the Royal Army, quoted in *Newsweek* (July 7, 1941).

The Battle of San Pietro (1944) ... a poignant on-the-spot account of Allied attempts to capture a German-held Italian village, contrasted military objectives with human courage and carnage and pulled no punches. Death in action is plainly seen and there are some telling sequences showing bodies being wrapped in white "shrouds" and heaved around like sacks of flour. "These lives were valuable," says [John] Huston [the director] himself on the soundtrack. "Valuable to their loved ones, to their country, and to the men themselves. . . ." The film's deep-seated humanity and scenes of slaughter (of American troops significantly, not the enemy) caused the War Department to condemn it as pacifist and demoralizing ["It's against war," a general is supposed to have complained to Huston, who replied: "Well, sir, whenever I make a picture that's for war—why, I hope you take me out and shoot me"].
  Clyde Jeavons, *A Pictorial History of War Films* (1974).

When Bing Crosby returned to America after his visit to the French front, he told reporters, according to one news dispatch, that entertainment is needed most by the dispirited troops of the rear echelon rather than by the front-line soldiers. Up there, it

seemed to him, "morale is sky-high, clothes are cleaner and salutes really snap." The dogfaces who read that dispatch in the foxholes didn't know what front Bing was talking about.
Bill Mauldin, *Up Front* (1945).

When the wind was blowing hard at ninety degrees to the runway, instead of straight down the length as it did in fine weather, I saw Tyrone Power make five passes in an R5c before he got it down safely. Every pilot on the island seemed to know that a movie star was at the controls, and they came out in the rain to watch him and to take pleasure in his troubles.
Samuel Hynes, *Flights of Passage: Reflections of a World War II Aviator* (1988).

[During World War II] John [Ford] couldn't get [John] Wayne in [Ford's naval photography unit] as an enlisted man, much less as an officer. Wayne tried other avenues but couldn't get a commission. The only way he could get in the service was to enlist in the army as a private. He says today: "I felt that it would be a waste of time to spend two years picking up cigarette butts. I thought I could do more for the war effort if I stayed in Hollywood."
Dan Ford, *Pappy: The Life of John Ford* (1979).

Battle scenes in films often make people who have been in battles restless. On the screen there are particular conventions to be observed. Men blown up by high explosives in real war, for example, are often torn apart quite hideously; in films, there is a big bang and bodies, intact, fly through the air with the greatest of ease. If they are shot . . . they fall down like children in a game to lie motionless. The most harrowing thing in real battles is that they usually *don't* lie still; only the lucky ones are killed outright.
General Sir John Hackett, *The Times* (London) (March 20, 1983).

honor, national

The nurse of manly sentiment and heroic enterprise, is gone! It is gone, that sensibility of principle, that chastity of honor, which felt a stain like a wound, which inspired courage whilst it mitigated ferocity, which ennobled whatever it touched, and under which vice itself lost half of its evil by losing all its grossness!
Edmund Burke, *Reflections on the Revolution in France* (1790).

That nation is worthless which does not joyfully stake everything in defense of her honor.
Friedrich von Schiller, *The Maid of Orleans* (1801).

National honor is national property of the highest value.
President James Monroe, first Inaugural Address, March 4, 1817.

War is not merely justifiable, but imperative, upon honorable men, upon an honorable nation, where peace can only be obtained by the sacrifice of conscientious conviction or of national welfare.
President Theodore Roosevelt, Message to Congress, December 4, 1906.

A really great people, proud and high-spirited, would face all the disasters of war rather than purchase that base prosperity which is bought at the price of national honor.
President Theodore Roosevelt, speech at Harvard, February 23, 1907.

It is a false conclusion that wars are waged for the sake of material advantage. Modern wars are not fought for the sake of booty. Here the high moral ideal of national

honor is a factor handed down from one generation to another, enshrining something positively sacred, and compelling the individual to sacrifice himself to it.
Heinrich von Treitschke, *Politics* (1916).

There may at any moment come a time when I cannot preserve both the honor and the peace of the United States. Do not exact of me an impossible and contradictory thing.
President Woodrow Wilson, speech at Milwaukee, Wisconsin, January 21, 1916.

The nation's honor is dearer than the nation's comfort; yes, than the nation's life itself.
President Woodrow Wilson, speech at Cleveland, January 29, 1916.

When [General] MacArthur put out an order forbidding confiscation of Japanese officers' swords, [Admiral] Halsey was indignant. The next time he saw the general he protested, saying he considered the order unwise for two reasons. First, the sword, a symbol of militarism, would keep its spirit alive. He gave the example of Germany, where he had served as an attaché shortly after World War I. In many homes there he had seen a bust of Napoleon with a sword hung above it. Such displays, he was convinced, helped preserve in Germany the spirit of militarism that exploded into World War II.
"That's true," said MacArthur, "but I was thinking of Appomattox, when Grant allowed Lee's troops to keep their side arms."
"That brings me my second point," Halsey replied. "Grant was dealing with an honorable foe. We are not."
The general pondered a few moments, pacing his office. "You're right!" he exclaimed. "You're right! I'll revoke the order." He did.
E. B. Potter, *Bull Halsey* (1985).

It is said that we must carry on the war in Vietnam in order to preserve and defend our national honor. Our national honor is not at stake, and should not so readily be offered. In every other great war of the century, we have had the support of what is generally accepted as the decent opinion of mankind. We do not have that today. We cannot, of course, depend only on this opinion to prove our honor; it may not be sound. But always in the past we have not only had this support, but we have used it as a kind of justification for our actions.
Eugene J. McCarthy, *The Limits of Power* (1967).

We are told that the justification for their sacrifice is that it is necessary for "our national honor." Can we not see the sophistry in this position, when in fact our national honor is daily being soiled in the mud of Indochina?
Clark M. Clifford, *The National Observer* (December 30, 1972).

Prior to the defeat in Vietnam, most Americans had been content to think of themselves as honorable people, unerringly drawn to the side of what was true and noble and right—not the kind of people to push women and children away from the last helicopter out of town. If the war proved them wrong in this judgment, it was because the war was never honestly declared and because, at the end of it, nobody, certainly none of its official sponsors, could say why 58,000 American soldiers were dead and another 300,000 wounded. What could be said was that America had lost not only a war but also the belief in its virtue.
Lewis H. Lapham, "Vietnam Diary," *Harper's* (May 1989).

honor, personal

A prophet is not without honor, save in his own country, and in his own house.
The Bible, Matthew 13:57.

Of all I had, only honor and life have been spared.
Francis I (of France) on his defeat at the Battle of Pavia, February 24, 1525 from a letter to his
mother, Louise of Savoy. Often quoted as "All is lost save honor."

Mine honor is my life; both grow in one;
Take honor from me and my life is done.
William Shakespeare, *Richard II*, Act I (1595).

Honor pricks me on. Yea, but how if honor
prick me off when I come on? How then?
Can honor set a leg? No: or take away the
grief of a wound? No. Honor hath no skill
in surgery, then? No. What is honor? A
word. What is that word honor? Air. Who
hath it? He that died o'Wednesday. Doth
he feel it? No. Doth he hear it? No. It is
insensible, then? Yes, to the dead. But will
it not live with the living? No. Therefore
I'll none of it. Honor is a mere scutcheon;
and so ends my catechism.
Falstaff in William Shakespeare, *Henry IV*, Part I, Act V (1597).

Set honor in one eye and death i' the other,
And I will look on both indifferently:
For let the gods so speed me as I love
The name of honor more than I fear death.
William Shakespeare, *Julius Caesar*, Act I (1600).

My honor is dearer to me than my life.
Miguel Cervantes, *Don Quixote* (1604).

I would not love thee, dear, so much.
Loved I not honor more.
Richard Lovelace, "To Lucasta, on Going to the Wars" (1649).

War, he sung, is toil and trouble;
Honor but an empty bubble.
John Dryden, *Alexander's Feast* (1697).

And for the support of this Declaration, with a firm reliance on the Protection of
Divine Providence, we mutually pledge to each other our Lives, our Fortunes and our
sacred Honor.
Declaration of Independence, July 4, 1776.

I have just been offered two hundred and fifty thousand dollars and the most beautiful woman I have ever seen to betray my trust. I am depositing the money with the
Treasury of the United States and request immediate relief from this command. They
are getting close to my price.
Civil War dispatch from Colonel Arthur MacArthur (father of General Douglas MacArthur)
to the President of the United States, quoted in General Douglas MacArthur, *Reminiscences*
(1964).

But who of us could endure a world . . . without the divine folly of honor? . . . In the midst of doubt, in the collapse of creeds, there is one thing I do not doubt, and that is that the faith is true and adorable which leads a soldier to throw away his life in obedience to a blindly accepted duty, in a cause which he little understands, in a plan of campaign of which he has no notion, under tactics of which he does not see the use.
    Oliver Wendell Holmes, Jr., "The Soldier's Faith," speech at Harvard, reprinted in his *Speeches* (1913).

He has honor if he holds himself to an ideal of conduct though it is inconvenient, unprofitable, or dangerous to do so.
    Walter Lippmann, *A Preface to Morals* (1929).

There may be very many reported missing who will come back home, someday, in one way or another. In the confusion of this fight it is inevitable that many have been left in positions where honor required no further resistance from them.
    Winston Churchill, speech to House of Commons on the Dunkirk evacuation, June 4, 1940.

[Field Marshal Douglas] Haig was an honorable man according to his lights—but his lights were dim.
    B. H. Liddell Hart, *Why Don't We Learn From History?* (1943).

The choice of death or dishonor is one which has always faced the professional fighting man, and there must be no doubt in his mind what his answer must be. He chooses death for himself so that his country may survive, or on a grander scale so that the principles for which he is fighting may survive. Now we are facing a somewhat different situation, when the reply is not to be given by individuals but by countries as a whole. Is it right for the Government of a country to choose complete destruction of the population rather than some other alternative, however unpleasant that alternative may be?
    Lt. General Sir John Cowley, "Future Trends in Warfare," *Journal of the Royal United Service Institution* (February 1960).

Not long ago, unexpectedly, I had a telegram from a very happy young man. I remembered this boy well because during my last year as president of the Citadel, the military college of South Carolina, he had been found guilty of an infraction of the honor system, and we had to dismiss him.
    The honor system, as it functions at the Citadel, does not bend. If you intentionally violate it, you have to leave. But I have never felt that one misstep should condemn a young man permanently. And so, in almost all cases, I did my best to help such youngsters—there weren't many—to gain admission to another college, or get another chance, where they could make a fresh start.
    This policy almost always was vindicated, and certainly it was in this case because the lad had just been commissioned in the U.S. Army. "Wish you could be here," the telegram said, "to help me celebrate my return to honor."
    General Mark Clark, "Recapturing What Honor Really Means," *Rocky Mountain News* (May 5, 1984). This article was originally written for the *North American Newspaper Alliance* in 1968.

I cannot give you an easy answer to the objections raised by those who consider intelligence work incompatible with democratic principles. The nation must to a degree take it on faith that we too are honorable men devoted to her service. I can assure you that we are, but I am precluded from demonstrating it to the public.
    Richard Helms, Director of the Central Intelligence Agency, *The New York Times* (April 15, 1971).

hostages

I do not fear England; Canada is a hostage for her good behavior; but I do fear some of the other powers.
Theodore Roosevelt, May 3, 1897 letter to Alfred T. Mahan, *The Letters of Theodore Roosevelt*, ed. E. E. Morison, I (1951).

[The doctrine of Mutual Assured Destruction] rests on a form of warfare universally condemned since the Dark Ages—the mass killing of hostages.
Fred C. Ikle, "Can Nuclear Deterrence Last Out the Century?" *Foreign Policy* (January 1973).

If I should ever be captured, I want no negotiation—and if I should request a negotiation from captivity they should consider that a sign of duress.
Henry Kissinger, *U.S. News and World Report* (October 7, 1985).

One difference between French appeasement and American appeasement is that France pays ransom in cash and gets its hostages back while the United States pays ransom in arms and gets additional hostages taken.
William Safire, *The New York Times* (November 13, 1986).

Huns

It was during the retreat from Orleans that a Christian hermit is reported to have approached the Hunnish king [Attila] and said to him "Thou art the Scourge of God for the chastisement of Christians." Attila instantly assumed this new title of terror, which thenceforth became the appellation by which he was most widely and most fearfully known.
Sir Edward Creasey, *Fifteen Decisive Battles of the Western World* (1851).

You must know, my men, that you are about to meet a crafty, well-armed cruel foe. Meet him and beat him! Give no quarter! Take no prisoners! Kill him, when he falls into your hands! Even as, a thousand years ago, the Huns under their King Attila made such a name for themselves as still resounds in terror . . . so may the name of Germany resound through Chinese history a thousand years from now.
Kaiser William II, in a speech to his troops at the time of the 1900 Boxer Rebellion in China, quoted in Emil Ludwig, *Wilhelm Hohenzollern* (1926). It was the Kaiser himself who first created the modern image of "the Hun."

For all we have and are,
for all our children's fate,
stand up and take the war.
The Hun is at the gate!
Rudyard Kipling, *For All We Have and Are* (1914).

A Hun alive is a war in prospect.
Winston Churchill, speaking on October 13, 1940, quoted in John Colville, *The Fringes of Power* (1985).

The Huns were Asiatic nomads who dashed into Europe on mangy little ponies in the fourth century A.D. and started a crime wave.
Will Cuppy, *The Decline and Fall of Practically Everybody* (1950).

I learned within a few seconds the truth of the old warning, "Beware of the Hun in the Sun." I was making pleasant little sweeps from side to side, and peering earnestly into my mirror when, from out of the sun and dead astern, bullets started appearing along my port wing. There is an appalling tendency to sit and watch this happen with-

out taking any action, as though mesmerized by a snake; but I managed to pull myself together and go into a spin.
Richard Hillary, RAF pilot writing on August 17, 1940, quoted in Len Deighton, *Battle of Britain* (1980).

The [British] government purchased 25,000 revolvers from the United States to distribute to constables and policemen to repel Nazi invaders. If the attack ever did come, Churchill had already decided upon the final sentence of his call to eternal resistance. "The hour has come; kill the Hun."
William K. Klingaman, *1941* (1988).

Every Hun has value—even if only to serve as a bad example.
Wess Roberts, *Leadership Secrets of Attila the Hun* (1989).

incompetence

There are field-marshals who would not have shone at the head of cavalry regiments, and vice versa.
Karl von Clausewitz, *On War* (1832).

There are plenty of carefree generals, who are never worried nor harassed. They do not bother about anything. They say, "I advance. Follow me." The result is an incredible disorder.
Ardant du Picq, *Battle Studies* (1868).

It is not that generals and admirals are incompetent, but that the task has passed beyond their competence. Their limitations are due not to a congenital stupidity—as a disillusioned public is so apt to assume—but to the growth of science, which has upset the foundations of their technique.
B. H. Liddell Hart, *Thoughts on War* (1944).

Men were taken on the Staff [in World War I] because they were liked and if a General was relieved of his command another post was immediately found for him. At first this had worried me, too often I saw the results on stretchers. Now I have come to see that this immense toleration is just English. It is not found among dominion troops, it is not Irish nor Scotch but only English. That is where we differ from the Prussians, we are tolerant of everything. And this attitude is impossible where there exists a relentless demand for efficiency.
Lord Moran, *The Anatomy of Courage* (1945).

Any historian of warfare knows it is in good part a comedy of errors and a museum of incompetence.
Richard Hofstadter, *The Paranoid Style in American Politics* (1965).

The supreme form of bad generalship, one might say, is to have every advantage in one's hands—the world's best army, not a few of its best generals, and enemies, such as Russia and the democracies, whose interests naturally diverge—and then

through pure arrogance, through actions which are mere wasteful display or wanton provocation, to blow the whole game. Hitler did so.
Charles Fair, *From the Jaws of Victory* (1971).

Normally, it is not possible for an army simply to dismiss incompetent generals. The very authority which their office bestows upon generals is the first reason for this. Moreover, the generals form a clique, tenaciously supporting each other, all convinced that they are the best possible representatives of the army. But we can at least give them capable assistants. Thus the General Staff officers are those who support incompetent generals, providing the talents that might otherwise be wanting among leaders and commanders.
General Gerhard von Scharnhorst quoted in T. N. Dupuy, *A Genius For War* (1977).

infantry

The infantry must ever be regarded and valued as the very foundation and nerve of an army.
Niccolò Machiavelli, *The Discourses* (1517).

Infantry is the nerve of an army.
Francis Bacon, *Essays* (1625).

Infantry is the Queen of Battles.
Attributed to Sir William Napier, 1785–1860.

The better the infantry is, the more it should be used carefully and supported with good batteries. Good infantry is, without doubt, the sinew of an army; but if it is forced to fight for a long time against a very superior artillery it will become demoralized and will be destroyed.
Napoleon I, *Military Maxims* (1827).

"There," said Wellington, pointing to the small scarlet figure [a British soldier], "There, it all depends upon that article whether we do the business or not. Give me enough of it, and I am sure."
Duke of Wellington, speaking a few weeks before the Battle of Waterloo, quoted in Thomas Creevey, *The Creevey Papers* (1934).

They dashed on towards that thin red line tipped with steel.
William Howard Russell, *The British Expedition to the Crimea* (1877). This was a description of a Russian cavalry charge at the 93rd Highlanders on October 25, 1854 at Balaclava. As Russell originally reported it in *The Times* (of London) on November 15, 1854: "Gathering speed at every stride, they dash on towards that thin red streak topped with a line of steel."

All great wars will, as heretofore, depend chiefly on the infantry. . . . Earth-forts, and especially field-works, will hereafter play an important part in wars, because they enable a minor force to hold a superior one in check for a time, and time is a most valuable element in all wars.
General William T. Sherman, *Memoirs* (1885).

When [General Walter] Krueger found an infantryman with untreated blisters, athlete's foot, or leaky socks, the soldier's noncoms lost their stripes and his officers got official reprimands. We in the lower echelons sort of loved the crusty old boy, were delighted to learn that he had enlisted as a private and risen through the ranks, and were not surprised when later he turned out to be one of the most distinguished generals in the Pacific.
Bill Mauldin, writing in 1941 in *The Brass Ring* (1971).

The successive steps of infantry combat are summarized by the expression "Find 'em, fix 'em, and fight 'em."
General Terry Allen, *The New Yorker* (April 24, 1943).

I love the infantry because they are the underdogs. They are the mud-rain-and-wind boys. They have no comforts, and they even learn to live without the necessities. And in the end they are the guys that wars can't be won without.
Ernie Pyle, *New York World Telegram* (May 5, 1943).

The way to remain prepared for any future war . . . is to keep a careful eye on the balance between firepower and mobility. In our time this means the recognition that ground warfare has become three-dimensional and that air mobility is a critical factor on the battlefield. The infantryman of future fights will take the high ground by air assault.
John R. Galvin, *Air Assault* (1969).

Being shelled is the real work of an infantry soldier, which no one talks about. Everyone has his own way of going about it. In general, it means lying face down and contracting your body into as small a space as possible. In novels you read about soldiers, at such moments, fouling themselves. The opposite is true. As all your parts are contracting, you are more likely to be constipated.
Louis Simpson, *Air with Armed Men* (1972).

One of my questions to the general [Mark Clark] was, "Could he see any similarities between the foot soldiers of World War I and II?"
There was a mark of sorrow in his eyes as he answered.
"They both did what a soldier has to know how to do very well."
"What is that?" I asked.
"Die," he answered.
Henry Berry, *Make the Kaiser Dance* (1978).

They were called grunts, and many of them, however grudgingly, were proud of the name. They were the infantrymen, the foot soldiers of the war.
Bernard Edelman, *Dear America: Letters Home from Vietnam* (1985).

The infantry doesn't change. We're the only arm [of the military] where the weapon is the man himself.
General C. T. Shortis quoted in *The New York Times* (February 4, 1985).

I am only a dumb infantryman trying to make a living as a commander in Europe, and with only 10 days to go [to retirement].
General Bernard W. Rogers, NATO Commander, *The Washington Post* (June 18, 1987).

Soldiers . . . don't have to be hit with bullets to respect them. The snap and crack of rounds going overhead is strong incentive toward keeping one's head down. Which prevents him from firing at you. Which allows a fire team to maneuver, then a squad, then a platoon. And that's how victories on the battlefield are fashioned when the war is between infantrymen.
J. D. Coleman, *Pleiku* (1988).

insubordination

"Do you know," said he [Admiral Horatio Nelson] to Mr. Ferguson, "what [signal flag] is shown on board the commander-in-chief? No. 39!" Mr. Ferguson asked what that meant?—"Why, to leave off action! Now damn me if I do! You know, Foley," turning to the captain, "I have only one eye,—I have a right to be blind sometimes,"—

and then putting the glass to his blind eye, in the mood of mind which sports with bitterness, he exclaimed, "I really do not see the signal!" Presently he exclaimed, "Damn the signal! Keep mine for closer battle flying! That's the way I answer such signals. Nail mine to the mast!"
Robert Southey, on the April 2, 1801 Battle of Copenhagen, *Life of Nelson* (1813).

Thousands of moralists have solemnly repeated the old saw that only he can command who has learnt to obey. It would be nearer the truth to say that only he can command who has the courage and the initiative to disobey.
William McDougall, *Character and Conduct of Life* (1937).

Rules are mostly made to be broken and are too often for the lazy to hide behind.
General Douglas MacArthur quoted in William A. Ganoe, *MacArthur Close-Up* (1962).

It's the orders you disobey that make you famous.
General Douglas MacArthur quoted in William Manchester, *American Caesar* (1978).

I felt uneasy but sometimes, like I said before, I believed in Colonel North and there was a very solid and very valid reason he must have been doing this for and sometimes you have to go above the written law, I believe.
Testimony of Fawn Hall, Lt. Colonel Oliver North's secretary, during the 1987 Iran-Contra Congressional hearings, quoted in William S. Cohen and George J. Mitchell, *Men of Zeal* (1988).

insurgency

Everybody . . . will seek a military solution to the insurgency problem, whereas by its very nature, the insurgency problem is militarily only in a secondary sense, and politically, ideologically, and administratively in a primary sense. Once we understand this, we will understand more of what is actually going on in Viet-Nam.
Bernard B. Fall, "The Theory and Practice of Insurgency. . .," *Naval War College Review* (April 1965).

The basic military strategy . . . must be to insert as many as possible of the government forces, both military and paramilitary, into the same element as the insurgent forces to which they are opposed. If they are not so engaged, then they are being wasted. . . .
Getting government forces into the same element as the insurgent is rather like trying to deal with a tomcat in an alley. It is no good inserting a large, fierce dog. The dog may not find the tomcat; if he does, the tomcat will escape to a tree; the dog will then chase the female cats in the alley. The answer is to put in a fiercer tomcat. The two cannot fail to meet because they are both in exactly the same element and have exactly the same purpose in life. The weaker will be eliminated.
Sir Robert G. K. Thompson, *Defeating Communist Insurgency* (1966).

insurrection

Insurrection—by means of guerrilla bands—is the true method of warfare for all nations desirous of emancipating themselves from a foreign yoke. This method of warfare supplies the want—inevitable at the commencement of the insurrection—of a regular army; it calls the greatest number of elements into the field, and yet may be sustained by the smallest number. It forms the military education of the people, and consecrates every foot of the native soil by the memory of some warlike deed.
Giuseppe Mazzini, *General Instructions for Members of Young Italy* (1831).

When an insurrection is justifiable, an answer can seldom be given beforehand. The result decides. When treason prospers, none dare call it treason.
James Bryce, *The American Commonwealth* (1888).

Insurrection is an art, and like all arts it has its laws.
Leon Trotsky, *History of the Russian Revolution* (1932).

Insurrection is an art quite as much as war.
Karl Marx quoted in J. F. C. Fuller, *The Conduct of War* (1961).

intelligence

It is essential to know the character of the enemy and of their principal officers—whether they be rash or cautious, enterprising or timid, whether they fight on principle or from chance.
Vegetius, *De Re Militari* (378 A.D.).

And in such indexes, although small pricks
to their subsequent volumes, there is seen
The baby figure of the giant mass
Of things to come at large.
William Shakespeare, *Troilus and Cressida*, Act I (1601).

Great advantage is drawn from knowledge of your adversary, and when you know the measure of his intelligence and character you can use it to play on his weaknesses.
Frederick the Great, *Instructions for His Generals* (1747).

Nothing is so contradictory and nonsensical as this mass of reports brought in by spies and officers sent on scouting missions. The former see corps in place of mere detachments, the latter report weak detachments in places where corps are present. Often they do not even report their own eyesight, but only repeat that which they have heard from panic-stricken or surprised people. To draw the truth from this mass of chaotic reports is something vouchsafed only to a superior understanding.
Napoleon I quoted in Martin van Creveld, *Command in War* (1985).

A great part of the information obtained in war is contradictory, a still greater part is false, and by far the greatest part somewhat doubtful. What is required of an officer in this case is a certain power of discrimination, which only knowledge of men and things and good judgment can give.
Karl von Clausewitz, *On War* (1832).

If I took your gloomy view, I should commence immediate inquiries as to the most painless form of suicide. But I think you listen too much to the soldiers. No lesson seems to be so deeply inculcated by the experience of life as that you never should trust in experts. If you believe the doctors nothing is wholesome; if you believe the theologians nothing is innocent; if you believe the soldiers nothing is safe. They all require to have their strong wine diluted by a very large admixture of insipid common sense.
Lord Salisbury, June 15, 1877 letter to Lord Lytton, Viceroy of India, quoted in Bernard Brodie, *War and Politics* (1973); Samuel P. Huntington, *The Soldier and the State* (1957).

Stimson, as Secretary of State, was dealing as a gentleman with the gentlemen sent as ambassadors and ministers from friendly nations, and, as he later said, "Gentlemen do not read each other's mail."
Henry L. Stimson and McGeorge Bundy, *On Active Service in Peace and War* (1948). This was Stimson's explanation for the 1929 dismantling of the U.S. government's only secret intelligence (code-breaking) capabilities.

When the fate of a nation and the lives of its soldiers are at stake, gentlemen do read each other's mail—if they can get their hands on it.
Allen Dulles, *The Craft of Intelligence* (1963).

[On June 7, 1944] "as we reached the middle of the [Utah] beach there was the drone of airplane motors and almost immediately afterwards machinegun fire as they swept immediately over us down the beach. The General [William J. Donovan, head of the OSS], accustomed to such emergencies, rolled nimbly off the hood where we were sitting, onto the sand. . . ."
While lying in the sand, Donovan remarked to [David] Bruce [of the OSS]: "By the way, David, have you arranged to be buried in Arlington Cemetery?"
Bruce replied: "Why, no."
"Well," said Donovan, as he was getting up and brushing off the sand, "I have; that's where I want to be buried. David, you've got to get a plot near mine. Then we can start an Underground together."
Anthony Cave Brown, *The Last Hero* (1982).

After the war, when I [a U-Boat captain] got to know the mysterious "Remy" [of the French Resistance] personally, I asked him among other things: "How did you actually get to know the exact dates when my boat returned from and sailed for patrol, which the British then trumpeted to all the world?"
He laughed. "We got the tip from the laundry."
"From the laundry? How was that possible?"
"Look," Remy continued. "One of our women agents worked there and kept her eye on you. From your boat's bed linen which you brought to be washed and fetched only when about to sail she could tell exactly when you had returned and that you were intending to go out again on a long patrol. Then she reported to us. . . ."
Peter Cremer, *U-Boat Commander* (1984).

Expect only five per cent of an intelligence report to be accurate. The trick of a good commander is to isolate the five per cent.
General Douglas MacArthur quoted in Courtney Whitney, *MacArthur* (1956).

Question: Senator, you were promised a military intelligence briefing from the President. Have you received that?
Mr. Kennedy: Yes. I talked on Thursday morning to General Wheeler from the Defense Department.
Question: What was his first name?
Mr. Kennedy: He didn't brief me on that.
Presidential candidate John F. Kennedy, press conference, September 4, 1960.

If someone comes in to tell me this or that about the minimum wage bill, I have no hesitation in overruling them. But you always assume that the military and intelligence people have some secret skill not available to ordinary mortals.
President John F. Kennedy quoted in Arthur M. Schlesinger, Jr., *A Thousand Days* (1965).

Americans have always had an ambivalent attitude toward intelligence. When they feel threatened, they want a lot of it, and when they don't, they regard the whole thing as somewhat immoral.
General Vernon A. Walters, *Silent Missions* (1978).

Intelligence traditionally represented the most gentlemanly war work. . . . At the higher levels, the cryptanalytic work was intensely enjoyable. Being paid, or otherwise rewarded, seemed almost a curiosity. It was also something of a holiday even from professional mathematics, for the kind of work required was more on the line of

ingenious application of elementary ideas, rather than pushing back the frontiers of scientific knowledge. It was like a solid diet of the hard puzzles in the New Statesman, with the difference that no one knew that solutions existed.
Andrew Hodges, *Alan Turing: The Enigma* (1983).

Just who "the gooks" were, they didn't know, and didn't want to know. You could have asked any American senior officer in Korea: "Who commands the Korean 42nd division—ROK or Communist—and what's his background?" He wouldn't have known what you were talking about. A good is a gook. But if the Germans had been the enemy, he'd have known.
Colonel Fred Ladd quoted in Max Hastings, *The Korean War* (1987).

intelligence agencies

So it was not until 1909, in Britain, that the first intelligence agency came into being, a government department, financed from government funds, its employees largely civilians, created to steal secrets from other countries and to protect its own, empowered to operate in peace as well as in war. Once invented, the intelligence agency turned out be a bureaucrat's dream.
Phillip Knightley, *The Second Oldest Profession* (1986).

Ah, those first OSS arrivals in London! How well I remember them, arriving like *jeunes filles en fleur* straight from a finishing school, all fresh and innocent, to start work in our frowsy old intelligence brothel.
Malcolm Muggeridge quoted in William Casey, *The Secret War Against Hitler* (1988).

It is the duty of every sophisticated intelligence service to keep open a channel of communication with the enemy's intelligence service. Perhaps it may sound strange that . . . I was able to keep such channels active during the Third Reich—although it might have cost me my neck.
General Reinhard Gehlen, *The Service* (1971).

CIA (Central Intelligence Agency)
In 2½ years of working with these men I have yet to meet a "007."
President Lyndon B. Johnson, speech at the White House, June 30, 1966.

The CIA has become a sort of mythical monster. When something happens, like the fall of [Prince Norodom] Sihanouk in Cambodia, the first reaction is to blame the CIA. And it is true that the United States has gone to the extreme of playing a dominating role almost everywhere in the world. People react to this role in different degrees—doubt, repulsion, hate, admiration, a mixture of all sorts of feelings. The CIA is the dark side of the American imperium.
Raymond Aron, *The Christian Science Monitor* (May 22, 1970).

Dirty tricks form about 5 per cent of the C.I.A.'s work—and we must have full control over dirty tricks.
Dean Rusk, *The New York Times* (January 22, 1971).

The CIA has three major functions: science and technological work, analysis, and the clandestine collection of intelligence. Now, there's been a fourth responsibility, and that is positively influencing a situation through political or paramilitary means. That's the one that goes up and down, depending on national policy. Right now it's way down.
William E. Colby, Director of the CIA, *Time* (September 30, 1974).

I think the American people support the concept of a strong Central Intelligence Agency, and if they don't, they'd better. . . .
George Bush, Director of the CIA, *The New York Times* (May 9, 1976).

The CIA is made up of boys whose families sent them to Princeton but wouldn't let them into the family brokerage business.
President Lyndon B. Johnson quoted in *People* (February 2, 1987).

The CIA is three-headed: The technical side, the analysts and the spooks.
Admiral Stansfield Turner, Former Director of the CIA, *Newsweek* (October 12, 1987).

Although the CIA attempts to disguise the identities of its rank-and-file officers in Moscow, the KGB knows who the station chief is—because it approves him in advance. Under a little-known practice the chief of the CIA's Moscow station is, in effect, subject to an *agreement* by Moscow, in much the same fashion that a new American ambassador must be approved before being dispatched to the Soviet Union. In turn, the CIA approves the KGB resident in Washington.
David Wise, *The Spy Who Got Away* (1988).

OSS (Office of Strategic Services)
Gen. "Wild Bill" Donovan—of the Office of Strategic Service, sometime called the "Cloak and Dagger Club," or "Oh So Social," will miss Roosevelt terribly. Donovan ran the giant espionage outfit which tried to find out what was going on behind enemy lines, and he had accumulated the most bizarre assortment of female spies, social register bluebloods and anti-Roosevelt haters ever seen in Washington. As an old personal friend, Roosevelt gave him free reign, including grandiose plans . . . for a postwar-espionage service. Truman does not like peacetime espionage and will not be so lenient.
Drew Pearson, *The Washington Post* (April 27, 1945).

[David] Bruce made [Ernest] Hemingway an honorary OSS officer and . . . they joined the advance units entering the capital in the hope of being the first Americans in Paris. While Generals de Gaulle and Leclerc, whose troops had decided the issue, formally received the German surrender, and while the communist resistance, which had begun the uprising and had borne the brunt of the casualties, buried its dead, the OSS officers took their men down the Champs-Elysees to the Ritz Hotel. The manager looked at them askance and asked if there was anything they wanted: "How about seventy-three dry martinis", Hemingway replied.
Phillip Knightley, *The Second Oldest Profession* (1986).

The OSS was always regarded as an amateur set-up, an unfair assessment because the Americans have always been quick to learn from their own mistakes. By the end of World War II the OSS was a force to be reckoned with. . . . There was no reason why the OSS should not have been maintained as a permanent intelligence service, but it was vetoed by President Truman, a Jekyll and Hyde character, despite all attempts to portray him as a normal well-balanced American.
Richard Deacon, *Spyclopaedia* (1987).

It is no exaggeration to say that Donovan created the OSS against the fiercest kind of opposition from everybody—the Army, Navy, and State Departments, the Joint Chiefs of Staff, regular army brass, the whole Pentagon bureaucracy, and, perhaps most devastatingly, the White House staff.
William Casey, *The Secret War Against Hitler* (1988).

intelligence, definitions of

All the business of war, and indeed all the business of life, is to endeavor to find out what you don't know by what you do; that's what I called "guessing what was at the other side of the hill".
Duke of Wellington quoted in John Wilson Croker, *The Croker Papers* (1884).

Military intelligence is a contradiction in terms.
Attributed to Groucho Marx, 1950s.

Intelligence is at best an imprecise science. It is not like counting beans; it is more like estimating cockroaches.
General William C. Westmoreland, *The Christian Science Monitor* (January 27, 1982).

The intelligence process is often like a jigsaw puzzle. That is, the picture becomes clear long before the last piece is put in.
William E. Colby, Former Director of the CIA, testimony before U.S. Senate Committee on Foreign Relations, January 15, 1987.

international relations

The features of history are virile, unsuited to sentimental or feminine natures. Brave people alone have an existence, an evolution or a future; the weak and cowardly perish, and perish justly. The grandeur of history lies in the perpetual conflict of nations, and it is simply foolish to desire the suppression of their rivalry.
Heinrich von Treitschke, *Politics* (1916).

Living next to you is in some ways like sleeping with an elephant. No matter how friendly and even-tempered is the beast, if I can call it that, one is affected by every twitch and grunt.
Pierre Elliott Trudeau, Prime Minister of Canada, speaking of U.S. relations, *The New York Times* (March 26, 1969).

The contracting parties undertake to refrain in their international relations from the threat or use of force, and to settle their international disputes by peaceful means so as not to endanger international peace and security.
Article 1 of The Warsaw Pact Treaty of 1955.

[In 1959 Vice President Richard] Nixon went to the Kremlin for a courtesy call on Khrushchev. . . .
He opened up by telling Nixon that he knew all about him—he was the enemy of the Soviet Union, the enemy of Communism, the white knight of Capitalism.
Nixon conceded that he didn't like Communism but as for Capitalism, well, he had grown up a poor boy, working in a small orchard, doing all the chores. Khrushchev snorted. He, Khrushchev, had grown up the poorest of the poor. He had walked barefoot. He had had no shoes. He had shoveled shit to earn a few kopeks. Nixon shot back that he'd been poor and barefoot, too—and had shoveled shit.
What kind of shit? Khrushchev demanded. Horseshit, Nixon said. That's nothing, Khrushchev replied. He had shoveled cow shit—loose, runny, stinking cow dung. It got between your toes. I too shoveled cow shit, Nixon said tightly.
Well, Khrushchev grumbled, maybe Nixon had shoveled cow shit once or twice, but he, Khrushchev, has shoveled human shit. That was the worst. Nixon couldn't top that.
Harrison E. Salisbury, *A Time of Change* (1988).

The Game of nations . . . differs from other games . . . in several important respects. First, each player has his own aims, different from those of the others, which constitute "winning"; second, every player is forced by his own domestic circumstances to make moves in the Game which have nothing to do with winning and which, indeed, might impair chances of winning; third, in the Game of nations there are no winners, only losers. The objective of each player is not so much to win as to avoid loss.

The common objective of players in the game of nations is merely to keep the Game going. The alternative to the Game is war.

Egyptian Vice President Zakaria Mohieddin, speaking before the Egyptian War College in 1962, quoted in Miles Copeland, *The Game of Nations* (1969).

We intend to remain alive. Our neighbors want to see us dead. This is not a question that leaves much room for compromise.

Golda Meir, Prime Minister of Israel, quoted in Israel and Mary Shenker, *As Good As Golda* (1970).

The central fact about international politics is that power is not controlled, since there is no authority capable of controlling it.

Abba Eban, *The New Diplomacy* (1983).

My view is that President Gorbachev is different from previous Soviet leaders. I think he knows some of the things wrong with his society and is trying to fix them. We wish him well. And we'll continue to work to make sure that the Soviet Union that eventually emerges from this process is a less threatening one.

What it all boils down to is this: I want the new closeness to continue. And it will so long as we make it clear that we will continue to act in a certain way as long as they continue to act in a helpful manner. If and when they don't—at first pull your punches. If they persist, pull the plug.

It's still trust—but verify.

It's still play—but cut the cards.

President Ronald Reagan, Farewell Address, January 11, 1989.

While keeping our alliances and friendships around the world strong, ever strong, we will continue the new closeness with the Soviet Union, consistent both with our security and with progress. One might say that our new relationship in part reflects the triumph of hope and strength over experience. But hope is good. And so is strength, and vigilance.

President George Bush, Inaugural Address, January 20, 1989.

interservice rivalry

But it [Pearl Harbor], and the subsequent lessons we learned, day by day, until September 1945, should have taught all military men that our military forces are one team—in the game to win regardless of who carries the ball. This is no time for "fancy dans" who won't hit the line with all they have on every play, unless they can call the signals. Each player on this team—whether he shines in the spotlight of the backfield or eats dirt in the line—must be an all-American.

General Omar Bradley, testimony before the House Armed Service Committee, October 19, 1949.

The President [Roosevelt]—who was an old Navy man—continually made it plain that in an even argument he would be inclined to favor the Navy's case against that of the Army. This nettled [General George C.] Marshall, but he kept his mouth shut until

one day Roosevelt's naval bias was so obvious that he blurted out, "At least, Mr. President, stop speaking of the Army as 'they' and the Navy as 'us.' "
Leonard Mosley, *Marshall* (1982).

When a breathless junior officer reported the enemy had just successfully launched the first man-made satellite, his superior, an Air Force general—so the story goes—blanched and asked which one, the Navy or the Army?
John C. Ries, *The Management of Defense* (1964).

My pet gripe is that we have four tactical air forces: Army, Navy and Marines, as well as the Air Force itself. This is one of the glaring examples of repetition that we don't need.... We're the only country that does. It's political. You have the Army fighting the idea that the Air Force should do it. The Air Force fights the idea that anybody else but the Air Force should do it.
Senator Barry Goldwater, *U.S. News and World Report* (October 15, 1973).

When I was in the Pentagon, I suppose that 80 to 90 percent of the secrecy in the Navy was to keep the secrets from the Army and the Air Force.
Admiral Gene LaRocque quoted in Gwynne Dyer, *War* (1985).

The rivalry among the branches of our services—the Navy, Army, Air Force, Marines—is legendary, as anyone who has served in the armed forces can tell you. Most Americans believe that one branch of our armed forces would rather win a fight with another branch than win a battle with one of our nation's adversaries.
Representative Toby Roth, speech in the House of Representatives, October 16, 1985.

[In Vietnam] there was the competition between the air force and navy, which sometimes led to the misuse of men and equipment, and, if not to outright lying, then to exaggerated claims about the damage inflicted during air strikes. One manifestation of the competition was in the sortie rate—a sortie being one round-trip combat flight by one airplane—which was used as a measuring stick to show how hard each service was working to win the war. When a bomb shortage occurred in early 1966, both the air force and the navy sent their planes up with only one or two bombs per plane, to keep their sortie rate high and prevent their competitor from getting ahead in the statistics game.
Zalin Grant, *Over the Beach* (1986).

intervention

We Americans can't seem to get it that you can't commit rape a little.
Lincoln Steffens on the 1914 U.S. intervention in Mexico, *The Autobiography of Lincoln Steffens* (1931).

It has seemed to us that it is our role to intervene in world affairs with sporadic and violent bursts of energy and with decisive and definitive effect—to appear on the scene in the nick of time like a knight errant, rescue the lady, and ride away.
But the experience brought its disillusionment. The lady did not remain as glamorous; she did not even seem particularly grateful; she became demanding. And then, too, there was no secure and serene place to ride to.
Former Secretary of State Dean Acheson, Introduction to Louis J. Halle, *Civilization and Foreign Policy* (1955).

It is only since the French Revolution of 1789 and the rise of the nation-state that the legitimacy of intervention has been questioned. Article 119 of the French Constitution of 1793 declared that the French people "do not interfere in the domestic affairs of other nations and will not tolerate interference by other nations in their affairs."

This declaration ushered in a period of interventions by all concerned on the largest possible scale.
Hans J. Morgenthau, "To Intervene or Not to Intervene," *Foreign Affairs* (April 1967).

The Soviet people are under no obligation to ask for permission to intervene when issues of world peace and the freedom and independence of peoples are involved. That is our right as a world power.
Soviet Foreign Minister Andrei A. Gromyko, speaking after the 1968 Soviet invasion of Czechoslovakia, quoted in *The New York Times* (July 4, 1989).

Social and political orders in one country or another changed in the past and may change in the future. But this change is the exclusive affair of the people of that country and is their choice. Any interference in domestic affairs and any attempts to restrict the sovereignty of states—friends, allies or any others—are inadmissible.
Mikhail Gorbachev, speech to the Council of Europe in Strasbourg, France, *The New York Times* (July 7, 1989).

invasion

It may be laid down as a principle that in invading a country with two or three armies, each of which has its own distinct line of operations extending towards a fixed point at which all are to unite, the union of the different corps should never be ordered to take place in the vicinity of the enemy, as by concentrating his forces he may not only prevent their junction but also defeat them one by one.
Napoleon I, *Military Maxims* (1827).

The first rule of invasion is "Establish your bridgehead." Until you have done that, you can't attack.
Quentin Reynolds, "Bloody Salerno," *Collier's* (October 23, 1943).

Invasions are magnificent things to watch but awful things to be in. Evidently the army likes to pick certain outfits, train them in landing operations, and then use the same men for every invasion. This is undoubtedly an efficient system, but it gets a little rough on the guys who do the invading.
Bill Mauldin, *Up Front* (1945).

Once one has decided to invade a country, one must not be afraid to deliver battle, and should seek out the enemy everywhere to fight him.
Napoleon I quoted in J. F. C. Fuller, *The Conduct of War* (1961).

Iron Curtain

[France is] a nation of 40 million with a deep rooted grievance and an iron curtain at its frontier.
George W. Creel, *A Mechanistic View of War and Peace* (1915).

We were behind the "iron curtain" at last.
Ethel Viscountess Snowden, *Through Bolshevik Russia* (1920).

If the German people lay down their arms, the whole of Eastern and Southern Europe, together with the Reich, will come under Russian occupation. Behind an iron curtain mass butcheries of people would begin.
Joseph Goebbels, *Manchester Guardian* (February 23, 1945).

From Stettin in the Baltic to Trieste in the Adriatic, an iron curtain has descended across the Continent. Behind that line lie all the capitals of the ancient states of central and eastern Europe. Warsaw, Berlin, Prague, Vienna, Budapest, Belgrade, Bucharest,

and Sofia, all these famous cities and the populations around them lie in what I must call the Soviet Sphere, and all are subject in one form or another, not only to Soviet influence, but to a very high and, in many cases, increasing measure of control from Moscow. Athens alone—Greece with its immortal glories—is free to decide its future at an election under British, American, and French observation.
Winston Churchill, speech at Westminster College, Fulton, Missouri, March 5, 1946.

From behind the iron curtain, there are signs that tyranny is in trouble and reminders that its structure is as brittle as its surface is hard.
President Dwight D. Eisenhower, State of the Union Address, January 7, 1954.

Italy

There are three different characters of troops. One combines warlike ardor with discipline: this produces true valor, like that of the Romans. All history shows that a proper discipline prevailed in their armies, and had done so for a long time. For in a well-ordered army no one should do anything except in accordance with the regulations.... And armies that do not observe such a system cannot in reality be called armies.... For good order sustains the courage and reanimates that ardor with the hope of victory, which will never fail if discipline be preserved. The reverse of this happens to armies that have ardor without discipline: such was the case with the Gauls, who were wholly wanting in discipline during combat. For if they did not overthrow the enemy by their first furious onset, upon which they relied for victory, not being sustained by a well-regulated valor, and having nothing besides their impetuosity to give them confidence, they failed when that first ardor was cooled. But with the Romans it was very different; less mindful of danger because of the good order which they preserved during battle, they felt assured of victory, and continued the fight.... The third kind of armies are such as have neither natural courage nor discipline. Of this kind are the Italian armies of our time, which are entirely useless.
Niccolò Machiavelli, *The Discourses* (1517).

Italy will never have a really firm army. The Italians are too civilized, too fine, too democratic in a certain sense of the word.
Ardant du Picq, *Battle Studies* (1868).

On this tenth day of June 1940, the hand that held the dagger has struck it into the back of its neighbor.... Neither those who sprang from that ancient stock nor those who have come hither in later years can be indifferent to the destruction of freedom in their ancestral lands across the seas.
President Franklin D. Roosevelt, speech at Charlottesville, Virginia, June 10, 1940. The "hand" here is that of Italy, which declared war on its neighbor (France) only after that country had been essentially defeated by Germany.

I need only a few thousand dead [in the Spring 1940 Battle of France] to ensure that I have the right to sit at the peace table in the capacity of a belligerent.
Benito Mussolini quoted in Alistair Horne, *To Lose a Battle: France 1940* (1960). Horne writes that Italy's attacks in France on June 10, 1940 "had little military consequence."

While the U.S. Navy drinks whisky and the British Navy prefers rum, the Italian Navy sticks to port.
World War II British Broadcasting Corporation humor quoted in Reynolds and Eleanor Packard, *Balcony Empire* (1942).

The last shred of self-respect that might have remained to Italy was removed when Mussolini dared not even send his army against the weak French forces on the Alps

until the Germans had advanced so far that the French were caught, hopelessly, in a vise. There was not even that much courage left in Fascist Italy! The word passed around by Roman wits was: "Don't fire until you see the whites of their flags." And that was exactly what happened. It was not until four days after Petain sued for peace that Mussolini sent his troops forward—only to have them severely mauled by the embittered French.
Herbert L. Matthews, *Fruits of Fascism* (1943).

The red light district of Naples was declared off-limits to GIs, posters warning against VD covered every wall in areas occupied by the Allies, and there were "pro stations," where prophylactics were distributed to the GIs free of charge, on every corner. In some cities, the American Red Cross issued a "Trust Pass" to women who were investigated and found to be of good character and free of disease.
E. B Shkert and B. S. Seibetta, *War Brides Of World War II* (1988).

If England wins, we are losers; if Germany wins, we are lost.
A quip summarizing the attitude of Italians toward the war quoted in *Time* (March 16, 1942).

The time has come for you to decide whether Italians shall die for Mussolini and Hitler—or live for Italy, and for civilization.
Joint message to the Italian people from President Franklin D. Roosevelt and Prime Minister Winston Churchill, July 16, 1943.

The withdrawal of Italy means little in a military sense because the struggle in that country has for months been sustained and carried on mainly by German forces. We will now continue the struggle free of all burdensome encumbrances.
Adolf Hitler, *Time* (September 20, 1943).

The dogfaces over here have pretty mixed feelings as far as Italy is concerned. A lot of them . . . remember that some of their best friends were killed by Italians, and many of our allies can't forget that Italy caused them some grief. I don't belong to that group, even though the first enemies I saw were Italians. You can't work up a good hate against soldiers who are surrendering to you so fast you have to take them by appointment.
Bill Mauldin, *Up Front* (1945).

Rommel saw none of the sights of Rome. He did, however, by invitation of the Italian command, see, on his birthday [November 15, 1941], the film *On from Benghazi*, which depicted the advance of the previous April. It showed the victorious Italians attacking with the bayonet; it showed some very scruffy British officers, played by Italian "bit players," running in panic before them; it did not show a single German soldier in action. "Very interesting and instructive," said Rommel to his hosts, "I often wondered what happened in that battle."
Desmond Young, *Rommel* (1950).

Hermann Göring had loathed the Italians. . . .
"You have no idea," he would tell U. S. General Carl F. Spaatz on May 10, 1945, "What a bad time we had in Italy. If they had only been our enemies instead of our allies, we might have won the war."
David Irving, *Göring* (1989).

I saw the new Italian Navy. Its boats have glass bottoms so they can see the old Italian Navy.
Peter Secchia, nominee for ambassador to Italy, *Newsweek* (June 5, 1989).

Japan

It will be the greatest mistake to be soft with the Japanese. The fact that you have been prevented from inflicting the crushing [defeat] . . . will, I fear, enable the Japanese leaders to delude their people into thinking they were defeated only by the scientists and not in battle, unless we can so humble them that the completeness of defeat is brought home to them.

Normally I am not a vindictive person, but I cannot help feeling that unless we really are tough with all the Japanese leaders they will be able to build themselves up eventually for another war.

Admiral Lord Louis Mountbatten, letter to General Douglas MacArthur, August 16, 1945, quoted in Philip Ziegler, *Mountbatten* (1985).

Prior to Pearl Harbor, the United States in general had rated Japan as no better than a class-C nation. After that one successful sneak attack, however, panicky eyes saw the monkeymen as supermen. I saw them as nothing of the sort, and I wanted my forces to know how I felt. I stand by the opinion that the Japs are bastards.

Admiral William F. Halsey and J. Bryan III, *Admiral Halsey's Story* (1947).

If you tell me that it is necessary that we fight, then in the first six months to a year of war against the U.S. and England, I will run wild, and I will show you an uninterrupted succession of victories; but I must also tell you that, should the war be prolonged for two or three years, I have no confidence in our ultimate victory.

Japanese Admiral Isoroku Yamamoto's pessimistic outlook on a war with the United States, quoted in John Dean Potter, *Yamamoto* (1965).

Aspiring sincerely to an international peace based on justice and order, the Japanese people forever renounce war as a sovereign right of the nation and the threat or use of force as means of settling international disputes.

In order to accomplish the aim of the preceding paragraph, land, sea, and air forces as well as other war potential, will never be maintained. The right of belligerency of the state will not be recognized.

Article 9 of the 1947 Constitution of Japan.

The American taxpayer has been paying unconsciously for the defense of Japan. We provide the nuclear umbrella; we provide the high-seas capability; we're defending their oil. They need it a hell of a lot more than we do. Yet they are spending only nine-tenths of 1 percent of their gross national product on defense. I'm embarrassed for the Japanese. I would think the Japanese honor would not allow them to be so supine.

Bob Komer, U.S. Under Secretary of Defense for Policy, *The Washington Post* (February 14, 1981).

Japan has an army, a navy and an air force, all constitutionally illegal. In fact, Japan has perhaps the most efficiently integrated military organization in the world. . . . What road the Japanese will travel in the future no one can say exactly, but it is apparent that they are on the move to world military power to match their economic strength, pushed by events. This movement is led by the politicians, not just the military. . . . As one Japanese told me, if militarism of the old *gunkokushugi* sort ever returns to Japan, it will be brought by the politicians, for there is none so fierce as he who does not have to fight in battle.

Edwin P. Hoyt, *The Militarists* (1985).

jingoism

We don't want to fight, but by jingo if we do,
We've got the ships, we've got the men,
We've got the money too.
We've fought the Bear before, and while
Britons shall be true,
The Russians shall not have Constantinople.
This English music-hall song of the late 1870s, usually credited to G. W. Hunt, is often cited as origin of the word *jingoism*. *Jingo* was a euphemism for "by God" or "by Jesus."

Greek history is a panorama of jingoism and imperialism—war for war's sake, all the citizens being warriors. It is horrible reading, because of the irrationality of it all— save for the purpose of making "history"—and the history is that of the utter ruin of a civilization in intellectual respects perhaps the highest the earth has ever seen.
William James, "The Moral Equivalent of War," *McClure's Magazine* (August 1910).

I have always been against the pacifists during the quarrel, and against the Jingoes at its close.
Winston Churchill, *My Early Life* (1930).

In the earlier part of the modern period, men massacred each other in the name of what they called religion; in the latter part the chief appeal has been chauvinism or jingoism, miscalled patriotism.
William Ralph Inge, *Christian Ethics and Modern Problems* (1932).

Joint Chiefs of Staff

Why, you take the most gallant sailor, the most intrepid airman, or the most audacious soldier, put them at a table together—what do you get? The sum of their fears.
Winston Churchill, on the Chiefs of Staff, during a shipboard lunch on November 16, 1943, en route to the Cairo Conference, quoted in Harold Macmillan, *The Blast of War* (1967).

After the Bay of Pigs, the Kennedys began to question the [Joint] Chiefs' professional competence. They also resented their public relations tactics. The new President was not one for men in uniform with pointers reading aloud sentences off flip charts he could read much faster himself. In the spring of 1961, Kennedy received the Net Evaluation, an annual doomsday briefing analyzing the chances of nuclear war. An Air Force general presented it, said Roswell Gilpatric, the deputy secretary of defense, "as though it were for a kindergarten class. ... Finally Kennedy got up and walked right out in the middle of it, and that was the end of it. And we never had another one."
Arthur M. Schlesinger, Jr., *Robert Kennedy and His Times* (1978).

The military in the United States is the dominant force in our society. We criticize our clergy, our judges, even our wives—but never the Joint Chiefs of Staff.
Admiral Gene R. LaRocque, *The New York Times* (April 28, 1981).

[The job of the Chairman of the Joint Chiefs of Staff is] to give the president and secretary of defense military advice before they know they need it.
General John W. Vessey, Jr., Chairman, Joint Chiefs of Staff, quoted in *The New York Times* (July 15, 1984).

Kahn, Herman (1922–1983)

Kahn's main purpose in writing OTW [*On Thermonuclear War*] was "to create a vocabulary" so that strategic issues can be "comfortably and easily" discussed, a vocabulary that reduces the emotions surrounding nuclear war to the dispassionate

cool of scientific thought. To the extent that many people today talk about nuclear war in such a nonchalant, would-be scientific manner, their language is rooted in the work of Herman Kahn. And to the extent that people have an image of defense analysts as mad-scientist Dr. Stangeloves who almost glorify the challenge of nuclear war, that image, too, comes from Herman Kahn.
Fred Kaplan, *The Wizards of Armageddon* (1983).

The most outspoken among Kahn's many critics was mathematician James Newman, who in March 1961 wrote a review of *On Thermonuclear War* for *Scientific American*. Newman confessed he had at first thought the book "a hoax in bad taste," and its authorship mythic. Upon learning that both were authentic, Newman dismissed the epic as "thermonuclear pornography," suggesting that Kahn's first name might more properly be "Genghis."
Gregg Herken, *Counsels of War* (1987).

During the civil defense furor of the early '60s, a neighbor accosted Jane Kahn [Herman's wife] at a reception at the Community Center: "So you really want your children to survive a thermonuclear war?"
"They are *very nice* children," said Jane.
B. Bruce-Briggs, *The Shield of Faith* (1988).

I attended [a briefing] in which Dr. Herman Kahn pontificated about the consequences of the Tet Offensive. Kahn, one of the gurus of American nuclear policy, felt he was an expert on Vietnam because, as he explained, he had visited the country every year since the early fifties. In fact this made him just another tourist, but the Defense guys and military men nonetheless gushed over everything he said. The military men were particularly enthusiastic, perhaps because, having been so conditioned by their own can-doism not to think, they were mesmerized by people who used their brains for a living.
David H. Hackworth, *About Face* (1989).

Kaiser William II (1859–1941)

All the long years of my reign my colleagues, the Monarchs of Europe, have paid no attention to what I have to say. Soon, with my great Navy to endorse my words, they will be more respectful.
Kaiser William II, speaking prior to World War I, quoted in E. F. Benson, *The Kaiser and English Relations* (1936).

When the war broke out she took down the signed photograph of the Kaiser and, with some solemnity, hung it in the men-servants' lavatory; it was her most combative action.
Evelyn Waugh, *Vile Bodies* (1930).

We hated with a common hate that was exhilarating. The writer . . . remembers attending a great meeting in New England, held under the auspices of a Christian Church—God save the mark! A speaker demanded that the kaiser, when captured, be boiled in oil, and the entire audience stood on chairs to scream its hysterical approval. This was the mood we were in.
James Duane Squires, *British Propaganda at Home and in the United States from 1914 to 1917* (1935).

The Kaiser, it was said, had referred to the British troops as "a contemptible little army." It is now known that the phrase emanated not from the German side but from the closets of British propagandists, who needed something memorable and incisive to inspirit the troops. The phrase was actually devised at the War Office by Sir Frederick Maurice and fathered upon the Kaiser.

Paul Fussell, *The Great War in Modern Memory* (1975). On October 1, 1914, *The Times* (London) quoted the Kaiser as saying, "It is my royal and imperial command that you . . . exterminate first the treacherous English, and . . . walk over General French's contemptible little army."

killing

He smote them hip and thigh, with a great slaughter.
The Bible, Judges 15:8.

The end of war is the destruction of the enemy State. One has the right to kill its defenders as long as they are armed, but as soon as they lay down their arms and surrender, they cease to be enemies, or rather instruments of the enemy, and one no longer has a right to their lives. One can kill the State without killing a single one of its members.
Jean-Jacques Rousseau, *The Social Contract* (1762).

Ninepence a day fer killin' folks comes kind o' low fer murder.
James Russell Lowell, *The Biglow Papers*, First Series (1848).

Yet each man kills the thing he loves,
By each let this be heard,
Some do it with a bitter look,
Some with a flattering word.
The coward does it with a kiss,
The brave man with a sword!
Oscar Wilde, *The Ballad of Reading Gaol* (1905).

Nothing is ever done in this world until men are prepared to kill each other if it is not done.
George Bernard Shaw, *Major Barbara* (1905).

Ask any soldier. To kill a man is to merit a woman.
Jean Giraudoux, *Tiger at the Gates*, Act I (1935).

We must hate with every fiber. . . . We must lust for battle; our object in life must be to kill; we must scheme and plan night and day to kill. There need be no pangs of conscience, for our enemies have lighted the way to faster, surer, crueler killing.
General Lesley J. McNair quoted in *Time* (December 7, 1942).

Why is it worse to kill civilians than soldiers? Obviously one must not kill children if it is in any way avoidable, but it is only in propaganda pamphlets that every bomb drops on a school or an orphanage. A bomb kills a cross-section of the population; but not quite a representative selection, because the children and expectant mothers are usually the first to be evacuated, and some of the young men will be away in the army. Probably a disproportionately large number of bomb victims will be middle-aged. . . . On the other hand, "normal" or "legitimate" warfare picks out and slaughters all the healthiest and bravest of the young male population. Every time a German submarine goes to the bottom about fifty young men of fine physique and good nerve are suffocated. Yet people who would hold up their hands at the very words "civilian bombing" will repeat with satisfaction such phrases as "We are winning the Battle of the Atlantic".
George Orwell, "As I Please," *Tribune* (May 19, 1944).

I don't give a damn what color you are so long as you get out there and kill those sonsofbitches in the green suits.
General George S. Patton, Jr., greeting a Negro battalion on the battlefront, quoted in *Time* (April 9, 1945).

Christmas [1944] dawned clear and cold; lovely weather for killing Germans, although the thought seemed somewhat at variance with the spirit of the day.
General George S. Patton, Jr., *War as I Knew It* (1947).

[General] MacArthur lit up his corncob pipe, waved out the match and explained that he wanted to get "a sense of the situation." A lieutenant touched him on the sleeve, pointed at a path, and said, "Excuse me, sir, but we killed a Jap sniper in there just a few minutes ago." The General nodded approvingly. "Fine," he said, "That's the best thing to do with them."
William Manchester, *American Caesar* (1978).

Before I had a chance in another war, the desire to kill people to whom I had not been introduced had passed away.
Mark Twain, referring to his brief career as a Confederate soldier in the Civil War, quoted in C. Neider, ed., *The Autobiography of Mark Twain* (1959).

Be peaceful, be courteous, obey the law, respect everyone; but if someone puts his hand on you, send him to the cemetery.
Malcolm X, *Malcolm X Speaks* (1965).

Patriots always talk of dying for their country and never of killing for their country.
Bertrand Russell, *Autobiography* (1967).

There's a consensus out that it's OK to kill when your government decides who to kill. If you kill inside the country you get in trouble. If you kill outside the country, right time, right season, latest enemy, you get a medal.
Joan Baez, *Daybreak* (1966).

Now it was a duty to shoot, and there was a splendid target.... One couldn't miss them. Every man I fired at dropped except one. Him, the boldest of the lot, I missed repeatedly. I was puzzled and angry.... Not that I wanted to hurt him or anyone else. It was missing I hated. That's the beastliest thing in war, the damnable frivolity. One's like a merry mischievous ape tearing up the image of God.
R. H. Tawney, on his experiences in World War I, quoted in Guy Chapman, ed., *Vain Glory* (1968).

[Air Marshal Arthur Harris, head of Bomber Command in World War II] spent much of the war racing his Bentley at breakneck speed between High Wycombe and the Air Ministry, and was the bane of motor-cycle policemen on the London road. "You might have killed somebody, sir," said a reproachful constable who stopped him late one night.
"Young man, I kill thousands of people every night!" snapped Harris.
Max Hastings, *Bomber Command* (1979).

Remember that every Boche you fellows kill is a point scored to our side; every Boche you kill brings victory one minute nearer and shortens the war by one minute. Kill them! Kill them! There's only one good Boche, and that's a dead one!
Major Campbell (British Army), World War I training lecture, quoted in Paul Fussell, *Siegfried Sassoon's Long Journey* (1983).

The sad idiom of the American soldier in Vietnam reflected the futility of his war. A man was not killed there. He was "wasted." He was "blown away."
Neil Sheehan, *A Bright Shining Lie* (1988).

kings

Had I but serv'd my God with half the zeal
I serv'd my king, He would not in mine age
Have left me naked to mine enemies.
William Shakespeare, *Henry VIII*, Act II (1613).

War is the trade of kings.
John Dryden, *King Arthur* (1691).

A French bastard landing with an armed banditti and establishing himself King of England against the consent of the natives is, in plain terms, a very paltry rascally original.... The plain truth is that the antiquity of English monarchy will not bear looking into.
Thomas Paine, *Common Sense* (1776).

Never strike a king unless you are sure you shall kill him.
Ralph Waldo Emerson, *Journals* (1909–14). Entry written during September 1843.

The sovereign has, under a constitutional monarchy such as ours, three rights—the right to be consulted, the right to encourage, the right to warn.
Walter Bagehot, *The English Constitution* (1867).

So long as you suffer any man to call himself your shepherd sooner or later you will find a crook round your ankle. We were not making war against Germany; we were being ordered about in the King's war with Germany.
H. G. Wells, *Experiment in Autobiography* (1934).

The kingly office is entitled to no respect. It was originally procured by the highwayman's methods; it remains a perpetuated crime, can never be anything but the symbol of a crime. It is no more entitled to respect than is the flag of a pirate.
Mark Twain, *Mark Twain's Notebooks* (1935).

Their majesties [the King and Queen of England] visited an Eighth Air Force Base. Rain began to fall and [General Carl] Spaatz removed his coat, putting it over the queen's shoulders, and said, "This makes you a major general in the U.S. Army Air Forces, Your Majesty." The reporters present made a story of it, having never pictured the stern-visaged general in the role of Sir Walter Raleigh.
David R. Mets, *Master of Airpower* (1988).

Let me tell you quite bluntly that this king business has given me personally nothing but headaches.
Shah of Iran quoted in *The New York Times* (October 27, 1967).

Korean War

In Korea the Government forces, which were armed to prevent border raids and to preserve internal security, were attacked by invading forces from North Korea. The Security Council of the United Nations called upon the invading troops to cease hostilities and to withdraw to the thirty-eighth parallel. This they have not done, but on the contrary have pressed the attack. The Security Council called upon all members of the United Nations to render every assistance to the United Nations in the execution of this resolution. In these circumstances I have ordered United States air and sea forces to give the Korean Government troops cover and support.

The attack upon Korea makes it plain beyond all doubt that Communism has passed beyond the use of subversion to conquer independent nations and will now use armed invasion and war.

President Harry S. Truman, statement of June 27, 1950 explaining American involvement in the Korean War.

United Nations forces are now being attacked from the safety of a privileged sanctuary. Planes operating from bases in China cross over into Korea to attack United Nations ground and air forces and then flee back across the border. . . .

The pretext which the Chinese Communists advance for taking offensive action against United Nations forces in Korea from behind the protection afforded by the Sino-Korean border is their professed belief that these forces intend to carry hostilities across the frontier into Chinese territory.

The resolutions and every other action taken by the United Nations demonstrate beyond any doubt that no such intention has ever been entertained.

President Harry S. Truman, press release, November 16, 1950. According to Frazier Hunt, *The Untold Story of Douglas MacArthur* (1954), this "was the first time that the phrase 'privileged sanctuary' had been used in a public document."

In the simplest terms, what we are doing in Korea is this: We are trying to prevent a third world war.

President Harry S. Truman, speech to the nation, April 16, 1951.

Red China is not the powerful nation seeking to dominate the world. Frankly, in the opinion of the Joint Chiefs of Staff, this strategy would involve us in the wrong war, at the wrong place, at the wrong time, and with the wrong enemy.

General Omar Bradley, testifying before Congress on the desirability of extending the Korean War into China, May 15, 1951.

That job [ending the Korean War] requires a personal trip to Korea. I shall make that trip. Only in that way could I learn how best to serve the American people in the cause of peace. I shall go to Korea.

Presidential candidate Dwight D. Eisenhower, speech in Detroit, October 24, 1952.

Qn: What are your views, Mr. Churchill, on the present stalemate in Korea?
Ans: Better a stalemate than a checkmate.

John Colville, *The Fringes of Power* (1985); diary entry for January 3, 1953.

I return with feelings of misgiving from my third war—I was the first American commander to put his signature on a paper ending a war when we did not win it.

General Mark Clark, *New York Herald Tribune* (October 21, 1953).

The principal reason we were able to obtain the armistice was because we were prepared for a much more intensive scale of warfare. It should not be improper to say at such a restricted gathering that we had already sent the means to the theater for delivering atomic weapons. This became known to the Chinese Communists through their good intelligence sources and in fact we were not unwilling that they should find out.

John Foster Dulles, speaking in December 1953, quoted in McGeorge Bundy, *Danger and Survival* (1988).

The lack of progress in the long-stalemated talks—they were then recessed—and the nearly stalemated war both demanded, in my opinion, definite measures on our part to put an end to these intolerable conditions. One possibility was to let the Communist authorities understand that, in the absence of satisfactory progress, we intended to move decisively without inhibition in our use of weapons, and would no longer be responsible for confining hostilities to the Korean Peninsula. We would not be limited by any worldwide gentleman's agreement . . . we dropped the word, discreetly, of our intention. We felt quite sure it would reach Soviet and Chinese Communist ears.

Soon the prospects for armistice negotiations seemed to improve.
President Dwight D. Eisenhower, *The White House Years*, I (1963).

The willingness to settle for a stalemate . . . was all that brought peace to Korea. . . . We had finally come to realize that military victory was not what it had been in the past—that it might even elude us forever if the means we used to achieve it brought wholesale devastation to the world or led us down the road of international immorality past the point of no return.
General Matthew B. Ridgway, *The Korean War* (1967).

This was a police action, a limited war, whatever you want to call it, to stop aggression and to prevent a big war. And that's all it ever was.
President Harry S. Truman quoted in Merle Miller, *Plain Speaking* (1973).

If the best minds in the world had set out to find us the worst possible location to fight a war, the unanimous choice would have to have been Korea.
Dean Acheson quoted in Walter Isaacson and Evan Thomas, *The Wise Men* (1986).

Korea merits close consideration as a military rehearsal for the subsequent disaster in Vietnam. So many of the ingredients of the Indochina tragedy were already visible a decade or two earlier in Korea: The political difficulty of sustaining an unpopular and autocratic regime; the problems of creating a credible local army in a corrupt society; the fateful cost of underestimating the power of an Asian Communist army. For all the undoubted benefits of air superiority and close support, Korea vividly displayed the difficulties of using air power effectively against a primitive economy, a peasant army. The war also demonstrated the problem of deploying a highly mechanized Western army in a broken country against a lightly equipped foe.
Max Hastings, *The Korean War* (1987).

Inchon

The enemy . . . has failed to prepare Inchon properly for defense. The very arguments you have made as to the impracticabilities involved will tend to ensure for me the element of surprise. For the enemy commander will reason that no one would be so brash as to make such an attempt. Surprise is the most vital element for success in war. . . .

The Navy's objections as to tides, hydrography, terrain, and physical handicaps are indeed substantial and pertinent. But they are not insuperable. My confidence in the Navy is complete, and in fact I seem to have more confidence in the Navy than the Navy has in itself. . . .

If my estimate is inaccurate and should I run into a defense with which I cannot cope, I will be there personally and will immediately withdraw our forces before they are committed to a bloody setback. The only loss then will be my professional reputation. But Inchon will not fail. Inchon will succeed. And it will save 100,000 lives.
General Douglas MacArthur, briefing of senior officers on proposed Inchon landing in Tokyo on August 23, 1950, reprinted in his *Reminiscences* (1964); D. Clayton James, *The Years of MacArthur*, III (1985).

We shall land at Inchon, and I will crush them.
General Douglas MacArthur on Inchon landing, quoted in J. Lawton Collins, *War in Peacetime* (1969).

Unlike the grueling and more nearly even ground battles between American and North Korean soldiers in the perimeter, the Inchon invasion displayed the overwhelming imbalance between the United States and a wholly outclassed North Korea.... Once American navel and air power was combined with well-equipped and well-trained amphibious assault forces, there was not a shadow of a doubt about the invasion's success. One example should suffice to show the disproportion between forces: the North Koreans had nineteen piston-driven aircraft; the United States had so much air power, jet and piston, there literally was not enough airspace over the battlefield and its approaches to accommodate it.

Bevin Alexander, *Korea: The First War We Lost* (1986).

For all its undisputed Korean provenance, the name of Inchon possesses a wonderfully resonant American quality. It summons a vision of military genius undulled by time, undiminished by more recent memories of Asian defeat. Inchon remains a monument to "can do," to improvisation and risk-taking on a magnificent scale, above all to the spirit of Douglas MacArthur.... The amphibious landings of September 15, 1950, were MacArthur's masterstroke.

Max Hastings, *The Korean War* (1987).

lancers

In May 1916 a French infantry officer was also treated to the sight of a regiment of lancers forming for the attack. One of his fellow officers turned to him and said resignedly: "They're holding back all these fellows for the breakthrough, the famous breakthrough that we've been waiting for for two years.... You know there's nothing like a lance against machine guns."

John Ellis, *The Social History of the Machine Gun* (1975).

Coming towards us were a troop of French cavalry. I should say a hundred and fifty or two hundred strong. Gosh, but they looked splendid.... They could never have been told about the machine-guns. They laughed and waved their lances at us, shouting "Le Bosch fini."

Before reaching the top of the hill they opened out to about six feet between each horse and in a straight line.... Over the top of the hill they charged, lances at the ready.

There was not a sound from us. Then, only a few seconds after they disappeared, the hellish noise of machine-guns broke out. We just looked at each other. The only words I heard spoken were "Bloody hell ...." That's what it must have been over that hill, for not one man came back. Several of their horses did.

William Pressey, writing of March 26, 1918 near Amiens, quoted in M. Mohnihan, ed., *People At War* (1973).

A story goes that an examiner once asked a junior officer in a famous regiment of lancers, "What is the purpose of cavalry in war?" And the young man replied, "To give tone to what would otherwise be a vulgar brawl."

Bernard Brodie, *A Guide to Naval Strategy* (1944).

law of war

Can anything be more ridiculous than that a man has a right to kill me because he dwells on the other side of the water, and because his prince has a quarrel with mine, although I have none with him?

Blaise Pascal, *Pensées* (1670).

They imagined a conqueror had a right to destroy the state; whence they inferred that he had a right to destroy the men that compose it: a wrong consequence from a false principle. For from the destruction of the state it does not at all follow that the people who compose it ought to be also destroyed. The state is the association of men, and not the men themselves; the citizen may perish, and the man remain.
Charles de Montesquieu, *The Spirit of the Laws* (1734).

The law of nations is naturally founded on this principle, that different nations ought in time of peace to do one another all the good they can, and in time of war as little injury as possible, without prejudicing their real interests.
The object of war is victory; that of victory is conquest; and that of conquest preservation. From this and the preceding principle all those rules are derived which constitute the law of nations.
Charles de Montesquieu, *The Spirit of the Laws* (1734).

A state shall not, during war, admit of hostilities of a nature that would render reciprocal confidence in a succeeding peace impossible: such as employing assassins, poisoners, violation of capitulations, secret instigations to rebellion, etc.
Immanuel Kant, *Perpetual Peace* (1795).

It cannot be too clearly stated that international law is no protection except to the strong, and that the only laws which great powers recognize as binding are those of power and expediency.
S. L. Murray, *The Future Peace of the Anglo-Saxons* (1905).

The fact that the law of war has been violated pursuant to an order of a superior authority, whether military or civil, does not deprive the act in question of its character as a war crime, nor does it constitute a defense in the trial of an accused individual, unless he did not know and could not reasonably have been expected to know that the act ordered was unlawful.
United States Army, *The Law of Land Warfare* (1956).

When he [Stalin] made one of his typical remarks, "I know sixty thousand German officers I'm going to shoot," Churchill became so agitated he paced the floor for several minutes, preaching about Christianity and civilization. It was against the laws of civilized warfare, he insisted, to shoot sixty thousand officers. Stalin waited patiently until he finished, then said again through his interpreter, "I know sixty thousand German officers I'm going to shoot when the war is over."
General Henry H. Arnold, *Global Mission* (1949); Thomas M. Coffey, *Hap* (1982).

Lawrence, T. E. "of Arabia" (1885–1935)

He had a genius for backing into the limelight.
Lowell Thomas, *With Lawrence in Arabia* (1924).

There are those who have tried to dismiss his story with a flourish of the Union Jack, a psycho-analytical catchword or a sneer; it should move our deepest admiration and pity. Like Shelley and like Baudelaire, it may be said of him that he suffered, in his own person, the neurotic ills of an entire generation.
Christopher Isherwood, *Exhumations* (1966).

The manner of his death was such that almost inevitably a series of legends have grown up about it. There are people who believe to this day that Lawrence was not killed, that the accident was faked so as to allow him to undertake, incognito, important work in the Middle East during World War II and that he died of old age (or is still alive) in a villa outside Tangier. Others believe that Lawrence committed suicide because life no longer held any appeal for him. . . . Other people are certain that Lawrence was killed by agents of a foreign power; some say French, some say German, some Arab. A more fanciful version is that he was killed by British agents because his next book would have exposed government secrets. A legend that has lingered longer than most is that Lawrence was a victim of his love of speed and of a death-wish. . . .

The facts are very different. They establish that Lawrence died after a road accident while trying to avoid a boy on a bike.
Phillip Knightley and Colin Simpson, *The Secret Lives of Lawrence of Arabia* (1969).

There can be no question of his personal pluck, gallantry and resources, but the money with which I was able to supply him in such large quantities has much more to do with the success of the Arab operation than is realized.
Sir Reginald Wingate quoted in Phillip Knightley and Colin Simpson, *The Secret Lives of Lawrence of Arabia* (1969).

leadership

When troops flee, are insubordinate, distressed, collapse in disorder, or are routed, it is the fault of the general. None of these disorders can be attributed to natural causes.
Sun Tzu, *The Art of War* (4th century B.C.).

Philip of Macedonia . . . put behind his army some of his most faithful cavalry and ordered them to kill whoever ran; hence his men, preferring to die fighting rather than running, conquered. Many Romans, not so much to stop a flight as to give their men a reason for making greater effort, have, while they were fighting, taken a banner from the hands of their men and thrown it among the enemy and offered rewards to any one who would regain it.
Niccolò Machiavelli, *The Art of War* (1520).

It is even better to act quickly and err than to hesitate until the time of action is past.
Karl von Clausewitz, *On War* (1832).

There go the people. I must follow them, for I am their leader.
Attributed to Alexandre Ledru-Rollin, a leader of the Revolution of 1848 in France. Alvin R. Calman, in *Ledru-Rollin and the Second French Republic* (1922), holds that this attribution is probably apocryphal.

In enterprise of martial kind
When there was any fighting,
He led his regiment from behind—
He found it less exciting.
But when away his regiment ran,
His place was at the fore, O—
That celebrated,
Cultivated,
Underrated
Nobelman, The Duke of Plaza-Toro!
William S. Gilbert, "The Duke of Plaza-Toro," *The Gondoliers* (1889).

The leader's first duty is to understand the mind of the enemy.
René Quinton, *Soldier's Testament* (1930).

A competent leader can get efficient service from poor troops, while on the contrary an incapable leader can demoralize the best of troops.
General of the Armies John J. Pershing, *My Experiences in the World War*, II (1931).

A man of diffident manner will never inspire confidence. A cold reserve cannot beget enthusiasm, and so with the others there must be an outward and visible sign of the inward and spiritual grace.

It then appears that the leader must be an actor, and such is the fact. But with him, as with his bewigged compeer, he is unconvincing unless he lives his part.

Major George S. Patton, Jr., "Success in War," [1931] *Infantry Journal Reader*, ed. J. I. Greene (1943).

I saw the Captain of a ship drinking a cup of tea on the bridge in the course of dive-bombing attacks that had gone on all day. While he was drinking the look-out reported "Aircraft on the starboard bow, sir." He did not even look up. At "Aircraft diving, sir," the Captain glanced up only. "Bomb released, sir," and the Captain gave the order "Hard a-starboard," and went on drinking his tea until the bomb hit the water nearby. The reaction to this episode was a kind of schoolboy hero-worship on the part of everyone who saw it. When the bombing had ceased the Captain went down to his cabin and when he was alone he wept.

Surgeon Commander McDowell quoted in Lord Moran, *The Anatomy of Courage* (1945).

Leadership . . . is the thing that wins battles. I have it—but I'll be damned if I can define it.

General George S. Patton, Jr., letter to his son of January 16, 1945, reprinted in Martin Blumenson, ed., *The Patton Papers*, II (1974).

Officers had to lead. Bruce Palmer, Jr., recalled how Krueger had once made his point. Chief of staff of the Sixth Infantry Division, Palmer encountered Krueger at Maffin Bay, New Guinea, shortly after the Twentieth Infantry had fought the bloody Battle of Lone Tree Hill. "How many officer casualties?" Krueger wanted to know. Palmer said that they had been heavy. "Good," Krueger responded. No doubt noticing the surprised look on Palmer's face, Krueger explained that the high toll indicated a fighting outfit with good leadership.

William M. Leary, "Walter Krueger: MacArthur's Fighting General," *We Shall Return!*, ed. William M. Leary (1988).

To a very high degree the measure of success in battle leadership is the ability to profit by the lessons of battle experience.

General Lucian K. Truscott, *Command Missions* (1954).

The most terrible job in warfare is to be a second lieutenant leading a platoon when you are on the battlefield.

President Dwight D. Eisenhower, news conference, March 17, 1954.

Men are neither lions nor sheep. It is the man who leads them turns them into either lions or sheep.

Jean Dutourd, *Taxis of the Marne* (1957).

General Ludendorff [during World War I]: The English soldiers fight like lions.
General Hoffman: True. But don't we know that they are lions led by donkeys.

Alan Clark, *The Donkeys* (1962).

Never tell people *how* to do things. Tell them *what* to do and they will surprise you with their ingenuity.

General George S. Patton, Jr., quoted in Porter B. Williamson, *Patton's Principles* (1979).

Just before the 1967 war, Premier Levi Eshkol [of Israel] delivered a radio address to his nation, and was criticized because he stumbled over his words. Golda [Meir] said

afterward: "A leader who doesn't hesitate before he sends his nation into battle is not fit to be a leader."
Israel and Mary Shenker, *As Good As Golda* (1970).

An atheist could not be as great a military leader as one who is not an atheist.
Admiral Thomas H. Moorer, as chairman-designate of the Joint Chiefs of Staff, testifying in U.S. District Court in support of the policy of compulsory chapel attendance at the service academies, *The Washington Post* (April 29, 1970).

I wouldn't make the slightest concession for moral leadership. It's much overrated.
Dean Rusk, U.S. Secretary of State, quoted in David Halberstam, *The Best and the Brightest* (1972).

You've got to keep distant from [your soldiers]. The officer-enlisted man distance helps. This is one of the most painful things, having to withhold sometimes your affection for them, because you know you're going to have to destroy them on occasion. And you do. You use them up: they're material. And part of being a good officer is knowing how much of them you can use up and still get the job done.
Paul Fussell quoted in Gwynne Dyer, *War* (1985).

Political leaders, whether civilian or military, had more influence in the outcome of the World Wars and the shape of policy in the interwar years than the military command. It was they who carried their countries to victory or doomed them to defeat.
Allan R. Millett and Williamson Murray, "Lessons of War," *National Interest* (Winter 1988–89).

leave

The Iron Duke [of Wellington] had a sound understanding of human nature; and he was being realistic, rather than cynical when, during the Peninsular campaigns he set a limit of forty-eight hours for his officers' leaves in Lisbon, or behind the lines. This, he said, was as long as any reasonable man could wish to spend in bed with any woman.
Harriette Wilson, *The Game of Hearts*, ed. Lesley Blanch (1955).

A gentleman called upon President Lincoln before the fall of Richmond and solicited a pass for that place. "I should be very happy to oblige you," said the President, "if my passes were respected; but the fact is, I have, within the past two years, given passes to two hundred and fifty thousand men to go to Richmond and not one has got there yet."
Paul Selby, *Anecdotal Lincoln* (1900).

[During the Civil War a confederate] soldier in W. H. T. Walker's division applied for a furlough. Gen'l Walker disapproved but respectfully forwarded to the HdQrtrs of Gen'l [D. H.] Hill where it was endorsed as follows: "Approved for the reason that a brave soldier ought to be allowed to go home whenever practicable, else all the children born during the war or within the usual period afterwards will be the offspring of the cowards who remain at home by reason of substitutes or other exemption."
Edwin H. Fay, *This Infernal War* (1958).

A young lieutenant [in the Navy] once asked . . . for permission to visit his home, for he expected his wife to have a baby soon. The Captain replied: "Not granted. It is customary that you should be there for the laying of the keel, but as for the launching, you are not needed."
Leland P. Lovette, *School of the Sea* (1941).

Time's correspondent [in Vietnam] Burt Pines related the case of a sergeant on patrol who shouted, "A three day pass for whoever gets that gook." After a moment's hesitation, most of the patrol opened up with their M-16s, ripping an old man, as well as the child he was carrying, into pieces.
Phillip Knightley, *The First Casualty* (1975).

liberty

Those who would give up essential liberty, to purchase a little temporary safety, deserve neither liberty nor safety.
Benjamin Franklin, writing in November 11, 1755, *The Papers of Benjamin Franklin*, ed. Leonard W. Labaree (1963). President Franklin D. Roosevelt used these words in a message to Congress, January 7, 1941.

The tree of liberty must be refreshed from time to time with the blood of patriots and tyrants. It is its natural manure.
Thomas Jefferson, November 13, 1787 letter to W. S. Smith, reprinted in *The Writings of Thomas Jefferson*, XI, ed. A. E. Bergh (1853).

He that would make his own liberty secure, must guard even his enemy from oppression; for if he violates this duty, he establishes a precedent that will reach to himself.
Thomas Paine, "Dissertation on First Principles of Government" (1795), *The Writings of Thomas Paine*, III, ed. D. Conway (1895). President Thomas Jefferson would write in an April 21, 1803 letter to Benjamin Rush: "It behoves every man who values liberty of conscience for himself, to resist invasions of it in the case of others; or their case may, by change of circumstances, become his own." *The Writings of Thomas Jefferson*, VIII, ed. Paul L. Ford (1897).

Eternal vigilance is the price of liberty—power is ever stealing from the many to the few. . . . The hand entrusted with power becomes . . . the necessary enemy of the people. Only by continual oversight can the democrat in office be prevented from hardening into a despot.
Wendell Phillips, speech in Boston, January 28, 1852, reprinted in his *Speeches Before the Massachusetts Anti-Slavery Society* (1853).

For the saddest epitaph which can be carved in memory of a vanished liberty is that it was lost because its possessors failed to stretch forth a saving hand while yet there was time.
Associate Justice George Sutherland of the U.S. Supreme Court, dissenting opinion in *Associated Press v. National Labor Relations Board* (1938).

My most cherished hope is that after Japan joins the Nazis in utter defeat, neither my country nor yours need ever again summon its sons and daughters from their peaceful pursuits to face the tragedies of battle. But—a fact important for both of us to remember—neither London nor Abilene, sisters under the skin, will sell her birthright for physical safety, her liberty for mere existence.
General Dwight D. Eisenhower, speech at Guildhall, London, June 12, 1945.

Let every nation know, whether it wishes us well or ill, that we shall pay any price, bear any burden, meet any hardship, support any friend, oppose any foe to assure the survival and the success of liberty.
President John F. Kennedy, Inaugural Address, January 20, 1961.

Extremism in the defense of liberty is no vice. And . . . moderation in the pursuit of justice is no virtue.
Senator Barry Goldwater, speech accepting the Republican Presidential nomination in San Francisco, July 16, 1964.

Libya

We know that this mad dog of the Middle East [Muammar Qaddafi of Libya] has a goal of a world revolution.
President Ronald Reagan, press conference, April 9, 1986.

Today we have done what we had to do. If necessary, we shall do it again.
President Ronald Reagan, address to the nation on the bombing of Libya in reprisal for terrorist acts, April 14, 1986.

The *News* says, Khadafy
The *Times* says, Qaddafi
Time says, Gaddafi
Newsweek, Kaddafi;
MOO-a-mar
Mo-AH-mar;
LIB-ya
LIB-ee-a;
Let's blow the whole thing off.
Jack Gescheidt, *The New York Times*, May 18, 1986.

Auschwitz-in-the-sand.
William Safire's name for the Libyan chemical weapons factory being built with the help of West German businesses, *The New York Times*, January 2, 1989.

Liddell Hart, Sir Basil H. (1895–1970)

I read a curious document by Liddell Hart who advocates peace with Germany since he believes we can only overthrow the Nazis by propaganda and cannot, in the military field, expect more than a stalemate, with exhaustion, disease and devastation on both sides, if indeed we are not defeated. This document, which has been privately circulated, is thought by the Admiralty to show traces of enemy propaganda and to be not spontaneous.
John Colville, *The Fringes of Power* (1985), diary entry for December 3, 1940.

I was . . . Military Attache in Berlin from April 1932 to May 1935, and during that time there I could not fail to be impressed by the extent to which both Liddell Hart's and "Boney" Fuller's books were being studied by Officers of all ranks and arms in the German Army. I knew both Blomberg (Minister for War) and Reichenau (Chief of the Defense Staff) very well, and they were both engaged in translating books by these two authors for use for non-English speaking German officers. . . .
Liddell Hart's themes and arguments had as stimulating an effect on the German military mentality as it had on ours, and I am not sure they even didn't get more value out of it than we did, as they were on the whole much better grounded in principles than we were.
General Sir Andrew Thorne, 1946 letter to Sir Maurice Hankey, quoted in Brian Bond, *Liddell Hart* (1977).

It was principally the books and articles of the Englishmen, Fuller, Liddell Hart and Martel, that excited my interest and gave me food for thought. These far-sighted soldiers were even then trying to make of the tank something more than just an infantry support weapon.

It was Liddell Hart who emphasized the use of armored forces for long-range strokes, operations against the opposing army's communications, and also proposed a type of armored division combining panzer and panzer-infantry units. Deeply impressed by these ideas I tried to develop them in a sense practicable for our own army.

General Heinz Guderian, *Panzer Leader* (1952).

We mostly studied the books of English tank experts like Captain Liddell Hart. German tank successes in the first year of the war were mainly due to the fact that we adopted the theories taught by Captain Liddell Hart while the enemy, in their thoughts, were still in the First World War.

General F. W. von Mellenthin, former Chief of Staff to Field Marshal Rommel, *Evening Standard* (August 27, 1959).

The walls of his study. . .are adorned with photographs of readers who found something of value in what the controversial Captain had to say. Heads of state are represented by Mussolini, Lloyd George, and John F. Kennedy; the British tank pioneers are there to a man; so, too, are many of the leading generals of the Second World War. But the photograph with the most appropriate inscription comes from the youthful commander of Israeli forces on the southern front against Egypt in 1948. General Yigal Allon wrote simply: "To Basil, the Captain who teaches Generals."

Jay Luvaas, *The Education of an Army* (1964).

[Liddell Hart] is now one of the most cogent critics of the strategic radicalism of today. The daring thinker of the thirties has become in the sixties the apostle of common sense, cautious and sceptical of the equally facile notions that deterrence is a substitute for defence, that nuclear weapons have made war impossible, or that they are a substitute for men at arms.

Alastair Buchan, *The Observer* (July 3, 1960).

No expert on military affairs has better earned the right to respectful attention than B.H. Liddell Hart. For two generations he has brought to the problems of war and peace a rare imaginative insight. His predictions and warnings have often proved correct.

Senator John F. Kennedy, *Saturday Review* (September 3, 1960).

Sir Basil Liddell Hart . . . is the military historian *non pareil*—very readable, absolutely clear, and an expert in analysis and comment. For over forty years I have known him personally and read his works; his military thinking has always appealed to me and it had a definite influence on my own conduct of war as I rose in military rank. Some historians are wise after the event; one has only to read the volumes of Liddell Hart's *Memoirs* to realize that he was wise before the event.

Field Marshal Viscount Montgomery of Alamein, *A History of Warfare (1968)*.

Liddell Hart firmly rejected the brainless human battering-ram tactics of General Haig and his fellows and reintroduced the notion that battles are won by ideas. There was always an indirect approach, he argued, always an unexpected place or unexpected way to hit the enemy.

Len Deighton, *Blitzkrieg* (1980).

line

[On May 11, 1864, General Grant] wrote a despatch of about two hundred words [to General Halleck]. In the middle of the communication occurred the famous words, "I propose to fight it out on this line if it takes all summer."

When the letter had been copied, he folded it and handed it to Mr. Washburne, who ... at once mounted his horse and rode off. The staff officers read the retained copy of the despatch, but neither the General himself nor any one at headquarters realized the epigrammatic character of the striking sentence it contained until the New York papers reached camp a few days afterward with the words displayed in large headlines.
Horace Porter, *Campaigning with Grant* (1897).

It is the line that gives you your high command, the line only, and very rarely the staff. The staff, however, dies infrequently, which is something. Do they say that military science can only be learned in the general staff schools? If you really want to learn to do your work, go to the line.
Ardant du Picq, *Battle Studies* (1868).

lines

An army should have but a single line of operations which it should carefully preserve, and should abandon only when compelled by imperious circumstances.
Napoleon I, *Military Maxims* (1827).

The roads which lead from the position of an army to those points in its rear at which its sources of subsistence and refitment are chiefly concentrated ... have a double purpose. In the first place they are its lines of communication for the constant sustenance of the forces and next, they are lines of retreat.
Karl von Clausewitz, *On War* (1832).

Simple and interior lines enable a general to bring into action, by strategic movements, upon the important point, a stronger force than the enemy. ... If the art of war consists in bringing into action upon the decisive point of the theater of operations the greatest possible force, the choice of the line of operations, being the primary means of attaining this end, may be regarded as the fundamental idea in a good plan of a campaign.
General Antoine Henri Jomini, *Summary of the Art of War* (1838).

The line that connects an army with its base of supplies is the heel of Achilles—its most vital and vulnerable point.
John S. Mosby, *War Reminiscences* (1887).

Interior lines are lines shorter in time than those the enemy can use.
Alfred Thayer Mahan, *Naval Strategy* (1911).

The national territory becomes the base of operations for the forces in the field, and the railways become their necessary lines of communication.
Marshal Ferdinand Foch, *Precepts and Judgments* (1920).

The unquestionable advantages of the inner line of operations are valid only as long as you retain enough space to advance against one enemy by a number of marches, thus gaining time to beat and to pursue him, and then to turn against the other who is in the meantime merely watched. If this space, however, is narrowed down to the extent that you cannot attack one enemy without running the risk of meeting the other

who attacks you from the flank or rear, then the strategic advantage of the inner line of operations turns into the tactical disadvantage of encirclement during the battle.
Field Marshal Helmuth von Moltke quoted in Hajo Holborn, "Moltke and Schlieffen," *Makers of Modern Strategy*, ed. E. M. Earle (1943).

"Interior lines" is a needlessly academic phrase to describe the simple fact of a central position.
B. H. Liddell Hart, *Thoughts on War* (1944).

logistics

The first man to call the baggage of an army "impedimenta" could not have found a better name. And whoever coined the phrase that says something "is more trouble than moving a camp," was very right. It is an endless task to get everything in a camp organized so that it can move.
Francesco Guicciardini, *Ricordi* (1530).

Understand that the foundation of an army is the belly. It is necessary to procure nourishment for the soldier wherever you assemble him and wherever you wish to conduct him. This is the primary duty of a general.
Frederick the Great, *Instructions for His Generals* (1747).

For the want of a nail the shoe was lost,
For the want of a shoe the horse was lost,
For the want of a horse the rider was lost,
For the want of a rider the battle was lost,
For the want of a battle the kingdom was lost—
And all for want of a horseshoe-nail.
Benjamin Franklin, *Poor Richard's Almanack* (1758).

What makes the general's function difficult is the necessity of nourishing so many men and animals; if he permits himself to be guided by administrators, he will never budge and his expeditions will fail.
Napoleon I, *Military Maxims* (1827).

It is very necessary to attend to detail, and to trace a biscuit from Lisbon into a man's mouth on the frontier, and to provide for its removal from place to place, by land and by water, or no military operations can be carried on.
Duke of Wellington quoted in Thomas Gilby, *Britain at Arms* (1953).

The word logistics is derived . . . from the title of the *major general des logis*, (translated in German by Quartiermeister,) an officer whose duty it formerly was to lodge and camp the troops, to give direction to the marches of columns, and to locate them upon the ground. Logistics was then quite limited. But when war began to be waged without camps, movements became more complicated, and the staff officers had more extended functions. The chief of staff began to perform the duty of transmitting the conceptions of the general to the most distant points of the theater of war.
General Antoine Henri Jomini, *Summary of the Art of War* (1838).

We can get along without anything but food and ammunition. The road to glory cannot be followed with much baggage.
Confederate General Richard S. Ewell quoted in Lynn Montross, *War Through the Ages* (1946).

I don't know what the hell this "logistics" is that [General] Marshall is always talking about, but I want some of it.
Attributed to Admiral Ernest J. King, during World War II.

To his headquarter staff, [General George] Patton raged that he was "up against two enemies—the Germans and our own high command. I can take care of the Germans, but I'm not sure I can win against Montgomery and Eisenhower." He tried. Convinced that he could bludgeon his way into Germany in a matter of days, Patton furiously appealed to Bradley and Eisenhower. "My men can eat their belts," he stormed, "but my tanks have gotta have gas."
Cornelius Ryan, *A Bridge Too Far* (1974).

The old aphorism that amateurs talk about strategy while professionals talk about logistics was validated again in the Falklands. The outcome of the battle may be seen to be a failure of Argentine logistics and a major success of British logistics. While a huge cache of supplies was built up after the initial Argentine invasion, the Argentine command in the Falklands was never able effectively to distribute the supplies and ammunition, and troops in the field were usually critically short of important items that were languishing close by in supply dumps.
John F. Lehman, Jr., *Command of the Seas* (1988).

loyalty

Very powerful in keeping the ancient soldiers well disposed were religion and the oath sworn when they were taken into service, because in all their transgressions they were threatened not alone with the ills they could fear from men but with those they could expect from God. This condition, mingled with other religious cushions, many times made every sort of undertaking easy for the ancient generals, and always will make them so, where religion is feared and observed.
Niccolò Machiavelli, *The Art of War* (1520).

My kind of loyalty was loyalty to one's country, not to its institutions or its office-holders. The country is the real thing, the substantial thing, the eternal thing; it is the thing to watch over, and care for, and be loyal to; institutions are extraneous, they are its mere clothing, and clothing can wear out, becomes ragged, cease to be comfortable, cease to protect the body from winter, disease, and death. To be loyal to rags, to shout for rags, to worship rags, to die for rags—that is a loyalty of unreason, it is pure animal; it belongs to monarchy, was invented by monarchy; let monarchy keep it.
Mark Twain, *A Connecticut Yankee in King Arthur's Court* (1889).

Loyalty is a noble quality, so long as it is not blind and does not exclude the higher loyalty to truth and decency. But the word is much abused. For "loyalty," analyzed, is too often a polite word for what would be more accurately described as "a conspiracy for mutual inefficiency."
B. H. Liddell Hart, *Why Don't We Learn From History?* (1943).

A good officer ought to recognize that there is a higher loyalty than that to his immediate superiors—loyalty to the army and the nation.
B. H. Liddell Hart, *Thoughts on War* (1944).

A good soldier is loyal to his Chief; it says so in the book. But what kind of loyalty is that—to fallible men above him, half the time dopes and cowards? What about loyalty to common sense . . . ?
William Wister Haines, *Command Decision* (1947).

Obedience is something a leader can command, but loyalty is something, an indefinable something, that he is obliged to win.
William A. Ganoe, *MacArthur Close-Up* (1962).

Numberless soldiers have died, more or less willingly, not for country or honor or religious faith or for any other abstract good, but because they realized that by fleeing their posts and rescuing themselves, they would expose their companions to greater danger. Such loyalty to the group is the essence of fighting morale.
I. Glenn Gray, *The Warriors* (1970).

I don't want loyalty. I want *loyalty*. I want him to kiss my ass in Macy's window at high noon and tell me it smells like roses. I want his pecker in my pocket.
President Lyndon B. Johnson, explaining what he meant by staff loyalty over Vietnam, quoted in Larry Berman, *Planning a Tragedy* (1982).

luck

The race is not to the swift, nor the battle to the strong, neither yet bread to the wise, nor yet riches to men of understanding, nor yet favor to men of skill; but time and chance happeneth to them all.
The Bible, Ecclesiastes 9:11.

The violence of war admits no distinctions; the lance that is lifted at guilt and power will sometimes fall on innocence and gentleness.
Samuel Johnson, *Rasselas* (1759).

War involves in its progress such a train of unforeseen and unsupposed circumstances that no human wisdom can calculate the end. It has but one thing certain, and that is to increase taxes.
Thomas Paine, *Prospects on the Rubicon* (1787).

War is composed of nothing but accidents and, although holding to general principles, a general should never lose sight of everything to enable him to profit from these accidents; that is the mark of genius.
Napoleon I, *Military Maxims* (1827).

[War is in] the province of chance. In no sphere of human activity is such a margin to be left for this intruder, because none is in such constant contact with it on every side.
Karl von Clausewitz, *On War* (1832).

I don't care for war, there's far too much luck in it for my liking.
Napoleon III, spoken after the Battle of Solferino, June 24, 1859, quoted in Edward Crankshaw, *The Fall of the House of Hapsburg* (1963).

Luck in the long run is given only to the efficient.
Field Marshal Helmuth von Moltke quoted in Alfred Vagts, *A History of Militarism*, rev. ed. (1959).

I also learned that in spite of all the training you get and precautions you take to keep yourself alive, its largely a matter of luck that decided whether or not you get killed. It doesn't make any difference who you are, how tough you are, how nice a guy you might be, or how much you may know, if you happen to be at a certain spot at a certain time, you get it.
James Jones, letter to Jeff Jones from Guadalcanal, January 28, 1943, reprinted in *The New York Times Magazine* (March 8, 1989).

That's the way it is in war. You win or lose, live or die—and the difference is just an eyelash.
General Douglas MacArthur, *Reminiscences* (1964).

I know what you're thinking. Did he fire six shots or only five? Well, to tell you the truth, in all this excitement I've kinda lost track myself. But being this is a .44 magnum, the most powerful handgun in the world, and would blow your head clean off— you've got to ask yourself one question: do I feel lucky? Well, do ya, punk?
Clint Eastwood in *Dirty Harry* (1971), directed by Don Siegel; screenplay by Harry Julian Fink, R.M. Fink, and Dean Riesner.

machine gun

I shall never forget the way
That Blood stood upon this awful day
Preserved us all from death.
He stood upon a little mound
Cast his lethargic eyes around,
And said beneath his breath:
"Whatever happens, we have got
The Maxim Gun, and they have not."
Hilaire Belloc, *The Modern Traveller* (1900).

In 1910 the [French] Director-General of Infantry complacently confided to a group of parliamentarians that the French General Staff was having machine guns manufactured merely as a sop to public opinion. "Make no mistake," he declared, "this weapon will change absolutely nothing."
William L. Shirer, *The Collapse of the Third Republic* (1969).

Take [Lord] Kitchener's maximum, square it, multiply the result by two—and when you are in sight of that, double it again for good luck.
Prime Minister David Lloyd George, insisting that World War I British troops have more machine guns, quoted in B. H. Liddell Hart, *The War in Outline* (1936). This was in response to the British Army's attitude in 1915 that "the machine gun is a much overrated weapon" and that "two per battalion is more than sufficient."

[Evidently] when you are twenty years old it is great fun to turn a machine-gun on a crowd of unarmed "natives".
George Orwell, *New Statesman and Nation* (August 18, 1937).

The machine gun was an essentially American invention. Not simply because the four greatest names of machine gun history—Gatling, Maxim, Browning and Lewis— were Americans, but also because it was in America that were first developed the material conditions that made automatic fire a feasible proposition.
John Ellis, *The Social History of the Machine Gun* (1975).

Like an automatic press, it would, when actuated by a simple trigger, begin and continue to perform its functions with the minimum of human attention, supplying its own power and only requiring a steady supply of raw material and a little routine maintenance to operate efficiently throughout a working shift. The machine-gunner is best thought of, in short, as a sort of machine-minder.... The appearance of the machine-gun, therefore, had not so much *disciplined* the act of killing—which was what seventeenth-century drill had done—as *mechanized* or *industrialized* it.
John Keegan, *The Face of Battle* (1976).

manifest destiny

The fulfillment of our manifest destiny [is] to overspread the continent allotted by Providence for the free development of our yearly multiplying millions.
John L. O'Sullivan, "Editorial," *U.S. Magazine and Democratic Review* (July 1845). The first use of the term "manifest destiny" was in this editorial supporting the annexation of Texas.

The annexationists argued [in 1898] that if the United States did not take Hawaii, Great Britain would, or alternatively Japan, who was already plotting to gain control by encouraging the influx of Japanese subjects subsidized by their government. Besides, it now lay clearly in the American path. "We need Hawaii just as much and a good deal more than we did California," [President] McKinley told his secretary, George Cortelyou, on May 4. "It is Manifest Destiny."
Barbara W. Tuchman, *The Proud Tower* (1966).

If America ever fought an unavoidable war, it was the conflict with Mexico over the delineation of the common boundary. The whole thrust of America's physical and cultural growth carried her inexorably westward.... Thrust in the way of this movement were three sparsely settled and inadequately protected Mexican provinces: Alta California, New Mexico, and Texas. If the inexorable demands of destiny drove the United States onto Mexican lands, similar demands of nationalism and self-respect prevented Mexico from parting with those areas except to overwhelming force.
K. Jack Bauer, *The Mexican War* (1974).

maps

Roll up that map; it will not be wanted these ten years.
William Pitt, on the map of Europe after hearing of Napoleon's 1805 victory at Austerlitz, quoted in Lord Stanhope, *Life of William Pitt* (1862).

Prussian Lieutenant: I want a globe.
Shopkeeper: Terrestrial or celestial?
Prussian Lieutenant: Oh, no! Don't you have any globes of Prussia?
Caption to an 1865 German Newspaper cartoon reprinted in Alfred Vagts, *A History of Militarism*, rev. ed. (1959).

General George B. McClellan had elaborate maps prepared for his Virginia campaign of 1862 and found to his dismay when he arrived on the scene that they were unreliable; "the roads are wrong...," he wailed.
T. Harry Williams, *Lincoln and His Generals* (1952).

While the battles the British fight may differ in the widest possible ways, they have invariably two common characteristics—they are always fought uphill and always at the junction of two or more map sheets.
Sir William Slim, *Unofficial History* (1959).

Time and again he [George C. Marshall] required that classes [at Fort Benning in the early 1930s] work with road maps, foreign maps, maps that were out of date. After World War II an officer who had been one of his students, General Charles Bolte, said: "I think he was so right, because that's exactly what we had—maps of North Africa that were no good, and as far as the Pacific was concerned, if you got a sketch you were lucky."
Forrest C. Pogue, *George C. Marshall: Education of a General* (1963).

The most remarkable escape story of all concerns Havildar [sergeant] Manbahadur Rai.... He escaped from a Japanese prison camp in southern Burma and in five

months walked 600 miles until at last he reached the safety of his own lines. Interrogated by British intelligence officers about his remarkable feat, Manbahadur told them that the Burmese had not helped him. . . . But all that had not mattered, for he had a map, which before his capture had been given him by a British soldier in exchange for his cap badge. He produced the much creased and soiled map. The intelligence officers stared at it in awe. It was a street map of London.
Byron Farwell, *The Gurkhas* (1984).

marches

An army is exposed to more danger on marches than in battles. In an engagement the men are properly armed, they see their enemies before them and are prepared to fight. But on a march the soldier is less on his guard, has not his arms always ready and is thrown into disorder by a sudden attack or ambuscade. A general, therefore, cannot be too careful and diligent in taking necessary precautions to prevent a surprise on the march.
Vegetius, *De Re Militari* (378 A.D.).

When the army is in column of march there must be advanced guards and flank guards to observe the enemy's movements in front, on the right, and on the left; and at sufficient distances to allow the main body of the arm to deploy and take up its position.
Napoleon I, *Military Maxims* (1827).

An army can march anywhere and at any time of the year, wherever two men can place their feet.
Napoleon I, *Military Maxims* (1827).

An army marches on its stomach.
Attributed to both Napoleon I and Frederick the Great.

Whether the march is of the one kind or the other, it is a fundamental principle of the modern art of war, in all cases in which even the possibility of an engagement is conceivable, that is, in the whole realm of real war, so to organize the columns that the mass of troops composing each column is capable of independent engagement.
Karl von Clausewitz, *On War* (1832).

As a general rule, the maxim of marching to the sound of the guns is a very wise one.
General Antoine Henri Jomini, *The Political and Military History of the Campaign of Waterloo* (1853).

I had rather lose one man in marching than five in fighting.
General Thomas J. "Stonewall" Jackson quoted in G. F. R. Henderson, *Stonewall Jackson and the American Civil War*, I (1926).

The columns should always support each other, and therefore, unless they have received a special mission, or are in conflict themselves, should march to the sound of the guns. This is an excellent rule, and, except under contrary and precise orders, it is the duty of the officer commanding a body of troops to direct his steps towards the cannonade so as to lend a hand to the troops engaged.
Colonel George Armand Furse, *The Art of Marching* (1901).

The General said to me: "The War Office is very nervous about an invasion, there are five million . . . sheep in Sussex, Kent and Surrey. When the enemy land, they will at once be moved by route march to Salisbury Plain." I knew that this was an impossible task. . . . But there was no arguing over it, so I spent days and days working out march tables for sheep. One day I said to him: "Do you realize, sir, that should all these sheep be set in movement, every road will be blocked?" "Of course," he answered; "at once arrange to have a number of signposts ready and marked, 'Sheep are not to use this road.' " "But," I replied, "what if the less well-educated sheep are unable to read them?" This brought our conversation to an end.

J. F. C. Fuller, *Memoirs of an Unconventional Soldier* (1936).

Marine Corps, U.S.

Resolved, That two Battalions of marines be raised, consisting of one Colonel, two Lieutenant Colonels, two Majors, and other officers as usual in other regiments; and that they consist of an equal number of privates with other battalions; that particular care be taken, that no person appointed to office, or enlisted into said Battalions, but such as are good seamen, or so acquainted with maritime affairs as to be able to serve to advantage by sea when required; that they be enlisted and commissioned to serve for and during the present war between Great Britain and the colonies, unless dismissed by order of Congress; that they be distinguished by the names of the first and second battalions of American marines, and that they be considered as part of the number which the continental Army before Boston is ordered to consist of.

The resolution of the Continental Congress that established the U.S. Marine Corps on November 10, 1775.

Tell that to the Marines—the sailors won't believe it.

Sir Walter Scott, *Redgauntlet*, II (1824). This referred to the Royal Marines, who sailors felt were lazy and stupid because aboard ship they functioned as prison guards for the sailors.

The hostility between the Marines and Sailors constitute in my judgment the strongest argument in favour of their great utility on board ships of war, and it should be the policy of Navy officers to promote that hostility in order to more effectively guard against mutiny of sailors.

Captain Samuel E. Watson, in a letter to Archibald Henderson, Commandant of the U.S. Marine Corps, March 17, 1830, quoted in Allan R. Millett, *Semper Fidelis* (1980).

From the halls of Montezuma to the shores
    of Tripoli,
We fight our country's battles in the air, on
    land and sea,
First to fight for rights and freedom,
And to keep our honor clean,
We are proud to claim the title
    Of United States Marine . . .
If the Army and the Navy
Ever gaze on Heaven's scenes,
They will find the streets are guarded
    By United States Marines.

The Marines Hymn, author anonymous (late 1800s).

The Marines are considered a sort of elite Corps, designed to go into action outside the United States. The high percentage of Marksmen, Sharpshooters, and Expert Riflemen, as perceived among our prisoners, allows a conclusion to be drawn as to the quality of the training in rifle marksmanship that the Marines receive. The prisoners are mostly members of the better class, and they consider their membership in the

Marine Corps to be something of an honor. They proudly resent any attempts to place their regiments on a par with other infantry regiments. . . .

World War I German report on Marine POWs quoted in Robert Debs Heinl, Jr., *Soldiers of the Sea* (1962).

We will not forget you. As we embrace you in uniform today, we will embrace you without uniform tomorrow.

Secretary of the Navy Josephus Daniels' inadvertently funny tribute to World War I female Marines as they were mustered out, quoted in Linda L. Hewitt, *Woman Marines in World War I* (1974).

They were the old breed of American regular, regarding the service as home and war as an occupation.

John W. Thomason, Jr., *Fix Bayonets!* (1926).

I helped make Mexico safe for American oil interests in 1914. I helped make Haiti and Cuba a decent place for the National City Bank boys to collect revenue in. I helped purify Nicaragua for the international banking house of Brown Brothers. . . . I brought light to the Dominican Republic and American sugar interests in 1916. I helped make Honduras "right" for American fruit companies in 1903. Looking back on it, I might have given Al Capone a few hints.

General Smedley D. Butler, U.S.M.C., *The New York Times* (August 21, 1931).

The Marine Corps, then, believes that it has earned this right—to have its future decided by the legislative body which created it—nothing more. Sentiment is not a valid consideration in determining questions of national security. We have pride in ourselves and in our past but we do not rest our case on any presumed gratitude owing us from the nation. The bended knee is not a tradition of our Corps. If the Marine as a fighting man has not made a case for himself after 170 years of service, he must go. But I think you will agree with me he has earned the right to depart with dignity and honor, not by subjugation to the status of uselessness and servility planned for him by the War Department.

General Alexander A. Vandegift, Commandant of the U.S. Marine Corps, testimony before the Senate Naval Affairs Committee, May 10, 1946.

A small bitched-up Army talking Navy lingo. We are going to put those Marines in the Regular Army and make efficient soldiers out of them.

Brigadier General Frank A. Armstrong, December 11, 1946, quoted in Demetrious Caraley, *The Politics of Military Unification* (1966).

The Marine Corps is the Navy's police force . . . and as long as I am President that is what it will remain. They have a propaganda machine that is almost equal to Stalin's.

President Harry S. Truman, August 29, 1950 letter to Representative Gordon L. McDonough, printed in *Time* (September 18, 1950). This was in response to McDonough's suggestion that the Marine Corps be represented on the Joint Chiefs of Staff. When Truman's letter was made public, he quickly apologized for "the unfortunate choice of language."

During the retreat from Chochin Reservoir, a Marine officer told his troops: We're going to come out of this as Marines, not as stragglers. We're going to bring out our wounded and our equipment. We're coming out, I tell you, as Marines or not as all.

Marguerite Higgens, *War in Korea* (1951).

Joe Owen, the mortar section leader, was a real Marine. We had asked, "Where you from, Joe?"

"Here."

"Naw, Joe. Where's home?"

"Right here. Wherever the Marines send me, that's home."

Dean Westberg quoted in Donald Knox, *The Korean War: Pusan to Chosin* (1985).

We're professional soldiers. We fight any enemy the President designates. We don't just keep talking Communism, Communism, Communism. You might build up hate against one enemy and find yourself fighting another.

General David M. Shoup, Commandant of the U.S. Marine Corps, *The New York Times* (October 29, 1961).

Whereas the American government generally approved of the Marine Corps' performance in Hispaniola, other articulate Americans became convinced that the Marine Corps was the tool of American overseas corporations and a bloodthirsty collection of sociopathic misfits who derived great satisfaction from gunning down helpless Dominicans and Haitians. This view was a caricature, but the Marine Corps was saddled with it until World War II.

Allan R. Millett, *Semper Fidelis* (1980).

The Marine Corps had always recruited a disproportionate number of men from the South. . . . They were born killers; in the Raider battalions, in violation of orders, they would penetrate deep behind Japanese lines at night, looking for two Nips sacked out together. Then they would cut the throat of one and leave the other to find the corpse in the morning. Their's was brilliant psychological warfare. . . . In combat these Southerners would charge fearlessly with the shrill rebel yell of their great-grandfathers, and they loved the bayonet. How my father's side defeated my mother's side in the Civil War will always mystify me.

William Manchester, *Good-bye, Darkness* (1980).

The basic secret of the Marine Corps is that every Marine is trained as a rifleman or a platoon leader.

General Leonard F. Chapman, Jr., Commandant, U.S. Marine Corps, *The Washington Post* (December 19, 1971).

If we didn't have a Marine Corps we would have to invent one.

General Louis H. Wilson, Commandant, U.S. Marine Corps, *The Washington Post* (November 9, 1975).

I'll let General [Paul] Kelley's words describe the incident. He spoke of a "young Marine with more tubes going in and out of his body than I have ever seen in one body. He couldn't see very well. He reached up and grabbed my four stars just to make sure I was who I said I was. He held my hand with a firm grip. He was making signals and we realized he wanted to tell me something. We put a pad of paper in his hand and he wrote, 'semper fi.' "

Well, if you've been a Marine, or if, like myself, you're an admirer of the Marines, you know those words are a battle cry, a greeting and a legend in the Marine Corps. They're marine shorthand for the motto of the Corps: Semper Fidelis, Always Faithful.

President Ronald Reagan, speech to the nation on Lebanon and Grenada, October 27, 1983.

I think the nation loves our Marine Corps, and I think they pray for us and they support us. But they also place some very special demands on us, and one is that we be the premier military organization in the world. I'm not sure if we're that good, but that's exactly where we're going to go if we aren't.

General Alfred M. Gray, Jr., Commandant, U.S. Marine Corps, *Los Angeles Times* (August 13, 1987).

McNamara, Robert Strange (b. 1916)

President Johnson . . . stated that he was the "best Secretary of Defense the nation ever had." But McNamara was a manager, not a leader. Unfortunately, as head of the largest establishment in America, where professional career officers considered leadership a pre-eminent qualification for high responsibility, the Secretary lacked the touch with his people which could create loyalty, enthusiasm, and high morale.
James A. Donovan, *Militarism, U.S.A.* (1970).

After McNamara killed the B-70 and a host of other Air Force weapons, and then stopped building Minuteman after reaching 1,000 missiles, [General] LeMay would often ominously inquire of his Air Force friends, "I ask you: would things be much worse if Khrushchev were Secretary of Defense?"
Fred Kaplan, *The Wizards of Armageddon* (1983).

At the end of November [1967], McNamara learned through a press leak of his appointment as the new president of the World Bank. Johnson decided that his secretary of defense, who had been at the Pentagon for the better part of seven years, had come unstrung from too many years of carrying the burden of the war. The man had deteriorated into "an emotional basket case," the president told his press secretary, George Christian.
Neil Sheehan, *A Bright Shining Lie* (1988). Johnson would also complain that "McNamara's gone dovish on me."

Another cause for wonder is the way anti-nuclear politics has served as a reentry vehicle into liberal respectability for dubious characters like Robert S. McNamara and McGeorge Bundy. A decade ago they were widely regarded as war criminals; now a couple of high-minded pronunciamentos about how awful a nuclear war would be, and they start winning peace awards.
Michael Kinsley, "TRB," *The New Republic* (November 28, 1983).

Medal of Honor

I would rather have that medal, the Congressional Medal of Honor, than to be president of the United States.
President Harry S. Truman, remarks upon presenting the Medal of Honor to fourteen men of the Navy and Marine Corps, October 5, 1945.

During the war I found that men who won the Medal of Honor—and survived—were so conscious of the distinction that when they returned to combat they showed even greater courage, took greater risks and were far more likely to be killed than their comrades. This tendency was so pronounced that I instituted a policy of sending such men back to the states to train and inspire our untried troops. Usually they would protest bitterly, but I never let myself be swayed.
General Mark Clark, "Recapturing What Honor Really Means," *Rocky Mountain News* (May 5, 1984). This article was originally written for the North American Newspaper Alliance in 1968.

medals

Washington . . . decreed that in reward for singular merit—"not only instances of unusual gallantry but also of extraordinary fidelity and essential services in any way"—a common soldier should be entitled to wear on his left breast "the figure of a heart in purple cloth or silk." This would empower him "to pass all guards and sentinels which officers are permitted to do." What Washington called the "Badge of Military Merit" was the first general decoration established in the American army.

Being limited to privates and noncommissioned officers, it revealed, Washington wrote, that "the road to glory in a patriot army and a free country is thus open to all."
James T. Flexner, *George Washington: In the American Revolution* (1967). This decoration was revived in 1933 as the Purple Heart and made available to officers as well as enlisted men who were wounded in action.

When [Antoine] Thibaudeau, an ex-revolutionary, objected in the Council of State that decorations were "baubles," Napoleon replied, "You are pleased to call them 'baubles': well, it is with 'baubles' that mankind is governed."
Felix Markham, *Napoleon* (1963).

The cross of the Legion of Honor has been conferred upon me. However, few escape that distinction.
Mark Twain, *A Tramp Abroad* (1880).

The number of medals on an officer's breast varies in inverse proportion to the square of the distance of his duties from the front lines.
Charles E. Montague, *Fiery Particles* (1923).

We have all seen self-seeking men go behind the lines to win decorations. But it is those who bestow them who are the more culpable.
René Quinton, *Soldier's Testament* (1930).

The old man [Air Marshal Hugh Trenchard] cast a powerful spell. Visiting 76 Squadron in 1942, he walked into the mess tent set for lunch in his honor, sidestepped his intended place among the "Brass" and sat down instead with the young pilots below the salt. He noticed one wearing the single ribbon of the DFC and glanced down at his own vastly decorated chest: "Don't worry, my boy," he boomed. "Once you've got one, they grow on you like measles."
Max Hastings, *Bomber Command* (1979).

The result of decorations works two ways. It makes the men who get them proud and determined to get more, and it makes the men who have not received them jealous and determined to get some in order to even up. It is the greatest thing we have for building a fighting heart.
General George S. Patton, Jr., quoted in Harry H. Semmes, *Portrait of Patton* (1955).

[Goering] The Reich-Marshal. . . . would send signals to his commanders advising them which units he proposed to visit on the following day. These signals shed an interesting light on the absence of spit and polish in the German squadrons [during the Battle of Britain]. Goering was fastidious and he had obviously found some of the pilots, to whom he was lavishly handing out decorations, not quite to his liking. As a result his signals now instructed the commanding officers to make quite sure that the men whom he was going to decorate were properly deloused; he had obviously had an unfortunate experience.
F. W. Winterbotham, *The Ultra Secret* (1974).

He really deserves some sort of decoration . . . a medal inscribed "For Vaguery in the Field."
John Osborne *Look Back in Anger*, Act I (1957).

No honor I have ever received moves me more deeply. Perhaps this is because I can recall no parallel in history where a great nation recently at war has so distinguished its former enemy commander.
General Douglas MacArthur, on receiving a decoration from Japan, *The New York Times* (June 22, 1960).

When Khrushchev [on meeting President Kennedy in Vienna in 1961] said that the medal he was wearing was for the Lenin Peace Prize, Kennedy retorted with a smile: "I hope you keep it."
Theodore C. Sorensen, *Kennedy* (1965).

medals—Vietnam War

How can they give you a medal for a war they don't even want you to fight?
Bruce Dern in *Coming Home* (1978), directed by Hal Ashby; screenplay by Waldo Salt and Robert C. Jones.

Disregard all Legions of Merit, Air Medals, Distinguished Service Medals. Discount Silver Stars if the officer was high-ranking when it was awarded and if unaccompanied by a Purple Heart.
A U.S. Marine Corps officer's method for interpreting military awards, quoted in *Newsweek*, July 9, 1984.

It got to be a game between the Communists [in Vietnam] and ourselves to see how many fingers and ears that we could capture from each other. After a kill we would cut his finger or ear off as a trophy, stuff our unit patch in his mouth, and let him die.
I collected about 14 ears and fingers. With them strung on a piece of leather around my neck, I would go downtown, and you would get free drugs, free booze, free pussy because they wouldn't wanna bother with you 'cause this man's a killer. It symbolized that I'm a killer. And it was, so to speak, a symbol of combat-type manhood.
Arthur E. "Gene" Woodly, Jr., quoted in Wallace Terry, *Bloods* (1984).

Judged by their medals, almost all officers sent to Vietnam must have been heroes.
Edward N. Luttwak, *The Pentagon and the Art of War* (1985).

In what could only be seen as a continued debasement of an awards system already thoroughly prostituted in Vietnam, for the Grenada operation 8,612 medals (almost 200 for bravery) were awarded when there were no more than seven thousand U.S. personnel on the tiny island at any time during the three days of sputtering combat against a few Cuban troops. Somehow I don't think that's what Napoleon had in mind when he suggested if he had enough ribbon he could conquer the world.
David H. Hackworth, *About Face* (1989).

medics

Daily practice of the military exercises is much more efficacious in preserving the health of an army than all the art of medicine.
Vegetius, *De Re Militari* (378 A.D.).

Keep two lancets; a blunt one for the soldiers, and a sharp one for the officers: this will be making a proper distinction between them.
Francis Grose, *Advice to the Officers of the British Army* (1782).

The sick rate of the Georgian [eighteenth-century British] navy is not on record. Captains did not care to report a noticeably long sick list and surgeons liked to keep captains happy. If the daily quota was twelve, the surgeon's mate might say to No. 13, "Avast, you bugger. I won't have any more today." One doctor dosed all patients with salt water to reduce complaints. While drunk, he fell overboard and his mate reported to the captain, "Sir, he drowned in his own medicine chest."
James Dugan, *The Great Mutiny* (1965).

My exodus from the [World War I] Front Line was a garrulous one. A German bullet had passed through me leaving a neat hole near my right shoulder-blade and this patriotic perforation had made a different man of me. I now looked at the War, which had been a monstrous tyrant, with liberated eyes. For the time being I had regained my right to call myself a private individual.

The first stage of my return journey took me to the Advanced Dressing Station, a small underground place crowded with groaning wounded. Two doctors were doing what they could for men who had paid a heavy price for their freedom. My egocentricity diminished among all that agony. I remember listening to an emotional padre who was painfully aware that he could do nothing except stand about and feel sympathetic. The consolations of the Church of England weren't much in demand at an Advanced Dressing Station.

Siegfried Sassoon, *Siegfried Sassoon's Long Journey*, ed. Paul Fussell (1983).

[In November 1941] Rommel ... visited a field hospital, full of a mixed bag of German and British wounded. Walking between the beds, he observed that the hospital was still in British hands and that British soldiers were all about. It was, indeed, a British medical officer who was conducting him round, having mistaken him, or so he imagined, for a Polish general. The German wounded goggled at him and began to sit up in bed. "I think we'd better get out of this," whispered Rommel. As he jumped into "Mammut," [his British-made armored command truck] he acknowledged a final salute.

Desmond Young, *Rommel* (1950).

When [Bob] Hope went into a hospital he was likely to go up to a poor guy swathed in bandages, and instead of spreading out the old sympathy he would shake hands and say something such as, "Did you see my show this evening, or were you already sick?"

Ernie Pyle, *Brave Men* (1944).

Behind an evil-looking barricade of barbed wire [in a U.S. Army hospital in Tunisia], was "Casanova Park." Back there were 150 soldiers with venereal disease.

"What's the barbed wire for?" I asked. "They wouldn't try to get out anyhow."

"It's just to make them feel like heels, " said the colonel. "There's no damned excuse for a soldier getting caught nowadays unless he just doesn't care. When he gets venereal disease he's no good to his country and somebody else has to do his work. So I want him to feel ashamed."

Ernie Pyle, *Here Is Your War* (1945).

Fanned by the fierce winds of war, medical science and surgical art have advanced unceasingly, hand in hand. There has certainly been no lack of subjects for the treatment. The medical profession at least cannot complain of unemployment through lack of raw material.

Winston Churchill, speech to the International Congress of Physicians at the Guildhall, London, September 10, 1947.

[On August 3, 1943 General Patton shouts at and hits a "shell shock" patient during a visit to a field hospital in Sicily.] Your nerves, Hell, you are just a goddammed coward, you yellow son of bitch. . . . You ought to be lined up against a wall and shot. . . . In fact I ought to shoot you myself right now, goddam you. . . . I won't have these other brave boys seeing such a bastard babied!

General George S. Patton, Jr., quoted in A. N. Garland and H. M. Smyth, *Sicily and the Surrender of Italy* (1965). This is the incident that nearly got Patton sent home for the duration.

"Major," [Sergeant Charles] Dohun told the doctor, "my captain needs attention right away." The major shook his head. "I'm sorry, sergeant. . . . He'll have to wait his turn." . . . Dohun pulled out his .45 and cocked the trigger. "It's not soon enough," he said calmly. "Major, I'll kill you right where you stand if you don't look at him right now." Astonished, the surgeon stared at Dohun. "Bring him in," he said.

In the operating theater Dohun stood by, his .45 in hand as the doctor and a medical team worked on Johnson. When the operation was completed . . . he handed over his .45. "O.K.," he said, "thanks. Now you can turn me in."

Dohun was . . . brought before the commanding officer. . . . he was asked if he was aware of exactly what he had done and that his action constituted a court-martial offense. Dohun replied, "Yes, sir, I do." Pacing up and down, the commander suddenly stopped. "Sergeant," he said, "I'm placing you under arrest"—he paused and looked at his watch—"for exactly one minute." The two men waited in silence. Then the officer look at Dohun. "Dismissed," he said. "Now get back to your unit."
Cornelius Ryan, *A Bridge Too Far* (1974).

Medics in the 101st carried M & M candies in their medical kits long before the psychiatrists found it necessary to explain away their actions. They offered them as placebos for their wounded who were too broken for morphine, slipping the sweets between their lips as they whispered to them over the noise of the fighting that it was for the pain. In a world of suffering and death, Vietnam is like a Walt Disney true-life adventure, where the young are suddenly left alone to take care of the young.
Ronald J. Glasser, *365 Days* (1971).

memorials

Go, tell the Spartans, thou who passeth by:
Carrying out their orders, here we lie.
Simonides, epitaph for the Spartan dead at Thermopylae, quoted in Herodotus, *Histories* (5th century B.C.).

As Caesar loved me, I weep for him; as he was fortunate, I rejoice at it; as he was valiant, I honor him: but as he was ambitious, I slew him. There is tears for his love; joy for his fortune; honor for his valor; and death for his ambition.
William Shakespeare, *Julius Caesar*, Act III (1600).

Fourscore and seven years ago, our fathers brought forth upon this continent a new nation, conceived in liberty, and dedicated to the proposition that all men are created equal. Now we are engaged in a great civil war, testing whether that nation, or any nation so conceived and so dedicated, can long endure. We are met on a great battlefield of that war. We are met to dedicate a portion of it as the final resting place of those who here gave their lives that that nation might live. It is altogether fitting and proper that we should do this. But in a larger sense we cannot dedicate—we cannot consecrate—we cannot hallow this ground. The brave men, living and dead, who struggled here, have consecrated it far above our poor power to add or detract. The world will little note, nor long remember, what we say here, but it can never forget what they did here. It is for us, the living, rather to be dedicated here to the unfinished work that they have thus far so nobly advanced. It is rather for us to be here dedicated to the great task remaining before us, that from these honored dead we take increased devotion to that cause for which they here gave the last full measure of devotion; that we here highly resolve that these dead shall not have died in vain; that this nation, under God, shall have a new birth of freedom, and that government of the people, by the people, for the people, shall not perish from the earth.
President Abraham Lincoln's Gettysburg Address, November 19, 1863.

To die at the height of a man's career, the highest moment of his effort here in this world, universally honored and admired, to die while great issues are still commanding the whole of his interest, to be taken from us at a moment when he could already see ultimate success in view—is not the most unenviable of fates.

Winston Churchill, speech on the death of Lord Lothian, British Ambassador to the United States (who died in Washington on December 11, 1940), in the House of Commons, December 19, 1940.

In memory of Peggy who in her lifetime kicked one brigadier, two colonels, four majors, ten captains, 24 lieutenants, 42 sergeants, 60 corporals, 436 other ranks and one bomb.

Peggy was a British Army mule. *Time* (December 18, 1944).

mercenaries

If any one supports his state by the arms of mercenaries, he will never stand firm or sure, as they are disunited, ambitious, without discipline, faithless, bold amongst friends, cowardly amongst enemies, they have no fear of God, and keep no faith with men. Ruin is only deferred as long as the assault is postponed; in peace you are despoiled by them, and in war by the enemy. The cause of this is that they have no love or other motive to keep them in the field beyond a trifling wage, which is not enough to make them ready to die for you. They are quite willing to be your soldiers so long as you do not make war.

Niccolò Machiavelli, *The Prince* (1513).

Let us therefore animate and encourage each other, and show the whole world, that a Freeman contending for LIBERTY on his own ground is superior to any slavish mercenary on earth.

General George Washington, General Orders of July 2, 1776, *The Writings of George Washington*, V, ed. J. C. Fitzpatrick (1931–44).

The analogy of the mercenary and the prostitute is apt. In each case economic power is abused to hire human bodies with the specific intentions of avoiding public association with them and responsibility for their welfare, and using money to exploit moral weakness. It was Gus Grillo, the captured American mercenary, who first coined the metaphor. As a former Mafia enforcer, he knew enough about both trades. In the mercenary business, too, it is the recruiters, the pimps of war, who deserve the greater blame. And if it were not for those who pay the money, the trade would not exist.

Wilfred Burchett and Derek Roebuck, *The Whores of War* (1977).

Purchasing military service is an old practice. Thucydides tells of commanders in the Peloponnesian War augmenting their forces by going to towns near their lines of march to engage bowmen or stone-slingers. Athens used its treasure to lure foreign and domestic rowers to its triremes, the battleships of the day. During the Renaissance, Switzerland was known throughout Europe as the exporter of its prime commodity: fine pikemen. A vestige of this tradition remains today in the Swiss Guards, who police the Vatican and serve as bodyguards of the Pope.

Paul Seabury and Angelo Codevilla, *War* (1989).

Mexican War

The cup of forbearance had been exhausted. . . . After reiterated menaces, Mexico has passed the boundary of the United States, has invaded our territory and shed

American blood upon American soil. She has proclaimed that hostilities have commenced, and that the two nations are now at war.
President James K. Polk, message on war with Mexico, May 11, 1846.

If I were a Mexican, I would tell you, "Have you not enough room in your own country to bury your dead men? If you come into mine, I will greet you with bloody hands and welcome you to hospitable graves."
Thomas Corwin, speech in the U.S. Senate opposing the Mexican War, February 11, 1846.

Though the United States were the aggrieved nation, Mexico commenced the war, and we were compelled in self-defense to repel the invader and to vindicate the national honor and interests by prosecuting it with vigor until we could obtain a just and honorable peace. . . .
It is well known that the only indemnity which it is in the power of Mexico to make in satisfaction of the just and long-deferred claims of our citizens against her and the only means by which she can reimburse the United States for the expenses of the war is a cession to the United States of a portion of her territory. Mexico has no money to pay, and no other means of making the required indemnity. If we refuse this, we can obtain nothing else.
President James K. Polk, third annual message to Congress, December 7, 1847.

I do not think there ever was a more wicked war than that waged by the United States in Mexico. I thought so at the time, when I was a youngster, only I had not moral courage enough to resign . . . It was an instance of a republic following the bad example of European monarchies, in not considering justice in their desire to acquire additional territory.
President Ulysses S. Grant, *Personal Memoirs* (1885).

[General U.S. Grant on first meeting General Robert E. Lee at Appomattox Court House, Virginia on April 9, 1865] "I met you once before, General Lee, while we were serving in Mexico, when you came over from General Scott's headquarters to visit Garland's brigade, to which I then belonged. I have always remembered your appearance, and I think I should have recognized you anywhere."
"Yes," replied General Lee, "I know I met you on that occasion, and I have often thought of it and tried to recollect how you looked, but I have never been able to recall a single feature."
Horace Porter, *Battles and Leaders of the Civil War* (1887).

Alas, poor Mexico! So far from God and so close to the United States.
Porfirio Diaz quoted in John S. D. Eisenhower, *So Far From God* (1989).

Mickey Mouse

"Mickey Mouse"—or "chicken regs," as they are called just as often—is a term that covers, for one thing, those self-serving regulations and practices by which some commanders attempt to give an appearance of efficiency or smartness but which in fact make no contribution to either of those desirable conditions. Hastily painting over rust spots the day before inspection is that kind of Mickey Mouse, and so is making a sailor change out of dungarees into a liberty uniform before going to the commissary for a candy bar. . . . Requiring a person going home on leave to prove he or she had the money for a round-trip ticket is that kind of Mickey Mouse, and so is refusing to provide parking spaces on naval stations for motorcycles on the grounds that motorcycles (unlike nuclear submarines or guided missile frigates or helicopters) are too dangerous for sailors to ride.
Elmo R. Zumwalt, Jr., *On Watch* (1976).

A summit must not labor and bring forth a mouse. Mickey Mouse things, like fishing rights and a new consulate in Kiev and commercial agreements, are fine. We had them at the first Moscow summit in 1972. They're the froth. But you've also got to have some good stout beer.
President Richard M. Nixon, *Time* (April 22, 1985).

militarism

We oppose militarism. It means conquest abroad and intimidation and oppression at home. It means the strong arm which has ever been fatal to free institutions. It is what millions of our citizens have fled from in Europe. It will impose upon our peace loving people a large standing army and unnecessary burden of taxation, and will be a constant menace to their liberties.
Democratic Party national platform, 1900.

The justification of militarism is that circumstances may at any time make it a true morality of the moment. It is by producing such moments that we produce violent and sanguinary revolutions, such as that in Russia.
George Bernard Shaw, *Major Barbara*, Preface (1905).

Militarism does not consist in the existence of any army, not even in the existence of a very great army. Militarism is a spirit. It is a point of view. It is a system. It is a purpose. The purpose of militarism is to use armies for aggression.
President Woodrow Wilson, speech at West Point, June 13, 1916.

The combination of a profound hatred of war and militarism with an innocent delight in playing soldiers is one of these apparent contradictions of American life that one has to accept.
Denis W. Brogan, *The American Character* (1944).

Modern militarism has, nevertheless, specific traits. Since modern armies are not so constantly engaged in combat as were the ancient armies, they are more liable to forget their true purpose, war, and the maintenance of the state to which they belong. Becoming narcissistic, they dream that they exist for themselves alone. An army so built that it serves military men, not war, is militaristic; so is everything in an army which is not preparation for fighting, but merely exists for diversion or to satisfy peacetime whims like the long-anachronistic cavalry. This was well expressed by the Russian grand duke who admitted that he hated war "because it spoils the armies."
Alfred Vagts, *A History of Militarism*, rev. ed. (1959).

Militarism will come in a new guise. The old militarism was characterized by Japanese as *gunkokushugi*, using the four characters that signify "army," "country," "master" and "justice" equaling national military rule. In the manner of the times, a resurgent militarism in Japan will, in the fashion of the U.S. and Soviets, be designated by a new, self-serving phrase that speaks only of "defense."
Edwin P. Hoyt, *The Militarists* (1985).

All through history, it has been the dictatorships and the tyrannies that have surrendered first to the cult of militarism and the pursuit of war. Countries based on the consent of the governed, countries that recognize the unalienable rights of the individual, do not make war on each other.
President Ronald Reagan, speech to the United Nations General Assembly, September 22, 1986.

militarists

We want to get rid of the militarist not simply because he hurts and kills, but because he is an intolerable thick-voiced blockhead who stands hectoring and blustering in our way to achievement.
H. G. Wells, *The Outline of History* (1920).

So long as men worship the Caesars and Napoleons, Caesars and Napoleons will duly rise and make them miserable.
Aldous Huxley, *Ends and Means* (1937).

The militarists of Berlin and Tokyo started this war, but the massed angered forces of common humanity will finish it.
President Franklin D. Roosevelt, speech to Joint Session of Congress, January 6, 1942.

When I come in contact with a militarist, his stupidity depresses me and makes me realize the amount of human obtuseness that has to be overcome before we can make much progress towards peace.
B. H. Liddell Hart, *Thoughts on War* (1944).

The military caste did not originate as a party of patriots, but a party of bandits.
H. L. Mencken, *Minority Report* (1956).

Militarists who mock the ballot only betray their own bloodthirsty proclivities. A ballot-form, like a treaty, is to them only a scrap of paper; that it has not been dipped in blood renders it contemptible in their eyes; for them the only valid decisions are those reached through blood.
Elias Canetti, *Crowds and Power* (1960).

military

The military, a profession which makes bad men worse.
Laurence Sterne, *A Sentimental Journey* (1768).

The services in wartime are fit only for desperadoes, but in peace are fit only for fools.
Benjamin Disraeli, *Vivian Grey* (1826).

Americans have a special affection for the man of peace—like Sergeant York in the World War—who leaves his trade only long enough to beat the military at their own game.
Dixon Wecter, *The Hero in America* (1941).

The military man rarely favors war. He will always argue that the danger of war requires increased armaments; he will seldom argue that increased armaments make war practical or desirable. He always favors preparedness, but he never feels prepared. Accordingly, the professional military man contributes a cautious, conservative, restraining voice to the formulation of state policy. This has been his typical role in most modern states including fascist Germany, communist Russia, and democratic America. He is afraid of war. He wants to prepare for war. But he is never ready to fight a war.
Samuel P. Huntington, *The Soldier and the State* (1957).

To blame the military for war makes about as much sense as suggesting that we get rid of cancer by getting rid of doctors.
Ronald Reagan, Governor of California, *Los Angeles Herald-Examiner* (June 8, 1970).

A democratic society and its military rise and fall together. In a free country the military cannot perform well, no matter how much is spent on it, when government, the banks, the big corporations, the schools, the colleges, the courts, the police and the media perform badly.
Geoffrey Perret, *A Country Made by War* (1989).

military audacity

To defeat them [our country's enemies] . . . we need audacity, yet more audacity, audacity at all times, and France will be saved.
French revolutionary George-Jacques Danton, speech in the legislative assembly, September 2, 1792, reprinted in André Fribourg, *Discours de Danton* (1910). Danton's famous "audacity" is sometimes translated as "boldness."

They want war too methodical, too measured; I would make it brisk, bold, impetuous, perhaps sometimes even audacious.
General Antoine Henri Jomini, *Summary of the Art of War* (1838).

Audacity may seem foolish to those who shrink back, but it is the only possible course for those who are capable of looking ahead.
René Quinton, *Soldier's Testament* (1930).

In war, audacity has often disproved calculations of what is possible.
B. H. Liddell Hart, *Thoughts on War* (1944).

There are only three principles of warfare—Audacity, *Audacity* and AUDACITY!
General George S. Patton, Jr., quoted in Brinton G. Wallace, *Patton and His Third Army* (1946).

In planning any operation, it is vital to remember, and constantly repeat to oneself, two things: "In war nothing is impossible, provided you use audacity," and "Do not take counsel of your fears." If these two principles are adhered to, with American troops victory is certain.
General George S. Patton, Jr., *War as I Knew It* (1947).

military discipline

The strength of an army lies in strict discipline and undeviating obedience to its officers.
Thucydides, *The Peloponnesian War* (5th century B.C.).

Discipline is the soul of an army. It makes small numbers formidable, procures success to the weak, and esteem to all.
Colonel George Washington, 1756 letter to his captains, quoted in James T. Flexner, *George Washington: The Forge of Experience* (1965).

After the organization of troops, military discipline is the first matter that presents itself. It is the soul of armies. If it is not established with wisdom and maintained with unshakable resolution you will have no soldiers. Regiments and armies will be only contemptible, armed mobs, more dangerous to their own country than to the enemy.
Marshal Maurice de Saxe, *Reveries Upon the Art of War* (1757).

Discipline is simply the art of inspiring more fear in the soldiers of their officers than of the enemy.
Claude-Adrien Helvetius, *De l'Esprit* (1758).

It was an inflexible maxim of Roman discipline that a good soldier should dread his own officers far more than the enemy.
Edward Gibbons, *The Decline and Fall of the Roman Empire* (1776).

Nothing can be more hurtful to the service, than the neglect of discipline; for that discipline, more than numbers, gives one army the superiority over another.
General George Washington, general orders of July 6, 1977, *The Writings of George Washington*, VIII, ed. John C. Fitzpatrick (1933).

[Flogging] invariably makes a tolerably good man bad, and a bad man infinitely worse. Once flog a man and you degrade him for ever, in his own mind; and thus take from him every possible incentive to good conduct.
Tom Morris, a private in Duke of Wellington's Army, quoted in Elizabeth Longford, *Wellington: The Years of the Sword* (1969).

Till the whole army were new modelled and governed under a stricter discipline, they must not expect any notable success in anything they were about.
Oliver Cromwell quoted in Antonia Fraser, *Cromwell* (1973).

The ultimate test of military training and the military discipline that results therefrom is the capacity of troops to suffer losses without being turned aside from the task before them.
Major James W. McAndrew, "Infantry Training," *Infantry Journal* (November–December 1913).

If one, only one, of all the myriad incidents of his [Robert E. Lee's] stirring life had to be selected to typify his message, as a man . . . who would hesitate in selecting that incident? It occurred in Northern Virginia, probably on his last visit there. A young mother brought her baby to him to be blessed. He took the infant in his arms and looked at it and then at her and slowly said, "Teach him he must deny himself."
Douglas S. Freeman, *R. E. Lee*, IV (1935).

Military discipline is instructive. More than fifty years ago I was marching in a procession which numbered at least a thousand men. It was broken up and scattered in hopeless confusion and terror by twenty pale nervous policemen armed with nothing more deadly than their clubs. Not one of the thousand knew what to do or what any of the others would do; so they all ran away, except those who were overtaken and knocked on the head. . . .
But each of the twenty policemen knew what the other nineteen were going to do, and had the law on his side. He had a uniform, a helmet, and a weapon, and could depend on the co-operation of nineteen uniformed, helmeted, weaponed comrades. It was a triumph of expected behavior over mistrust and anarchy.
George Bernard Shaw, *Everybody's Political What's What* (1944).

There is only one sort of discipline—PERFECT DISCIPLINE. Men cannot have good battle discipline and poor administrative discipline.
General George S. Patton, Jr., *War as I Knew It* (1947).

Discipline is teaching which makes a man do something which he would not, unless he had learnt that it was the right, the proper, and the expedient thing to do. At its best, it is instilled and maintained by pride in oneself, in one's unit, in one's profession; only at its worst by a fear of punishment.
Field Marshal Archibald P. Wavell, *Soldiers and Soldiering* (1953).

Mr. Maryk, you may tell the crew for me there are four ways of doing things on board my ship: the right way, the wrong way, the Navy way—and my way. If they do things my way, we'll get along.
Humphrey Bogart in *The Caine Mutiny* (1954), directed by Edward Dmytryki; screenplay by Stanley Roberts from the novel by Herman Wouk.

Dreaming won't get you to Damascus, sir, but discipline will.
Anthony Quayle in *Lawrence of Arabia* (1962), directed by David Lean; screenplay by Robert Bolt.

The Three Main Rules of Discipline are as follows:
(1) Obey orders in all your actions.
(2) Do not take a single needle or piece of thread from the masses.
(3) Turn in everything captured.
The Eight Points for Attention are as follows:
(1) Speak politely.
(2) Pay fairly for what you buy.
(3) Return everything you borrow.
(4) Pay for anything you damage.
(5) Do not hit or swear at people.
(6) Do not damage crops.
(7) Do not take liberties with women.
(8) Do not ill-treat captives.
Mao Tse-tung, *Selected Military Writings* (1968).

military doctrine

The doctrines of strategy do not go beyond the rudimentary propositions of common sense; they can hardly be called a science; their value lies almost entirely in their application to the concrete case.
Field Marshal Helmuth von Moltke quoted in Rudolf von Caemmerer, *The Development of Strategical Science During the Nineteenth Century* (1905).

A doctrine of war does not impose itself; it is born of the unanimous concurrence of understandings under the empire of convictions *progressively* acquired.
Henri Bonnal quoted in Gabriel Darrieus, *War on the Sea* (1908).

A doctrine of war consists first in a common way of objectively approaching the subject; second, in a common way of handling it.
Marshal Ferdinand Foch, *Precepts and Judgments* (1920).

Adherence to dogmas has destroyed more armies and cost more battles than anything in war.
J. F. C. Fuller quoted in Dale D. Smith, *U.S. Military Doctrine* (1955).

Generals and admirals stress the central importance of "doctrine." Military doctrine is the "logic" of their professional behavior. As such, it is a synthesis of scientific knowledge and expertise on the one hand, and traditions and political assumptions on the other.
Morris Janowitz, *The Professional Soldier* (1960).

We Vietnamese have no military doctrine because the command of all operations in Vietnam is in the hands, is the responsibility, of the American side. We followed the American military doctrine.
General Cao Van Vien, speaking in 1969 as Chairman of the South Vietnamese Joint General Staff, quoted in Harry G. Summers, Jr., *On Strategy* (1982).

Sometimes strategic doctrines may be widely held which cannot be attributed to any specific thinkers, but represent simply the consensus of opinion among a large number of professionals who have undergone a formative common experience.
Michael Howard, *Studies in War and Peace* (1972).

The amazing fact is that the Germans did so well for so long; even at the close of 1944, just as in September 1918, they were still occupying territories far larger than the Reich's own boundaries at the onset of war. To this question military historians have offered a virtually unanimous response: that German operational doctrine, emphasizing flexibility and decentralized decision-making at the battlefield level, proved far superior to the cautious, set-piece tactics of the British, the bloody, full-frontal assaults of the Russians, and the enthusiastic but unprofessional forward rushes of the Americans.
Paul Kennedy, *The Rise and Fall of the Great Powers* (1987).

military history

Of the events of war, I have not ventured to speak from any chance information, nor according to any notion of my own; I have described nothing but what I saw myself, or learned from others of whom I made the most careful and particular inquiry. The task was a laborious one because eyewitnesses of the same occurrence gave different accounts of them as they remembered, or were interested in the actions of one side or the other. And very likely the strictly historical character of my narrative may be disappointing to the ear. But if he who desires to have before his eyes a true picture of the events which have happened, and of the like events which may be expected to happen hereafter in the order of human things, shall pronounce what I have written to be useful, then I shall be satisfied. My history is an everlasting possession, not a prize composition which is heard and forgotten.
Thucydides, *The Peloponnesian War* (5th century B.C.).

Cato the elder, who was often Consul and always victorious at the head of the armies, believed he could do his country more essential service by writing on military affairs, than by all his exploits in the field. For the consequences of brave actions are only temporary, while whatever is committed to writing for public good is of lasting benefit.
Vegetius, *De Re Militari* (378 A.D.).

History . . . is, indeed, little more than the register of the crimes, follies, and misfortunes of mankind.
Edward Gibbon, *The Decline and Fall of the Roman Empire* (1776).

The most glorious hero that ever desolated nations might have smouldered into oblivion among the rubbish of his own monument, did not some historian take him into favor, and benevolently transmit his name to posterity.
Washington Irving, *Diedrich Knickerbocker's History of New York* (1809). The Roman poet Horace wrote in his *Odes* (1st century B.C.): "Many brave men lived before Agamemnon's time; but they are all, unmourned and unknown, covered by the long night, because they lack their sacred poet."

Military history, accompanied by sound criticism, is indeed the true school of war.
General Antoine Henri Jomini, *Summary of the Art of War* (1838).

It is not the statesman, the warrior, or the monarch that survives, but the despised poet, whom they may have fed with their crumbs, and to whom they owe all that they now are or have—a name.
Nathaniel Hawthorne, *Our Old Home* (1863).

The real war will never get into the books.
Walt Whitman, *Specimen Days* (1882).

Wars produce many stories of fiction, some of which are told until they are believed to be true.
President Ulysses S. Grant, *Personal Memoirs* (1885).

The military historian is a naturalist. He collects wars as specimens, he dissects them, he compares and classifies them. His laboratory is a collection of documents and maps. He examines the correspondence of governments, to discover the aims with which they made war, the records of armies and navies to find out how they were constituted, the secret dispatches of commanders to understand their motives, the reports they received about the enemy and the orders they issued, which enable him to put himself in their place, to see with their eyes, and to think their thoughts.
Field Marshal Viscount Wolseley, 1891 letter quoted in Jay Luvaas, *The Education of an Army* (1964).

My argument is that War makes rattling good history; but Peace is poor reading.
Thomas Hardy, *The Dynasts*, II (1906).

Those who cannot remember the past are condemned to repeat it.
George Santayana, *The Life of Reason* (1906).

History [is] an account mostly false, of events mostly unimportant, which are brought about by rulers mostly knaves, and soldiers mostly fools.
Ambrose Bierce, *The Devil's Dictionary* (1911).

To be able to enumerate the blades of grass in the Shenandoah Valley and the yards marched by Stonewall Jackson's men is not an adequate foundation for leadership in a future war where conditions and armament have radically changed.
B. H. Liddell Hart, *The Remaking of Modern Armies* (1927).

Not a few military historians have admitted that they feel compelled by position, interest or friendship, to put down less than they know to be true. Once a man surrenders to this tendency the truth begins to slip away like water down a waste-pipe—until those who want to learn how to conduct war in the future are unknowingly bathing their minds in a shallow bath.
B. H. Liddell Hart, *The Ghost of Napoleon* (1933).

The Prime Minister [Churchill] said that it was foolish to keep a day-by-day diary because it would simply reflect the change of opinion or decision of the writer, which, when and if published, makes one appear indecisive and foolish. . . . He would much prefer to wait until the war is over and then write impressions, so that, if necessary, he could correct or bury his mistakes.
Captain Harry C. Butcher, writing of May 30, 1943, *My Three Years With Eisenhower* (1946).

Two Confederate veterans were reminiscing about the days during the war when Paducah was being fought over by the Northern and Southern forces. "I remember," one veteran said, "when we pushed those damyankees all the way across the Ohio and up into Illinois!" The other old soldier regretfully corrected him. "I was there, old

friend," he said, "and I'm afraid that wasn't the way it happened at all. Those Yankees drove us out of Paducah and almost to the Tennessee line." The first veteran reflected a bit, then sourly remarked, "Another good story ruined by an eyewitness!"
Alben W. Barkley, *That Reminds Me* (1954).

Most official accounts of past wars are deceptively well written, and seem to omit many important matters—in particular, anything which might indicate that any of our commanders ever made the slightest mistake. They are therefore useless as a source of instruction.
Field Marshal B. L. Montgomery, *Memoirs* (1958).

Some of us think it wise to associate as much as possible with historians and culti-vate their good will, though we always have the remedy which Winston Churchill once suggested when he prophesied during World War II that history would deal gently with us. "Because," Mr. Churchill said, "I intend to write it!"
President John F. Kennedy, speech, Washington D.C., October 3, 1961.

The popularity of books and films dealing with war and violence (particularly evi-dent after a prolonged period of peace), like that for pornography following an age of sexual repression, attests to the pleasure provided by the vicarious satisfaction of hith-erto frustrated drives.
Norman Dixon, *On the Psychology of Military Incompetence* (1976).

Unless history can teach us how to look at the future, the history of war is but a bloody romance.
J. F. C. Fuller, quoted in Hew Strachan, *European Armies and the Conduct of War* (1983).

Russian-language military history literature is designed both to instruct and to mis-inform Soviet youth. . . . as to the whole course of European and world history over the last three hundred years. For the Soviet leadership has for many years been teach-ing its peoples that nearly all world progress over the last century or more originated with communism: and where this origin must obviously predate the October 1917 revolution . . . imperial Russia, must be given the credit. . . . This is carried to such grotesque lengths in the rewriting of history, that present-day Soviet officers . . . are taught that modern naval expertise began in Russia . . . that there was apparently no battle of Waterloo since Napoleon was destroyed in 1812 and 1813, that all military inventions, radio, radar, the tank, the tank-destroyer, rocketry, the jet engine and so on, originated in Russia, and that the Soviet Union, largely by its own efforts, defeated not only Nazi Germany but also imperialistic Japan.
Albert Seaton and Joan Seaton, *The Soviet Army* (1986).

When one gets to the core of military history and the exercises in manipulation that spring from it, one finds that all strategies and all tactics remain more or less ageless: One side attempts to mass its manpower and weapons in such a way as to defeat the other in the attack or in the defense. This is true for land armies, and it is true for navies.
Eric Hammel, *Guadalcanal: The Carrier Battles* (1987).

military history, study of

For it is history, and history alone, which, without involving us in actual danger, will mature our judgement and prepare us to take right views, whatever may be the crisis or the posture of affairs.
Polybius, *The Histories* (2nd century B.C.).

But as to exercise for the mind, the prince ought to read history and study the actions of eminent men, see how they acted in warfare, examine the causes of their victories and defeats in order to imitate the former and avoid the latter.
Niccolò Machiavelli, *The Prince* (1513).

Knowledge of the grand principles of warfare can be acquired only through the study of military history and of the battles of the great captains and through experience. There are no precise, determinate rules: everything depends on the character that nature has bestowed on the general, on his qualities and defects, on the nature of the troops, on the range of the weapons, on the season of the year, and on a thousand circumstances which are never twice the same.
Napoleon I quoted in J. C. Herold, *The Mind of Napoleon* (1955).

I consider remembrances of old campaigns a disadvantage. . . . War is progressive.
President Ulysses S. Grant quoted in William Conant Church, *Ulysses S. Grant* (1897).

It is well known that military history, when superficially studied, will furnish arguments in support of any theory or opinion.
Bronsart von Schellendorf quoted in Jay Luvaas, *The Military Legacy of the Civil War* (1959). Luvaas notes that the "same might apply to other fields of history as well, but in military history, unfortunately, more than an academic reputation is often at stake."

Although famous politicians and generals of the twentieth century have given impressive testimony about the utility of military history, they have been vague about just how their reading helped to prepare them for high military responsibilities. Perhaps the most specific testimony is Winston Churchill's dependence on the experiences of Marlborough and the two Pitts, or George S. Patton's mystical belief that he was the reincarnation of earlier soldiers (a conceit probably grounded in his voracious reading of military classics).
Allan R. Millett and Williamson Murry, "Lessons of War," *National Interest* (Winter 1988–89).

military-industrial complex

Avoid the necessity of those overgrown military establishments which, under any form of government, are inauspicious to liberty, and which are to be regarded as particularly hostile to republican liberty.
President George Washington, Farewell Address, September 17, 1796.

The military men who dominate a modern technical society will be very different from the officers of history and tradition. It is probable that the specialists on violence will include in their training a large degree of expertness in many of the skills that we have traditionally accepted as part of modern civilian management.
Harold Lasswell, *The Garrison State* (1941).

In response to the machine gun the tank was developed and mechanized warfare advanced one stage further. Increasingly the quality of a country's weaponry and the capacity of its industrial output became the determinants of success, rather than any will to win born of idealism, faith or personal self-respect.
John Ellis, *The Social History of the Machine Gun* (1975).

In the councils of government we must guard against the acquisition of unwarranted influence, whether sought or unsought, by the military-industrial complex. The potential for the disastrous rise of misplaced power exists and will persist.
President Dwight D. Eisenhower, Farewell Address, January 17, 1961.

You know, we only have a military-industrial complex until a time of danger: then it becomes "the arsenal of democracy."
President Ronald Reagan, State of the Union Address, February 6, 1985.

When you vote for a strong defense, you're also voting for the employment of literally hundreds of thousands of Californians, a fact to which I am not indifferent. What it means is, our national-security interest coincides with our self-interest.
Senator Pete Wilson, *The Los Angeles Times* (May 12, 1985).

Critics of national-defense policies often refer to the military-industrial complex as if it were a conspiracy imposed from above against the will and desires of the American people. But even Eisenhower actually suggested a subtler, more insidious meaning. . . . the military-industrial complex is ourselves.
Nick Kotz, *Wild Blue Yonder* (1988).

military minds

If my soldiers began to think, not one would remain in the ranks.
Frederick the Great quoted in G. F. Nicolai, *The Biology of War* (1919).

The professional military mind is by necessity an inferior and unimaginative mind; no man of high intellectual quality would willingly imprison his gifts in such a calling.
H. G. Wells, *The Outline of History* (1920).

As soon as any man started to talk about the theory of war one could be nearly sure that he would bring forward some idiotic suggestion, to the effect that cavalry had had its day and that dismounted action was all that could be expected of it, or that machine-guns and barbed wire had wrought a fundamental change in tactics, or even—wildest lunacy of all—that these rattletrap aeroplanes were going to be of some military value.
C. S. Forester, *The General* (1936).

There are over two thousand years of experience to tell us that the only thing harder than getting a new idea into the military mind is to get an old one out.
B. H. Liddell Hart, *Thoughts on War* (1944).

Nothing so comforts the military mind as the maxim of a great but dead general.
Barbara W. Tuchman, *The Guns of August* (1962).

The Military Mind is, of course, a catch phrase. For a good many years it has been used to suggest a pedantic, rather dull, professional soldier who was either monumentally stupid or unbelievably wrong about one thing or another. It was a caricature that was only occasionally accurate.
Rear Admiral J. C. Wylie, *Military Strategy* (1967).

When faced with obtuse arrogance in military men, [Edward R.] Murrow would tell of the time General Mark Clark opened a conversation with, "Of course, you civilians. . . ." [Winston] Churchill cut him short with, "Young man, I was killing people when you were puling and puking in your blanket."
Joseph E. Persico, *Edward R. Murrow* (1988).

military music

The Spartans came on slowly and to the music of many flute-players in their ranks. This custom of theirs has nothing to do with religion: it is designed to make them keep

in step and move forward steadily without breaking their ranks, as large armies often do when they are just about to join battle.
Thucydides, *History of the Peloponnesian War* (5th century B.C.).

Noble and manly music invigorates the spirit, strengthens the wavering man, and incites him to great and worthy deeds.
Homer, *The Iliad* (1000 B.C.).

Music regulates the army, which by moving in paces that correspond to its beats, easily keeps in rank. Thence it is that the ancients had whistles and fifes and musical instruments perfectly modulated; because, just as one who dances moves in time with music and keeping with it does not err, so an army moving in obedience to music does not get disordered. And therefore they varied the music according as they wished to vary the movement and according as they wished to stir up or to quiet or to make firm the spirits of the men.
Niccolò Machiavelli, *The Art of War* (1520).

I don't believe we can have an army without music.
General Robert E. Lee quoted in Burke Davis, *Gray Fox* (1956).

General Lee's surrender had been announced. . . . Delirious multitudes surged to the White House, calling the President out for a speech. It was a moment for easy betrayal into words that might widen the breach between sections. He said in his quaint way that he had no speech ready, and concluded humorously: "I have always thought 'Dixie' one of the best tunes I ever heard. I insisted yesterday that we had fairly captured it. I presented the question to the Attorney-General and he gave his opinion that it is our lawful prize. I ask the band to give us a good turn upon it." In that little speech, he claimed of the South by right of conquest a song—and nothing more.
Myrta Lockett Avary, *Dixie After the War* (1937).

How good bad music and bad reasons sound when one marches against an enemy!
Friedrich Nietzsche, *The Dawn* (1881).

Over hill, over dale, we have hit the dusty
   trail
And those caissons go rolling along.
Countermarch! Right about! Hear those
   wagon soldiers shout
While those caissons go rolling along.
Edmund L. Gruber, *The Caisson Song* (1908).

military pensions

I haven't been able to get anything done on military retirement. It's a scandal. It's an outrage. The institutional forces in the military are more concerned about protecting their retirement benefits than they are about protecting the security of the American people. When push comes to shove, they'll give up on security before they'll give up on retirement.
David A. Stockman, Director, Office of Management and Budget, testimony before the Senate Budget Committee, February 5, 1985.

We want to encourage more people to serve longer. The current system has such generous benefits at the 20-year mark that it simply encourages them to get out at 20 years. In fact, there's a saying in the services that you're crazy to stay longer than 20 years because you're effectively working only for half pay after that.
Representative Les Aspin, *The New York Times* (March 22, 1986).

military science

War, like most things, is a science to be acquired and perfected by diligence, by perseverance, by time, and by practice.
Alexander Hamilton, *The Federalist*, No. 25 (1787).

Military science consists in first calculating all the possibilities accurately and then in making an almost mathematically exact allowance for accident. It is on this point that one must make no mistake; a decimal more or less may alter everything.
Napoleon I quoted in J. C. Herold, *The Mind of Napoleon* (1955).

It is in military history that we are to look for the source of all military science. In it we shall find those exemplifications of failure and success by which alone the truth and value of the rules of strategy can be tested.
Dennis Hart Mahan, *Advanced-Guard, Outpost, and Detachment Service of Troops* (1864).

Mathematics is the dominant science in war, just as battle is its only purpose.
Ardant du Picq, *Battles Studies* (1868).

There is no "science" of war, and there never will be any. There are many sciences war is concerned with. But war itself is not a science; war is practical art and skill.
Leon Trotsky, *How the Revolution Was Armed* (1923).

Military science is based on principles that have been deduced from the application of common sense in the conduct of military affairs. . . . Military genius is really only the capacity to understand and apply simple principles founded on experience and sound reasoning.
General of the Armies John J. Pershing, *My Experiences in the World War*, I (1931).

At the present time [the late nineteenth century], it will enter no one's head to assert that there can be a military science; it is just as unthinkable as are the sciences of poetry, painting and music.
General M. I. Dragomirov quoted in Vasili Savkin, *The Basic Principles of Operational Art and Tactics* (1972).

Because military science until recent times had been exclusively controlled by kings and nobles, no theorist had dared go beyond the mental horizons of his prince. [Baron Dietrich von] Bulow [1757–1808], the well-known Prussian military writer, had committed this error and later had good cause to complain that "military writings which are found to contain truth, novelty, and originality, or to bear proofs of genius and talent, invariably exclude their author from all promotion and employment, whether civil or military."
Jay Luvaas, *The Education of an Army* (1964).

What is commonly called "military science" is not scientific in the same sense as law or medicine or engineering. It encompasses no agreed-upon body of knowledge, no prescribed curriculum, no universally recognized principles that one must master to qualify as a military professional. (The so-called "principles of war" are really a set of platitudes that can be twisted to suit almost any situation.)
Alain C. Enthoven and K. Wayne Smith, *How Much Is Enough* (1971).

The most important [aspect of Soviet military science] is referred to in the West as military art. However, the established translation of *iskusstvo* as art is misleading because of the word's connotations in English, particularly the tendency to contrast the colloquial meanings of art and science. The sense in Russian is conveyed better by the original meaning of art as technics or applied knowledge, which is a subset of

science or knowledge. The Russian term is perhaps best translated as the military craft or the craft of war. The semantics are important because they highlight the very different way that Westerners and the Soviets approach the problem of waging war. The Soviets tend to see is as an applied science with immutable laws; Westerners tend to see it as an art form executed by great captains.
Michael MccGwire, *Military Objectives in Soviet Foreign Policy* (1987).

military service

The leisure of army life attracts three out of four officers, laziness, if you like. But such is the fact.
Ardant du Picq, *Battle Studies* (1868).

The chief attraction of military service has consisted and will consist in this compulsory and irreproachable idleness.
Leo Tolstoy, *War and Peace* (1869).

The Captain of an American frigate once told Midshipman A. T. Mahan: "There is one reply to objections; if they do not wish to conform they can leave the Service."
Leland P. Lovette, *School of the Sea* (1941).

You have made patriotism fashionable again, and serving in the armed forces attractive.
Admiral William J. Crowe, Jr., Chairman of the Joint Chiefs of Staff, speaking to President Ronald Reagan, quoted in *The New York Times* (January 13, 1989).

militia

To place any dependence upon militia, is, assuredly, resting upon a broken staff.
General George Washington, letter to the President of Congress, September 24, 1776, reprinted in J. C. Fitzpatrick, ed., *The Writings of George Washington*, VI (1931–44).

The Congress shall have power. . . To provide for calling forth the Militia to execute the Laws of the Union, suppress Insurrections and repel Invasions; To provide for organizing, arming, and disciplining, the Militia, and for governing such Part of them as may be employed in the Service of the United States, reserving to the States respectively, the Appointment of the Officers, and the Authority of training the Militia according to the discipline prescribed by Congress.
Constitution of the United States, Section I, Article 8 (1789).

A well regulated Militia, being necessary to the security of a free State, the right of the people to keep and bear Arms, shall not be infringed.
Constitution of the United States, Amendment II (1791).

For a people who are free, and who mean to remain so, a well-organized and armed militia is their best security.
President Thomas Jefferson, annual message to Congress, November 8, 1808.

Always remember that an armed and trained militia is the firmest bulwark of republics—that without standing armies their liberty can never be in danger, nor with large ones safe.
President James Madison, first Inaugural Address, March 4, 1809.

The bulwark of our defense is the national militia, which in the present state of our intelligence and population must render us invincible.
President Andrew Jackson, Inaugural Address, March 3, 1829.

Militia and armed civilians cannot and should not be employed against the main force of the enemy, or even against sizeable units. They should not try to crack the core, but only nibble along the surface and on the edges.
Karl von Clausewitz, *On War* (1832).

I longed for more Regular troops with which to rebuild and expand the Army. Wars are not won by heroic militia.
Winston Churchill, *The Second World War: Their Finest Hour* (1949).

mines

This is about the lowest form of warfare that can be imagined. It is the warfare of the I.R.A., leaving the bomb in the parcels' office at the railway station. The magnetic mine ... may perhaps be Herr Hitler's much vaunted secret weapon. It is certainly a characteristic weapon, and one that will no doubt be for ever associated with his name.
Winston Churchill, speech in the House of Commons, December 6, 1939.

Elsewhere in the world mine detection is divided into two phases; first the problem of detecting the mine and second that of rendering it harmless. Here [the Soviet Union during World War II] they are combined in the following manner. They send a lot of Russians poking into the weeds with a lot of poles. Presently you hear a loud bang and see a Russian rising out of the air on a column of smoke. This indicates not only the detection of the mine, but the fact that it is simultaneously rendered harmless.
William L. White, *Report on the Russians (1945)*.

There are two kinds of mines; one is the personnel mine and the other is the vehicular mine. When we come to a mine field our infantry attacks exactly as if it were not there. The losses we get from personnel mines we consider only equal to those we would have gotten from machine guns and artillery if the Germans had chosen to defend that particular area with strong bodies of troops instead of with mine fields. The attacking infantry does not set off the vehicular mines, so after they have penetrated to the far side of the field they form a bridgehead, after which the engineers come up and dig out channels through which our vehicles can go.
Marshal Grigori K. Zhukov, describing Russian mine clearing operations in World War II, quoted in Dwight D. Eisenhower, *Crusade in Europe* (1948).

When we'd go into a possible VC village and the elder said no VC, no mines, we'd say fine, and push him along in front of us till we got out again. If he hesitated, we'd just keep pushing him till he set off the first one.
Paratrooper, 101st Airborne, quoted in Ronald J. Glasser, *365 Days* (1971).

Mining [parts of Nicaragua] was unacceptable. The debate asked the question: Have we, as a nation, no decency? It was almost as though the mining was a "national" act, a statement of national character. Mining was sneaky, a shadowy endeavor, akin to planting a bomb in a restaurant, a trap for the unsuspecting and innocent. [Senator Barry] Goldwater's disapproval magnified the issue. He loomed as an arbiter of toughness and common sense. Privately he called the mining "the dumbest fucking idea I ever heard of."
Bob Woodward, *Veil: The Secret Wars of the CIA* (1987).

missiles

David put his hand in his bag, and took thence a stone, and slang it, and smote the Philistine in his forehead, that the stone sunk into his forehead; and he fell upon his face to the earth.
The Bible, I Samuel 17:49.

Oh, yes, we shall get to the moon—but of course I daren't tell Hitler yet.
Wernher von Braun, Technical Director of the World War II German V-2 project, quoted in Donald M. Kaplan and Armand Schwerner, *The Domesday Dictionary* (1963).

Londoners had a new name for the German rocket bombs: "Bob Hopes." The name was contraction of "Bob down, and hope for the best."
Time (December 25, 1944).

People . . . have been talking about a 3,000-mile high angle rocket shot from one continent to another carrying an atomic bomb, and so directed as to be a precise weapon which would land on a certain target such as this city.
I say technically I don't think anybody in the world knows how to do such a thing, and I feel confident it will not be done for a very long period of time to come. I think we can leave that out of our thinking.
Vannevar Bush, the federal government's chief scientist during World War II, testifying at a December 1945 Senate hearing, quoted in Edmund Beard, *Developing the ICBM* (1976).

An analysis of the performance of the V-2 proves conclusively that it is possible to build liquid-fuel rockets of almost any size. There is little question that their size, range, and accuracy will be enormously improved. We must look forward to the possibility, in time, of our cities being accurately bombed from across the seas.
Harrison Brown, *Must Destruction Be Our Destiny?* (1946).

Our scientific power has outrun our spiritual power. We have guided missiles and misguided men.
Martin Luther King, *Strength Through Love* (1963).

You are endangering the defense of the country by depending on this weapon system [strategic missiles] alone because you have no flexibility. You only have two choices. You are either off the button and are at peace or you are on the button and you are at war.
General Curtis E. LeMay, testimony before Congress, February 25, 1964, quoted in James M. Roherty, *Decisions of Robert S. McNamara* (1970).

These doomsday warriors look no more like soldiers than the soldiers of the Second World War looked like conquistadors. The more expert they become the more they look like lab assistants in small colleges.
Alistair Cooke, on U.S. Air Force missilemen, *America* (1973).

There is indeed grave risk in using ballistic missiles, but that risk is not uncertainty of accuracy.
Charles Stark Draper, *The New York Times* (September 20, 1981).

I want to make it clear that we welcome the day when the Soviet Union can shoot down any incoming missile, so long as the United States can shoot down any incoming missile, too.
President Ronald Reagan, radio address to the nation, October 12, 1985.

When a formation of enemy armored vehicles is detected, a missile is launched. . . . Small sub-munitions are then released by the main missile to attack the enemy forces.

Each sub-munition is a smart missile. It can scan the target area with its own sensor and seek out, for example, a tank. When it has found one, the sensor guides the sub-munition down towards the turret of the tank. . . .

As the sub-munition approaches the tank it is attacking it fires a high-speed projectile into the turret. The turret is chosen for attack because it is the weakest part of the tank (it is the weakest part because it has to rotate rapidly carrying a heavy gun and, therefore, cannot carry such heavy armour as the rest of the tank). If each warhead carried twenty sub-munitions, a typical number, and it took, on average, two sub-munitions to destroy a main battle tank, then each main missile could destroy ten tanks.
Frank Barnaby, *The Automated Battlefield* (1986).

Missiles are not only becoming more accurate; they are becoming "autonomous." Once fired, an autonomous missile can seek out its target, identify it and attack it without any further instructions from the person or platform that fired the missile. . . . This means that once the pilot has fired the missile he can turn his aircraft round and go home. Autonomous missiles are also called "fire-and-forget" or "launch-and-leave" missiles.
Frank Barnaby, *The Automated Battlefield* (1986).

I found missile research utterly demoralizing. . . . I was not alone in realizing that the missile system was unlikely ever to be built. It was a folly, a monument to British self-delusion. In any case this kind of science was ultimately negative. Why spend a life developing a weapon you hope and pray will never be used?
Peter Wright, *Spycatcher* (1987).

He has got so many ratholes over there in Eastern Europe that 500 is a pittance.
Dick Cheney, U.S. Secretary of Defense, response to Mikhail S. Gorbachev's announcement that the Soviet Union would be unilaterally withdrawing 500 short-range nuclear missiles from Eastern Europe, *The New York Times* (May 18, 1989).

Eisenhower was right to say the problem of defense is how far can you go without destroying from within what you're trying to protect from without. Already we've gone too far when, on any given night, 100,000 American children go to sleep homeless. And we house our missiles so much better than we do our homeless.
William Sloane Coffin, *Time* (June 5, 1989).

missile gap
The idea of a "missile gap" had been first set forth publicly by Eisenhower's second Secretary of Defense, Neil McElroy, who forecast in 1959 that the Soviet Union would probably have a 3-1 superiority in intercontinental ballistic missiles by the early sixties. This estimate rested on the best intelligence then available and was shared by General James Gavin, who conveyed it to Stuart Symington, Kennedy and other Senators. By 1960 it was a staple of Democratic oratory.
Arthur M. Schlesinger, Jr., *A Thousand Days* (1965).

If the phrase referred to the Soviets' lead in 1957 in rocketry and engine thrust, to their capacity to convert that lead into the world's first sizable force of ICBMs, or to the total number of missiles of all sizes and ranges targeted by either side, then clearly a "missile gap" did exist at one time. But if the phrase referred to a Soviet missile-based over-all military superiority capable of reducing on first strike America's retaliatory capacity to an insignificant lever, then clearly no such "missile gap" ever existed.
Theodore C. Sorensen, *Kennedy* (1965).

The gap was chiefly the product of Air Force intelligence. The Air Force was riding the crest of its own missile-building program, and a higher assessment of Soviet capability naturally reinforced its position. . . . The missile gap, it turned out, had been calculated largely by anticipating all the weapons Soviet technology could produce. There had been little allowance for physical evidence, anything short of total strategic commitment, or the economic burden for the Soviets.
Henry L. Trewhitt, *McNamara* (1971).

The missile-gap was indeed a myth, if only because the Soviet Union was overambitious and tried to deploy too quickly a huge and most impractical first ICBM. But a myth has also been created about the myth—that the missile-gap overestimate was the result of unreasoned, groundless hysteria or even deliberate fabrication. In fact, it was induced by elementary prudence, for once misapplied. And there is worse, much worse: the missile-gap myth lasted only for three years, but the myth about the myth endures still. As do its evil consequences.
Edward N. Luttwak, *Strategy and History*, II (1985).

In many ways, 1980 seemed like a replay of 1960. The phrase "window of vulnerability" carried the same political message that "missile gap" had twenty years earlier: the United States urgently needed to build more nuclear weapons.
Nick Kotz, *Wild Blue Yonder* (1988).

MX missile system
Our deployed nuclear forces were built before the age of microcircuits. It is not right to ask our young men and women in uniform to maintain and operate such antiques. . . . We must replace and modernize our forces and that is why I have decided to proceed with the introduction of the new ICBM known as the MX.
President Ronald Reagan, address to the nation, November 22, 1982.

I recently watched a filmed launching of an MX missile. It rose slowly out of the ground, surrounded by smoke and flames and elongated into the air—it was indeed a very sexual sight, and when armed with the ten warheads it will explode with the most almighty orgasm. The names that the military uses are laden with psychosexual overtones: missile erector, thrust-to-weight ratio, soft lay down, deep penetration, hard line and soft line. A McDonnell-Douglas advertisement for a new weapons system proudly proclaims that it can "shoot down whatever's up, and blow up whatever's down."
Helen Caldicott, *Missile Envy* (1984).

The vote on the Peacekeeper [the MX] is also a vote on Geneva. Rejecting the Peacekeeper will knock the legs out from under the negotiating table.
President Ronald Reagan quoted in *Newsweek* (March 18, 1985).

[The MX is an] unnecessary piece of goldplated military junk that serves no useful military purpose and is intended solely to serve political perceptions.
Senator Alan Cranston, *The New York Times* (March 20, 1985).

Are the Soviets going to get upset by the American people spending money they don't have for a missile they don't need and putting it in silos that are vulnerable?
Representative Byron Dorgan, speech in the House of Representatives, March 25, 1985.

mobilization

Your Majesty, it cannot be done. The deployment of millions cannot be improvised. If Your Majesty insists on leading the whole army to the East it will not be an army ready for battle but a disorganized mob of armed men with no arrangement for supply. Those arrangements took a whole year of intricate labor to complete and once settled, it cannot be altered.

General Helmuth von Moltke, explaining to the Kaiser in 1914 why Germany could not redeploy its Army to attack Russia instead of Belgium and France, quoted in Barbara Tuchman, *The Guns of August* (1962).

The politician should fall silent the moment that mobilization begins.

Field Marshal Helmuth von Moltke quoted in Roger Parkinson, *Clausewitz* (1970).

In theory, mobilization is a military precaution and a diplomatic warning.... In practice, once the first European power mobilized, every country [in 1914] found itself on a nonstop train to war. The general staffs elsewhere demanded that their own governments mobilize immediately in response.... And then, whenever the increasingly frightened governments tried to draw back from the headlong rush to war, the general staff planners pointed out that the mobilization schedules would be hopelessly disrupted if they were stopped midway....

The operation was successful, but the patient died (as a different profession would put it). The governments of Europe believed what they were told by their military professionals, and the trains delivered them punctually into World War I.

Gwynne Dyer, *War* (1985).

Monroe Doctrine

The American continents, by the free and independent condition which they have assumed and maintain, are henceforth not to be considered as subjects for future colonization by any European powers....

We owe it, therefore, to candor, and to the amicable relations existing between the United States and those powers to declare that we should consider any attempt on their part to extend their system to any portion of this hemisphere as dangerous to our peace and safety. With the existing colonies or dependencies of any European power we ... shall not interfere. But with the governments ... whose independence we have ... acknowledged, we could not view any interposition for the purpose of oppressing them, or controlling, in any other manner, their destiny, by any European power, in any other light than as a manifestation of an unfriendly disposition towards the United States.

President James Monroe, message to Congress, known as the Monroe Doctrine, December 2, 1823.

The United States, sincerely desirous of preserving relations of good understanding with all nations, cannot in silence permit any European interference on the North American continent, and should any such interference be attempted will be ready to resist it at any and all hazards.

President James K. Polk, first annual message to Congress, December 2, 1845.

The rights, security, and repose of this Confederacy reject the idea of interference or colonization on this side of the ocean by any foreign power beyond present jurisdiction as utterly inadmissible.

President Franklin Pierce, Inaugural Address, March 4, 1853.

Hereafter no territory on this continent shall be regarded as subject of transfer to a European power.

President Ulysses S. Grant, speech to Congress, May 31, 1870.

The government of the United States is not entitled to affirm as a universal proposition, with reference to a number of independent States for whose conduct it assumes

no responsibility, that its interests are necessarily concerned in whatever may befall those States simply because they are situated in the Western Hemisphere.
British Prime Minister Lord Salisbury, November 26, 1895 letter to Sir Julian Pauncefote, reprinted in U.S. Department of State, *Papers Relating to the Foreign Relations of the United States* (1896).

There is a homely adage which runs, "Speak softly and carry a big stick; you will go far." If the American nation will speak softly and yet build and keep at a pitch of the highest training a thoroughly efficient navy, the Monroe Doctrine will go far.
President Theodore Roosevelt, speech at the Minnesota State Fair, September 2, 1901.

In the Western hemisphere the adherence of the United States to the Monroe Doctrine may force the United States, however reluctantly, in flagrant cases of wrongdoing or impotence, to the exercise of an international police power.
President Theodore Roosevelt, annual message to Congress, December 6, 1904. This statement is often called the Roosevelt Corollary to the Monroe Doctrine.

We consider that the Monroe Doctrine has outlived its time, has outlived itself, has died, so to say, a natural death. Now the remains of this doctrine should best be buried as every dead body is so that it should not poison the air by its decay.
Nikita Khrushchev, *The New York Times* (July 13, 1960).

It was not the Monroe Doctrine that kept all Europe away from this hemisphere—it was the strength of the British fleet and the width of the Atlantic Ocean.
President John F. Kennedy, speech prepared for delivery in Dallas, November 22, 1963, the day of his death.

[The Monroe Doctrine means]
1. Other nations are *not allowed* to mess around with the internal affairs of nations in this hemisphere.
2. But we are.
3. Ha-ha-ha.
Dave Barry, *Dave Barry Slept Here* (1989).

morale

[It is] the *morale* of armies, as well as of nations, more than any thing else, which makes victories and their results decisive.
General Antoine Henri Jomini, *Summary of the Art of War* (1838).

In the last analysis, success in battle is a matter of morale. In all matters which pertain to an army, organization, discipline and tactics, the human heart in the supreme moment of battle is the basic factor.
Ardant du Picq, *Battle Studies* (1868).

He who knows the morale of the infantryman, which is put to the hardest proof, knows the morale of all the combatants.
Ardant du Picq, *Battle Studies* (1868).

Battles are beyond everything else struggles of morale. Defeat is inevitable as soon as the hope of conquering ceases to exist. Success comes not to him who has suffered the least but to him whose will is firmest and morale strongest.
French Army Field Regulations adopted in 1913, quoted in Barbara W. Tuchman, *The Guns of August* (1962).

That unhumorous race, the Germans, held an investigation after the late War [World War I] into the causes of morale, and attributed much of the British soldier's

staying power to his sense of humor. They therefore decided to instill this sense into their own soldiers, and included in their manuals an order to cultivate it. They gave as an illustration in the manual one of Bairnsfather's pictures of "Old Bill" sitting in a building with an enormous shell-hole in the wall. A new chum asks: "What made that hole?" "Mice," replies Old Bill. In the German manual a solemn footnote of explanation is added: "It was not mice, it was a shell."
General Sir Archibald Wavell, *Generals and Generalship* (1941).

The driving force of a nation lies in its spiritual purpose, made effective by free, tolerant but unremitting national will.
President Franklin D. Roosevelt, message to Congress, April 14, 1938.

When things are really bad the people's morale is greatly sustained by the knowledge that we are giving back as good as we are getting, and this engenders a sort of combatant pride, like that of the charlady in a government office who was asked during the London blitz where her husband was—"he's in the Middle East, the bloody coward!"
Sir John Slessor, *Strategy for the West* (1954).

The general [Jimmy Doolittle] went with his chief, Lieutenant General Spaatz, to visit a bomber station which had been having bad luck and heavy losses. They thought maybe their presence would pick the boys up a bit. So they visited around awhile. And when they got ready to leave, a veteran Fortress [B-17] pilot walked up to them. "I know why you're out here," he said. "You think our morale is shot because we've been taking it on the nose. Well, I can tell you our morale is all right. There is only one thing that hurts our morale. And that's having three-star generals coming around to see what's the matter with it."
Ernie Pyle, *Brave Men* (1944).

When the general complains of the morale of his troops, the time has come to look into his own.
General Omar Bradley, speaking of General Douglas MacArthur during the Korean War, quoted in Mark Perry, *Four Stars* (1989).

Nothing raises morale better than a dead general.
John Masters, *The Road Past Mandalay* (1961).

"Jody" is an Army invention, used to keep the troops fired up. At this writing Jody is sleeping with every trainee's wife, mother or sister—whichever is the girl he left behind—drinking his liquor, watching his TV, driving his car, spending his money, and, in a few limited cases, wearing his ties. . . .[Another soldier] tells me that he thinks that Jody's last name is Maggio.
Peter Tauber, *The Sunshine Soldiers* (1971).

moral factors

In war, moral factors account for three quarters of the whole; relative material strength accounts for only one quarter.
Napoleon I, writing in 1808, quoted in J.C. Herold, *The Mind of Napoleon* (1955).

If general moral superiority enables one opponent to intimidate and out-distance the other, he can use surprise to greater effect, and may even reap the fruits of victory where ordinarily he might expect to fail.
Karl von Clausewitz, *On War* (1832).

Absolute bravery, which does not refuse battle even on unequal terms, trusting only to God or to destiny, is not natural in man; it is the result of moral culture.
Ardant du Picq, *Battle Studies* (1868).

The most solid moral qualities melt away under the effect of modern arms, if one allows the enemy to use all his power.
Marshal Ferdinand Foch, *Precepts and Judgments* (1902).

The strength of an army depends on its moral foundation more than its numbers; the strength of an armed nation depends on the morals of its citizens. If this crumbles the resistance of their armies will also crumble, as an inevitable sequel.
B. H. Liddell Hart, *Thoughts on War* (1944).

Generals who become depressed when things are not going well, who lack the "drive" to get things done, and who lack the resolution, the robust mentality and the moral courage to see their plan through to the end—are useless. They are, in fact, worse than useless—they are a menace—since any sign of wavering or hesitation has immediate repercussions down the scale when the issue hangs in the balance. No battle is ever lost till the general in command thinks it so.
Field Marshal B. L. Montgomery, *Memoirs* (1958).

motivation

In a battle all you need to make you fight is a little hot blood and the knowledge that it's more dangerous to lose than win.
George Bernard Shaw, *Man and Superman*, Act III (1903).

It was said in the First World War that the French fought for their country, the British fought for freedom of the seas, and the Americans fought for souvenirs.
President Harry S. Truman quoted in Margaret Truman, *Harry S. Truman* (1973).

A wise commander knows that the moral "drive" of a body of troops is akin to the spring of an alarm clock, and that, once it has "gone off", it must be wound up and set afresh.
B. H. Liddell Hart, *Thoughts on War* (1944).

One man, his face covered with blood and dirt, his eyes two bitter holes, was saying, "I used to wonder what I was doing in the army. I didn't have anything personal against the Krauts, even if they were making me live in a freezing, frigging foxhole. But I learned something today. Now I want to kill every goddam Kraut in the world. You know why? To save my own ass."
John Toland, *Battle: The Story of the Bulge* (1959).

Other problems which plagued the French Army in Indochina were the native common-law wives of the soldiers. . . . This problem was partly solved through the creation of the *camps des maries*, settlements for local dependents either within or near a French Army base. . . .
In other cases, the wives and children of the Frenchmen, North Africans or Senegalese, would just travel with the unit, in the old tradition of the camp followers and share the fate of the unit, for better or for worse. Here again, this arrangement could work out well or prove disastrous. Some officers felt that a man who had his family near him in a fort could not afford to run away; hence, he would stand and fight, for the family's survival depended on him.
Bernard B. Fall, *Street Without Joy* (1961).

There was within the flying fraternity, particularly military flying, a brotherhood based on the idea that all that counted in life was the excellent performance of routine duties, which consisted of defying death daily in the air. Rank meant nothing. Money meant nothing. Yeager, when he ascended to the top of this pyramid, was a captain in the Air Force. Excellent performance of your duty was all that mattered. He told me at that time, "Everything I ever did I did for this blue suit," and he grasped the lapel of his blue Air Force officer's uniform.
Tom Wolfe, "The Meaning of Freedom," *Parameters* (March 1988).

mottos

Pax Quaeritur Bello (Let Peace be sought through War)
Oliver Cromwell's personal motto.

I will quote the motto of one, I believe, of the regicides of Charles I, "Rebellion to tyrants is obedience to God."
Thomas Jefferson, letter to Edward Everett, February 24, 1823, printed in *The Writings of Thomas Jefferson*, XV, ed. A. E. Bergh (1853).

Semper Paratus (Always ready)
U.S. Coast Guard.

Ex scientia, tridens. (From knowledge, sea power)
U.S. Naval Academy.

Semper Fidelis (Ever faithful)
U.S. Marine Corps.

Duty, honor, country
U.S. Military Academy, West Point.

Man's flight through life is sustained by the power of his knowledge.
Motto of the U.S. Air Force Academy.

Hit hard, hit fast, hit often.
Admiral William F. Halsey, *Time* (November 30, 1942).

Grab 'em by the nose and kick 'em in the tail.
General George S. Patton's favorite motto, quoted in *Time* (March 29, 1943).

Go for broke.
Motto of the 442nd Regimental Combat team in World War II. This U.S. Army unit was composed of Americans of Japanese ancestry. According to Bill Hosokawa, *Nisei* (1969), the motto was "a Hawaiian dice-roller's pidgin phrase meaning 'shoot the works' or 'go all out.'"

Lightning speed, more lightning speed; boldness, more boldness.
Motto of North Vietnamese General Van Tien Dung, quoted in Harry G. Summers, Jr., *On Strategy* (1982).

musical analogies

No man can properly command an army from the rear. . . . Some men think that modern armies may be so regulated that a general can sit in an office and play on his several columns as on the keys of a piano; this is a fearful mistake. The directing mind must be at the very head of an army.
General William T. Sherman, *Memoirs* (1885).

A perfected modern battle plan is like nothing so much as a score for an orchestral composition, where the various arms and units are the instruments, and the tasks they perform are their respective musical phrases. Every individual unit must make its entry precisely at the proper moment, and play its part in the general harmony.
General Sir John Monash, Commander Australian Corps, France, 1918, quoted in Len Deighton, *Blitzkrieg* (1980).

Our thousand-stringed artillery began to play its battle-tune.
Field Marshal Paul von Hindenburg, *Out of My Life* (1920).

Diplomacy without armaments is like music without instruments.
Frederick the Great quoted in G. P. Gooch, *Studies in Diplomacy and Statecraft* (1942).

Whereas the other arts are, at their height, individual, the art of war is essentially orchestral.
B. H. Liddell Hart, *Thoughts on War* (1944).

The game of strategy can, like music, be played in two "keys." The major key is direct strategy, in which force is the essential factor. The minor key is indirect strategy, in which force recedes into the background and its place is taken by psychology and planning. Naturally any strategy may make use of both these keys in varying degree and the result is a large number of "patterns" of strategy.
André Beaufre, *An Introduction to Strategy* (1965).

Mussolini, Benito (1883–1945)

Professor Morell, Hitler's personal physician, overhauled Mussolini in the autumn of 1943 and reported "slight blood pressure", nervous exhaustion and weak bowels; this opinion exasperated [Joseph] Goebbels who exclaimed, "In fact, just about what we've all got."
Hugh L'Etang, *The Pathology of Leadership* (1970).

It is said that when Mussolini's corpse was exhibited in public, an old woman drew a revolver and fired five shots into it, exclaiming, "Those are for my five sons!" It is the kind of story that the newspapers make up, but it might be true. I wonder how much satisfaction she got out of those five shots.
George Orwell, "As I Please," *Tribune* (November 9, 1945). This incident was reported in *Time* (May 7, 1945).

Mussolini's end is deserved but ghastly. Democracies may treat their ex-leaders carelessly and frequently without respect, but the way Mussolini and his mistress were executed and publicly displayed in the square at Milan should be a warning to all future would-be dictators. The pictures are revolting.
Captain Harry C. Butcher, *My Three Years With Eisenhower* (1946).

Hitler showed surprising loyalty to Mussolini, but it never extended to trusting him.
Alan Bullock, *Hitler* (1952).

Disloyal as he had been to some of his closest associates, a number of whom he had had murdered . . . , Hitler maintained a strange and unusual loyalty to his ridiculous Italian partner that did not weaken, that indeed was strengthened when adversity and then disaster overtook the strutting, sawdust Roman Caesar. It is one of the interesting paradoxes of this narrative.
William L. Shirer, *The Rise and Fall of the Third Reich* (1959).

mutiny

A multitude never broke out into open sedition at once and with unanimous consent. They are prepared and excited by some few mutineers, who hope to secure impunity for their crimes by the number of their associates. But if the height of the mutiny requires violent remedies, it will be most advisable, after the manner of the ancients, to punish the ringleaders only in order that, although few suffer, all may be terrified by the example.
Vegetius, *De Re Militari* (378 A.D.).

And though public justice and the public safety can allow no vindication of any species of Mutiny, yet reason and humanity will distinguish the sudden unpremeditated act of desperation and frenzy, from the foul deliberate contempt of every religious duty and honorable sentiment; and will deplore the uncertainty of human prospects, when they reflect that a young man is condemned to perpetual infamy, who, if he had served on board any other ship, or had perhaps been absent from the *Bounty* a single day, or one ill-fated hour, might still have been an honor to his country, and a glory and comfort to his friends.
Edward Christian (Fletcher's brother), *A Short Reply to Captain Bligh's Answer* (1795), quoted in Richard Hough, *Captain Bligh and Mr. Christian* (1973).

Casting me adrift 3,500 miles from a port of call! You're sending me to my doom, eh? Well, you're wrong, Christian. I'll take this boat, as she floats, to England if I must. I'll live to see you—all of you—hanging from the highest yardarm in the British fleet.
Charles Laughton as Captain William Bligh in *Mutiny on the Bounty* (1935), directed by Frank Lloyd; screenplay by Talbot Jennings and others from the novel by Charles Nordhoff and James Norman Hall.

Most mutinies are led by officers, not enlisted men. The reason for this is simply that the enlisted men do not know how to navigate the ship. Moreover, officers have the advantages and educational background to know that successful rebellion is a possibility. Both of these factors would be even more true in the Soviet Navy.
Tom Clancy, *The Hunt for Red October* (1984).

napalm

Napalm, or jellied gasoline, is the most familiar of the antipersonnel weapons. Napalm is "delivered" on villages in aluminum tanks triggered by white phosphorus bombs. On impact the bomb explodes and the now flaming jellied gasoline consumes everything it comes in contact with. The effect on flesh is similar to that of a blowtorch or flamethrower but more tenacious. Nothing is wasted. Fragments of the phosphorus bomb itself, if they penetrate the body, will not stop burning for days, even after death, even in the grave. Military terminology makes it hard for people to visualize the effects of these raids but the terminology at air bases is more vivid. Villages are bathed in napalm; "Charlie" is barbecued.
Robert Crichton quoted in C. Woolf and J. Bagguley, *Authors Take Sides on Vietnam* (1967).

Napalm has become "Incinderjell," which makes it sound like Jello. And defoliants are referred to as weed-killers—something you use in your driveway. The resort to euphemism denotes, no doubt, a guilty conscience or—the same thing nowadays—a twinge in the public-relations nerve.
Mary McCarthy, *Vietnam* (1967).

Strafe the town and kill the people

Drop your napalm in the square
Get out early in the morning
Catch them at their Sunday prayer.
A song reportedly sung by some pilots in Vietnam quoted in Charles Fair, *From the Jaws of Victory* (1971).

I love the smell of napalm in the morning.
Robert Duvall in *Apocalypse Now* (1979), directed by Francis Ford Coppola. Those words were spoken by Lt. Colonel Kilgore as he attacked a Vietcong village with Richard Wagner's "Ride of the Valkyries" blasting from his helicopter's loudspeakers.

Napoleon I, Emperor of France (1769–1821)

Napoleon is a torrent which as yet we are unable to stem. Moscow will be the sponge that will suck him dry.
Field Marshal Michael Kutuzov, speech to Russian Army officers at Fili, September 13, 1812.

The tiger has broken out of his den.
The monster was three days at sea.
The wretch has landed at Fréjus.
The Brigand has arrived at Antibes.
The Invader has reached Grenoble.
The General has entered Lyons.
Napoleon slept last night at Fontainebleau.
The Emperor proceeds to the Tuileries to-day.
His Imperial Majesty will address his loyal subjects to-morrow.
An anonymously written skit of 1815 showing how Napoleon's progress from Elba to Paris was viewed, reprinted in Louis Cohen, *Napoleonic Anecdotes* (1925).

Thirteen and a half years of success turned Alexander the Great into a kind of madman. Good fortune of exactly the same duration produced the same disorder in Napoleon. The only difference was that the Macedonian hero was lucky enough to die.
Marie-Henri Beyle ("Stendhal"), *A Life of Napoleon* (1818).

Although too much of a soldier among sovereigns, no one could claim with better right to be a sovereign among soldiers.
Sir Walter Scott, *Life of Napoleon* (1827).

He was sent into this world to teach generals and statesmen what they should avoid. His victories teach what may be accomplished by activity, boldness, and skill; his disasters what might have been avoided by prudence.
General Antoine Henri Jomini, *Summary of the Art of War* (1838).

[Napoleon] directed Bourrienne to leave all his letters unopened for three weeks, and then observed with satisfaction how large a part of the correspondence had thus disposed of itself, and no longer required an answer.
Ralph Waldo Emerson, *Representative Men* (1850).

It is very true that I have said that I considered Napoleon's presence in the field equal to forty thousand men in the balance. This is a very loose way of talking; but the idea is a very different one from that of his presence at a battle being equal to a reinforcement of forty thousand men.
Duke of Wellington quoted in Philip Henry Stanhope, *Notes of Conversations with the Duke of Wellington, 1831–1851* (1888).

I always hate to compare Napoleon with Hitler, as it seems an insult to the great Emperor and warrior to connect him in any way with a squalid caucus boss and butcher.
Winston Churchill, speech in the House of Commons, September 28, 1944.

Napoleon was a contemporary of Kant, Goethe, Mozart, and Beethoven. Compare their tombs, and you will get an aesthetic measure of how more we admire a great soldier than a great philosopher, poet, or composer.
George Bernard Shaw, *Everybody's Political What's What?* (1944).

Napoleon looking across the Channel was faced by a problem so vast that he never understood it in all its magnitude. He simply turned away. Perhaps one of his spies had relayed to him the classic comment ascribed to the Earl of St. Vincent at a meeting of the war council discussing the prospect of French invasion of the British Isles. The First Sea Lord is reported to have said, "I do not say the Frenchman will not come, I only say he will not come by sea."
Rear Admiral J. C. Wylie, *Military Strategy* (1967).

Napoleon ... was Cesare Borgia with twice the brains, and Machiavelli with half the caution and a hundred times the will. He was an Italian made skeptical by Voltaire, subtle by the ruses of survival in the Revolution, sharp by the daily duel of French intellects. All the qualities of Renaissance Italy appeared in him: artist and warrior, philosopher and despot; unified in instincts and purposes, quick and penetrating in thought, direct and overwhelming in action, but unable to stop. Barring that vital fault, he was the finest master of controlled complexity and coordinated energy in history. Tocqueville put it well: he was as great as a man can be without virtue, and he was as wise as a man can be without modesty.
Will and Ariel Durant, *The Age of Napoleon* (1975).

Napoleon's ultimate contribution to the development of the modern concept of principles of war, however, consists not of references that can be gleaned from his writings or conversations but in his example, which inspired the belief that success in war can be simply and consistently achieved.
John I. Alger, *The Quest for Victory* (1982).

Napoleon was always a genius at contriving to use the weapons at hand. So, with his last weapon, the will, Napoleon aimed a shaft at those who sent him to die on that lonely island in the South Atlantic, and at his detested jailer, the English governor Hudson Lowe: "I die prematurely, murdered by the English oligarchy and its hired assassin."
Ben Weider and David Hapgood, *The Murder of Napoleon* (1982). According to Weider and Hapgood, "someone had administered periodic large, but not immediately fatal, doses [of arsenic] to the victim [Napoleon]."

national interest

Though peace be made, yet it is interest that keeps peace.
Oliver Cromwell, speech in Parliament, September 4, 1654.

I am heartily disposed to entertain the most favorable sentiments of our new ally [France] but it is a maxim founded on the universal experience of mankind, that no nation is to be trusted farther than it is bound by interest.
President George Washington quoted in Samuel B. Griffith II, *In Defense of the Public Liberty* (1976).

We have no eternal allies, and we have no perpetual enemies. Our interests are eternal, and those interests it is our duty to follow.
Lord Palmerston, speech in the House of Commons, March 1, 1848.

Foreign policies are not built upon abstractions. They are the result of practical conceptions of national interest arising from some immediate exigency or standing out vividly in historical perspective.
Charles E. Hughes, speaking as Secretary of State, quoted in Charles A. Beard, *The Idea of National Interest* (1934).

The concept of the national interest presupposes neither a naturally harmonious, peaceful world nor the inevitability of war as a consequence of the pursuit by all nations of their national interest. Quite to the contrary, it assumes continuous conflict and threat of war to be minimized through the continuous adjustment of conflicting interest by diplomatic action.
Hans J. Morgenthau, "Another 'Great Debate'," *American Political Science Review* (December 1952).

We must recognize that every nation determines its policies in terms of its own interests.
President John F. Kennedy, speech at Salt Lake City, September 26, 1963.

No nation has friends—only interests.
Charles de Gaulle, *U.S. News and World Report* (September 19, 1966).

Men may be linked in friendships. Nations are linked only by interests.
Rolf Hochhuth, *The Soldiers* (1967).

The many different strands that make up American thinking on foreign policy have so far proved inhospitable to an approach based on the calculation of the national interest and relationships of power. Americans are comfortable with an idealistic tradition that espouses great causes, such as making the world safe for democracy, or human rights.
Henry Kissinger, *Years of Upheaval* (1982).

nationalism

Patriotism is a lively sense of responsibility. Nationalism is a silly cock crowing on its own dunghill.
Richard Aldington, *The Colonel's Daughter* (1931).

Nationalism is an infantile disease. It is the measles of mankind.
Albert Einstein, *The World As I See It* (1934).

Internationalism is nonsense. Pushing all the nations into Geneva is like throwing all the fishes into the same pond: They just begin eating one another. We need something higher than nationalism: a genuine political and social Catholicism. How are you to get that from these patriots, with their national anthems and flags and dreams of war and conquest rubbed into them from their childhood? The organization of nations is the organization of world war.
George Bernard Shaw, *Geneva*, Act II (1938).

The advent of "automatic warfare" should make plain the absurdity of warfare as a means of deciding nations' claims to superiority. It blows away romantic vaporings about the heroic virtues of war, utilized by aggressive and ambitious leaders to generate a military spirit among their people. They can no longer claim that war is any test of a people's fitness, or even of its national strength. Science has undermined the foun-

dations of nationalism, at the very time when the spirit of nationalism is most rampant.
B. H. Liddell Hart, *The Revolution in Warfare* (1946).

Patriotism is when love of your own people comes first; nationalism, when hate for people other than your own comes first.
Charles de Gaulle, *Life* (May 9, 1969).

Nationalism represents a profound value for Latin Americans simply because of the fact that our nationhood is still in question. In New York, Paris or London, no one loses sleep asking themselves whether the nation exists. In Latin America you can wake up and find that the nation is no longer there, usurped by a military junta, a multinational corporation or an American ambassador surrounded by a bevy of technical advisers.
Carlos Fuentes, *Time* (June 21, 1982).

national security

The chief foundations of all states, whether new, old, or mixed, are good laws and good arms. And as there cannot be good laws where there are not good arms, and where there are good arms there must be good laws.
Niccolò Machiavelli, *The Prince* (1513).

If all that Americans want is security, they can go to prison. They'll have enough to eat, a bed and a roof over their heads. But if an American wants to preserve his dignity and his equality as a human being, he must not bow his neck to any dictatorial government.
Dwight D. Eisenhower, President of Columbia University, *The New York Times* (December 9, 1949).

If you believe the doctors, nothing is wholesome: if you believe the theologians, nothing is innocent: if you believe the soldiers, nothing is safe.
Lord Salisbury quoted in Samuel P. Huntington, *The Soldier and the State* (1957).

National security is a condition which cannot be qualified. We shall either be secure, or we shall be insecure. We cannot have partial security. If we are only half secure, we are not secure at all. We cannot lock the front door and leave the back door ajar.
General Jacob L. Devers quoted in Bernard Brodie, *Strategy in the Missile Age* (1959).

The Xerox machine is one the biggest threats to national security ever devised.
Admiral Thomas Moorer quoted in *Time* (June 17, 1985).

My feeling has always been that if we rest our security on the answer to the question of whether we trust the General Secretary of the Communist Party of the Soviet Union, then we have already lost our security.
Caspar W. Weinberger, *The New York Times* (July 16, 1989).

NATO

The Parties agree than an armed attack against one or more of them in Europe or North America shall be considered an attack against them all; and consequently they agree that, if such an armed attack occurs, each of them, in exercise of the right of individual or collective self-defense recognized by Article 51 of the Charter of the United Nations, will assist the Party or Parties so attacked by taking forthwith, individually and in concert with the other Parties, such action as it deems necessary,

including the use of armed force, to restore and maintain the security of the North Atlantic area.
Article 5 of the North Atlantic Treaty of April 4, 1949.

I want to make it absolutely clear that we at SHAPE are basing all our planning on using atomic and thermonuclear weapons in our defence. With us it is no longer: "They may possibly be used." It is very definitely: "They will be used, if we are attacked."
Field Marshal B. L. Montgomery, "A Look Through a Window at World War III," *Journal of the Royal United Services Institute* (November 1954).

I had no intention of allowing Europe to be overrun, as it had been in 1940. But we knew that the Soviets maintained something in the neighborhood of 175 divisions active in Europe at all times. The United States had twenty divisions, only five of which were in Europe. Therefore, in view of the disparity in the strengths of the opposing ground forces, it seemed clear that only by the interposition of our nuclear weapons could we promptly stop a major Communist aggression in that area. Two more divisions or ten more divisions, on our side, would not make very much difference against this Soviet ground force.
President Dwight D. Eisenhower, *White House Years*, I (1963).

There will be no peace, no lasting peace, until you get the armed forces of different countries back behind their borders and get the Russians back into Russia. Keep the Germans in Germany, get the Americans back to America, the Canadians back to Canada, and the British back to Britain.... I don't believe the people who say that once the Americans go home they will never come back to Europe in a war. I have never known the Americans to break their word. They have signed a treaty. They will stick to it.
Field Marshal B. L. Montgomery, March 22, 1963, quoted in D. L. Sulzberger, *The Last of the Giants* (1970).

NATO is an aggressive military bloc. The defensive efforts of the Socialist countries, the national liberation movements, the revolutionary and working class movement and the peace movement in NATO countries have thus far restrained NATO from acting in keeping with its aggressive nature.
M. Kulanov, *NATO—Threat to World Peace* (1972).

One could argue—and many did—that nations whose combined populations and Gross National Products were at least three times the Soviet Union's should be able to mount a conventional defense against the Warsaw Pact. The difficulty was that no member of the [NATO] Alliance, including the United States, was prepared to make the effort.
Henry Kissinger, *White House Years* (1979).

The prospect of [General Alexander] Haig as SACEUR, a potentially important foreign-policy proconsul in Europe, had initially enraged the other indispensable figure of the infant [Ford] administration, Secretary Kissinger. When Kissinger threatened to veto the posting .... Haig then "stormed into Henry's office and had a little talk about what could come out" in a Senate hearing or a series of leaks. Looming over that conversation with his old boss were all the shadows they had cast together, yet so far publicly escaped—the truth of the wiretaps; Kissinger's (and Haig's) liaison with the plumbers, which the secretary had solemnly denied to the Foreign Relations Committee under oath; the long trail of sordid policies not yet exposed. "It took about a

half an hour" said one Kissinger confidante of the talk that September, "and Henry saw what a great NATO supreme commander Al would make."
  Roger Morris, *Haig: The General's Progress* (1982).

I rather look upon this effort as about the last remaining chance for the survival of Western civilization.
  General Dwight D. Eisenhower, on the creation of NATO, quoted in Stephen E. Ambrose, *Eisenhower*, I (1983).

According to a popular joke at NATO headquarters in Brussels, one of the most difficult decisions confronting Soviet military planners in the event that they attack Western Europe will be whether to bomb the Alliance's headquarters of not. They probably won't, say the corridor experts, so as to ensure a maximum degree of confusion with in NATO.
  Daniel Charles, *Nuclear Planning in NATO* (1987).

And when ... we encountered speculation as to whether Moscow was planning a trick and wanted to split NATO, to lull Western Europe's vigilance and then overrun it, when the idea of a nuclear-free Europe began to be attacked as harmful and dangerous, I said publicly to all these people: "What are you afraid of, gentlemen? Is it so difficult to rise to the level of real assessments for the truly historic processes which are taking place in the Soviet Union and the entire socialist world? Can you not understand the objective, unbreakable connection of these processes with genuinely good intentions in foreign policy?"
  Mikhail Gorbachev, *Perestroika* (1987).

Do you think 320 million Europeans can continue forever to ask 240 million Americans to defend us against 280 million Soviets?
  Jean-Pierre Bechter, French NATO official, *Insight* (December 26–January 2, 1989).

NATO is a subject that drives the dagger of boredom deep, deep into the heart. Perhaps in elite circles in Europe people pay attention to its workings; some few may even feel an improbable tingle of transnational patriotism over "the Alliance." But in the United States NATO is the exclusive property of academics who hold conferences at European resorts, or at the kind of American resort that should be in Europe, where they read turgid reports on why the United States must spend more tax dollars on an alliance to which not one American in ten has ever given a moment's thought.
  Jack Beatty, "The Exorbitant Anachronism," *The Atlantic* (June 1989).

Navy, British

The dominion of the sea, as it is an ancient and undoubted right of the Crown of England, so it is the best security of the land. The wooden walls are the best walls of this kingdom.
  Thomas Coventry, speech on the Royal Navy, June 17, 1635, quoted in Admiral Sir Herbert Richmond, *The Navy as an Instrument of Policy* (1953).

It is upon the navy under the Providence of God that the safety, honor, and welfare of this realm do chiefly attend.
  Charles II, preamble to the *Articles of War* (1666).

In this high century [eighteenth] of naval sail, an uncompromising sea battle was a horror unsurpassed by modern machine warfare. The compulsion of commanders was to bring the big wooden vessels physically together, forming a compact butcher shop. The grappling of two matched warships was like a collision of overcrowded poorhouses, whose lousy, half-starved and choking inmates fired cannons point-blank

through the windows at each other. Men literally shot each other to pieces, and saw the pieces.
James Dugan, The *Great Mutiny* (1965).

When Britain first, at heaven's command,
Arose from out the azure main,
This was the charter of the land,
And guardian angels sung this strain:
"Rule, Britannia, rule the waves;
Britons never will be slaves."
James Thomson, *The Masque of Alfred*, Act II (1740).

[The eighteenth-century British] navy was not a home for innovative minds, being considered the place to dispose of the unteachable or stupid son of a family whose more promising brothers qualified for the army or clergy.
Barbara W. Tuchman, *The First Salute* (1988).

I do not say, my lords, that the French will not come. I only say they will not come by sea.
Admiral John Jervis [Earl St. Vincent], to the British Cabinet in 1803 concerned with a possible invasion from France, quoted in G. J. Marcus, *The Age of Nelson* (1971).

There were gentlemen and there were seamen in the navy of Charles the Second. But the seamen were not gentlemen; and the gentlemen were not seamen.
Thomas Babington Macaulay, *History of England*, I (1848).

I cleaned the windows and I swept the floor,
And I polished up the handle of the big front door.
Then I was promoted to the post of junior clerk.
I served the writs with a smile so bland,
And I copied all the letters in a big round hand.
Finally I became a lawyer and was given a partnership which was the only *ship*
  I'd ever seen!
I grew so rich I was sent to Parliament.
I always voted at my party's call,
And I never thought of thinking for myself at all.
As a matter of fact—
I thought so little, they rewarded me
By making me the Ruler of the Queen's Na-vy!
Now landsmen all, whoever you may be,
If you want to rise to the top of the tree,
Stick close to your desks and never go to sea,
And you *all* may be Rulers of the Queen's Navy!
William S. Gilbert, *H. M. S. Pinafore* (1878).

The world has never seen a more impressive demonstration of the influence of sea power upon its history. Those far distant, storm-beaten ships, upon which the Grand Army [of Napoleon] never looked, stood between it and the dominion of the world.
Alfred Thayer Mahan, *The Influence of Sea Power Upon the French Revolution and Empire* (1892).

If blood be the price of admiralty,
Lord God, we ha' paid in full!
Rudyard Kipling, *The Song of the English* (1893).

Strangely enough, the British Admiralty was opposed to the introduction of steamships, and when the Colonial Office asked the First Lord for a steam packet to convey mails from Malta to the Ionian Islands, the following reply was received: "Their Lordships felt it their bounden duty to discourage, to the utmost of their ability, the employment of steam vessels, as they considered that the introduction of steam was calculated to strike a fatal blow at the naval supremacy of the Empire."
J. F. C. Fuller, *The Conduct of War* (1961).

The Navy is the 1st, 2nd, 3rd, 4th, 5th . . . ad infinitum Line of Defense! If the Navy is not supreme, no Army however large is of the slightest use.
Admiral Sir John Fisher, speaking before World War I, quoted in Arthur J. Marder, *The Anatomy of British Sea Power* (1940).

Although the British thought of their [World War I] navy in terms of "the Nelson touch"—that is, of adventurous initiative—it was in fact ruled by a discipline more rigid and pointless than that of the Prussian army. This discipline was based on the principle of absolute, unquestioning obedience of, and subordination to, one's superiors. Any discussion of service problems, however innocently remote from real insubordination, was treated as subversion. . . . A ship's captain could not even give permission for his crew to hang up their washing to dry without obtaining the approval of the senior officer present.
Correlli Barnett, *The Swordbearers* (1963).

There's something wrong with our bloody ships today.
Admiral Earl Beatty, during the May 30, 1916 Battle of Jutland, quoted in Winston Churchill, *The World Crisis* (1927). What was "wrong" was that British ships were being sunk more easily than opposing German ships, because the British ships tended to lack watertight subdivisions and efficient damage-control systems. The British won the battle; but some German battleships with greater damage than some of the sunk British ships stayed afloat because of better damage-control capabilities.

My only great qualification for being put in charge of the Navy is that I am very much at sea.
Sir Edward Carson, remark to Admiralty staff on his 1917 appointment as First Lord of the Admiralty, quoted in H. Montgomery Hyde, *Carson* (1974).

For the Royal Navy, the watchword should be, "Carry on, and dread nought."
Winston Churchill, speech in the House of Commons, December 6, 1939.

And to Nelson's signal of 135 years ago, "England expects that every man will do his duty," there may now be added last week's no less proud reply: "The Navy is here!"
Winston Churchill, speech at Guildhall, London on February 23, 1940, in which he extolled the rescue in Norwegian waters of British seamen on the German prison ship *Altmark*, quoted in William Manchester, *The Last Lion*, II (1988).

Don't talk to me about naval tradition. It's nothing but rum, sodomy, and the lash.
Winston Churchill, responding during World War II to an admiral's observation that a combined operation under consideration "would be entirely against the traditions of the Royal Navy," quoted in Sir Peter Gretton, *Former Naval Person* (1968).

Most of the ships of an Arctic convoy had been sunk, and Stalin, who knew only that the convoy had failed to bring into Murmansk much needed equipment, said: "Has the British Navy no sense of glory?"
"You must take it from me that what was done was right," Churchill replied. "I really do know a lot about the Navy and sea war."

"Meaning," said Stalin, "that I know nothing."
"Russia is a land animal," Churchill answered. "The British are sea animals."
Robert Payne, *The Rise and Fall of Stalin* (1965).

The Mosquito Armada as a whole was unsinkable. In the midst of our defeat glory came to the Island people, united and unconquerable; and the tale of the Dunkirk beaches will shine in whatever records are preserved of our affairs.
Winston Churchill, *The Second World War: Their Finest Hour* (1949).

Navy, U.S.

Without a Respectable Navy—alas America!
John Paul Jones, letter to Robert Morris, October 17, 1776, quoted in Samuel Eliot Morison, *John Paul Jones* (1959).

It is by no means enough that an officer of the Navy should be a capable mariner. . . . He should be as well a gentleman of liberal education, refined manners, punctilious courtesy, and the nicest sense of personal honor.
John Paul Jones quoted in Leland P. Lovette, *School of the Sea* (1941).

To aim at such a navy as the greater European nations possess would be a foolish and wicked waste of the energies of our countrymen. It would be to pull on our own heads that load of military expense which makes the European laborer go supperless to bed, and moistens his bread with the sweat of his brow.
Thomas Jefferson, *Notes on the State of Virginia* (1785).

It is no part of our policy to create and maintain a navy able to cope with that of the other great powers of the world.
President Chester A. Arthur, message to Congress, December 4, 1883.

At the present moment it must be conceded that we have nothing which deserves to be called a navy. . . . it is questionable whether we have a single naval vessel finished and afloat at the present time that could be trusted to encounter the ships of any important power.
William C. Whitney, Secretary of the Navy, *Annual Report*, 1885, quoted in Leonard D. White, *The Republican Era* (1958).

It is not the business of naval officers to write books.
Admiral Francis M. Ramsay's 1892 response to a request that Captain Alfred Thayer Mahan be given shore duty to complete a book, quoted in W. D. Puleston, *Mahan* (1939).

In no event will there be money in it; but there may always be honor and quietness of mind and worthy occupation—which are far better guarantees of happiness.
Alfred Thayer Mahan, "The Navy as a Career," *The Forum* (November 1895).

A thoroughly good navy takes a long time to build up. . . . Ships take years to build, crews take years before they become thoroughly expert, while the officers not only have to pass their early youth in a course of special training, but cannot possibly rise to supreme excellence in their profession unless they make it their life-work.
Theodore Roosevelt, "Admiral Dewey," *McClure's Magazine* (October 1899).

Was talking to a lady congressman and she said to me why do all those men say that a big navy will bring peace, I told her well even if it don't bring peace, it will come in mighty handy in case of war.
Will Rogers, writing in 1934, *The Autobiography of Will Rogers*, ed. D. Day (1949).

Admiral Ernest J. King is the new Commander in Chief of the U.S. Fleet, but he will not be called CINCUS, the traditional Navy abbreviation of this big title. At his own stern, thin-lipped request, CINCUS (pronounced "sink-us") was abandoned. Official new nickname for the job: COMINSH.
Time (January 19, 1942).

The burden the Navy has carried so brilliantly in the Pacific will inevitably be shared more and more with the Army and its air forces. But the Navy has performed its historic duty; the Navy got them there.
Ralph D. Paine, Jr., "The War: The Pacific Sweep," Fortune (July 1945).

You should go through the experience of trying to get any changes in the thinking . . . and action of the career diplomats and then you'd know what a real problem was. But the Treasury and the State Department put together are nothing as compared with the Na-a-vy. . . . To change anything in the Na-a-vy is like punching a feather bed. You punch it with your right and you punch it with your left until you are finally exhausted, and then you find the damn bed just as it was before you started punching.
President Franklin D. Roosevelt quoted in Marriner Eccles, Beckoning Frontiers (1951).

The Navy is a machine invented by geniuses, to be run by idiots.
Herman Wouk, The Caine Mutiny (1951).

What is a navy in the absence of a strategy? It is, in effect, a priesthood. Ships, aircraft and facilities are maintained, as temples are kept clean, repaired and repainted. Fleets are rotated from home bases to overseas deployment areas, and then back again, as liturgical services are performed at set hours, in the days set by the priestly calendar. Routine ceremonies alternate with the consecration of new ships, and with the intro- duction of new devices, much as new temples are from time to time commissioned to replace those beyond repair, or to augment their number when faith is on the rise, and the harvest gods have been kind.
Edward N. Luttwak, "War, Strategy, and Maritime Power," Naval War College Review (February 1979).

Destroyer sailors were of a different breed from the rest of the Navy. Their ships were faster and rolled more than the squat battleships and cruisers. And so the men rolled too, walking with a swagger on land, boasting of storms in which destroyers heeled so far that they took seawater in their stacks. Battleship sailors looked down at the ocean; destroyer sailors said they looked the ocean in the eye. Destroyers were tactically used like bullets. A man aboard a destroyer in battle knew that he and his ship were expendable. That kind of knowledge gave a man a certain bravado.
Norman Polmar and Thomas B. Allen, Rickover (1982).

For the past two decades, consultants and systems analysts have endlessly studied and debated the relative merits of nuclear and non-nuclear ships, and the proper com- position of our future Navy. Contracts for studies frequently waste the time of agency personnel who often must educate the so-called experts doing the study, assist them in gathering the data, and then respond to their reports and recommendations—which often defy common sense.
Admiral Hyman Rickover, testimony before the Joint Economic Committee of the Congress, January 28, 1982.

We are a one-and-a-half ocean Navy with a three ocean commitment.
Admiral Thomas B. Hayward, Chief of Naval Operations, The New York Times (April 11, 1982).

I asked around the ship whether the Soviets carried women on their helicopter carriers and other warships. Nobody seemed to know. But the Soviets do have luxurious looking white hospital ships that go from ship to ship. I was to fly over them later in the deployment as they were tied to anchored Soviet warships in the Mediterranean. The scuttlebutt on the *Kennedy* was that these white ships are literally love boats as well as hospitals in which attractive women on board tend to all the needs of the sex-starved Russian officers and sailors in romantic surroundings. A floating brothel for the boys at sea. I could confirm with high ranking Navy officers that this was indeed a suspicion in the U.S. intelligence community but not an established fact. Fact or fiction, everyone looked down lustfully at the white ships whenever any of us flew over them.
George C. Wilson, *Super Carrier* (1986).

I sat in on a briefing by a navy planner on the strategic rationale for the U.S. Navy. Slide after slide portrayed the Soviet naval threat to U.S. interests around the world, and there followed slide after slide depicting how the U.S. Navy was countering the threat. When he finished, the planner, an admiral, asked my boss, an army major general, what he thought of the presentation.
"Very interesting," the general said. "But what you've just said is that if the Soviet navy sank tomorrow, we could do away with the U.S. Navy."
The admiral laughed. "You don't understand," he said. "If the Soviet navy sank tomorrow, I'd get me a new set of slides."
Colonel Harry G. Summers, Jr., "A Bankrupt Military Strategy," *The Atlantic* (June 1989).

Navy wife: It's the toughest job in the Navy.
Slogan on shopping bags in towns with concentrations of U.S. Navy personnel.

neutrality

A prince is further esteemed when he is a true friend or a true enemy, when, that is, he declares himself without reserve in favor of some one or against another. This policy is always more useful than remaining neutral. For if two neighboring powers come to blows, they are either such that if one wins, you will have to fear the victor, or else not. In either of these two cases it will be better for you to declare yourself openly and make war, because in the first case if you do not declare yourself, you will fall prey to the victor, to the pleasure and satisfaction of the one who has been defeated, and you will have no reason nor anything to defend you and nobody to receive you.
Niccolò Machiavelli, *The Prince* (1513).

To be neutral when others are at war is a wise course for the strong, who need not fear the victor, for the strong man can maintain himself without trouble, and he can hope to gain from the disorders of the others. In any other case, neutrality is ill-considered and harmful, for the neutral party remains the prey of both victor and vanquished. Worst of all is neutrality born, not of judgment, but of irresolution. . . . This mistake is committed more often by republics than by princes, because it is often caused by divisions among those who must make decisions. One advises this, the other that, and there are never enough who agree to make one opinion prevail over the other.
Francesco Guicciardini, *Recordi* (1530).

Just for a word—"neutrality", a word which in wartime has so often been disregarded—just for a scrap of paper, Great Britain is going to make war on a kindred nation which desires nothing better than to be friends with her.
German Chancellor Theobald von Bethmann-Hollweg, speaking to the British Ambassador, Sir Edward Goshen, on August 4, 1914, on Britain's declaration of war against Germany because of the German invasion of neutral Belgium, *The New York Times* (August 19, 1914); *The Cambridge History of British Foreign Policy*, III (1923).

The United States must be neutral in fact as well as in name during these days that are to try men's souls. We must be impartial in thought as well as in action, must put a curb upon our sentiments as well as upon every transaction that might be construed as a preference of one party to the struggle before another.
President Woodrow Wilson, proclamation of neutrality during World War I, August 18, 1914.

The Republican party maintains the traditional American policy of noninterference in the political affairs of other nations. This government has definitely refused membership in the League of Nations and to assume any obligations under the covenant of the League.
Plank in the Republican Party national platform, 1928.

Neutrals, gazing at the spectacle of nations at each other's throats, always contrive to collect entertainment tax.
René Quinton, *Soldier's Testament* (1930).

As long as Europe prepares for war, America must prepare for neutrality.
Walter Lippmann, *New York Herald Tribune* (May 17, 1934).

My ministers are pro-German, my wife is pro-Italian, and my people are pro-Russian. I am the only neutral in the country.
King Boris III of Bulgaria quoted in *Time* (January 20, 1941). Shortly thereafter Bulgaria would end her neutrality and join the Axis.

The principle of neutrality pretends that a nation can best gain safety for itself by being indifferent to the fate of others. This has increasingly become an obsolete conception, and, except under very special circumstances, it is an immoral and shortsighted conception.
John Foster Dulles, speech of June 9, 1956, printed in *Department of State Bulletin* (June 18, 1956).

That expression "positive neutrality" is a contradiction in terms. There can be no more positive neutrality than there can be a vegetarian tiger.
V. K. Krishna Menon quoted in *The New York Times* (October 18, 1960).

A government can be neutral but no *man* can be.
Walter Hines Page, American Ambassador to London in 1914, quoted in Barbara W. Tuchman, *The Guns of August* (1962).

"Prince Sihanouk [U.S. Secretary of State John Foster Dulles said in 1958], you are very young. You must choose between the free world and the Communist world." Today I pay homage to his grave. John Foster Dulles was right: There is no nonalignment.
Norodom Sihanouk, Former Chief of State of Cambodia, *The New York Times* (September 5, 1981).

We need to educate our children on why we need strong armed forces. Neutrality is a great thing but who is going to enforce neutrality?
General Lewis W. Walt, USMC, speaking in 1971, quoted in *The New York Times* (March 28, 1989).

armed neutrality

The most sincere neutrality is not a sufficient guard against the depredations of nations at war. To secure respect to a neutral flag requires a naval force organized and ready to vindicate it from insult or aggression. This may even prevent the necessity of going to war.
President George Washington, in his eighth annual message to Congress, December 7, 1796.

Since it has unhappily proved impossible to safeguard our neutral rights by diplomatic means against the unwarranted infringements they are suffering at the hands of Germany, there may be no recourse but to armed neutrality.
President Woodrow Wilson, speech before Congress, February 26, 1917.

Armed neutrality is ineffectual enough at best; in such circumstances and in the face of such pretensions it is worse than ineffectual: it is likely only to produce what it was meant to prevent; it is practically certain to draw us into the war without either the rights or the effectiveness of belligerents.
President Woodrow Wilson, speech to a joint Session of Congress to request a declaration of war against Germany, April 2, 1917.

Nicaragua

The average American doesn't know the difference between a Contra and a caterpillar or between a Sandinista and a sardine.
Senator John P. East, *The New York Times* (October 12, 1984).

The freedom fighters of Nicaragua [the Contras] ... are the moral equal of our Founding Fathers and the brave men and women of the French Resistance.
President Ronald Reagan, speech to the National Conservative Political Action Conference, March 1, 1985.

The little dictator [Daniel Ortega, President of Nicaragua] who went to Moscow in his green fatigues to receive a bear hug did not forsake the doctrine of Lenin when he returned to the West and appeared in a two-piece suit.
President Ronald Reagan quoted in *Time* (June 17, 1985).

If we don't want to see the map of Central America covered in a sea of red, eventually lapping at our own borders, we must act now.
President Ronald Reagan, statement to Congress asking aid for Contras, March 5, 1986.

The United States government saw Nicaragua variously as a case of gangrene, or cancer, or as a dagger pointed at the Rio Grande. . . . But the vision contained a contradiction. While their country was a menace, Nicaraguans themselves were seen as barely able to tie their shoelaces, much less run their own affairs.
Peter Davis, *Where is Nicaragua?* (1987).

The nun asked the men [Contras] why they had launched a raid on San Juan de Limay some days before and burned the town's only bus. She explained that it had taken a very long time to raise the money for that bus and for many it was the only means of transportation. If they won the war, she asked, would they buy the town another bus? "You won't need the bus," a soldier replied. "After democracy comes, everyone will drive a big car."
Leslie Cockburn, *Out of Control* (1987).

If no act of genuine violence could be committed, what about a symbolic one? According to CIA experts, there were some mines available (so-called firecracker mines) that would make a very loud noise, frighten ships' crews half out of their minds, but not cause any serious damage, and certainly not kill anyone. Perhaps this was the answer. It was brought to Casey, who loved it. He instructed . . . others to brief Congress, and this was done on several occasions. . . . There was no objection from any of the [oversight] committee members, and the program went ahead.

The mining program was every bit as effective as its sponsors had hoped. Insurance was cancelled, ships ceased to sail into Nicaraguan harbors, and the Sandinistas faced economic catastrophe. While the *comandantes* launched their usual accusation that the CIA was at the root of all their troubles, little credence was given to their claims in the American media until April 5, 1984, when Senator Barry Goldwater, who had either forgotten or had failed to pay attention to the briefing he had received on the subject, grabbed a classified memorandum on the mining operation, raced to the Senate floor, and began to read the secret information. The next morning, the *Wall Street Journal* had a report on the subject, and within a few days the CIA's role in organizing the mining was on all the front pages.

Michael A. Ledeen, *Perilous Statecraft* (1988).

Dear Bill . . . I am pissed off . . . this is no way to run a railroad. . . . It is an act of war. For the life of me, I don't see how we are going to explain it.

Senator Barry Goldwater, 1984 letter to CIA Director William Casey on the mining of Nicaraguan harbors by the CIA, quoted in David Wise, *The Spy Who Got Away* (1988).

no-man's land

This was a kind of Border, that might be called No Man's Land, being a part of Grand Tartary.

Daniel Defoe, *Robinson Crusoe* (1719).

The [tank] had been conceived, but before it could be born and waddle across no-man's land to browse upon the barbed wire of the Germans, it had first to get through the barbed wire of the bureaucrats.

Sir Ian Hamilton, *The Soul and Body of an Army* (1921).

The Krauts sometimes used herds of livestock for cover and drove them ahead of the infantry in an attack. Whether the attack was successful or not, both sides usually got fresh meat out of it. A dead cow in No Man's Land sometimes was a major objective for patrol activity.

Bill Mauldin, *Up Front* (1945).

Rather than a stage for posturing and heroics, the battlefield would become a no-man's-land where the enemy was invisible and the killing accomplished at extreme ranges in a spirit of methodical indifference.

Robert L. O'Connell, *Of Arms and Men* (1989).

noncommissioned officers

If a soldier during an action looks about as if to flee, or so much as sets foot outside the line, the non-commissioned officer standing behind him will run him through with his bayonet and kill him on the spot.

Frederick the Great, a standing order of 1745 quoted in R. R. Palmer, "Frederick the Great, Guibert, Bulow," *Makers of Modern Strategy*, ed. Peter Paret (1986).

As a rule it is easy to find officers, but it is sometimes very hard to find noncommissioned officers.
Napoleon I, writing in 1809, quoted in J. C. Herold, *The Mind of Napoleon* (1955).

The backbone of the Army is the non-commissioned man!
Rudyard Kipling, *The 'Eathen* (1896).

nuclear weapons

Ever since the invention of gunpowder ... I continually tremble lest men should, in the end, uncover some secret which would provide a short way of abolishing mankind, of annihilating peoples and nations in their entirety.
Charles de Montesquieu, *The Persian Letters* (1721).

[Atmospheric nuclear] tests do not seriously endanger either present or future generations.
Edward Teller, "Compelling Needs for Nuclear Tests," *Life* (February 10, 1958).

Once, when Herman Kahn was briefing [Air Force General Thomas S.] Power [in 1960] on the long-term genetic effects of nuclear weapons, Power suddenly chuckled, leaned forward in his chair and said, "You know, it's not yet been proved to me that two heads aren't better than one." Even Kahn was outraged.
Fred Kaplan, *The Wizards of Armageddon* (1983).

Make no mistake. There is no such thing as a conventional nuclear weapon.
President Lyndon B. Johnson, speech in Detroit, September 7, 1964.

Each nuclear-weapon State party to the treaty undertakes not to transfer to any recipient whatsoever nuclear weapons or other nuclear explosive devices or control over such weapons or explosive devices directly, or indirectly; and not in any way to assist, encourage, or induce any non-nuclear-weapon State to manufacture or otherwise acquire nuclear weapons or other nuclear explosive devices, or control over such weapons or explosive devices.
Article 1 of the Treaty on the Non-Proliferation of Nuclear Weapons, June 12, 1968.

When later I achieved a wholly undeserved reputation for expertise in nuclear matters, no one knew better than Robert Oppenheimer how fraudulent this was. At the beginning of our work he came to stay with us and after dinner each evening would lecture [John J.] McCloy and me with the aid of a borrowed blackboard on which he drew little figures representing electrons, neutrons, and protons, bombarding one another, chasing one another about, dividing and generally carrying on in unpredictable ways. Our bewildered questions seemed to distress him. At last he put down the chalk with gentle despair, saying "It's hopeless! I really think you two believe neutrons and electrons are little men!" We admitted nothing.
Dean Acheson, *Present at the Creation* (1969).

Nuclear weapons are controlled by unimaginably complex electronic systems. It is almost statistically inevitable that one day one of the systems will malfunction, and its complexity will make it almost impossible to trace the fault in time. By then the missiles will have left the silos. The world will go [out with] neither a whimper nor a bang, just a simple short-circuit.
John Ellis, *The Social History of the Machine Gun* (1975).

What are we to make of terms like "nuclear exchange," "nuclear yield," "counterforce".... ? These words provide a way of talking about nuclear weapons without really talking about them. In them we find nothing about billions of human

beings being incinerated or literally melted, nothing about millions of corpses. Rather, the weapons come to seem ordinary and manageable or even mildly pleasant: a "nuclear exchange" sounds something like mutual gift-giving.
Robert J. Lifton and Richard Falk, *Indefensible Weapons* (1982).

We are saying that the decisions about nuclear weapons are among the most pressing moral questions of our age. While these decisions have obvious military and political aspects, they involve fundamental moral choices. In simple terms, we are saying that good ends (defending one's country, protecting freedom, etc.) cannot justify immoral means (the use of weapons which kill indiscriminately and threaten whole societies).
U.S. Catholic Bishops' letter, *The Challenge of Peace* (1983).

I don't think there'll be an Armageddon war, but I'll put it this way. There has never been any weapon yet invented or perfected that hasn't been used.
General Bruce Holloway quoted in Michael Parfit, *The Boys Behind the Bombs* (1983).

Try to reduce the dangers of nuclear war within the relevant future time period as best you can. . . . You just get depressed [if you worry] about the long-term future.
Paul Nitze quoted in R. Brownstein and N. Easton, *Reagan's Ruling Class* (1983).

The secret of the cheapness of the strategic forces is that they mostly consist of weapons and not people: they are "capital intensive," in the language of the economists. Although the bombers, missile submarines, and the rest are even more expensive pound for pound than other weapons, their use of manpower is by contrast very frugal.
Edward N. Luttwak, *The Pentagon and the Art of War* (1985).

When Phyllis Schlafly argues that nuclear weapons are good because God gave them to us, one can ask why He allowed the atheistic Soviet Union also to get them.
Joseph S. Nye, Jr., *Nuclear Ethics* (1986).

If I were a Soviet General and were told that nuclear weapons were out of the picture, I would say, "Comrade, we would be in a dominant position in the world." We don't want to make the world safe for a massive conventional war.
Senator Sam Nunn, *U.S. News and World Report* (October 27, 1986).

A world without nuclear weapons would be less stable and more dangerous for all of us.
Margaret Thatcher quoted in *Time* (April 27, 1987).

atomic bomb
. . . it may become possible to set up a nuclear chain reaction in a large mass of uranium, by which vast amounts of power and large quantities of new radium-like elements would be generated . . . . This new phenomenon would also lead to the construction of bombs, and it is conceivable—though much less certain—that extremely powerful bombs of a new type may thus be constructed. A single bomb of this type, carried by boat and exploded in a port, might very well destroy the whole port together with some of the surrounding territory. However, such bombs might very well prove to be too heavy for transportation by air.
Albert Einstein, letter to President Franklin D. Roosevelt, August 2, 1939. According to Richard Rhodes in *The Making of the Atomic Bomb* (1988), the final draft of this letter was prepared by Leo Szilard, who initially wrote it in German so Einstein could better understand it.

We waited until the blast had passed, walked out of the shelter and then it was extremely solemn. We knew the world would not be the same. A few people laughed, a few people cried. Most people were silent. I remembered the line from the Hindu scripture, the *Bhagavad-Gita:* Vishnu is trying to persuade the Prince that he should do his duty and to impress him he takes on his multi-armed form and says, "Now I am become Death, the destroyer of worlds." I suppose we all thought that, one way or another.
J. Robert Oppenheimer quoted in Len Giovannitti and Fred Freed, *The Decision to Drop the Bomb* (1965).

If only I had known, I should have become a watchmaker.
Albert Einstein, on his role in the development of the atom bomb, quoted in Gerald Leach, "Einstein's Legacy," *New Statesman* (April 16, 1965).

[Kenneth] Bainbridge went around congratulating the leaders on the success of the implosion method. "I finished by saying to Robert [Oppenheimer], 'Now we are all sons of bitches.' . . . [He] told my younger daughter that it was the best thing anyone said after the test."
Richard Rhodes, *The Making of the Atomic Bomb* (1988).

After all this new bomb is just going to be bigger than our present bombs. It involves no difference in the principles of war. And as for any post-war problems there are none that cannot be amicably settled between me and my friend, President Roosevelt.
Winston Churchill to physicist Niels Bohr, May 16, 1944, quoted in Ronald W. Clark, *The Greatest Power on Earth* (1980).

That [the Manhattan Project] is the biggest fool thing we have ever done. The bomb will never go off, and I speak as an expert in explosives.
Admiral William Leahy to President Harry S. Truman, a few hours after Truman assumed the presidency on the death of Roosevelt, April 12, 1945, quoted in Harry S. Truman, *Memoirs,* I (1955).

The Atomic Age began at exactly 5:30 Mountain War Time on the morning of July 16, 1945, on a stretch of semi-desert land about fifty airline miles from Alamogordo, New Mexico. At that great moment in history, ranking with the moment in the long ago when man first put fire to work for him and started on his march to civilization, the vast energy locked within the hearts of the atoms of matter was released for the first time in a burst of flame such as had never before been seen on this planet.
William L. Laurence, *The New York Times* (September 26, 1945).

Nuclear weapons, in a sense, just happened. . . . Indeed, the military's first reaction was one of fear—not so much dismay at the awesome power of the "The Bomb," but concern that such extremely destructive weaponry could put them out of business: [in that] it might do away with the need for large conventional forces. General Curtis LeMay, who would later become head of the Strategic Air Command, referred to the atomic bomb in September 1945 as "the worst thing that ever happened to the Army Air Force."
Daniel Ford, *The Button* (1985).

If you ask, "Can we make them more terrible?" the answer is yes. If you ask, "Can we make a lot of them?" the answer is yes.
J. Robert Oppenheimer, on atomic bombs, *Time* (October 29, 1945).

I do not believe that civilization will be wiped out in a war fought with the atomic bomb. Perhaps two thirds of the people of the earth might be killed, but enough men

capable of thinking, and enough books, would be left to start again, and civilization could be restored.
Albert Einstein, *The Atlantic Monthly* (November 1945).

We have often been asked ... why Germany made no attempt to produce atomic bombs. The simplest answer one can give to this questions is this: because the project could not have succeeded under German war conditions. In particular, a German atomic bomb project could not have succeeded because of the military situation. In 1942, German industry was already stretched to the limit. ... The immediate production of armaments could be robbed neither of personnel nor of raw materials, nor could the enormous plants required have been effectively protected against air attack. Finally—and this is a most important fact—the undertaking could not even be initiated against the psychological background of the men responsible for German war policy. These men expected an early decision of the war, even in 1942, and any major project which did not promise quick returns was specifically forbidden.
Werner Heisenberg, "Research in Germany on the Technical Applications of Atomic Energy," *Nature* (August 16, 1947). Edward N. Luttwak writes in *Strategy* (1987) that the "postwar claim of the leading German nuclear physicists (Heisenberg and others) that they deliberately refrained from developing a bomb was fraudulent."

Stimson, what was gunpowder? Trivial. What was electricity? Meaningless. This atomic bomb is the second coming in wrath!
Winston Churchill quoted in Henry L. Stimson and McGeorge Bundy, *On Active Service in Peace and War* (1948).

No country without an atom bomb could properly consider itself independent.
Charles de Gaulle, *The New York Times Magazine* (May 12, 1968).

You think of the lives which would have been lost in an invasion of Japan's home islands—a staggering number of Americans but millions more of Japanese—and you thank God for the atomic bomb.
William Manchester, *Goodbye, Darkness* (1980).

John Kenneth Galbraith ... thinks the A-bombs were unnecessary and unjustified because the war was ending anyway. The A-bombs meant, he says, "a difference, at most, of two or three weeks." But at the time, with no indication that surrender was on the way ... Allied casualties were running to over 7,000 per week. Two weeks more means 14,000 more killed and wounded, three weeks more, 21,000. Those weeks mean the world if you're one of those thousands or related to one of them. ... What did he do in the war? He worked in the Office of Price Administration in Washington. I don't demand that he experience having his ass shot off. I merely note that he didn't.
Paul Fussell, *Thank God for the Atom Bomb* (1988).

counterforce
The United States has come to the conclusion that to the extent feasible, basic military strategy in a general nuclear war should be approached in much the same way that more conventional military operations have been regarded in the past. That is to say, principal military objectives, in the event of a nuclear war stemming from a major attack on the Alliance, should be the destruction of the enemy's military forces, not of its civilian population.
Robert S. McNamara, Secretary of Defense, "National Security and NATO," *Department of State Bulletin* (July 9, 1962).

We have no announced counterforce strategy, if by counterforce one infers that one is going to attempt to destroy silos. We have a new targeting doctrine that emphasizes selectivity and flexibility.
James Schlesinger, testimony before the Senate Armed Services Committee, February 5, 1974.

If either side is striving for or appears to be striving for an effective counterforce first strike capability, then there is no hope for strategic arms control.
Gerard Smith, *Doubletalk* (1980).

first strike
In any fight, it's the first blow that counts; and if you keep it up hot enough, you can whip 'em as fast as they come up.
Confederate General Nathan Bedford Forrest quoted in John W. Morton, *The Artillery of Nathan Bedford Forrest's Cavalry* (1909).

In order to make atomic retaliation effective as a deterrent to aggression, we must decide now and prepare to strike first whenever we have positive evidence that an attack is being mounted against the United States. Such a policy does not contemplate preventive war or a sneak attack. We would only strike if the prospective enemy did not cease preparing to attack us or our allies by a certain time.
W. D. Puleston, *The Influence of Force in Foreign Relations* (1955).

Almost every analyst is now agreed that the first use of nuclear weapons—even if against military targets—is likely to be less for the purpose of destroying the other's military forces or handicapping its operations, than for redress, warning, bargaining, punitive, fining or deterrence purposes.
Herman Kahn, *On Escalation* (1965).

There is no level of superiority which will make a strategic first strike between the two great states anything but an act of utter folly.
McGeorge Bundy, "To Cap the Volcano," *Foreign Affairs* (October 1969).

Each day brings new evidence that U.S. foreign policy is becoming pervaded more and more with a spirit of militarism. A first nuclear strike is being talked about as if it were something casual or routine.
Andrei A. Gromyko, Foreign Minister of the Soviet Union, *Los Angeles Times* (June 16, 1982).

The first-use option is a vital factor . . . because the Soviet Union has to continue to be faced with the prospect that if she aggresses against us that we will use nuclear weapons as we believe necessary and appropriate, which could very well escalate to a strategic nuclear exchange. I happen to believe it would, and I happen to believe it would do so quite quickly. And that's the one thing she fears.
General Bernard W. Rogers, NATO Commander, *The Christian Science Monitor* (April 23, 1987).

H-Bomb
There is an immense gulf between the atomic and the hydrogen bomb. The atomic bomb, with all its terrors, did not carry us outside the scope of human control or manageable events in thought or action, in peace or war. But [with the hydrogen bomb], the entire foundation of human affairs was revolutionized, and mankind placed in a situation both measureless and laden with doom.
Winston Churchill, speech in the House of Commons, March 1, 1955.

This [the hydrogen bomb] brings us a long way from the subtleties of a Clausewitz, a Jomini, or a Mahan. It brings us, in short, to the end of strategy as we have known it.
Bernard Brodie, "Strategy Hits a Dead End," *Harper's* (October 1955).

Those who oppose the hydrogen bomb are behaving like ostriches if they think they are going to promote peace in that way.
Edward Teller quoted in Robert Jungk, *Brighter than a Thousand Suns* (1958).

I happened to read recently a remark by the American nuclear physicist W. Davidson, who noted that the explosion of one hydrogen bomb releases a greater amount of energy than all the explosions set off by all countries in all wars known in the entire history of mankind. And he, apparently, is right.
Soviet Premier Nikita Khrushchev, speech at the United Nations, *The New York Times* (September 19, 1959).

The H-bomb rather favors small nations that don't as yet possess it; they feel slightly more free to jostle other nations, having discovered that a country can stick its tongue out quite far these days without provoking war, so horrible are war's consequences.
E. B. White, *The Points of My Compass* (1962).

mutual assured destruction (MAD), doctrine of
If the United States is to deter a nuclear attack on itself or its allies, it must possess an actual and a credible assured-destruction capability.

When calculating the force required, we must be conservative in all our estimates of both a potential aggressor's capabilities and his intentions. Security depends upon assuming a worst plausible case, and having the ability to cope with it. In that eventuality we must be able to absorb the total weight of nuclear attack on our country—on our retaliatory forces, on our command and control apparatus, on our industrial capacity, on our cities, and on our population—and still be capable of damaging the aggressor to the point that his society would be simply no longer viable in twentieth-century terms. That is what deterrence of nuclear aggression means. It means the certainty of suicide to the aggressor, not merely to his military forces, but to his society as a whole.
Robert S. McNamara, *The Essence of Security* (1968).

The concept of mutual assured destruction provides one of the few instances in which the obvious acronym for something yields at once the appropriate description; for it, that is, a Mutual Assured Destruction posture as a goal is, almost literally, mad. MAD.
Donald Brennan, "When the SALT Hits the Fan," *National Review* (June 23, 1972).

Thus, "assured destruction" fails to indicate what is to be destroyed; but then, "assured genocide" would reveal the truth too starkly .... Tomas de Torquemada [head of the Spanish Inquisition], who burned 10,000 heretics at the stake, could claim principles more humane than our nuclear strategy.
Fred C. Ikle, "Can Nuclear Deterrence Last Out the Century?" *Foreign Policy* (January 1973).

The only weapon we have is MAD—Mutual Assured Destruction. Why don't we have MAS instead—Mutual Assured Security?
President Ronald Reagan, in advocating SDI, quoted in *The New York Times* (February 12, 1985).

no first use

The argument is now put forward that we must never use the atomic bomb until, or unless, it has been used against us first. In other words, you must never fire until you have been shot dead. That seems to me a silly thing to say and a still more imprudent position to adopt.
Winston Churchill, speech in the House of Commons, December 14, 1950.

Every time we conduct a nuclear test, which is necessary in a limited way, we issue a statement as follows: "We will not at any time and under any circumstances be the first to use nuclear weapons. Never! Secondly, we advocate that all countries of the world regardless of their size sit down together and agree on the complete prohibition and complete destruction of nuclear weapons."
Chou En-Lai, Premier of the People's Republic of China, *The New York Times* (June 23, 1971).

In long private conversations with successive Presidents—Kennedy and Johnson—I recommended, without qualification, that they never initiate, under any circumstances, the use of nuclear weapons. I believe they accepted my recommendation.
Robert S. McNamara, "The Military Role of Nuclear Weapons," *Foreign Affairs* (Fall 1983).

First use became irrational when the Russians developed the ability to respond in kind. . . . They have already renounced first use in every way they conceivably could. They've done so unilaterally. They've done so publicly, and with every indication of meaning it. We are the ones who are dragging our feet. If there is no first use of these weapons, there will never be any use of them.
George F. Kennan, *Esquire* (January 1985).

NATO's current political guidelines for nuclear use, in contrast to other elements of its nuclear posture, may actually imply a de facto no-first-use policy.
Daniel Charles, *Nuclear Planning in NATO* (1987).

For the last thirty years, the United States has promised to use nuclear weapons if they are needed to defend Western Europe against an attack from the Soviet Union, even if the Soviet Union has not used [nuclear] weapons up to that point. Few Americans seem aware of this fact.
Daniel Charles, *Nuclear Planning in NATO* (1987).

If the U.S. were to adopt a clear policy to use nuclear weapons in response to—and not in anticipation of—a nuclear attack, we would make very different choices than those advocated by a military focused on preemption and "launch on warning."
The degree to which we need to modernize our nuclear production facilities depends on whether we envision fighting large-scale nuclear wars on battlefields throughout the world. If, instead, we view our nuclear arsenal solely as a means to deter nuclear attacks on ourselves and our allies, then we need many fewer nuclear weapons.
Morton H. Halperin and Jane Wales, "Unchecked Thumbs On Nuclear Buttons," *The New York Times* (February 12, 1989).

NSC-68

At the end of January 1950, President Truman issued a directive to the Secretaries of State and Defense "to undertake a re-examination of our objectives in peace and war and of the effect of these objectives on our strategic plans, in the light of the probable fission bomb capability and possible thermo-nuclear bomb capability of the Soviet Union." The main drafting of the report was undertaken by Paul Nitze. . . . The result, known as NSC-68, was presented to the National Security Council (NSC) in April 1950.

NSC-68's main purpose was to impress upon its bureaucratic readership the Soviet threat to world peace, best blocked through increased military preparedness in the non-Soviet world. This role, of getting over the message of the seriousness of the Soviet challenge to all responsible sections of the State and Defense Departments, may account for the turgidity of the style.
Lawrence Freedman, The *Evolution of Nuclear Strategy* (1981).

NSC-68 greatly exaggerated Soviet superiority. Henry Kissinger, though generally approving of Acheson's strategy of containment, asserts that "it was based on a flawed premise; that we were weaker than the Soviets. . . . In fact, we were stronger than they were."
Walter Isaacson and Evan Thomas, *The Wise Men* (1986).

[George] Kennan strongly objected to NSC-68. He argued that Stalin had no grand scheme for world conquest, that the Soviet sphere of influence lay in Eastern Europe, and that American diplomacy was already too rigid and militaristic. But Acheson and Truman were watching the home front too. Wary of domestic rumblings over apparent Soviet successes, they overrode Kennan's objections and used NSC-68 to quadruple defense spending and accelerate United States military build-up, including development of the hydrogen bomb. NSC-68, a durable document, lived on to become the rationale for America's intervention in the Korean War.
John Patrick Diggins, *The Proud Decades* (1988).

nuclear parity
Atomic equality may soon result in the neutralization of the terrifying weapon. When it does, the superiority of strategic position, of land forces, and of human potential will come into full play in favor of the Soviet Union.
Then the permanent armies of the West will not merely have to threaten reprisals in order to stifle any fancy for aggression, but will have to be capable of stopping the Russian armies.
Raymond Aron, *The Century of Total War* (1954).

[Secretary of Defense Robert McNamara] talked of "superiority" over the Soviets without the leavening that placed a ceiling on the arms race. "I don't believe that any time in our lifetime they will reach parity with us in the total power of their system versus ours," he told Congress in 1963. He was wrong, of course.
Henry L. Trewhitt, *McNamara* (1971).

The purpose of SALT is to create conditions of mutual stability, parity.
Zbigniew Brzezinski, *U.S. News and World Report* (May 30, 1977).

It was clear to me by 1969 that there could never be absolute parity between the U.S. and the U.S.S.R. . . . Consequently, at the beginning of my administration I began to talk in terms of *sufficiency* rather than *superiority* to describe my goals for our nuclear arsenal.
President Richard Nixon, *RN: Memoirs* (1978).

Everybody must realize and agree: Parity in the potential to destroy one another several times over is madness and absurdity.
Mikhail Gorbachev, *The Christian Science Monitor* (March 18, 1987).

nuclear superiority
"Nuclear superiority" as the United States maintains [it] is of little significance, since we do not know how to use it to achieve our national security objectives. In other words, since the Soviet Union has an assured-destruction capability against the United States, "superior" U.S. nuclear forces are extremely difficult to convert into real politi-

cal power. The blunt, unavoidable fact is that the Soviet Union could effectively destroy the United States even after absorbing the full weight of a U.S. first strike, and vice versa.
Alain C. Enthoven and K. Wayne Smith, *How Much is Enough* (1971).

Nuclear superiority was very useful to us when we had it.
Richard M. Nixon, *The Real War* (1980).

It is a copybook principle in strategy that, in actual war, advantage tends to go to the side in a better position to raise the stakes by expanding the scope, duration or destructive intensity of the conflict. By the same token, at junctures of high contention short of war, the side better able to cope with the potential consequences of raising the stakes has the advantage. The other side is the one under greater pressure to scramble for a peaceful way out. To have the advantage at the utmost level of violence helps at every lesser level. In the Korean war, the Berlin blockades, and the Cuban missile crisis the United States had the ultimate edge because of our superiority at the strategic nuclear level. That edge has slipped away.
Paul Nitze quoted in Charles Tyroler II, ed., *Alerting America* (1984).

I have spoken on a number of occasions of the declining relative value of our nuclear superiority. I am continually surprised at the complaints which such statements arouse, as though the problem would go away if we stopped talking about it. Yet of course we are not talking about a policy . . . it is not a policy which we can choose to follow or not to follow, but a fact of life and a fact which we can ignore only at great peril to our national security. The increasing numbers of survivable missiles in the hands of both the United States and the Soviet Union are a fact of life.
Robert S. McNamara quoted in McGeorge Bundy, *Danger and Survival* (1988).

nuclear war
The way to win an atomic war is to make certain it never starts.
General Omar Bradley, quoted in *The Observer* (April 20, 1952).

It is not fair. No one in the Southern Hemisphere ever dropped a bomb, a hydrogen bomb or a cobalt bomb or any other sort of bomb. We had nothing to do with it. Why should we have to die because other countries nine or ten thousand miles away from us wanted to have a war? It's so bloody unfair.
Nevil Shute, *On the Beach* (1957).

And we will all go together when we go,
What a comforting fact that is to know.
Universal bereavement,
An inspiring achievement,
Yes, we all will go together when we go.
Tom Lehrer, *We Will All Go Together When We Go* (1958).

It would indeed be the ultimate tragedy if the history of the human race proved to be nothing more noble than the story of an ape playing with a box of matches on a petrol dump.
David Ormsby-Gore quoted in *The Christian Science Monitor* (October 25, 1960).

When one examines the possible effects of thermonuclear war carefully, one notices that there are indeed many postwar states that should be distinguished. If most people do not or cannot distinguish among these states it is because the gradations occur as a result of a totally bizarre circumstance—a thermonuclear war. The mind recoils from thinking hard about that; one prefers to believe it will never happen. If asked, "How

does a country look on the day of the war?" the only answer a reasonable person can give is "awful." It takes an act of iron will or an unpleasant degree of detachment or callousness to go about the task of distinguishing among the possible degrees of awfulness.
Herman Kahn, *On Thermonuclear War* (1961).

[A] nuclear disaster . . . could well engulf the great and the small, the rich and the poor, the committed and the uncommitted alike. Mankind must put an end to war or war will put an end to mankind.
President John F. Kennedy, address to the United Nations, September 25, 1961.

[Bernard] Brodie objected to [Herman] Kahn's coining of the term "wargasm" to describe an all-out nuclear conflict. "So grim a subject does not exclude an appropriate kind of humor used very sparingly," Brodie scolded, "but levity is never legitimate."
Gregg Herken, *Counsels of War*, expanded edition (1987), quoting a Brodie letter to Kahn of February 16, 1962.

[The] principal military objectives in the event of a nuclear war stemming from a major attack on the [Atlantic] Alliance, should be the destruction of the enemy's military forces, not his civilian population.
Robert S. McNamara, commencement address at the University of Michigan, June 16, 1962, reprinted in the *Department of State Bulletin* (July 9, 1962).

In 1963 he would cite the 1914 conversation between two German leaders on the origins and expansion of that war, a former chancellor asking, "How did it all happen?" and his successor saying, "Ah, if only one knew." "If this planet," said President Kennedy, "is ever ravaged by nuclear war—if the survivors of that devastation can then endure the fire, poison, chaos and catastrophe—I do not want one of those survivors to ask another, 'How did it all happen?' and to receive the incredible reply: 'Ah, if only one knew.' "
Theodore C. Sorensen, *Kennedy* (1965).

Uneasy is the peace that wears the nuclear crown.
President Lyndon B. Johnson, speech in Arco, Idaho, August 26, 1966.

We are, to put it mildly, in a mess, and there is a strong chance that we shall have exterminated ourselves by the end of the century. Our only consolation will have to be that, as a species, we have had an exciting term of office.
Desmond Morris, *The Naked Ape* (1967).

We came to the conclusion that thermonuclear war was unfeasible. Not impossible, in the sense that, technically, it couldn't happen. In that sense it was all too possible. But unfeasible in the sense that you couldn't fight such a war and hope to win in any meaningful sense.
Robert McNamara quoted in Norman Moss, *Men Who Play God* (1968).

The primary purpose of our strategic forces is to prevent nuclear war. Let us be very clear just what this means. If we are attacked, it is likely that over half of our people will be killed and most of our cities will be destroyed. We will not have to worry about the unemployed—they will no longer be with us.
Senator Barry Goldwater, speech in the Senate, September 12, 1969.

If you have a crisis, both sides say something like this: "Look, nothing at issue is worth the serious risk of nuclear war. It's just crazy for us to continue this terrible crisis. One of us has to be reasonable *and it isn't going to be me.*"
Herman Kahn, *Newsweek* (April 22, 1974).

During my years with the Atomic Energy Commission and the State Department I tried to find some moral basis for the use of and even for planning to use nuclear weapons. I could not reconcile my understanding of Christian belief about justifiable use of force and my knowledge of the blast, heat and radiation effects of nuclear explosions. I finally gave up the effort.... Recently I was asked to lecture on the moral use of nuclear weapons. I declined. I knew of none.
Gerard Smith, *Doubletalk* (1980).

In an all-out nuclear war, more destructive power than in all of World War II would be unleashed every second for the long afternoon it would take for all the missiles and bombs to fall. A World War II every second—more people killed in the first few hours than [in] all the wars of history put together. The survivors, if any, would live in despair amid the poisoned ruins of a civilization that had committed suicide.
President Jimmy Carter, Farewell Address, January 14, 1981.

A nuclear war cannot be won and must never be fought.
President Ronald Reagan, radio address, April 17, 1982.

General, I have fought just as many nuclear wars as you have.
Alain Enthoven, Pentagon systems analyst, quoted in Fred Kaplan, *The Wizards of Armageddon* (1983).

To those who tell us we should mind our own business [on nuclear weapons], I say: If the superpowers fight a nuclear war, we, too, will be wiped out.
Olaf Palme, Prime Minister of Sweden, *The Christian Science Monitor* (February 27, 1986).

nuclear war, limited
The secret dream of every European was, . . . if there had to be nuclear war, to have it conducted over their heads by the strategic forces of the United States and the Soviet Union.
Henry Kissinger, "NATO Defense and the Soviet Threat," *Survival* (November–December 1979).

The United States officially adheres to a strategic doctrine in accordance with which a future nuclear war could be conducted in a limited manner: the other power, the Soviet Union, officially denounces such a posture but is thought, by some analysts, to be likely to limit its own operations if once it found itself in a nuclear exchange with the United States. Whereas once we were assured of mutual destruction in a nuclear war, officialdom now encourages us to believe in the possibility of limited nuclear survival.
Ian Clark, *Limited Nuclear War* (1982).

One technical problem is that they [the Russians] would have great difficulty distinguishing a "limited" U.S. strike against military targets in the USSR, such as their ICBM silos, from an all-out attack against their cities. Whereas the U.S. Minuteman bases . . . are relatively far away from the nation's major cities, Soviet ICBM fields are located close to heavily populated areas, including Moscow. Unless the Soviets had very advanced computer capabilities—and this is an area in which they are notably behind the West—they would not know whether incoming U.S. warheads were heading toward their missile bases or their cities. Hence, if the United States wants to encourage the Soviets to stick to limited exchanges against military targets, does it have to donate new supercomputers to them to make sure they keep to the rules?
Daniel Ford, *The Button* (1985).

The talk of limited [nuclear] war also raised other problems. It required yet more sophisticated capabilities for command, control, communication and intelligence (C^3I).

It is also suggested that some form of nuclear war might be "safe" (i.e. safely fought in Europe and not on the territories of the Superpowers).
Gerald Segal, *Guide to the World Today* (1988).

nuclear warfighting

We've got to be *prepared* to fight a nuclear war—horrible though it may be—in order really to prevent a nuclear war. If you're really not *prepared* to do so, then your deterrent is not persuasive.
U. Alexis Johnson, *U.S. News and World Report* (April 4, 1977).

Land-based missiles give America a true war-fighting nuclear force. What I'm saying is this: If we want to deter war, we must prepare for the chance that deterrence may fail—meaning we must be ready to actually fight a nuclear war and win. I call this "thinking the unthinkable." If we are unwilling to make this leap of imagination, our deterrent system is not credible. Minutemen [missiles] are by far the best weapons we have for this mission. . . . The MX missile is even better.
Herman Kahn, *U.S. News and World Report* (September 21, 1981).

There are contingency plans in the NATO doctrine to fire a nuclear weapon for demonstrative purposes to demonstrate to the other side that they are exceeding the limits of toleration in the conventional area, all designed to maintain violence at the lowest level possible.
Alexander M. Haig, Jr., U.S. Secretary of State, testimony before U.S. Senate Committee on Foreign Relations, November 4, 1981.

I have said that the principal reason for the United States to maintain a strategic triad is deterrence, but a deterrent force without war-fighting capability is hollow.
George V. Orr, Jr., Secretary of the Air Force, quoted in R. Brownstein and N. Easton, *Reagan's Ruling Class* (1983).

Basically, American nuclear policy has been a stated policy of war-fighting with nuclear weapons from the beginning.
Robert S. McNamara quoted in Gregg Herken, *Counsels of War* (1985).

nuclear weapons, tactical

In any combat where these things [small atomic weapons] can be used on strictly military targets and for strictly military purposes, I see no reason why they shouldn't be used just exactly as you would use a bullet or anything else.
President Dwight D. Eisenhower, news conference, March 16, 1954.

I could see where you could have the exchange of tactical [nuclear] weapons against troops in the field without it bringing either one of the major powers to pushing "the button."
President Ronald Reagan, addressing newspaper editors in Washington, D.C., October 16, 1981.

Nuclear weapons are, foremost, political weapons for both sides, controlled by political leaders. This limits their battlefield utility. A decision to use an atomic warhead in a tactical environment must be passed on by those leaders. By the time approval is granted, the tactical situation will almost certainly have changed, and the weapon is no longer useful.
Tom Clancy, *Red Storm Rising* (1986).

The West German Army . . . trains only a few of its artillery teams to handle and fire nuclear shells. U.S. nuclear custody units are integral parts of these specially trained nuclear artillery teams. Once conflict starts, the West German nuclear teams will move to the field with their accompanying U.S. nuclear warhead custodians but will stay in hiding until ordered to carry out a nuclear strike. At that time, they will go to one of a number of designated howitzers, bump the other firing squad from the gun, fire the nuclear rounds, and leave again.

Daniel Charles, *Nuclear Planning in NATO* (1987).

Small yield and short-range tactical nuclear weapons were hailed as a means of providing firepower with less manpower. The nuclear genie, as it had solved Allies' needs in World War II, could rescue them again. Now packaged in a tactical bottle, it was believed that this atomic wonder could provide the needed "beef up to NATO's punch," but at much less cost than conventional forces.

Robert Kromer, *New Weapons and NATO* (1987).

Presidential Directive-59

The Carter doctrine, embodied in the executive order PD-59, was swiftly embraced by the new Reagan team, with one important addition. Reagan said that American nuclear forces had to be able not only to fight a prolonged nuclear war, but also to *prevail.*

The single world "prevail" was to cause quite a stir—fueling the fears of many that Ronald Reagan, the ex-Hollywood cowboy, suffered from an itchy trigger finger. To prevail in a nuclear war meant to win. Even though the military's top generals accepted that there could be no "winners" in a nuclear war, the loose-lipped Reagan defense team sounded disturbingly confident about the concept of nuclear victory.

Peter Pringle and William Arkin, *SIOP* (1983).

PD-59 is *not* a new strategic doctrine; it is *not* a radical departure from US strategic policy over the past decade or so. It *is*, in fact, a refinement, a codification of previous statements of our strategic policy. . . . Previous Administrations, going back well into the 1960s, recognized the inadequacy of a strategic doctrine that would give us too narrow a range of options.

Harold Brown quoted in Robert C. Aldridge, *First Strike* (1983).

Paul Warnke . . . claimed that with PD-59 [President] Carter had gone "from MAD to worse."

Gregg Herken, *Counsels of War* (1987).

[President Carter's] PD-59 had introduced into the SIOP an explicit option for striking at the Soviet command structure. Earlier SIOPs hadn't made a point of avoiding "the head," but neither had they provided for decapitation. The new thinking assumed that the Soviets had targeted America at its weakest link—the command system. Emulation (if that's what it was) seemed only prudent. The incoming Reagan people liked PD-59, and they gave it a thrust of their own. They made decapitation a stouter option than before, even though it was—is—widely deplored.

John Newhouse, *War and Peace in the Nuclear Age* (1988).

SIOP (Single Integrated Operations Plan)

In the present SIOP, only one choice before the president is still convincing. That choice is the Major Attack Option, releasing more than a thousand warheads in a single strike against Soviet forces. It is the same option that was open to the president in the 1950s. All the limited options, which are subject to the generals' instant interpretations, have as their purpose fighting and winning.

Peter Pringle and William Arkin, *SIOP* (1983).

As General [Robert] Herres described the precise time schedules that have been worked out in the S.I.O.P. in the last two decades, he could just as well have been describing the famous Schlieffen plan. This was the meticulously crafted war plan that the German General Staff began to develop in 1893 and finally saw implemented at the outset of World War I. The Schlieffen plan was exceedingly rigid and mechanical, as were the plans of the other opposing powers. . . .

The present S.I.O.P. is such a machine, and once an alert began it could quickly proceed toward what retired Lieutenant General Brent Scowcroft referred to as "the automatic phase of the war. That is the time at which the quick response systems are discharged against predetermined targets and so on, and the battle plan unfolds more or less automatically."
Daniel Ford, *The Button* (1985).

occupation

A capital which is occupied by an enemy is like a girl who loses her virginity.
Karl von Clausewitz, 1812 letter to his wife, quoted in Roger Parkinson, *Clausewitz* (1970).

As the officers and soldiers of the United States have been subject to repeated insults from the women (calling themselves ladies) of New Orleans, in return for the most scrupulous noninterference and courtesy on our part, it is ordered that hereafter when any female shall, by word, gesture, or movement, insult or show contempt for any officer or soldier of the United States, she shall be regarded and held liable to be treated as a woman of the town plying her avocation.
General Benjamin F. Butler's notorious General Order No. 28 of May 15, 1862, issued as the military commander of occupied New Orleans during the Civil War, reprinted in *Butler's Book: Autobiography* (1892). According to Butler, "The order executed itself. No arrests were ever made under it or because of it. All the ladies in New Orleans forbore to insult our troops because they didn't want to be deemed common women, and all the common women forbore to insult our troops because they wanted to deemed ladies, and of those two classes were all the women secessionists of the city."

I have no desire for personal revenge, nor do I believe that others who suffered with me have the feeling. . . . But it must not be a soft occupation [of Japan] nor a soft peace.
General Jonathan M. Wainwright, *Newsweek* (September 24, 1945).

Atomic warfare is bad enough; biological warfare would be worse; but there is something that is worse than either. The French can tell you what it is; or the Czechs, or the Greeks, or the Norwegians, or the Filipinos; it is subjection to an alien oppressor.
Elmer Davis, "No World, If Necessary," *Saturday Review* (March 30, 1946).

The Italians will laugh at me; every time Hitler occupies a country he sends me a message.
Benito Mussolini quoted in Alan Bullock, *Hitler* (1952).

In France during the war, passivity or collaboration with the German occupiers was the norm. Gen. Charles de Gaulle, after a few years of serious collaborator hunting in liberated France, decided that the country did not need an extended period of strife and recrimination. "France needs all its sons and daughters," he insisted, and allowed the myth to be created that everybody had taken part in the Resistance, some operating under a cover so deep that not even the Resistance had been aware of their contribution.
Henrik Bering-Jensen, "A Nation Haunted Still," *Insight* (March 20, 1989).

officers

I had rather have a plain russet-coated captain that knows what he fights for and loves what he knows, than that which you call a "gentleman" and is nothing else. I honor a gentleman that is so indeed.
Oliver Cromwell, writing of qualities he most desires in his officers, in a letter to Sir William Spring, September 1643, quoted in Thomas Carlyle, *Oliver Cromwell's Letters and Speeches* (1845).

If your pay and allowances for officers will not support them decently, then you will have only rich men who serve for pleasure or adventure, or indigent wretches devoid of spirit.
Marshal Maurice de Saxe, *Reveries Upon the Art of War* (1757).

War must be carried on systematically, and to do it, you must have good officers; there are, in my judgement, no other possible means to obtain them but by establishing your Army upon a permanent footing; and giving your officers good pay; this will induce gentlemen, and men of character to engage.
General George Washington, letter to the President of Congress, September 24, 1776, reprinted in J. C. Fitzpatrick, ed., *The Writings of George Washington*, VI (1931–44).

Let death be shared like prize money—the lion's share to the officers.
An 18th-century British seaman before a battle quoted in James Dugan, *The Great Mutiny* (1965).

Recollect that you must be a seaman to be an officer; and also that you cannot be a good officer without being a gentleman.
Admiral Horatio Nelson, speaking to a new midshipman, quoted in Leland P. Lovette, *School of the Sea* (1941).

It is very difficult for a nation to create an army when it has not already a body of officers and non-commissioned officers to serve as a nucleus, and a system of military organization.
Napoleon I, *Military Maxims* (1827).

An active, intelligent officer, with an imagination fertile in the expedients of his profession, will seldom be at a loss as to his best course when the occasion offers; to one without these qualities, opportunities present themselves in vain.
Dennis Hart Mahan, *An Elementary Treatise on Advanced-Guard* (1861).

In every military system which has triumphed in modern war the officers have been recognized as the brain of the army, and to prepare them for their trust, governments have spared no pains to give them special education and training.
Emory Upton, *The Military Policy of the United States* (1904).

The night was chilly. Colonel Byng and I shared a blanket. When he turned over I was in the cold. When I turned over I pulled the blanket off him and he objected. He was the Colonel. It was not a good arrangement. I was glad when morning came.
Winston Churchill, *My Early Life* (1930).

You neither want to be killed nor to kill anybody. Officers, you feel, shouldn't engage in the rough-and-tumble—that's for the men.
Lieutenant-Colonel A. A. Hanbury-Sparrow, *The Land-Locked Lake* (1932).

Positively no alcoholic beverages will be sold to Air Corps lieutenant colonels under 21 unless accompanied by their parents.
Sign in U.S. Officers Club quoted in *Time* (July 6, 1942).

I divide my officers into four classes as follows: The clever, the industrious, the lazy, and the stupid. Each officer always possesses two of these qualities. Those who are clever and industrious I appoint to the General Staff. Use can under certain circumstances be made of those who are stupid and lazy. The man who is clever and lazy qualifies for the highest leadership posts. He has the requisite nerves and the mental clarity for difficult decisions. But whoever is stupid and industrious must be got rid of, for he is too dangerous.

German General Freiherr von Hammerstein-Equord quoted in Arcades Ambo, "All God's Chillun Ain't Got Wings," *Infantry Journal Reader*, ed. J. I. Greene (1943).

Please see *The Times* of February 4. Is it really true that a seven-mile cross-country run is enforced upon all in this division, from generals to privates? . . . It looks to me rather excessive. A colonel or a general ought not to exhaust himself in trying to compete with young boys running across country seven miles at a time. The duty of officers is no doubt to keep themselves fit, but still more to think for their men, and to take decisions affecting their safety or comfort. Who is the general of this division, and does he run the seven miles himself? If so, he may be more useful for football than war. . . . In my experience based on many years' observation, officers with high athletic qualifications are not usually successful in the highest ranks.

Winston Churchill, February 4, 1941 inquiry to the Secretary of State for War, reprinted in his *The Second World War: The Grand Alliance* (1950).

I then said, that if he was thinking of dying it would be better to do it now, as he could be replaced easily and smoothly; it is always a nuisance if officers die when the battle starts and things are inclined to be hectic. His state of health was clearly not very good, and I preferred him to do the run and die.

Field Marshal B. L. Montgomery, to an overweight officer who said he would die if forced to run seven miles in training, recounted in his *Memoirs* (1958).

An officer should avoid any expression of dissatisfaction or indication of unhappiness because this invariably gives him a bad reputation. . . . Everybody recoils from a whiner.

General Dwight D. Eisenhower, letter to his son, John, January 22, 1947, quoted in Stephen E. Ambrose, *Eisenhower*, I (1983).

Ah, but the strawberries! That's—that's where I had them. They laughed and made jokes, but I proved beyond a shadow of a doubt, and with geometric logic, that a duplicate key to the wardroom icebox did exist. And I'd have produced that key if they hadn't have pulled the *Caine* out of action. I know now they were out to protect some fellow officer.

Humphrey Bogart in *The Caine Mutiny* (1954), directed by Edward Dmytryk; screenplay by Stanley Roberts from the novel by Herman Wouk.

The modern officer corps is a professional body and the modern military officer a professional man.

Samuel P. Huntington, *The Soldier and the State* (1957).

Our radioman [on a B-17 in World War II Europe] had style. I have seen Duke, wearing his fatigues, with a mess kit hanging from his belt, lean forward and toss a salute. In the process he would so patronize a hapless officer that the latter would slink away to hide his brass. I have heard other men say that when they salute an officer it is their way of sending the message "Fuck you." Duke delivered that message with punctilio.

Elmer Bendiner, *The Fall of Fortresses* (1980).

The officer corps comprised only 2.86 percent of the German army's total strength at the beginning of the Second World War and declined in relative strength as the war went on. In contrast, officers represented 7 percent of the overall strength of the American army (and were to grow to 15 percent of the army during the Vietnam War).
Russell F. Weigley, *Eisenhower's Lieutenants* (1981).

Horses played such an important part in the lives of most officers that some tended to think of humans in horsy terms. A Royal Horse Artillery officer, reporting on a subordinate, noted: "Personally, I would not breed from this officer."
Byron Farwell, *Mr. Kipling's Army* (1981).

The Italian officers' corps went into battle with a huge baggage train. Waiters from the best Roman hotels served as orderlies to higher-ranking officers; even near the front, Italian generals were waited on hand and foot. There were even mobile officers' brothels for their use in the field. Rommel was especially horrified to learn that the Italians had different field rations for officers, NCOs, and enlisted men, in sharply descending order. While officers received a three-course cooked meal, even in active campaigning, the private had to be content with a can of [something] which was barely edible. The Italian soldiers were shocked to find German generals and German privates eating the same field rations.
Samuel W. Mitcham, Jr., *Triumphant Fox* (1984).

Soldiers are the tradesmen of killing, but officers are the managers of violence.
Harold Lasswell quoted in Gwynne Dyer, *War* (1985).

Several of the lieutenants in the battalion were "snide and mean." In combat [in France] they became "shy, quiet, and frightened." "They were afraid of the enemy, and they were also afraid of the enlisted men"—not without some reason. The officers who got on well were the friendly, easygoing officers from barracks days. "In combat these men became the tigers and leaders," according to Sergeant [William] Ogden.
Edwin P. Hoyt, *The GI's War* (1988).

Some men are born mediocre, some men achieve mediocrity, and some men have mediocrity thrust upon them. With Major Major it had been all three.
Joseph Heller, *Catch-22* (1961).

order of battle

The art of encamping on a position is nothing else than the art of forming in order of battle on that position. For this purpose the artillery should all be in readiness and favorably placed; a position should be selected which is not commanded, cannot be turned, and from which the ground in the vicinity is covered and commanded.
Napoleon I, *Military Maxims* (1827).

The decisively important points in any order of battle, land or sea, are (1) that the line can not be pierced and (2) that the flanks can not be turned.
Alfred Thayer Mahan, *Naval Strategy* (1911).

Bringing up forces piecemeal ... amounts to throwing drops of water into a sea.
Marshal Ferdinard Foch, *Precepts and Judgments* (1920).

One of Napoleon's marshals once brought him a plan of campaign in which the French Army was neatly and evenly lined up from one end of the frontier to the other. "Are you trying to stop smuggling?" Napoleon asked heartlessly.
Theodore Draper, *The Six Weeks War* (1946).

Since the [1944] attempt on his life Hitler had himself attempted to bluff on the grand scale. He ordered the formation of artillery corps which in fact were no stronger than brigades. Panzer brigades were two battalions, that is to say with the strength of regiments. Tank-destroyer brigades consisted of only one battalion. In my opinion these methods served rather to confuse our own military organization than to conceal our real weakness from the enemy.
General Heinz Guderian, *Panzer Leader* (1952).

Like Hitler, Stalin had a mania for impressive orders of battle. Both dictators tried to keep in being on the Russo-German front an enormous number of infantry divisions, so that each had a grossly inflated order of battle that had little relevance to its real strength and effectiveness. Many of these divisions on both sides were mere shells. . . . The probability is that this was done by both to deceive the other's intelligence.
Albert Seaton and Joan Seaton, *The Soviet Army* (1984).

orders

Our business in the field of fight,
Is not to question, but to prove our might.
Homer, *Iliad* (9th century B.C.).

When the king is on the field ... he in person gives general orders to the polemarches, which they convey to the commanders of divisions; these again to the commanders of fifties, the commanders of fifties to the commanders of *enomoties*. . . . In like manner any more precise instructions are passed down through the army, and quickly reach their destination. For almost the whole Lacadaemonian army are officers who have officers under them, and the responsibility of executing an order devolves upon many.
Thucydides, *Peloponnesian War* (5th century B.C.).

What you cannot enforce, do not command.
Sophocles, *Oedipus at Colonus* (401 B.C.).

He who has never learned to obey cannot be a good commander.
Aristotle, *Politics* (4th century B.C.).

For I am a man under authority, having soldiers under me; and I say to this man, Go, and he goeth; and to another, Come, and he cometh; and to my servant, Do this, and he doeth it.
The Bible, Matthew 8:9.

Many times imperfect understanding or bad interpreting of the generals' orders has caused confusion in their armies; therefore the words in which orders are given in time of peril should be clear and distinct. . . . You ought to take care to avoid general words and use special ones, and of the special ones, avoid those that can be wrongly interpreted.
Niccolò Machiavelli, *The Art of War* (1520).

Remember, gentlemen, an order than can be misunderstood will be misunderstood.
Attributed to Field Marshal Helmuth von Moltke (1800–1891).

A general-in-chief cannot exonerate himself from responsibility for his faults by pleading an order of his sovereign or the minister, when the individual from whom it proceeds is at a distance from the field of operations, and but partially, or not at all, acquainted with the actual condition of things. Hence it follows that every general-in-

chief who undertakes to execute a plan which he knows to be bad, is culpable. He should communicate his reasons, insist on a change of plan, and finally resign his commission rather than become the instrument of his army's ruin.
Napoleon I, *Military Maxims* (1827).

There is nothing in war which is of greater importance than obedience.
Karl von Clausewitz, *On War* (1832).

For short periods after the Civil War both Grant and Sherman actually occupied simultaneously the offices of Secretary of War and General of the Army. This personal union temporarily resolved conflict but led to curious consequences. Referring to Grant's experience, his biographer [William B. Hesseltine] wrote, "To preserve the line between his two offices, he followed the practice of issuing orders as Secretary of War from the War Department. Then having sent the orders across the street to army headquarters by messenger, he trudged after them to obey the orders as General of the Army."
Leonard D. White, *The Republican Era* (1958).

The spirit of obedience, as distinguished from its letter, consists in faithfully forwarding the general object to which the officer's particular command is contributing.
Alfred Thayer Mahan, *Retrospect and Prospect* (1902).

In handling your men in the presence of actual conditions, you absolutely must use the same commands and the same movements that they have been taught on the drillfield. The men are going to be sensitive to disturbance, and to anything unusual. If they think that you cannot control them by the usual methods, that their training has failed, they are likely to believe that everything has gone to the bad, and their morale will go with it.
Lincoln C. Andrews, *Fundamentals of Military Service* (1916).

Presently fresh air, hard training, and clean living begin to weave their spell. Incredulous at first, we find ourselves slowly recognizing the fact that it is possible to treat an officer deferentially, or carry out an order smartly, without losing one's self-respect as a man and a Trades Unionist.
George Coppard, writing of World War I, *With a Machine Gun to Cambrai* (1969).

If it were merely enough to give an order the battalion officers would be superfluous. The officer of the line exists to transform the orders he receives, to make them possible. The verbal transmission of an order as it is is a heresy; it must be adapted to every rank in the scale.
René Quinton, *Soldier's Testament* (1930).

The officers of a panzer division must learn to think and act independently within the framework of the general plan and not wait until they receive orders.
Field Marshal Erwin Rommel, *The Rommel Papers*, ed. B. H. Liddell Hart (1953).

The good soldier will lie under orders as bravely as he will die under them.
Murray Kempton, *The New Republic* (November 30, 1963).

No man in uniform, be he private or five-star general, may decide for himself whether an order is consonant with his personal views. While the loyalty he owes his superiors is reciprocated with equal force in the loyalty owed him from above, the authority of his superiors is not open to question.
General Matthew B. Ridgway, *The Korean War* (1967).

The squadron rode in double file and "passing on of orders" was practiced, an order spoken in a low voice being passed on from man to man. Now, if the order given in front was: "Sergeant-major move to the head of the column," what came out at the rear was: "Eight troopers to be shot immediately," or something of that sort. And it is in a similar manner that world history came about.
Robert Musil, *The Man Without Qualities* (1980).

Gurkhas are apt to obey orders literally, so that officers must exercise care if trouble, even tragedy, is not to result from a scrupulous obedience to the letter of their commands. After a hard-fought battle at Mozzagrogna [in Italy] ... Major R. W. Morland-Hughes ordered a detail of men to carry out nine German corpses from the cellar [of a house] and bury them. ... As they were carrying up the ninth, he suddenly sprang to life and leaped to his feet. *Kukris* were drawn and the screaming German, his hands over his head, was about to be dispatched when some English anti-aircraft gunners happened by and saved him. One called, "Hey Johnny! You can't kill him like that." But the Gurkhas not only knew that they could, they were sure that they should. They had been ordered to bury nine dead Germans, and if one was not dead they had the means for making him so. Besides, they could not be expected to bury one alive.
Byron Farwell, *The Gurkhas* (1984).

I haven't, in the 23 years that I have been in the uniformed services of the United States of America ever violated an order—not one.
Lt. Colonel Oliver L. North, USMC, testimony before the Joint Iran-Contra Committee of the U.S. Congress, July 7, 1987.

pacifism

We utterly deny all outward wars and strife, and fightings with outward weapons, for any end, or under any pretence whatever: this is our testimony to the whole world.
The Quakers' Declaration to King Charles II (1660).

As long as armies exist, any serious conflict will lead to war. A pacifism which does not actively fight against the armament of nations is and must remain impotent.
Albert Einstein, *The World as I See It* (1934).

Rational pacifism must be based on a new maxim—"If you wish for peace, understand war."
B. H. Liddell Hart, *Thoughts on War* (1944).

pacifists

The professional pacifist is merely a tool of the sensual materialist who has no ideals, whose shrivelled soul is wholly absorbed in automobiles, and the movies, and money making, and in the policies of the cash register and the stock ticker, and the life of fatted ease.
President Theodore Roosevelt, speech at Kansas City, Missouri, May 30, 1916.

That this house will in no circumstances fight for its King and country.
Motion passed at the Oxford Union, an undergraduate student debating society at Oxford University, February 9, 1933. In *The Times* (London) of February 18, 1933, Winston Churchill commented,"One can almost [feel the curl of contempt upon the lips of the manhood of ... [Germany, Italy, and France] when they read this message sent out by Oxford University in the name of young England."

General Crozier is a professional soldier and by his own showing spent the years between 1899 and 1921 in almost ceaseless slaughter of his fellow creatures; hence as

a pacifist he makes an impressive figure, like the reformed burglar at a Salvation Army meeting.
George Orwell, review of *The Men I Killed* by F. P. Crozier, *New Statesman and Nation* (August 28, 1937).

The Socialist who finds his children playing with soldiers is usually upset, but he is never able to think of a substitute for the tin soldiers; tin pacifists somehow won't do.
George Orwell, *New English Weekly* (March 21, 1940).

The surest way to become a pacifist is to join the infantry.
Bill Mauldin, *Up Front* (1945).

There is no greater pacifist than the regular officer.
General Dwight D. Eisenhower, *The New York Times* (June 20, 1945).

I am not a pacifist. I was very much for the war against Hitler and I supported the intervention in Korea. But in this war, we went in to steal Viet Nam.
Dr. Benjamin Spock, *Time* (January 12, 1968).

Panama

Last night I ordered U.S. military forces to Panama. . . . For nearly two years, the United States, nations of Latin America and the Caribbean have worked together to resolve the crisis in Panama. The goals of the United States have been to safeguard the lives of Americans, to defend democracy in Panama, to combat drug trafficking and to protect the integrity of the Panama Canal Treaty. Many attempts have been made to resolve this crisis through diplomacy and negotiations. All were rejected by the dictator of Panama, Gen. Manuel Noriega, an indicted drug trafficker.
Last Friday, Noriega declared his military dictatorship to be in a state of war with the United States and publicly threatened the lives of Americans in Panama. The very next day forces under his command shot and killed an unarmed American serviceman, wounded another, arrested and brutally beat a third American serviceman and then brutally interrogated his wife, threatening her with sexual abuse. That was enough.
President George Bush, address to the nation, December 20, 1989.

I need to get on a wire there—in a telegram or something—explain this to Mr. Gorbachev. It's not altogether surprising that he doesn't understand some of the special arrangements that the United States has in Panama. . . . and I also need to let him know . . . if they kill an American Marine, that's real bad. And if they threaten and brutalize the wife of an American citizen, sexually threatening the lieutenant's wife while kicking him in the groin over and over again, then, Mr. Gorbachev, please understand, this President is going to do something about it.
President George Bush, news conference, December 21, 1989.

This was not the result of an accused wimp's need to prove himself macho; we've had too much of that personal-motive pap since Lyndon Johnson.
William Safire, *The New York Times* (December 21, 1989).

It was just like walking into a John Wayne movie.
Sergeant David Parish, U.S. Army ranger, describing his combat experience in Panama, *The Washington Post* (December 24, 1989).

This intervention is a good-neighbor policy. America's role in Panama . . . is an act of hemispheric hygiene.
George F. Will, *The Washington Post National Weekly* (December 25–31, 1989).

His [General Manuel Noriega's] reign of terror is over.
Marlin Fitzwater, White House Spokesman, on Noriega's seeking of asylum at the Vatican Embassy in Panama, *The New York Times* (December 25, 1989).

For ten years, beginning in 1959, the U.S. had been converting the police force [of Panama] into a full-fledged military. . . .
Whichever U.S. official decided that the U.S. should endow Panama with an army ought to have been submitted to psychiatric examination and, if found sane, shot for treason.
R. M. Koster, *The New York Times* (December 29, 1989).

People [in Latin America] will protest, but at the same time they'll applaud—quietly.
Senator Richard Lugar, *Newsweek* (January 1, 1990).

paratroopers

What would be the security of the good, if the bad could at pleasure invade them from the sky? Against an army sailing through the clouds neither walls, nor mountains, nor seas, could afford any security.
Samuel Johnson, *Rasselas* (1759).

Where is the Prince who can afford so to cover this country with troops for its defense, as that 10,000 men descending from the clouds, might not, in many places, do an infinite deal of mischief before a force could be brought together to repel them?
Benjamin Franklin's 1784 quotation on the World War II desk of General Lewis J. Brereton quoted in Cornelius Ryan, *A Bridge Too Far* (1974).

What the hell. When you jump you've only got two things to worry about: whether your 'chute opens or whether it doesn't. If it doesn't open you've got nothing to worry about.
Lieutenant Ralph Miller quoted in Lowell Benett, *Assignment to Nowhere* (1943).

Now and then a paratrooper would rise, lumber heavily to the little bathroom in the tail of the plane, find he could not push through the narrow doorway in his bulky gear, and come back, mumbling his profane opinion of the designers of the C-47 airplane. Soon the crew chief passed a bucket around, but this did not entirely solve our problem. A man strapped and buckled into full combat gear finds it extremely difficult to reach certain essential portions of his anatomy, and his efforts are not made easier by the fact that his comrades are watching him, jeering derisively and offering gratuitous advice.
General Matthew B. Ridgway, describing his flight to France on the night before D-Day, *Soldier* (1956).

The Americans found humor even in the terrifying approach to the drop zones [at Arnhem during World War II]. Just after Captain Cecil Lee stood to hook up, his plane was hit. Shrapnel ripped a hole through the seat he had just vacated. Nearby, a trooper shouted disgustedly, "Now they give us a latrine!"
Cornelius Ryan, *A Bridge Too Far* (1974).

A standard question for a new man was why he had volunteered for parachuting and whether he enjoyed it. On one occasion, a bright-eyed recruit startled me by replying to the latter question with a resounding "No, sir." "Why then, if you don't like jumping did you volunteer to be a parachutist?" I asked. "Sir, I like to be with people who do like to jump," was the reply. I shook his hand vigorously and assured him that there were at least two of us of the same mind in the Division.
General Maxwell D. Taylor, *Swords and Plowshares* (1972).

Hitler . . . remarked: "General Student, I believe that the days of the paratroopers are over. They have no surprise value any more."

Student looked at him amazed. "Why, *mein Fuhrer?*"

"Because the surprise effect is no longer there. Crete has shown that the days of the paratrooper are finished. The parachute force is purely and simply a weapon of surprise. The factor of surprise has now been used up."

And there the conversation ended. Adolf Hitler, the man who would soon rule all of Europe from the Channel to the Urals, had passed sentence. . . .

Crete, their greatest victory, was to prove, as Student told British military historian Sir Basil Liddell Hart in captivity after the war, "the graveyard of the paratroopers."
Charles Whiting, *Hunters From the Sky* (1974).

A parachute is merely a means of delivery but not a way of fighting.
Bernard Fall, *Street Without Joy* (1964).

The basic tactic used by all countries employing parachutists and gliderborne troops in World War II was the strike-hold concept, in which the initial air assault quickly devolved into a static defense of the objective. Parachute and glider assaults from their earliest beginnings were characterized by this lack of flexibility. The airborne forces traveled light, without much firepower and with very few ground vehicles, and for this reason were like ducks out of water when they got on the ground.
John R. Galvin, *Air Assault* (1969).

partisan warfare

One of the most conspicuous and advantageous departures from the so-called rules of warfare is the independent action of men acting separately against men huddled together in a mass. Such independent activity is always seen in a war that assumes a national character. In this kind of warfare, instead of forming in a crowd to attack a crowd, men disperse in small groups, attack singly and at once fly, when attacked by superior forces, and then attack again, when an opportunity presents itself. Such were the methods of the guerillas in Spain; of the mountain tribes in the Caucasus, and of the Russians in 1812.

War of this kind has been called partisan warfare.
Leo Tolstoy, *War and Peace* (1865–69).

The military value of a partisan's work is not measured by the amount of property destroyed, or the number of men killed or captured, but by the number he keeps watching.
John S. Mosby, *War Reminiscences* (1887).

I endeavored . . . to diminish. . . the aggressive power of the army of the Potomac, by compelling it to keep a large force on the defensive. . . . I wanted to use and consume the Northern cavalry in hard work. I have often thought that their fierce hostility to me was more on account of the sleep I made them lose than the number we killed and captured.
John S. Mosby, *War Reminiscences* (1887).

patriotism

A patriot, sir! Why, patriots spring up like mushrooms! I could raise fifty of them within the four and twenty hours. I have raised many of them in one night. It is but refusing to grant an unreasonable or an insolent demand, and up starts a patriot.
Sir Robert Walpole, speech in the House of Commons, February 13, 1741.

Be England what she will,
With all her faults, she is my country still.
Charles Churchill, *The Farewell* (1763).

Patriotism is the last refuge of a scoundrel.
Samuel Johnson quoted in James Boswell, *Life of Johnson* (1791).

Breathes there the man, with soul so dead,
Who never to himself has said,
This is my own, my native land!
Sir Walter Scott, *The Lay of the Last Minstrel* (1805).

That kind of patriotism which consists in hating all other nations.
Elizabeth Gaskell, *Sylvia's Lovers* (1863).

Remember . . . behind officers and government and people even, there is the country herself, your country, and that you belong to her as you belong to your own mother.
Edward Everett Hale, *The Man Without a Country* (1863).

Patriotism is, fundamentally, a conviction that a particular country is the best in the world because you were born in it.
George Bernard Shaw, *Music in London* (1890–94), III (November 15, 1893).

"My country, right or wrong," is a thing that no patriot would think of saying except in a desperate case. It is like saying, "My mother, drunk or sober."
G. K. Chesterton, *The Defendant* (1901).

Patriotism has becomes a mere national self-assertion, a sentimentality of flag-cheering with no constructive duties.
H. G. Wells, *The Future in America* (1906).

Patriotism [is] combustible rubbish ready to the torch of any one ambitious to illuminate his name. In Dr. Johnson's famous dictionary patriotism is defined as the last resort of a scoundrel. With all due respect to an enlightened but inferior lexicographer I beg to submit that it is the first.
Ambrose Bierce, *The Devil's Dictionary* (1911).

Patriotism is easy to understand in America. It means looking out for yourself by looking out for your country.
President Calvin Coolidge, speech at Northampton, Massachusetts, May 30, 1923.

Patriotism is often an arbitrary veneration of real estate above principles.
George Jean Nathan, *Testament of a Critic* (1931).

Talking of patriotism, what humbug it is; it is a word which always commemorates a robbery. There isn't a foot of land in the world which doesn't represent the ousting and re-ousting of a long line of successive owners.
Mark Twain, *Mark Twain's Notebooks* (1935).

Ask not what your country can do for you, ask what you can do for your country.
President John F. Kennedy, Inaugural Address, January 20, 1961.

He majored in English history, which was a mistake.
"*English history!*" roared the silvermaned senior Senator from his state indignantly. "What's the matter with American history? American history is as good as any history in the world!"
Joseph Heller, *Catch-22* (1961).

"Our Country, right or wrong. . . ." Have you not perceived that that phrase is an insult to the nation? . . . Only when a republic's life is in danger should a man uphold his government when it is in the wrong. There is no other time.
Mark Twain quoted in Bernard DeVoto, ed., *Letters from the Earth* (1962).

I don't think the United States needs super-patriots. We need patriotism, honestly practiced by all of us, and we don't need these people that are more patriotic than you or anybody else.
President Dwight D. Eisenhower, *The New York Times* (November 24, 1962).

Patriotism to the Soviet State is a revolutionary duty, whereas patriotism to a bourgeois State is treachery.
Leon Trotsky quoted in Fitzroy Maclean, *The Disputed Barricade* (1966).

When Dr. Johnson defined patriotism as the last refuge of a scoundrel, he ignored the enormous possibilities of the word reform.
Roscoe Conkling quoted in David M. Jordan, *Roscoe Conkling of New York* (1971).

I have never understood why one's affections must be confined, as once with women, to a single country.
John Kenneth Galbraith, *A Life in Our Times* (1981).

Don't let yourselves be convinced by some jackass that patriotism has something to do with Nazism or national socialism. Love of fatherland is a virtue that becomes every people, the Germans as well.
West German Chancellor Helmut Kohl, *Insight* (March 20, 1989).

peace

I prefer the most unfair peace to the most righteous war.
Marcus Tullius Cicero, *Letters to Atticus* (1st century B.C.).

They make a desert and call it peace.
Tacitus, *Agricola* (1st century A.D.).

It is not that they love peace less, but that they love their kind of peace more.
Saint Augustine of Hippo, *City of God* (426).

Deliver to the army this news of peace;
let them have pay, and part.
William Shakespeare, *Henry IV, Part II*, Act IV (1597).

What we dignify with the name of peace is really only a short truce, in accordance with which the weaker party renounces his claims, whether just or unjust, until such time as he can find an opportunity of asserting them with the sword.
Marquis de Vauvenargues, *Reflections and Maxims* (1746).

What my enemies call a general peace is my destruction. What I call peace is merely the disarmament of my enemies. Am I not more moderate than they?
Napoleon I, speaking in 1813, quoted in J. C. Herold, *The Mind of Napoleon* (1955).

Buried was the bloody hatchet;
Buried was the dreadful war-club;
Buried were all warlike weapons,
And the war-cry was forgotten.
Then was peace among the nations.
Henry Wadsworth Longfellow, *The Song of Hiawatha* (1855).

Peace is generally good in itself, but it is never the highest good unless it comes as the handmaid of righteousness; and it becomes a very evil thing if it serves merely as a mask for cowardice and sloth, or as an instrument to further the ends of despotism or anarchy.

President Theodore Roosevelt, speech on receiving the Nobel Peace Prize in 1910.

"Peace" in military mouths today is a synonym for "war expected."

William James, "The Moral Equivalent of War," *McClure's* (August 1910).

Only a peace between equals can last. Only a peace the very principle of which is equality and a common participation in a common benefit.

President Woodrow Wilson, address to the Senate, January 22, 1917.

Don't tell me peace has broken out.

Bertolt Brecht, *Mother Courage*, Act VIII (1939).

Speaking for the Allied forces, we are going to have peace if we have to fight for it.

General Dwight D. Eisenhower, speech in Germany, June 10, 1945, quoted in Captain Harry C. Butcher, *My Three Years With Eisenhower* (1946).

[Peace is] an idea which seems to have originated in Switzerland but had never caught hold in the United States. Supporters of this idea are frequently accused of being unpatriotic and trying to create civil disorder.

Dick Gregory, *Dick Gregory's Political Primer* (1972).

peace conferences

I have never known a peace made, even the most advantageous, that was not censured as inadequate, and the makers condemned as injudicious or corrupt. "Blessed are the peacemakers" is, I suppose, to be understood in the other world; for in this they are frequently cursed.

Benjamin Franklin, letter to John Adams, October 12, 1781, *The Complete Works of Benjamin Franklin*, ed. J. Bigelow, 7 (1885).

I originated a remark many years ago that I think has been copied more than any little thing that I've said, and I used it in the FOLLIES of 1922. I said America has a unique record. *We never lost a war and we never won a conference* in our lives. I believe that we could without any degree of egotism, single-handed lick any nation in the world. But we can't confer with Costa Rica and come home with our shirts on.

Will Rogers quoted in Paula M. Love, *The Will Rogers Book* (1972).

When the war of the giants is over the wars of the pygmies will begin.

Winston Churchill, *The Second World War: Triumph and Tragedy* (1953).

It is normal in this imperfect world that you can appoint the members of your delegation to a peace conference, but not the members of the other side. Talking with others is not a grace to be conferred but a convenience to be used.

Abba Eban, on Israel talking to the Palestine Liberation Organization, *The New York Times* (February 3, 1989).

peace with honor

Peace is . . . desirable with all men, as far as it may be had with conscience and honor!

Oliver Cromwell, speech to Parliament, September 4, 1654, reprinted in Maurice Ashley, ed., *Cromwell* (1969).

While we endeavor to maintain peace, I certainly should be the last to forget that, if peace cannot be maintained with honor, it is no longer peace.
Lord John Russell, *The Times* (London) (September 21, 1853).

Peace without honor is not only a disgrace, but, except as a temporary respite, it is a chimera.
Lord Salisbury, *Quarterly Review* (April 1864).

Lord Salisbury and myself have brought you back peace—but a peace I hope with honor.
Benjamin Disraeli, on the Treaty of Berlin, speech in the House of Commons, July 16, 1878.

For the second time in our history, a British Prime Minister has returned from Germany bringing peace with honor. I believe it is peace for our time.
Neville Chamberlain, speech to a crowd in front of 10 Downing Street after returning from the Munich Conference, September 30, 1938, quoted in *The New York Times* (October 1, 1938).

At the price of our honor we could only purchase a precarious peace which would be revocable.
Edouard Daladier, Premier of France, at the outbreak of World War II, speech in the Chamber of Deputies, September 2, 1939, reprinted in *Vital Speeches* (September 15, 1939).

As this long and difficult war [Vietnam] ends, I would like to address a few special words to . . . the American people: Your steadfastness in supporting our insistence on peace with honor has made peace with honor possible.
President Richard M. Nixon, speech to the nation, January 23, 1973.

Pentagon

[The Pentagon] was a sorry place to light after having commanded a theater of war.
General Dwight D. Eisenhower, letter to his son, John, December 15, 1945, quoted in Stephen E. Ambrose, *Eisenhower*, I (1983).

I had been to lunch in the general officers' mess . . . a considerable distance from my new office. Ordinarily, I went there with other officers and returned with them . . . . This time, I ventured on the return trip alone.
Although I reached E. ring safely, I discovered that this ring, the outermost corridor of the building, was an endless vista of doors, every one of them identical in appearance. I had not the slightest idea which was mine.
So, . . . trying to look as if I were out for a carefree stroll around the building, I walked. I walked and walked, encountering neither landmarks nor people who looked familiar. One had to give the building his grudging admiration; it had apparently been designed to confuse any enemy which might infiltrate it. Finally, I gave up.
Immediately ahead was a group of girls, stenographers, I supposed, and I went up to one of them quietly and said, "Can you tell me where the office of the Chief of Staff is?"
She immediately said, "You just passed it about a hundred feet back. . . ."
By grapevine . . . the word got around the Pentagon quickly. Then it got to the press offices. . . . The headlines may not have been so impressive as during the war, but they were just as bold and large. I'm afraid that any confidence in my ability, as new Chief of Staff, to manage the Army may have been considerably shaken.
President Dwight D. Eisenhower, *At Ease* (1967).

The Pentagon, that immense monument to modern man's subservience to the desk.
Lord Franks, *The Observer* (November 30, 1952).

The Pentagon is like a log going down the river with 25,000 ants on it, each thinking he's steering the log.
Henry S. Rowen, *The Washington Post* (December 10, 1961).

This place is a jungle—a jungle.
Robert S. McNamara, Secretary of Defense, speaking of the Pentagon after his first few weeks in office, quoted in Arthur M. Schlesinger, Jr., *A Thousand Days* (1965).

Jokes about the Pentagon quickly became a staple of bureaucratic humor. It was so huge people were said to spend days and even weeks wandering its endless corridors trying to find their way out. One woman was said to have told a guard she was in labor and needed help in getting to a maternity hospital. He said, "Madam, you should not have come in here in that condition."
"When I came in here," she answered, "I wasn't."
David Brinkley, *Washington Goes to War* (1988).

Peter Principle

In a hierarchy every employee tends to rise to his level of incompetence.
Laurence J. Peter, *The Peter Principle: Why Things Always Go Wrong*, with Raymond Hull (1969). Peter further observes that "in time, every post tends to be occupied by an employee who is incompetent to carry out his duties." In answer to the logical question of who then does the work that has to be done, Peter asserts that "work is accomplished by those employees who have not yet reached their level of incompetence."

I have seen some extremely good colonels become very bad generals.
Marshal Maurice de Saxe, *Reveries Upon the Art of War* (1757).

Almost all Generals whom history presents . . . as merely having attained to mediocrity, and as wanting in decision when in supreme command, are men who had distinguished themselves in the lower ranks.
Karl von Clausewitz, *On War* (1832).

Every officer has his ceiling in rank, beyond which he should not be allowed to rise—particularly in war-time.
Field Marshal B. L. Montgomery, *Memoirs* (1950).

Philippines

On December 10 [1898] the Treaty of Paris was signed, transferring sovereignty of the Philippines to the United States, with the $20,000,000 to follow upon ratification. "We have bought ten million Malays at $2.00 a head unpicked," remarked [Speaker of the House Thomas B.] Reed acidly, and in the most prescient comment made by anyone at the time, he added, "and nobody knows what it will cost to pick them."
Barbara W. Tuchman, *The Proud Tower* (1966).

[President] McKinley had no intention of seizing territory—which, he had intoned, would "by our code of morality . . . be criminal aggression." In any case, he confessed, he could not locate the Philippines on the map.
Dewey sank the decrepit Spanish fleet in Manila Bay on May 1. American troops soon captured Manila. After waffling for months, McKinley reversed himself and decided to keep the islands. Unaware that the Filipinos were Roman Catholic, he later explained that God had instructed him to "uplift and Christianize them."
Stanley Karnow, "America's Forgotten War in the Philippines," *The New York Times* (April 1, 1989).

If old Dewey had just sailed away when he smashed the Spanish fleet, what a lot of trouble he would have saved us.
President William McKinley quoted in Foster Rhea Dulles, *America's Rise to World Power: 1898–1954* (1955).

Jonathan, I want you to understand my position very plainly. I'm leaving for Australia pursuant to repeated orders of the President. Things have gotten to such a point that I must comply with these orders or get out of the Army. I want you to make it known throughout all elements of your command that I'm leaving over my repeated protests. . . .
General Douglas MacArthur, speaking to General Jonathan Wainright on March 10, 1942, quoted in Jonathan M. Wainright, *General Wainright's Story* (1946).

The President of the United States ordered me to break through the Japanese lines . . . for the purpose, as I understand it, of organizing the American offensive against Japan, a primary object of which is the relief of the Philippines. I came through and I shall return.
General Douglas MacArthur, "I shall return" statements made on March 17, 1942 after escaping from the Philippines and arriving in Australia, quoted in *The Times* (London) (March 21, 1942); Douglas MacArthur, *Reminiscences* (1964); and D. Clayton James, *The Years of MacArthur*, II (1975).

People of the Philippines: I have returned. By the grace of Almighty God, our forces stand again on Philippine soil—soil consecrated in the blood of our two peoples. . . .
The hour of your redemption is here. Your patriots have demonstrated an unswerving and resolute devotion to the principles of freedom. . . . I now call upon your supreme effort that the enemy may know, from the temper of an aroused people within, that he has a force there to contend with no less violent than is the force committed from without.
Rally to me. Let the indomitable spirit of Bataan and Corregidor lead on. As the lines of battle roll forward to bring you within the zone of operations, rise and strike. Strike at every favorable opportunity. For your homes and hearths, strike! For future generations of your sons and daughters, strike! In the name of your sacred dead, strike! Let no heart be faint. Let every arm be steeled.
General Douglas MacArthur, radio address to the people of the Philippines as American forces invaded Leyte, October 20, 1944, reprinted in his *Reminiscences* (1964).

You have spent many lives and much treasure to bring freedom to many lands that were reluctant to receive it. And here you have a people who won it by themselves and need only the help to preserve it.
President Corazon Aquino of the Philippines, Address to Joint Session of Congress, *Time* (September 29, 1986).

Filipinos have long bristled at the colonialistic implications of calling their country the Philippines, in honor of Philip II of Spain. During the regime of Ferdinand Marcos, there was a campaign to rename the country Maharlika, a native word meaning noble or aristocratic. Plans for the rechristening proceeded apace until an academic pointed out that the word was probably derived from Sanskrit. Fine, its proponents said, Sanskrit is a non-imperialist language. Yes, replied the scholar, but Maharlika was most likely derived from the words *maha lingam* meaning "great phallus." That was the end of the campaign.
Time (June 19, 1989).

pill-boxes (fortified defensive positions)

Attack become[s] far easier and more menacing to the defender if "infiltrating pill-boxes" [tanks] replace infiltrating foot-sloggers.
B. H. Liddell Hart, *Thoughts on War* (1944).

[On Tarawa], the Marines took the blockhouse their own way. Bulldozers were moved up, the drivers sheltering behind the blades, and buried the entrance in coral and dirt. As the height of the rubble increased, gunports and other apertures were closed, immobilizing all Japanese resistance and completing the process of entombment. Marines then climbed on top ... and poured gasoline down the air vents. A few hand grenades, and incineration followed. ... The Marines took out 300 bodies.
General Holland M. Smith and Percy Smith, *Coral and Brass* (1948).

We fired high explosives at the embrasures [of a pill-box on the Siegfried Line], and sometimes this was sufficient to persuade the pill-box crew that the war held no future for them. But if not, we had a very effective weapon in the shape of one of the funnies ... [a kind of tank with] a petard which hurled a dustbin sized charge of high explosive. This usually succeeded in blasting the embrasure wide open and causing the occupants to lose all further interest in the campaign. Yet sometimes it didn't, and then we carried out the third movement of the drill which was to bring up a flame-throwing tank. ... There was no fourth movement to this drill; it wasn't really necessary.
John Foley, *Mailed First* (1957).

I'll never forget one of the last classes at basic school, they brought us out to a fortified bunker and they said, "Remember if you ever see one of these, you can always send some guys around the back with grenades. You don't have to hit it head on." Why? Because they had a lieutenant that had recently graduated, who had his Marines assault a fortified bunker head on, because their basic mentality is "Charge!"
Bobby Muller quoted in Kim Willenson, *The Bad War* (1987).

pilots

These planes [DC-3s] are familiarly dubbed by their pilots "the flying box car." Because they are transports and therefore virtually unarmed, the pilots' motto is "In clouds we trust."
Hanson W. Baldwin, "Flight to Guadalcanal," *The New York Times Magazine* (November 1, 1942).

Despite the proliferation of military technology, all three services are dependent on the initiative of a very small percentage of the fighting personnel, who are willing to press the attack under all circumstances. The Air Force during World War II discovered that less than one percent of its military pilots accounted roughly for 30 to 40 per cent of the enemy aircraft destroyed in the air.
Morris Janowitz, *Sociology and the Military Establishment*, 3rd ed. (1974).

The air ace was the object of limitless envy among infantry, mired in mud and seeming helplessness. Soldiers looked up from their trenches and saw in the air a purity of combat that the ground war had lost. The "knights of the sky" were engaged in a conflict in which individual effort still counted, romantic notions of honor, glory, heroism and chivalry were still intact. ... The most significant technological achievement of the modern world was thus also seen as a means of affirming traditional values.
Modris Eksteins, *Rites of Spring: The Great War and the Birth of the Modern Age* (1989).

On March 28, 1931 he [Lieutenant Curtis LeMay] took a young lady friend up for a ride in a PT-3, with the group commander's permission, and was cruising around at five hundred feet, showing her the local countryside, when the engine quit. He chose ... [an] open field, sliced the plane in, ran through a fence, washing out the landing gear, and slid to a stop in a manure pile. Neither he nor the girl was injured and the plane was easily repairable. ... After this incident, LeMay didn't see much more of his lady passenger. Perhaps she didn't enjoy impromptu landings in manure piles.
Thomas M. Coffey, *Iron Eagle* (1986).

But it was not bravery in the simple sense of being willing to risk your life. The idea seemed to be that any fool could do that, if that was all that was required, just as any fool could throw away his life in the process. No, the idea here. . .seemed to be that a man should have the ability to go up in a hurtling piece of machinery and put his hide on the line and then have the moxie, the reflexes, the experience, the coolness, to pull it back in the last yawning moment—and then to go up again the next day, and the next day, and every next day. ... A career in flying was like climbing one of those ancient Babylonian pyramids made up of a progression of steps and ledges, a ziggurat, a pyramid extraordinarily high and steep; and the idea was to prove at every foot of the way up that pyramid that you were one of the elected and anointed ones who had the right stuff.
Tom Wolfe, *The Right Stuff* (1979).

I turned my back on lousy fliers as if their mistakes were catching. When one of them became a grease spot on the tarmac, I almost felt relieved: it was better to bury a weak sister in training than in combat, where he might not only bust his ass, but do something (or, more than likely, fail to do something) that would bust two or three other asses in addition to his own.
General Chuck Yeager and Leo Janos, *Yeager* (1985).

The press treated pilots who were shot down with respect, almost as heroes, like an injured football player carried off the field. But their squadron mates, who knew what was involved, tended to divide shootdowns into two categories, the ones that could have been prevented and those that could not.
Zalin Grant, *Over the Beach* (1986).

The controller [at Edwards Air Force Base] said, "Oh, that's that Yeager voice. They can come from Sunnyside, Queens, Bangor, Maine, Long Beach, California, or Portland, Oregon. You let them up in the skies over Edwards Air Force Base, and they are all going to talk like Chuck Yeager."
Tom Wolfe, "The Meaning of Freedom," *Parameters* (March 1988).

pistols

A calm, cool "dead-shot" behind a Colt's revolver or a Spencer repeating rifle has more moral force than a gatling gun. The average soldier has an unconquerable prejudice against a pistol which he knows is going to hit somebody when it goes off.
John H. Alexander, *Mosby's Men* (1907).

It is difficult to leave the shelter of a shell-hole for a final rush in the face of a deadly shower of bullets and the certain knowledge that cold steel awaits. It is less difficult, however, if there is the knowledge that a loaded revolver for use against the enemy is also loaded for use against you if you fail to jump forward when the barrage lifts.
F. P. Crozier, *The Men I Killed* (1937).

[On August 11, 1940, Winston Churchill] fired his revolver, still smoking a cigar, with commendable accuracy. . . . The whole time he talked of the best method of killing Huns. Soft-nose bullets were the thing to use and he must get some. But, said Randolph [his son], they are illegal in war; to which the P. M. replied that the Germans would make very short work of him if they caught him, and so he didn't see why he should have any mercy on them.
John Colville, *The Fringes of Power* (1985).

Oh, that. That's just part of my clothes. I hardly ever shoot anybody with it.
Dick Powell, referring to his pistol in *Murder, My Sweet* (1944), directed by Edward Dmytryk; screenplay by John Paxton, from the novel *Farewell, My Lovely* by Raymond Chandler.

Ike said he had chuckled at Patton at luncheon for the King at Liége. General Patton had told the King with gusto, when asked how frequently he used his famous pearl-handled revolvers:
"I personally have killed thirty Germans."
"How many?" said Ike.
Patton replied, "Five."
Captain Harry C. Butcher, writing on November 20, 1944, *My Three Years With Eisenhower* (1946).

I spy my service revolver. Automatically I pick it up, remove the clip, and check the mechanism. It works with buttered smoothness. I weigh the weapon in my hand and admire the cold, blue glint of its steel. It is more beautiful than a flower; more faithful than most friends.
Audie Murphy, *To Hell and Back* (1949).

plunder

When a hostile army had been defeated, all the booty was put in a central place and then distributed to one Roman after another according to the rank of each man. This method caused the soldiers to attend to winning and not to robbing.
Niccolò Machiavelli, *The Art of War* (1520).

Friends! I promise you these conquests! But you must swear to me in return to observe one condition. You must show consideration for the peoples to whom you bring liberty, you must keep down that plundering which scoundrels indulge in, of which our enemies have given the example. Unless you do this, you will be called not liberators but scourges of the nations.
General Napoleon Bonaparte, address to his army in Italy, April 26, 1796, reprinted in Houston Peterson, ed., *A Treasury of the World's Great Speeches* (1965).

Fire authorizes looting, which the soldier permits himself in order to save the remnants from the flames.
Napoleon I, writing of the burning of Moscow on September 20, 1812, quoted in J. C. Herold, *The Mind of Napoleon* (1955).

Nothing can be designed better to disorganize and destroy an army than pillage.
Napoleon I, *Military Maxims* (1827).

Looting the enemy's dead was a soldier's right, and fortunes were lying on the field for anyone cold-blooded enough to take them. Dead officers, in particular, had purses, watches, pistols, swords, lockets and sentimental charms. . . . When all those were gone, there were clothes and equipment, and when even the clothes were gone there were teeth. False teeth were either carved out of ivory or made up of human teeth, and

dentists would pay well for the raw materials. Such a haul was made from the field of Waterloo that dentures for years afterwards were often called Waterloo teeth.
David Howarth, *A Near Run Thing* (1971).

They resemble the Democratic party at least in one particular, for they are held together by the cohesive power of public plunder.
John S. Mosby's description of his irregular forces during the Civil War quoted in John Scott, *Partisan Life with Col. John S. Mosby* (1867).

They fight all day and march all night, covering impossible distances and appearing in incredible places, not because every soldier carries a field marshal's baton in his knapsack, but because he hopes to carry at least half a dozen silver forks there next day.
George Bernard Shaw, *The Man of Destiny* (1897).

Modern war is so expensive that we feel trade to be a better avenue to plunder.
William James, "The Moral Equivalent of War," *McClure's* (August 1910).

When a rich city was captured there was often looting, but the victorious commanders usually tried to put it on an organized basis. An officer was appointed prize agent, the troops were shaken down to disgorge their pickings, and the plunder was auctioned. The resulting cash was then divided according to a system whereby the lion's share went to the commanding general.
Byron Farwell, *Mr. Kipling's Army* (1981).

The looting [of the Winter Palace in St Petersburg on November 7, 1917] was just beginning when somebody cried, "Comrades! Don't take anything. This is the property of the People!" Immediately twenty voices were crying "Stop! Put everything back! Don't take anything! Property of the People!" Many hands dragged the spoilers down. Damask and tapestry were snatched from the arms of those who had them. . . . Roughly and hastily the things were crammed back in their cases, and self-appointed sentinels stood guard. It was all utterly spontaneous. Through corridors and up staircases the cry could be heard growing fainter and fainter in the distance, "Revolutionary discipline! Property of the People . . . ."
John Reed, *Ten Days That Shook the World* (1926).

point position

We got eight new replacements into my platoon. We were supposed to make a little feeling attack that same day. Well, by next day, all eight of them replacements were dead, buddy. But none of us old guys were. We weren't going to send our own guys out on point in a damnfool situation like that. . . . We sent the replacements out ahead.
U.S. Army sergeant quoted in James Jones, *WWII* (1977).

I would dress like a Montagnard. I wouldn't wear conventional camouflage fatigues in the field. I wore a dark-green loincloth, a dark-green bandana to blend in with the foliage, and a little camouflage paint on my face. And Ho Chi Minh sandals. And my grenades and ammunition. That's the way I went to the field.
I dressed like that specifically as the point man, because if the enemy saw anyone first, they saw myself. They would just figure I was another jungle guy that was walking around in the woods. And I would catch 'em off guard.
Arthur E. "Gene" Woodley, Jr. quoted in Wallace Terry, *Bloods* (1984).

policing

Policemen are soldiers who act alone; soldiers are policemen who act in unison.
Herbert Spencer, *Social Statics* (1851).

Neither conscience nor sanity itself suggests that the United States is, should or could be the global gendarme.
Robert S. McNamara, U.S. Secretary of Defense, quoted in *The New York Times* (May 19, 1966).

We may well be unable to afford to be the world's policeman, but neither can we afford to fail to live up to the responsibilities that the accidents of a bountiful land and a beneficent fate have placed upon us.
General William C. Westmoreland, *A Soldier Reports* (1976).

Observers have faulted our intervention in Vietnam as evidence of American arrogance of power—attempts by the United States to be the World's Policeman. But there is another dimension to American arrogance, the international version of our domestic Great Society programs where we presumed that we knew what was best for the world in terms of social, political, and economic development and saw it as our duty to force the world into the American mold—to act not so much the World's Policeman as the World's Nanny. It is difficult today to recall the depth of our arrogance.
Harry G. Summers, Jr., *On Strategy* (1982).

power

To reign is worth ambition, though in Hell:
Better to reign in Hell than serve in Heaven.
John Milton, *Paradise Lost* (1667).

Unlimited power is apt to corrupt the minds of those who possess it.
William Pitt the Elder, speech in the House of Lords, January 9, 1770.

The greater the power, the more dangerous the abuse.
Edmund Burke, speech in the House of Commons, February 7, 1771.

Power is my mistress. I have worked too hard at her conquest to allow anyone to take her away from me or even covet her.
Napoleon I, speaking in 1804, quoted in J. C. Herold, *The Mind of Napoleon* (1955).

I have never been so well pleased, as when I could shift power from my own, on the shoulders of others; nor have I ever been able to conceive how any rational being could propose happiness to himself from the exercise of power over others.
Thomas Jefferson, letter to Monsieur Destutt de Tracy, January 26, 1811, reprinted in *The Writings of Thomas Jefferson*, XIII, ed. A. E. Bergh (1853).

War is simply power unrestrained by constitution or compact.
General William T. Sherman, speaking in 1865, quoted in Russell F. Weigley, *History of the United States Army*, enlarged ed. (1984).

Power tends to corrupt, and absolute power corrupts absolutely. Great men are almost always bad men. . . . There is no worse heresy than that the office sanctifies the holder of it.
Lord Acton (John Dahlberg), letter to Bishop Mandell Creighton, April 5, 1887, reprinted in *Life and Letters of Mandell Creighton* (1904).

You cannot have power for good without having power for evil too. Even mother's milk nourishes murderers as well as heroes.
George Bernard Shaw, *Major Barbara*, Act III (1905).

Our next war will be fought for the highest interests of our country and of mankind. This will invest it with importance in the world's history. "World power or downfall" will be our rallying cry.
General Friedrich von Bernhardi, *Germany and the Next War* (1914).

Power without responsibility—the prerogative of the harlot throughout the ages.
Stanley Baldwin, 1931 speech, quoted in G. M. Young, *Stanley Baldwin* (1952). Tom Stoppard, *Loes Malquist and Mr. Moon* (1966), described the House of Lords as a place of "responsibility without power, the prerogative of the eunuch throughout the ages."

Power politics is the diplomatic name for the law of the jungle.
Ely Culbertson, *Must We Fight Russia?* (1946).

We have the power to do any damn fool thing we want to do, and we seem to do it about every 10 minutes.
J. William Fulbright, on the U.S. Senate, *Time* (February 4, 1952).

The very fact that those men, by their own design, are in the Kremlin, means that they love power. They want to be there. Whenever they start a war, they are taking the great risk of losing that power. They study history pretty well. They remember Mussolini. They remember Hitler. They have even studied Napoleon very seriously. When dictators over-reach themselves and challenge the whole world, they are very likely to end up in any place except a dictatorial position. And those men in the politburo know that.
President Dwight D. Eisenhower, address to the nation, April 5, 1954.

The official world, the corridors of power, the dilemmas of conscience and egotism—she disliked them all.
C. P. Snow, *Homecomings* (1956). Snow later used the phrase "corridors of power" as the title of a 1964 novel.

We often say how impressive power is. But I do not find it impressive at all. The guns and the bombs, the rockets and the warships, are all symbols of human failure. They are necessary symbols. They protect what we cherish. But they are witness to human folly.
President Lyndon B. Johnson, speech at Johns Hopkins University, April 7, 1965.

Political power grows out of the barrel of a gun.
Mao Tse-tung, *Quotations from Chairman Mao* (1966).

You only have power over people so long as you don't take everything away from them. But when you've robbed a man of everything he's no longer in your power—he's free again.
Alexander Solzhenitsyn, *The First Circle* (1968).

If a man can accept a situation in a place of power with the thought that it's only temporary, he comes out all right. But when he thinks that he is the cause of the power, that can be his ruination.
President Harry S. Truman, quoted in Merle Miller, *Plain Speaking* (1973).

Power is the ultimate aphrodisiac.
Henry A. Kissinger, *The New York Times* (October 28, 1973).

Being powerful is like being a lady. If you have to tell people you are, you ain't.
Jesse Carr, *Newsweek* (September 27, 1976).

We are the greatest power in the world—if we behave like it.
Walt Rostow quoted in William Shawcross, *Sideshow* (1979).

balance of power

Into the discussion of human affairs the question of justice only enters where there is equal power to enforce it, and that the powerful exact what they can, and the weak grant what they must.
Thucydides, *The Peloponnesian Wars* (5th century B.C.).

We were not in honor obliged to take any share in the war which the Emperor brought upon himself in the year 1733, nor were we in interest obliged to take a share in that war as long as neither side attempted to push its conquests farther than was consistent with the balance of power in Europe, which was a case that did not happen.
Sir Robert Walpole, speech in the House of Commons, February 13, 1741.

A new disease is spreading over Europe; it has seized upon our princes and induces them to maintain an inordinate number of soldiers. The disease is attended by complications and it inevitably becomes contagious; for, as soon as one state increases what it calls its forces, the others immediately increase theirs; so that nothing is gained except mutual ruination.
Charles de Montesquieu, *The Spirit of the Laws* (1748).

I have ever deemed it fundamental for the United States never to take active part in the quarrels of Europe. Their political interests are entirely distinct from ours. Their mutual jealousies, their balance of power, their complicated alliances, their forms and principles of government, are all foreign to us. They are nations of eternal war.
Thomas Jefferson, June 11, 1823 letter to President James Monroe, reprinted in *The Writings of Thomas Jefferson*, XV, ed. A. E. Bergh (1853).

I resolved that if France had Spain it should not be Spain with the Indies; I called a New World into existence to redress the balance of the Old.
George Canning, speech in the House of Commons on the independence of former Spanish colonies in South America, December 12, 1826.

The idea of an equilibrium cannot explain a suspension of hostilities ... all it amounts to is waiting for a more favorable moment.
Karl von Clausewitz, *On War* (1832).

This whole notion of the "balance of power" is a mischievous delusion which has come down to us from past times; we ought to drive it from our minds, and to consider the solemn question of peace and war in more clear, more definite, and on far higher principles than any that are involved in the phrase.
John Bright, speech in the House of Commons, March 31, 1854.

What is it to me who is a judge or who is a bishop? It is my business to make kings and emperors, and to maintain the balance of Europe.
John Carteret, eighteenth-century British Secretary of State, quoted in John Morley, *Walpole* (1889).

So the celebrated encirclement of Germany has finally become an accomplished fact, in spite of all efforts by our politicians to prevent it. ... A magnificent achievement which even those for whom it means disaster are bound to admire.... Our dilemma over keeping faith with the old and honorable Emperor [of Austria-Hungary] has been exploited to create a situation which gives England the excuse she has been seeking to

annihilate us with a spurious appearance of justice on the pretext that she is helping France and maintaining the well-known Balance of Power in Europe, i.e. playing off all European States for her own benefit against us.
Kaiser William II, writing on the eve of World War I (July 30–31, 1914), quoted in Michael Balfour, *The Kaiser and His Times* (1964).

There must be, not a balance of power, but a community of power; not organized rivalries, but an organized common peace.
President Woodrow Wilson, address to the U.S. Senate, January 22, 1917.

A single demand of you, comrades, provide us with atomic weapons in the shortest possible time. You know that Hiroshima has shaken the whole world. The equilibrium has been destroyed. . . . Provide the bomb—it will remove a great danger from us.
Joseph Stalin, speaking in 1945, quoted in David Holloway, "Entering the Nuclear Arms Race," *Social Studies of Science*, II (1981).

It was during my visit to Bulgaria [May 1962] that I had the idea of installing missiles with nuclear warheads in Cuba without letting the United States find out they were there until it was too late to do anything about them . . . our missiles would have equalized what the West likes to call the "balance of power." The Americans had surrounded our country with military bases and threatened us with nuclear weapons, and now they would learn just what it feels like to have enemy missiles pointing at you.
Nikita Khrushchev, *Khrushchev Remembers: The Last Testament* (1970).

Those who scoff at "balance of power diplomacy" on the world scene should recognize that the only alternative to a balance of power is an imbalance of power—and history shows us that nothing so drastically escalates the danger of war as such an imbalance.
President Richard M. Nixon, press conference, June 25, 1972.

The management of a balance of power is a permanent undertaking, not an exertion that has a foreseeable end.
Henry A. Kissinger, *White House Years* (1979).

Balance of power theory has been around in one guise or another since Thucydides' account of the Peloponnesian War.
Barry R. Posen, *The Sources of Military Doctrine* (1984).

preparedness

To be prepared for war is one of the most effectual means of preserving peace.
A free people ought not only to be armed, but disciplined; to which end a uniform and well-digested plan is requisite; and their safety and interest require that they should promote such manufactories as tend to render them independent of others for essential, particularly military, supplies.
President George Washington, first annual message to Congress, January 8, 1790.

Whatever enables us to go to war, secures our peace.
Thomas Jefferson, letter to James Monroe, July 11, 1790.

We need to keep in a condition of preparedness, especially as regards our navy, not because we want war, but because we desire to stand with those whose plea for peace is listened to with respectful attention.
President Theodore Roosevelt, speech in New York City, November 11, 1902.

Just because we have won victory, we must never relax our vigilance against the frenzied plots for revenge by the imperialists and their running dogs.
Mao Tse-tung, speaking on June 15, 1949, *Quotations from Chairman Mao* (1966).

For all your days prepare,
    And meet them all alike:
When you are the anvil, bear—
    When you are the hammer, strike.
Edwin Markham, "Preparedness," *Poems* (1950).

Patriotism means equipped forces and a prepared citizenry.
President Dwight D. Eisenhower, first Inaugural Address, January 20, 1953.

A war regarded as inevitable or even probable, and therefore much prepared for, has a very good chance of eventually being fought.
George F. Kennan, *The Cloud of Danger* (1977).

None of the four wars in my lifetime came about because we were too strong. It is weakness—it is weakness that invites adventurous adversaries to make mistaken judgments.
President Ronald Reagan, speech to the Republican National Convention, Dallas, Texas, August 23, 1984.

principles of war

Now an army may be likened to water, for just as flowing water avoids the heights and hastens to the lowlands, so an army avoids strength and strikes weakness. And as water shapes its flow in accordance with the ground, so an army manages its victory in accordance with the situation of the enemy. And as water has no constant form, there are in war no constant conditions.
Sun Tzu, *The Art of War* (4th century B.C.).

All sciences have principles and rules. War has none.
Marshal Maurice de Saxe, *Reveries Upon the Art of War* (1757).

These three things you must always keep in mind: concentration of strength, activity, and a firm resolve to perish gloriously. They are the three principles of the military art which have disposed luck in my favor in all my operations.
Napoleon I, 1804 letter to General Lauriston, quoted in J. C. Herold, *The Mind of Napoleon* (1955).

No rule of war is so absolute as to allow no exceptions.
Napoleon I, *Military Maxims* (1827).

The destruction of the enemy's military force is the leading principle of war.
Karl von Clausewitz, *On War* (1832).

There exists a small number of fundamental principles of war, which may not be deviated from without danger, and the application of which . . . has been in all times crowned with glory.
General Antoine Henri Jomini, *Summary of the Art of War* (1838).

War is not, as some seem to suppose, a mere game of chance. Its principles constitute one of the most intricate of modern sciences.
General Henry W. Halleck, *Elements of Military Art and Science*, 3rd ed. (1863).

If men make war in slavish obedience to rules, they will fail.
President Ulysses S. Grant, *Personal Memoirs* (1885).

Correct military principles are learned from a study of the important campaigns of history, and from comments and criticisms of those campaigns by their participants, or by able military students. Military principles are to the art of war what the principles of mechanics are to the art of engineering.
   Gustave J. Fiebeger, *Elements of Strategy* (1906).

To some men the first rule of war is that they shall not expose themselves to it.
   René Quinton, *Soldier's Testament* (1930).

The truths of war are absolute, but the principles governing their application have to be deduced on each occasion from the circumstances, which are always different; and in consequence no rules are any guide to action.
   Winston Churchill, *The World Crisis* (1931).

A little study and reflection will lead us to realize that all past strategy and tactics has been governed, consciously or unconsciously, as it may be, by the principles of war, and we may deduce from this that this government will continue. Economy of force, surprise, security, offensive action, movement and cooperation hold good whether an army is composed of foot soldiers, horse soldiers or machine soldiers.
   J. F. C. Fuller, *Lectures on F. S. R. III* (1932).

The so-called "principles of war" derive from the work of a handful of theorists, most of them long since dead. Their specific contributions to living doctrine are not widely known, because their works are seldom read.
   Bernard Brodie, *Strategy in the Missile Age* (1959).

[Official principles of war are] a catalogue of commonplaces that ... has served generations of soldiers as an excuse not to think things through for themselves.
   Peter Paret, *Innovation and Reform in Warfare* (1966).

All military laws and military theories which are in the nature of principles are the experience of past wars summed up by people in former days or in our own times. We should seriously study these lessons, paid for in blood, which are a heritage of past wars. That is one point. But there is another. We should put these conclusions to the test of our own experience, assimilating what is useful, rejecting what is useless, and adding what is specifically our own. The latter is very important, for otherwise we cannot direct a war.
   Mao Tse-tung, *Selected Military Writings* (1968).

Don't march on Moscow. That is rule one of war. Lots of people have tried it. But nobody has succeeded. Napoleon got there but he had to get out. Hitler didn't even get there. You can destroy Moscow without invading it. You can destroy it with atomic rockets. The function of an army is to hold. The offensive is for the air.
   Rule two of war is don't march on China. China is like a sponge. You can squeeze it and everything is forced out of it. Any army that gets into China will be squeezed and forced out. Just like a sponge.
   Field Marshal B. L. Montgomery, January 18, 1957, quoted in C. L. Sulzberger, *The Last of the Giants* (1970).

It may be well that the consideration of a catalog of numbered principles (usually fewer than a dozen) with the barest definition of the meaning of each may be necessary to communicate to second-order minds (or minds too busy with the execution of plans to worry much about the specific validity of the ideas behind them) some conception of what the business is all about.
   Bernard Brodie, *War and Politics* (1973).

One day an Australian fighter pilot was shot down quite near us. Monty [General B. L. Montgomery] saw a parachute going down, so he said, "Send somebody out, bring him back to lunch...."

Now Monty had decided to rewrite the Principles of War—at least to introduce his new principle of war...which was: Win the air battle first. And he was very proud of this and kept telling everybody, "You know the first principle of war? Win the air battle first!"

About halfway through lunch he turned to this Australian and said, "Now, do you know what the first and greatest Principle of War is?"

"Well, I don't know much about principles of war, but I should say it's stop frigging about!"

Monty was speechless.
Sir William Mather quoted in Nigel Hamilton, *Master of the Battlefield* (1983).

I'm talking about strategic direction plus violation of the fundamental principles of war—of which there are nine. Those were violated, not all of them, but most of them. We could have won by more correct adherence to those principles, such as the principle of objective, the principle of unity of command, the principle of surprise and security, all of which were violated. The United States can never afford again to allow itself to be at such a vast strategic disadvantage as we were in Vietnam. I sincerely hope we've learned. We were defeated by an eighth-rate power.
Major General George S. Patton III, quoted in Kim Willenson, *The Bad War* (1987).

maneuver
Both advantage and danger are inherent in maneuver.
Sun Tzu, *The Art of War* (4th century B.C.).

Never did I see such a pounding match. Both were what the boxers call gluttons. Napoleon did not maneuver at all. He just moved forward in the old style, in columns, and was driven off in the old style.
Duke of Wellington on the Battle of Waterloo quoted in Elizabeth Longford, *Wellington: The Years of the Sword* (1969).

Arrange maneuvers in peacetime to include . . . causes of friction, in order that the judgment, circumspection, even resolution, of the separate leaders may be exercised, ... It is of immense importance that the soldier . . . whatever be his rank, should not see for the first time in war those phenomena of war which, when seen for the first time, astonish and perplex him.
Karl von Clausewitz, *On War* (1832).

Maneuvers are threats; he who appears most threatening, wins.
Ardant du Picq, *Battle Studies* (1868).

While maneuver is the key to victory, it is maneuver of the units of fire power and not of masses of cannon fodder. We must learn to depend for success, not on the physical weight of the infantry attack, but on the skillful offensive used in combination of all available weapons, based on the principle of maneuver.
B.H. Liddell Hart, "The Essential Principles of War . . . ," *United Service Magazine* (April 1920).

Battles are won by slaughter and maneuver. The greater the general, the more he contributes in maneuver, the less he demands in slaughter.
Winston Churchill, *The World Crisis*, II (1923).

Under the protection of . . . [an] artificially generated fog of war, the advanced forces . . . will move forward as rapidly as possible with the one idea of engaging the

enemy, not to annihilate him but to fix him, not so much by hitting him as by maneuvering him into difficult ground or against an obstacle. Infantry are normally pinned down by fire, but fire will seldom pin down a mechanized force, it will have to be boxed up by maneuver.
J. F. C. Fuller, *Armoured Warfare* (1943).

Battles are won by fire and by movement. The purpose of the movement is to get the fire in a more advantageous place to play on the enemy. This is from the rear or flank.
General George S. Patton, Jr., *War as I Knew It* (1947).

We are not interested in real estate. We are interested only in inflicting maximum casualties on the enemy with minimum losses to ourselves. To do this, we must wage a war of maneuver—slashing at the enemy when he withdraws and fighting delaying actions when he attacks.
General Matthew Ridgway, on Korean War tactics, quoted in R. Ernest Dupry and Trevor N. Dupry, *Military Heritage of America* (1956).

mass

The strength of an army, like the momentum in mechanics, is estimated by the weight multiplied by the velocity. A rapid march exerts a beneficial moral influence on the army and increases its means of victory.
Napoleon I, *Military Maxims* (1827).

Do not let my opponents castigate me with the blather that Waterloo was won on the playfields of Eton, for the fact remains geographically, historically and tactically, whether the Great Duke uttered such undiluted nonsense or not, that it was won on the fields in Belgium by carrying out a fundamental principle of war, the principle of mass; in other words by marching on to those fields three Englishmen, Germans or Belgians to every two Frenchmen.
J. F. C. Fuller, 1916 *RUSI Journal* article, paraphrased in A. J. Trythall, *'Bony Fuller'* (1977).

I see only one thing, the *mass*; I try to destroy it, feeling sure that the *accessories* will then tumble down of themselves.
Napoleon I quoted by Marshal Ferdinand Foch in *Precepts and Judgements* (1920).

The theory of human mass has dominated the military mind from Waterloo to the World War. This monster was the child of the French Revolution by Napoleon. The midwife who brought it into the modern world was the Prussian philosopher of war, Clausewitz.
B. H. Liddell Hart, *When Britain Goes to War* (1935).

Force, in Napoleon's well-known dictum, is mass multiplied by speed; and, with the development in mechanical fire-weapons, mass is best interpreted by the term "firepower."
B. H. Liddell Hart, *Thoughts on War* (1944).

The peculiar Russian style of war is based on the use of numbers, of mass, not mass employed mechanically to overwhelm the enemy but rather the creative, inventive use of mass. During the Second World War the Red Army ... advanced all across the front, at least in a theater of war, with regiments that were like the fingers of a hand ...; their job was to advance as far as they could. The high command behind them kept back the reinforcements in a pool and would then reinforce opportunistically—whichever finger, whichever regiment or division happened to find a path through. They then would let all the reinforcements flow through that path, thereby condemning the Germans who were holding out on the line to encirclement when the successful

torrent breaking out behind them hit. So this was a case of the high command's making a highly fluid, elastic and flexible use of numbers, not just using mass in waves of attack.
Edward Luttwak, "The Strategy of Survival," *American Heritage* (July/August 1988).

objective

It is not the object of war to annihilate those who have given provocation for it, but to cause them to mend their ways.
Polybius, *Histories* (2nd century B.C.).

It is the object only of war that makes it honorable. And if there was ever a just war since the world began, it is this in which America is now engaged.
Thomas Paine, *The American Crisis*, V (March 21, 1778).

Destruction of the enemy's military forces is in reality the object of all combats.
Karl von Clausewitz, *On War* (1832).

Defense is the stronger form with the negative object, and attack the weaker form with the positive object.
Karl von Clausewitz, *On War* (1832).

"Lee's Army will be your objective point. Wherever Lee goes, there will you go also."
General U. S. Grant, to General George Meade during the Civil War, quoted in James M. McPherson, *Battle Cry of Freedom* (1988).

In war, the proper objective of the Navy is the enemy's navy.
Alfred Thayer Mahan, *Naval Strategy* (1911).

I maintain that Congress has the right and the duty to declare the object of the war, and the people have the right and the obligation to discuss it.
Robert M. Lafollette, Sr., speech in the U.S. Senate, October 6, 1917.

The objective of war is specifically "to preserve oneself and destroy the enemy" (to destroy the enemy means to disarm him or "deprive him of the power to resist", and does not mean to destroy every member of his forces physically).
Mao Tse-tung, *On a Prolonged War* (1938).

Objectives must not be confused with the decisive point of attack, for objectives are like the rounds on a ladder, they are but means towards attaining a decision.
J. F. C. Fuller, *Armoured Warfare* (1943).

The Navy Department dragooned me into giving an interview, and among the questions asked me [Admiral William F. Halsey] was, "Is the Mikado's palace a military objective?"
I replied, "No. If by chance the B-29's or somebody came over there in an undercast, they might hit it by mistake, but it would have been a mistake." Instead of letting well enough alone, I added with thoughtless flippancy, "I'd hate to have them kill Hirohito's white horse, because I want to ride it."
The White Horse promptly jumped into the headlines, and soon I found myself connected with it as inseparably as if I were a centaur. The Chamber of Commerce of Reno sent me a beautiful saddle. The Lions Club of Montrose, Colorado, sent another, with a bridle, blanket, and lariat. . . . The Military Order of the World Wars sent a toy horse. A Texas Sheriff sent a pair of spurs. My cabin on the *Missouri* began to look like a tack room.
William F. Halsey and J. Bryan III, *Admiral Halsey's Story* (1947).

The object in war is to attain a better peace—even if only from your own point of view.
B. H. Liddell Hart, *Strategy* (1967).

For the military historian failure to maintain the objective is among the easiest mistakes to detect. For the soldier, it is among the most difficult blunders to avoid.
Robert G. Tanner, *Stonewall in the Valley* (1976).

offensive
When you have once undertaken the offensive, it should be maintained to the last extremity.
Napoleon I, *Military Maxims* (1827).

If at any time you feel able to take the offensive, you are not restrained from doing so.
President Abraham Lincoln, letter of July 4, 1862 to General George McClellan, quoted in J. G. Nicolay and J. Hay, *Complete Works of Abraham Lincoln*, VII (1905). Considering McClellan's famous reluctance to attack, this comment is probably meant to be ironic.

The offensive alone is suited to the temperament of French soldiers. . . . We are determined to march straight against the enemy without hesitation.
Armand Fallieres, President of France, speaking in 1913, quoted in Marshal Joseph Joffre, *Memoirs* (1932).

The motor car and the tank re-establish the offensive as the stronger form of war. Nevertheless, this fact does not justify us in supposing that mobile warfare will endure for ever; but rather that, sooner or later, means of slowing down tank offensives will be resorted to, and once again the castle, in modified form, will appear. Once again armies will be faced by siege warfare, but in what forms?
J. F. C. Fuller, *Armoured Warfare* (1943).

A revolution or a revolutionary war is on the offensive, yet it has its defensive and retreat. To defend in order to attack, to retreat in order to advance, to take a flanking position in order to take a frontal position, and to follow a corkscrew path in order to go directly to the objective—these are inevitable phenomena in the development of all events, and why should we suppose that military events are otherwise?
Mao Tse-tung quoted in Robert Payne, *Mao Tse-tung* (1950).

Once on land we must be offensive, and more offensive, and ever more offensive as the hours go by. We must call on the soldiers for an all out effort. . . .
Inaction, and a defensive mentality, are criminal in any officer— however senior.
Field Marshal B. L. Montgomery, instructions to his officers before D-Day, quoted in his *Memoirs* (1958).

French leadership [prior to World War I] became victim of its own public relations: its strategy, its military organization and equipment and its tactical doctrine were influenced by . . . myth. Hence the offensive, *whatever the circumstances*. But this was not to be based on the careful use of ground or on the fire power of modern rifles and machine guns, or on modern artillery preparation; it was merely an abstract idea. *Elan* and *cran* ("guts") would do it all by succession of charges—by attack pushed "body to body."
Correlli Barnett, *The Swordbearers* (1963).

Two squadrons each of the 20th Deccan Horse and the 7th Dragoon Guards carried out a charge against unshaken German infantry in High Wood. As they came out of the cornfields in front of the wood a German machine gun opened up and the attackers were forced to retire. As many eye-witnesses testified afterwards, it was certainly magnificent. One would like to complete the cliché and say that even so it was not war. But the tragedy is that for those who had ordered this futile gesture it was the very essence of the correct offensive spirit.

John Ellis, *The Social History of the Machine Gun* (1975).

A German ex-soldier . . . I talked to in the DDR in 1958 . . . had fought on the East Front throughout, from 1941 on, and talked of waves of "human sea" attacks, only the first wave of Russians being armed. It was, he told me, "sickening" to shoot them down. Eventually, there were so many Russians to so few Germans that it was impossible to shoot them all down. He saw young boys, with coat-sleeves too long for their arms, wandering dazed and weaponless among the German positions, and old men also—all expected to pick up rifles or tommy-guns from the dead and so continue the Stalin offensive.

Alexander McKee, *Dresden 1945* (1984).

surprise

The first blow is half the battle.

Oliver Goldsmith, *She Stoops to Conquer*, Act II (1773).

For ever keep in view the necessity of guarding against surprises. In all your marches, at times, at least, even when there is no possible danger, move with front, rear, and flank guards, that they may be familiarized to the use; and be regular in your encampments, appointing necessary guards for the security of your camp. In short, whether you expect an enemy or not, this should be practised; otherwise your attempts will be confused and awkward, when necessary.

General George Washington, letter of November 10, 1775 to Colonel William Woodford, reprinted in J. C. Fitzpatrick, ed., *The Writings of George Washington*, IV (1931–44).

Who can surprise well must conquer.

John Paul Jones, letter to Benjamin Franklin of February 10, 1778, quoted in Lincoln Lorenz, *John Paul Jones* (1943).

An ordinary general occupying a bad position, if surprised by a superior force, seeks safety in retreat; but a great captain displays the utmost determination and advances to meet the enemy. By this movement he disconcerts his adversary; and if the march of the latter evinces irresolution, an able general, profiting by the moments of indecision, may yet hope for victory.

Napoleon I, *Military Maxims* (1827).

To be defeated is pardonable; to be surprised—never!

Napoleon I, *Military Maxims* (1827).

Whatever its aims, the side which decides to go to war will unleash all its aerial forces in mass against the enemy nation the instant the decision is taken, without waiting to declare war formally.

Giulio Douhet, *The Command of the Air* (1921).

A military man can scarcely pride himself on having "smitten a sleeping enemy"; in fact, to have it pointed out is more a matter of shame.

Japanese Admiral Isoroku Yamamoto, January 9, 1942 letter to Ogata Taketora, quoted in Hirosuki Asawa, *The Reluctant Admiral* (1979). Yamamoto commanded the Japanese surprise attack on Pearl Harbor on December 7, 1941.

[A] surprise attack by a large nation on a small one, entailing many civilian casualties, would go against America's traditions.
Robert F. Kennedy, writing of the Cuban Missile Crisis, *Thirteen Days* (1969).

With modern intelligence, it is not possible to make a surprise attack from a world situation that is perfectly calm. We are not going to look up suddenly and see all those weapons falling on Washington.
Admiral Thomas J. Moorer, *U.S. News & World Report* (September 5, 1977).

Surprise is the greatest factor in war. There are two kinds, tactical and strategic. Tactical surprise is an operational art. A skilled unit commander can generally achieve it. Strategic surprise is attained on the political level.
Tom Clancy, *Red Storm Rising* (1986).

unity of command

It is better to confide any expedition to a single man of ordinary ability, rather than to two, even though they are men of the highest merit and both having equal authority.
Niccolò Machiavelli, *The Discourses* (1517).

Nothing is more important in war than unity in command. When, therefore, you are carrying on hostilities against a single power only, you should have but one army acting on one line and led by one commander.
Napoleon I, *Military Maxims* (1827).

Of all the faulty decisions of the war [World War II] perhaps the most inexplicable one was the failure to unify the command in the Pacific. The principle involved is perhaps the most fundamental one in the doctrine and tradition of command. In this instance it did not involve an international problem. It was accepted and entirely successful in the other great theaters.
The failure to do so in the Pacific cannot be defended in logic, in theory or even in common sense. Other motives must be ascribed.
It resulted in divided effort, the waste of diffusion and duplication of force, undue extension of the war with added casualties and cost.
General Douglas MacArthur quoted in Charles Willoughby and John Chamberlain, *MacArthur, 1941–1951* (1954).

[General George C.] Marshall's most persistent concern was the need for unity of command. This concept had arisen among the Americans during World War I, and Marshall and Fox Conner had both come to hold a passionate belief in it. They felt that the forces would have been used more effectively under a single commander. In its simplest terms, the idea was that one commander should be in command of all forces within a given theater of operations. Few military officers accepted this doctrine; for example, in 1941, the British used the committee system, with the commander of each branch serving as a member of a council of equals.
Joseph Patrick Hobbs, *Dear General* (1971).

I consistently resisted suggestions that a single, combined command could more efficiently prosecute the war [in Vietnam]. I believed that subordinating the Vietnamese forces to U.S. control would stifle the growth of leadership and acceptance of responsibility essential to the development of Vietnamese Armed Forces capable eventually of defending their country.
General William C. Westmoreland quoted in Harry G. Summers, Jr., *On Strategy* (1982).

When [General Matthew] Ridgway commanded in Korea ... Ridgway also commanded the South Korean Army; and whenever the president sought his advice during

the Vietnam War, Ridgway always wondered aloud why [General William] West-moreland didn't command the South Vietnamese Army as well as the American Army.
Colonel Jim R. Paschall quoted in Ivan Prashker, *Duty, Honor, Vietnam* (1988).

prisoners of war

The information obtained from prisoners ought to be estimated at its proper value. A soldier seldom looks beyond his own company and an officer can, at most, give account of the position or movements of the division to which his regiment belongs. A general, therefore, should not allow himself to be confirmed in his conjectures as to the enemy's position, by attaching any weight to the statements of prisoners, except when they coincide with the reports of the advance guards.
Napoleon I, *Military Maxims* (1827).

When news of the [General Robert E. Lee's] surrender first reached our lines our men commenced firing a salute of a hundred guns in honor of the victory. I at once sent word, however, to have it stopped. The Confederates were now our prisoners, and we did not want to exult over their downfall.
President Ulysses S. Grant, *Personal Memoirs* (1885).

But mark this, Caesar. Clemency is very well for you; but what is it for your soldiers, who have to fight to-morrow the men you spared yesterday? You may give what orders you please; but I tell you that your next victory will be a massacre, thanks to your clemency. I, for one, will take no prisoners. I will kill my enemies in the field; and then you can preach as much clemency as you please: I shall never have to fight them again.
George Bernard Shaw, *Caesar and Cleopatra*, Act II (1900).

The town was carried by storm the eleventh day. All the inhabitants were forced to come out, and were divided up among the Mongol companies to be slaughtered. One old woman, just about to receive the fatal blow, cried out that, if they did not kill her, she would give a fine pearl. They asked her for it. She replied that she had swallowed it. At once they slit open her stomach, and pulled out, in fact, several pearls. Thinking others might perhaps have swallowed pearls, Chingis-khan gave the order to slit open all the dead.
René Grousset, *Conqueror of the World* (1966).

In May 1864, Stanton reduced prisoner rations to the same level that the Confederate army issued to its own soldiers. In theory this placed rebel prisoners on the same footing as Yankee prisoners in the South, who in theory received the same rations as Confederate soldiers. But in practice few southern soldiers ever got the official ration by 1864—the Union prisoners inevitably got even less—so most rebel captives in the North probably ate better than they had in their own army.
James M. McPherson, *Battle Cry of Freedom* (1988).

I wouldn't take prisoners. What sense is there in taking prisoners? That's chivalry. The French have destroyed my home and are coming to destroy Moscow; they have outraged and are outraging me at every second. They are my enemies, they are all criminals to my way of thinking. They must be put to death.
Leo Tolstoy, *War and Peace* (1865–69).

I have the honor to inform you that as I do not consider that your government has any right to detain me as a military prisoner, I have decided to escape from your custody. I have every confidence in the arrangements I have made with my friends outside, and I do not therefore expect to have another opportunity of seeing you. I therefore

take this occasion to observe that I consider your treatment of prisoners is correct and humane, and that I see no grounds for complaint. When I return to the British lines I will make a public statement to this effect. I have also to thank you personally for your civility to me, and to express the hope that we may meet again at Pretoria before very long, and under different circumstances. Regretting that I am unable to bid you a more ceremonious or a personal farewell. . . .
Winston Churchill's letter of December 10, 1899, to the Secretary of War of the South African Republic published after he made good his escape in his *London to Ladysmith via Pretoria* (1900).

The Egyptians had tortured him [Jonathan Etkes, an Israeli pilot] as a prisoner [during the 1956 Sinai Campaign]. "They were very rough. . . . They burned me with cigarettes." He pointed to a white spot on his cheek. "All my lips were burned, my nose, eyebrows, and ears. This was the easy part. They put surgical clamps on my tongue and started to turn them as you would open a sardine can, until you can't breathe anymore." They used syringes to give him shots all over his body, of what he did not know. They cut away dead flesh from his wounded leg without using anesthetic. "My head was as big as a watermelon. Electric shocks. I was completely naked. They put water on me to have good connections.
". . . they deserve some credit for the amount of hatred and the amount of satisfaction they drew from the torture." His eyes burned intensely beneath his bushy eyebrows. Then suddenly he guffawed as he remembered the positive side. After his release, a false rumor circulated that the Egyptians had castrated him, he said. A lot of Israeli women wanted to find out firsthand whether it was true.
David K. Shipler, *Arab and Jew* (1986).

prisoners of war, Korea
There were heroes in those prison camps, great heroes. There were but few rats.
General Mark Clark on North Korean POW camps, *U.S. News and World Report* (August 19, 1955).

Most shocking of all to American sensibilities in Korea and at home in the United States, the Communists proved ruthlessly indifferent to the taking of prisoners. A shudder of revulsion ran through the American nation at the discovery, in Korea, of the first groups of American prisoners shot dead by the roadside, their hands tied behind their back with barbed wire. It rapidly became apparent that the North Koreans served prisoners in such fashion whenever they had no explicit need for them alive, for propaganda or intelligence purposes.
Max Hastings, *The Korean War* (1987).

prisoners of war, Vietnam
When Major Kushner arrived at First Camp in January 1968, Robert had already been captive for two years. He was a rugged and intelligent corporal from a crack marine unit. . . .
Robert was convinced that he would soon be released. The Viet Cong had made it a practice to release, as examples, a few men who had cooperated with them and adopted the correct attitudes. Robert had done so. . . .
[Then] it dawned on him that he had been deceived—that he had already served his captor's purpose, and he wasn't going to be released. He stopped working and showed signs of severe depression: he refused food and lay on his bed in a fetal position, sucking his thumb. His fellow prisoners tried to bring him around. They hugged him, babied him and when this didn't work, tried to bring him out of his stupor with their fists. . . . After a few weeks it was apparent to Kushner that Robert was moribund:

although otherwise his gross physical shape was still better than most of the others. . . .
In the early hours of a November morning he lay dying in Kushner's arms. . . .

Hope of release sustained Robert. When he gave up hope, when he believed that all his efforts had failed and would continue to fail, he died.

Can a psychological state be lethal? I believe it can.
Martin E. P. Seligman, *Helplessness* (1975).

The next thing I knew, the man was out of the helicopter.
I turned around and I asked the folks what happened to him.
They told me he jumped out.
I said, "Naw, man. The man ain't jumped out."
The brother said, "Yes, he did. He one of those tough VC."
I didn't believe it. The brother was lying to me, really.
Haywood T. "The Kid" Kirkland quoted in Wallace Terry, *Bloods* (1984).

This future author of *Don Quixote* was a young officer in the Spanish army taken prisoner after the Battle of Lepanto in the 16th century. He spent seven years in an Algiers political prison. Same story: "Confess your crimes," "Discredit yourself," "Disavow your roots." He was tortured to disavow Christianity; he could get amnesty and go home if he would disavow it. I was made much the same offer. I was to disavow "American Imperialism." Good boy, Cervantes, you hung in too.
James Bond Stockdale, "In War, In Prison, In Antiquity," *Parameters* (December 1987).

Sometimes we'd get wounded prisoners, and we'd have to carry them to the medevac. The helicopters would take them away, but by that time they'd be dead, because we'd kill them first. If there was a firefight and some of us died, there'd be a lot of pain and hatred. Someone would shout, "VC wounded, we need some medicine." Whoever was pissed off that day—maybe they killed his friend—would say, "I've got the medicine for him." Psshow. It was difficult to protect a wounded prisoner. Sometimes we'd get them to the helicopters and the crew would throw them out. You'd see them flying down, like birds.
Angel Quintana quoted in Harry Mauer, *Strange Ground* (1989).

prisoners of war, World War II

At one place along the way we passed a band of Scottish Highlanders marching toward internment, blowing lustily all the while on bagpipes. A monocled officer led them, sporting a cane in place of his saber. Not one face carried a shadow of sadness. The more I see of them the more these men amaze me.
A Japanese reporter's description of British POWs from Singapore quoted in *Time* (March 2, 1942).

In a Tunisian town, American soldiers who could speak Italian heckled a batch of Italian prisoners. Finally, one Italian could contain himself no longer. "All right, laugh," he said, "but we're going to America. You're only going to Italy."
Time (May 10, 1943).

I got slugged in the jaw about every day, mostly for not being polite. To get to the toilet you had to ask the guard's permission politely, then thank him politely for the favor when you came back. If you were having dysentery, as most of us did at times, it meant a hell of a lot of politeness day and night.
Major Gregory "Pappy" Boyington, on his experience as a prisoner of the Japanese, quoted in *Time* (September 10, 1945).

Sorta rough, one American squealing on another American. Then again, Cookie, maybe that stoolie's not an American at all. Maybe he's a German the Krauts planted in this barracks. They do that sometimes. They put an agent in on us, a trained special-ist. Lots of loose information floating around a prison camp—not just whether some-body's trying to escape—what outfit we were with, where we were stationed, how our radar operates. Could be, couldn't it?

William Holden in *Stalag 17* (1953), directed by Billy Wilder; screenplay by Billy Wilder and Edwin Blum from the play by Donald Bevan and Edmund Trzcinski.

The men who greeted me were scarcely more than skeletons. . . .

Here was all that was left of my men of Bataan and Corregidor. The only sound was the occasional sniffle of a grown man who could not fight back the tears. As I passed slowly down the scrawny, suffering column, a murmur accompanied me as each man barely speaking above a whisper, said, "You're back," or "You made it," or "God bless you." I could only reply, "I'm a little late, but we finally came."

General Douglas MacArthur, on liberating American POWs in the Philippines, *Reminiscences* (1964).

[Stalin] spoke of having interviewed German prisoners and asking them why they killed women and children. When he received no satisfactory reply, he ordered them to be shot out of hand. It was one of his minor pleasures.

Robert Payne, *The Rise and Fall of Stalin* (1965).

One of the more effective things I found in dealing with the German prisoners [in North Africa] was to quote their German soldier's oath to them. A prisoner is always in a state of shock and somewhat ashamed of his position. If the interrogator struck the right chord, he often received co-operation. For instance, I would ask a German prisoner a question. He would refuse to answer and say that his soldier's duty would not let him answer. I would recite slowly to him the German soldier's oath, which said, "I swear before God and the German people unconditional obedience to my Fuhrer Adolf Hitler who has united the German people in National Socialism. I further swear that I will at all times be ready as a gallant soldier to lay down my life in fulfillment of this oath." I would then say to him, "But you didn't lay down your life. You have not fulfilled the oath. Stop talking to me about your soldier's duty." This was harsh but effective. Some broke down and then talked freely.

General Vernon Walters, *Silent Missions* (1978).

The word to kill [American] prisoners reached almost all subordinate units [during the Battle of the Bulge]. One company commander enjoined his men to "fight in the old SS spirit," and added: "I am not giving you orders to shoot prisoners of war, but you are all well-trained SS soldiers. You know what you should do with prisoners without me telling you that." A private recalled that not only were they to take no prisoners but "civilians who show themselves on the streets or at the windows will be shot without mercy." One non-commissioned officer urged his men to think of the thousands of German women and children buried in the rubble of German cities; then they would know "what you as SS men have to do in case you capture American soldiers."

Charles B. MacDonald, *A Time for Trumpets* (1985).

The greatest of all Hitler's mistakes was his treatment of Soviet POWs. Since the USSR had not signed the Geneva Convention, he felt under no obligation to treat them according to the rules of war, nor did he, allowing them to starve to death in appalling conditions. Once news of this reached the front, surrender ceased to be an attractive option. The last word on the whole sorry subject has been attributed to General

Guderian, who is said to have observed sadly: "We started to mistreat them too soon."
Alex de Jonge, *Stalin* (1986).

The Americans wanted their prisoner-of-war camps to operate smoothly, even if that meant allowing ardent Nazis to run German affairs inside the camps. When life in the camps failed to run smoothly, the problems, which usually stemmed from the struggles of anti-Nazi prisoners of war to avoid the harsh domination of the Nazis who controlled them, led the American authorities to associate the anti-Nazis with disorder. Order became more important than individual rights. From the beginning, American commanders and guards tended to brand anti-Nazis as trouble-makers.
Allen V. Koop, *Stark Decency* (1988).

At Stalag XXA, Rifleman Porter experienced the lengths to which starving men will go to steal food. While out on a working party one day he was offered two loaves of black bread in return for his shirt. Wolfing one down immediately he smuggled the other back into camp. That night he rested his head on his precious loaf but discovered next morning that someone had neatly sawn off both ends while he slept, leaving only the center portion. "In future I always ate anything as soon as I got it," he said.
David Rolf, *Prisoners of the Reich* (1988).

Ruggerio Purin, an Italian POW captured in Tunis, Africa, in June, 1943 . . . was sent to Camp Hill Field, Utah. . . . "I was treated better by the American Army than by my own Italian Army."
E. B. Shukert and B. S. Scibetta, *War Brides of World War II* (1988).

procurement

If you are going to try to go to war, or to prepare for war, in a capitalist country, you have got to let business make money out of the process or business won't work.
Henry L. Stimson and McGeorge Bundy, *On Active Service in Peace and War* (1947). This was Secretary of War Stimson's diary entry for August 28, 1940.

You just sat there thinking that this piece of hardware had 400,000 components, all of them built by the lowest bidder.
Apollo 15 Astronaut David Scott, thought while waiting for blastoff, *Time* (May 19, 1978).

Take the profit out of war.
Bernard M. Baruch, "Taking the Profit out of War," *Atlantic Monthly* (January 1926).

Move over, $7,000 coffeepots! Stand aside, $400 hammers! We now have the $792 doormat. . . .
The poor taxpayer may wipe his shoes on a $3 doormat when he goes home, but not the Navy. It is, damn the cost, full feet ahead on a doormat you would be ashamed to get muddy.
Senator William Proxmire, quoted in *The New York Times* (October 4, 1985).

Fraud has never been, and is not now, the major problem. For every dollar diverted by fraud, there may be a hundred wasted by congressional patronage and micro-management, military intransigence and inefficiency, contractor mismanagement and cost padding, and pure bureaucratic bungling at the Pentagon.
Robert Higgs, "Military Scandals Again," *The Wall Street Journal* (June 27, 1988).

profession of arms

The man who devotes himself to war should regard it as a religious order into which he enters. He should have nothing, know no concern other than his troops, and should hold himself honored in his profession.
Marshal Maurice de Saxe, *Reveries Upon the Art of War* (1757).

I'm a professional soldier: I fight when I have to, and am very glad to get out of it when I haven't to. You're only an amateur: You think fighting's an amusement.
George Bernard Shaw, *Arms and the Man*, Act III (1894).

Neither war nor love should be made a profession. Professional armies beside national armies are like courtesans beside mothers.
René Quinton, *Soldier's Testament* (1930).

It has often been remarked that the soldier, unlike the followers of other professions, has but rare opportunities to practice his profession. Indeed it might even be argued that in a literal sense the profession of arms is not a profession at all but merely "casual employment."
B. H. Liddell Hart, *Thoughts on War* (1944).

Your mission remains fixed, determined, inviolable—it is to win our wars. Everything else in your professional career is but a corollary to this vital dedication. All other public purposes, all other public projects, all other public needs, great or small, will find others for their accomplishment; but you are the ones who are trained to fight; yours is the profession of arms—the will to win, the sure knowledge that in war there is no substitute for victory; that if you lose, the nation will be destroyed; that the very obsession of your public service must by Duty-Honor-Country. Others will debate the controversial issues, national and international, which divide man's minds; but serene, calm, aloof, you stand as the nation's war guardian, as its lifeguard from the raging tide of international conflict; as its gladiator in the arena of battle. . . .
You are the leaven which binds together the entire fabric of our national system of defense. From your ranks come the great captains who hold the nation's destiny in their hands the moment the war tocsin sounds.
General Douglas MacArthur, speech at West Point, May 12, 1962, reprinted in his *Reminiscences* (1964).

The quintessential "strategic lesson learned" from the Vietnam war is that we must once again become masters of the profession of arms. The American people deserve, demand and expect nothing less of their Army.
Harry G. Summers, Jr., *On Strategy* (1982).

To a man, professional soldiers despised terrorists, and each would dream about getting them in an even-up-battle—the idea of the Field of Honor had never died for the real professionals. It was the place where the ultimate decision was made on the basis of courage and skill, on the basis of manhood itself, and it was this concept that marked the professional soldier as a romantic, a person who truly believed in the rules.
Tom Clancy, *Patriot Games* (1987).

promotion

'Tis the curse of service,
Preferment goes by letter and affection,
And not by old gradation, where each second
Stood heir to the first.
William Shakespeare, *Othello*, Act I (1605).

Every French soldier carries in his cartridge-pouch the baton of a marshal of France.
Attributed to Napoleon I.

All the ambitious minds in a democratic army ardently long for war, because war makes vacancies [for promotion] available and at last allows violations of the rule of seniority, which is the one privilege natural to a democracy. We thus arrive at the strange conclusion that of all the armies those which long for war most ardently are the democratic ones, but that of all people those most deeply attached to peace are the democratic nations.
Alexis de Tocqueville, *Democracy in America* (1835).

The judicious selection of generals is one of the most delicate points in the science of government and one of the most essential parts of the military policy of a state. Unfortunately, this choice is influenced by so many petty passions, that chance, rank, age, favor, party spirit, jealousy, will have as much to do with it as the public interest and justice.
General Antoine Henri Jomini, *Summary of the Art of War* (1838).

Forward! If any man is killed, I'll made him a corporal!
Captain Anda R. Chaffee, order to men of the 6th Cavalry in 1874, quoted in Fairfax Downey, *Indian Fighting Army* (1943).

I am free to confess to you that my hope and ambition in life is to live long enough to see this son made a General Officer, and I feel I am placing my entire life, as it were, in your hands for consideration, and I trust you can see your way clear, dear General Pershing, to give him the recommendation necessary to advance him to the grade of Brigadier General.
Mary P. MacArthur, letter of June 12, 1918 to General John J. Pershing on behalf of her son, Colonel Douglas MacArthur. After the promotion was made, she wrote again to Pershing on June 29, 1918, thanking him and assuring him that "You will *not* find our Boy wanting!" quoted in D. Clayton James, *The Years of MacArthur*, I (1970).

Soldiers pay with their lives for mistakes in promotion.
René Quinton, *Soldier's Testament* (1930).

[After the fall of France, Hitler awarded] field marshals' batons to twelve generals and a special king-size one to Goering, who was given the newly created rank of Reich Marshal of the Greater German Reich, which put him above all the others. . . . This promiscuous award of field-marshalships—the Kaiser had named only five field marshals from the officer corps during all of World War I and not even Ludendorff had been made one—undoubtedly helped to stifle any latent opposition to Hitler among the generals such as had threatened to remove him on at least three occasions in the past. In achieving this and in debasing the value of the highest military rank by raising so many to it, Hitler acted shrewdly to tighten his hold over the generals.
William L. Shirer, *The Rise and Fall of the Third Reich* (1959).

The Secretary of the Army has just told me of Major Walters' promotion to Lieutenant Colonel and I am delighted to pass on this information to you. As you may or may not know the old Army custom is to place the insignia in a glass of hard liquor and require the newly promoted officer to drain the glass in one swallow. Since Walters is a teetotaler, you may have to use milk or water.
General George C. Marshall, 1950 letter to W. Averell Harriman, quoted in Vernon Walters, *Silent Missions* (1978).

By good fortune in the game of military snakes and ladders, I found myself general.
Sir William Slim, *Unofficial History* (1959).

Those of you who regard my profession of political life with some disdain should remember that it made it possible for me to move from being an obscure lieutenant in the United States Navy to Commander-in-Chief in fourteen years with very little technical competence.
President John F. Kennedy, speech at University of North Carolina, October 12, 1961.

We make generals today on the basis of their ability to write a damned letter. Those kinds of men can't get us ready for war.
General Lewis B. "Chesty" Puller, USMC, quoted in Burke Davis, *Marine!* (1962).

propaganda

Good propaganda must keep well ahead of actual political events. It must act as a pacemaker of policy and mold public opinion, without appearing to do so.
German General Erich Ludendorff, *Ludendorff's Own Story* (1919).

Propaganda, as inverted patriotism, draws nourishment from the sins of the enemy. If there are no sins, invent them! The aim is to make the enemy appear so great a monster that he forfeits the rights of a human being. He cannot bring a libel action, so there is no need to stick at trifles.
Sir Ian Hamilton, *The Soul and Body of an Army* (1921).

"The freedom of Europe," "The war to end war," "The overthrow of militarism," "The cause of civilization"—most people believe so little now in anything or anyone that they would find it hard to understand the simplicity and intensity of faith with which these phrases were once taken among our troops, or the certitude felt by hundreds of thousands of men who are now dead that if they were killed their monument would be a new Europe.
Charles E. Montague, *Disenchantment* (1922).

The great mass of the people ... will more easily fall victim to a big lie than to a small one.
Adolf Hitler, *Mein Kampf* (1924).

But no amount of genius spent on the creation of propaganda will lead to success if a fundamental principle is not forever kept in mind. Propaganda must confine itself to a very few points, and repeat them endlessly. Here, as with so many things in this world, persistence is the first and foremost condition of success.
Adolf Hitler, *Mein Kampf* (1924).

Think of the press as a great keyboard on which the government can play.
Paul Joseph Goebbels, *Time* (March 27, 1933).

The propagandist's purpose is to make one set of people forget that certain other sets of people are human.
Aldous Huxley, *The Olive Tree* (1937).

It does not greatly matter that nearly all books by Communists are propaganda. Most books are propaganda, direct or indirect. The trouble is that Communist writers are obliged to claim infallibility for their Party Chiefs. As a result Communist literature tends more and more to become a mechanism for explaining away mistakes.
George Orwell, *New Leader* (July 8, 1938).

Why is propaganda so much more successful when it stirs up hatred than when it tries to stir up friendly feeling?
Bertrand Russell, *The Conquest of Happiness* (1936).

The story that he [Rommel] had kept up his classics and was a keen archaeologist who spent his scanty leisure in digging for Roman remains was a production of the propagandists. [General] von Esebeck was responsible for it. "Some of us had been scratching about and had turned up some bits of Roman pottery," he told me. "We were looking at them when Rommel came along. What he actually said, when we showed them to him, was: 'What the hell do you want with all that junk?' But you can't tell that from the photograph!"

Desmond Young, *Rommel* (1950).

The British also dropped a few leaflets [on Berlin early in World War II] saying that "the war which Hitler started will go on, and it will last as long as Hitler does." This was good propaganda, but the thud of exploding bombs was better.

William L. Shirer, *The Rise and Fall of the Third Reich* (1959).

Modern man is aggressive because he is fearful. Almost all propaganda is designed to create fear. Heads of governments and other officials know that a frightened people is easier to govern, will forfeit rights it would otherwise defend, is less likely to demand a better life, and will agree to millions and millions being spent on "Defense".

J. B. Priestley, *Outcries and Asides* (1974).

Propaganda is that branch of the art of lying which consists in nearly deceiving your friends without quite deceiving your enemies.

F. M. Cornford, *New Statesman* (September 15, 1978).

It is almost impossible to locate an offensive-minded, realistic, hard-boiled thinker in the [American] army high command. To a suggestion that propaganda might be utilized as a military weapon, they throw up their arms in horror, exclaiming: "Of course, we wouldn't think of using a Nazi method!"

Harrison E. Salisbury, writing of the period immediately following the Pearl Harbor attack, in *A Journey for Our Times* (1983).

Jane Fonda had gone to Hanoi [during the Vietnam War] to propagandize with the Communists and had become a liberal heroine. I believe she was a political whore.

Barry M. Goldwater, *Goldwater* (1988).

The battle of Okinawa began on Easter Sunday, April 1st [1945]. We heard about it at Ulithi, standing around outside of the ready room, where a loudspeaker had been hung on palm tree. Tokyo Rose told us that the assault forces had landed, but had been repulsed; many ships had been sunk. On the second day she addressed our squadron specifically; she knew that 232 was coming, she said, but they would be ready for us. I felt ridiculously melodramatic, standing there being threatened on the radio; it was like stumbling onto the set of a B-grade spy movie, where an Oriental hisses, "Yankee dog, you die!" But I also felt a bit important—at least in Tokyo they had heard of us. It made up a little for not having bombed Tokyo.

Samuel Hynes, *Flights of Passage* (1988).

public opinion

Nothing is more dangerous in wartime than to live in the temperamental atmosphere of a Gallup Poll, always feeling one's pulse and taking one's temperature.

Winston Churchill, speech in the House of Commons, September 30, 1941.

In our democracy where the government is truly an agent of the popular will, military policy is dependent on public opinion, and our organization for war will be good

or bad as the public is well informed or poorly informed regarding the factors that bear on the subject.
General George C. Marshall, "Our Most Serious Military Problem," *Harper's* (November 1950).

Eisenhower explained to Montgomery that, whatever the merits of a single thrust, he could hardly hold back Patton and stop the U.S. Third Army in its tracks. "The American people," said the Supreme Commander, "would never stand for it, and public opinion wins wars." Montgomery heatedly disagreed. "Victories win wars," he announced. "Give people victory and they won't care who won it."
Cornelius Ryan, *A Bridge Too Far* (1974).

Some members of the military profession have come to believe that the armed forces of the United States should not be ordered into war without a prior guarantee of irrevocable public support. They insist on a letter of credit of the sort that is demanded before shipping merchandise to dubious importers from lawless countries. The implicit belief is, of course, that there was no causal link between the *manner* in which the Vietnam War was fought and the increasing aversion of the decently patriotic among the public.
Edward N. Luttwak, "Low-Intensity Warfare," *Parameters* (December 1983).

public relations

Ancient generals, as soon as . . . an accident happened, either showed that it resulted from some natural cause or interpreted it to their advantage. Caesar, falling in Africa as he left his ship, said: "Africa, I seize you."
Niccolò Machiavelli, *The Art of War* (1520).

The publishers have to understand that we're never more than a miscalculation away from war and that there are things we're doing that we just can't talk about.
President John F. Kennedy quoted in Pierre Salinger, *With Kennedy* (1966).

Personal publicity in war can be a drawback because it may affect a man's thinking. A commander may not have sought it; it may have been forced upon him by zealous subordinates or imaginative war correspondents. Once started, however, it is hard to keep in check. In the early days of a war, when little about the various commanders is known to the public, and some general or admiral does a good and perhaps spectacular job, he gets a head start in publicity. Anything he does thereafter tends towards greater headline value than the same thing done by others, following the journalistic rule that "names make news." Thus his reputation snowballs, and soon, probably against his will, he has become a colorful figure, credited with fabulous characteristics over and above the competence in war command for which he had been conditioning himself all his life.
His fame may not have gone to his head, but there is nevertheless danger of this. Should he get to identifying himself with the figure as publicized, he may subconsciously start thinking in terms of what his reputation calls for, rather than of how best to meet the actual problems confronting him.
Admiral Raymond Spruance quoted in Oliver Warner, *Command at Sea* (1976).

Unchallenged, the air briefer was able to present the air war [in Vietnam] in terms of the Pentagon's choosing. Thus the bridge at Co Trai became part of the "Phu Ly-Co Trai military complex"; a fishing junk was a "waterborne logistics craft"; targets were hit with "surgical precision." Not once did he say, "Today U. S. planes ran into such heavy antiaircraft fire that they dumped their bombs which landed God knows where and got out of there as fast as possible." Instead, he intoned: "Today U. S. warplanes

cratered the approaches to the Co Trai bridge." There were frequent announcements of "cratered approaches," which journalists duly reported.
Zalin Grant, *Over the Beach* (1986).

When the Soviets make unilateral announcements, Moscow reaps a tremendous p.r. benefit, and I'm left with the reality—continued huge Soviet military capabilities. It's difficult to get the public to realize that unilateral pronouncements uncodified by treaty are easy to turn around. ... I'm routinely criticized for a supposedly overly simplistic insistence on assessing capabilities rather than intentions. Well, we hope Gorbachev means what he says, but if he changes his mind and we have reduced our own military strength on the basis of a rhetoric of intentions when his capabilities haven't really changed much at all, then we could be in big trouble fast.
General John Galvin, NATO Commander, *Time* (May 29, 1989).

pursuit

When an enemy army is in flight, you must either build a golden bridge for it or stop it with a wall of steel.
Napoleon I, speaking in 1813, quoted in J. C Herold, *The Mind of Napoleon* (1955).

Next to victory, the act of pursuit is the most important in war.
Karl von Clausewitz, *On War* (1832).

Never give up the pursuit so long as your men have strength to follow, for an army routed, if hotly pursued becomes panic stricken, and can be defeated by half their numbers. To move swiftly, strike vigorously, and secure all the fruits of victory is the secret of successful war.
G. F. R. Henderson, *The Science of War* (1905). Henderson credited General "Stonewall" Jackson as the originator of this principle.

Strenuous, unrelaxing pursuit is therefore as imperative after a battle as is courage during it.
Alfred Thayer Mahan, *Naval Strategy* (1911).

In pursuit you must always stretch the possibilities to the limit. The troops, having beaten the enemy, will want to rest. They must be given as objectives not those you think they will reach, but the farthest they can possibly reach.
General Archibald Wavell quoted in Allan A. Michie, *Retreat to Victory* (1942).

In a pursuit ship you're a one-man army, not a taxi driver. You're on your own— you don't have to wait for orders from a guy who can't fly they call a bombardier.
A fighter pilot in *Air Force* (1943), directed by Howard Hawks; screenplay by Dudley Nichols.

The zest of the Gurkhas in their pursuit of the retreating Japanese [in Burma] has been compared to that of terriers after rats. One battalion commander offered a reward for each head brought in, and one havildar [sergeant] returned with six bloody ears in his haversack. These he placed in a neat row on the ground. The commandant inspected them and asked what had happened to the rest of the heads. "Too heavy to carry, sahib," said the havildar.
Byron Forwell, *The Gurkhas* (1984).

quarters

No soldier shall, in time of peace be quartered in any house, without the consent of the Owner, nor in time of war, but in a manner to be prescribed by law.
Constitution of the United States, Amendment III (1791).

Single men in barricks don't grow into plaster saints.
Rudyard Kipling, *Tommy* (1890).

And, even in peace and at home, what was the sanitary condition of the [British] Army [at mid-nineteenth century]? The mortality in the barracks was, she [Florence Nightingale] found, nearly double the mortality in civil life. "You might as well take 1100 men every year out upon Salisbury Plain and shoot them," she said.
Lytton Strachey, *Eminent Victorians* (1918).

Here the Field Marshal has slept, before the battle of Tannenberg, after the battle of Tannenberg and, between you and me, during the battle of Tannenberg also.
Colonel Max Hoffman, showing a visitor Field Marshal Hindenburg's quarters on the World War I Russian front, quoted in Rudolf Olden, *Hindenburg* (1935); Barbara W. Tuchman, *The Guns of August* (1962).

Bomber Command is in the building of a famous old school for girls. . . . When the Americans arrived . . . the famous story about the bells originated. The men moved into the girls' dormitory, and after they had retired the first night, the officers heard buzzes and bells ringing in their quarters, they being in the old administrative offices. They roused themselves and traced the calls until they found their origin, which was in the sleeping rooms formerly occupied by the girl students. In these rooms were little signs above the push buttons, reading, "If mistress is desired, ring bell."
Captain Harry C. Butcher, *My Three Years With Eisenhower* (1946).

As tents were in short supply, the maximum number of recruits were allotted to each one. . . . I had no idea that it had twenty-two separate pieces of canvas sewn together to form the roof. The flap was the point of entry and, with twenty-two men stampeding to get in, somebody had to get the flap division as his portion of territory. I got it. This meant that I couldn't lie down at night until everyone was in the tent. There were forty-four feet built up in tangled layers converging in the general direction of the center pole. Nights were a nightmare to me and I dreaded them. Outside the tent flap within a yard of my head stood a urinal tub, and throughout the night boozy types would stagger and lunge towards the tent flap in order to urinate. I got showered every time and, worst of all, it became a joke. At last revulsion overcame me, and one night I suddenly went berserk and lashed out violently at someone. There followed a riotous eruption and the tent collapsed. Luckily more tents became available, and from then on I managed to avoid the entry flap.
George Coppard, *With a Machine Gun to Cambrai* (1969).

There was a joke that made the rounds of wartime Washington. A man crossing the Fourteenth Street bridge looked down into the Potomac and saw another man drowning. "What's your name and address?" he shouted to him and then ran off to see the drowning man's landlord. He asked to rent the now-vacant room and was told it was already taken. "But I just left him drowning in the river," he protested. "That's right," the landlord replied, "but the man who pushed him in got here first."
David Brinkley, *Washington Goes to War* (1988).

racism

It is the declared policy of the President that there shall be equality of treatment and opportunity for all persons in the armed services without regard to race, color, religion or national origin.
President Harry S. Truman, Executive Order No. 9981 of July 26, 1948. This order formally ended racial segregation in the United States Armed Forces.

Prewitt . . . sat down in one of the backless chairs and leaned against the wall . . . fingering the mouthpiece in his pocket that was his own and that he always carried with him. He had bought it . . . with a crapgame winnings and it was the mouthpiece he had used to play the Taps at Arlington. Pulling it out now and looking into the ruby bell as if it were a crystal ball brought that day back to him. The President himself had been there, with all his aides and guards, leaning on the arm of one of them. There had been a colored bugler who played the echo to his own Taps from the stand. The Negro was a better bugler, but because he was not white he had been stationed in the hills to play the echo.
James Jones, *From Here to Eternity* (1951).

There are no white or colored signs on the foxholes or graveyards of battle.
President John F. Kennedy, message to Congress, June 19, 1963.

Dan Inouye was a chubby-faced eighteen-year-old when he volunteered for military service in early 1943 along with 10,000 other Hawaiian *Nisei*. . . . He was barely twenty when he won a battlefield commission. Nine days before the end of the war in Italy he led an assault against a German position. . . . Forty yards from the German bunkers, he stood up and threw a grenade into a machine gun nest, cutting down the crew with his tommy gun, but taking a bullet in the abdomen in return. . . . A German fired a rifle grenade from 10 yards range and it all but tore off Inouye's right arm. . . . Inouye, who lost his arm, received the Distinguished Service Cross. Earlier he had been awarded the Bronze Star. His hopes of becoming a physician shattered by the loss of his arm, Inouye turned to law, became the first Congressman from Hawaii and was elected to the Senate in 1962. But on his way home in 1945, Capt. Dan Inouye, his empty sleeve pinned to a beribboned tunic, was denied a haircut in a San Francisco barbership. "We don't serve Japs here," the barber said.
Bill Hosokawa, *Nisei* (1969).

Unlike the American Deep South, where many of the blacks lived, Britain was not a segregated country. Blacks could enter pubs, shops, dance halls and other public facilities. But the [World War II] U.S. Army authorities in Britain were sure that this would lead to trouble. White GIs were use to traveling, drinking and dating girls without coming into contact with blacks. The Army therefore practiced its own form of discreet segregation by giving black and white units leave passes on different days of the week. Towns near American bases were "black" one night and "white" the next.
David Dimbleby and David Reynolds, *An Ocean Apart* (1988).

rape

Have they not divided the prey; to every man a damsel or two?
The Bible, Judges 5:30.

The greatest pleasure is to vanquish your enemies and chase them before you, to rob them of their wealth and see those dear to them bathed in tears, to ride their horses and clasp to your bosom their wives and daughters.
Genghis Khan, quoted in James Chambers, *The Devil's Horsemen* (1979).

War is pusillanimously carried out in this degenerate age; quarter is given; towns are taken and people spared; even in a storm, a woman can hardly hope for the benefit of a rape.
Lord Chesterfield, in a 1757 letter, quoted in Dale O. Smith, *U.S. Military Doctrine* (1955).

Attorney General Knox, having been asked by Roosevelt to construct a defense [of taking the Isthmus of Panama from Colombia in 1903] is said to have remarked, "Oh, Mr. President, do not let so great an achievement suffer from any taint of legality." At another point, during a Cabinet meeting, Roosevelt talked of the bitter denunciations in the press, then entered into a long formal statement of his position. When he had finished, the story goes, he looked about the table, finally fixing his eye on Elihu Root. "Well," he demanded, "have I answered the charges? Have I defended myself?"
"You certainly have, Mr. President," replied Root, who was known for his wit. "You have shown that you were accused of seduction and you have conclusively proved that you were guilty of rape."
David McCullough, *The Path Between the Seas* (1977).

Certainly the most ironic sexual assault of this entire period [1945] of rape and plunder occurred in the village of Prieros [near Berlin].... The village had been bypassed by ... advancing troops.... Finally the [Red Army] soldiers arrived. Among the Germans they found were two women.... Else Kloptsch and her friend Hildegard Radusch, "the man of the house," [who] had almost starved to death waiting for this moment. Hildegard had dedicated her whole life to furthering Marxism: the arrival of the Russians meant the realization of a dream. When the Soviet troops entered the village one of their first acts was the brutal rape of Communist Hildegard Radusch.
Cornelius Ryan, *The Last Battle* (1966).

People who are vigorous and brutal often find war enjoyable, provided that it is a victorious war and that there is not too much interference with rape and plunder. This is a great help in persuading people that wars are righteous.
Bertrand Russell, *Unpopular Essays* (1950).

readiness

There has been a constant struggle on the part of the military element to keep the end—fighting, or readiness to fight—superior to mere administrative considerations.... The military man, having to do the fighting, considers that the chief necessity; the administrator equally naturally tends to think the smooth running of the machine the most admirable quality.
Alfred Thayer Mahan, *Naval Administration and Warfare* (1908).

If we continue [training] at a lowered tempo, there will be progressive deterioration of combat readiness. We're just like a football team, and if you don't practice during the week, you may not be able to play the game on Saturday.
Admiral Thomas H. Moorer, Chairman, Joint Chiefs of Staff, *Time* (December 10, 1973).

Admiral Gorshkov, the head of the Soviet Navy, once said that the job of senior people in defense is to try to make the total capability greater than the sum of individual parts. The way we have developed over many years, in the Pentagon and in Congress, we have just the opposite. Our total capability is less than the sum of the individual parts.
General David C. Jones, *The Washington Post* (November 30, 1982).

[The U.S. military] for the last 40 years have concentrated on deterring nuclear conflict and the "big war" on the plains of Europe. . . . We are well prepared for the least likely conflicts and poorly prepared for the most likely.
Representative Dan Daniel, *U.S. News and World Report* (November 3, 1986).

Our force posture is back where it used to be: pathetic.
John Thompson of the Canadian Institute for Strategic Studies, *The New York Times* (June 30, 1989).

rebellion

A little rebellion, now and then, is a good thing, and as necessary in the political world as storms in the physical. . . . It is a medicine necessary for the sound health of government.
Thomas Jefferson, January 30, 1787 letter to James Monroe, reprinted in *The Writings of Thomas Jefferson*, VI, ed. A. E. Bergh (1853).

The only justification of rebellion is success.
Thomas B. Reed, speech in the House of Representatives, April 12, 1878.

reconnaissance

Agitate the enemy and ascertain the pattern of his movement. Determine his dispositions and so ascertain the field of battle. Probe him and learn where his strength is abundant and where deficient.
Sun Tzu, *The Art of War* (4th century B.C.).

Knowledge of the country is to a general what a rifle is to an infantryman and what the rules of arithmetic are to a geometrician. If he does not know the country he will do nothing but make gross mistakes. Without this knowledge his projects, be they otherwise admirable, become ridiculous and often impracticable.
Frederick the Great, *Instructions for His Generals* (1747).

To inform, and, therefore, to reconnoiter, this is the first and constant duty of the advance guard.
Marshal Ferdinand Foch, *Precepts and Judgments* (1920).

They called the operation a "reconnaissance in force," a term often used to minimize disappointment over the failure of an attack.
Ned Russell, *Springboard to Berlin* (1943).

One young fellow from New York . . . he'd gotten into a tiff with his captain, some disagreement, and he'd stood his ground. So the captain saw to it that he went out on every patrol. He'd come in from one and go right out on the next one. That meant he was condemned to death, and eventually he caught one in the butt, and it ranged up through his stomach. He died two days later. I saw him when they brought him in. Just pitiful.
Isadore Feldman, speaking of the U.S. Army in the Pacific during World War II, quoted in Peter Manso, *Mailer* (1985).

I'm not against the militarization of space. We have been militarizing space with reconnaissance satellites since the 1960s, and they're worth their weight in gold.
Carl Sagan, *The Christian Science Monitor* (January 15, 1985).

recruitment

I beseech you be careful what captains of Horse you choose, what men be mounted: a few honest men are better than numbers.
Oliver Cromwell, 1643 letter to William Springe, reprinted in Thomas Carlyle, *Letters and Speeches of Oliver Cromwell* (1845).

A few good men are preferable to a number of recruits of inferior material.
Brigadier General Jacob Zeihin, Commandant of the U.S. Marine Corps, admonishing an officer who met his recruit quota with men of low quality on April 1, 1872, quoted in Allan R. Millett, *Semper Fidelis* (1980).

Your King and Country need you.
Text of a 1914 British World War I recruiting poster, which had a portrait of Field Marshal Horatio Kitchener pointing a finger at the viewer. This led Margot Asquith, then the wife of the British Prime minister, to remark, "If Kitchener was not a great man, he was, at least, a great poster"; quoted in Philip Magnus, *Kitchener* (1958).

The Army is very full just at present. Things will be much easier when we have had some casualties.
Evelyn Waugh, *Put Out More Flags* (1942).

If we persuade intelligent youth to hold aloof from the Army in peace, we ought not to complain if we are not properly led in war.
Lord Moran, *The Anatomy of Courage* (1945).

I was in the Victoria Library in Toronto in 1945, studying a Latin poet, and all of a sudden I thought, "War can't be this bad." So I walked out and enlisted.
Lester B. Pearson quoted in Robinson Beal, *The Pearson Phenomenon* (1964).

Join the Army, see the world, meet interesting people and kill them.
Anti-Vietnam War slogan of the late 1960s.

The Army's been criticized for enlisting poor-quality people. . . . Roughly one third can't make it through a three-year enlistment. That's because we have high standards. We're pretty demanding. We discharge one third because they can't meet those standards, then make our Army out of the two thirds who can.
General Frederick J. Kroesen, *U.S. News & World Report* (August 9, 1982).

regular army and navy

They aren't forgotten because they haven't died. They're living right out there—Collingwood and the rest—and they'll keep on living as long as the regiment lives. The pay is $13 a month. The diet, beans and eggs—may be horsemeat before this campaign is over. They fight over cards or rot-gut whiskey but share the last drop in their canteens. The faces may change. Names. But they're there. They're the regiment—the regular Army—now and 50 years from now.
John Wayne in *Fort Apache* (1948), directed by John Ford; screenplay by Frank S. Nugent.

While I was studying law 'n' old Keefer here was writing his play for the Theater Guild, and Willie here was on the playing fields of Princeton, all that time these birds we call regulars—these stuffy, stupid Prussians, in the Navy and the Army—were manning guns. Course they weren't doing it to save mom from Hitler, they were doing it for dough, like everybody else does what they do. Question is, in the last analysis—last analysis—*what* do you do for dough? Old Yellowstain, for dough, was standing guard on this fat dumb and happy country of ours. Meantime me, I was advancing my little free non-Prussian life for dough. Of course, we figured in those days, only fools

go into armed service. Bad pay, no millionaire future, and you can't call your mind or body your own. Not for sensitive intellectuals. So when all hell broke loose and the Germans started running out of soap and figured, well it's time to come over and melt down old Mrs. Greenwald—who's gonna stop them? Not her boy Barney. Can't stop a Nazi with a law book. So I dropped the law books and ran to learn how to fly. Stout fellow. Meantime, and it took a year and a half before I was any good, who was keeping Mama out of the soap dish? Captain Queeg.
Herman Wouk, *The Caine Mutiny* (1951).

research and development

[The U.S. Army] Air Corps ... does not, at this time, feel justified in obligating funds for basic jet propulsion research and experimentation.
Brigadier General George H. Brett, 1941 letter to Robert Goddard, quoted in Milton Lehman, *This High Man: The Life of Robert Goddard* (1963).

We have spent $2 billion on the greatest scientific gamble in history—and won.
President Harry S. Truman on the atomic bomb, *Time* (August 13, 1945).

If you turned over the problem of stopping Soviet tanks to small engineering outfits and machine shops, to little companies in Silicon Valley, they'd figure out a way to do it. I don't know what it could look like. I couldn't begin to imagine. But I'll tell you one thing: It wouldn't look anything like what the Pentagon is doing now.
Edward Luttwak, "The Strategy of Survival," *American Heritage* (July/August 1988).

reserves

It is better to have several bodies of reserves than to extend your front too much.
Vegetius, *De Re Militari* (378 A.D.).

If a little help reaches you in the action itself, it determines the turn of fortune for you . The enemy is discouraged and his excited imagination sees the help as being at least twice as strong as it really is.
Frederick the Great, *Instructions for His Generals* (1747).

The system of holding out a reserve as long as possible for independent action when the enemy has used his own, ought to be applied downwards. Each battalion should have its own, each regiment its own, firmly maintained.
Ardant du Picq, *Battle Studies* (1868).

Success in battle turns, as a rule, upon the skillful employment of reserves.
G. F. R. Henderson, *The Battle of Spicheren (1909)*.

In the battle in line ... [reserves] become warehouses into which one dips to replace the wear and tear as it occurs. ...
In the battle of maneuvers, the reserve is a sledgehammer planned and carefully preserved to execute the only action from which any decisive result is expected: the final attack. The reserve is meanwhile husbanded with the utmost caution, in order that the tool may be as strong, the blow as violent, as possible.
General Ferdinand Foch, *The Principles of War* (1918).

It is in the use and withholding of their reserves that the great commanders have generally excelled. After all, when once the last reserve has been thrown in, the commander's part is played. ... The event must be left to pluck and the fighting troops.
Winston Churchill, *Painting as a Pastime* (1932).

On May 16 [1940] Prime Minister Churchill flew to Paris to find out [about the Battle of France]. By the afternoon, when he drove to the Quai d'Orsay to see Premier Reynaud and General Gamelin, German spearheads were sixty miles west of Sedan, rolling along the undefended open country. Nothing very much stood between them and Paris, or between them and the Channel, but Churchill did not know this. "Where is the strategic reserve?" he asked Gamelin and, breaking into French, "*Où est la masse de manoeuvre?*" The Commander in Chief of the Allied armies turned to him with a shake of the head and a shrug and answered, "*Aucune*—there is none."

"I was dumbfounded," Churchill later related. It was unheard of that a great army, when attacked, held no troops in reserve. "I admit," says Churchill, "that this was one of the greatest surprises I have had in my life."
William L. Shirer, *The Rise and Fall of the Third Reich* (1959).

In mechanized warfare the value of a reserve force cannot be exaggerated, for increased mobility carries with it the power of effecting innumerable surprises, and the more the unexpected becomes possible the stronger must be the reserves.
J. F. C. Fuller, *Armoured Warfare (1943).*

retaliation

Union field commanders in South Carolina and Virginia carried out the only official retaliation for southern treatment of black prisoners. When Confederates at Charleston and near Richmond put captured Negroes to work on fortification under enemy fire in 1864, northern generals promptly placed an equal number of rebel prisoners at work on Union facilities under fire. This ended the Confederate practice.
James M. McPherson, *Battle Cry of Freedom* (1988).

Local defense will always be important. But there is no local defense which alone will contain the mighty land power of the Communist world. Local defense must be reinforced by the further deterrent of massive retaliatory power. A potential aggressor must know that he cannot always prescribe battle conditions that suit him. . . . The basic decision was to depend primarily upon a great capacity to retaliate, instantly, by means and at times of our own choosing.
Secretary of State John Foster Dulles, speech at the Council on Foreign Relations, January 12, 1954, quoted in Henry L. Trewhitt, *McNamara* (1971).

We had no use for the policy of the Gospels: if someone slaps you, just turn the other cheek. We had shown that anyone who slapped us on our cheek would get his head kicked off.
Nikita Khrushchev, *Khrushchev Remembers* (1970).

If the Soviet Union opted for a massive nuclear war, our option must be to return that hell in kind. And this option we would need to choose for so simple a reason as that we would not then have died for nothing, because it is better than nothing to rid the world of such monsters as would unleash such a war.
William F. Buckley, Jr., *The Wall Street Journal* (May 21, 1982).

retreat

When soldiers run away in war they never blame themselves; they blame their general or their fellow-soldiers.
Demosthenes, *Third Olynthiac* (4th century B.C.).

To a flying enemy, a silver bridge.
Miguel de Cervantes, *Don Quixote* (1605). It was a maxim of the ancient Roman army that "a golden bridge should be made for a flying enemy."

Retreats are always disastrous. They cost more lives and materiel than the bloodiest battles, with this additional difference, that in a battle the enemy loses approximately as much as you, while in a retreat you lose and he does not.
Napoleon I quoted in J. C. Herold, *The Mind of Napoleon* (1955).

[The test of a great general is] to know when to retreat; and to dare to do it.
Duke of Wellington quoted in Sir William Fraser, *Words on Wellington* (1889).

The officers should feel ... that firmness amid reverses is more honorable than enthusiasm in success,—since courage alone is necessary to storm a position, while it requires heroism to make a difficult retreat before a victorious and enterprising enemy, always opposing to him a firm and unbroken front. A fine retreat should meet with a reward equal to that given for a great victory.
General Antoine Henri Jomini, *Summary of the Art of War* (1838).

Napoleon's army was flying in disorder at its utmost possible speed out of Russia; that is to say, doing the very thing that every Russian most desired. What object was there in conducting all sorts of operations against the French when they were running away as fast as they could already? It would have been idle to stop men on the road, whose whole energies were bent on flight. Thirdly, it would have been absurd to lose men in destroying the French army when it was already, without external interference, perishing at such a rate.
Leo Tolstoy, *War and Peace* (1865–69).

Ulysses S. Grant, upon hearing of Jefferson Davis's prediction that the fate that crumpled Napoleon in Russia now awaited Sherman outside Atlanta, inquired: "Who is to furnish the snow for this Moscow retreat?"
Shelby Foote, *The Civil War*, III (1974).

Retreat, hell! We just got here.
Captain Lloyd S. Williams, USMC, at Belleau Wood, to a French officer who advised withdrawal, June 5, 1918, quoted in Allan R. Millet, *Semper Fidelis* (1980).

Retreat, hell! We're just attacking in another direction.
General Oliver P. Smith of the U.S. Marine Corps during the 1950 withdrawal from the Chosin Reservoir in Korea. According to Jim Wilson in *Retreat, Hell!* (1988), this statement was first made in response to a comment to the general by Lieutenant Colonel Winecoff: "This is a new experience for Marines, retreating." The general later repeated the remark at a press conference. According to Wilson, "hell" was never used by the general. "So somewhere between the press conference and headlines in the United States, the rallying cry, 'Retreat, hell....,' was born, and it is inaccurate." Donald Knox, in *The Korean War: Pusan to Chosin* (1985), quotes Smith: "You can't retreat or withdraw when you are surrounded. The only thing you can do is break out. When you break out, you attack. That's what we were doing."

In case of a forced retreat of Red Army units, all rolling stock must be evacuated; to the enemy must not be left a single engine, a single railway car, not a single pound of grain or a gallon of fuel.... In occupied regions conditions must be made unbearable for the enemy and all his accomplices.
Joseph Stalin, "scorched earth" radio broadcast on the German invasion of Russia, July 3, 1941, quoted in Isaac Deutscher, *Stalin*, 2nd ed. (1967).

The Egyptians could run to Egypt, the Syrians into Syria. The only place we could run was into the sea, and before we did that we might as well fight.
Golda Meir, Prime Minister of Israel, quoted in *Life* (October 3, 1969).

revenge

Vengeance is mine, I will repay, saith the Lord.
The Bible, Romans 12:19.

Thou shalt not avenge.
The Bible, Leviticus 19:18.

If you prick us, do we not bleed? if you tickle us, do we not laugh? if you poison us, do we not die? and if you wrong us, shall we not revenge?
William Shakespeare, *The Merchant of Venice*, Act III (1596).

In taking revenge, a man is but even with his enemy; but passing it over, he is superior.
Francis Bacon, "Of Revenge," *Essays* (1625).

When the hour of liberation strikes Europe, as strike it will, it will also be the hour of retribution.
Winston Churchill, speech in the House of Commons, September 8, 1942.

Properly speaking, there is no such thing as revenge. Revenge is an act which you want to commit when you are powerless and because you are powerless: as soon as the sense of impotence is removed, the desire evaporates also.
George Orwell, *Tribune* (November 9, 1945).

We had several thousand prisoners [in the 1967 six-day war], despite all our efforts not to accept them. The adjutant general assured me that the behavior of our troops toward them was good and that possible revenge takes only one form—the prisoners are being fed Israeli army "rations"!
Moshe Dayan, *Story of My Life* (1976).

reviews

I don't know what effect these men will have on the enemy, but, by God, they frighten me.
Duke of Wellington, traditionally attributed remark made upon reviewing his troops in Spain (1809).

There is no use in trying to elicit any complaint from the men after the manner the hurley burley inspecting officer does when he comes publicly through the quarters attended by his staff with the captain and first sergeant trooping at his heels; woe betide the unfortunate who was bold enough to step out and say he did not get enough to eat. The gimlet eye of the first sergeant would pierce him like an augur into a pine board; the angry captain would mark him, mark him for life. He might as well desert right away; it would be far better than the life he would get afterwards.
Letter from an ex-soldier to General John M. Schofield, January 15, 1890, quoted in Edward M. Coffman, *The Old Army* (1986).

In the 1914/18 war Sir Douglas Haig would inspect troops in complete silence. There is a story told that one of his staff suggested it would create a good impression if he would occasionally stop and speak to one or two men. He took the advice and asked one man: "Where did you start this war?" The astonished soldier replied: "I didn't start this war, sir; I think the Kaiser did." I understand that Haig gave it up after this encounter!
Field Marshal Viscount Montgomery of Alamein, *A History of Warfare* (1968).

General Pershing would have undoubtably accepted a nomination for the presidency, but the "Iron Commander" just didn't have the needed charisma to sell himself to the American public. As so many of the Doughboys put it, "I wasn't about to vote for a man who kept our regiment waiting three hours in the rain so he could review us."
Henry Berry, *Make the Kaiser Dance* (1978).

You may ask the reason for this display of military strength. It is to show that the Government has armed forces at its disposal. It may happen perchance, that armed forces may help some people to make up their minds.
Benito Mussolini, *Time* (March 17, 1923).

revolution

We hold these truths to be self-evident, that all men are created equal, that they are endowed by their Creator with certain unalienable Rights, that among these are Life, Liberty and the pursuit of Happiness. That to secure these rights, Governments are instituted among Men, deriving their just powers from the consent of the governed. That whenever any Form of Government becomes destructive of those ends, it is the Right of the People to alter or abolish it, and to institute a new Government, laying its foundation on such principles and organizing its power in such form, as to them shall seem most likely to effect their Safety and Happiness.
Thomas Jefferson, *Declaration of Independence*, July 4, 1776.

The right of revolution is an inherent one. When people are oppressed by their government, it is a natural right they enjoy to relieve themselves of the oppression, if they are strong enough, either by withdrawal from it, or by overthrowing it and substituting a government more acceptable.
President Ulysses S. Grant, *Personal Memoirs* (1885).

This country, with its institutions, belongs to the people who inhabit it. Whenever they shall grow weary of the existing government, they can exercise their constitutional right of amending it, or their revolutionary right to dismember or overthrow it.
President Abraham Lincoln, first Inaugural Address, March 4, 1861.

No people in the world ever did achieve their freedom by goody-goody talk and moral suasion: it being the immutable law that all revolution that will succeed must begin in blood.
Mark Twain, *A Connecticut Yankee at King Arthur's Court* (1889).

Revolutions are always verbose.
Leon Trotsky, *History of the Russian Revolution* (1932).

Revolution is delightful in the preliminary stages. So long as it's a question of getting rid of the people at the top.
Aldous Huxley, *Eyeless in Gaza* (1936).

A non-violent revolution is not a programme of seizure of power. It is a programme of transformation of relationships, ending in a peaceful transfer of power.
Mahatma Gandhi, *Non-violence in Peace and War* (1948).

Revolution is not a dinner party, not an essay, or a painting, nor a piece of embroidery; it cannot be advanced softly, gradually, carefully, considerately, respectfully, politely, plainly and modestly.
Mao Tse-tung quoted in *Time* (December 18, 1950).

The successful revolutionary is a statesman, the unsuccessful one a criminal.
Erich Fromm, *Escape from Freedom* (1941).

I began revolution with 82 men. If I had [to] do it again, I'd do it with 10 or 15 and absolute faith and plan of action.
Fidel Castro, *The New York Times* (April 22, 1959).

Every revolution evaporates and leaves behind only the slime of a new bureaucracy.
Franz Kafka, *Newsweek* (October 14, 1968).

Those who make peaceful revolution impossible will make violent revolution inevitable.
President John F. Kennedy, speech at the White House, March 13, 1962.

The most radical revolutionary will become a conservative the day after the revolution.
Hannah Arendt, *The New Yorker* (September 12, 1970).

All successful revolutions are the kicking in of a rotten door.
John Kenneth Galbraith, *The Age of Uncertainty* (1977).

Richthofen, Baron Manfred von (1892–1918)

The pilot of one of the hostile machines which was brought down in combat was the well-known German airman and fighter Rittmeister Freiherr von Richthofen, who claimed to have brought down eighty Allied machines. His body has today been buried with full military honors.
British communiqué of April 22, 1918, announcing the death of the "Red Baron," quoted in William E. Burrows, *Richthofen* (1969). According to Burrows, "Many letters were sent to London newspapers, however, which protested what their writers considered too elaborate a burial for a Hun, even a noble Hun. Some German newspapers attacked the burial for the opposite reason, charging that it had been an act of hypocrisy."

What a man he was! The others, admittedly, were doing their share, but they had wives at home, children, a mother or a profession. And only on rare occasions could they forget it. But Richthofen always lived on the other side to the boundary which we crossed only in our great moments. When he fought, his private life was thrust ruthlessly behind him. Eating, drinking and sleeping were all he granted life, and then only the minimum that was necessary to keep flesh and blood in working order. He was the simplest man I ever met. He was a Prussian through and through.
Ernst Udet, *Ace of the Black Cross* (1937).

Richthofen's fighting methods were typically German. That is not to belittle the Baron's qualifications [as the ace of aces], but it is certainly not said in admiration of his qualities either. . . . He flew with a cold calculating skill and his great trick was to withhold from battle himself until his flying mates had set up a target for him. Then Richthofen would come whisking down out of the sun for the kill, pop off the lame duck, and fly away home with another great victory under his belt.
Canadian "ace" Billy Bishop quoted in William A. Bishop, *The Courage of the Early Morning* (1965).

rifles

The rifle is the best engine of war ever invented by man.
Napoleon I quoted in J. C. Herold, *The Mind of Napoleon* (1955).

The outward and visible sign of the end of war was the introduction of the magazine rifle. . . . The soldier by natural evolution has so perfected the mechanism of slaughter that he has practically secured his own extinction.
W. T. Stead, Preface to I. S. Block, *Is War Impossible?* (1899).

[Private] Jones then stood there, holding his "gun" [penis] in his right hand and his rifle in his left and recited:
"This is my rifle,
   This is my gun,
This is for fighting,
   This is for fun."
Leon M. Uris, *Battle Cry* (1953).

We cleaned and recleaned our weapons; then we cleaned them again. We were filthy, but our rifles gleamed. I used to remember a drill instructor in Boot Camp telling us, "If you get killed, no one can pick you up and use you again. But your clean rifle might save a fellow Marine's life."
David Johnson quoted in Donald Knox, *The Korean War: Uncertain Victory* (1988).

My rifle has a plastic stock, to make it lighter in the jungle, but that only adds to the sense of unreality. A certified weapon of death is in my hands, and it resembles nothing more than a highly stylized Christmas toy.
Peter Tauber, *The Sunshine Soldiers* (1971).

The U.S. Army and Marine Corps both happen to favor the lightest, cheapest, and least capable of the automatic rifles on the world market. That is an understandable preference for armed forces which actually plan to fight their "real" wars by artillery and airpower. . . . Our late allies in Indochina were given M-16s, and now the troops of El Salvador receive the same flimsy and unsoldierly rifle, with the same millimetric tolerances that require standards of cleanliness unknown to peasants. Acres of computer printouts may prove the excellence of the weapon, but one should not expect high self-confidence from soldiers who are sent into action carrying a weapon that feels like a large toothbrush. But then, of course, there is no mathematical designation for "feel," and no system preoccupied with "real" war can be expected to pay attention to such petty things as mere rifles.
Edward N. Luttwak, "Low-Intensity Warfare," *Parameters* (December 1983).

I talked to Bill Bennett about that, because I said, "Bill, what can be worked out with finality on AK-47s? What can be done and still, you know, do what's right by the legitimate sportsman?"
President George Bush, *Newsweek* (March 20, 1989).

robots

No one seems to be talking about putting two-legged mechanical men such as C3-PO of *Star Wars* or Robby the Robot of *Forbidden Planet* onto the battlefield to replace human foot soldiers. . . . Military engineers talk about automatic fire-control systems, capable of spotting enemy forces and automatically shooting at them. They talk about "fire and forget" weapons, which need a soldier only to find a target and push a button. . . . They devise elaborate schemes for "identification of friend or foe" that could automatically discriminate between enemy targets and friendly forces. . . . . They envision scenarios of war in space in which automated battle satellites take on fleets of self-guided intercontinental ballistic missiles. The coming generation of military hardware won't include any mechanical men, but there are plans for systems that

could be labeled "robots" just as the term is used for bolt-tightening automatons on production lines.
Jeff Hecht, *Beam Weapons* (1984).

The concept of automated warfare raises basic questions. How would victory be defined in an automated battle? Is it necessary for blood to be spilled in war? If warfare is becoming a battle between unmanned vehicles and robots, on the one hand, and automated missiles on the other, why not simply decide the issue by having the generals play computer games?
Frank Barnaby, *The Automated Battlefield* (1986).

Royal Air Force

Miss [Mae] West sent a letter to the RAF, on hearing that her name had been attached to a life-saving jacket. The last two paragraphs read: "If I do get in the dictionary—where you say you want to put me—how will they describe me? As a warm clinging life-saving garment worn by aviators? Or an aviator's jacket that supplies the woman's touch while the boys are flying around nights? I've been in *Who's Who* and I know what's what, but it'll be the first time I ever made the dictionary."
A. Marjorie Taylor, *The Language of World War II* (1948).

The theory which [Air Marshal Hugh] Trenchard fortified was this: the heart of air power lay in strategic bombing of an independent character. Operations in direct support of the army and navy, however necessary they might be from time to time, were subsidiary and diversionary. Fighter defence against enemy bombing was fruitless, and had to be catered for mainly as a sop to politicians and other civilians. This theory had certain defects, but it had one crowning merit. It kept the Royal Air Force in being [between the wars] when nearly every other circumstance favored its disbandment.
Noble Frankland, *The Bombing Offensive Against Germany* (1965).

Many RAF fighter pilots. . . clamored for a chance to go after the German fighters. Young men, they had been nourished upon schoolboy fiction of another age. But like aviators of that previous generation, they had to come to terms with a grimmer reality: they were ordered to kill the men of the slower, more vulnerable bombers. They were to run away from enemy fighters unless instructed to pursue them.
Len Deighton, *Fighter* (1978).

Nor were English profiteers above turning out execrable products. A brand called "RAF" [cigarettes] were amongst the worst. It was discovered that they were made from cigarette butts swept up from cinema floors and the manufacturer was eventually sent to prison, though this did not stop them turning up at the front for some months afterwards.
John Ellis, *The Sharp End: The Fighting Man in World War II* (1980).

rules of engagement

We got in more trouble for killing water buffalo than we did for killing people. That was something I could never adjust to.
Lee Childress, quoted in Al Santoli, *Everything We Had: An Oral History of the Vietnam War* (1981).

The people in Washington setting [Vietnam War] policy . . . were listening to certain people who didn't really know what we were dealing with. That's why we had all those stupid restrictions. Don't fight across this side of the DMZ, don't fire at women unless they fire at you, don't fire across this area unless you smile first or unless somebody shoots at you. If they attack you and run across this area, you could not go back over there and take them out. If only we could have fought it in a way that we had been taught to fight.

Archie "Joe" Biggers, quoted in Wallace Terry, *Bloods* (1984).

You are a young lieutenant in Vietnam. The rules of engagement say that you can call in air support if you are confronted with more than twenty of the enemy. Less than twenty enemy you and your men have to handle by yourselves. One morning you count fifteen "Charlies" advancing through the rice paddy in front of you. I can tell you with total assurance that Lieutenant Future General claims he sees thirty enemy, calls in an air strike, kills the enemy with less effort, and saves his men. The overall war effort may suffer because somewhere else Lieutenant Total Honesty, facing nineteen Viet Cong, is still counting and hoping to get twenty.... And those who condemn Lieutenant Future General as they read this had best ask themselves quickly which officer they would prefer to walk with on patrol.

Arthur T. Hadley, *The Straw Giant* (1986).

runners

The point I wish to make is this: [President William] McKinley gave Rowan a letter to be delivered to Garcia; Rowan took the letter & did not ask, "Where is he at?" By the Eternal! there is a man whose form should be cast in deathless bronze & the statue placed in every college of the land. It is not book-learning young men need, nor instruction about this and that, but a stiffening of the vertebrae which will cause them to be loyal to a trust, to act promptly, concentrate their energies: do the thing—"Carry a message to Garcia!"

Elbert Hubbard, "A Message to Garcia," *The Philistine* (March 1899).

As a runner, finding your way around that sea of mud was the worst part.

The moment you set off you felt that dreadful suction. It was forever pulling you down, and you could hear the sound of your feet coming out in a kind of sucking "plop" that seemed much louder at night when you were on your own. In a way, it was worse when the mud didn't suck you down; when it yielded under your feet you knew that it was a body you were treading on. It was terrifying. You'd tread on one on the stomach, perhaps, and it would grunt all the air out of its body.... The smell could make you vomit. And you could always tell whether it was a dead Jerry or a dead Tommy. The Germans smelt different in death.

Private Charlie Miles, reminiscence of World War I, quoted in Trevor Wilson, *The Myriad Faces of War* (1986).

Communication trenches were often sketchy excavations, waterlogged and liable to collapse by shelling. Precisely when a runner most needed shelter, therefore, urgency might drive him above ground, forcing him to get forward by leaps and bounds from one point of dead ground or shell hole to another. Runner casualties, in consequence, were always heavy during heightened periods of trench warfare.... Hitler's worst wound came to him in that way. Sent forward on October 7, 1916, near Bapaume, when the weight of the British fire was so heavy that his officer had called for volunteers, he was hit.... The wound was so serious that he was sent to hospital in Germany, where he took five months to recover.

John Keegan, *The Mask of Command* (1987).

Ruse de Guerre

As to new stratagems, when the armies are engaged in conflict, every captain should endeavor to invent such as will encourage his own troops and dishearten those of the enemy.... In proof of which I will cite the example of the Roman Dictator C. Sulpicius, who, being about to come to battle, with the Gauls, armed all the teamsters and camp-followers, and mounted them upon the mules and other beasts of burden, and supplied them with standards, so as to seem like regular cavalry. These he placed behind a hill, with orders to show themselves to the enemy at a given signal during the heat of battle. The artifice, being carried out as ordered, so alarmed the Gauls as to cause them to lose the day.

Niccolò Machiavelli, *The Discourses* (1517).

Ruses are of great usefulness. They are detours which often lead more surely to the objective than the wide road which goes straight ahead.... Thus one feigns the contrary to what one wishes to do.

Frederick the Great, *Instructions for His Generals* (1747).

German aerial rearmament reveals a concern for appearances. Werner von Blomberg, the German defense minister in 1935, instructed his subordinates, "We must feign as much armed strength as we can, in order to look as powerful as possible to the Western powers." This became air force policy. As late as 1939, when told that ammunition stocks were painfully low, Hitler retorted, "Nobody inquires whether I have any bombs or ammo, it is the number of aircraft and guns that counts."

Barry R. Posen, *The Sources of Military Doctrine* (1984).

In war the power to use two fists is an inestimable asset. To feint with one fist and strike with the other yields an advantage, but a still greater advantage lies in being able to interchange them—to convert the feint into the real blow if the opponent uncovers himself.

B. H. Liddell Hart, *Thoughts on War* (1944).

[Prior to D-Day] there were dozens of men keeping up a shuttle service from one part of the southeast [of England] to another. They arrived at night in their trucks and unloaded their equipment: piles and piles of folded rubber. These were pumped up, and became tanks, guns and halftracks. They were left camouflaged on the edge of a forest, but not too well camouflaged. The last job was to leave tank tracks leading to the forest, and the men had special machines for the purpose. So when dawn came, there was an armored division opposite Pas-de-Calais, all ready to be sighted by a German reconnaissance plane. When the pilot had taken his pictures, the equipment was packed up and taken somewhere else.

Gilles Perrault, *The Secret of D-Day* (1965).

I had also suggested to Hitler that we use amplified phonograph records of tank tracks, marching feet, and other sound effects of massive reinforcement arriving to persuade the Russians that we had built up a particularly powerful and impregnable line of defense between the river Oder and Berlin.... There was little else that we could offer.

General Reinhard Gehlen, *The Service* (1971).

The unusual feature of the Israeli raid [in 1982 in Lebanon] was that it began with the use of a wave of remotely piloted vehicles (pilotless aircraft) as decoys. The Syrians fell for this ruse and attacked the drones with surface-to-air missiles. When the Syrians switched on their radars to attack the Israeli drones, the missiles carried by the Israeli aircraft were able to detect the rays emitted by the radars and home in on them.

Frank Barnaby, *The Automated Battlefield* (1986).

Russia

This is a hard climate, and an American finds many things to try his patience, and but few that are capable of winning his affections. One of the most disagreeable features that he has to encounter, is the secrecy with which everything is done. He can rarely obtain accurate information, until events have transpired, and he may rely upon it, that his own movements are closely observed by eyes that he never sees. The Russian mind seems naturally distrustful, and this is especially so with the government officials. . . .

Nothing is made public that is worth knowing. You will find no two individuals agreeing in the strength of the Army and Navy, in the amount of the public debt, or the annual revenue. In my opinion it is not intended that these things should be known.

Neil S. Brown, United States Minister to Russia, writing to Secretary of State Daniel Webster in 1853, quoted in Frederick H. Hartman, *The Relations of Nations*, 6th ed. (1983).

The idea of Russian diplomatic supremacy owes its efficacy to the imbecility and timidity of the Western Nations, and . . . the belief in Russia's superior military power is hardly less a delusion.

Karl Marx, *New York Tribune* (December 30, 1853), quoted in Paul W. Blackstock and Bert F. Hoselitz, *The Russian Menace to Europe* (1952).

It is a *sine qua non* of successful dealing with Russia that the foreign government in question should remain at all times cool and collected and that its demands on Russian policy should be put forward in such a manner as to leave the way open for a compliance not too detrimental to Russian prestige.

"X" [George F. Kennan], "The Sources of Soviet Conduct," *Foreign Affairs* (July 1947).

He [President Eisenhower] said that as regards the P. M.'s [Winston Churchill] belief that there was a New Look in Soviet Policy, Russia was a woman of the streets and whether her dress was new, or just the old one patched, it was certainly the same whore underneath. America intended to drive her off her present "beat" into the back streets.

John Colville, *The Fringes of Power* (1985), diary entry for December 4, 1953.

There is nothing in the world that the Communists want badly enough to risk losing the Kremlin.

President Dwight D. Eisenhower quoted in Stephen E. Ambrose, *Eisenhower*, II (1984).

We cannot afford to delude ourselves about the danger in the continuing Soviet military buildup. As has been said, it is useless for sheep to pass resolutions in favor of vegetarianism while the wolf remains of a different opinion.

Helmut Schmidt, Chancellor of West Germany, *Reader's Digest* (September 1975).

There is no Soviet domination of Eastern Europe and there never will be any under a Ford Administration.

President Gerald Ford, second debate with presidential candidate Jimmy Carter, October 6, 1976.

The Soviet Union can choose either confrontation or cooperation. The United States is adequately prepared to meet either choice. We would prefer cooperation.

President Jimmy Carter, commencement address at the United States Naval Academy, Annapolis, June 7, 1978.

Nowadays the Politburo in Moscow wears Western suits and speaks a variant of the Western political dialectics. But the Soviet leaders are—as much as any Sultan or

Mahdi—the product of centuries of history very different from our own, and of a long-standing political psychology alien to ours in its motives, judgments and intentions.

Robert Conquest, *Present Danger* (1979).

It's my belief that you should sell the Russians anything they can't shoot back at you. If they buy our grain, they'll have less money to do mischief with.

Senator Rudolph E. Boschwitz, *U.S. News and World Report* (August 23, 1982).

My fellow Americans: I'm pleased to tell you today that I've signed legislation that will outlaw Russia forever. We begin bombing in five minutes.

President Ronald Reagan, comments while testing a microphone before a national radio broadcast, August 11, 1984.

[The Reagan] administration's foreign policy has been to kiss the Russian bear's bottom, and he keeps turning the other cheek.

Howard Phillips quoted in *Time* (October 13, 1986).

[The] Soviet Union has become the personification of ethical and moral norms in international relations . . . a great torch which emits hope for the preservation of peace on our planet.

Miguel D'Escoto, Foreign Minister of Nicaragua, speech accepting the Lenin Peace Prize in Moscow, *U.S. News and World Report* (December 21, 1987).

Official Soviet spokesmen have always condemned terrorism. . . . Yet, at the same time, the Soviet Union has provided arms, financial aid, military training, and, on occasion, political support to various terrorist groups. . . . Furthermore, it has closely cooperated with the countries which have been the main sponsors of international terrorism, Libya and Syria.

Walter Laqueur, *Terrorism* (1987).

What we are witnessing today in Russia is the break-up of much, if not all, of the system of power by which that country has been held together and governed since 1917.

George F. Kennan, "Just Another Great Power," *The New York Times* (April 9, 1989).

The United States now has as its goal much more than simply containing Soviet expansionism. We seek the integration of the Soviet Union into the community of nations. And as the Soviet Union itself moves toward greater openness and democratization, as they meet the challenge of responsible international behavior, we will match their steps with steps of our own. Ultimately, our objective is to welcome the Soviet Union back into the world order.

President George Bush, speech at Texas A & M University, May 12, 1989.

evil empire

The man beside me was saying, "We have a different regard for human life than those monsters do." He was referring to what he said was the Soviets' belief in winning nuclear war despite casualties that we would find unacceptable. And he added that they are "godless" monsters. It is this theological defect "that gives them less regard for humanity or human beings." The man telling me all this was Ronald Reagan, as I interviewed him [in 1980].

Robert Scheer, *With Enough Shovels* (1982).

Let us pray for the salvation of all those who live in totalitarian darkness, pray they will discover the joy of knowing God.

But until they do, let us be aware that while they preach the supremacy of the state, declare its omnipotence over individual man, and predict its eventual domination of all peoples of the earth—they [the Soviet Union] are the focus of evil in the modern world.
President Ronald Reagan, speech to the National Association of Evangelists, Orlando, Florida, March 8, 1983.

The idea that our country is an "evil empire," the October Revolution a blunder of history and the post-revolutionary period a "zigzag in history," is coming apart at the seams. That kind of perestroika really does not suit some people.
Mikhail Gorbachev, *Perestroika* (1987).

Russia, World War II
Day by day I followed, on a large map of Russia that hung on the wall of my office, the advance of Hitler's army across the great regions of forest and swamp to the west of Moscow, comparing it at every turn with the similar advance of Napoleon's army in the year 1812. (The similarities in timing and geography were often striking.)
George F. Kennan, *Memoirs, 1925–1950* (1967).

I cannot forecast to you the action of Russia. It is a riddle wrapped in a mystery inside an enigma; but perhaps there is a key. That key is Russian national interest.
Winston Churchill, BBC Broadcast, October 1, 1939.

I hope for only one thing, that in this war in the East the Germans lose a lot of feathers.
Benito Mussolini, quoted in Count Galeazzo Ciano, *The Ciano Diaries* (1946).

Kill! There is nothing that is innocent in the German. Neither in the living nor in the unborn. Follow the directive of Comrade Stalin and trample into the ground forever the Fascist beast in his cave. Break by force the racial haughtiness of German women! Take them as your lawful prey! Kill, you brave advancing Red soldiers!
Ilya Ehrenburg, speaking to the Red Army as it advanced into Germany, quoted in Alfred Vagts, *A History of Militarism*, rev. ed. (1959).

The worst and most suicidal errors were committed in the early stages of the war, when Stalin simply threw down the reins of government, absented himself from military headquarters, surrendered to despair and drank himself into a stupor. Khrushchev declared that it was a well-known fact that after the first severe disasters and reverses Stalin abandoned all hope, saying at a meeting of the Politburo: "All that Lenin created we have lost forever."
Robert Payne, *The Rise and Fall of Stalin* (1965).

Hitler's astonishing triumph over France was to be directly the source of his greatest disaster. After France, the mighty warrior nation which had defeated Germany in 1918, had been overthrown with such ease, what nation on earth could stand up to the Wehrmacht? So Hitler in 1941 was convinced that—while reducing his war production and demobilizing part of his forces, and without furnishing his cohorts with any winter equipment—he could knock out Russia in one lightning campaign.
Alistair Horne, *To Lose a Battle: France 1940* (1969).

You have only to kick in the door, and the whole rotten structure will come crashing down.
Hitler's advice to his generals on the 1941 invasion of Russia, quoted in Robert Payne, *The Life and Death of Adolf Hitler* (1973).

Certainly in the midst of surrounding darkness and storm, signs of light appear which lift up our hearts with great and holy expectations— these are those magnanimous acts of valor which now defend the foundations of Christian culture, as well as the confident hope in victory.

Pope Pius XII, radio address of June 29, 1941, quoted in Anthony Rhodes, *The Vatican in the Age of the Dictators* (1972). This was one week after the German invasion of Russia. The Pope saw the Nazis as defenders of "Christian culture."

I had remembered the first dispatch of my friend Cy Sulzberger when he got into Russia in late summer 1941. It started out: "The Russians have shoes." A curious fact to report, with the Germans pounding toward Moscow, but a significant one. What Cy meant was that despite Hitler's attack and the terrible losses, Russia was still able to feed and clothe itself. If the Russians wore shoes they were capable of fighting. This was big news.

Harrison E. Salisbury, *A Journey for Our Times* (1983).

I expect little of the Russian resistance, so that any resistance they do put up will be clear gain. We, on our part, must act on the assumption that they can't last through the summer.

Walter Lippmann, writing shortly after the 1941 German invasion of Russia, *Public Philosopher: Selected Letters of Walter Lippmann* (1985).

Not all of us will kill children, you won't and I won't. But to be honest, if you like, let those who *will* do it also kill the little Fritzes in their frenzy until they've had enough—that's war, Comrade, and not philosophy or literature. Of course in books there are such things as morality, humanism, internationalism. All O.K., theoretically correct. But right now we want to let Germany go up in smoke, and when that's done we'll behave correctly again, we'll write nice little books about humanism and internationalism.

Leo Kopelev, *No Jail For Thought* (1977).

[During World War II, Edgar Snow] admired Russian determination and energy, the way people regarded national defense as a personal responsibility. His reporting skills powerfully romanticized people like Zina. With the need for able-bodied men at the front, women assumed great responsibility for wartime industrial and agricultural production. Zina, a classic example of these Amazons, worked in a munitions plant. Snow described her wide grin, her arms like pistons, and her patriotism. "Her husband was at the front, and every time she finished a shell she felt he was nearer her."

John Maxwell Hamilton, *Edgar Snow* (1988).

Russian Army

Though our country is in no danger of invasion, no sooner is peace concluded than plans are laid for a new war, which has generally no other foundation than the ambition of the Sovereign, or perhaps merely the ambition of one of his ministers. . . . In a word, we are so exhausted and ruined by the keeping up of a standing army, and by the consequences flowing therefrom, that the most cruel enemy, though he should devastate the whole Empire, could not cause us one half of the injury.

Russian nobles complaining to Vockerodt, a Prussian diplomatic agent during the reign of Peter the Great, quoted in D. MacKenzie Wallace, *Russia* (1877).

[Peter the Great] was willing to be promoted from drummer boy to bombardier, from bombardier to sergeant and eventually up to general . . . but only when he felt that his competence and service merited promotion. In part, at the beginning, he did this because in peacetime exercises drummer boys and artillerymen had more fun and made more noise than majors and colonels. But there was also his continuing belief

that he should learn the business of soldiering from the bottom up. And if he, the Tsar, did this, no nobleman would be able to claim command on the basis of title.
Robert K. Massie, *Peter the Great* (1980).

[Marshal Zhukov] was a harsh disciplinarian. Senior commanders who failed to measure up were often fired on the spot and then punished for failing. The punishment usually took one of two forms: the officer either was sent to join a penal battalion or was ordered to serve on the most exposed part of the front line—as a private. . . .
Once during the Polish campaign of 1944 Zhukov had stood with Marshal Konstantin Rokossovskii and General Pavel Batov . . . watching the troops advance. Suddenly Zhukov, viewing the scene through binoculars, yelled at Batov: "The corps commander and the commander of the 44th Rifle Division—penal battalion!" Both Rokossovskii and Batov began to plead for the two generals. Rokossovskii was able to save the corps commander. But Zhukov remained firm regarding the second officer. The general was immediately reduced in rank, sent to the front lines, and order to lead a suicidal attack. He was killed almost instantly.
Cornelius Ryan, *The Last Battle* (1966).

There was a lot of lazy thinking by Americans before the Red Army began moving into Europe, and consequently, a lot of people are now "disillusioned" to find that the Kremlin has its own ideas about how to make friends and influence people in Eastern Europe.
Edgar Snow, *The Saturday Evening Post* (March 3, 1945).

She [a twelve-year-old] was lying in bed, exceedingly ill with dysentery, when a Russian soldier came through the door, demanding alcohol. This was the first Red army man she had ever seen who was not a prisoner. Seeing only a bottle of ink, he picked it up and drank it. . . . Some of the Russians drank petrol, she recalled.
Alexander McKee, *Dresden 1945* (1984).

The commissar was the party's representative with the army and was the immediate executive of the Bolshevik government: his position was unassailable by the military of any rank, and an insult to the commissar was a serious criminal offense. One of the commissar's most important responsibilities was that of safeguarding against conspiracy and counter-revolution, and "to see that the army should not become a thing apart" from the party and state. In order to accomplish this the commissar was required "to receive, jointly with the military commander specialist, all orders and correspondence and to countersign all orders", for according to the Bolshevik regulation only countersigned orders were valid.
Albert Seaton and Joan Seaton, *The Soviet Army* (1986).

The defense needs of the Soviet Union hardly call for maintaining more combat divisions in East Germany today than were in the whole allied invasion force that landed in Normandy on D-Day.
President Ronald Reagan, speech in Washington, D.C., November 18, 1981.

Russians
I wish someone could tell me about the Russians. I don't know a good Russian from a bad Russian. I can tell a good Frenchman from a bad Frenchman, I can tell a good Italian from a bad Italian, I know a good Greek when I see one. But I don't understand the Russians.
President Franklin D. Roosevelt quoted in Frances Perkins, *The Roosevelt I Knew* (1947).

I always regard myself as the real author of the Russian Revolution, because I said that the best thing the soldiers could do in the 1914–18 war was to shoot their officers

and go home; and the Russians were the only soldiers who had the intelligence to take my advice.
  George Bernard Shaw quoted in Hesketh Pearson, *G. B. S.: A Postscript* (1951).

Somebody said the second most stupid thing in the world that a man could say was that he could understand the Russians. I've often wondered what in hell was the first.
  President Ronald Reagan quoted in Hugh Sidey, "The Presidency," *Time* (October 20, 1986).

Charles Bohlen, one of the State Department's top experts on the Soviet Union between the 1930's and 1960's, once observed that it is well to beware of several "famous last words." One is, "Liquor doesn't affect me." The other is, "I understand the Russians."
  Walter LaFeber, *Chronicle of Higher Education* (May 24, 1989).

sabotage

The reprisal measures imposed in response to acts of sabotage and ambush have, despite their severity, failed to achieve any noteworthy success, since our own measures have been only transitory, so that the punished communities or territories soon have to be abandoned once more to the [partisan] bands. On the contrary, exaggerated reprisal measures undertaken without a more precise examination of the objective situation have only caused embitterment and have been useful to the bands.
  Lieutenant Kurt Waldheim, report on enemy activities in Greece sent to the Chief of the general staff of Army Group E, May 25, 1944, quoted in Robert Edwin Hertzstein, *Waldheim: the Missing Years* (1988). Hertzstein notes that "Waldheim's criticism of the reprisal policy was a singular gesture. Though many in the Wehrmacht may have felt the same way privately, Waldheim was one of the only junior staff officers willing to put his opposition on record. . . ." [Waldheim] didn't argue that the German policy of reprisals was evil or criminal, merely that it was counterproductive. And whatever motivated it, there is no evidence that Waldheim ever openly criticized or otherwise protested against Nazi brutality on any other occasion."

Sabotage allowed a precision the most sophisticated bomb sight could not achieve. Damage from plastic explosives often exceeded that of bombs, took longer to repair, and civilian casualties were lower, even if the Nazis did take hostages and punish civilians.
  William Casey, *The Secret War Against Hitler* (1988).

sacrifice

It is not a question of who are the Prime Minister's friends. It is a far bigger issue. He has appealed for sacrifice. The nation is prepared for every sacrifice so long as the Government show clearly what they are aiming at, and so long as the nation is confident that those who are leading it are doing their best. I say solemnly that the Prime Minister should give an example of sacrifice, because there is nothing which can contribute more to victory in this war than that he should sacrifice the seals of office.
  David Lloyd George, speech in the House of Commons on whether Neville Chamberlain should remain as prime minister, June 8, 1940.

I consider it no sacrifice to die for my country. In my mind we came here to thank God that men like these have lived rather than to regret that they have died.
  General George S. Patton, Jr., speech at an Allied cemetery in Italy, November 11, 1943, quoted in Harry H. Semmes, *Portrait of Patton* (1955).

A nation which makes the final sacrifice for life and freedom does not get beaten.
Kemal Ataturk, first president of the Republic of Turkey, quoted in M. M. Mousharrafa, *Ataturk* (1944).

Humility must always be the portion of any man who receives acclaim earned in the blood of his followers and the sacrifices of his friends.
General Dwight D. Eisenhower, speech at Guildhall, London, June 12, 1945, reprinted in R. L. Treuenfels, *Eisenhower Speaks* (1948).

The soldier, above all other men, is required to practice the greatest act of religious training—sacrifice. In battle and in the face of danger and death, he discloses those divine attributes which his Maker gave when He created man in His own image. No physical courage and no brute instinct can take the place of the Divine help which alone can sustain him. However horrible the incidents of war may be, the soldier who is called upon to offer and to give his life for his country is the noblest development of mankind.
General Douglas MacArthur, speech at West Point, May 12, 1962, reprinted in his *Reminiscences* (1964).

I do not believe any man's son is worth sacrificing in order to achieve merely tactical advantages in the endless skirmishing between the great powers. There is nothing elemental to the American identity at stake in Vietnam.
Paddy Chayefsky quoted in C. Woolf and J. Bagguley, *Authors Take Sides on Vietnam* (1967).

Often the individual infantryman [in Vietnam] would spend days in the field in search of the enemy only to witness upon his return large numbers of clean-shaven and starch-fatigued officers going about their business in their secure environments. The troops developed a series of terms for these officers, the most derisive of which was "rear-echelon motherfucker." In the end it was not only a case of too many officers, too much rank, and too low quality. It was the searing awareness on the part of the troops that large numbers of officers—often those occupying the higher ranks—simply did not share the burden of sacrifice that was expected of them.
Richard A. Gabriel and Paul L. Savage, *Crisis in Command* (1978).

Sandhurst

The suggestion that I recommend is, therefore, to get gentlemen with a gentleman's education from the public schools and do away with your military schools for boys as a competing nursery for the Army. Test their qualifications and then give them two years at a military college.
Prince Albert's 1856 recommendation for the reform of Sandhurst (which were eventually implemented) quoted in Hugh Thomas, *The Story of Sandhurst* (1961).

Really I feel less keen about the Army every day. I think the Church would suit me better.
Winston Churchill, letter home while a student at Sandhurst, quoted in William Manchester, *The Last Lion: Visions of Glory; 1874–1932* (1983).

Cheating, which caused trouble for so many members of the West Point football squad a few years back, was recognized as a form of work and had it own customs. It was permissible [in the 1930s], indeed almost laudable, to cheat if that was your only hope of passing out and getting your commission. What did book learning matter, anyway, to a subaltern of a fighting regiment? It was not permissible to cheat in the hope of improving an already secure position, and most especially not in order to get a reward. . . . On the other hand it was my duty, at an examination, to put my worked

papers in such a position that a desperate neighbor could look at them if he needed to cheat to avoid dropping a term. Whether he did look or not was his business. And if he was stupid enough to get caught, that was his business too. Damn it, a chap had to be good at something!
John Masters, *Bugles and a Tiger* (1956).

school solution

It is a very easy matter for a school-man to make a plan for outflanking a wing or threatening a line of communications upon a map, where he can regulate the positions of both parties to suit himself; but when he has opposed to him a skillful, active, and enterprising adversary, whose movements are a perfect riddle, then his difficulties begin, and we see an exhibition of the incapacity of an ordinary general with none of the resources of genius.
General Antoine Henri Jomini, *Summary of the Art of War* (1838).

There is no approved solution to any tactical situation.
General George S. Patton, Jr., *War As I Knew It* (1947).

Incongruously, during the firefight Campbell remembered some doggerel on a tombstone in a fake cemetery at the Infantry School in Ft. Benning, Georgia.
    Here lie the bone of Lt. Jones,
    A graduate of this institution.
    He died on the night of his very first fight,
    While using the school solution.
Harold P. Leinbaugh and John D. Campbell, *The Men of Company K* (1985).

We're training our students to work in the strategic environment. Most of them have never done that before. They've spent their careers in the operating forces, where they competed with their peers and problems usually had right answers. Now we have to teach them to work more cooperatively and to tolerate ambiguity. Lots of big problems have several answers, or none at all.
Colonel Donald Lunday of the Army War College, *Insight* (December 14, 1987).

scrounging

Officers watched them carefully. They had to, lest the men from one outfit grab supplies assigned to another outfit. Our Army is great for that. They will steal a battleship if they can get away with it. At night, every jeep driver cannibalizes his car—removes the magneto. Otherwise, his jeep would be gone. Our boys don't call it stealing. They call it "moonlight requisitioning."
Quentin Reynolds, "Bloody Salerno," *Collier's* (October 23, 1943).

Stealing was not, of course, called stealing; you called it scrounging, and nobody had any qualms about doing it. In a world where everything belonged to the government, nothing belonged to anybody, and we quickly lost our back-home sense of the inviolability of personal property. If an object was portable and no one was guarding it, it was as much yours as anybody else's.
Samuel Hynes, *Flights of Passage* (1988).

The slang word from the food supplies was "organize": [corporal] Hitler [during World War I] "organized" flour, but his great coup involved a supply of zwieback. Taking his turn standing guard at night over the staff living quarters, he found nearby a few large boxes that proved to be filled with the sweet biscuits. He devised a way of opening the boxes from the bottom; taking some for himself and the other runners each night he was on guard, he was able to keep the continuing pilferage undetected. When meat ran short later in the war, no one was better than Hitler at finding dogs and cats for the cooking pot.

Charles B. Flood, *Hitler: The Path to Power* (1989).

secrets

Consult with many on proper measures to be taken, but communicate the plans you intend to put in execution to few, and those only of the most assured fidelity. Or better, trust no one but yourself.

Vegetius, *De Re Militari* (A.D. 378).

To keep your actions and your plans secret always has been a very good thing. For that reason Metellus, when he was with the armies in Spain, replied to one who asked him what he was going to do the next day, that if his shirt knew he would burn it. Marcus Crassus said to one who asked him when he was going to move the army: "Do you believe that you will be the only one not to hear the trumpet?"

Niccolò Machiavelli, *The Art of War* (1520).

There's the one thing no nation can ever accuse us of and that is secret diplomacy. Our foreign dealings are an open book, generally a check book.

Will Rogers, writing in 1922, *The Autobiography of Will Rogers*, ed. D. Day (1949).

If my coat knew my plans, as Frederick the Great once said, I would take it off and burn it. And if I can deceive my friends, I can make certain of deceiving my enemies.

General Thomas J. "Stonewall" Jackson quoted in Burke Davis, *Gray Fox* (1956).

sentries

Issuing from his tent, by twilight, he [the King, Richard III] observed a sentinel asleep, and is said to have stabbed him, with this remark, "I found him asleep, and have left him as I found him." Perhaps this was the only person Richard ever put to death, who deserved it.

William Hutton, *The Battle of Bosworth Field* (1813).

Sometimes you'd end up putting a young fellow on guard duty who hadn't had any rest for a night or two. Then if we had a quiet spell, the lad was very apt to doze off.... We had this happen a few times, but I didn't feel I should report the soldier.... So I worked out my own scheme of punishment. I had this big paper sign made out that read as follows: "I fell asleep on post last night, endangering the lives of my buddies. For the next thirty days I'll do anything that is asked of me."

Well, everyone thought that was very fair. And they'd make the fellow run all types of errands for them all month. But it was a lot better than giving him a general court-martial. I'll tell you something else: It never happened to the same man twice.

Hamilton Fish, U.S. Army Captain, World War I, quoted in Henry Berry, *Make the Kaiser Dance* (1978).

sergeants

The sergeant *is* the Army.

President Dwight D. Eisenhower, *The New York Times* (December 24, 1972).

Hold the sergeant responsible for his section and all its equipment, to include the gun truck. Hold the lieutenant responsible for his platoon, and so on. When you see something wrong don't correct the individual soldier. Give the sergeant hell for failing to see trouble before you did and make him correct it.

Colonel Ray Chandler, letter to O. Chandler, May 18, 1943, explaining General Robert L. Eichelberger's "chain of command" concept, quoted in J. Luvaas and John F. Shortal, "Robert L. Eichelberger: MacArthur's Fireman," *We Shall Return!*, ed. William M. Leary (1988).

Milton Anthony Warden was thirty-four years old. In the eight months he had been topkicker of G Company he had wrapped that outfit around his waist like a money belt and buttoned his shirt over it.

James Jones, *From Here to Eternity* (1951).

A sergeant in the Soviet Army is not a professional soldier as is the case in most armies. He is a conscript, just like the privates, selected early in his enlistment term for special training due to his intelligence, political reliability, or perceived leadership ability. He is sent to a tough six-month course to make him an instant sergeant, then returned to his operational unit. In fact he has about as little practical experience as his subordinates.

Tom Clancy, *Red Storm Rising* (1986).

ships

They that go down to the sea in ships, that do business in great waters;
These see the works of the Lord, and his wonders in the deep.
The Bible, Psalms 107: 23–24.

I don't think much of these naval combats, *C'est piff poff* on one side and the other, and leaves the sea afterwards as salty as before.

Jean-Frederic Maurepas, head of the French Navy (1723–49), quoted in George Martelli, *Jemmy Twicher* (1962).

No man will be a sailor who has contrivance enough to get himself into a jail; for being in a ship is being in a jail, with the chance of being drowned.

Samuel Johnson quoted in James Boswell, *Life of Johnson* (1791).

Since medieval days of the sixty-pound suit of armor, in which, for the sake of combat, men roasted and could not arise if they fell, no contrivance for fighting has matched in discomfort and inconvenience and use contrary to nature the floating castle called a ship of the line in the age of fighting sail. With its motor power dependent on the caprice of heaven and direction-finding on the distant stars, and its central piece of equipment—the mast—dependent on seasoned timber that was rarely obtainable, and control of locomotion dependent on rigging and ropes of a complexity to defy philosophers of the Sorbonne, much less the homeless untutored poor off the streets who made up the crews, and communication from commander to his squadron dependent on signal flags easily obscured by distance or smoke from the guns or by pitching of the ship, these cumbersome vehicles were as convenient as if dinosaurs had survived to be used by cowboys for driving cattle.

Barbara W. Tuchman, *The First Salute* (1988).

Taken all in all, a ship-of-the-line is the most honorable thing that man, as a gregarious animal, has produced.

John Ruskin, speaking in 1830, quoted in Lewis Mumford, *Technics and Civilization* (1934).

[A ship is always referred as "she"] because it costs so much to keep one in paint and powder.

Admiral Chester W. Nimitz, *The New York Times* (February 15, 1940).

A happy and efficient ship. A very happy and very efficient ship. Some of you might think I'm a bit ambitious wanting both, but in my experience you can't have one without the other. A ship can't be happy unless she's efficient, and she certainly won't be efficient unless she's happy.
Noel Coward in *In Which We Serve* (1942), directed by Noel Coward and David Lean; screenplay by Noel Coward. This film was a fictionalized account of Admiral Louis Mountbatten's adventures while captain of the destroyer *HMS Kelly*.

You spend a couple of weeks in the troop compartment of a Liberty ship and you'll fight anyone to come ashore.
Attitude of World War II troops quoted in John G. Bunker, *Liberty Ships* (1972).

It is cheering to see that the rats are still around—the ship is not sinking.
Eric Hoffer, *The New York Times Magazine* (April 25, 1971).

We sink ships and try to pretend that they're just ships—things without people in them. It's dishonest, but we do it anyway.
Tom Clancy, *Red Storm Rising* (1986).

shooting

We have wished to avoid shooting, but the shooting has started. And history has recorded who fired the first shot. In the long run, however, all that will matter is who fired the last shot.
Franklin D. Roosevelt, Navy Day speech, Washington, D.C., October 27, 1941.

A bit of shooting takes your mind off your troubles—it makes you forget the cost of living.
Brendan Behan, *The Hostage* (1958).

signals

One if by land, and two if by sea;
And I on the opposite shore will be,
Ready to ride and spread the alarm
Through every Middlesex village and farm.
Henry Wadsworth Longfellow, "Paul Revere's Ride," *Tales of a Wayside Inn* (1863).

[At Kenesaw Mountain in Georgia on June 27, 1864] General Sherman made his way to the top of a high hill, where we were lying, to enable him to overlook the country and see operations better. He sat on a stump with a map spread out on his knees, and was giving General Cox directions as to his line of march. After doing this, he mounted his horse and started away, but after having gone away a little distance he shouted back, "See here, Cox, burn a few barns occasionally, as you go along. I can't understand those signal flags, but I know what smoke means."
Washington Davis, *Campfire Chats of the Civil War* (1888).

By May 1942 they [the British] were breaking every Enigma key system of the African theater. In August this was joined by . . . the breaking of the system used by Mediterranean surface ships. Rommel was now losing one quarter of his supplies through British attacks which were almost totally dependent on detailed Enigma information—sometimes enabling them to pick out the more important cargoes for destruction.
Andrew Hodges, *Alan Turing: The Enigma* (1983).

The second battle of Alamein started on October the twenty-third [1942]. . . . On November the second Hitler sent his now famous signal to Rommel saying that "there could be no other course but that of holding out to the last man and that for the

German troops there was only the choice, victory or death." Alamein was the first real German defeat of the war and also the first of this type of signal to come from Hitler.... This signal was immediately picked up by us and was in the hands of Montgomery and Churchill within minutes of its transmission by Hitler. Apparently Rommel had either got sand in his cypher machine or was deliberately stalling because, instead of acknowledging the signal, he sent a request for a repeat. It was probably the only time that a British commander has received a signal from the enemy's commander-in-chief before the enemy's commander in the field had got it, or at least admitted that he had.
F. W. Winterbotham, *The Ultra Secret* (1974).

Signals travel alone and, like telegrams, have to be carefully worded to be readily understood. Unlike telegrams, however, they are impersonal and public. They carry the authority of a ship or squadron. They are paid for with reputations, sometimes even with human lives.
Captain Jack Broome, *Make a Signal* (1955).

"The Russians," he [General Guenther Blumentritt] subsequently wrote, "were taken entirely by surprise on our front." As dawn broke German signal stations picked up the Red Army radio networks. "We are being fired on. What shall we do?" Blumentritt quotes one Russian message as saying. Back came the answer from headquarters: "You must be insane. And why is your signal not in code?"
William L. Shirer, *The Rise and Fall of the Third Reich* (1959).

Admiral Nimitz . . . wanted information [during the October 1944 Battle for Leyte Gulf] and sent a dispatch asking for it. The encoding yeoman at Pearl Harbor . . . put in as padding (to throw off possible enemy decrypters), "the world wonders." The decoding yeoman on board *New Jersey,* taking this to be a part of the message, handed it to Admiral Halsey . . . in this form:
FROM CINCPAC ACTION COM THIRD FLEET INFO COMINCH CTF 77 X WHERE IS RPT WHERE IS TASK FORCE THIRTY-FOUR RB THE WORLD WONDERS.
Halsey was furious. He thought that Nimitz was criticizing him, and that, too, before Admirals King and Kinkaid (CTF77) by making them addressees.
Samuel Eliot Morison, *The Two-Ocean War* (1963).

slogans

Don't give up the ship.
Commander James Lawrence, last orders to the crew of the *Chesapeake* as he lay dying after a brief battle with the British ship *Shannon* on June 1, 1813, quoted in Glenn Tucker, *Poltroons and Patriots*, I (1954). This phrase, of dubious authenticity, has been a watchword of the U.S. Navy ever since. A blue battle-flag with these words inscribed was used by Oliver Hazard Perry during the Battle of Lake Erie, September 10, 1813.

Remember the Alamo!
Attributed to Colonel Sidney Sherman at the Battle of San Jacinto, April 21, 1836.

A bayonet is a weapon with a worker at each end.
A pre-World War II British pacifist slogan.

The difficult we do immediately. The impossible takes a little longer.
Slogan of United States Army Air Force quoted in *Newsweek* (March 8, 1943). Other units also used a variant of this. *The New York Times* (November 4, 1945) reports the motto of the Army Service Corps to be: "The impossible we do at once; the miraculous takes a little longer." The inscription on a memorial to the U.S. Navy's Seabees (construction batallions)

of World War II, located between Memorial Bridge and Arlington National Cemetery in Virginia, reads: "with willing hearts and skillful hands, the difficult we do at once; the impossible takes a bit longer."

First to fight.
U.S. Marine Corps slogan.

Remember Pearl Harbor.
World War II slogan.

I'd rather be Red than dead.
Slogan of Britain's Campaign for Nuclear Disarmament quoted in *Time* (September 15, 1961).

Nobody wants to fight, but somebody has to know how.
U.S. Marine Corps recruiting slogan of the mid-1960s.

Hey, hey LBJ, how many kids did you kill today?
Anonymous anti-Vietnam War chant commonly used by demonstrators in the mid-1960s, *Time* (January 5, 1968).

Win the hearts and the minds of the people.
The slogan that described the objectives of American counterinsurgency efforts in Vietnam. According to Barbara J. Tuchman, *The March of Folly* (1984), this effort was "known as WHAM to Americans in the field." The U.S. troop response to the "hearts and mind" slogan was typically "Grab them by the balls, and their hearts and minds will follow."

There was this slogan about hearts and minds—the idea that we were trying to sell the war to the Vietnamese, who were reluctant to buy it. But our assumption was that we had their hearts and minds—that we were there because they wanted us to be there.
Douglas Pike quoted in Harry Mauer, *Strange Ground* (1989).

snipers

Snipers killed as many Americans as they could, and then when their food and ammunition ran out they surrendered. Our men felt that wasn't quite ethical. The average American soldier had little feeling against the average German soldier who fought an open fight and lost. But his feelings about the sneaking snipers can't very well be put into print. He was learning how to kill the snipers before the time came for them to surrender.
Ernie Pyle, *Brave Men* (1944).

Cautiously moving from house to house, we search for snipers. Leaping from the sunlight into the dim rooms, we must wait for our eyes to become adjusted to the change. As we stand in one house, the door of a room creaks open. Suddenly I find myself faced by a terrible looking creature with a tommy gun. His face is black; his eyes are red and glaring. I give him a burst and see the flash of his own gun, which is followed by the sound of shattering glass.
The horrible being that I shot at was the reflection of my own smoke-blackened self in a mirror. Kerrigan doubles with laughter. "That's the first time I ever saw a Texan beat himself to the draw," says he.
Audie Murphy, *To Hell and Back* (1949).

I knew a major who dropped his pants in the bush on Guadalcanal and squatted to defecate. A shot rang out. Another Marine had spotted a Nip sniper in a coconut tree overhead. The dead sniper dropped thirty feet and plopped right in front of the major. Starting right then he developed an extraordinary case of constipation. Every time he

tried to empty his bowels he saw Japs above him. Three weeks later he was flown to Noumea for surgery.
William Manchester, *Goodbye, Darkness* (1980).

A colonel: "You go through those hamlets [in Vietnam] in company and battalion strength and you get a sniper round and hell, yes, you level the place." But unarmed women and children? What if there was no sniper round? "The distinction's pretty slight," said the colonel. "Pretty damn slight."
Ward Just, *Military Men* (1970).

soldiers

The Lord is a man of war.
The Bible, Exodus 5: 3.

Peasants are the most fit to bear arms for they from their infancy have been exposed to all kinds of weather and have been brought up to the hardest labor. They are able to endure the most intense heat of the sun, are unacquainted with use of baths, and they are strangers to the other luxuries of life. They are simple, content with little, inured to fatigue, and prepared in some measure for a military life.
Vegetius, *De Re Militari* (A.D. 378).

If you wish to be loved by your soldiers, do not lead them to slaughter. They can be spared . . . by the skill with which you choose weakest points of attack, in not breaking your head against impracticable things which are ridiculous to attempt, in not fatiguing the soldier uselessly and in sparing him in sieges and in battles. When you seem to be most prodigal of the soldier's blood, you spare it, however, by supporting your attacks well and by pushing them with the greatest vigor to prevent time from augmenting your losses.
Frederick the Great, *Instructions for His Generals* (1747).

When we assumed the soldier, we did not lay aside the citizen; and we shall most sincerely rejoice with you in that happy hour when the establishment of American liberty, upon the most firm and solid ground, shall enable us to return to our private stations.
General George Washington, address to the legislature of New York, June 26, 1775.

Every man thinks meanly of himself for not having been a soldier, or not having been at sea.
Samuel Johnson quoted in James Boswell, *Life of Samuel Johnson* (1791).

Soger (soldier) is the worst term of reproach that can be applied to a sailor. It signifies a *skulk*, a *shirk*,—one who is always trying to get clear of work, and is out of the way, or hanging back, when duty is to be done.
Richard H. Dana, Jr., *Two Years Before the Mast* (1840).

You are a very poor soldier: a chocolate cream soldier!
George Bernard Shaw, *Arms and the Man* (1898).

The soldier is an anachronism of which we must get rid.
George Bernard Shaw, *John Bull's Other Island*, preface (1904).

A soldier is a slave—he does what he is told to do—everything is provided for him—his head is a superfluity. He is only a stick used by men to strike other men.
Elbert Hubbard, *The Roycroft Dictionary and Book of Epigrams* (1923).

They're changing guard at Buckingham Palace

Christopher Robin went down with Alice.
Alice is marrying one of the guard.
"A soldier's life is terrible hard,"
Says Alice.
A. A. Milne, *When We Were Very Young* (1924).

We are soldiers. It is a great brotherhood, which adds something of the good-fellow-ship of the folk-song, of the feeling of solidarity of convicts, and of the desperate loy-alty to one another of men condemned to death, to a condition of life arising out of the midst of danger, out of the tension and forlorness of death.
Erich Maria Remarque, *All Quiet on the Western Front* (1929).

In the long run "good party men" make the best soldiers. . . . Old soldiers are of course more useful at the beginning of a campaign, and they are all right when there is any fighting, but they have more tendency to go to pieces under inaction and physical exhaustion. A man who has fully identified with some political party is reliable in *all* circumstances.
George Orwell, "Notes on the Spanish Militias (1939)," *The Collected Essays, Journals and Letters of George Orwell*, eds. S. Orwell and I. Angus (1968).

A good soldier has his heart and soul in it. When he receives an order, he gets a hard on, and when he drives his lance into the enemy's guts, he comes.
Bertolt Brecht, *The Caucasian Chalk Circle*, Act III (1945).

We have . . . the worst individual fighting soldiers of any big power. Or at least in their natural state they are. They're comparatively wealthy, they're spoiled, and as Americans they share, most of them, the peculiar manifestation of our democracy. They have an exaggerated idea of the rights due themselves as individuals and no idea at all of the rights due others. It's the reverse of the peasant, and I'll tell you right now it's the peasant who makes the soldier.
Norman Mailer, *The Naked and the Dead* (1948).

"Why me?" That is the soldier's first question, asked each morning as the patrols go out and each evening as the night settles around the foxholes.
William Broyles, Jr., *The New York Times* (May 26,1986).

space-age weapons

It is still a matter of wonder how the Martians are able to slay men so swiftly and so silently. Many think that in some way they are able to generate an intense heat in a chamber of practically absolute nonconductivity. This intense heat they project in a parallel beam against any object they choose by means of a polished parabolic mirror of unknown composition, much as the parabolic mirror of a lighthouse projects a beam of light. But no one has absolutely proved these details. However, it is done, it is certain that a beam of heat is the essence of the matter. Heat, and invisible, instead of visible light. Whatever is combustible flashes into fame at its touch, lead runs like water, it softens iron, cracks and melts glass, and when it falls upon water, that explodes into steam.
H. G. Wells, *The War of the Worlds* (1898).

I won't go so far as to say that the suggestion that the Soviets have a new Manhattan Project capability breakthrough in the charged particle beam weapon is a piece of advance flackery for the new science fiction movie, "Star Wars."
Secretary of Defense Harold Brown, *Aviation Week and Space Technology* (May 30, 1977).

All in all the problem is much more complex than asking Luke Skywalker to "trust the Force" before blowing the Death Star to oblivion with "proton torpedoes."
Jeff Hecht, *Beam Weapons* (1984).

Spanish-American War

We want no war of conquest.... War should never be entered upon until every agency of peace has failed.
President William McKinley, Inaugural Address, March 4, 1897.

Stout hearts, my laddies! If the row comes, REMEMBER THE MAINE, and show the world how American sailors can fight.
Clifford K. Berryman, cartoon caption, *The Washington Post* (April 3, 1898). According to Edward T. Folliard, "Thus was born the slogan and battle cry of the Spanish-American War"; *The Washington Post* (September 24, 1972).

Everything is quiet. There is no trouble here. There will be no war. I wish to return.
Artist Frederic Remington's 1898 cable from Cuba to publisher William Randolph Hearst. Hearst cabled back: "Please remain. You furnish the pictures and I'll furnish the war." W. A. Swanberg, *Citizen Hearst* (1961). According to Joyce Milton, in *The Yellow Kids* (1989), "Hearst always denied sending such a telegram, and there is no proof that he did, even though it accurately reflects his views at the time."

I have already transmitted to Congress the report of the naval court of inquiry on the destruction of the battleship *Maine* in the harbor of Havana during the night of the 15th of February. The destruction of that noble vessel has filled the national heart with inexpressible horror. Two hundred and fifty-eight brave sailors and marines and two officers of our Navy, reposing in the fancied security of a friendly harbor, have been hurled to death, grief and want brought to their homes and sorrow to the nation.... The destruction of the *Maine*, by whatever exterior cause, is a patent and impressive proof of a state of things in Cuba that is intolerable....
I ask the Congress to authorize and empower the President to take measures to secure a full and final termination of hostilities between the government of Spain and the people of Cuba, and to secure in the island the establishment of a stable government, capable of maintaining order and observing its international obligations, insuring peace and tranquility and the security of its citizens as well as our own, and to use the military and naval forces of the United States as may be necessary for these purposes.
William McKinley, war message to Congress, April 11, 1898.

Don't cheer, men; those poor devils are dying.
Captain John "Jack" Philip of the USS *Texas*, asking his men to feel compassion for the sailors on the burning Spanish ship *Vizcaya* during the Battle of Santiago, July 4, 1898, quoted in Frank Freidel, *The Splendid Little War* (1959).

It has been a splendid little war; begun with the highest motives, carried on with magnificent intelligence and spirit, favored by that fortune which loves the brave. It is now to be concluded, I hope, with that fine good nature, which is, after all, the distinguishing trait of the American character.
John Hay, letter to Theodore Roosevelt, July 27, 1898, reprinted in *The Life and Letters of John Hay*, II ed., William R. Thayer (1915).

Someone has said that "God takes care of drunken men, sailors, and the United States." This expedition apparently relied on the probability that that axiom would prove true.
Richard Harding Davis, *The Cuban and Puerto Rican Campaigns* (1898).

When [in 1898] Senator [Redfield] Proctor, who owned marble quarries in Vermont, made a strong speech for war [Speaker of the House Thomas B.] Reed commented, "Proctor's position might have been expected. A war will make a large market for gravestones."
Barbara W. Tuchman, *The Proud Tower* (1966).

If we had not had a war with a nation that was already licked and looking for an excuse to quit, we would have had hell licked out of us.
General Smedley Butler, USMC, *The New York Times* (August 21, 1931).

I really do believe that if we had been up against a first-rate power, they would have whaled the mischief right out of us.
General Billy Mitchell, quoted in Isaac Don Levine, *Mitchell, Pioneer of Air Power* (1943).

After the *Maine* went down in 1898, war became virtually inevitable. In a Broadway bar a man raised his glass and said solemnly, "Gentlemen, remember the *Maine*." Through the streets of cities and towns, one suspects even down country roads and lanes, went the cry, "Remember the *Maine*! To hell with Spain!"
Curtis V. Hard, *Banners in the Air* (1988).

Spanish Armada

[On July 19, 1588] a match at bowls was being played, in which [Sir Francis] Drake and other high officers of the fleet were engaged, when a small armed vessel was seen running before the wind into Plymouth harbor with all sails set. Her commander landed in haste, and eagerly sought the place where the English lord admiral and his captains were standing. . . . He told the English officers that he had that morning seen the Spanish Armada off the Cornish coast. At this exciting information the captains began to hurry down to the water, and there was a shouting for the ships' boats; but Drake coolly checked his comrades, and insisted that the match should be played out. He said there was plenty of time both to win the game and beat the Spaniards. The best and bravest match that ever was scored was resumed accordingly. Drake and his friends aimed their last bowls with the same steady, calculating coolness with which they were about to point their guns.
E. S. Creasy, *The Fifteen Decisive Battles of the World* (1851).

Let tyrants fear. I have always so behaved myself that, under God, I have placed my chiefest strength and safeguard in the loyal hearts and good will of my subjects; and therefore I am come amongst you, as you see, at this time, not for my recreation and disport, but being resolved, in the midst and heat of the battle, to live or die amongst you all, to lay down for my God, and for my kingdom, and for my people, my honor and my blood, even in the dust. I know I have the body of a weak and feeble woman, but I have the heart and stomach of a king, and of a king of England too; and think foul scorn that Parma or Spain, or any prince of Europe, should dare to invade the borders of my realm.
Elizabeth I, speech to her army at Tilbury in anticipation of a Spanish invasion, August 8, 1588, reprinted in Joel Hurstfield, *Elizabeth I and the Unity of England* (1960). Hurstfield writes: "If we did not know that these words were written by Queen Elizabeth, we should be inclined to wonder whether they were written by William Shakespeare."

You are especially to take notice that the enemy's object will be to engage at a distance, on account of the advantage which they have from their artillery and the offensive fireworks with which they will be provided; and on the other hand, the object of our side should be to close and grapple and engage hand to hand.

Philip II of Spain, advice to Admiral Medina Sidonia before he sailed with the Spanish Armada, quoted in J. F. C. Fuller, *A Military History of the Western World*, II (1955).

Their force is wonderful, great and strong, yet we pluck their feathers by little and little.

Sir William Howard, *Of the Spanish Armada* (1588).

A tempest and the efforts of the English caused the failure of this expedition, which, although of considerable magnitude for the period when it appeared, was by no means entitled to the high-sounding name it received.

General Antoine Henri Jomini, *Summary of the Art of War* (1838).

Philip knew nothing whatever about ships, so he built the Spanish Armada and placed it in charge of the Duke of Medina-Sidonia, who knew even less. The Duke of Medina-Sidonia had never sailed a ship, but he said he would try.

Will Cuppy, *The Decline and Fall of Practically Everybody* (1950).

The defeat of the Spanish Armada really was decisive. It decided that religious unity was not to be reimposed by force on the heirs of medieval Christendom, and if, in doing so, it only validated what was already by far the most probable outcome, why, perhaps that is all that any of the battles we call decisive have ever done.

Garrett Mattingly, *The Armada* (1959).

Sparta

The Spartans remained secure as long as they were at war; but they collapsed as soon as they acquired an empire. They did not know how to use the leisure which peace brought; and they had never accustomed themselves to any discipline other and better than that of war.

Aristotle, *Politics* (4th century B.C.).

The Spartans . . . did not permit their city to be protected by walls, for they wanted to rely solely upon the valor of their men for their defense, and upon no other means. And therefore when a Spartan was asked by an Athenian whether he did not think the walls of Athens admirable, he replied, "Yes, if the city were inhabited by women."

Niccolò Machiavelli, *The Discourses* (1517).

Spartans not only conscripted and trained girls as well as boys, but they went far towards an identical treatment of both sexes. For Spartan girls, as well as for Spartan boys, conscription was universal; and the Spartan girls were not trained in special female accomplishments, nor kept in seclusion from the men. Spartan girls, like Spartan boys, were trained on a competitive system in athletics; and girls, like boys, competed naked in public before a male audience.

Arnold J. Toynbee, *War and Civilization* (1950).

speed

Rapidity is the essence of war.

Sun Tzu, *The Art of War* (4th century B.C.).

If the Army be not put into another method, and the War more vigorously prosecuted, the People can bear the War no longer, and will enforce you to a dishonorable peace.

Oliver Cromwell quoted in Antonia Fraser, *Cromwell* (1973).

All delays are dangerous in war.
John Dryden, *Tyrannic Law* (1669).

If you wage war, do it energetically and with severity. This is the only way to make it shorter, and consequently less inhuman.
Napoleon I, writing in 1799, quoted in J. C. Herold, *The Mind of Napoleon* (1955).

Go, sir, gallop, and don't forget that the world was made in six days. You can ask me for anything you like, except time.
Napoleon I, speaking to an aide in 1803, quoted in R. M. Johnston, *The Corsican* (1910).

Strategically, time and space are relative, and as the history of war has shown again and again, a handful of men at a certain spot at a certain hour is frequently a far more powerful instrument of war than ten times the number on the same spot twenty-four hours later.
J. F. C. Fuller, *Armoured Warfare* (1943).

The true speed of war is not headlong precipitancy, but the unremitting energy which wastes no time.
Alfred Thayer Mahan quoted in Bernard Brodie, *A Guide to Naval Strategy* (1944).

Nearly every attack involves some sort of regrouping or change of line.... With seasoned troops this can be done without loss of momentum . . ., but when the soldiers or their junior leaders are inexperienced and bewildered the pause to regroup can be fatal to success. This is not just due to the fact that if one goes to ground under fire it requires a real effort of will to stand up again; it is also because in all the noise and danger of action one is inclined to think the worst. Any pause, therefore, can be taken by raw troops as a sign that the attack has already failed, where the old sweats will sit tight until the next command reaches them.
Peter Cochrane, *Charlie Company* (1977).

spies and espionage

In general it is necessary to pay spies well and not be miserly in that respect. A man who risks being hanged in your service merits being well paid.
Frederick the Great, *Instructions for His Generals* (1747).

One of the most astonishing documents to come to light ... is an intercept dated December 12, 1940. Transmitted by the Japanese naval attaché in Berlin to ... Tokyo, the translation ... reads: "I have received from the GERMAN Navy minutes of a meeting of the BRITISH War Cabinet held on 15 August this year dealing with operations against JAPAN ...."
... this document's existence must raise the astonishing question of how the most confidential decisions of the British War Cabinet were being leaked to Berlin at the very height of the Battle of Britain.
John Costello, *The Pacific War* (1981).

The sense of bungling and futility cast a shadow over Washington and over political life generally. In the country at large, said one observer, a profound cynicism had developed toward "the system." Roosevelt was still popular, but not the major political and economic institutions which affected people's lives. In the late months of 1942 a joke was being told of a Japanese spy sent to discover which agencies of American government could be sabotaged and thereby cripple the American war effort. He reported back: "Suggested plan hopeless. Americans brilliantly prepared. For each

agency we destroy two more are already fully staffed and doing exactly the same work."
Geoffrey Perrett, *Days of Sadness, Years of Triumph: The American People 1939–1945* (1973).

Sometimes the cryptographers [at Bletchley Park] would labor for hours over a message, only to discover it was of mind-numbing banality, as in the following case. The Abwehr sent a message to its head of station in Algeciras, Spain, an officer code named "Cesar." The decoded message said: "Be careful of Axel. He bites." Was this a code within a code? It turned out to refer to the arrival of a guard dog for the station compound, a theory confirmed a few days later with the decrypting of an Enigma reply which read: "Cesar is in hospital. Axel bit him."
Phillip Knightley, *The Second Oldest Profession* (1986).

I was to go down to the deciphering headquarters at Bletchley Park in Buckinghamshire. On no account was I to go in uniform, it was far too secret. Having arrived at Bletchley Junction I asked the taxi-driver to take me to Bletchley Park. "Oh, the cloak and dagger center," he replied—so much for secrecy!
Ewen Montagu, *Beyond Top Secret Ultra* (1977).

At this time I had a complete confidence in Russian policy and I believed that the Western Allies deliberately allowed Russia and Germany to fight each other to the death. I had, therefore, no hesitation in giving all the information I had....
At first I thought that all I would do would be to inform the Russian authorities that work upon the atom bomb was going on. They wished to have more details and I agreed to supply them. I concentrated at first mainly on the products of my own work, but in particular at Los Alamos I did what I consider to be the worst I have done, namely to give information about the principles of the design of the plutonium bomb.
Klaus Fuchs, from his formal confession of January 27, 1950, reprinted in Norman Moss, *Klaus Fuchs: The Man Who Stole the Atom Bomb* (1987).

There are no rules in such a game. Hitherto acceptable norms of human conduct do not apply. If the US is to survive, longstanding American concepts of "fair play" must be reconsidered. We must develop effective espionage and counterespionage services and must learn to subvert, sabotage and destroy our enemies by more clever, more sophisticated, and more effective methods than those used against us. It may become necessary that the American people be made acquainted with, understand and support this fundamentally repugnant philosophy.
Commission in the Organization of the Executive Branch (Hoover Commission), *Report on the Intelligence Community* (July 4, 1954).

"I knew that flying over the Soviet Union without permission was spying," Francis Gary Powers said much later [after the 1960 U-2 incident]. "I *knew* that it was. But I really didn't think that in the true sense of the word spy I ever considered myself a spy. I was a pilot flying an airplane and it just so happened that where I was flying made what I was doing spying."
Michael R. Beschloss, *Mayday* (1986).

Espionage is undoubtedly a deplorable practice. But how can it be avoided when two rival powers, heavily over-armed, give each other the impression that they may reach for their guns at any moment?
Charles de Gaulle, *Memoirs of Hope: Renewal and Endeavor* (1971).

For better or worse, spy satellites serve a stabilizing function, reassuring each side that the other is not in the process of launching an attack. Taking potshots at such

satellites in peacetime, and especially during a period of international tension, doesn't make sense. The other side is far too likely to interpret those potshots as the first shots of a war and react accordingly.
Jeff Hecht, *Beam Weapons* (1984).

Espionage is the world's second oldest profession and just as honorable as the first.
Michael J. Barrett, "Honorable Espionage," *Journal of Defence and Diplomacy* (February 1984).

Today, in the United States certainly and in Britain possibly, spying is done for money, sex, revenge or just for the hell of it by tawdry little people of no discernible talent beyond showing up the nation's counterintelligence organizations. How elegant Donald Maclean, Guy Burgess, Kim Philby and Anthony Blunt seem by contrast, with their Cambridge educations, proper accents and high motives.
Robin W. Winks, "Traitors of Their Class," *The New York Times Book Review* (April 16, 1989).

staff

But I remember, when the fight was done,
When I was dry with rage and extreme toil,
Breathless and faint, leaning upon my sword,
Came there a certain lord, neat and trimly dress'd,
Fresh as a bridegroom; and his chin new reap'd
Show'd like a stubble-land at harvest-home;
He was perfumed like a milliner;
And 'twixt his finger and his thumb he held
A pouncet-box, which ever and anon
He gave his nose and took't away again;
Who therewith angry, when it next came there,
Tok it in snuff; and still he smiled and talk'd,
And as the soldiers bore dead bodies by,
He call'd them untaught knaves, unmannerly,
To bring a slovenly unhandsome corse
Betwixt the wind and his nobility. . . .

To see him shine so brisk, and smell so sweet,
And talk so like a waiting-gentlewoman
Of guns and drums and wounds—God save the mark!—
And telling me the sovereign'st thing on earth
Was parmaceti for an inward bruise;
And that it was great pity, so it was,
This villanous salt-petre should be digg'd
Out of the bowels of the harmless earth,
Which many a good tall fellow had destroy'd
So cowardly; and but for these vile guns,
He would himself have been a soldier.
William Shakespeare, *Henry IV, Part I*, Act I, Scene iii. General James M. Gavin, in his memoirs of World War II, *On to Berlin* (1978), said that this was his "favorite description of a staff officer from a higher command."

I am opposed to officers surrounding themselves with sons and relatives. It is a wrong principle, and in that case selections would be made from private and social relations, rather than for the public good.
General Robert E. Lee quoted in Captain Robert E. Lee, Jr., *Recollections and Letters of General Robert E. Lee* (1924).

The almost entire separation of the staff from the line, as now practised by us, has proved mischievous, and the great retinues of staff-officers with which some of our earlier generals began the war were simply ridiculous. . . . A bulky staff implies a division of responsibility, slowness of action, and indecision, whereas a small staff implies activity and concentration of purpose.
General William T. Sherman, *Memoirs* (1885).

"Good morning; good morning!" the general said
When we met him last week on our way to the line.
Now the soldiers he smiled at are most of 'em dead,
And we're cursing his staff for incompetent swine.
Siegfried Sassoon, *The General* (1918).

Staff officers should be the philosophers of war.
René Quinton, *Soldier's Testament* (1930).

[During a lunch with General George C. Marshall in 1944, General Douglas MacArthur] began a sentence, "My staff—" and Marshall cut him short, saying, "You don't have a staff, General. You have a court."
William Manchester, *American Caesar* (1978).

The old theory that a staff must limit itself to broad policy and planning activities has been proved unsound in this war [World War II]. . . . Unless a staff officer is able to assist his commander in getting things done, in addition to coordinating, planning and policy making, he is not serving his full usefulness.
General Alexander M. Patch quoted in Ray S. Cline, *Washington Command Post* (1951).

Alex [Field Marshal Harold Alexander] wouldn't do any work, except when he had to, and when he had to, it was on big exercises. . . He was ambitious to do his duty. He was lazy, but not over the essentials. He relied on his staff. If they did something wrong he would pull them up. His laziness was a virtue. It meant a capacity to delegate, and in wartime it became a tremendous asset, because it meant that he could relax and unhook.
Field Marshal Sir Gerald Templar quoted in Nigel Nicolson, *Alex* (1973).

Staff officers were separated from line officers the same way officers in general were separated from other ranks, by uniform. Their cap-bands and lapel-tabs were bright scarlet. The flamboyant unsuitability of this color as camouflage served to emphasize that the place of the Staff was distinctly not in the line.
Paul Fussell, *The Great War in Modern Memory* (1975).

[General Henry A. "Hap"] Arnold decreed a seven-day week for the duration. He wanted to make sure everyone around him knew there was war in progress, and everyone soon did. Whenever a member of his staff asked to be sent out for combat duty, someone was likely to accuse him of wanting a rest.
Thomas M. Coffey, *Hap* (1982).

chief of staff
To know the country thoroughly; to be able to conduct a reconnaissance with skill; to superintend the transmission of orders promptly; to lay down the most complicated

movements intelligibly, but in a few words and with simplicity: these are the leading qualifications which should distinguish an officer selected for the head of the staff.
Napoleon I, *Military Maxims* (1827).

When one congressman, noting the army's budget for toilet paper, asked him [General MacArthur as Army Chief of Staff in the early 1930s] with heavy irony, "General, do you expect a serious epidemic of dysentery in the U.S. Army?" MacArthur rose. "I have humiliated myself," he said bitterly. "I have almost licked the boots of some gentlemen to get funds for the motorization and mechanization of the army. Now, gentlemen, you have insulted me. I am as high in my profession as you are in yours. When you are ready to apologize, I shall be back." Before he could stalk from the room, they expressed their regrets.
William Manchester, *American Caesar* (1978).

Dean Acheson told me a characteristic story about Marshall when he first took over as Secretary of State. Marshall had asked Dean Acheson to stay on as Under Secretary and said, "I want the most complete and blunt truths from you, particularly about myself." Dean Acheson replied, "Do you, General?" "Yes," Marshall said. "I have no feelings except a few which I reserve for Mrs. Marshall."
Harry S. Truman, *Memoirs*, II (1956). This story is also told in Walter Isaacson and Evan Thomas, *The Wise Men* (1986). They add that "Marshall told Acheson that he would be his chief of staff—and the only channel to the secretary of state."

general staff
No part of our military organization requires more attention in peace than the general staff. It is in every service invariably the last in attaining perfection; and, if neglected in peace, when there is leisure, it will be impossible, in the midst of the hurry and bustle of war, to bring it to perfection.
John C. Calhoun, Secretary of War (1817–25), quoted in Russell F. Weigley, *History of the United States Army*, enlarged ed. (1984).

In times of peace the general staff should plan for all contingencies of war. Its archives should contain the historical details of the past, and all statistical, geographical, topographical, and strategic treatises and papers for the present and future.
General Antoine Henri Jomini, *Summary of the Art of War* (1838).

Our system makes no adequate provision for the directing brain which every army must have to work successfully. Common experience has shown that this cannot be furnished by any single man without assistants, and that it requires a body of officers working together under the direction of a chief and entirely separate from and independent of the administrative staff of an army (such as the adjutants, quartermasters, commissaries. . . .) This body of officers, in distinction from the administrative staff, has come to be called a general staff.
Secretary of War Elihu Root argues for a general staff for the U.S. Army in *The Annual Report of the Secretary of War for the Year 1902*.

When [in 1914, President] Wilson read in the Baltimore *Sun* that the General Staff was working on a war plan which was based on hostilities between Germany and the United States, he directed the Secretary of War to launch "an immediate investigation, and if it proved true, to relieve at once every officer of the General Staff and order him out of Washington," claimed General Bliss, the acting chief of staff at the time. . . . Once Bliss explained to Wilson that preparation of theoretical war plans had been a primary function of the war college division since 1903, the President dropped the matter.
D. Clayton James, *The Years of MacArthur*, I (1970).

The ideal General Staff should, in peace time, do nothing! They deal in an intangible stuff called thought. Their main business consists in thinking out what an enemy may do and what their Commanding Generals ought to do, and the less they clank their spurs the better.
Sir Ian Hamilton, *The Soul and Body of an Army* (1921).

The General Staff was essentially intended to form a collective substitute for genius, which no army can count on producing at need.
B. H. Liddell Hart, *The Defense of Britain* (1940).

The General Staff still lives in the world of pure staff planning.... It stakes its chances of success on the notion that if any project is given enough top-level direction, it just won't dare fail. Every program or project must be minutely planned from the beginning. The future holds no uncertainties, or if it does, they must be anticipated and treated as certainties. One of the basic faiths of the hierarchical general staff system is that there are no insoluble problems. Goals are viewed as puzzles for which there is only one right answer. The answer may not be obvious, but there is no doubt that it exists.
John C. Ries, *The Management of Defense* (1964).

German general staff
Me a Doctor? Then they should at least make Gneisenau an apothecary, for we two belong together always.
Prussian Field Marshal Gebhard von Blücher (Wellington's ally at Waterloo), on learning in June 1914 that Oxford University wished to award him an honorary doctorate; quoted in Roger Parkinson, *Clausewitz* (1970). Gneisenau was his Chief of Staff.

If people in Germany think I am the Supreme Commander, they are grossly mistaken. The General Staff tells me nothing and never asks my advice. I drink tea, go for walks and saw wood.... The only one who is a bit kind to me is the Chief of the Railway Department who tells me all he does and intends to do.
Kaiser William II, speaking during the fall of 1914, quoted in Michael Balfour, *The Kaiser and His Times* (1964).

The Great German General Staff and all similar organizations shall be dissolved and may not be reconstituted in any form.
Treaty of Versailles, Article 160 (1919).

Twice, after the loss of a World War, the General Staff has been dissolved on the orders of the victors. Both these actions show the unwilling respect in which our former enemies hold that most excellent organization.
General Heinz Guderian, *Panzer Leader* (1952).

Just a club of intellectuals.
Adolf Hitler's description of the German General Staff quoted in Walter Coerlitz, *History of The German General Staff* (1953).

There were vociferous objections to the general-staff principle following World War I, because it was written into the Treaty of Versailles that war guilt rested with the German General Staff. This superficial analysis of war cause is typical of those who make no systematic study of war. Knowing little about the subject they can quickly dispose of it by agreeing that such and such a cause, like "pernicious militarism," or "imperialism," or "the German General Staff," was responsible for the whole unpleasant business.
Dale O. Smith, *U.S. Military Doctrine* (1955).

While forbidding the existence of the Great General Staff, the Treaty of Versailles permitted the continued existence of the staff systems in the ten Reichwehr divisions of the postwar Germany Army. In these divisions the general staff officers continued their duties, still wearing their old insignia, thus forming an effective means of keeping alive the methods and traditions of the general staff during the years that passed between the treaty of Versailles and the rearmament of Germany.
J. D. Hittle, *The Military Staff*, 3rd ed. (1961).

The General Staff was always one of Hitler's pet hates, and not only because he knew very well that originally the Army regarded him as a jumped-up corporal. As a genuine, embittered veteran of the trenches to whom the defeat of 1918 had come as a shattering blow, Hitler never stopped "cursing the Staff for incompetent swine."
Richard Humble, *Hitler's Generals* (1974).

Stalin, Joseph (1879–1953)

Stalin is too rude, and this fault, entirely supportable in relations among us Communists, becomes insupportable in the office of General Secretary. Therefore, I propose to the comrades to find a way to remove Stalin from that position and appoint to it another man who in all respects differs from Stalin only in superiority—namely, more patient, more loyal, more polite and more attentive to comrades, less capricious, etc.
V. I. Lenin, letter to the Central Committee of the Communist Party, December 25, 1922, postscript of January 4, 1923, quoted in Robert Payne, *The Rise and Fall of Stalin* (1965).

[Stalin during World War II] had no strategic dogmas to impose upon others. He did not approach his generals with operational blue-prints of his own. He indicated to them his general ideas, which were based on an exceptional knowledge of all aspects of the situation, economic, political, and military. But beyond that he let his generals formulate their views and work out their plans, and on these he based his decisions. His role seems to have been that of the cool, detached, and experienced arbiter of his own generals.
Isaac Deutscher, *Stalin*, 2nd ed. (1967).

For Stalin the discovery of Hitler's body by Russian troops was the sweetest of all triumphs. Against Hitler he had waged a strange vendetta which could only end with the death of one of them. . . . Inevitably for Stalin the vendetta took a Georgian form; he would not rest until he had the body of his adversary in his power, until he had insulted it, and until he had left upon it the indelible sign of his victory.
According to the ritual of a Georgian vendetta the body of the dead enemy becomes a trophy, and the victor can do with it whatever he pleases. Usually the skull was kept and fashioned into a drinking cup, while the dismembered body was thrown into a ravine. . . . No one knows what punishment Stalin inflicted on the charred body of Hitler. What is certain is that it came within the circle of his power and that he was able to do with it as he pleased.
Robert Payne, *The Rise and Fall of Stalin* (1965).

My father died a difficult and terrible death. . . . God grants an easy death only to the just.
Svetlana Alliluyeva (Stalin's daughter), *Twenty Letters to a Friend* (1967).

There are still some people who think that we have Stalin to thank for all our progress, who quake before Stalin's dirty underdrawers, who stand at attention and salute them.
Nikita Khrushchev quoted in Strobe Talbott, *Khrushchev Remembers* (1970).

I always thought they made a mistake of treating Stalin [as if he were] a product of the Foreign Service. He was a rough SOB who made his way by murder and everything else and should be talked to that way.
General George C. Marshall quoted in Forrest C. Pogue, *George C. Marshall: Organizer of Victory* (1973).

Stalin was an SOB but of course he thinks I'm one, too.
President Harry S. Truman quoted in James MacGregor Burns, *The Crosswinds of Freedom* (1989).

strategic analysis

We may be likened to two scorpions in a bottle, each capable of killing the other, but only at the risk of his own life.
J. Robert Oppenheimer, "Atomic Weapons and American Policy," *Foreign Affairs* (July 1953).

The superpowers often behave like two heavily armed blind men feeling their way around a room, each believing himself in mortal peril from the other whom he assumes to have perfect vision. Each side should know that frequently uncertainty, compromise, and incoherence are the essence of policymaking. Yet each tends to ascribe to the other side a consistency, foresight, and coherence that its own experience belies. Of course, over time even two armed blind men in a room can do enormous damage to each other, not to speak of the room.
Henry Kissinger, *White House Years* (1979).

War is unthinkable but not impossible, and therefore we must think about it.
Bernard Brodie quoted in Fred Kaplan, *The Wizards of Armageddon* (1983).

Welcome to the world of strategic analysis, where we program weapons that don't work against threats that don't exist.
Ivan Selin quoted in Andrew Cockburn, *The Threat* (1983).

Much of the criticism concerning today's Navy stems from career-academic strategists and so-called "defense analysts" who have never set foot on a Navy deckplate. It is folly for these individuals, who have the responsibility neither to deploy a military force nor face the threat, to attempt to determine military requirements needed to meet that threat.
Admiral Carlisle A. H. Trost, Chief of Naval Operations, *Philadelphia Inquirer* (August 22, 1987).

Strategic Defense Initiative

As soon as they signal a flight of offensive rockets speeding towards them, the defensive rockets will automatically be released by radar, to speed into the heavens and explode in whatever cubic space in the stratosphere radar decides the enemy's offensive rockets will enter at a calculated time. Then, hundreds of miles above the surface of the earth, noiseless battles will be fought between blast and counter-blast. Now and again an invader will get through when up will go London, Paris or New York in a 40,000 feet high mushroom of smoke and dust, and as nobody will know what is happening above or beyond, or be certain who is fighting whom—let alone what for— the war will go on in a kind of bellicose perpetual motion until the last laboratory blows up. Then should any life be left on earth, a conference will undoubtedly be held to decide who was victor and who was vanquished, the latter being forthwith liquidated by the former as war "criminals".
J. F. C. Fuller anticipating SDI development in *Armament and History* (1945).

The rulers in the Kremlin are as eager as Hitler was to get power over the whole world. But, unlike Hitler, they are not gamblers. If we can put up a missile defense that makes their attack dubious, chances are they will never try the attack.
Edward Teller, *Time* (March 29, 1982).

Tonight, consistent with our obligations under the ABM Treaty and recognizing the need for close consultation with our allies, I am taking an important first step. I am directing a comprehensive and intensive effort to define a long-term research and development program to begin to achieve our ultimate goal of eliminating the threat posed by strategic nuclear missiles. This could pave the way for arms control measures to eliminate the weapons themselves. We seek neither military superiority nor political advantage. Our only purpose—one all people share—is to search for ways to reduce the danger of nuclear war.
President Ronald Reagan, speech to the nation on the Strategic Defense Initiative, March 23, 1983.

The inescapable reality is that there is literally no hope that Star Wars can make nuclear weapons obsolete. . . . [But] as long as the American people believe that Star Wars offers real hope of reaching the President's asserted goal, it will have a level of political support unrelated to reality.
McGeorge Bundy, George F. Kennan, Robert S. McNamara, and Gerard Smith, "The President's Choice," *Foreign Affairs* (Winter 1984–85).

Some say it will bring war to the heavens, but its purpose is to deter war, in the heavens and on earth.
President Ronald Reagan, State of the Union address, February 6, 1985.

It is the Edsel of the 1980s. It is overpriced, it has been oversold, it will not perform as advertised.
Congressman Gerry E. Studds quoted in *The New York Times* (June 21, 1985).

We're talking about a weapon that won't kill people. It'll kill weapons.
President Ronald Reagan quoted in *Newsweek* (September 30, 1985).

These [SDI support in the Congress] are the kind of things you don't measure by votes—you put your nose in the air and smell. If you give it the old sniff test, there's an awful lot of uneasy feeling about SDI.
Senator Sam Nunn, *Los Angeles Times* (June 7, 1985).

[SDI] cannot be implemented effectively in a military-strategic sense. I think that a potential enemy with highly developed technology always can find a means to overcome space defenses. It is much easier and cheaper to overcome space defenses than to create them. If the SDI is created, the U.S.S.R. will find ways to make it ineffective at every stage.
Andrei D. Sakharov, *U.S. News and World Report* (January 12, 1987).

The notion of a defense that will protect American cities is one that will not be achieved, but it is that goal that supplies the political magic, as it were, in the president's vision.
James R. Schlesinger, testimony before the Senate Foreign Relations Committee, quoted in *The New York Times* (February 7, 1987).

[The SDI] has been a singularly effective instrument for bringing the Soviets to the bargaining table.
President Ronald Reagan, speech in Washington, D.C., March 23, 1987.

We cannot succumb to [those] who would pull a "Star Wars" cover over our heads—a modern Maginot Line—ravaging our economic capital, nuclearizing the heavens and yielding the fate of our children's world to the malfunction of a computer.
Senator Joseph R. Biden, Jr., *Los Angeles Times* (June 10, 1987).

SDI is a bit like the French folk story of the Pope's mule. The Pope offered vast sums of money to anyone who could teach his mule to speak. One day a simple peasant went to see the Pope and returned with the prize. The peasant had promised to teach the mule to speak within ten years. When asked how he could make such a pledge since mules cannot speak, the peasant replied: "In ten years either the Pope will be dead, or I will be dead or the mule will be dead."
Gerald Segal, *Guide to the World Today* (1988).

During the Reagan Administration it [SDI] was described in terms that, frankly, I think oversold the concept. We have this notion that occasionally was mentioned, the idea of a total, complete shield that would be absolutely leak-proof and block all incoming missiles.
If you think about it in those terms, it's going to be an extremely remote proposition. If, on the other hand, you look at it as a system that could interfere with a Soviet first strike on the United States, that would be able to knock out a lot of incoming warheads and thereby increase deterrence, then it becomes a very different proposition.
Dick Cheney, Secretary of Defense, *The New York Times* (March 29, 1989).

strategic superiority

The so-called "defense intellectuals" of the Kennedy-Johnson Administration advocate parity as an ultimate goal, although not many admit it publicly. . . . Others, notably military men, think that deterrence is only possible in an atmosphere of strategic superiority. . . .
General Curtis E. LeMay, *America Is in Danger* (1968).

What in the name of God is strategic superiority? What is the significance of it, politically, militarily, operationally, at these levels of numbers? What do you do with it?
Secretary of State Henry A. Kissinger, *Department of State Bulletin* (July 29, 1974).

Our country has never sought, nor is it seeking, military superiority. But we will not permit others to become superior to us.
Andrei A. Gromyko, Foreign Minister of the Soviet Union, *The New York Times* (September 23, 1981).

A truly paradoxical situation has now developed. Even if one country engages in a steady arms buildup while the other does nothing, the side that arms itself will all the same gain nothing. The weak side may simply explode all its nuclear charges, even on its own territory, and that would mean suicide for it and a slow death for the enemy. This is why any striving for military superiority means chasing one's own tail. It can't be used in real politics.
Mikhail Gorbachev, *Perestroika* (1987).

strategy

The best way to defeat an enemy is to defeat his strategy. The best way to defeat his strategy is to adopt it.
Sun Tzu, *The Art of War* (4th century B.C.).

A vigilant and prudent general will carefully weigh in council the state of his own forces and of those of the enemy, as a civil magistrate judging between two contending parties. If he finds himself in many respects superior to his adversary, he must by no means defer bringing on an engagement. But if he knows himself to be inferior, he must avoid general actions and endeavor to succeed by surprises, ambuscades and stratagems. These, when skillfully managed by good generals, have often given them the victory over enemies superior both in numbers and strength.

Vegetius, *De Re Militari* (A.D. 378).

Recently there have been people getting on in the world as strategists, but they are usually just sword-fencers.

Miyamoto Musashi, *A Book of Five Rings* (1645).

[Strategy is] the art of the employing of battles to gain the object of the war.... Strategy forms the plan of the war, maps out the proposed course of the different campaigns which compose the war, and regulates the battles to be fought in each.

Karl von Clausewitz, *On War* (1832). According to B. H. Liddell Hart, *Strategy*, 2nd ed. (1967), "One defect of this definition is that it intrudes on the sphere of policy, or the higher conduct of the war, which must necessarily be the responsibility of the government and not of the military leaders it employs as its agents.

The object of warfare is murder; the means employed in warfare—spying, treachery, and the encouragement of it, the ruin of a country, the plundering of its inhabitants and robbery for the maintenance of the army, trickery and lying ... are called military strategy.

Leo Tolstoy, *War and Peace* (1865–69).

Strategy is a game.

Ardant du Picq, *Battle Studies* (1868).

The main thing in true strategy is simply this: first deal as hard blows at the enemy's soldiers as possible, and then cause so much suffering to the inhabitants of a country that they will long for peace and press their Government to make it. Nothing should be left to the people but eyes to lament the war.

General Philip H. Sheridan quoted in Archibald Forbes, *Memories and Studies in War and Peace* (1895).

War, once declared, must be waged offensively, aggressively. The enemy must not be fended off, but smitten down. You may then spare him every exaction, relinquish every gain; but till down he must be struck incessantly and remorselessly.

Alfred Thayer Mahan, *The Interest of America in Sea Power* (1897).

Atrocities are the last resource of strategy in its efforts to force an enemy to his knees.

Captain Charles Ross, *Representative Government and War* (1903).

If I am in command when war breaks out I shall issue as my orders: The essence of war is violence. Moderation in war is imbecility. Hit first, hit hard, and hit everywhere.

Admiral Sir John Fisher, April 25, 1912, letter to Lord Esher, quoted in Ruddock F. MacKay, *Fisher of Kilverstone* (1973).

Range is more to strategy than force. The invention of bully-beef has modified land-war more profoundly than the invention of gunpowder.

T. E. Lawrence, "Evolution of a Revolt," *Army Quarterly* (October 1920), reprinted in *Evolution of a Revolt* (1968).

The aim of strategy is to clinch a political argument by means of force instead of words. Normally this is accomplished by battle, the true object of which is not physical destruction, but mental submission on the part of the enemy.
J. F. C. Fuller, *Armoured Warfare* (1943).

There is a stark simplicity about an unrestricted nuclear war that almost enables it to be summed up in one short sentence: Be quick on the draw and the trigger squeeze, and aim for the heart. One then has to add: but even if you shoot first, you will probably die too.... This brings us a long way from the subtleties of a Clausewitz, Jomini, or a Mahan.... It brings us even a long way from Douhet, the prophetic theorist of strategic air power. It brings us, in short, to the end of strategy as we have known it.
Bernard Brodie, "Strategy Hits a Dead End," *Harper's* (October 1955).

A great deal of argument about military strategy ... postulates the "rational action" of a kind of "strategic man," a man who on further acquaintance reveals himself as a university professor of unusual intellectual subtlety.
Hedley Bull, *The Control of the Arms Race* (1961).

The history of strategy is, fundamentally, a record of the application and evolution of the indirect approach.
B. H. Liddell Hart, *Strategy*, 2nd ed. (1967).

The one gleaming lesson of twentieth-century warfare is that strategy follows, and does not precede, the scientist and the technician.
Robert Rhodes James, *The British Revolution* (1976).

Strategy is a system of expediencies.... In war, as in the arts, there is no general standard, in neither can talent be replaced by a rule.
Field Marshal Helmuth von Moltke quoted in John I. Alger, *The Quest for Victory* (1982).

Strategy has become fashionable in the United States, though only the demand for that elusive commodity is in evidence, there being no perceptible supply. It was Vietnam that did it of course, by proving that good intentions and the sheer outpouring of means need not suffice to achieve even the half-victory that was desired.
Edward N. Luttwak, *Strategy and History*, II (1985).

Consider an ordinary tactical choice, of the sort frequently made in war. An advancing force can move toward its objective on one of two roads, one good and one bad.... Only in the conflictual realm of strategy would the choice arise at all, for it is only if combat is possible that a bad road can be good *precisely because it is bad* and may therefore be less strongly held or even left unguarded by the enemy. Equally, the good road is apt to be bad because it is the better road, whose use by the advancing force is more likely to be anticipated and opposed.
In this case, then, the paradoxical logic of strategy reaches the extreme of a full reversal.
Edward N. Luttwak, *Strategy* (1987).

Strategy is a fancy word for a road map for getting from here to there, from the situation at hand to the situation one wishes to attain.
Paul Seabury and Angelo Codevilla, *War* (1989).

center of gravity

A center of gravity is always found where the mass is concentrated most densely. It presents the most effective target for a blow; furthermore, the heaviest blow is that struck by the center of gravity.

Karl von Clausewitz, *On War* (1832). Clausewitz later delineates the wide variety of possible centers of gravity: "For Alexander, Gustavus Adolphus, Charles XII, and Frederich the Great, the center of gravity was their army. If the army had been destroyed, they would all have gone down in history as failures. In countries subject to domestic strife, the center of gravity is generally the capital. In small countries that rely on large ones, it is usually the army of their protector. Among alliances, it lies in the community of interest, and in popular uprisings it is the personalities of the leaders and public opinion."

There are in Europe many good generals, but they see too many things at once. I see only one thing, namely the enemy's main body. I try to crush it, confident that secondary matters will then settle themselves.

Napoleon I quoted in David G. Chandler, *The Campaigns of Napoleon* (1968). According to Chandler, this statement is "the kernel, the central theme, of Napoleon's concept of warfare: the blitzkrieg attack aimed at the main repository of the enemy's power—his army."

Among all the combat agencies of war, the Infantry remains the center of gravity of battle. Only the infantryman can hold ground and protect himself. But no longer can the Infantry alone win ground. The tragic Queen of Battles, without her servitors, is no longer queen. She remains at the center of military power but is powerless without her stanch supporters.

Thomas R. Phillips, "The New Face of War," *Infantry Journal Reader*, ed. J. I. Greene (1943).

By seeing the Viet Cong as a separate entity rather than as an instrument of North Vietnam, we chose a center of gravity which in fact did not exist. The proof that the Viet Cong guerrillas were not a center of gravity was demonstrated during Tet-68, when, even though they were virtually destroyed, the war continued unabated.

Harry G. Summers, Jr., *On Strategy* (1982).

In war we often see the collision of centers of gravity, great concentrations of combat power at decisive points. These collisions—these battles—can occur sporadically throughout the depths of the theater of war with one ultimate moral objective. This is the raw destruction of the enemy's will to resist. For it is the strength of will to resist that provides the cohesion, the coherence, to these centers of gravity in collision.

James J. Schneider and Lawrence L. Izzo, "Clausewitz's Elusive Center of Gravity," *Parameters* (September 1987).

concentration

If I am able to determine the enemy's dispositions while at the same time I conceal my own, then I can concentrate and he must divide.

Sun Tzu, *The Art of War* (4th century B.C.).

One should never risk one's whole fortune unless supported by one's entire forces.

Niccolò Machiavelli, *The Discourses* (1517).

There is no more dangerous form than to extend the front of your army greatly if you do not clearly have a very effective and a very large army; on the contrary, you ought to make it deep and not very wide rather than very wide and thin.

Niccolò Machiavelli, *The Art of War* (1520).

There is an ancient rule of war that cannot be repeated often enough: hold your forces together, make no detachments, and, when you are ready to fight the enemy,

assemble all your forces and seize every advantage to make sure of success. This rule is so certain that most of the generals who have neglected it have been punished promptly.
Frederick the Great, *Instructions for His Generals* (1747).

The art of war consists, with a numerically inferior army, in always having larger forces than the enemy at the point which is to be attacked or defended. But this art can be learned neither from books nor from practice; it is an intuitive way of acting which properly consitutes the genius of war.
Napoleon I, writing in 1797, quoted in J. C. Herold, *The Mind of Napoleon* (1955).

It is the same with strategy as with the siege of fortresses; concentrate fire on a single point; when the breach is made the equilibrium is broken; all the rest becomes useless and the fortress is taken.
Napoleon I quoted in Felix Markam, *Napoleon* (1963).

There is no more imperative and no simpler law for strategy than to keep the forces concentrated. No portion is to be separated from the main body.... On this maxim we stand firm.
Karl von Clausewitz, *On War* (1832).

Concentration is the secret of strength in politics, in war, in trade, in short in all management of human affairs.
Ralph Waldo Emerson, *The Conduct of Life* (1860).

[Confederate General] Nathan Bedford Forrest, who had but a single year of formal education, is occasionally cited as a contributor to the popularity of terse aphorisms that express the highest truths of the military art. Any mention of either Forrest or military fundamentals brings to mind the advice associated with his name: "Git thar furst with the mostest." This phrase is an astute, albeit homey, rewording of Jomini's fundamental principle to be strong at the decisive point.
John I. Alger, *The Quest for Victory* (1982).

Very large concentrations of troops are in themselves a calamity. The army which is concentrated at one point is difficult to supply and can never be billeted; it cannot march, it cannot operate, it cannot exist at all for any length of time; it can only fight.
To remain separated as long as possible while operating and to be concentrated in good time for the decisive battle, that is the task of the leader of large masses of troops.
Field Marshal Helmuth von Moltke, 1869 instructions, quoted in Rudolf von Caemmerer, *The Development of Strategical Thought in the 19th Century* (1905).

The fundamental object in all military combinations is to gain local superiority by concentration.
Alfred Thayer Mahan, *Naval Strategy* (1911).

To win, we must endeavor to be the stronger of the two at the point of impact. Our only hope of this lies in making *our own choice* of operations, not in waiting *passively* for whatever the *enemy chooses* for us.
Field Marshal Alfred von Schlieffen quoted in Gerhard Ritter, *The Schlieffen Plan* (1979).

All through history, from the days of the great phalanx of the Roman Legion, the master law of tactics remains unchanged; this law is that to achieve success you must be superior at the point where you intend to strike the decisive blow.
Major B. L. Montgomery, "The Growth of Modern Infantry Tactics," *Antelope* (January 1925); also in Nigel Hamilton, *Monty* (1981).

Oppose the strategy of striking with two "fists" in two directions at the same time, and uphold the strategy of striking with one "fist" in one direction at a time.
Mao Tse-tung, *Selected Military Writings* (1963).

The principles of war, not merely one principle, can be condensed into a single word—"concentration." But for truth this needs to be amplified as the "concentration of strength against weakness." And for any real value it needs to be explained that the concentration of strength against weakness depends on the dispersion of your opponent's strength, which in turn is produced by a distribution of your own that gives the appearance, and partial effect of dispersion. Your dispersion, his dispersion, your concentration—such is the sequence, and each is a sequel. True concentration is the fruit of calculated dispersion.
B. H. Liddell Hart, *Strategy*, 2nd ed. (1967).

grand strategy
The management of operations so as to determine the times, areas, and results of campaigns in order to win the war is called grand strategy.
Quincy Wright, *A Study of War* (1942).

It is the function of grand strategy to discover and exploit the Achilles' heel of the enemy nation; to strike not against its strongest bulwark but against its most vulnerable spot.
B. H. Liddell Hart, *Thoughts on War* (1944).

While the horizon of strategy is bounded by the war, grand strategy looks beyond the war to the subsequent peace.
B. H. Liddell Hart, *Strategy*, 2nd ed. (1967).

indirect approach
In all fighting, the direct method may be used for joining battle, but indirect methods will be needed in order to secure victory.
Sun Tzu, *The Art of War* (4th century B.C.).

A direct approach to the . . . objective along the "line of natural expectation" has ever tended to negative results. The reason being that the strength of an enemy country or force lies far less in its numbers or resources than in its stability or equilibrium—of control, morale and supply. . . . The decisive victories in military history have come from the strategy of indirect approach, wherein the dislocation of the enemy's moral, mental, or material balance is the vital prelude to an attempt at his overthrow. The strategy of indirect approach is, indeed, the highest and widest fulfillment of the principle of surprise.
B. H. Liddell Hart, *Thoughts on War* (1944).

Under [Field Marshal B. L.] Montgomery's theory the old slogging match was out. Stealth and cunning were far more important than the massing of overwhelming numbers. One must never strike directly at important objectives, but go around them. The cutting edge of the Army must consist of strong highly trained and highly mobile columns, capable of making narrow but deep penetrations and then fanning out in the rear of the enemy line.
Alan Moorehead, *Montgomery* (1946).

This system of warfare [allowed me] to avoid the frontal attack with its terrible loss of life; to by-pass Japanese strongpoints and neutralize them by cutting their lines of supply, to thus isolate their armies and starve them on the battlefield; to, as Willie

Keeler [a baseball player] used to say, "hit 'em where they ain't"—that from this time forward guided my movements and operations.
General Douglas MacArthur speaking of his World War II tactics in the Pacific in his *Reminiscences* (1964).

The strategy of the indirect approach is a "must" for the side which cannot be certain of being strong enough to beat the enemy in battle on ground of the enemy's choosing.
Andre Beaufre, *An Introduction to Strategy* (1965).

maritime strategy

The United States is a naval power by necessity, critically dependent on the transoceanic import of vital strategic materials. Over 90 percent of our commerce between continents moves in ships. Freedom to use the seas is our nation's lifeblood. For that reason our navy is designed to keep the sea lanes open worldwide—a far greater task than closing those sea lanes at strategic choke points. Maritime superiority for us is a necessity. We must be able in time of emergency to venture in harm's way, controlling air, surface, and subsurface areas to assure access to all the oceans of the world. Failure to do so will leave the credibility of our conventional defense forces in doubt.
We are . . . building a six-hundred-ship fleet, including fifteen carrier battle groups.
President Ronald Reagan, speech at Long Beach, California, December 28, 1982.

[The U.S. Navy's] leaders have then produced a so-called maritime strategy to justify the 600-ship goal, even though the strategy is unrealistic and the forces "required" do not relate to it in any coherent way. Thus the navy boasts of its ability to provide forward deployments in the Sea of Japan and the Norwegian Sea, to attack enemy fleets in their home ports, and to project naval firepower by means of aircraft, cruise missiles, and guns against targets on land, sea, and air. Indeed, if one were to believe all this, the Navy and the Marine Corps would be the decisive offensive factor in defeating the Soviet Union in a conventional war.
William W. Kaufmann and Lawrence J. Korb, *The 1990 Defense Budget* (1989).

An analysis of the content of the maritime strategy suggests that it is a carefully woven fabric of substrategies that more clearly serves the Navy's institutional interests in rationalizing its existing force mix than it does the U.S. national strategy or security interests.
Carl H. Builder, *The Masks of War* (1989).

strategy and tactics

Strategy is the art of making war upon the map, and comprehends the whole theater of operations. Grand Tactics is the art of posting troops upon the battlefield according to the accidents of the ground, of bringing them into action, and the art of fighting upon the ground, in contradistinction to planning upon a map. Its operations may extend over a field of ten or twelve miles in extent. Logistics comprises the means and arrangements which work out the plans of strategy and tactics. Strategy decides where to act; logistics brings the troops to this point; grand tactics decides the manner of execution and the employment of the troops.
General Antoine Henri Jomini, *Summary of the Art of War* (1838).

Only great tactical results can lead to great strategical results.
Alfred Thayer Mahan, *Naval Strategy* (1911).

Tactical results are the only things that matter in war. . . . Where there is no battle, there is no award, nothing is accomplished. . . . No strategy can henceforth prevail over that which aims at ensuring tactical results, victory by fighting.
Marshal Ferdinand Foch, *The Principles of War* (1918).

In peace we concentrate so much on tactics that we are apt to forget that it is merely the handmaiden of strategy.
B. H. Liddell Hart, *Thoughts on War* (1944).

Our strategy is one against ten, while our tactics is ten against one—such contradictions provide the laws by which we overcome the enemy.
Mao Tse-tung quoted in Robert Payne, *Mao Tse-tung* (1950).

I hold that tactics, the art of handling troops on the battlefield, is and always will be a more difficult and more important part of the general's task than strategy, the art of bringing forces to the battlefield in a favorable position. A homely analogy can be made from contract bridge. The calling is strategy, the play of the hand tactics. I imagine that all experienced card-players will agree that the latter is the more difficult part of the game, and gives more scope for the skill of the good player. Calling is to a certain degree mechanical and subject to conventions: so is strategy, the main principles of which are simple and easy to grasp. . . . But in the end it is the result of the manner in which the cards are played or the battle is fought that is put down on the score sheets of the pages of history. Therefore, I rate the skillful tactician above the skillful strategist, especially him who plays the bad cards well.
Field Marshal Archibald Wavell, *Soldiers and Soldiering* (1953).

The task of the science of strategy is to study those laws for directing a war that govern a war situation as a whole. The task of the science of campaigns and the science of tactics is to study those laws for directing a war that govern a partial situation.
Mao Tse-tung, *Selected Military Writings* (1963).

As regards the relation of strategy to tactics, while in execution the borderline is often shadowy, and it is difficult to decide exactly where a strategical movement ends and a tactical movement begins, yet in conception the two are distinct. Tactics lines in and fills the province of fighting. Strategy not only stops on the frontier, but has for its purpose the reduction of fighting to the slenderest possible proportions.
B. H. Liddell Hart, *Strategy*, 2nd ed. (1967).

There is more truth than jest in the statement that, to any soldier, what he does is tactical and what his next senior does is strategic. This is generally expressive from the private all the way up to the theater commander.
Rear Admiral J. C. Wylie, *Military Strategy* (1967).

In theater strategy, political goals and constraints on one hand and available resources on the other determine projected outcomes. At a much lower level, tactics deal with specific techniques. In the operational dimension, by contrast, schemes of warfare such as blitzkrieg or defense in depth evolve or are exploited. Such schemes seek to attain the goals set by theater strategy through suitable combinations of tactics.
Edward N. Luttwak, "The Operational Level of War," *International Security* (Winter 1980/81).

"Strategic" war is a nonsense term, for strategy is a feature not a type of war. To talk of "strategic" war is like talking about a political election or a musical concert; the use of the word "strategic" is redundant. Similarly, to talk of a "tactical" weapon is nonsensical. The use of any weapons in battle involves judgments on targeting, the avoidance of counter-measures and concentration on immediate objectives, i.e. tactics. It is as difficult to imagine a non-tactical weapon as it is to imagine a non-strategic war.
Lawrence Freedman, *The Evolution of Nuclear Strategy* (1981).

The plan, Zeppelin, was based on Allied knowledge of German misconceptions, that Churchill favored a Balkan invasion in World War II, as he had in World [War] I. The object of Zeppelin: to force Hitler to defend Fortress Europe everywhere so that on D-Day he would not be strong enough at the point of actual attack to resist effectively. Zeppelin was the modern application of the Duke of Wellington's reply to Blucher before Waterloo about what his strategy and tactics were to be when they met Napoleon's army: "Sir, my strategy is one against ten, my tactics ten against one."
    Anthony Cave Brown, *The Last Hero* (1982).

strength

Even the bravest cannot fight beyond his strength.
    Homer, *The Iliad* (1000 B.C.).

We all have enough strength to endure the misfortunes of others.
    François de La Rochefoucauld, *Maxims* (1665).

The first quality of a soldier is constancy in enduring fatigue and hardship. Courage is only the second. Poverty, privation, and want are the school of the good soldier.
    Napoleon I, *Military Maxims* (1827).

My good blade carves the casques of men,
    My tough lance thrusteth sure,
My strength is as the strength of ten,
    Because my heart is pure.
    Alfred, Lord Tennyson, *Sir Galahad* (1842).

No one should get into this fight [World War I combat] who hasn't the physical endurance and stamina. Courage is the smallest part of it. Physical endurance will give one control of one's nerves long after the breaking point seems to have been reached.
    Major William J. "Wild Bill" Donovan, letter to his wife, August 7, 1918, quoted in Anthony Cave Brown, *The Last Hero* (1982).

To insist on strength . . . is not war-mongering. It is peace-mongering.
    Senator Barry M. Goldwater, *The New York Times* (August 11, 1964).

We will maintain strength so sufficient that it need not be proven in combat—a quiet strength based not merely on the size of an arsenal but on the nobility of ideas.
    President Jimmy Carter, Inaugural Address, January 20, 1977.

submarines

The whole manner of its attack implied skulking, treachery and deception—qualities warriors traditionally had disdained. British Admiral A. K. Wilson spoke for the entire naval establishment when he described the submarine as "underhanded, unfair and damned un-English."
    Robert L. O'Connell, *Of Arms and Men* (1989).

[The] submarines may be the cause of bringing battle to a stoppage altogether, for fleets will become useless, and as other war materiel continues to improve, war will become impossible.
    Jules Verne, "The Future of the Submarine" (1904), *Fifty Years of Popular Mechanics*, ed. E. L. Throm (1951).

But the Royal Navy has immediately attacked the U-boats, and is hunting them night and day—I will not say without mercy, because God forbid we should ever part company with that—but at any rate with zeal and not altogether without relish.
Winston Churchill, BBC broadcast as First Lord of the Admiralty, October 1, 1939.

When you see a rattlesnake poised to strike, you do not wait until he has struck before you crush him.
President Franklin D. Roosevelt, address to the nation, September 11, 1941. The "rattle-snakes" were German U-boats in the Atlantic and he had just ordered the U.S. Navy to attack them on sight.

Sighted sub, sank same.
Contact report during the Battle of the Atlantic, sent on January 28, 1942 by Donald F. Mason of the U.S. Navy, quoted in the *The New York Times* (April 2, 1942).

Sturgeon no longer virgin.
U.S. submarine *Sturgeon*, a signal that it has sunk its first enemy ship, *Time* (October 12, 1942).

If the Bureau of Ordnance can't provide us with torpedoes that will hit and explode, or with a gun larger than a peashooter, then, for God's sake get the Bureau of Ships to design a boathook with which we can rip the plates off the target's sides.
Admiral Charles Lockwood, complaining about the U.S. Navy's torpedoes during the first part of World War II, quoted in Clay Blair, Jr., *Silent Victory* (1975).

Will Rogers once said that the way to end World War I, I believe, was to drain the Atlantic Ocean and there would not be any German submarines. Somebody asked him how he was going to do it. He said: "Well, that is a detail. I am not a detail man."
Senator Sam Nunn, speech in the Senate, June 3, 1975.

At Nuremberg [German] Admirals Erich Raeder and Karl Doenitz, successively commanders in chief of the German navy, were charged with war crimes in that they were responsible for U-boat operations. . . . But the evidence at the trial, which included testimony by the U. S. naval commander in the Pacific, Admiral Chester W. Nimitz, established that in this regard the Germans had done nothing that the British and Americans had not done.
Telford Taylor, *Nuremberg and Vietnam* (1971).

submarines, nuclear
One of the most wonderful things that happened in our Nautilus [the first nuclear-powered submarine] program was that everybody knew it was going to fail—so they let us completely alone so we were able to do the job.
Admiral Hyman G. Rickover, *Reader's Digest* (July 1958).

I don't see why some people think the world is coming to an end just because the Russians decide to build 43 missile submarines when we have 41.
John H. Chafee, Secretary of the Navy, *The Washington Post* (November 26, 1971).

I see no reason why we have to have just as many as the Russians do. At a certain point you get where it's sufficient. What's the difference whether we have 100 nuclear submarines or 200? I don't see what difference it makes. You can sink everything on the oceans several times over with the number we have, and so can they.
Admiral Hyman G. Rickover, testimony before Congressional Joint Economic Committee, January 28, 1982.

Anyone who tells me he prefers one more division of soldiers to a missile-launching submarine is living in the wrong age.
Charles Hernu, French Minister of Defense, *The Christian Science Monitor* (November 17, 1982).

Submarines running at high speed from one point to another were blind and unable to harm anyone. As a result, the operating pattern of an attack submarine was much like that of a combat infantryman. With a rifleman it was called dash-and-cover; with a sub, sprint-and-drift. After detecting a target, a sub would race to a more advantageous position, stop to reacquire her prey, then dash again until a firing position had been achieved. The sub's quarry would be moving too, and if the submarine could gain position in front of it, she had then only to lie in wait like a great hunting cat to strike.
Tom Clancy, *The Hunt for Red October* (1984).

Suez crisis

We are not at war with Egypt. We are in an armed conflict.
Anthony Eden, speech in the House of Commons, November 4, 1956.

There were stories floating around the embassy in London that . . . Ike had telephoned Eden and had given him unshirted hell. Eden denied this, and Eisenhower does not mention it in his memoirs. Eden's memory may have been selective on this score, however, and Eisenhower's account may have been discreet. Ike, it appears, did call Downing Street, but mistook one of the prime minister's aides, who answered the call, for Eden himself. By the time Eden got to the phone, Ike had finished his tirade and hung up.
Chester L. Cooper, *The Lion's Last Roar* (1978).

On Thursday, November 29th [1956], Winston [Churchill] had told me in reply to a direct question that he thought the whole operation the most ill-conceived and ill-executed imaginable. . . . I had begun by asking him if he would have acted as Eden had if he had still been Prime Minister. He replied, "I would never have dared; and if I had dared, I would certainly never have dared stop."
John Colville, *The Fringes of Power* (1985).

Sun Tzu (4th century B.C.)

His principles became the fundamentals of warfare for many military thinkers, including Mao Tse-tung. It is interesting that, during World War II, one of Chiang Kai-shek's military aides told the noted British historian and theoretician Basil Liddell Hart that, in Chiang's army, Sun Tzu's *The Art of War* was considered a classic but out of date. A few years later, Chiang fell to Sun Tzu's tactics—employed at the hands of Mao.
James Coates and Michael Kilian, *Heavy Losses* (1985).

There's an ancient Chinese military notion found in Sun Tzu's treatise on *The Art of War*. . .which we ran into in Burma with the Chinese troops during the war. And that is the notion that you should never completely surround an enemy, because if you do he will fight too hard. You must always leave him a route of escape. Now, in World War II we found that a little frustrating and slightly amusing, but in the nuclear world this ancient Chinese doctrine takes on special significance. We aren't going to have nuclear war because a nuclear government makes a deliberate, calm decision to start one. They all realize that that is mutual suicide. But you could have nuclear war if a group of men and women find themselves driven into a corner from which they see no

escape and they elect to play the role of Samson and pull down the temple around themselves and everyone else at the same time.
Dean Rusk quoted in James G. Blight and David A. Welch, *On the Brink* (1989).

superpowers

There are now two great nations in the world which, starting from different points, seem to be advancing toward the same goal: the Russians and the Anglo-Americans.
Alexis de Tocqueville, *Democracy in America* (1835).

We may be likened to two scorpions in a bottle, each capable of killing the other, but only at the risk of his own life.
J. Robert Oppenheimer, "Atomic Weapons and American Policy," *Foreign Affairs* (July 1953).

In the nuclear age, superpowers make war like porcupines make love— carefully.
Richard E. Neustadt and Graham T. Allison, "Afterword" to Robert F. Kennedy, *Thirteen Days* (1971).

Were it not for the fact that they [the Russians] are Communists—and, therefore, "bad" people—while we are Americans—and, therefore, "good" people—our [foreign] policies would be nearly indistinguishable.
Senator J. William Fulbright, *The New York Times* (April 5, 1971).

The superpowers often behave like two heavily armed blind men feeling their way around a room, each believing himself in mortal peril from the other, whom he assumes to have perfect vision.
Henry A. Kissinger, *The Observer* (September 30, 1979).

I conclude that the true and accurate state of the military relationship [between the U.S. and the Soviet Union] is that of strategically ambiguous equivalence. . . . Neither side can be very certain about the consequences of a military engagement, and even less so about the consequence of quick pre-emption.
Zbigniew Brzezinski, *The Washington Post* (October 6, 1982).

Despite the absence of general conflict between the superpowers, the *pax atomica* has not ensured peace throughout the international system. A strong case can even be made for the proposition that peace in the northern industrial sector has been achieved by the "export" of limited wars to areas in which vital superpower interests have not been vitally engaged.
Abba Eban, *The New Diplomacy* (1983).

I can tell you it's going to be a lot more fun than going over and over again the same arguments about the window of vulnerability, first strike capacity and the 24 notches of nuclear deterrence.
François Heisbourg, Director of the International Institute for Strategic Studies in London, on the fading of superpower rivalry, *The New York Times* (December 27, 1988).

supplies

I will end . . . by recording a remark of Napoleon which may appear whimsical, but which is still not without reason. He said that in his first campaigns the enemy was so well provided that when his troops were in want of supplies he had only to fall upon the rear of the enemy to procure every thing in abundance. This is a remark upon which it would be absurd to found a system, but which perhaps explains the success of many a rash enterprise, and proves how much actual war differs from narrow theory.
General Antoine Henri Jomini, *Summary of the Art of War* (1838).

We should not depend upon our own war industry, but on that of the imperialists and our enemy at home. We have a claim on the output of the arsenals of London and Hanyang, to be delivered by the enemy's transport corps. This is not a joke, but the truth.

Mao Tse-tung quoted in Robert Payne, *Mao Tse-tung* (1950).

The history of war proves that nine times out of ten an army has been destroyed because its supply lines have been cut off.

General Douglas MacArthur, *Time* (September 25, 1950).

At a Patton press conference, one questioner touched the raw nerve: "Is it true that Third Army has outrun its supplies?" he asked. And: "Are you getting your share?"

"Yes," snapped Patton with heavy irony. "But unfortunately we cannot make five barley loaves and three small fishes expand as they used to."

Somebody else asked: "Will the Nazis go underground when the Allies get to Germany?" Patton said: "Six feet."

David Irving, *The War Between the Generals* (1981).

surrender

The Guards die but do not surrender. [*La Garde meurt, mais ne se rend pas.*]
Attributed to French General Pierre-Jacques Cambronne, when asked to surrender the Imperial Guard at the 1815 Battle of Waterloo. His actual reply is said to be "Merde!" [Shit!], which has come to be known as "Le mot de Cambronne."

It is always better, therefore, to grant an honorable capitulation to a garrison which has resisted vigorously than to run the risk of an attempt to storm.
Napoleon I, *Military Maxims* (1827).

"Sir: yours of this date proposing armistice and appointment of Commissioners to settle terms of capitulation, is just received. No terms except an unconditional and immediate surrender can be accepted. I propose to move immediately upon your works." Buckner replied that the overwhelming size of the Union force made it necessary for him "to accept the ungenerous and unchivalrous terms."
Union General Ulysses S. Grant's response to Confederate General Simon Bolivar Buckner's request for surrender terms at Fort Donaldson during the American Civil War, quoted in Ulysses S. Grant, *Personal Memoirs*, I (1885–86).

I know they will say hard things of us. They will not understand how we were overwhelmed by numbers. But that is not the question, Colonel: The question is, is it right to surrender this army. If it is right, then I will take all the responsibility.... How easily I could be rid of this [his life] and be at rest! I have only to ride along the line and all will be over. But it is our duty to live. What will become of the women and children of the South if we are not here to protect them?
General Robert E. Lee quoted in A. L. Long, *Memoirs of Robert E. Lee* (1886).

[Grant] wrote into the terms of surrender one of the great sentences in American history. Officers and men were to sign paroles, and then they were to go home, "not to be disturbed by the United States authority so long as they observe their paroles and the laws in force where they reside."

... Grant knew very well that powerful men in Washington were talking angrily of treason and of traitors, and wanting to draw up proscription lists, so that leading Confederates could be jailed or hanged.

The sentence Grant had written would make that impossible. They could proceed against Robert E. Lee, for instance, only by violating the pledged word of U. S. Grant,

who had both the will and the power to see his word kept inviolate. If they could not hang Lee they could hardly hang anybody.
Bruce Catton, *U. S. Grant and the American Military Tradition* (1954).

I caught the bright face of a soldier leaning out from the lines as far as possible into the road, to catch the message that fell from my lips. "What is it! What is it!" he anxiously shouted. "Lee has surrendered with his whole army to Grant," was the reply. Clear and loud, above all the voices, and quick as the message fell upon his ears, was his answer: "Great God! You're the man I've been looking for for the last four years."
Captain A. J. Ricks quoted in B. A. Botkin, *A Civil War Treasury* (1960).

I report the order to defend Tunisia to the last cartridge has been carried out.
Colonel General Jurgen von Arnim, last message to Berlin before his surrender to the British, quoted in *Newsweek* (May 24, 1943).

German prisoners with dead eyes stumbled among the corpses, carting them off to endless trenches under the tommy guns of sullen Red Army men. I could not tell whether either Russians or Germans knew what they were doing. The Germans moved like sleepwalkers. The hardest thing, they told us, was the moment of surrender. Unless you were in a big group, a hundred or a thousand, you didn't have a chance. The Soviet tommy gunners just mowed you down.
Harrison E. Salisbury, *A Journey for Our Times* (1983).

One of the first platoon's squad leaders, Max Sobel, spoke some German. "Both sides were yelling back and forth, and the lieutenant wanted someone to holler to the Germans to put down their weapons and come out with their hands up." Although Max felt his German was a bit rusty, he gave it a try. "I started yelling for them to surrender, but a lot of good it did. After they picked up my Jewish accent they redoubled their fire."
Harold P. Leinbaugh and John D. Campbell, *The Men of Company K* (1985).

The cost of freedom is always high, but Americans have always paid it. And one path we shall never choose, and that is the path of surrender, or submission.
President John F. Kennedy, speech during the Cuban Missile Crisis, October 22, 1962.

I think that this is the first war in history that on the morrow the victors sued for peace and the vanquished called for unconditional surrender.
Abba Eban, Foreign Minister of Israel, on the Six Day War, *The New York Times* (July 9, 1967).

It happened during the international rescue effort in earthquake-stricken Armenia. A uniform-wearing French military contingent, aided by a team of trained dogs, detected the presence of a group of people trapped underneath the rubble. The rescuers summoned a crane, and, as the rubble was cleared, they kept talking among themselves in French. When the Armenians finally surfaced, they looked at the dogs, saw the uniforms, listened to the conversations in a strange language and assumed they were victims of a foreign attack. They put their arms up in the air and "surrendered" to the French.
Charles Fenyvesi, "Washington Whispers," *U.S. News and World Report* (February 20, 1989).

survival

Standing before a grave, who can be sure that he has done his duty? It is a hard thing to have survived when we owe our place to the dead.
René Quinton, *Soldier's Testament* (1930).

This kind of cache [a pilot's survival kit] was later immortalized in Stanley Kubrick's classic *Dr. Strangelove* when the redneck pilot portrayed by Slim Pickens read fellow airmen the contents of their survival packs: "In them you'll find one forty-five-caliber automatic, two boxes amma-ni-shun, four days' concentrated emergency rations, one drug isha containin' annabah-yotics, *mor*-phine, *vah*-tamin pills, *pep* pills, *sleep*-in' pills, *trank*-willizin' pills, one minitcher Roo-shin phrase book and Bah-ble, one hundred dollars in rubles, one hundred dollars in gold, five packs o' chewin' gum, one isha prophylactics, three pair o' nah-lon stockin's—
"Shoot, a guy could have a pretty good weekend in Vegas with all *that* stuff!"
Michael R. Beschloss, *Mayday* (1986).

survivors

As for me dear sister, fear nothing from this war. Only the worthy get killed; my type always survives.
Frederick the Great, 1756 letter to his sister, Wilhelmina, quoted in Ludwig Reiners, *Frederick the Great* (1960).

The 82nd Airborne Division ... troopers who could be spared were given short furloughs, and most of them were off to Paris. They made a good impression. General J. C. H. Lee later told me of a brief conversation he had overheard at SHAEF. One staff officer commented to another, "Those paratroopers are the smartest, most alert-looking soldiers I have seen." The other replied, "Hell, man, they ought to be, you are looking at the survivors."
General James M. Gavin, *On To Berlin* (1978).

I feel like a fugitive from th' law of averages.
Bill Mauldin, *Up Front* (1946).

Yesterday, German fighters flew by my [B-17] plane so close I could have hit them with a Colt .45. My gunners must have fired a thousand rounds, but most of the ME-109s escaped. If we don't shoot better than that tomorrow, we won't come back. . . . So this evening, the gunners are down at the range learning how to hit a moving target, and some of the pilots who flew raggedly on the mission today are now out practicing formation flying. I don't mind being called tough. In this racket it's the tough guys who lead the survivors.
General Curtis E. LeMay quoted in Thomas M. Coffey, *Iron Eagle* (1986).

The survivors would envy the dead.
Nikita Krushchev, on the aftermath of nuclear war, quoted in Ed Zuckerman, "Hiding from the Bomb—Again," *Harper's* (August 1979).

swords

Then said Jesus unto him, Put up again thy sword into his place: for all they that take the sword shall perish with the sword.
The Bible, Matthew 26:52.

One of his captains, it is said, who was sent by him [Julius Caesar] to Rome, standing before the senate house one day, and being told that the senate would not give

Caesar longer time in his government, clapped his hand on the hilt of his sword and said, "But this shall."
Plutarch, *The Lives* (A.D. 106).

The conduct of war, in its great outlines, is, therefore, politics itself, which takes up the sword in place of the pen, but does not on that account cease to think according to its own laws.
Karl von Clausewitz, *On War* (1832).

Save in defense of my native State, I have no desire ever again to draw my sword.
Colonel Robert E. Lee, letter of April 20, 1861 to General Winfield Scott resigning his commission in the U.S. Army, quoted in Burke Davis, *Gray Fox* (1956).

I draw the sword that with God's help I have kept all these years in the scabbard. I have drawn the sword, which without victory and without honor, I cannot sheath.
Kaiser William II, speaking at the beginning of World War I, *The Times* (London) (August 20, 1914).

I found a young Marine on guard among the blasted pillboxes at the base of the volcano. He had a Japanese samurai sword at his belt. "We flushed a Jap officer out of a cave over there," he told me, indicating a fire-blackened hole in the face of the cliff where a flame thrower had been used. "He came out waving his sword and we shot him. There were three of us and when we took his sword we couldn't decide which one had killed him and whose sword it was. So we decided to share." Drawing the blade from the scabbard, he added proudly, "It's my turn to wear it today, sir."
General Holland M. Smith and Percy Smith, *Coral and Brass* (1948).

Unlike Christianity, which preached a peace that it never achieved, Islam unashamedly came with a sword.
Sir Steven Runciman, *History of the Crusades* (1951).

We [Kamikaze pilots] were forbidden to take swords into the cockpits of our planes as they might affect the gyroscope.
Ryuji Nagatsuka, *I Was A Kamikaze* (1972).

Waving my sword I ran forward in front of my platoon, but unfortunately I had only gone six paces when I tripped over my scabbard, the sword fell from my hand (I hadn't wound that sword strap round my wrist in the approved fashion!) and I fell flat on my face on very hard ground. By the time I had picked myself up and rushed after my men I found that most of them had been killed.
Field Marshal B. L. Montgomery, on one of his first combat experiences in World War I, quoted in Brian Montgomery, *A Field-Marshal in the Family* (1973).

During one phase of the Dnieper campaign, after his troops had surrounded several German divisions, [Soviet Marshal Ivan] Koniev demanded their immediate surrender. When the Germans refused he ordered his saber-wielding Cossacks to attack. "We let the Cossacks cut for as long as they wished," he told Milovan Djilas, head of the Yugoslav Military Mission to Moscow, in 1944. "They even hacked off the hands of those who raised them to surrender."
Cornelius Ryan, *The Last Battle* (1966).

systems analysis

Unhappy the general who comes on the field of battle with a system.
Napoleon I, *Military Maxims* (1827).

No soldier who has made himself conversant with the resources of his art, will allow himself to be trammeled by any exclusive system.
Dennis Hart Mahan, *Advanced Guard, Out-Post, and Detachment Service* . . ., rev. ed. (1864).

Courage comes from the exact computation of the probabilities.
René Quinton, *Soldier's Testament* (1930).

The cult of numbers is the supreme fallacy of modern warfare. The way it persists is testimony to the tenacity of stupidity.
B. H. Liddell Hart, *Thoughts on War* (1944).

The story is told about the high defense official, confident in the methods of systems analysis, and faced with a personal decision. He owned two self-winding watches . . . that had both become defective. The first lost four seconds every day; the second had stopped completely. So he called in his Chief Systems Analyst, and asked him to evaluate these two chronological "systems" and recommend what to do.
After study, the recommendation was clear: throw away the first watch and keep the second. Calculation showed that the first watch was correct only once every fifty-nine years, and the second was correct twice a day.
This is something more than a bad joke. It illustrates that systems analysis, while it is a superb decision-making tool, operates in a broader setting that requires human judgment.
Wesley W. Posvar, "The Easy Magic of Systems Analysis," *American Defense Policy*, 2nd ed., ed. M. E. Smith III and C. J. Johns, Jr. (1968).

Misuse of systems analysis apart, there was a truth which senior military officers had learned in a lifetime of service that did not lend itself to formal articulation: that power has a psychological and not only a technical component. Men can be led by statistics only up to a certain point and then more fundamental values predominate.
Henry A. Kissinger, *White House Years* (1979).

Many of the "systems analysis" techniques introduced by McNamara . . . are based on mathematical models which treat warfare as a cumulative exchange of fire-power. . . . Even though the historical record of war shows quite conclusively that superior firepower is often associated with defeat, and that winners more often than not were actually inferior in firepower, these mathematical models continue to be devastatingly influential because they capture all that is conveniently measurable about warfare. Thus bookkeepers may fancy themselves strategists.
Edward N. Luttwak, "The American Style of Warfare," *Survival* (March/April 1979).

The new breed of the "systems analysts" introduced new standards of intellectual discipline and greatly improved bookkeeping methods, but also a trained incapacity to understand the most important aspects of military power, which happen to be nonmeasurable. Because morale is nonmeasurable it was ignored, in large and small ways, with disastrous effects.
Edward N. Luttwak, *The Pentagon and the Art of War* (1985).

tactics

[A general] should also, as a matter of course, know his tactics; for a disorderly mob is no more an army than a heap of building materials is a house.
Socrates quoted in Xenophon, *Memorabilia* (4th century B.C.).

When the enemy is at ease, be able to weary him; when well fed, to starve him; when at rest, to make him move.
Sun Tzu, *The Art of War* (4th century B.C.).

Good officers decline general engagements where the odds are too great, and prefer the employment of stratagem and finesse to destroy the enemy as much as possible in detail and intimidate them without exposing their own forces.
Vegetius, *De Re Militari* (A.D. 378).

The ancient commanders of armies, who well knew the powerful influence of necessity, and how it inspired the soldiers with the most desperate courage, neglected nothing to subject their men to such a pressure, whilst, on the other hand, they employed every device that ingenuity could suggest to relieve the enemy's troops from the necessity of fighting. Thus they often opened the way for the enemy to retreat, which they might easily have barred; and closed it to their own soldiers for whom they could with ease have kept it open.
Niccolò Machiavelli, *The Discourses* (1517).

Petty geniuses attempt to hold everything; wise men hold fast to the most important points. They parry great blows and scorn little accidents. There is an ancient apothegm: he who would preserve everything, preserves nothing. Therefore, always sacrifice the bagatelle and pursue the essential! The essential is to be found where big bodies of the enemy are.
Frederick the Great, *Instructions for His Generals* (1747).

In tactics every engagement, great or small, is a defensive one if we leave the initiative to the enemy.
Karl von Clausewitz, *On War* (1832).

In future, sir, I must ask you to be a little less generous with the blood of your men, and a little more generous with your own brains.
General Burgoyne in George Bernard Shaw's *The Devil's Disciple* (1901).

[Grand tactics are] those stratagems, maneuvers, and devices by which victories are won, and concern only those officers who may find themselves in independent command.
G. F. R. Henderson, *Science of War* (1906).

What can't be done by main courage, in war, must be done by circumvention.
James Fenimore Cooper, *The Last of the Mohicans* (1826).

I perceived at once, however, that [William J.] Hardee's tactics [*Rifle and Light Infantry Tactics* (1855)]—a mere translation from the French with Hardee's name attached—was nothing more than common sense.... I found no trouble in giving commands that would take my regiment where I wanted it to go.... I do not believe that the officers of the regiment ever discovered that I had never studied the tactics that I used.
President Ulysses S. Grant, *Memoirs* (1885).

In war we resemble a man endeavoring to seek an enemy in the dark, and the principles which govern our action will be similar to those which he would naturally adopt. The man stretches out one arm in order to grope for his enemy (Discover). On touching his adversary he feels his way to the latter's throat (Reconnoiter). As soon as he has reached it, he seizes him by the collar or throat so that his antagonist cannot wriggle away or strike back at him effectively (Fix). Then with his other fist he strikes his enemy, who is unable to avoid the blow, a decisive knock-out blow (Decisive Attack).

Before his enemy can recover, he follows up his advantage by taking steps to render him finally powerless (Exploit).
B. H. Liddell Hart, "The Essential Principles of War . . .," *United Service Magazine* (April 1920).

[General B. L. Montgomery talked] of his continuous struggle since the war began to infuse both public officials and Army officers with the necessity for an affirmative instead of a defensive attitude. "I tell you, Willkie, it's the only way to defeat the Boches"—he always spoke of the Germans as the Boches. "Give them no rest, give them no rest. These Boches are good soldiers. They are professionals."
When I asked him about Rommel he said: "He's a trained, skilled general, but he has one weakness. He repeats his tactics— and that's the way I'm going to get him."
Wendell Willkie, *One World* (1943).

Hit the enemy twice: First, to find out what he's got; then, to take it away from him.
General Omar Bradley quoted in *Reader's Digest* (July 1944).

In modern mobile warfare the tactics are not the main thing. The decisive factor is the organization of one's resources—*to maintain the momentum.*
German General Ritter von Thoma quoted in B. H. Liddell Hart, *The Other Side of the Hill* (1948).

In almost any battle situation he [George C. Marshall] believed leaders of troops would be required to make up their minds quickly with scant information. He sought, therefore, to teach the art of improvisation, to extricate tactical principles from the procedural formulas in which they had become fixed by the schoolmen. One way to do that was to set problems in rapidly moving situations where even a mediocre solution arrived at in time was better than the perfect tactic discovered hours after the opportunity to use it had passed.
Forrest C. Pogue, *George C. Marshall: Education of a General* (1963).

The art of the indirect approach can only be mastered, and its full scope appreciated, by study of and reflection upon the whole history of war. But we can at least crystallize the lessons into two simple maxims, one negative, the other positive. The first is that in the face of the overwhelming evidence of history no general is justified in launching his troops to a direct attack upon an enemy firmly in position. The second, that instead of seeking to upset the enemy's equilibrium by one's attack, it must be upset before a real attack is, or can be successfully, launched.
B. H. Liddell Hart, *Memoirs* (1965).

[Colonel Claire Chennault] told his new pilots: You will face Japanese pilots superbly trained in mechanical flying. They have been drilled for hundreds of hours in flying precise formations and rehearsing set tactics for each situation they may encounter. Japanese pilots fly by the book. They have plenty of guts but lack initiative and judgment.
They go into battle with a set tactical plan and they stick to it. Their bombers will fly a tight formation through the toughest pursuit as precisely as though they were in an air show over Tokyo. Their pursuits always pull the same tricks. God help the American pilot who tries to fight them according to their plans.
The object of our tactics is to break their formations and make them fight according to our style. Once the Japanese pilot is forced to deviate from his plan, he is in trouble. They lack the ability to improvise and react instinctively to new situations. Their rigid air discipline can be used as a strong weapon against them.
Duane Schultz, *The Maverick War: Chennault and the Flying Tigers* (1987).

Hutier tactics

As dictated by General von Manteuffel, the troops were to make direct attacks on American positions at only two places. . . . Units not designated for those attacks were to practice what had become known in World War I as "Hutier tactics" (after a German general, Oscar von Hutier), whereby the troops advanced in small units avoiding prepared enemy positions, leaving them to be mopped up by other units coming later.
Charles B. MacDonald, *A Time for Trumpets* (1985).

In fact it was the Germans who led in this respect. Under the guidance of General Hutier, serving in Russia, they developed so-called "infiltration tactics." An attack was preceded only by a very short bombardment, and the leading infantry, usually attacking at night, were made up of small groups of "storm troopers," whose main equipment was composed of light machine guns or automatic rifles. Such units were told to push forward as rapidly as possible, and to leave the reduction of any strongpoints to the infantry behind.
John Ellis, *The Social History of the Machine Gun* (1975).

naval tactics

Most men were in fear that the French would invade; but I was always of another opinion, for I always said that whilst we had a fleet in being, they would not dare to make an attempt.
Admiral Sir Arthur Torrington, 1690 letter defending his actions toward the superior French fleet. According to Bernard Brodie, *A Guide to Naval Strategy* (1944), Torrington would "harry the French force, but he had declined to engage decisively." He justified his tactic of maintaining a "fleet in being" (the first use of this phrase) by asserting that "had I fought otherwise, our fleet had been totally lost, and the kingdom laid open to invasion." Brodie quotes Alfred Thayer Mahan comparing a "fleet in being" to "a position on the flank and rear" of the enemy in land warfare: "When such a force is extremely mobile, its power of mischief is very great."

Because individual captains of the time had formerly used their own tactics, often resulting in unmanageable confusion, the Admiralty [during the seventeenth century] issued the *Fighting Instructions* to give a fleet greater effect by requiring its ships to act in concert under signaled orders of the commanding officer and prohibiting action on personal initiative. In general, the result did make for greater efficiency in combat, though in particular instances . . . it could cause disaster by persuading a too submissive captain to stick by the rule when crisis in a situation could better have been met by a course determined by the particular circumstances. As deviations from the rule were always reported by some disgruntled officer and tried by a court-martial, the *Instructions* naturally reduced, if not destroyed, initiative except when a captain of strong self-confidence would act to take advantage of the unexpected. . . . In allowing no room for the unexpected that lies in wait in the waywardness of men, not to mention the waywardness of winds and ocean, *Fighting Instructions* was a concept of military rigidity that must forever amaze the layman.
Barbara W. Tuchman, *The First Salute* (1988).

I wish to have no connection with any ship that does not sail fast, for I intend *to go in harm's way.*
John Paul Jones, letter of November 1778 to Le Ray de Chaumont, quoted in Samuel Eliot Morison, *John Paul Jones* (1959).

What I want you to preserve is honor, and not a few planks and men.
Napoleon I, 1804 letter to the head of his French Navy, quoted in J. C. Herold, *The Mind of Napoleon* (1955).

I believe my arrival was most welcome, not only to the Commander of the Fleet but almost to every individual in it; and when I came to explain to them the "Nelson touch", it was like an electric shock. Some shed tears, all approved—"It was new—it was singular—it was simple!" . . . Some may be Judas's; but the majority are much pleased with my commanding them.

Admiral Horatio Nelson, letter to Lady Emma Hamilton, October 1, 1805. According to David Howarth in *Trafalgar: The Nelson Touch* (1969), Nelson used the phrase "the Nelson touch" only in private letters to his mistress, Lady Hamilton. "But in after years, when his letters to her were made public, it came to mean two things: in general, his touch of genius and in particular the tactical plan he made before Trafalgar."

Unless you have a supreme navy, it is not worth while having one at all, and a navy that is not supreme is only a hostage in the hands of the Power whose fleet is supreme.

I. S. Bloch, *Is War Impossible?* (1899).

[There are] always two moments of greatest importance in a seafight; one which determines the method of the main attack, the other the bringing up and directing [of] the effort of the reserve. If the first is more important, the second perhaps requires the higher order of ability; for the former may and should proceed on a pre-determined plan, while the latter may, and often must, be shaped to meet unforeseen emergencies.

Alfred Thayer Mahan, *Naval Strategy* (1911).

The whole principle of naval fighting is to be free to go anywhere with every damned thing the Navy possesses.

Sir John Fisher, *Memories* (1919).

In character these operations were more like the naval warfare than ordinary land operations, in their mobility, their ubiquity, their independence of bases and communications, their lack of ground features, of strategic areas, of fixed directions, of fixed points. "He who commands the sea is at great liberty, and may take as much or as little of the war as he will": he who commands the desert is equally fortunate. Camel raiding-parties, as self-contained as ships, could cruise without danger along any part of the enemy's land frontier, just out of sight of his posts along the edge of cultivation, and tap or raid into his lines where it seemed fittest or easiest or most profitable, with a sure retreat always behind them into an element which the Turks could not enter.

T. E. Lawrence, "Evolution of a Revolt," *Army Quarterly* (October 1920), reprinted in *Evolution of a Revolt* (1968). Note how this 1920 article contradicts Desmond Young's contention in *Rommel: The Desert Fox* (1950) that in the early 1940s Rommel "was the first to identify desert war with war at sea."

Thus ended the first major engagement in naval history [the May 1942 Battle of the Coral Sea] in which surface ships did not exchange a shot.

Admiral Ernest J. King, *A Report to the Secretary of the United States Navy* (1944). This was a fight between aircraft carriers.

We want to get the big ones first.

Admiral Daniel J. Callaghan's November 13, 1942 order to his gunnery officers upon closing with a Japanese task force, *The New York Times* (December 12, 1942). A few minutes after giving this order, he was killed by enemy fire.

We do the unexpected. . . . We expose ourselves to shore-based planes. We don't stay behind the battle with our carriers. But . . . whatever we do, we do fast.

Admiral William F. Halsey's description of his tactics in naval warfare, *Newsweek* (October 8, 1945).

You will be governed by the principle of calculated risk, which you will interpret to mean the avoidance of exposure of your force to attack by superior enemy forces without the prospect of inflicting, as a result of such exposure, greater damage to the enemy.
Admiral Raymond Spruance's orders as he sailed toward the Battle of Midway, quoted in Thomas B. Buell, *The Quiet Warrior* (1974).

tanks

I can make armored wagons carrying artillery, which shall break through the most serried ranks of the enemy, and so open a safe passage for . . . infantry.
Leonardo da Vinci, describing his ability to make weapons in a letter to the Duke of Milan asking for employment, quoted in *The World's Great Letters* (1940).

I managed to get astride one of the German trenches . . . and opened fire with the Hotchkiss machine-guns. There were some Germans in the dug-outs and I shall never forget the look on their faces when they emerged. . . .
Captain H. W. Mortimore, commander of the first tank to go into battle on September 15, 1916, quoted in Trevor Wilson, *The Myriad Faces of War* (1986).

Once appreciate that tanks are not an extra arm or a mere aid to infantry but the modern form of heavy cavalry and their true military use is obvious— to be concentrated and used in as large masses as possible for a decisive blow against the Achilles' heel of the enemy army, the communications and command centers which form its nerve system. Then not only may we see the rescue of mobility from the toils of trench-warfare, but with it the revival of generalship and the art of war, in contrast to its mere mechanics.
B. H. Liddell Hart, *Paris, or the Future of War* (1925).

They [the first tanks] carried these particular guns because they were naval guns which the Admiralty found it possible to spare; the War Office did not find it possible to spare, or to make, any such armaments for tanks. In fact the War Office attitude to tanks was mainly confined to cancelling the orders given to construct them, whittling down the construction programmes when these were forced through by Cabinet Ministers, and staffing the Tank Corps with officers who had in some way gained a reputation for "difficulty." Luckily this type of officer was, under the social conditions then reigning in the British Army, often the best available for a new arm developing new tactics.
Tom Wintringham, *Weapons and Tactics* (1943).

[In Poland in 1939] Hitler asked about casualties. I gave him the latest figures that I had received, some 150 dead and 700 wounded for all the four divisions under my command during the Battle of the Corridor. He was amazed at the smallness of these figures . . . . I was able to show him that the smallness of our casualties in this battle against a tough and courageous enemy was primarily due to the effectiveness of our tanks. Tanks are a life-saving weapon.
General Heinz Guderian, *Panzer Leader* (1952).

There is, in general, little chance of success in a tank attack over country where the enemy has been able to take up defensive positions.
Field Marshal Erwin Rommel, *The Rommel Papers*, B. H. Liddell Hart, ed. (1953).

"The Panther [German tank] can slice through a Churchill [British tank] like butter from a mile away."
"And how does a Churchill get a Panther?"

"It creeps up on it. When it reaches close quarters, the gunner tries to bounce a shot off the underside of the Panther's gun mantlet. If he's lucky, it goes through a piece of thin armor above the driver's head."

"Has anybody ever done it?"

"Yes. Davis in 'C' Squadron. He's back with headquarters now trying to recover his nerve."

"What's next on the list?"

"Tigers. The Tiger can get you from a mile and a half."

"And how does a Churchill get a Tiger?"

"It's supposed to get within 200 yards and put a shot through the periscope."

"Has anyone ever done it?"

"No."

Andrew Wilson, recalling a conversation prior to D-Day, *Flamethrower* (1956).

"Call Colonel Boos and ask for tank destroyers," [Lt. Col.] Mildren shouted above the din.

A junior staff officer made radio contact with Colonel Boos. "Sir, we've got to have TDs. We're being overrun by Jerry Tanks!"

"How many tanks?" Boos asked calmly, "And just how close are they to you?"

There was a roar. The house shook, plaster fell in hunks.

"Well, Colonel," said the officer at the radio, "if I went up to the second floor, I could piss out the window and hit at least six!"

John Toland, *Battle: The Story of the Bulge* (1959).

The bodies [in the tanks] were indistinguishable from one another, simply a mass of cooked flesh welded together in the great heat; we had to sift through this for identity tags. Each tank told the same story—broken legs, broken arms, open chest wounds, and so on, had trapped many, so that they had burnt alive. The screams I thought I had heard during the action had not been imaginary after all.

Sergeant L. R. Gariepy quoted in A. McKee, *Caen* (1966).

The mathematics of combat operate with peculiar force for tanks, which are easily identified, easily engaged, discrete, much-feared targets which attract all the fire on the battlefield. When all is said and done, a tank is a small steel box crammed with inflammable or explosive substances which is easily converted into a mobile crematorium for its highly skilled crew.

Shelford Bidwell, *Modern Warfare* (1973).

He (the recruiting officer) asked me, "Why tanks?" I replied that I preferred to go into battle sitting down.

Peter Ustinov, recalling his service in the World War II British Army, *Dear Me* (1977).

The fighting on the far side of the [Moselle] river was fierce, but I must admit that I cherish its memory. One of those incidents occurred that humanizes war as much as possible, that injects a humor, however grim, into the otherwise purely brutal proceedings.

A monster of a Tiger 6 [tank] was pivoting not thirty yards in front of me. I fired three shots at it, figuring to force it backward. All three shots bounced off the side and ricocheted harmlessly. What do I see but a German officer stick his head out of the turret and smile at me! He then proceeded to pull a white handkerchief out of his pocket and wipe it against the side of his machine, where my bullets had skidded. He smiled again as if to forgive me for scratching his property; then he replaced his handkerchief in his pocket.

General George S. Patton quoted in Nat Frankel and Larry Smith, *Patton's Best* (1978).

His [Air Marshal Arthur Harris] dry, cutting, often vulgar wit was legendary throughout the RAF, as was his hatred of the British army and the Royal Navy. He was fond of saying that the army would never understand the value of tanks until they could be modified to "eat hay and shit."
Max Hastings, *Bomber Command* (1979).

"Aspirine" did little for headaches but a lot to motors. Chemical pills, they knocked out engines when put into gasoline tanks. "Aspirine" tablets are credited with giving 50 German Panzers engine trouble and delaying their passage to the Normandy beaches in June.
William Casey, *The Secret War Against Hitler* (1988).

Tanks are more suited than other types of military equipment to combat actions where nuclear weapons are used. In particular they are suited to enduring powerful dynamic pressure. The advantage of the tank is that its armor protects the crew against thermal radiation and decreases the effect of penetrating radiation, while the tank's actual weight gives it stability which protects it against the shock wave. As a result of this, the use of tanks when nuclear weapons have been employed makes it possible to wage active combat action on contaminated terrain immediately after an atomic explosion.
Marshal P. A. Rotmistrov, *Time and Tanks* (1972).

The antitank missile can also be made mobile . . . by the simple expedient of providing a helicopter to carry the missiles and its firing crew —but then, of course, the weapon will no longer be cheap. . . . If we are more modest, and merely seek to equal the mobility of armored forces . . ., we must provide a cross-country vehicle for our missile, and then armor to protect its crew. Next we would find that the missile firing armored vehicle will usually be inferior to gun-armored vehicles. . . . Having wrapped our antitank missile in armor and given it cross-country mobility, we would then find it advantageous to replace or supplement the missile launcher with a gun—and we would thus reinvent the tank.
Edward N. Luttwak, *Strategy and History*, II (1985).

There's no better thing to have if you're going to be attacked or overrun than some tanks. They have good radios, so you can communicate with them. They have a variety of rounds that can be effective if you're overrun, fleshettes or shrapnel. And they're a security blanket for the troops.
Walter Mack quoted in Harry Mauer, *Strange Ground* (1989).

Inscriptions indicate that the pharoahs and the warrior kings of Mycenae kept track of their chariots no less anxiously than NATO commanders fret over the tank ratio in Europe.
Robert L. O'Connell, *Of Arms and Men* (1989).

targets

The selection of [target] objectives, the grouping of zones, and determining the order in which they are to be destroyed is the most difficult and delicate task in aerial warfare, constituting what may be defined as aerial strategy. Objectives vary considerably in war, and the choice of them depends chiefly upon the aim sought, whether the command of the air, paralyzing the enemy's army and navy, or shattering the morale of civilians behind the lines.
Giulio Douhet, *The Command of the Air* (1921).

The real target in war is the mind of the enemy command, not the bodies of his troops.
  B. H. Liddell Hart, *Thoughts on War* (1944).

The intelligence officer of the U.S. Fifth Air Force declared on July 21, 1945, that "the entire population of Japan is a proper military target," and he added emphatically, *"There are no civilians in Japan."*
  Paul Fussell, *Thank God for the Atom Bomb* (1988).

Submariners lived by a simple motto: There are two kinds of ships, submarines . . . and targets.
  Tom Clancy, *The Hunt for Red October* (1984).

Attrition is war waged by industrial methods. The enemy is treated as a mere array of targets, and success is to be obtained by the cumulative effect of superior firepower and material strength, eventually to destroy the full inventory of enemy targets, unless retreat or surrender terminates the process (as is usually the case).
  Edward N. Luttwak, *Strategy* (1987).

The tendency in the Army today is to avoid the phrase "killing the enemy." They call it "servicing the target."
  Fred Downs, "Death and the Dark Side of Command," *The Washington Post* (August 16, 1987).

In Japan we dropped 502,000 tons and we won the war. In Vietnam we dropped 6,162,000 tons of bombs and we lost the war. The difference was that McNamara chose the targets in Vietnam and I chose the targets in Japan.
  General Curtis E. LeMay quoted in Thomas M. Coffey, *Iron Eagle* (1986).

[Bernard Brodie] branded as senseless the competition among and between the military services to destroy targets in Russia not once but many times— characterizing the result with a new word: "overkill".
  Gregg Herken, *Counsels of War* (1987).

terrorism

He was that extraordinary product—a Terrorist for moderate aims. A reasonable and enlightened policy—the Parliamentary system of England . . . freedom, toleration and good will—to be achieved wherever necessary by dynamite at the risk of death.
  Winston Churchill, on Boris Savinkov (the Russian Vice Minister of War in the 1917 government of Alexander Kerensky), *Great Contemporaries* (1937).

The success of a terrorist operation depends almost entirely on the amount of publicity it receives. This was one of the main reasons for the shift from rural guerilla to urban terror in the 1960s; in the cities the terrorist could always count on the presence of journalists and TV cameras.
  Walter Laqueur, *Terrorism* (1977).

Let terrorists beware that when the rules of international behavior are violated, our policy will be one of swift and effective retribution.
  President Ronald Reagan, speech in Washington, D.C., January 27, 1981.

We put the production of nuclear weapons at the top of the list of terrorist activities. As long as the big powers continue to manufacture atomic weapons, it means they are continuing to terrorize the world. . . . This is one reason why the U.S. is a top terrorist force in the world.
  Muammar al-Qaddafi, *Time* (June 8, 1981).

At the wheel was a young man on a suicide mission. The truck carried some 2,000 pounds of explosives, but there was no way our marine guard could know this. Their first warning that something was wrong came when the truck crashed through a series of barriers, including a chain link fence and barbed wire entanglements. The guards opened fire but it was too late.

The truck smashed through the doors of the headquarters building in which our marines were sleeping and instantly exploded. The four-story concrete building collapsed in a pile of rubble.

More than 200 of the sleeping men were killed in that one hideous insane attack.
President Ronald Reagan, speech to the nation on Lebanon and Grenada, October 27, 1983.

We also must recognize that although we may make moral distinctions between dropping bombs on a city from 20,000 feet and car bombs driven into embassies by suicidal terrorists, the world may not share that fine distinction.
Brian Jenkins, *U.S. News and World Report* (July 1, 1985).

We have an obligation to punish murder of American citizens in places where courts of law cannot reach. My conviction is that we will save a lot more lives in the long run by being tough and steady.
Lawrence S. Eagleburger, *U.S. News and World Report* (July 1, 1985).

International publicity is the mother's milk of terrorism.
Senator John Glenn, *U.S. News and World Report* (July 8, 1985).

The American people are not—I repeat, not—going to tolerate intimidation, terror and outright acts of war against this nation and its people. And we are especially not going to tolerate these attacks from outlaw states run by the strangest collection of misfits, Looney Tunes and squalid criminals since the advent of the Third Reich.
President Ronald Reagan, speech in Washington, July 8, 1985.

These [U.S. forces that captured in midair a planeload of terrorists] young Americans sent a message to terrorists everywhere. The message: You can run but you can't hide.
President Ronald Reagan, news conference, October 11, 1985.

I'm a participant in the doctrine of constructive ambiguity. I don't think we should tell them [terrorists] what we're going to do in advance. Let them think. Worry. Wonder. Uncertainty is the most chilling thing of all.
General Vernon Walters, on dealing with terrorists, *Christian Science Monitor* (April 18, 1986).

For us to ignore, by inaction, the slaughter of American civilians and American soldiers, whether in nightclubs or airline terminals, is simply not in the American tradition. When our citizens are abused or attacked anywhere in the world, on the direct orders of a hostile regime, we will respond, so long as I'm in this Oval Office. Self-defense is not only our right, it is our duty.
President Ronald Reagan, speech in Washington, D.C., April 14, 1986.

theater of war

He [Candide] clambered over heaps of dead and dying men and reached a neighboring village, which . . . the Bulgarians had burned in accordance with international law. Here, old men dazed with blows watched the dying agonies of their murdered wives who clutched their children to their bleeding breasts; there, disemboweled girls who had been made to satisfy the natural appetites of heroes gasped their last sighs; others, half-burned begged to be put to death. Brains were scattered on the ground among

dismembered arms and legs. Candide fled to another village as fast as he could; it belonged to the Bulgarians, and Abarian heroes had treated it in the same way. Candide, stumbling over quivering limbs or across ruins, at last escaped from the theatre of war.
Voltaire, *Candide* (1759).

The theater of a war comprises all the territory upon which the parties may assail each other, whether it belong to themselves, their allies, or to weaker states who may be drawn into the war through fear or interest. When the war is also maritime, the theater may embrace both hemispheres. . . . The theater of a war may thus be undefined, and must not be confounded with the theater of operations [which]. . . . embraces all the territory it [an army] may desire to invade and all that it may be necessary to defend.
General Antoine Henri Jomini, *Summary of the Art of War* (1838).

There must be one man in command of an entire theater—air, ground, and ships. We cannot manage by cooperation.
General George C. Marshall, speaking in 1942, quoted in Forrest C. Pogue, *George C. Marshall: Ordeal and Hope, 1939–1942* (1966).

The most obvious reason why "theater" and modern war seem so compatible is that modern wars are fought by conscripted armies, whose members know they are only temporarily playing their ill-learned parts.
Paul Fussell, *The Great War in Modern Memory* (1975).

think tanks

The Contractor will perform a program of study and research on the broad subject of intercontinental warfare, other than surface, with the object of recommending to the Army Air Forces preferred techniques and instrumentalities for this purpose.
The letter of contract of March 2, 1946, which first created the RAND Corporation, quoted in Bruce L. R. Smith, *The RAND Corporation* (1966).

It is poor business for a non-profit think-tank to come up with an analysis contrary to the interests of their paymaster.
William R. Corson, *The Betrayal* (1968).

There is an enormous gulf between what political leaders really think about nuclear weapons and what is assumed in complex calculations of relative "advantage" in simulated strategic warfare. Think tank analysts can set levels of "acceptable" damage well up in the tens of millions of lives. They can assume that the loss of dozens of great cities is somehow a real choice for sane men. They are in an unreal world. In the real world of real political leaders—whether here or in the Soviet Union—a decision that would bring even one hydrogen bomb on one city of one's own country would be recognized in advance as a catastrophic blunder.
McGeorge Bundy, "To Cap the Volcano," *Foreign Affairs* (October 1969).

tigers

In peace, there's nothing so becomes a man
As modest stillness and humility;
But when the blast of war blows in our ears,
Then imitate the action of the tiger.
William Shakespeare, *Henry V*, Act III (1598).

Dictators ride to and fro upon tigers which they dare not dismount. And the tigers are getting hungry.
Winston Churchill, *While England Slept* (1936).

No man can tame a tiger into a kitten by stroking it. There can be no appeasement with ruthlessness. There can be no reasoning with an incendiary bomb.
President Franklin D. Roosevelt, speech to the nation, December 29, 1940.

I have said that all the reputedly powerful reactionaries are merely paper tigers. The reason is that they are divorced from the people. Look! Was not Hitler a paper tiger? Was Hitler not overthrown? I also said that the tsar of Russia, the emperor of China and Japanese imperialism were all paper tigers. As we know, they were all overthrown. U.S. imperialism has not yet been overthrown and it has the atom bomb. I believe it also will be overthrown. It, too, is a paper tiger.
Mao Tse-tung, speech in Moscow (November 18, 1957), *Quotations from Chairman Mao* (1966).

In the past, those who foolishly sought power by riding on the back of the tiger ended up inside.
President John F. Kennedy, Inaugural Address, January 20, 1961.

Khruschev reminds me of the tiger hunter who has picked a place on the wall to hang the tiger's skin long before he has caught the tiger. This tiger has other ideas.
President John F. Kennedy, *The New York Times* (December 24, 1961).

Once on the tiger's back we cannot be sure of picking the place to dismount.
George Ball in 1964, quoted in Leslie H. Gelb, *The Irony of Vietnam* (1979).

toasts

Our country! In her intercourse with foreign nations, may she always be in the right; but our country, right or wrong.
Stephen Decatur, in a toast offered at Norfolk, Virginia, April 4, 1816, quoted in Alexander S. Mackenzie, *Life of Stephen Decatur* (1848). Samuel Flagg Bemis, *John Quincy Adams and the Union* (1956), quotes John Quincy Adams in an August 1, 1816 letter to his father (John Adams) concerning Decatur's toast: "I can never join with my voice in the toast which I see in the papers attributed to one of our gallant naval heroes. I cannot ask of heaven success, even for my country, in a cause where she should be in the wrong. *Fiat justitia, pereat caelum* [Let justice be done though the heavens fall]. My toast would be, may our country be always successful, but whether successful or otherwise, always right." Carl Schurz, in a speech in the U.S. Senate, modified this sentiment in 1872: "Our country, right or wrong! When right, to be kept right; when wrong, to be put right!"

So 'ere's to you, Fuzzy-Wuzzy, at your 'ome in the Soudan;
You're a poor benighted 'eathen but a first-class fightin' man.
Rudyard Kipling, *Fuzzy-Wuzzy* (1890).

To the Officers, may they get killed, wounded or promoted!
Toast of the Rough Riders before the 1898 Battle of San Juan, quoted in Edmund Morris, *The Rise of Theodore Roosevelt* (1979).

I've drunk your health in company;
I've drunk your health alone;
I've drunk your health so many times

I've damned near ruined my own.
Admiral F. "Bull" Halsey's favorite toast. He was often quoted as saying "There are exceptions, of course, but as a general rule I never trust a fighting man who doesn't smoke or drink."

We want you to know that all the world realizes it was the Red Army that clawed the guts out of the filthy Nazi war machine. To the Red Army.
Winston Churchill to Joseph Stalin, during a World War II meeting in Moscow, quoted in *Time* (October 23, 1944).

I want to drink a toast to you, Mr. Keefer. From the beginning, you hated the Navy. You thought up the whole idea, and you kept your skirts all starched and clean. Steve Maryk will be remembered as a mutineer—but you! You'll publish a novel, you'll make a million bucks, you'll marry a big movie star, and, for the rest of your life, you'll have to live with your conscience, if you have any. Now, here's to the real author of "The Caine Mutiny." Here's to you, Mr. Keefer.
Jose Ferrer in *The Caine Mutiny* (1954), directed by Edward Dmytryk; screenplay by Stanley Roberts from the novel by Herman Wouk.

[The World War I British] officers assembled in the headquarters mess. ... Recent strain between the commanding officer and some of the others led to an embarrassing pause when the senior company commander was called on to propose a toast to the C. O. On a sudden inspiration, he raised his glass and gave the toast with the words: "Gentlemen, when the barrage lifts."
B. H. Liddell Hart, *Memoirs* (1965).

torpedoes

Damn the torpedoes [nineteenth-century naval mines]! Full speed ahead!
Admiral David Farragut, at the Battle of Mobile Bay, August 5, 1864, quoted in Alfred T. Mahan, *Admiral Farragut* (1892).

Whoever imagines he can aid England must, in all circumstances, know one thing. Every ship, whether with or without escort, that comes before our torpedo tubes will be torpedoed.
Adolf Hitler, making a thinly veiled threat to the then neutral United States, quoted in *Time* (February 10, 1941).

Our military-naval command did not keep abreast of new developments in warfare, notably the use of torpedoes from planes in shallow water. This was how the Japs did most of their damage at Pearl Harbor, and naval intelligence warned of this possibility months in advance.
I. F. Stone, "Brass Hats Undaunted," *The Nation* (September 8, 1945).

That the United States tolerated for so long the Mark 13 torpedo is difficult to fathom. The defects of this miserable weapon that made torpedo-plane attack well-nigh worthless until the Philippine Sea battle (and perhaps not good then) were recognized but not soon remedied. Why could not the United States Navy, by reverse lease-lend, have acquired British 18-inch aerial torpedoes of the type that hit the Bismarck? Though smaller, these weapons had at least one virtue—they exploded.
James H. Belote and William M. Belote, *Titans of the Seas* (1975).

training

To lead an untrained people to war is to throw them away.
Confucius, *Analects* (6th century B.C.).

A handful of men, inured to war, proceeds to certain victory, while on the contrary numerous armies of raw and undisciplined troops are but masses of men dragged to slaughter.
Vegetius, *De Re Militari* (A.D. 378).

Whoever wishes to form a good army must, by real or sham fights, train his troops to attack the enemy sword in hand, and to seize hold of him bodily; and he must rely more upon infantry than upon cavalry.
Niccolò Machiavelli, *The Discourses* (1517).

The more a leader is in the habit of demanding from his men, the surer he will be that his demands will be answered.
Karl von Clausewitz, *On War* (1832).

A government is the murderer of its citizens which sends them to the field uninformed and untaught, where they are to meet men of the same age and strength, mechanized by education and discipline for battle.
General Henry "Light Horse Harry" Lee quoted in Emery Upton, *The Military Policy of the United States* (1912).

The war was won by the American spirit. . . . You know what one of our American wits said, that it took only half as long to train an American army as any other, because you only had to train them to go one way.
Woodrow Wilson, speech in Kansas City, Missouri, September 6, 1919. The "wit" was Will Rogers.

Make 'em so mad they'll eat steel rather than get another dressing from you. Make 'em hard but don't break 'em.
Laurence Stallings, *What Price Glory?* (1926).

Train in difficult, trackless, wooded terrain. War makes extremely heavy demands on the soldier's strength and nerves. For this reason make heavy demands on your men in peacetime.
Erwin Rommel, *Infantry Attacks* (1937).

Every officer is a teacher. The greater his proficiency as a teacher, the greater his efficiency as an officer. This has been true in all armies and for all time. Training is the paramount duty of officers at all times except when engaged in combat.
L. A. Pennington and others, *The Psychology of Military Leadership* (1943).

Fools say they learn by experience. I prefer to profit by other people's experience.
Otto von Bismarck quoted in B. H. Liddell Hart, *Why Don't We Learn From History?* (1943).

Before a raid he [Mountbatten] would often tell the assembled Commandos, weary from training, "Well, you have done it here, now you've got to do it over there. It reminds me of a sailor who had a girl friend at home and then was posted overseas. He wrote to her for a while, then stopped. Her letters remained unanswered. Eventually, in desperation she wrote: "I am sure you have found another girl, but I can't understand what she has got that I haven't!" To this he replied: "She hasn't got anything that you haven't got. You've got everything that she's got, but she's got it here!' "
Richard Hough, *Mountbatten* (1981).

The academy's long-range mission will be to train generals, not second lieutenants.
General Hubert R. Harmon, Superintendent of the U.S. Air Force Academy, quoted in *Newsweek* (June 6, 1955).

The whole training of an officer seeks to accomplish one purpose—to instill in him the ability to take over in battle in a time of crisis.
General Matthew B. Ridgway, *Soldier* (1956).

"You have been a splendid body of men to train, well worthy of the division to which you belong, well worthy of the objective for which you have been trained. . . . And I only wish I was coming with you . . . ."
"You can have my fucking place, for one." That was Dusty Miller.
"No talking in the ranks," [Sergeant] Meadows said.
Brian W. Aldiss, *A Soldier Erect* (1971).

[The soldier] who had been a Stateside civilian six months earlier and a member of K Company for only four days, was clued in by a couple of old-timers before the attack started. His briefing was short, to the point, and easy to remember: "When we duck, you duck."
Harold P. Leinbaugh and John P. Campbell, *The Men of Company K* (1985).

It has been over a century since mass formations of men were of any use on the battlefield, but every army in the world still drills its troops, especially during basic training, because marching in formation, with every man moving his body in the same way at the same moment, is a direct physical way of learning two things a soldier must believe: that orders have to be obeyed automatically and instantly, and that you are no longer an individual, but part of a group.
Gwynne Dyer, *War* (1985).

basic training
The first day I was at camp I was afraid I was going to die. The next two weeks my sole fear was that I wasn't going to die. And after that I knew I'd never die because I'd become so hard that nothing could kill me.
Anonymous soldier quoted in Kemper F. Cowing, *Dear Folks at Home* (1919).

Today we have naming of parts. Yesterday,
We had daily cleaning. And tomorrow morning
We shall have what to do after firing. But today,
Today we have naming of parts.
Henry Reed, *A Map of Verona* (1946).

When a recruit arrives he is plunged into an alien environment, and is enveloped in a situation without relief. He is stunned, dazed and frightened. The severity of shock is reflected in 17-hydroxycorticosteroid levels comparable to those in schizophrenic patients in incipient psychosis and which exceeds levels in other stressful situations. The recruit receives little, or erroneous, information about what to expect, which tends to maintain his anxiety. . . . Basic Training is unique in American society.
Peter B. Bourne, "Some Observations on the Psychosocial Phenomena Seen in Basic Training," *Psychiatry*, XXX, No. 2 (1967).

Our first evening as soldiers is devoted to the science of brushing the teeth. We are given a lecture by a captain who shows us a film on the vertical, or "the up-and-down," method. . . . We are all seated at tables facing each other, practicing what we have just learned with a free, disposable toothbrush, a ration of one squiggle of toothpaste and a small paper cup filled with water. Each desk has been covered with a paper towel so that nothing will dribble onto it, and we are each given a large paper cup to spit into. Soon the giggles being to reign, and spittle and toothpaste drip down the chins and onto the shirts of the men. Whole mouthfuls are shot forward as convulsive

laughter pries clamped teeth open. A corporal walks around the room taking the name of anyone who had dripped onto a desk.
Peter Tauber, *The Sunshine Soldiers* (1971).

We're still turning out hard and competent Marines, but we're doing it by motivating a recruit, not by scaring him half to death.
Colonel J. T. Bowlin, USMC, *U.S. News & World Report* (January 12, 1981).

The whole of basic training has evolved in the guise of a masculine initiation rite that often has particular appeal to the late adolescent struggling to establish a masculine identity for himself in society.
Peter Bourne, quoted in Richard Holmes, *Acts of War* (1985).

[Basic training] has been so consistently successful and so universal that we fail to notice it as remarkable. In countries where the army must extract its recruits in their late teens, whether voluntarily or by conscription, from a civilian environment that does not share the military values, basic training involves a brief but intense period of indoctrination whose purpose is not really to teach the recruits basic military skills, but rather to change their values and their loyalties.
Gwynne Dyer, *War* (1985).

I don't think boot camp is tough enough. [The Marine of the future is] going to be a tough guy. He's going to be what his idea of a Marine was in the first place . . . what he joined to be. . . . This nation desperately needs at least one outfit that can call themselves truly military professionals.
General Alfred M. Gray, Jr., Commandant of U.S. Marine Corps, *USA Today* (November 27, 1987).

traitors

The generals, officers and soldiers who in a battle have saved their lives by capitulating, ought to be decimated. He who commands the arms to be surrendered and those who obey him, are alike traitors, and deserve capital punishment.
Napoleon I, *Military Maxims* (1827).

[Stalin] observed to a foreign correspondent that there was no such thing as a Russian prisoner of war, only Russian traitors, with whom he would deal when the war was over.
Alex de Jonge, *Stalin* (1986).

I hate the idea of causes, and if I had to choose between betraying my country and betraying my friend, I hope I should have the guts to betray my country.
E. M. Forster, *Two Cheers for Democracy* (1951).

treason

Treason against the United States, shall consist only in levying War against them, or in adhering to their Enemies, giving them aid and comfort. No person shall be convicted of Treason unless on the Testimony of two witnesses to the same overt act, or on confession in open court.
Constitution of the United States, Article III, Section 3 (1787).

He [John S. Mosby] admitted that he, like Lee and all Confederates, had been guilty of treason in bearing arms against the United States government. It rankled him, however, to hear ex-Confederates deny the charge, as if it were somehow dishonorable. "Treason . . .," he said, "is a legal and technical but not necessarily a moral

offense. . . . When I hear Confederates deny that they were guilty of treason I tell them that the difference between us is that I am proud of it and they are ashamed."
Kevin H. Siepel, *Rebel* (1983).

treaties

Alliances are broken from considerations of interest; and in this respect republics are much more careful in the observance of treaties than princes. . . . I speak of the breaking of treaties from some extraordinary cause; and here I believe, from what has been said, that the people are less frequently guilty of this than princes, and are therefore more to be trusted.
Niccolò Machiavelli, *The Discourses* (1517).

Covenants, without the sword, are but words, and of no strength to secure a man at all.
Thomas Hobbes, *Leviathan* (1651).

Treaties at best are but complied with so long as interest requires their fulfillment. Consequently, they are virtually binding on the weaker party only; or, in plain truth, they are not binding at all.
Washington Irving, *Diedrich Knickerbocker's History of New York* (1809).

Treaties are observed as long as they are in harmony with interests.
Napoleon I, *Military Maxims* (1827).

Petkoff: But of course we saw to it that the treaty was an honorable one. It declares peace—
Catherine: Peace!
Petkoff:— but not friendly relations: remember that. They wanted to put that in; but I insisted on its being struck out.
George Bernard Shaw, *Arms and the Man* (1898).

The European waste-paper basket is the place to which all treaties eventually find their way. . . . There is no such thing as International law, for the thing so miscalled is merely international custom.
Stewart L. Murray, *The Future Peace of the Anglo-Saxons* (1905).

This doctrine of the scrap of paper, this doctrine which is proclaimed by Bernhardi, that treaties only bind a nation as long as it is to its interest, goes under the root of all public law. It is the straight road to barbarism. It is as if you were to move the Magnetic Pole because it was in the way of a German cruiser. The whole navigation of the seas would become dangerous, difficult, and impossible; and the whole machinery of civilization will break down if this doctrine wins in this way. We are fighting against barbarism, and there is one way of putting it right. If there are nations that say they will only respect treaties when it is to their interest to do so, we must make it to their interest to do so for the future.
David Lloyd George, speech in Queen Hall, London, September 19, 1914.

The high contracting parties solemnly declare in the names of their respective peoples that they condemn recourse to war for the solution of international controversies, and renounce it as an instrument of national policy in their relations with one another. The high contracting parties agree that the settlement or solution of all disputes or

conflicts of whatever nature or of whatever origin they may be, which may rise among them, shall never be sought except by pacific means.
The Kellogg-Briand Pact, signed in Paris by all of the major military powers on August 27, 1928. It was co-sponsored by Frank B. Kellogg, U.S. Secretary of State, and Aristide Briand, the French Foreign Minister. This is the treaty that "outlawed" war.

I am unwilling to have anybody in Virginia suppose that I am simple enough to imagine that this treaty is worth a postage stamp in bringing about peace . . . but it would be psychologically bad to defeat it.
Senator Carter Glass on the Kellogg-Briand Multilateral Treaty for the Renunciation of War as an Instrument of National Policy, *Time* (January 28, 1929).

I am willing to sign anything. I will do anything to facilitate the success of my policy. . . . there has never been a sworn treaty which has not sooner or later been broken or become untenable. . . . Why should I not make an agreement in good faith today and unhesitatingly break it tomorrow if the future of the German people demands it?
Adolf Hitler quoted in Richard Humble, *Hitler's Generals* (1974).

We have no intention of forgetting our rights or of deserting a free people. Soviet rulers should remember that free men have, before this, died for so-called "scraps of paper" which represented duty and honor and freedom.
President Dwight D. Eisenhower, address to the nation, March 16, 1959.

Treaties are like roses and young girls. They last while they last.
Charles de Gaulle, President of France, on a Franco-German treaty, *Time* (July 12, 1963).

If we are trying to trick one another, why do we need a piece of paper?
Soviet General Secretary Leonid Brezhnev to President Richard Nixon at the 1972 Moscow Summit, quoted in Richard A. Scribner, *The Verification Challenge* (1985).

No nation that placed its faith in parchment paper, while at the same time it gave up its protective hardware, ever lasted long enough to write many pages in history.
President Ronald Reagan, speech at West Point, May 27, 1981.

The fidelity of the United States to security treaties is not just an empty matter. It is a pillar of peace in the world.
Dean Rusk quoted in *The New York Times* (April 30, 1985).

There is a secret agreement between the United States and the Soviet Union . . . a simple but lucid treaty holding that when one side does something particularly fatheaded and self-destructive the other will respond by shooting itself in the foot within a period of from 17 to 30 days.
A. M. Rosenthal, *The New York Times* (December 14, 1986).

Lenin said treaties were like pie crusts—made to be broken.
John Lofton, *U.S. News and World Report* (June 1, 1987). According to Richard Shenkman, *Legends, Lies, and Cherished Myths of American History* (1988), this sentiment will be found in Lenin's published works "in the course of a bitter denunciation of socialist colleagues who wrongly believed, said Lenin, that promises are made to be broken."

I cherish no illusions about the Soviets. . . . For them, past arms-control treaties were like diets: The second day was always the best, for that's when they broke them.
President Ronald Reagan, speech in Washington, D.C., November 18, 1987.

trench warfare

To bury an army in entrenchments, where it may be outflanked and surrounded or forced in front even if secure from a flank attack, is manifest folly.
General Antoine Henri Jomini, *Summary of the Art of War* (1838).

Put a man in a hole and a good battery on a hill behind him, and he will beat off three times his number, even if he is not a very good soldier.
Colonel Theodore Lyman, writing of the Civil War, *Meade's Headquarters* (1922).

In the 1920s I used to catch myself despising men of my own age who had not been in the trenches.
Charles Carrington quoted in Richard Holmes, *Acts of War* (1985).

Without mobility an army is but a corpse—awaiting burial in a trench.
B. H. Liddell Hart, *Remaking of Modern Armies* (1927).

There was a kind of cascading movement in the battle [at Gallipoli in 1914]; directly one line of soldiers had come over the parapet and been destroyed another line formed up, emerged into view and was cut down. For the first hour it was simply a matter of indiscriminate killing, but presently the Australians and New Zealanders began to adopt more systematic methods: when a Turkish officer appeared they deliberately withheld their fire until he had assembled the full company of his men in the open. Then all were destroyed together. At some points it became a kind of game to pick off the survivors as they ran back and forth across the battlefield like terrified rabbits in search of cover. . . .
As daylight broke the battle assumed the character of a hunt, with the Turkish officers serving in the role of beaters driving the game on to the guns.
Alan Moorehead, *Gallipoli* (1956).

Throughout the [Civil] war, the spade increasingly became the complement of the rifle, until, in 1864, every battle fought between Grant and Lee in the Wilderness of Virginia was an entrenched one and when Grant neared Petersburg and Richmond, both sides became so extensively entrenched that siege warfare set in and lasted for nearly ten months. Even in Sherman's simultaneous advance on Atlanta, the mobility of his campaign was due not only to his skill in maneuvering his men, but also in his ability to maneuver their entrenchments with them.
J. F. C. Fuller, *The Conduct of War* (1961).

We set to work to bury people. We pushed them into the sides of the trench but bits of them kept getting uncovered and sticking out, like people in a badly made bed. Hands were the worst; they would escape from the sand, pointing, begging—even waving! There was one which we all shook when we passed, saying "Good morning," in a posh voice. Everybody did it. The bottom of the trench was springy like a mattress because of all the bodies underneath. . . . The flies entered the trenches at night and lined them completely with a density which was like moving cloth. We killed millions by slapping our spades along the trench walls but the next night it would be just as bad. We were all lousy and we couldn't stop shitting because we had caught dysentery. We wept, not because we were frightened but because we were so dirty.
Leonard Thompson, writing of Gallipoli in 1915, quoted in Ronald Blythe, *Akenfield* (1969).

Confronted with this deadlock [trench warfare], military art remained dumb; the Commanders and their General Staffs had no plan except the frontal attack which all

their experience and training had led them to reject; they had no policy except the policy of exhaustion.
Winston Churchill, *The World Crisis, 1915* (1923).

There was no patriotism in the trenches. It was too remote a sentiment, and rejected as fit only for civilians. A new arrival who talked patriotism would soon be told to cut it out.
Robert Graves, *Good-bye to All That* (1929).

In the summer of 1918 the first working model of the Thompson sub-machine gun had appeared. The gun had been designed by Colonel J. T. Thompson specifically as a weapon for trench warfare, and he dubbed it the "trench broom," to be used in close-quarter combat when troops were trying to clear an enemy trench.
John Ellis, *The Social History of the Machine Gun* (1975).

I don't know what is to be done . . . this isn't war.
Field Marshal Horatio Kitchener, British Secretary of State for War, speaking of trench warfare, quoted in Trevor Wilson, *The Myriad Faces of War* (1986).

Any distinction between belligerents and nonbelligerents is no longer admissible today either in fact or theory. . . .When nations are at war, everyone takes part in it; the soldier carrying his gun, the woman loading shells at a factory, the farmer growing wheat, the scientist experimenting in his laboratory. . . . It begins to look now as if the safest place may be the trenches.
Giulio Douhet, *The Command of the Air* (1921).

tripwires

Of course, twice the Americans came into the war too late and people suspect them. . . . Maybe it would be a good idea to have just a few Americans and British in the front line to get killed right away if the Russians attack, just to bring everybody in immediately. I used to say when I was at NATO that I would shoot an American myself if a war started, just to make sure.
Field Marshal B. L. Montgomery, March 22, 1963, quoted in C. L. Sulzberger, *The Last of the Giants* (1970).

You are the tripwire across which the forces of aggression and tyranny must stumble in their quest for global domination.
President Ronald Reagan, speech to CIA employees, June 23, 1982.

tyranny

The people always have some champion whom they set over them and nurse into greatness . . . . This and no other is the root from which a tyranny springs. When he first appears above ground he is a protector. In the early days of his career he is full of smiles . . . wanting to be so kind and good to everyone! But when he has disposed of foreign enemies by conquest or treaty, and there is nothing to fear from them, then he is always stirring up some war or other, in order that the people may require a leader. He has another object, which is that they may be impoverished by payment of taxes and thus compelled to devote themselves to their daily wants and therefore less likely to conspire against him. And if any of them are suspected by him of having notions of freedom and of resistance to his authority, he will have a good pretext for destroying them by placing them at the mercy of the enemy; and for all these reasons the tyrant must always be getting up a war.
Plato, *The Republic* (370 B.C.).

Taxation without representation is tyranny.
Attributed to James Otis in the 1760s. As "No taxation without representation," this became a slogan of the American Revolution.

Where law ends, tyranny begins.
William Pitt, Earl of Chatham, speech in the House of Lords, January 9, 1770.

Tyranny, like hell, is not easily conquered; yet we have this consolation with us, that the harder the conflict, the more glorious the triumph. What we obtain too cheap, we esteem too lightly: it is dearness only that gives every thing its value.
Thomas Paine, *The American Crisis* (1776).

The accumulation of all power, legislative, executive, and judiciary, in the same hands, whether of one, a few, or many, and whether hereditary, self-appointed, or elective, may justly be pronounced the very definition of tyranny.
James Madison, *The Federalist*, No. 47 (1788).

I have sworn upon the altar of God, eternal hostility against every form of tyranny over the mind of man.
Vice President Thomas Jefferson, September 23, 1800 letter to Benjamin Rush, *The Writings of Thomas Jefferson*, ed. A. Lipscomb (1903).

uniforms

On May 31, 1740, Frederick William I died, and when those around him sang the hymn, "Naked I came into the world and naked I shall go," he had just sufficient strength to mutter, "No, not quite naked; I shall have my uniform on."
J. F. C. Fuller, *A Military History of the Western World*, II (1955).

My pants sit as tight to my skin as the bark to a tree. And if I do not walk *military*, that is if I bend over quickly or run, they are very apt to crack with a report as loud as a pistol.
West Point Cadet Ulysses S. Grant, letter to a cousin, quoted in William S. McFeely, *Grant* (1981).

The Army at that time [during the Civil War] was less totalitarian—or at least less standardized—than it is now, particularly in the matter of clothing. At West Point a cadet wearing unauthorized gear would be skinned, but a private on active duty might not even be reprimanded. Officers in the field enjoyed still more freedom. [General George A.] Custer took advantage of this. He began to wear a tightly fitted hussar jacket, gold lace on his pants, and rebel boots. One staff member likened him to a circus rider. . . . [Another] recalled him wearing a dark blue sailor shirt that he got from a gunboat on the James, a bright red tie, a velveteen jacket with gold loops on the sleeve, and a Confederate hat.
About the hat there remains some question. During the battle for Aldie his wild charge took him so deep inside Confederate ranks that he was lucky to get out and he attributed his escape to the fact that they mistook him for one of their own, not because he wore a rebel hat but because it looked like one.
E. S. Connell, *Son of the Morning Star* (1984).

The secret of [the] uniform was to make a crowd solid, dignified, impersonal: to give it the singleness and tautness of an upstanding man. This death's livery which walled its bearers from ordinary life, was sign that they had sold their wills and bodies to the State: and contracted themselves into a service not the less abject for that its beginning was voluntary.
T. E. Lawrence, *Revolt in the Desert* (1927).

I am decidedly in favor of retention of the Sam Browne belt as an article of uniform for officers serving in Europe. Without it there is difficulty, particularly for troops of our Allied nations, in recognizing our officers. The American uniform without the belt does not lend itself readily to easily distinguishable insignia for our officers. I am satisfied the wearing of the Sam Browne belt adds to esprit and to discipline.
General of the Armies John J. Pershing quoted in Frank E. Vandiver, *Black Jack*, II (1977).

Our appearance [U-boat crews] ... gave us the look of pirates rather than military men, and unintentionally marked us off from the personnel at the base with their military bearing. It was not merely the matted growth of hair and unkempt beards which inevitably arose in the conditions on board. ... It was also the uniform. We went to sea with only a kit bag containing a change of underclothes, socks, handkerchiefs and little else. During a patrol all other effects were crammed into a bag that stayed behind at the base. ... When the blue number one suit came to light it would be crumpled (if not musty), anything but corresponding to regulation, and would need ironing. But the U-boat man, with the sea and its storms behind him, would be above such niceties.
Peter Cremer, *U-Boat Commander* (1984).

"I want the ungarbled truth from you. You weren't really stupid enough to threaten to shoot that labor leader [John L. Lewis, who led a strike of coal miners during World War II] with six fifty-caliber guns, were you?"
"Sir, I said it," I answered, "but I explained both before and afterward that it was just my personal opinion and not that of the War Department."
General [Hap] Arnold's face turned red. He did not say a word until he was standing and had his face practically in mine.
"Personal opinion, hell!" he said, really letting me have it. "Son, as long as you wear that uniform, remember this—*you don't have a personal opinion!*"
General Robert Lee Scott, Jr., *The Day I Owned the Sky* (1988).

The Navy, the Air Force and the Army must be one unit. If I had my way they all would be in the same uniform.
General Dwight D. Eisenhower, speech at West Point, June 20, 1945.

When you put on a uniform, there are certain inhibitions that you accept.
General Dwight D. Eisenhower, commenting on General Douglas MacArthur being relieved of command by President Truman, *The New York Times* (April 12, 1951).

unit cohesion

Four brave men who do not know each other will not dare to attack a lion. Four less brave, but knowing each other well, sure of their reliability and consequently of mutual aid, will attack resolutely. There is the science of organization of armies in a nutshell.
Ardant du Picq, *Battle Studies* (1868).

When under fire, the man in the rank and file obeys the voice of the officers he knows: company-commanders; section-commanders. The line soon turns into separate small batches of individuals who cannot be carried forward unless they are led individually and are known by name to their commanders.
Marshal Ferdinand Foch, *Precepts and Judgments* (1920).

Men are inclined to do what their comrades expect them to do or, more accurately, because nobody actually wants to fight, they do what they imagine their comrades

expect them to do. Whether this be mutual deception or mutual support it does the trick.
Peter Cochrane, *Charlie Company* (1977).

Troops in Vietnam served for a year (marines for thirteen months), a tacit admission that they had no personal stake in the war. The one-year tour meant that soldiers were individuals; they arrived in-country alone, and they left alone, not as part of a cohesive unit.
Harry Mauer, *Strange Ground* (1989).

United Nations

A general association of nations must be formed under specific covenants for the purpose of affording mutual guarantees of political independence and territorial integrity to great and small states alike.
President Woodrow Wilson, address to Congress (this was the last of the "Fourteen Points"), January 8, 1918.

The League [of Nations] exists as a foreign agency. We hope it will be helpful. But the United States sees no reason to limit its own freedom and independence of action by joining it.
President Calvin Coolidge, message to Congress, December 6, 1923.

Leagues of Nations are leagues of nonsense, as they cannot control the causes of war.
J. F. C. Fuller, *Foundations of the Science of War* (1926).

The Purposes of the United Nations are:
1. To maintain international peace and security, and to that end: to take effective collective measures for the prevention and removal of threats to the peace, and for the suppression of acts of aggression or other breaches of the peace, and to bring about by peaceful means, and in conformity with the principles of justice and international law, adjustment or settlement of international disputes or situations which might lead to a breach of the peace;
2. To develop friendly relations among nations based on respect for the principle of equal rights and self-determination of peoples. . . .
3. To achieve international cooperation in solving international problems of an economic, social, cultural, or humanitarian character.
Article 1 of the 1945 Charter of the United Nations.

Our instrument and our hope is the United Nations, and I see little merit in the impatience of those who would abandon this imperfect world instrument because they dislike our imperfect world.
President John F. Kennedy, State of the Union Message, January 11, 1962.

They'd [Third World nations] vote against the United States 100 per cent and nobody ever said a word to them, and suddenly I was saying, "You're sitting here, asking us for bread; you're sitting here, asking us for food; you're sitting here, asking us to help you against your traditional and mortal enemies, the mugwumps on the other side of the border; and there's your guy back there voting against us. How can we help you if you're not going to help us out?" And suddenly, these Ambassadors were getting cables from home saying, "What in the hell are you doing? We need help against those mugwumps."
Daniel P. Moynihan, *Playboy* (March 1977).

The UN is the only place the U.S. can turn to in time of crisis, when there's the risk of a serious confrontation between the nuclear powers. It makes no sense to throw away the key to the shelter.
Brian E. Urquhart, *The New York Times Magazine* (December 19, 1982).

In September 1982 Secretary General Javier Perez de Cuellar forced his way to public attention by an unexpected exercise in candor. He said in simple words that the United Nations is not amounting to very much, that few governments take notice of its resolutions and that the international system is marked by a "new anarchy." The background for this somber judgment was the fact that the year in review had been crowded with conflicts, and most of them had unfolded, for good or ill, exactly as they would have done if no international organization had existed.
Abba Eban, *The New Diplomacy* (1983).

If in the judicious determination of the members of the United Nations they feel they are not welcome and treated with the hostly consideration that is their due, the United States strongly encourages member states to seriously consider removing themselves and this organization from the soil of the United States. We will put no impediment in your way and we will be at dockside bidding you a farewell as you set off into the sunset.
Charles M. Lichenstein, U.S. delegate to the U.N., speaking on September 19, 1983, *The New York Times* (September 20, 1983).

Maybe all those delegates should have six months . . . in Moscow and then six months in New York, and it would give them an opportunity to see two ways of life. . . . I think the gentleman [Charles Lichenstein] who spoke the other day had the hearty approval of most people in America in his suggestion that we weren't asking anyone to leave, but if they chose to leave, good-bye.
President Ronald Reagan, press conference, September 21, 1983.

[The United Nations] provides first of all a place where people can let off steam. That's to say, where you make a strong verbal reaction which releases you from the necessity of doing very much.
Conor Cruise O'Brien, *The Christian Science Monitor* (March 14, 1985).

There are moments when I feel that only an invasion from outer space will re-introduce into the Security Council the unanimity and spirit which the founders of the Charter were talking about.
Brian E. Urquhart, Under Secretary General of the United Nations, *The New York Times* (September 23, 1985).

[The United Nations] has surely degenerated into a complaints bureau and an international registry for the mere recording of international political problems.
Spyros Kyprianou, President of Cyprus, *The New York Times* (October 16, 1985).

They all profess to love the UN and to be law-abiding countries, but when their interests are at stake they trample these noble principles and return to the law of the jungle where might means right.
Javier Perez de Cuellar, Secretary General of the United Nations, *The Christian Science Monitor* (October 17, 1985).

At the UN everybody wins a few, loses a few, settles for half a loaf. No one, not the U.S., not the U.S.S.R., not Japan, not China, not India can get away with playing the Big Bully or the Lone Ranger.
Natarajan Krishnan, Indian Ambassador to the United Nations, *The Christian Science Monitor* (October 17, 1985).

valor

The better part of valor is discretion.
William Shakespeare, *Henry IV, Part I*, Act V (1597).

Perfect valor consists in doing without witnesses that which we would be capable of doing before everyone.
François de la Foucauld, *Maxims* (1665).

So sensible were the Romans of the imperfections of valor without skill and practice that, in their language, the name of an Army [Exercitus] was borrowed from the word which signified exercise.
Edward Gibbon, *Decline and Fall of the Roman Empire* (1776).

The chief virtues of a soldier are constancy and discipline. Valor comes only in second place.
Napoleon I, writing in 1799, quoted in J. C. Herold, *The Mind of Napoleon* (1955).

Valor is secured by discipline.
Ardant du Picq, *Battle Studies* (1868).

Valor is necessary now as ever in war, but disciplined, subordinated valor, admitting the courage and energies of all be welded and directed to a common end.
Richard Taylor, *Destruction and Reconstruction* (1879).

verification

Verification is not something new. It is a continuation of our normal intelligence processes, because we are going to know about Soviet military forces and weapons, whatever it takes to learn of them, whether there is a treaty or not.
William Colby, Director of the CIA (1973–1976), quoted in Richard A. Scribner and others, *The Verification Challenge* (1985).

The Navy stands ready to accept whatever intrusive means of arms-control inspection, including allowing Soviet inspection teams aboard our ships, whatever is negotiated.
John F. Lehman, Jr., Secretary of the Navy, testimony before U.S. Senate Armed Service Committee, February 6, 1985.

I think it important to have a clear understanding of the purpose of verification. It is not to give us evidence to use in a court of law against the Soviets, but rather to protect our country against surprise. . . .
William Colby, testimony before the U.S. Senate Committee on Foreign Relations, January 15, 1987.

The verification of an agreement [with the Soviets] to abolish all nuclear weapons is not difficult, or very difficult: It is impossible. What Western leader would turn in his country's last remaining nuclear weapons on the strength of assurances—mere words—that the Soviets had done the same?
Richard N. Perle, *The Washington Post* (February 5, 1987).

veterans

OCTAVIUS: But he's a tried and valiant soldier.
ANTONY: So is my horse, Octavius, and for that I do appoint him store of provender.
William Shakespeare, *Julius Caesar*, Act IV (1599). A "store of provender" was a person in charge of food for the horses.

A man who is good enough to shed his blood for his country is good enough to be given a square deal afterwards. More than that no man is entitled to, and less than that no man shall have.
President Theodore Roosevelt, speech at Springfield, Illinois, July 4, 1903.

It takes very little yeast to leaven a lump of dough. . . . It takes a very few veterans to leaven a division of doughboys.
General George S. Patton, Jr., *War as I Knew It* (1947).

That's what you are. That's what you all are. All of you young people who served in the war. You are a lost generation.
Gertrude Stein quoted in Ernest Hemingway, *A Moveable Feast* (1964).

Some of your countrymen were unable to distinguish between their native dislike for war [Vietnam] and the stainless patriotism of those who suffered its scars. But there has been a rethinking [and] now we can say to you, and say as a nation, thank you for your courage.
President Ronald Reagan, Veterans Day speech, November 11, 1984.

victory

Thus we may know that there are five essentials for victory: (1) He will win who knows when to fight and when not to fight. (2) He will win who knows how to handle both superior and inferior forces. (3) He will win whose army is animated by the same spirit throughout all the ranks. (4) He will win who, prepared himself, waits to take the enemy unprepared. (5) He will win who has military capacity and is not interfered with by his sovereign. Victory lies in the knowledge of these five points.
Sun Tzu, *The Art of War* (4th century B.C.).

The two armies separated; and we are told that Pyrrhus said to one who was congratulating him on his victory, "If we are victorious in one more battle with the Romans, we shall be utterly ruined."
Plutarch, *The Lives* (A.D. 106).

They said it was a shocking sight
    After the field was won;
For many thousand bodies here
    Lay rotting in the sun;
But things like that, you know, must be
    After a famous victory.
Robert Southey, *The Battle of Blenheim* (1798).

I return you many thanks for the honor you have done me. But Europe is not to be saved by any single man. England has saved herself by her exertions, and will, as I trust, save Europe by her example.
William Pitt (the Younger), Prime Minister of Britain, on being toasted as "the savior of Europe" after the English victory at Trafalgar, November 9, 1805.

For the victor the engagement can never be decided too quickly, for the vanquished it can never last too long. The speedy victory is a higher degree of victory.
Karl von Clausewitz, *On War* (1832).

The next greatest misfortune to losing a battle is to gain such a victory as this.
Duke of Wellington on the Battle of Waterloo, quoted in *Recollections of Samuel Roberts*, ed. W. Sharpe (1859).

It must be a peace without victory. . . . Victory would mean peace forced upon the loser, a victor's terms imposed upon the vanquished. It would be accepted in humiliation, under duress, at an intolerable sacrifice, and would leave a sting, a resentment, a bitter memory upon which terms of peace would rest, not permanently, but only as upon quicksand. Only a peace between equals can last.
President Woodrow Wilson, speech to the U.S. Senate, January 22, 1917.

The earth is still bursting with the dead bodies of the victors.
George Bernard Shaw, *Heartbreak House*, preface (1920).

Victory is an inclined plain. On condition that you do not check your movement the moving mass perpetually increases its speed.
Marshal Ferdinand Foch, *Precepts and Judgments* (1920).

What we call victory is never won save by bits and scraps. The two trays of the scales counterbalance for a long time, and the slightest additional touch suffices to weigh one of them down.
Marshal Ferdinand Foch quoted in Raymond Recouly, *Marshal Foch* (1929).

Victory was never in doubt. Its cost was. What was in doubt, in all our minds, was whether there would be any of us left to dedicate our cemetery at the end, or whether the last Marine would die knocking out the last Japanese gun and gunner.
Major General Graves B. Erskine, at the dedication of the Third Marine Division Cemetery on Iwo Jima, March 14, 1945, quoted in Bill D. Ross, *Iwo Jima* (1985).

No one can guarantee success in war, but only deserve it.
Winston Churchill, *The Second World War: Their Finest Hour* (1948).

But once war is forced upon us, there is no other alternative than to apply every available means to bring it to a swift end. War's very object is victory, not prolonged indecision.
In war there is no substitute for victory.
General Douglas A. MacArthur, address to Joint Session of Congress, April 19, 1951.

Once upon a time our traditional goal in war—and can anyone doubt that we are at war?—was victory. Once upon a time we were proud of our strength, our military power. Now we seem ashamed of it. Once upon a time the rest of the world looked to us for leadership. Now they look to us for a quick handout and a fence-straddling international posture.
Senator Barry M. Goldwater, *Why Not Victory?* (1962).

With the development of modern technology, "victory" in war has become a mockery. What victory—victory for what or for whom?
Adlai E. Stevenson, "The Hard Kind of Patriotism," *Harper's* (July 1963).

Victory is no longer a truth. It is only a word to describe who is left alive in the ruins.
President Lyndon B. Johnson, speech in New York City, February 6, 1964.

We must come to grips with the fact that the nature of victory has changed in our lifetime. It seems almost a millennium between Roosevelt's call for "unconditional surrender" and Johnson's call for "unconditional negotiations." Victory in the military middle ages of the 1940s meant the smashing of the enemy and the occupation of

his territory. In the atomic era, military victory has come to mean the repulsion of an invader and the restoration of freedom.
Richard M. Nixon, speech to the National Association of Manufacturers, New York, December 3, 1965.

The greatest victory lies not in the battle which is fought and won, but in the battle which was never fought. As Milton said so simply, "Peace has her victories, no less renowned than war."
Caspar W. Weinberger, U.S. Secretary of Defense, *The Christian Science Monitor* (June 11, 1982).

This generation of American statesmen, who believe that victory is an archaic concept and that military power must be carefully graduated to send signals for securing specific objectives, have been proven wrong both in Korea and in Vietnam.
Paul Seabury and Angelo Codevilla, *War* (1989).

Vietnam War

aftermath
"You know you never defeated us on the battlefield," said the American colonel [Harry G. Summers, Jr.].
The North Vietnamese colonel pondered this remark a moment. "That may be so," he replied, "but it is also irrelevant."
Conversation in Hanoi, April 25, 1975, quoted in Harry G. Summers, Jr., *On Strategy* (1982).

Among the many [foreign aid] claims on American resources, I would put those of Vietnam in alphabetical order.
Henry A. Kissinger, *Newsweek* (May 16, 1977).

Vietnam is still with us. It has created doubts about American judgment, about American credibility, about American power—not only at home, but throughout the world. It has poisoned our domestic debate. So we paid an exorbitant price for the decisions that were made in good faith and for good purpose.
Henry A. Kissinger quoted in Stanley Karnow, *Vietnam* (1983).

The customary reward of defeat, if one can survive it, is in the lessons thereby learned, which may yield victory in the next war. But the circumstances of our defeat in Vietnam were sufficiently ambiguous to deny the nation the benefit of a well-understood military failure.
Edward N. Luttwak, *The Pentagon and the Art of War* (1985).

The decade of neglect [1970s] was fed, really, by a most insidious idea—that somehow American power was immoral. We began by doubting the war in Vietnam, and we ended by doubting ourselves.
Caspar W. Weinberger, farewell address as U.S. Secretary of Defense, November 17, 1987, *The New York Times* (November 18, 1987).

assessments
One country may support another's cause, but will never take it so seriously as it takes its own. A moderately-sized force will be sent to its help; but if things go wrong the operation is pretty well written off, and one tries to withdraw at the smallest possible cost.
Karl von Clausewitz, *On War* (1832).

I knew that Harry Truman and Dean Acheson had lost their effectiveness from the day that the Communists took over in China. I believed that the loss of China had

played a large role in the rise of Joe McCarthy. And I knew that all these problems, taken together, were chickenshit compared with what might happen if we lost Vietnam.
President Lyndon B. Johnson, speaking in 1970, quoted in Doris Kearns, *Lyndon Johnson and the American Dream* (1976).

From a historian's standpoint, the significant feature of Vietnam is not that the methods we have used there are immoral; it is that they have not worked.
Charles Fair, *From the Jaws of Victory* (1971).

I think we went wrong by intervening in the civil war in the first place and by involving ourselves so deeply on behalf not of a democracy but on behalf of a corrupt dictatorship that could not win the allegiance of its own people.
Senator Alan Cranston, *Los Angeles Times* (April 1, 1975).

When before has a great country stopped in the middle of a war, assessed the wisdom of its participation, decided it was wrong, asserted the judgment against all of the chauvinist tendencies aroused by armed conflict, dismissed from power those responsible and brought its participation to an end? The answer is never.... The country corrected the error of its leaders on Vietnam. It was not a defeat but a triumph of good sense.... Does it not say something for democracy?
John Kenneth Galbraith, *The New York Times* (July 12, 1975).

Wrong and morally wrong in its conduct and consequences, it was nevertheless not evil in intent or origin. What propelled us into this war was a corruption of the generous, idealistic, liberal impulse.
Alexander M. Bickel, *The Morality of Consent* (1975).

The ... lesson [of Vietnam] is that America must never commit its power and authority in defense of a country of only marginal strategic interests when that country lacks a broadly based government, or the will to create one.
George W. Ball, *Diplomacy for a Crowded World* (1976).

Psychologists or sociologists may explain some day what it is about that distant monochromatic land, of green mountains and fields merging with an azure sea, that for millennia has acted as a magnet for foreigners who sought glory there and found frustration, who believed that in its rice fields and jungles some principle was to be established and entered them only to recede in disillusion.
Henry A. Kissinger, *White House Years* (1979).

They came home without a victory not because they had been defeated but because they had been denied permission to win.
President Ronald Reagan, speech in Washington, D.C., February 24, 1981.

In the end, we simply cut and ran. The American national will had collapsed.
Graham A. Martin, the last American Ambassador to South Vietnam, quoted in *The New York Times* (April 30, 1985).

The biggest lesson I learned from Vietnam is not to trust [United States] government statements. I had no idea until then that you could not rely on [them].
J. William Fulbright, *The New York Times* (April 30, 1985).

The legacy of Vietnam ... is that the United States spends $300 billion a year for armed forces that American leaders are unable to use effectively.... As the smoke from that long conflict has drifted away, it has become clear that Americans distrust their government's ability to apply military power prudently. It has become equally

clear that most Americans feel they have no ties to their armed forces, other than paying enormous sums in taxes for their upkeep.
Richard Halloran, *To Arm a Nation* (1986).

The United States had not been in Vietnam for ten years but one year ten times.
John Paul Vann quoted in Roger Kaplan, "Army Unit Cohesion in Vietnam," *Parameters* (September 1987).

[The Vietnam War] will be important in history mostly for what it did, internally, to the United States, not what difference it made in Indochina.
James Fallows, *More Like Us* (1989).

People don't want to remember anything about that awful mess.
J. William Fulbright, *The New York Times Book Review* (February 19, 1989).

That war cleaves us still. But, friends, that war began in earnest a quarter of a century ago; and surely the statute of limitations has been reached. This is a fact: The final lesson of Vietnam is that no great nation can long afford to be sundered by a memory.
President George Bush, Inaugural Address, January 20, 1989.

It is an article of faith among the military that the American soldier was not defeated on the battlefield.
Those who actually fought at the squad, platoon and company level know this is largely myth. Far too often, Vietcong and regulars of the North Vietnamese Army savaged American units in battle before withdrawing and leaving Americans in command of a battlefield strewn with their own dead.
Bernard E. Trainor, *The New York Times Book Review* (April 30, 1989).

attitudes
No general was going to admit that the U. S. couldn't win this lousy little war against a couple of hundred thousand peasants in pajamas.
Hans J. Morgenthau quoted in James A. Donovan, *Militarism, U. S. A.* (1970).

We should declare war on North Vietnam. We could pave the whole place over by noon and be home for dinner.
Ronald Reagan, quoted in Edmund G. Brown, *Reagan: The Political Chameleon* (1976).

When I visited French units, almost as soon as I found myself alone with the commander, he would say to me, "Our government is not enthusiastic about what you are doing in Vietnam, but I want you to know that the people you are fighting killed our people, murdered our wounded and whenever you have a success against them, we feel warmth in our heart for you." This feeling was widespread throughout the French Army.
General Vernon Walters, *Silent Missions* (1978).

Within the soul of each Vietnam veteran there is probably something that says "Bad war, good soldier."
Max Cleland, *Time* (November 22, 1982).

After months in the hostile alien land most grunts despised the people— "gooks," "dinks," "slopes." An ugly joke circulated around the GI bars in 1968 that the solution of the Vietnam mess was to "load all the Friendlies onto ships and take them out to the South China Sea. Then you bomb the country flat. Then you sink the ships."
Irwin Unger and Debbi Unger, *Turning Point: 1968* (1988).

body count

There were slain in this battle about 6,000 men, which, to people that are unwilling to lie, may seem very much; but in my time I have been in several actions, where for one man that was really slain, they reported a hundred, thinking by such an account to please their masters.
Philip de Commines, *Memoirs* (1498).

The only measure of the war the Americans were interested in was quantitative; and quantitatively, given the immense American fire power, helicopters, fighter-bombers and artillery pieces, it went very well. That the body count might be a misleading indicator did not penetrate the command; large stacks of dead Vietcong were taken as signs of success. That the French statistics had also been very good right up until 1954, when they gave up, made no impression.
David Halberstam, *The Best and the Brightest* (1972).

The body counts that had been so prominent a feature of our estimates of enemy damage had been enormously exaggerated. The My Lai incident, where the victims were at first reported as slain Viet Cong, gave only one among many hints about the identity of the bodies counted.
Bernard Brodie, *War and Politics* (1973).

Since the only means of "scoring" the war lay in the accumulation and comparison of body counts (if the evening news reported 750 Vietcong killed and 75 Americans, America was "winning" 10 to 1), it was to the military's advantage to keep the reported casualty figures as low as possible. North Vietnamese and Vietcong losses were inflated, American casualties disguised. Men who died in the hospitals as a result of wounds were likely to be listed as having died from postoperative complications; they were nonbattle casualties and not counted.
C. D. B. Bryan, *Friendly Fire* (1976).

In Vietnam, the only measure of victory was one of the most hideous, morally corrupting ideas ever conceived by the military mind—the body count.
Philip Caputo quoted in David L. Bender, *The Vietnam War* (1984).

Body count was also well on its way to destroying whatever was left of the moral code of soldiers and officers in the zero-defect Army. Leaders did not challenge suspect figures reported by subordinate units (who themselves knew the importance of a significant count) and too often actively inflated their scores to please their ER raters or just to get higher HQ off their backs. Sometimes a body count was completely made up to mask a screwed-up mission. In just one instance, a battalion commander asked one of his company COs over the radio to tell him his college football jersey number to have something to report for a botched operation ("Eighty-six," said the company commander; "Eighty-six!" exclaimed the battalion commander. "Great body count!").
David H. Hackworth, *About Face* (1989).

Eisenhower years

The United States is carrying 78 percent of the cost of the Indo-Chinese war.
Christian Pineau, Deputy in the French National Assembly, speaking in Paris on March 16, 1954, quoted in William G. Effros, *Quotations Vietnam* (1970).

Pouring money, materiel and men into the jungles [of Vietnam] without at least a remote prospect of victory would be dangerously futile and self destructive.
Senator John F. Kennedy, speech in the U.S. Senate, April 6, 1954.

If to avoid further Communist expansion in Asia and Indochina, we must take the risk now of putting our boys in, I think the Executive has to take the politically unpopular decision and do it.
Vice President Richard M. Nixon, speaking on April 16, 1954, quoted in Dwight D. Eisenhower, *Mandate for Change* (1963).

The loss of South Vietnam would set in motion a crumbling process that could, as it progresses, have grave consequences for us and for freedom.
President Dwight D. Eisenhower, speech at Gettysburg College, April 4, 1959.

Ford years
The basic difficulty with the South Vietnamese forces is that they had everything with which to fight but really nothing to fight for.
Clark M. Clifford, *Los Angeles Times* (April 9, 1975).

The North Vietnamese in recent months began sending even their reserve divisions into South Vietnam. Eighteen divisions, virtually their entire army, are now in South Vietnam. The government of South Vietnam, uncertain of further American assistance, hastily ordered a strategic withdrawal to more defensible positions. This extremely difficult maneuver, decided upon without consultations, was poorly executed, hampered by floods of refugees, and thus led to panic. The results are painfully obvious and profoundly moving.
President Gerald R. Ford, speech to the nation, April 10, 1975.

"There was a period when no helicopters landed . . . [at the American Embassy]," [Kenneth] Moorefield noted. "I remember looking down at the court-yard and counting the people left—a little over four hundred, just a few more chopper loads. Not all were Vietnamese. . . .
"During this hiatus I went down to the sixth floor. Major Kean had just received a message from the fleet through his tactical net. There were a few of us standing there, and the major said to us, very dramatically, that the message was from the White House: 'I've just received an order from the President. Only Embassy staffers are to be evacuated from this point on. Don't panic!' He was very dramatic about it. 'Don't panic,' he said, as if any of us had the mind or the strength to panic at this point. And I remember turning to Jay Blowers and saying sardonically, 'Don't panic! Only Americans will be evacuated from here on. We're not evacuating anyone else!'
"I then went back to the roof and made another eyeball estimate of the bodies in the courtyard: just over four hundred. I knew now that none of them would ever get out."
At that moment Brunson McKinley, the Ambassador's aide, oblivious of Whitmire's decision to shut off the flow, strode out into the courtyard and promised . . . more choppers would be coming in.
Frank Snepp, *Decent Interval* (1977).

Johnson years
I'd drop a low-yield atomic bomb on the Chinese supply lines in North Vietnam.
Senator Barry M. Goldwater, *Look* (April 21, 1964).

I don't object to its being called "McNamara's war." I think it is a very important war and am pleased to be identified with it and do whatever I can to win it.
Robert S. McNamara, Secretary of Defense, quoted in *The New York Times* (April 25, 1964).

But we are not about to send American boys nine or ten thousand miles away from home to do what Asian boys ought to be doing for themselves.
President Lyndon B. Johnson, campaign speech, Akron, Ohio, October 21, 1964.

People ask me who my heroes are. I have only one—Hitler. I admire Hitler. . . . We need four or five Hitlers in Vietnam.
South Vietnamese Prime Minister Nguyen Cao Ky, *Sunday Mirror* (London) (July 4, 1965).

The more we Americanize the war . . . the more we make the war unwinnable.
Arthur M. Schlesinger, Jr., *Look* (July 25, 1966).

The United States could well declare unilaterally that this stage of the Vietnam War is over—that we have "won" in the sense that our armed forces are in control of most of the field and no potential enemy is in a position to establish its authority over South Vietnam. . . . It may be a far-fetched proposal, but nothing else has worked.
Senator George D. Aiken, speech in the Senate, October 19, 1966.

I just had the greatest brainwashing that anyone can get when you go over to Vietnam, not only by the generals, but also by the diplomatic corps over there, and they do a very thorough job.
George Romney, Governor of Michigan, speaking in Detroit, Michigan, September 4, 1967. This statement destroyed Romney's chances for the Republican presidential nomination in 1968. According to General William C. Westmoreland, *A Soldier Reports* (1976): "I cannot . . . understand the about-face on the war of Michigan's Governor George Romney, except that as a man prominently mentioned as a presidential candidate he listened to too many antiwar dissidents and deemed it politically expedient to say he had been 'brainwashed' while visiting Vietnam." According to David Halberstam, *The Best and the Brightest* (1972), Romney would be "jumped on by all sorts of people, like Robert Kennedy, who had been brainwashed themselves and never known it or admitted it."

We are very definitely winning in Vietnam. . . . I estimate that somewhere in the next year to a year and a half there will be a restoration of government control over most of the country—we can expect to see a gradual reduction of U. S. forces—as the Viet Cong are reduced to banditry.
General Harold J. Johnson, Chairman, Joint Chiefs of Staff, *U.S. News and World Report* (September 11, 1967).

I am not going to be the first President of the United States to lose a war.
President Lyndon B. Johnson quoted by James Reston in *The New York Times* (October 1, 1967).

The war in Vietnam is Johnson's mistake, and through the power of his office he has made it a national mistake.
Editorial, *The Saturday Evening Post* (November 18, 1967).

Lyndon Johnson should go on nationwide TV and say to the American people, "Ah have goofed," thus ending the only real aggression in Vietnam: our own.
If he brings to his withdrawal speech the same tears and regret he brings to his escalation speeches, the American people might very well unite behind him and he probably will not be impeached.
Jules Feiffer, quoted in C. Woolf and J. Bagguley, *Authors Take Sides on Vietnam* (1967).

The conflict in Vietnam can only be resolved by the complete and unconditional withdrawal of American troops. If Britain had intervened in the American Civil War on the side of the South—at one time it seemed possible—would Abraham Lincoln have agreed to negotiate the future of his country with a British government? Hanoi is just as close in blood to Saigon as New York to Richmond. The presence of foreign troops prevents negotiations between North and South.
Graham Greene quoted in C. Woolf and J. Bagguley, *Authors Take Sides on Vietnam* (1967).

To win in Vietnam, we will have to exterminate a nation.
Benjamin Spock, *Dr. Spock on Vietnam* (1968).

I bet that Russian Army is jealous as hell. Our troops are here [in Vietnam] getting all this experience, we're learning about guerrilla warfare, helicopters, vertical envelopment, close artillery support. . . . Those Russian generals would love to be here. . . . Any true professional wants to march to the sound of gunfire.
General William Westmoreland quoted in Ernest B. Furgurson, *Westmoreland* (1968).

[President Johnson] told an almost incredible story about his last visit to see General Douglas A. MacArthur in Walter Reed Hospital. The aged warrior might be a world-wide symbol of American belligerence in the Far East but as LBJ repeated the conversation, the General had counseled him, "Son, don't get into a land war in Asia."
Eric F. Goldman, *The Tragedy of Lyndon Johnson* (1968).

We think the American people should be getting ready to accept, if they have not already, the prospect that the whole Vietnam effort may be doomed.
Editorial, *The Wall Street Journal* (February 23, 1968).

Called to the White House in February 1968, [Dean] Acheson found Johnson obsessed with the ongoing siege of American Marines at the Vietnamese town of Khe Sanh. . . . Acheson attempted to voice his worries, but Johnson was not interested in doubts, and the President's unwillingness to listen eventually caused Acheson to walk out of the meeting and return to his law office. When Johnson's assistants called him there and said that the President wanted to know why he had walked out, Acheson answered acidly, "You tell the President—and you tell him in precisely these words—that he can take Vietnam and stick it up his ass."
James Chace and Caleb Carr, *America Invulnerable* (1988).

Victory in Vietnam—or even a favorable settlement—may simply be beyond the grasp of the world's greatest power.
Time (March 15, 1968).

There were brief moments when the reality seemed to flash through. Once during the [Vietnam] discussions the President turned to General Wheeler and said, "Bus, what do you think it will take to do the job?" And Wheeler answered, "It all depends on what your definition of the job is, Mr. President."
David Halberstam, *The Best and the Brightest* (1972).

Kennedy cooked the soup that Johnson had to eat.
Konrad Adenauer, Chancellor of West Germany, quoted in *The New York Times* (January 24, 1973).

I knew from the start that I was bound to be crucified either way I moved. If I left the woman I really loved—the Great Society—in order to get involved with that bitch of a war on the other side of the world, then I would lose everything at home. . . . But if I let the Communists take over South Vietnam, then I would be seen as a coward and my nation would be seen as an appeaser. . . . Oh, I could see it coming all right. History provided too many cases where the sound of the bugle put an immediate end to the hopes and dreams of the best reformers.
Lyndon B. Johnson quoted in Doris Kearns, *Lyndon Johnson and the American Dream* (1976).

Had President Johnson provided reinforcements, and had he authorized the operations I had planned in Laos and Cambodia and north of the DMZ, along with intensified bombing and the mining of Haiphong Harbor, the North Vietnamese would have

been broken. But that was not to be. Press and television had created an aura not of victory but of defeat, and timid officials in Washington listened more to the media than to their own representatives on the scene.
William C. Westmoreland, Commander of U.S. forces in Vietnam, 1964–68, *A Soldier Reports* (1976).

Supported by Marine Corps and Navy commanders, in September 1964 [General Curtis] LeMay recommended a classic strategic-bombing campaign against North Vietnam. It would knock out the military bases, transportation system, and industry that permitted North Vietnam to supply the Viet Cong in the South. "We should stop swatting flies and go for the manure pile," LeMay advised.
Nick Notz, *Wild Blue Yonder* (1988).

In that region there is nothing that we covet. There is nothing that we seek. There is no territory or no military position or no political ambition. Our one desire and our one determination is that the people of Southeast Asia be left in peace to work out their own destinies in their own ways.
President Lyndon B. Johnson, press conference, March 13, 1965.

The present U.S. objective in Vietnam is to avoid humiliation. The reasons we *went into* Vietnam to the present depth are varied; but they are now largely academic. Why we have *not withdrawn* from Vietnam is, by all odds, *one* reason: to preserve our reputation as a guarantor, and thus to preserve our effectiveness in the rest of the world.
John McNaughton, Assistant Secretary of Defense, memorandum of January 19, 1966, quoted in *The Pentagon Papers*, as published by *The New York Times* (1971).

Our purpose in Vietnam is to prevent the success of aggression. It is not conquest, it is not empire, it is not foreign bases, it is not domination. It is, simply put, just to prevent the forceful conquest of South Vietnam by North Vietnam.
President Lyndon B. Johnson, *Time* (March 4, 1966).

The bombs in Vietnam explode at home; they destroy the hopes and possibilities for a decent America.
Martin Luther King, *Where Do We Go from Here?* (1967).

I wanna be a Airborne Ranger
I wanna live a life of danger
I wanna be a fighting man
I wanna go to Vietnam
I wanna jump out of the sky
I wanna make the V.C. die.
U.S. Army Vietnam-era marching/running chant.

Believing this as I do, I have concluded that I should not permit the presidency to become involved in the partisan divisions that are developing in this political year.

With America's sons in the fields far away, with America's future under challenge right here at home, with our hopes and the world's hopes for peace in the balance every day, I do not believe that I should devote an hour or a day of my time to any personal partisan causes or to any duties other than the awesome duties of this office—the presidency of your country.

Accordingly, I shall not seek, and I will not accept, the nomination of my party for another term as your president.
President Lyndon B. Johnson, speech to the nation on Vietnam, March 31, 1968.

I'm tired. I'm tired of feeling rejected by the American people. I'm tired of waking up in the middle of the night worrying about the war.
President Lyndon B. Johnson quoted in *Newsweek* (April 15, 1968).

[The North Vietnamese] were determined to do one thing, and that's take over this little country [South Vietnam]. And if they take that one over, they were determined to take over others, in my judgment, just as Hitler was.
President Lyndon B. Johnson, *The Washington Post* (February 7, 1970).

Every day there were those whispering in his ear, "No President ever lost a war." That was red meat for a Texan.
W. Averell Harriman, *The Washington Post* (December 7, 1975).

It is because of their love of justice and humanity that many progressive Americans from all walks of life, hundreds of thousands of youths, students, professors, scientists, lawyers, writers, artists, clergymen, and working people ... staged huge demonstrations against the Johnson Administration's policy of aggression in Vietnam. For their part the American youth resolutely refuse to be sent to Vietnam as cannon fodder for the U.S. imperialists.
Ho Chi Minh, speaking on December 16, 1965, quoted in *Ho Chi Minh On Revolution*, ed. B. B. Fall (1967).

When we marched into the rice paddies ... , we carried, along with our packs and rifles, the implicit convictions that the Vietcong could be quickly beaten. We kept the packs and rifles; the convictions, we lost.
Philip Caputo, *A Rumor of War* (1977).

Vietnam was a fungus, slowly spreading its suffocating crust over the great plans of the president, both here and overseas. No matter what we turned our hands and minds to, there was Vietnam, its contagion infecting everything that it touched, and it seemed to touch everything.
Jack Valenti, aide to President Lyndon B. Johnson, quoted in Stanley Karnow, *Vietnam* (1983).

[Secretary of State] Dean Rusk also applied pressure. Rusk was an Anglophile and a former Rhodes scholar, who was deeply distressed by the British attitude. According to Louis Heren, a British correspondent in Washington, Rusk asked him at a cocktail party why the British couldn't manage [to send] "just one battalion of the Black Watch?" Patiently Heren explained British policy. Rusk glowered: "When the Russians invade Sussex, don't expect us to come and help you."
David Dimbleby and David Reynolds, *An Ocean Apart* (1988).

As [President] Johnson and [Secretary of Defense] McNamara upped the ante in Vietnam, an ironic twist from the presidential campaign came to haunt them. It was an anonymous quote on Johnson's claim that, if elected, Barry Goldwater would lead the nation into a massive war in Southeast Asia. The quote was: "I was told that, if I voted for Goldwater, we were going to war in Vietnam. I did, and damned if we didn't."
Barry M. Goldwater, *Goldwater* (1988).

[Marine General Victor H. Krulak] came into my office one day after briefing the president. Krulak was visibly shaken. After being briefed on the difficulties the Marines were encountering in locating and engaging the Vietcong, the president had

risen from his chair, his face dark with anger, and with his fist pounding the desk for emphasis, exclaimed: "Kill the goddamn bastards, kill'em, kill'em, kill'em!"
Paul Nitze, *The Washington Monthly* (July/August 1989); excerpted from *From Hiroshima to Glasnost* (1989).

Kennedy years

The United States is now involved in an undeclared war in South Vietnam. This is well known to the Russians, the Chinese Communists, and everybody else concerned except the American people.
James Reston, *The New York Times* (February 13, 1962).

We have not sent combat troops there—in the generally understood sense of the word. We have increased our training mission. We've increased our logistics support.
President John F. Kennedy, news conference, February 14, 1962.

The death of three American flyers and the injury of another this week revealed to the American people what the Communists have known for a long time—that United States Air Force planes, manned by United States pilots, as well as many Army light planes and helicopters have been engaged in active combat against the Vietminh guerillas.
Editorial, *The New York Times* (October 17, 1962).

The President said [in March 1963] . . . that he was beginning to agree about a complete military withdrawal. "But I can't do it until 1965—until after I'm re-elected." To do it before would cause "a wild conservative outcry" against him. . . .
His position was realistic, if not a profile in courage. Re-election was more than a year and a half away. To continue for that time to invest American resources and inevitably lives in a cause in which he no longer had much faith, rather than risk his own second term, was a decision in his own interest, not the country's. Only an exceedingly rare ruler reverses that order.
Barbara W. Tuchman, *The March of Folly* (1984).

South Vietnam's military situation in the vital Mekong Delta has deteriorated in the past year, and informed officials are warning of ominous signs. Essentially, these military sources say, a Communist Vietcong build-up is taking place in the Delta. They find it particularly disturbing because it has persisted since an American build-up twenty months ago.
David Halberstam, *The New York Times* (August 15, 1963). Halberstam would later write in his book *The Making of a Quagmire* (1965): "No story I ever wrote drew a more violent reaction. The President of the United States was angry, his generals were angry and his civilian officials were angry. At a press conference Dean Rusk specifically criticized the story."

In the final analysis, it is their war. They are the ones who have to win it or lose it. We can help them, we can give them equipment, we can send our men out there as advisers, but they have to win it, the people of Vietnam.
President John F. Kennedy, press conference, September 3, 1963.

It took us eight years of bitter fighting to defeat you French in Indochina. Now the Diem regime is well armed and helped by many Americans. The Americans are stronger than the French. It might perhaps take ten years, but our heroic compatriots in the south will defeat them in the end. We shall marshal world public opinion about this unjust war against the South Vietnamese people.
Ho Chi Minh, President of North Vietnam, interviewed by Bernard B. Fall, *The New Republic* (October 12, 1963).

Two old Vietnam hands, General Victor Krulak of the Marines and Joseph Mendenhall of State . . . disagreed on what should be done about Vietnam. They reported . . . to the National Security Council [on August 24, 1963]. Krulak told the assembled dignitaries the war was going beautifully, that the regime was beloved by the people and that we need have no undue concern. . . . Mendenhall told them that South Vietnam was in a desperate state, that the regime was on the edge of collapse. . . . The President listened politely and finally said, "Were you two gentlemen in the same country?"
Arthur M. Schleslinger, Jr., *A Thousand Days* (1965).

John Kennedy gave me to understand that the American aim was to establish a bulwark against the Soviets in the Indo-Chinese peninsula. But instead of giving him the approval he wanted, I told the President that he was taking the wrong road.
"You will find," I said to him, "that intervention in this area will be an endless entanglement. Once a nation has been aroused, no foreign power, however strong, can impose its will upon it. . . . We French have had more experience of it. You Americans wanted to take our place in Indochina. Now you want to take over where we left off and revive a war which we brought to an end. I predict that you will sink step by step into a bottomless military and political quagmire, however much you spend in men and money."
Charles de Gaulle, *Memoirs of Hope: Renewal and Endeavor* (1971).

The troops will march in [to Vietnam], the bands will play, the crowds will cheer, and in four days everyone will have forgotten. Then we will be told we have to send in more troops. It's like taking a drink. The effect wears off, and you have to take another.
President John F. Kennedy quoted in Stanley Karnow, *Vietnam: A History* (1983).

If it were ever converted into a white man's war, we should lose it as the French had lost a decade earlier.
President John F. Kennedy quoted in Barbara W. Tuchman, *The March of Folly* (1984). Tuchman has this as a direct quote from Kennedy; however, Arthur M. Schlesinger, Jr., *A Thousand Days* (1965), has those exact words as paraphrase.

General [Douglas] MacArthur, when he came down to see the President, was strongly against sending any troops into Southeast Asia. He said that you'd just get lost there, that it would be a very bad mistake. . . . The President [Kennedy] had been there in 1951 and had been impressed with the toughness of the French soldiers. A lot of them were Foreign Legion. There were paratroopers, and they were very impressive. They had several hundreds of thousands. And they were beaten.
Robert Kennedy quoted in Edwin O. Guthman and Jeffrey Shulman, editors, *Robert Kennedy In His Own Words* (1988).

light at the end of the tunnel
A year ago none of us could see victory. There wasn't a prayer. Now we can see it clearly—like light at the end of a tunnel.
General Henri Navarre, commander of French troops in Indochina, *Time* (September 28, 1953).

Every quantitative measurement we have shows we are winning this war.
Robert S. McNamara, Secretary of Defense, speaking in 1962 after his first visit to Vietnam, quoted in Arthur M. Schlesinger, Jr., *A Thousand Days* (1965).

We don't see the end of the tunnel, but I must say I don't think it is darker than it was a year ago, and in some ways lighter.
President John F. Kennedy, press conference, December 12, 1962.

For the first time since we spun into the Vietnam mess, there is hope for the United States. . . . The credit justly belongs to President Lyndon B. Johnson. He has made the war "unlosable."
Sam Caston, *Life* (November 30, 1965).

I urge you to remember that Americans often grow impatient when they cannot see light at the end of the tunnel.
President Lyndon B. Johnson, *Time* (June 17, 1966).

The North Vietnamese cannot take the punishment anymore in the South. . . . I think we can bring the war to a conclusion within the next year, possibly within the next six months.
S. L. A. Marshall, *Newsweek* (September 12, 1966).

Their casualties are going up at a rate they cannot sustain. . . . I see light at the end of the tunnel.
Walt W. Rostow, head of the Policy Planning Council of the Department of State, quoted in *Look* (December 12, 1967).

We have the enemy licked now. . . . We have the initiative in all areas. The enemy cannot achieve a military victory; he cannot even mount another major offensive. . . . My optimism is based on hard military realism.
Admiral John S. McClain, U.S. Commander-in-Chief, Pacific Theater, *Reader's Digest* (February 1969).

We are running out of time in Vietnam. The light at the end of the tunnel has gone out. The corner around which victory was supposed to appear has turned into an abyss.
Representative Abner J. Mikva, speech in the House of Representatives, October 14, 1969.

media coverage

[Morley] Safer [of CBS News] didn't tell them to burn the huts down with their lighters. He just photographed it [in 1965 in Vietnam]. He could have got a picture of me burning a hut, too. It was just the way they did it. When you say level a village, you don't use torches. It's not like in the 1800s. You use a Zippo. Now you would use a Bic. That's just the way we did it. You went in there with your Zippos. Everybody. That's why people bought Zippos. Everybody had a Zippo. It was for burnin' shit down.
Reginald "Malik" Edwards, quoted in Wallace Terry, *Bloods* (1984).

"I [said Arthur Sylvester, Assistant Secretary of Defense for Public Affairs] can't understand how you fellows can write what you do while American boys are dying out here."

Then he went on to the effect that American correspondents had a patriotic duty to disseminate only information that made the United States look good.

A network television correspondent said, "Surely, Arthur, you don't expect the American press to be handmaidens of government."

"That's exactly what I expect. . . . Look, if you think any American official is going to tell you the truth, then you're stupid. Did you hear that?—Stupid."
Morley Safer, *Dateline 1966*, publication of the Overseas Press Club of America, reporting a conversation that took place in Saigon, July 17, 1965, quoted in William G. Effros, *Quotations Vietnam* (1970). David Halberstam, *The Best and the Brightest* (1972), reports that in 1964 in Saigon "Arthur Sylvester, McNamara's officer, was arguing with a young *New York Times* reporter named Jack Langguth over the government's lack of credibility in its Vietnam statements. Sylvester said that although it was unfortunate, there were times when a government official had to lie, but that he, Sylvester, as a former newsman, had a genuine objection

to lying. Langguth answered that if you had a real objection to lying, you would quit, and the failure to resign meant that you had a soft job where you could exercise power, and that your principles were secondary. Sylvester looked at him almost shocked. 'If you believe that, you're stupid and naïve, and you didn't seem that way at lunch earlier today.' "

Your approach to the questions of the press should emphasize the positive aspects of your activities and avoid gratuitous criticism . . . .
As songwriter Johnny Mercer put it, you've got to accentuate the positive and eliminate the negative.
U.S. Army briefing given to all servicemen going to South Vietnam, quoted in William G. Effros, *Quotations Vietnam* (1970).

The problem was trying to cover something every day as news when in fact the real key was that it was all derivative of the French Indo-China war, which is history. So you really should have had a third paragraph in each story which would have said, "All of this is shit and none of this means anything because we are in the same footsteps as the French and we are prisoners of their experience." But given the rules of newspaper reporting you can't really do that. Events have to be judged by themselves, as if the past did not really exist.
David Halberstam quoted in Phillip Knightley, *The First Casualty* (1975).

Television brought the brutality of war into the comfort of the living room. Vietnam was lost in the living rooms of America—not on the battlefields of Vietnam.
Marshall McLuhan, *Montreal Gazette* (May 16, 1975).

Press and television had created an aura not of victory but of defeat, which, coupled with the vocal antiwar elements, profoundly influenced timid officials in Washington. It was like two boxers in a ring, one having the other on the ropes, close to a knockout, when the apparent winner's second inexplicably throws in the towel.
General William C. Westmoreland, *A Soldier Reports* (1976).

No event in American history is more misunderstood than the Vietnam War. It was misreported then, and it is misremembered now.
President Richard M. Nixon, *No More Vietnams* (1985).

My Lai massacre
I have reviewed what we know of the incident at My Lai with a number of officers who have served in Vietnam. It is their judgment—a judgment which I personally endorse and share—that what apparently occurred at My Lai is wholly unrepresentative of the manner in which our forces conduct military operations in Vietnam.
Stanley R. Resor, Secretary of the Army, speaking on November 26, 1969, quoted in Seymour M. Hersh, *Cover-up* (1972).

When we go into My Lai, it's open season. When we leave nothing will be living. Everything's going to go.
Captain Ernest Medina quoted in Seymour Hersh, *My Lai 4* (1970).

Guilty as Lieutenant Calley may have been of the actual act of murder, the verdict does not single out the real criminal. Those of us who have served in Vietnam know that the real guilty party is the United States of America.
John F. Kerry, speaking for Vietnam Veterans Against the War, *The New York Times* (April 2, 1971).

I'm not so sure that in those days, having been indoctrinated to a fever pitch, I might not have committed the same error—and I prefer to call it an error—that Lieutenant Calley did.
Audie Murphy, most decorated U.S. soldier in World War II, *The New York Times* (April 2, 1971).

[Calley's conviction is] ultimately hypocritical—it's too bad that one man is being made to pay for the brutality of the whole war.
Dr. Benjamin Spock, *The New York Times* (April 3, 1971).

The obedience of a soldier to orders is not the obedience of an automaton. When a man wears a soldier's uniform, he is still required to think, to make moral decisions, to know what is right and wrong. We know that the accused in fact never received orders to round up and execute civilians.
Captain Aubrey M. Daniel III, Army prosecutor in the court martial of Lieutenant William L. Calley, *The New York Times* (March 17, 1971).

What Calley and others who participated in the massacre did that was different was to kill hundreds of unarmed Vietnamese in two hamlets in a single morning and to kill point-blank with rifles, pistols, and machine guns. Had they killed just as many over a larger area in a longer period of time and killed impersonally with bombs, shells, rockets, white phosphorus, and napalm, they would have been following the normal pattern of American military conduct.
Neil Sheehan, *A Bright Shining Lie* (1988).

Somebody killed a baby, that son of a bitch ought to be in jail right now. Calley got everything he deserved, and unfortunately, his battalion commander was later killed in combat. But he should have been in jail, too. You don't do that as a soldier, and you don't permit that as an officer.
Colonel Jim R. Paschall quoted in Ivan Prashker, *Duty, Honor, Vietnam* (1988).

Nixon years
Never has so much military and economic and diplomatic power been used so ineffectively. And if after all of this time, and all of this sacrifice, and all of this support, there is still no end in sight, then I say the time has come for the American people to turn to new leadership. . . .
And I pledge to you tonight that the first priority foreign policy objective of our next Administration will be to bring an honorable end to the war in Vietnam.
Richard M. Nixon, presidential nomination acceptance speech at the Republican National Convention, Miami Beach, Florida, August 6, 1968.

We have not carved out this Republic, complete with ideals and promise, to send the flower of our youth to Vietnam any longer to perish for an Asian despotism whose jails bulge with non-Communist opponents of its autocratic rule. Calling them a freely elected government is like accusing Walter Ulbricht [East Germany's dictator] of being the prima ballerina of the Bolshoi Ballet.
Representative Bertram L. Podell, speech in the House of Representatives, October 14, 1969.

A "no-win" policy is disastrous and unknown in American history. I am confident that we could have won the Vietnam war a long time ago if our efforts had not been throttled by civilians.
Senator Strom Thurmond, speech in the Senate, July 10, 1969.

It simply does not matter very much for the United States, in cold unadorned strategic terms, *who* rules the states of Indochina.
Senator J. William Fulbright, speech in the Senate, April 2, 1970.

I would rather be a one-term President and do what is right than a two-term President at the cost of seeing America become a second-rate power and see this nation accept the first defeat of its proud 190-year history.
President Richard M. Nixon, address to the nation, April 30, 1970.

Every senator in this chamber is partly responsible for sending 50,000 young Americans to an early grave; and, in one sense, this chamber literally reeks of blood. Every senator here is partly responsible for that human wreckage at Walter Reed [Hospital] and all across this land. . . . If we don't end this damnable war, those young men will some day curse us for our pitiful willingness to let the Executive carry the burden that the Constitution places on us.
Senator George McGovern, speech in the Senate, September 1, 1970.

I rate myself as a deeply-committed pacifist.
President Richard M. Nixon, *The New York Times* (March 10, 1971).

According to Administration spokesmen, Cambodia was a success, Laos was a success. How many more successes will it take for the Nixon Administration to recognize failure?
Charles E. Goodell, *The New York Times* (March 28, 1971).

My people used to say, "Win the war." Then they said, "Win it or get out." Now, with one voice, they say, "Get out."
Representative John J. Flynt, Jr., speech in the House, April 1, 1971.

Private Doby asks the sergeant, with an unsarcastic honesty and simplicity that only he seems capable of making believable, if, as the sergeant says, we have never lost a war, how come we haven't won in Vietnam yet. The sergeant offers that we are trying to "fight a polite war."
Peter Tauber, recalling basic training, *The Sunshine Soldiers* (1971).

I say if a Russian ship is bombed at Haiphong, that's too damn bad. I hope we hit them all. They have no business being in Haiphong. They are our enemies when they supply our enemies with ammunition and weapons to kill our men.
Senator Barry M. Goldwater, speech in the Senate, April 19, 1972.

We are in Vietnam today only because we got into Vietnam yesterday.
Clark M. Clifford, testimony before the House Foreign Affairs Committee, May 18, 1972.

We have finally stopped wasting lives in Vietnam. We must now stop wasting American dollars there, too.
Senator Alan Cranston, *The New York Times* (April 18, 1974).

I call it the Madman Theory. . . . I want the North Vietnamese to believe that I've reached the point where I might do anything to stop the war. We'll just slip the word to them that, "for God's sake, you know Nixon is obsessed about Communists. We can't restrain him when he's angry—and he has his hand on the nuclear button"—and Ho Chi Minh himself will be in Paris in two days begging for peace.
President Richard M. Nixon quoted in H. R. Haldeman, *The Ends of Power* (1978).

I refuse to believe that a little fourth-rate power like North Vietnam doesn't have a breaking point.
Henry A. Kissinger quoted in Tad Szulc, *The Illusion of Peace* (1978).

[Henry] Kissinger was asked at a [White House Staff] meeting whether the invasion did not expand the war. "Look," he replied, "we're not interested in Cambodia. We're only interested in it not being used as a base." The wider justifications he cited dealt

with superpower relations. "We're trying to shock the Soviets into calling a conference," he said, "and we can't do this by appearing weak." William Safire asked if it did not breach the Nixon Doctrine, and Kissinger replied, "We wrote the goddam doctrine, we can change it."
William Shawcross, *Sideshow* (1979).

When the Nixon Administration took over in 1969 all the data on North Vietnam and on the United States was fed into a Pentagon computer—population, gross national product, manufacturing capability, number of tanks, ships, and aircraft, size of the armed forces, and the like.
The computer was then asked, "When will we win?"
It took only a moment to give the answer: "You won in 1964!"
Harry G. Summers, Jr., retelling a "bitter little story [which] made the rounds during the closing days of the Vietnam War," *On Strategy* (1982).

opposition

United States foreign policy is going through its most difficult phase. Not only are we having trouble convincing our Western allies and our Latin American friends that we are doing the right thing, but we're having a heck of a time persuading our own university students and professors.
Art Buchwald, syndicated column (May 20, 1965).

This [the destruction of Vietnam] is the crime our country is committing. And this is what we must condemn, lest a later generation ask of us, as they ask of the Germans, who spoke up?
I. F. Stone, *I. F. Stone's Weekly* (October 17, 1966).

We seem bent upon saving the Vietnamese from Ho Chi Minh, even if we have to kill them and demolish their country to do it. . . . I do not intend to remain silent in the face of what I regard as a policy of madness which, sooner or later, will envelop my son and American youth by the millions for years to come.
Senator George S. McGovern, speech in the U.S. Senate, April 25, 1967.

America's war on Vietnam makes me, for the first time in my life, ashamed of being an American. . . .
I am in complete agreement with Bertrand Russell's statement that "Vietnam is an acid test for this generation of Western intellectuals."
Susan Sontag quoted in C. Woolf and J. Bagguley, *Authors Take Sides on Vietnam* (1967).

Warming to his theme, President Johnson pounded knees, mine and others, "Liberal critics! It's the Russians who are behind the whole thing." He extolled the FBI and the CIA; they kept him informed about what was "really going on." It was the Russians who stirred up the whole agitation for a suspension of the bombing of North Vietnam. . . .
I was staggered. Did President Johnson really believe that his critics were Soviet puppets? Was he thinking in such Joseph McCarthyite terms that he found it impossible to understand why many Americans, in or out of the Senate, were so concerned over his Vietnam policy? Or was he letting off steam, as he sometimes did, enjoying shocking his listeners and testing how much he could get away with? But when he went on in the same vein in a grimly serious tone, I became convinced that he did indeed mean what he was saying, at least in part.
Eric F. Goldman, *The Tragedy of Lyndon Johnson* (1968).

I understand that there has been, and continues to be, opposition to the war in Vietnam on the campuses and also in the nation. As far as this kind of activity is

concerned, we expect it. However, under no circumstances will I be affected whatever by it.
    President Richard M. Nixon, news conference, September 26, 1969.

Nothing we are doing to help or harm our friends or foes in Southeast Asia can compare with what we are doing to ourselves as a nation. The erosion of spirit that we have experienced is beyond calculation. Weighed against that erosion, any possible geopolitical advantages in the war must be seen as pitifully small.
    John W. Gardner, *The New York Times* (May 14, 1970).

Each day to facilitate the process by which the United States washes its hands of Vietnam, someone has to give up his life so that the United States doesn't have to admit something the entire world already knows, so that we can't say we have made a mistake. Someone has to die so that President Nixon won't be—and these are his words—"the first American President to lose a war."
    Navy Lieutenant John Kerry, testimony before U.S. Senate Committee on Foreign Relations, April 22, 1971.

I would not want to leave the impression that those [Vietnam War protesters] who came to demonstrate were not listened to; it's rather hard not to hear them as a matter of fact.
    President Richard M. Nixon, at a press conference, on being asked if antiwar demonstrations in Washington will affect his policies, quoted in *The New York Times* (April 30, 1971).

I think it is reasonable that if we must continue to fight wars, they ought to be fought by those people who really want to fight them. Since it seems to be the top half of the generation gap that is the most enthusiastic about going to war, why not send the Old Folks Brigade to Vietnam . . .?
    Dick Gregory, *Dick Gregory's Political Primer* (1972).

Pentagon Papers
Hardly mentioned in the voluminous discussion of those papers, is the fact that shortly before his death President Kennedy approved a plan for the phased withdrawal of U.S. military personnel from Vietnam. They were supposed to be reduced to about 12,000 by the middle of 1964, bottoming out by the middle of 1968 at the level of 1,500, which would simply provide for a headquarters for the Military Assistance Advisory Group (MAAG).
    Bernard Brodie, *War and Politics* (1973).

Democratic government's capacity for Byzantine deviousness is probably best told by that epochal best-teller, the Pentagon Papers—that "hemorrhage" of classified matter, as Henry Kissinger ruefully called it—which dramatized, in 47 volumes, just how far a government would go in clandestine and illicit duplicity.
    Frank Tippett, *Time* (January 17, 1983).

strategy
You must be getting somewhat weary of teaching the Yanks the perils of war. . . . What a mess they seem to have made in Vietnam. In one of your talks you might run in Clausewitz's little-heeded maxim, that no war should be begun without first replying to the question "What is to be gained by it" and that the first step should not be taken without considering what may be the last one.
    J. F. C. Fuller, January 16, 1966, letter to B. H. Liddell Hart, quoted in A. J. Trythall, *"Boney Fuller"* (1977).

I do not believe in "gradualism" in fighting a war. I believe in putting in the kind of military strength we need to win, and getting it over with as soon as possible.
President Dwight D. Eisenhower, *U.S. News and World Report* (November 7, 1966).

I say when you get into a war, you should win as quick as you can, because your losses become a function of the duration of the war. I believe when you get in a war, get everything you need and win it.
President Dwight D. Eisenhower, speaking on March 15, 1968, *The New York Times* (March 16, 1968).

The North Vietnamese used their main forces the way a bullfighter uses his cape—to keep us lunging in areas of marginal political importance.
Henry A. Kissinger, "The Vietnam Negotiations," *Foreign Affairs* (January 1969).

To me it seems that our waging a ground war in a little Asiatic country torn by internal insurrection could be termed madness. Vietnam is of no importance whatever to the defense of the United States. It is an act of international insanity that the Johnson Administration involved us on a huge scale in this immoral, undeclared war which is the most unpopular foreign war in the history of this Republic.
Senator Stephen M. Young, speech in the Senate, September 30, 1969.

There is great irony in the fact that the North Vietnamese finally won by purely conventional means, using precisely the kind of warfare at which the American army was best equipped to fight.
W. Scott Thompson and Donaldson D. Frizzell, *The Lessons of Vietnam* (1977).

The Johnson Administration had already barricaded the one sure route to victory— to take the strategic offensive against the source of the war. Memories of Mao Tse-tung's reaction when North Korea was overrun by United Nations troops in 1950 haunted the White House. America's fear of war with Red China protected North Vietnam from invasion more surely than any instrument of war Hanoi could have fielded.
General Dave Richard Palmer, *Summons of the Trumpet* (1978).

Much of the criticism of the Vietnam war has to do with "political interference" in military operations. Such criticism is off the mark. Our problem was not so much political interference as it was the lack of a coherent military strategy—a lack for which our military leaders share a large burden of responsibility.
Harry G. Summers, Jr., *On Strategy* (1982).

tactics

Like us, Hanoi had failed to win the "hearts and minds" of the South Vietnamese peasantry. Unlike us, Hanoi's leaders were able to compensate for this failure by playing their trump card—they overwhelmed South Vietnam with a twenty-two division force.
Stuart Herrington, *Silence Was a Weapon* (1982).

One of the most frustrating aspects of the Vietnam War from the army's point of view is that as far as logistics and tactics were concerned we succeeded in everything we set out to do.... How could we have succeeded so well, yet failed so miserably?
Harry G. Summers, Jr., *On Strategy* (1982).

Should the hamlet elder reply in a negative way, the VC will rapidly and efficiently disembowel him, along with his wife and children, and then calmly ask the people to point out the next-ranking man. Indeed, it is likely that the newly designated hamlet

chief will see a logic in the VC arguments not perceived by his late predecessor, and an apathetic neutral or even pro-government hamlet has become a VC hamlet.
Charles M. Simpson III, *Inside the Green Berets* (1983).

Whether or not people were for or against [the Vietnam War], I'm sure we have very similar views about how America ought to make judgments about putting soldiers into places of risk. I think a universal theme for all of us would be: Don't ever put soldiers in that position again, asking them to make those sacrifices without guaranteeing that you're going to follow through and give them the capacity to win.
Senator John Kerry, *The New York Times* (May 28, 1987).

I knocked the barrel of the weapon up in the air as I saw the sergeant taking the slack up on the trigger. "Hold it, man!" I said. "They're South Vietnamese."
"A gook's a gook," the sergeant replied, shrugging. . . .
A *gook's a gook*, he said. Otherwise known in the 9th Division as the *mere gook rule*. I couldn't even chew the guy's ass. He was wrong, but I knew why he thought he was right, and I knew he was not alone in his feelings. . . . Day after day these Viet troops went out and never found the Viet Cong. Yet, if we followed in their tracks, we had to fight it out every step of the way. The ARVN unit had reached a "you don't shoot us, we won't shoot you" accommodation with the enemy. If they saw a contact brewing, they just walked around it. My guys saw this, and when they saw the medevac ships carrying away their buddies who'd been wounded or killed while ARVN sat back and let us fight their war, it bred tremendous resentment. The kind of resentment that made "a gook a gook."
David H. Hackworth, *About Face* (1987).

Second Lieutenant North arrived in Vietnam in camouflage fatigues, ready to do battle. He wore a flak jacket and black greasepaint under his eyes to cut the glare, and in the field he always kept his helmet buckled. He was squared away. In addition to the .45-caliber revolver issued each officer, Ollie opted to carry a 12-gauge shotgun for extra firepower. And if that wasn't enough protection, he also wore a crucifix.
Ben Bradlee, Jr., *Guts and Glory* (1988).

Tet offensive
A sense of disaster pervaded the United States, sharpened by the most widely quoted remark of the war: "It becomes necessary to destroy the town in order to save it." The American major meant that the town had to be razed in order to rout the Viet-Cong, but his phrase seemed to symbolize the use of American power—destroying the object of its protection in order to preserve it from Communism.
Barbara W. Tuchman, *The March of Folly* (1984). The anonymous major was interviewed by Peter Arnett of the Associated Press during Tet. The story had the dateline: Ben Tre, Vietnam, February 7, 1968.

I have in mind, for example, the recent disclosure that during the fighting in Hue a thousand Vietnamese soldiers were in the city on Tet leave, but instead of joining the fighting for their own city they disguised themselves as refugees and stayed in the university grounds for three weeks. Among them was a full colonel of the South Vietnamese Army. They were at all times behind U. S. lines yet they made no effort to rejoin their units or to join in the battle to save their own city.
Now, my question is: How can we win with allies like these?
Senator Frank Church, testimony before the U.S. Senate Committee on Foreign Relations, March 11, 1968.

The Tet Offensive shocked a citizenry which had been led to believe that success in Vietnam was just around the corner. Tet was the final blow to the sagging credibility

of the Johnson administration and to the waning patience of the American people with this remote and inconclusive war.
Don Oberdorfer, *Tet!* (1971).

[Tet was] an allied intelligence failure ranking with Pearl Harbor in 1941 or the Ardennes Offensive in 1944.
General Bruce Palmer, Jr., *The Twenty-Five-Year War* (1984).

Tonkin Gulf Resolution

We Americans know—although others appear to forget—the risk of spreading conflict. We still seek no wider war.
President Lyndon B. Johnson in a speech to the nation after ordering retaliatory attacks against North Vietnam after the Tonkin Gulf incidents, August 4, 1964.

Whereas naval units of the Communist regime in Vietnam . . . have deliberately and repeatedly attacked United States naval vessels lawfully present in international waters, and have thereby created a serious threat to international peace; and
Whereas these attacks are part of a deliberate and systematic campaign of aggression that the Communist regime in North Vietnam has been waging against its neighbors . . . and
Whereas the United States is assisting the people of southeast Asia to protect their freedom and has no territorial, military or political ambitions in that area, but desires only that these peoples should be left in peace to work out their own destinies in their own way: Now, therefore be it
Resolved by the Senate and House of Representatives of the United States of America in Congress assembled, That the congress approves and supports the determination of the President, as Commander in Chief, to take all necessary measures to repel any armed attack against the forces of the United States and to prevent further aggression.
Joint [the Tonkin Gulf] Resolution of Congress: Public Law 88-408, August 10, 1964.

With 450,000 U.S. troops now in Vietnam, it is time that Congress decided whether or not to declare a state of war exists with North Vietnam. Previous congressional resolutions of support provide only limited authority. The issue of a declaration of war should at least be put before the Congress for decision.
Dwight D. Eisenhower, summary of his remarks of July 15, 1967, *The Washington Post* (July 22, 1967).

The language of the Gulf of Tonkin resolution was far more sweeping than the congressional intent. In voting unlimited presidential power most members of Congress thought they were providing for retaliation for an attack on our forces; and preventing a large-scale war in Asia, rather than authorizing its inception.
Senator Jacob K. Javits, *Who Makes War* (1973).

With evidence accumulating of confusion by radar and sonar technicians in the second clash, [President] Johnson said privately, "Well, those dumb stupid sailors were just shooting at flying fish." So much for *casus belli.*
Barbara W. Tuchman, *The March of Folly* (1984).

The Tonkin Gulf Resolution would later become the focus of a furious storm. The administration would treat it as the moral and legal equivalent of a declaration of war; its antiwar opponents would denounce it as a colossal fraud and deception. Yet few people opposed it in August 1964. The House of Representatives passed it unanimously. In the Senate the curmudgeony Republican senator from Oregon, Wayne Morse, and Democratic Senator Ernest Gruening of Alaska cast the only dissenting

votes. Gruening presciently denounced the resolution as a "predated declaration of war."
Irwin Unger and Debbi Unger, *Turning Point: 1968* (1988).

veterans

In the latter years of the American involvement a large number of veterans . . . came back hating something or someone: the Vietnamese for being so unfathomable, so generally "fucked up"; American politicians for lying to them about why they had to go to Vietnam; hippies for "stabbing us in the back"; and the Joe Blows and their housewives who went about life as usual while the grunts had been counting off their hours and days in the paddies and hills. Along with the hatred were mixed generous amounts of fear and suspicion. Was it true that hippies were going around shooting every Vietnam veteran they could find? Was it true all the girls thought the veterans were babykillers and would have nothing to do with them? When the veteran learned those rumors were not true, his suspicion still remained; and it was, he felt, justified.
Charles Anderson, *The Grunts* (1976).

There were no homecoming parades for the million men and women who served in combat in the longest war America has ever fought and the only war it has ever lost. There were no brass bands or crowds cheering at the dock or celebratory speeches floating across village greens. The veterans of the failed United States mission in Vietnam returned instead to a kind of embarrassed silence, as if, one of them thought, everybody was ashamed of us. They were obliged to bear an inordinate share of the blame for having fought at all and for not having won.
Peter Goldman and Tony Fuller, *Charlie Company* (1983).

The Vietnam veteran returned to find that the country was not only not behind him, it was at best indifferent to him, at worst against him. Flown in a jet plane that took him from the front line to his front porch in only 48 hours, leaving him no time to make sense out of what he'd been through, he was ignored by the mainstream of American society, stigmatized by the liberal left and by the media as a dope-crazed killer, an accomplice of a criminal foreign policy. . . . Johnny didn't come marching home from Vietnam; he crept back, furtive, secretive and alone, like a convict just released from prison.
Philip Caputo, "Post-War Stress is Afflicting Veterans," *The Vietnam War*, ed. David L. Bender (1984).

Vietnamization

They [French officials] say this does not mean abandonment or withdrawal by the French in a defeatist mood. It means gradual transfer of the defense from French to native troops accompanied by an effort to solve the Indo-Chinese war . . . by ultimate local negotiation.
Harold Callender, *The New York Times* (July 22, 1953).

This must be just about the first time in the history of warfare that a nation has thought it could prevail by withdrawing combat troops and reducing its military presence.
Walter Lippmann, *Newsweek* (December 1, 1969).

The defense of freedom is everybody's business—not just America's business. And it is particularly the responsibility of the people whose freedom is threatened. In the previous administration, we Americanized the war in Vietnam. In this administration, we are Vietnamizing the search for peace.
President Richard M. Nixon, speech to the nation, November 3, 1969.

The policy of Vietnamization is a cruel hoax designed to screen from the American people the bankruptcy of a needless military involvement in the affairs of the Vietnamese people. Instead of Vietnamizing the war let us encourage the Vietnamization of the government in South Vietnam. We can do that by removing the embrace that now prevents other political groups from assuming a leadership role in Saigon, groups that are capable of expressing the desire for peace of the Vietnamese people.
Senator George S. McGovern, testimony before U.S. Senate Committee on Foreign Relations, February 4, 1970.

Vietnamization is an old idea. It was the basis of my own plan when I was sent to Indochina in 1952. In my days, the South Vietnamese did not fight well.
Henri Navarre, Former Commander of French Forces in Vietnam, *The New York Times* (May 10, 1970).

volunteers

I am not influenced by the expectation of promotion or pecuniary reward. I wish to be useful, and every kind of service necessary for the public good, becomes honorable by being necessary.
Captain Nathan Hale, remarks during September 1776 to Captain William Hull, who was seeking to dissuade him from volunteering to be a spy, quoted in Isaac William Stuart, *Life of Captain Nathan Hale* (1856).

The patriot volunteer, fighting for country and his rights, makes the most reliable soldier on earth.
Attributed to General Thomas J. "Stonewall" Jackson in Hunter McGuire, *Stonewall Jackson* (1897).

war

There is no instance of a country having benefited from prolonged warfare.
Sun Tzu, *The Art of War* (4th century B.C.).

Laws are silent in time of war. [*Silent enim leges inter arma.*]
Marcus Tullius Cicero, *Pro Milone*, IV (52 B.C.).

And ye shall hear of wars and rumors of wars: see that ye be not troubled: for all these things must come to pass, but the end is not yet.
The Bible, Matthew 24:6.

When the appeal is made to the sword, highly probable it is that the punishment will exceed the offense; and the calamities attending on war outweigh those preceding it.
John Dickinson, *Letters from a Farmer in Pennsylvania* (1768).

To make war with those who trade with us is like setting a bulldog upon a customer at the shop-door.
Thomas Paine, *The Age of Reason* (1794).

War justifies everything.
Napoleon I, writing in 1808, quoted in J. C. Herold, *The Mind of Napoleon* (1955).

War, war is still the cry,—"war even to the knife!"
Lord Byron, *Childe Harold's Pilgrimage*, Canto I (1812). "War even to the knife" was the Spanish reply to the French demand that they surrender the besieged city of Saragossa in 1808.

For what are the triumphs of war, planned by ambition, executed by violence, and consummated by devastation? The means are the sacrifice of many, the end, the bloated aggrandizement of the few.
Charles Caleb Colton, *Lacon* (1825).

To introduce in the philosophy of war. . . a principle of moderation would be an absurdity.
Karl von Clausewitz, *On War* (1832).

A long war almost always reduces nations to the wretched alternative of being abandoned to ruin by defeat, or to despotism by success.
Alexis de Tocqueville, *Democracy in America* (1835).

War is an integral part of God's ordering of the Universe. In war, man's noblest virtues come into play. Courage and renunciation, fidelity to duty and a readiness for sacrifice that does not stop short of offering up life itself. Without war the world would become swamped in materialism.
Field Marshal Helmuth von Moltke quoted in Arnold J. Toynbee, *War and Civilization* (1950).

It is well that war is so terrible, or we should get too fond of it.
General Robert E. Lee, statement made at the Battle of Fredericksburg after seeing his troops stop a charge of Union troops, quoted in Henry Steele Commager, ed., *The Blue and the Grey*, I (1950).

War is not altogether an evil. . . . It teaches obedience and contentment under privations; it fortifies courage; it tests loyalty; it gives occasion for showing mercifulness of heart; moderation in victory; endurance and cheerfulness under defeat. The brave who do battle victoriously in their country's cause leave a legacy of honor to their children.
William Makepeace Thackeray, *Denis Duval* (1864).

War on the one hand is such a terrible, such an atrocious, thing, that no man, especially no Christian man, has the right to assume the responsibility of beginning it.
Leo Tolstoy, *Anna Karenina* (1875).

Against war it may be said that it makes the victor stupid and the vanquished revengeful.
Friedrich Nietzsche, *Human, All Too Human* (1878).

War, to sane men at the present day, begins to look like an epidemic insanity, breaking out here and there like the cholera or influenza, infecting men's brains instead of their bowels.
Ralph Waldo Emerson, *Miscellanies* (1884).

Experience proves that the man who obstructs a war in which his nation is engaged, no matter whether right or wrong, occupies no enviable place in life or history. Better for him, individually, to advocate "war, pestilence, and famine," than to act as obstructionist to a war already begun.
President Ulysses S. Grant, *Personal Memoirs*, I, (1885–86).

As long as war is regarded as wicked, it will always have its fascination. When it is looked upon as vulgar it will cease to be popular.
Oscar Wilde, *The Critic as Artist* (1890).

They were going to look at war, the red animal—war, the blood-swollen god.
Stephen Crane, *The Red Badge of Courage* (1895).

A single glass of champagne imparts a feeling of exhilaration. The nerves are braced; the imagination is agreeably stirred; the wits become more nimble. A bottle produces a contrary effect. Excess causes a comatose insensibility. So it is with war; and the quality of both is best discovered by sipping.
Winston Churchill, *The Story of the Malakand Field Force* (1898).

What we now need to discover in the social realm is the moral equivalent of war: something heroic that will speak to men as universally as war does, and yet will be as compatible with their spiritual selves as war has proved itself to be incompatible.
William James, *The Varieties of Religious Experience* (1902).

To delight in war is a merit in the soldier, a dangerous quality in the captain, and a positive crime in the statesman.
George Santayana, *The Life of Reason* (1905–06).

War is too important to be left to the generals.
Usually credited to French Prime Minister Georges Clemenceau.

A belligerent state permits itself every such misdeed, every such act of violence as would disgrace the individual. It makes use against the enemy not only of the accepted *ruses de guerre*, but of deliberate lying and deception as well—and to a degree which seems to exceed the usage of former wars. The state exacts the utmost degree of obedience and sacrifice from its citizens, but at the same time it treats them like children by an excess of secrecy and a censorship upon news and expressions of opinion which leaves the spirits of those whose intellects it thus suppresses defenceless against every unfavorable turn of events and sinister rumor.
Sigmund Freud, *Reflections on War and Death* (1915).

Everything, everything in war is barbaric. . . . But the worst barbarity of war is that it forces men collectively to commit acts against which individually they would revolt with their whole being.
Ellen Key, *War, Peace and the Future* (1916).

Without war no State could be. All those we know of arose through war, and the protection of their members by armed force remains their primary and essential task. War, therefore, will endure to the end of history, as long as there is a multiplicity of States.
Heinrich von Treitschke, *Politics* (1916).

While you may not be interested in war, war is interested in you.
Leon Trotsky quoted in Gregg Herken, *Councils of War* (1987).

Many young men in it, mostly in messrooms and wardrooms, used to say to each other—"It's a damned bad war, but it's better than no war at all."
Joseph Conrad, *The Tale* (1917).

It was my fortune recently to see a demonstration of modern warfare. It is no longer a conflict in chivalry, no more a test of militant manhood. It is only cruel, deliberate, scientific destruction. There was no contending enemy, only the theoretical defense of a hypothetic objective.
President Warrren G. Harding, speech at the Tomb of the Unknown Soldier, Arlington National Cemetery, November 11, 1921.

The more horrible a depersonalized scientific mass war becomes, the more necessary it is to find universal ideal motives to justify it.
John Dewey, *Human Nature and Conduct* (1922).

The war against death ... is always a beautiful, noble and wonderful and glorious thing, and so, it follows, is the war against war. But it is always hopeless and quixotic too.
Hermann Hesse, *Steppenwolf* (1927).

I tell you how it should all be done. Whenever there's a big war coming, you should rope off the field and sell tickets. And, on the big day, you should take all the kings and cabinets and their generals, put them in the center dressed in their underpants and let them fight it out with clubs. The best country wins.
Louis Wolheim in *All Quiet on the Western Front* (1930), directed by Lewis Milestone; screenplay by Dell Andrews and others from the novel by Erich Maria Remarque.

I have seen war. I have seen war on land and sea. I have seen blood running from the wounded. I have seen men coughing out their gassed lungs. I have seen the dead in the mud. I have seen cities destroyed. ... I have seen children starving. I have seen the agony of mothers and wives. I hate war.
President Franklin D. Roosevelt, speech at Chautauqua, New York, August 14, 1936.

Sometime they'll give a war and nobody will come.
Carl Sandburg, *The People, Yes* (1936).

The most shocking fact about war is that its victims and its instruments are individual human beings, and that these individual beings are condemned by the monstrous conventions of politics to murder or be murdered in quarrels not their own.
Aldous Huxley, *The Olive Tree* (1937).

We are for the abolition of war, we do not want war; but war can only be abolished through war and to get ride of the gun, we must first grasp it in our own hands.
Mao Tse-tung, *Problems of War and Strategy* (1938).

War creates such a strain that all the pettiness, jealousy, ambition, greed, and selfishness begin to leak out the seams of the average character. On top of this are the problems created by the enemy.
General Dwight D. Eisenhower, letter to his wife, Mamie, December 16, 1942, quoted in *Letters to Mamie* (1978).

Confident prophecy [on war] is best left to generals, who as a class have a traditional fondness for it, and as prophets have no reputation to lose.
B. H. Liddell Hart, *Thoughts on War* (1944).

I have never met anybody who wasn't against War. Even Hitler and Mussolini were, according to themselves.
David Low, *The New York Times* (February 10, 1946).

We must conquer war, or war will conquer us.
Ely Culbertson, *Must We Fight Russia* (1946).

I hate war as only a soldier who has lived it can, only as one who has seen its brutality, its futility, its *stupidity*.
Dwight D. Eisenhower, speech of January 15, 1946, quoted in John Gunther, *Eisenhower: The Man and the Symbol* (1952).

Wars, conflict, it's all business. One murder makes a villain. Millions a hero. Numbers sanctify.
Charlie Chaplin, *Monsieur Verdoux* (1947).

The quickest way of ending a war is to lose it.
George Orwell, *Shooting an Elephant* (1950).

I know war as few other men now living know it, and nothing to me is more revolting. I have long advocated its complete abolition, as its very destructiveness on both friend and foe has rendered it useless as a means of settling international disputes.
General Douglas A. MacArthur, Address to Joint Session of Congress, April 19, 1951.

When the rich wage war, it is the poor who die.
Jean-Paul Sartre, *The Devil and the Good Lord* (1951).

War on land today is land-air warfare.
Sir John Slessor, *Strategy for the West* (1954).

War will never cease until babies begin to come into the world with larger cerebrums and smaller adrenal glands.
H. L. Mencken, *Minority Report: H. L. Mencken's Notebooks* (1956).

But that was war. Just about all he could find in its favor was that it paid well and liberated children from the pernicious influence of their parents.
Joseph Heller, *Catch-22* (1961).

We used to wonder where war lived, what it was that made it so vile. And now we realize that we know where it lives, that it is inside ourselves.
Albert Camus, *Notebooks 1935–1942* (1962).

War under modern conditions is bereft of even that dubious logic it may have had in the past.
Adlai E. Stevenson, "The Hard Kind of Patriotism," *Harper's* (July 1963).

Once upon a time even large-scale wars could be waged without risking the end of civilization. But what was once upon a time is no longer so, because general war is impossible.
President Lyndon B. Johnson, speech in Washington, D.C., March 24, 1964.

Men love war because it allows them to look serious. Because it is the one thing that stops women from laughing at them.
John Fowles, *The Magus* (1965).

Great horror as war itself is, every honest soldier knows that it has its moments of joy—joy in the fellowship of one's fighting comrades, joy and pride in the growth of a fighting spirit and the conviction of invincibility that shines out of the faces of well-led and well-disciplined troops; and the small but treasured joy of a warm fire and a plain hot meal at the end of a cold and difficult day.
General Matthew B. Ridgway, *The Korean War* (1967).

Blood is the currency of war. It's just like money really. You try to invest yours—to get as high a return as possible. And you try to spend the enemy's.
Charles Coe, *Young Man in Vietnam* (1968).

I have never understood this liking for war. It panders to instincts already catered for within the scope of any respectable domestic establishment.
Alan Bennett, *Forty Years On*, Act I (1969).

All great civilizations, in their early stages, are based on success in war.
Sir Kenneth Clark, *Civilization* (1969).

Either man is obsolete or war is.
R. Buckminster Fuller, *I Seem To Be a Verb* (1970).

In war man is much more a sheep than a wolf. He follows, he obeys. War is servility, rather—a certain fanaticism and credulity—but not aggressiveness.
Jean Rostand, *The New York Times* (May 30, 1971).

Force must only be used in extreme cases. If you happen to be the mother of three "war age" sons, then you think a lot about it. I do believe that having sons affects the way one thinks about war, or concretizes it.
Jeane J. Kirkpatrick, *Newsweek* (January 14, 1985).

Since 1945, the term "war" itself has acquired an unsavory connotation. Following the rules that govern the usage of all dirty words, it has tended to be taken out of the vocabulary and to give way to euphemisms. Beginning around 1950, and quite regardless of the nature of the ideology that they claimed to represent, most governments were no longer prepared to admit that they included a department, or office, or ministry, whose function was to take care of everything pertaining to war. Instead they spoke of defense or security.
Martin van Creveld, *Technology and War* (1989).

accidental war

The Soviets have made much of the possibility that a deranged or irresponsible American pilot on airborne alert might take it into his head to attack Russia alone. Not only are there many safeguards against this, but it is most unlikely that a single-plane attack would touch off a war. A more ominous possibility is illustrated in the novel *Red Alert*. A determined SAC general, who, unknown to his superiors, is sick with an incurable ailment (and whose judgment and sense of discipline are thus affected), personally decides to end the Soviet problem once and for all. The clever way he gets around the elaborate system set up to prevent exactly this kind of behavior suggests that no system is proof against everything.
Herman Kahn, *Thinking About the Unthinkable* (1962).

The duty officer asked General Ripper to confirm the fact that he had issued the go-code, and he said, "Yes, gentlemen. They are on their way in, and no one can bring them back. For the sake of our country and our way of life, I suggest you get the rest of SAC in after them; otherwise, we will be totally destroyed by Red retaliation. Uh, my boys will give you the best kind of start: 1,400 megatons worth. And you sure as hell won't stop them now. So let's get going. There's no other choice. God willing, we will prevail in peace and freedom from fear and in true health through the purity and essence of our natural fluid. God bless you all." Then he hung up. We—we're still trying to figure out the meaning of that last phrase, sir.
George C. Scott in *Dr. Strangelove* (1964), directed by Stanley Kubrick; screenplay by Stanley Kubrick and others from the novel *Red Alert* by Peter George.

You may reasonably expect a man to walk a tightrope safely for ten minutes; it would be unreasonable to do so without accident for two hundred years.
Bertrand Russell quoted in Desmond Bagley, *The Tightrope Men* (1973).

An "accidental war" is more likely if the non-accidental factors are strong. Translated from war to law, the concept means that a murder is more likely to be unintentional if the prisoner had strong intentions of committing murder.
Geoffrey Blainey, *The Causes of War* (1973).

Every man, woman, and child lives under a nuclear sword of Damocles, hanging by the slenderest of threads, capable of being cut at any moment by accident, miscalculation, or madness.
President John F. Kennedy quoted in David P. Barash, *The Arms Race and Nuclear War* (1987).

causes of war

A man blushes with shame when he recalls the scandalous and frivolous motives Christian princes invoke to persuade their peoples to take up arms. One proves, or affects to prove, he possesses some antiquated right, as if it mattered very much which particular prince governs a State, provided that its administration is in the public interest. Another takes as a pretext some item omitted in a treaty of a hundred chapters. This one bears a grudge against that one because of the rejection or abduction of some bride-to-be or of some over-bold piece of raillery.
Desiderius Erasmus, *Quelera Pacis* (1515).

The same reasons that make us quarrel with a neighbor cause war between two princes.
Michel de Montaigne, *Essays* (1580).

In the nature of man we find three principal causes of quarrel. First, competition; secondly, diffidence; thirdly, glory. The first maketh men invade for gain; the second, for safety; the third, for reputation.
Thomas Hobbes, *Leviathan* (1651).

War is only caused through the political intercourse of governments and nations.
Karl von Clausewitz, *On War* (1832).

War is never brought about by newspapers. The majority has usually no inclination for war. War is kindled by the minority, or in absolute states by the ruler or cabinet.
Otto von Bismarck, speech to the Reichstag, *The Times* (London) (February 16, 1876).

Our ancestors have bred pugnacity into our bone and marrow, and thousands of years of peace won't breed it out of us.
William James, "The Moral Equivalent of War," *McClure's* (August 1910).

Lenin was the first to discover that capitalism "inevitably" caused war; and he discovered this only when the First World War was already being fought. Of course he was right. Since every great state was capitalist in 1914, capitalism obviously "caused" the First World War; but just as obviously it had "caused" the previous generation of Peace.
A. J. P. Taylor, *The Origins of the Second World War* (1961).

Sooner or later every war of trade becomes a war of blood.
Eugene V. Debs, June 16, 1918 speech in Canton, Ohio, reprinted in *Eugene V. Debs Speaks*, ed. Jean Tussey (1970).

Let the officers and directors of our armament factories, our gun builders and munitions makers and shipbuilders all be conscripted—to get $30 a month, the same wage paid to the lads in the trenches. . . . Give capital thirty days to think it over and you will learn by that time that there will be no war. That will stop the racket—that and nothing else.
General Smedley D. Butler, USMC, "War Is a Racket," *The Forum and Century* (September 1934).

The chief reason warfare is still with us is neither a secret death wish of the human species, nor an irrepressible instinct of aggression, nor, finally and more plausibly, the

serious economic and social dangers inherent in disarmament, but the simple fact that no substitute for this final arbiter in international affairs has yet appeared on the political scene.
Hannah Arendt, *On Violence* (1970).

We do research to get rid of sewage, reduce air pollution and build better bridges. What makes us think we do not need to understand what really causes war—it's clearly something more complicated that the absence of good will.
J. David Singer, *The New York Times* (May 6, 1971).

People don't start wars, governments do.
President Ronald Reagan quoted in *Time* (March 18, 1985).

I'm sure that President Johnson would never have pursued the war in Vietnam if he'd ever had a Fulbright to Japan, or say Bangkok, or had any feeling for what these people are like and why they acted the way they did. He was completely ignorant.
J. William Fulbright, *The New York Times* (June 26, 1986).

cold war

War consists not in battle only, or the act of fighting; but in a tract of time, wherein the will to contend by battle is sufficiently known: and therefore the notion of time, is to be considered in the nature of war; as it is in the nature of weather. For as the nature of foul weather, lyeth not in a shower or two of rain; but in an inclination thereto of many days together; so the nature of war, consists not in actual fighting; but in the known disposition thereto, during all the time there is no assurance to the contrary. All other time is peace.
Thomas Hobbes, *Leviathan* (1651).

It may even reasonably be said that the intensely sharp competitive preparation for war by the nations is the real war, permanent, unceasing; and that the battles are only a sort of public verification of the mastery gained during the "peace" interval.
William James, "The Moral Equivalent of War," *McClure's* (August 1910).

At issue [in 1945] was the Soviet willingness to carry out the Yalta agreement. All that remained, the President insisted with a mule farmer's firmness, was "for Marshal Stalin to carry it out in accordance with his word."
[Soviet Foreign Minister] Molotov, [Charles] Bohlen recalled, "turned a little ashy" and tried to steer the conversation to the Japanese war. Truman cut him off. "That will be all, Mr. Molotov. I would appreciate it if you would transmit my views to Marshal Stalin."
"I've never been talked to like that in my life," protested Molotov, who had long labored under Stalin and thus surely had been.
"Carry out your agreements," Truman barked back, "and you won't get talked to like that."
"How I enjoyed translating those words," Bohlen later recalled. "They were probably the first sharp words uttered during the war by an American President to a high Soviet official."
Walter Isaacson and Evan Thomas, *The Wise Men* (1986).

Let us not be deceived—we are today in the midst of a cold war.
Bernard M. Baruch, speech before the South Carolina Legislature, April 16, 1947. Baruch always acknowledged that Herbert Bayard Swope coined the "cold war" expression. In an August 17, 1949 letter to Swope, quoted in *Safire's Political Dictionary* (1978), Baruch wrote "you coined the expression and I gave it currency."

Now we are in a period which I can characterize as a period of cold peace.
Trygve Lie, UN Secretary General, *The Observer* (August 21, 1949).

The cold war is a good war. It is the only war in history where the question of destruction doesn't enter into it at all. Everything we are doing is building up. We have rebuilt Europe, not destroyed it.
Paul Hoffman, *Time* (May 29, 1950).

We cannot win the cold war by military means alone. We cannot be confident of our ability to destroy International Communism as we destroyed National Socialism, because International Communism is armed with weapons that would very likely destroy us too. We cannot liquidate the cold war; we must live with it and fight it on terms that make sense.
James King, "Limited War," *Army* (August 1957).

There is but one sure way to avoid total war—and that is to win the cold war.
President Dwight D. Eisenhower, State of the Union Message, January 9, 1958.

Today we may have reached a pause in the cold war—but that is not a lasting peace. A test-ban treaty is a milestone—but that is not the millennium.
President John F. Kennedy, speech to United Nations General Assembly, September 20, 1963.

While our citizens may take pride in the solid front of high morality that our nation presents, they can also sleep more easily at night from knowing that behind this front we are in fact capable of matching the Soviets perfidy for perfidy.
Miles Copeland, *The Game of Nations* (1970).

I don't know why you use a fancy French word like *detente* when there's a good English phrase for it—cold war.
Golda Meir, Prime Minister of Israel, quoted in *Newsweek* (January 19, 1976).

I stand before you tonight in my green chiffon evening gown, my face softly made up, my fair hair gently waved . . . the Iron Lady of the Western World. Me? A cold war warrior? Well, yes—if that is how they [the Soviet Press] wish to interpret my defense of values and freedoms fundamental to our way of life.
Prime Minister Margaret Thatcher, *The Times* (London) (February 1, 1976).

The competition [should] be shaped into "a substitute for war," rather than "a prelude to war." The West cannot escape the military competition, but it can compete in ways that make war less likely.
General William Odom, "Soviet Force Posture," *Problems of Communism* (July/August 1985).

The intelligence community has a direct interest in the continuation of the Cold War. Careers, promotion, pensions, travel, expenses, and a largely agreeable and stimulating way of life depend on it. So when all this is threatened by detente, the intelligence agencies open their doors to show the public that the menace still exists, that the need for timely warning has not ended, and that the efficient, reliable and patriotic intelligence agency is there to serve the nation.
Phillip Knightley, *The Second Oldest Profession* (1986).

Helen Thomas of UPI . . . decided to ask a more general question: "Could you declare the Cold War over?"
[Paul] Nitze had only a split second to reply: "I hope it isn't over in the sense of becoming hot."
Strobe Talbott, *The Master of the Game* (1988).

I want to try to avoid words like cold war if I can because . . . that doesn't properly give credit to the advances that have taken place in this relationship. So I wouldn't use that term.
President George Bush, news conference, January 27, 1989.

The cold war of poisonous Soviet-American feelings, of domestic political hysteria, of events enlarged and distorted by East-West confrontation, of almost perpetual diplomatic deadlock is over.
Editorial, *The New York Times* (April 2, 1989).

I think we have come out of a period of cold war, even if there are still some chills and drafts.
Mikhail S. Gorbachev, *The New York Times* (June 16, 1989).

The cold war happened because we moved from the hot war to the cold war with the same team on both sides. The manners of open hostility became the manners of covert hostility.
John le Carré, *U.S. News and World Report* (June 19, 1989).

For all its risks and uncertainties, the cold war was characterized by a remarkably stable and predictable set of relations among the great powers.
Lawrence S. Eagleburger, *The New York Times* (September 29, 1989).

conventional war
The last thing we want to do is make Europe safe for a conventional war.
General Bernard Rogers quoted in *Time* (March 16, 1987).

Even a conventional war, to say nothing of a nuclear one, would be disastrous for Europe today. This is not only because conventional weapons are many times more destructive than they were during the Second World War, but also because there are nuclear power plants consisting of a total of some 200 reactor units and a large number of major chemical works. The destruction of those facilities in the course of conventional hostilities would make the continent uninhabitable.
Mikhail Gorbachev, *Perestroika* (1987).

definitions of war
During the time men live without a common power to keep them all in awe, they are in that condition which is called war: and such as is of every man against every man.
Thomas Hobbes, *Leviathan* (1651).

[War is] an immense art which comprises all others.
Napoleon I, quoted in J. Christopher Herold, *The Mind of Napoleon* (1955).

War is an act of violence whose object is to constrain the enemy to accomplish our will.
Karl von Clausewitz, *On War* (1832).

War is not merely a political act, but also a political instrument, a continuation of political relations, a carrying out of the same by other means.
Karl von Clausewitz, *On War* (1832).

War is the science of destruction.
John S. C. Abbott, *The History of Napoleon Bonaparte* (1855).

War is not a polite recreation, but the vilest thing in life, and we ought to understand that and not play at war. It all comes to this: have done with lying, and if it's

war, then it's war and not a game, or else warfare is simply the favorite pastime of the idle and frivolous.
Leo Tolstoy, *War and Peace* (1865–69).

I am tired and sick of war. Its glory is all moonshine. It is only those who have neither fired a shot nor heard the shrieks and groans of the wounded who cry aloud for blood, more vengeance, more desolation. War is hell.
General William T. Sherman, speech at the Michigan Military Academy, June 19, 1879.

War is a biological necessity.
General Friedrich von Bernhardi, *Germany and the Next War* (1911).

War is a transfer of property from nation to nation.
Leon Samson, *The New Humanism* (1930).

War is like love, it always finds a way.
Bertolt Brecht, *Mother Courage*, Act VI (1939).

War is not an adventure. It is a disease. It is like typhus.
Antoine de Saint-Exupéry, *Flight to Arras* (1942).

War? War is an organized bore.
Oliver Wendell Holmes, Jr., quoted in Catherine Bowen, *Yankee from Olympus* (1944).

War is evil, but it is often the lesser evil.
George Orwell, *Looking Back on the Spanish War* (1945).

War to an individual is hardly ever bigger than a hundred yards on each side of him.
Ernie Pyle, *Time* (April 30, 1945).

War is like a giant pack rat. It takes something from you, and it leaves something behind in its stead. It burned me out in some ways, so that now I feel like an old man, but still sometimes act like a dumb kid. It made me grow up too fast.
Audie Murphy, most-decorated American soldier in World War II, quoted in *The New York Journal-American* (August 30, 1955).

War is, after all, the universal perversion. We are all tainted: if we cannot experience our perversion at first hand we spend our time reading war stories, the pornography of war; or seeing war films, the blue films of war; or titillating our senses with the imagination of great deeds, the masturbation of war.
John Rae, *The Custard Boys* (1960).

War may be a very grim and tragic "game" but it must nevertheless remain a game, in the sense that the participants accept limitations upon their behavior.
R. W. Tucker, *The Just War* (1960).

[War is] the high end of the spectrum of conflict.
Attributed to Robert S. McNamara when Secretary of Defense during the administration of President John F. Kennedy (1961–63).

War is the unfolding of miscalculations.
Barbara W. Tuchman, *The Guns of August* (1962).

War is the highest form of struggle for resolving contradictions.
Mao Tse-tung, *Selected Military Writings* (1963).

War is capitalism with the gloves off.
Tom Stoppard, *Travesties* (1975).

War is just like bush-clearing—the moment you stop, the jungle comes back even thicker, but for a little while you can plant and grow a crop in the ground you have won at such terrible cost.
Kenneth Kaunda, *Kaunda on Violence* (1980).

As every combat veteran knows, war is primarily sheer boredom punctuated by moments of stark terror.
Harry G. Summers, Jr., *On Strategy* (1982).

just war
Lucky are soldiers who strive in a just war; for them it is an easy entry into heaven.
Bhagavad Gita, II.

For a war to be just, three conditions are necessary—public authority, just cause, right motive.
St. Thomas Aquinas, *Summa Theologica* (1267–73).

The most disadvantageous peace is better than the most just war.
Desiderius Erasmus, *Adagia* (1500).

The peace of heaven is theirs that lift their swords
In such a just and charitable war.
William Shakespeare, *King John*, Act I (1597).

War is only a regrettable expedient for asserting one's rights by force within a state of nature, where no court of justice is available to judge with legal authority. In such cases, neither party can be declared an unjust enemy, for this would already presuppose a judge's decision; only the outcome of the conflict, as in the case of a so-called "judgement of God", can decide who is in the right.
Immanuel Kant, *Perpetual Peace* (1795).

A just war is in the long run far better for a nation's soul than the most prosperous peace obtained by acquiescence in wrong or injustice.
President Theodore Roosevelt, message to Congress, December 4, 1906.

History shows that wars are divided into two kinds, just and unjust. All wars that are progressive are just, and all wars that impede progress are unjust. We Communists oppose all unjust wars that impede progress, but we do not oppose progressive, just wars. Not only do we Communists not oppose just wars, we actively participate in them.
Mao Tse-tung, *On a Prolonged War* (1938).

Statesmen will invent cheap lies, putting blame upon the nation that is attacked, and every man will be glad of those conscience-smoothing falsities, and will diligently study them, and refuse to examine any refutations of them; and thus he will by and by convince himself that the war *is* just, and will thank God for the better sleep he enjoys after this process of grotesque self-deception.
Mark Twain quoted in F. Anderson, ed., *A Pen Warmed Up in Hell* (1972).

Some writers believe that nuclear weapons have exploded the just war doctrine. They argue that no end can justify nuclear war, and that nuclear weapons are immoral means. In that view, the two main aspects of just war doctrine, *jus ad bellum* or the right to go to war, and *jus in bello* or limits on the means used in war, are both called in question by the unprecedented destructiveness of nuclear weapons.
Joseph S. Nye, Jr., *Nuclear Ethics* (1986).

limited war

A great country cannot wage a little war.
Duke of Wellington, speech in the House of Lords, January 16, 1838. According to Elizabeth Longford, *Wellington: Pillar of State* (1972), "This famous remark was first made to Fitzroy Somerset on January 5 [1838] by letter."

The day of total war has passed. . . . From now on limited military operations are the only ones which could conceivably serve any coherent purpose.
George F. Kennan, *The Realities of American Foreign Policy* (1954).

In practice, the limitation of war is morally and emotionally repugnant to the American people.
Robert E. Osgood, *Limited War* (1957).

If wars are limited in ages past, the reasons why they were so have little relevance for us today. . . . wars were kept limited by the small margin of the national economic resources available for mobilization and by the small capability for destruction that could be purchased with that narrow margin.
Bernard Brodie, *Strategy in the Missile Age* (1959).

Never corner an opponent, and always assist him to save his face. Put yourself in his shoes—so as to see things through his eyes. Avoid self-righteousness like the devil—nothing is so self-binding. Cure yourself of two commonly fatal delusions—the idea of victory and the idea that war cannot be limited.
B. H. Liddell Hart, *Deterrent or Defense* (1960).

At the heart of the West's military thought lies the belief that machines must be used to save its men's lives; Korea would progressively become a horrific illustration of the effects of a limited war where one side possessed the firepower and the other the manpower.
David Rees, *Korea: The Limited War* (1964).

The greatest contribution Vietnam is making . . . is developing an ability in the United States to fight a limited war, to go to war without arousing the public ire.
Robert S. McNamara, Secretary of Defense, quoted in Barbara W. Tuchman, *The March of Folly* (1984).

A proper concept of limited war is one in which the objectives are limited to something less than the total destruction of the enemy but which carries no implication of curtailed resources or restricted tactics. The resources allocated and their use in combat should be limited only by the requirements of prompt victory.
General Maxwell D. Taylor, *Swords and Plowshares* (1972).

preemptive war

A just fear of imminent danger, though there be no blow given, is lawful cause of war.
Francis Bacon, "Of Empire," *Essays* (1625).

I would . . . never advise . . . to declare war forthwith, simply because it appeared that our opponent would begin hostilities in the near future. One can never anticipate the ways of divine providence securely enough for that.
Otto von Bismarck quoted in Gordon A. Craig, *The Politics of the Prussian Army* (1955).

At one point he [Secretary of Defense Robert McNamara, in 1962] snapped at an Air Force General, "Damn it, if you keep talking about [building] ten thousand missiles, you are talking about preemptive attack. Why don't you just say so?"
Henry L. Trewhitt, *McNamara* (1971).

"If I see that the Russians are amassing their planes for an attack," [General Curtis] LeMay continued, "I'm going to knock the shit out of them before they take off the ground."

[Robert C.] Sprague was thunderstruck by the revelation.... Most startling was LeMay's final bit of news [as SAC commander in the late 1950s], that he would order a preemptive attack against Soviet air bases.

"But General LeMay," Sprague said, "that's not national policy."

"I don't care," LeMay replied. "It's my policy. That's what I'm going to do."

Fred Kaplan, *The Wizards of Armageddon* (1983).

preventive war

[A preventive war against the Soviet Union] would win for us a proud title—we would become the first aggressors for peace.

Francis P. Matthews, Secretary of the Navy, speaking on August 25, 1950, quoted in *The Nation* (September 9, 1950). Shortly thereafter Matthews was appointed Ambassador to Ireland by President Truman.

A preventive war, to my mind, is an impossibility today. How could you have one if one of its features would be several cities lying in ruins, several cities where many, many thousands of people would be dead and injured and mangled, the transportation systems destroyed, sanitation implements and systems all gone? That isn't preventive war; that *is* war.

I don't believe there is such a thing; and frankly, I wouldn't even listen to anyone seriously that came in and talked about such a thing.

President Dwight D. Eisenhower, 1954 press conference, quoted in McGeorge Bundy, *Danger and Survival* (1988).

I have always been opposed even to the thought of such a [preventive] war. There is nothing more foolish than to think that war can be stopped by war. You don't "prevent" anything by war except peace.

Harry S. Truman, *Memoirs*, II (1956).

proxy war

Vietnamization is basically an effort to tranquilize the conscience of the American people while our government wages a cruel and needless war by proxy.

Senator George S. McGovern, testimony before the Foreign Relations Committee of the U.S. Senate, February 4, 1970.

The most effective Soviet weapon used against us in recent years has been unarmed transport aircraft, full of Cubans and East Germans sent to exploit the turmoil in the Third World.

William E. Colby, Former Director of the CIA, *The Washington Post* (February 22, 1981).

The new reliance on covert paramilitary action as a normal instrument of foreign policy—even as a substitute for foreign policy—has strained the current [Congressional] oversight process to the breaking point.... It involves a most basic question which can only be resolved in open debate, with the full awareness of the American people. That question is: Can a democracy like the United States engage in large-scale, so-called covert paramilitary operations, using our intelligence agencies as instruments in waging proxy wars against the Soviet Union or its clients?

Senator Patrick J. Leahy, *The New York Times* (April 22, 1986).

study of war

War should be the only study of a prince. He should look upon peace only as a breathing time which affords him the leisure to contrive, and furnishes him with ability to execute military plans.

Niccolò Machiavelli, *The Prince* (1513).

I must study politics and war, that my sons may have liberty to study mathematics and philosophy. My sons ought to study mathematics and philosophy, geography, natural history and naval architecture, navigation, commerce, and agriculture, in order to give their children a right to study painting, poetry, music, architecture, statuary, tapestry and porcelain.

John Adams, letter of May 12, 1780 to his wife, Abigail, reprinted in *Adams Family Correspondence*, III, eds. L. H. Butterfield and M. Friedlaender (1973).

total war

The whole art of war is being transformed into mere prudence, with the primary aim of preventing the uncertain balance from shifting suddenly to our disadvantage and half-war from developing into total war.

Karl von Clausewitz, *On War* (1832).

It is not an army that we must train for war: it is a nation.

President Woodrow Wilson, speech in Washington, D.C., May 12, 1917.

If the term "absolute war" has any meaning it is that of a fight until the capacity of one side for further resistance is exhausted. In practice, this may well mean that its conqueror is on the verge of exhaustion, too weak to reap the harvest of his victory. In other words, absolute war is war in which the conductor allows the fighting instinct to usurp control of his reason.

B. H. Liddell Hart, *Thoughts on War* (1944).

When both sides possess atomic power, "*total* warfare" makes nonsense. Total warfare implies that the aim, the effort, and the degree of violence are unlimited. Victory is pursued without regard to the consequences.... Any unlimited war waged with atomic power would be worse than nonsense; it would be mutually suicidal.

B. H. Liddell Hart, *The Revolution in Warfare* (1946).

A mere increase in the deadliness of armaments would not bring peace. The difficulty is that the action of explosives is too limited; to overcome this deficiency war must be made as deadly for all the civilians back home as for the troops on the front lines . . . . War will instantly stop if the weapon is bacteriology.

Alfred Nobel quoted in Robert Shaplen, "Annals of Science," *The New Yorker* (March 22, 1958).

war aims

We go to gain a little plot of ground,
That hath in it no profit but the name.

William Shakespeare, *Hamlet*, Act IV (1600).

No war should be commenced . . . without first seeking a reply to the question, What is to be attained by and in the same.

Karl von Clausewitz, *On War* (1832).

Our aim is directed upon the destruction of the enemy's power.

Karl von Clausewitz, *On War* (1832).

The legitimate object of war is a more perfect peace.
Inscription on General William T. Sherman's statue in Washington, D. C. This was also J. F. C. Fuller's definition of the object of war in *The Conduct of War* (1961).

Modern war, in order to reach its purpose: to impose one's will on the enemy, knows of but one means: the destruction of the opponent's organized forces.
General Ferdinand Foch, *The Principles of War* (1918).

I would say to the House, as I said to those who have joined this Government: "I have nothing to offer but blood, toil, tears and sweat."
We have before us an ordeal of the most grievous kind. We have before us many, many long months of struggle and of suffering. You ask what is our policy? I will say: It is to wage war, by sea, land and air, with all our might and with all the strength that God can give us: to wage war against a monstrous tyranny, never surpassed in the dark, lamentable catalogue of human crime. That is our policy. You ask, What is our aim? I can answer in one word: Victory—victory at all costs, victory in spite of all terror, victory, however long and hard the road may be; for without victory, there is no survival.
Winston Churchill, speech to the House of Commons on becoming Prime Minister, May 13, 1940.

To kill an enemy was an effective action; to bring in one of our own wounded was praiseworthy, but unrelated to our war-aims.
Siegfried Sassoon, *Siegfried Sassoon's Long Journey*, Paul Fussell, ed. (1983).

war and chess
The secret of Napoleon was to meet events half-way so that he could control them, instead of waiting and allowing them to over-ride him. But it is important to note that he first of all carefully studied the field of operations and the conditions under which he was to fight. He knew in advance what events were inevitable. He may be compared to a chess-player who takes in at a glance the state of the chess-board: he does not stop at what I may call its static condition, but he also notes its dynamic potentialities; he sees the relative positions of the chess-men, but he also pays attention to their possible moves whenever any one of them is placed elsewhere. Napoleon and the chess-player appear to improvise, but the improvisation is never undertaken in a haphazard fashion.
Marshal Ferdinand Foch quoted in Raymond Recouly, *Marshal Foch* (1929).

The issue of any operation of war is decided not by what the situation actually is, but by what the rival commanders think it is. Historically, and practically, it is far more important to discover what information they had, and the times at which it reached them, than to know the actual situation of the "pieces." A battlefield is not a chessboard.
B. H. Liddell Hart, *Thoughts on War* (1944).

International relations have traditionally been compared to a chess game in which each nation tries to outwit and checkmate the other.
President Harry S. Truman, speech in Mexico City, March 3, 1947.

Warfare certainly isn't chess. You might make a case for the Navy, where it's all maneuvering on open flat surfaces with different units of fire power, where it's all Force, Space and Time, but war is like a bloody football game. You start off with a play and it never quite works out as you figured it would.
Norman Mailer, *The Naked and the Dead* (1948).

The atomic queens may never be brought into play; they may never actually take one of the opponent's pieces. But the position of the atomic queens may still have a decisive bearing on which side can safely advance a limited-war bishop or even a cold-war pawn.
Paul Nitze, "Atoms, Strategy and Policy," *Foreign Affairs* (January 1956).

As in chess, so in war.
Mao Tse-tung, *Selected Military Writings* (1963).

war and peace
In peace, sons bury their fathers; in war, fathers bury their sons.
Herodotus, *History* (5th century B.C.).

The paramount aim of any social system should be to frame military institutions, like all its other institutions, with an eye to the circumstances of peace-time, when the soldier is off duty; and this proposition is borne out by the facts of experience. For militaristic states are apt to survive only so long as they remain at war, while they go to ruin as soon as they have finished making their conquests. Peace causes their metal to lose its temper; and the fault lies with a social system which does not teach its soldiers what to make of their lives when they are off duty.
Aristotle (4th century B.C.) quoted in Arnold J. Toynbee, *War and Civilization* (1950).

This is to make an end of all wars, to conclude an eternal and perpetual peace.
Duke of Somerset, open letter to the people of Scotland, which sought to justify the English invasion, January 1548.

To reap the harvest of perpetual peace
By this one bloody trial of sharp war.
William Shakespeare, *Richard III*, Act V (1592).

An honorable peace is and always was my first wish! I can take no delight in the effusion of human blood; but, if this war should continue, I wish to have the most active part in it.
John Paul Jones, September 2, 1782 letter to Gouverneur Morris, quoted in Lincoln Lorenz, *John Paul Jones* (1943).

May we never see another war! For in my opinion, there never was a good war or a bad peace.
Benjamin Franklin, letter to Josiah Quincy, September 11, 1783, reprinted in *The Complete Works of Benjamin Franklin*, VIII, ed. John Bigelow (1888).

Since reason condemns war and makes peace an absolute duty, and since peace cannot be effected or guaranteed without a compact among nations, they must form an alliance of a peculiar kind, which may be called a pacific alliance (*foedus pacificum*), different from a treaty of peace (*pactum pacis*), inasmuch as it would forever terminate all wars, whereas the latter only ends one.
Immanuel Kant, *Perpetual Peace* (1795).

An honorable peace is attainable only by an efficient war.
Henry Clay, speech in the House of Representatives, January 8, 1813.

Wars are, of course, as a rule to be avoided; but they are far better than certain kinds of peace.
Theodore Roosevelt, *Thomas Hart Benton* (1897).

An analysis of the history of mankind shows that from the year 1496 B.C. to the year 1861 of our era, that is, a cycle of 3357 years, were but 227 years of peace and 3130

years of war: in other words, there were thirteen years of war for every year of peace. Considered thus, the history of the lives of people presents a picture of uninterrupted struggle. War, it would appear, is a normal attribute to human life.
Jean De Bloch, *The Future of War* (1903).

In international affairs, [peace is] a period of cheating between two periods of fighting.
Ambrose Bierce, *The Devil's Dictionary* (1911).

The working class who fight all the battles, the working class who make the supreme sacrifices, the working class who freely shed their blood and furnish the corpses, have never yet had a voice in either declaring war or making peace. It is the ruling class that invariably does both. They alone declare war and they alone make peace.
Eugene V. Debs, June 16, 1918 speech in Canton, Ohio, reprinted in *Eugene V. Debs Speaks*, ed. Jean Tussey (1970).

Peace is not only better than war, but infinitely more arduous.
George Bernard Shaw, *Heartbreak House*, Preface (1919).

I was once asked to devise an inscription for a monument in France. I wrote, "In war, Resolution. In defeat, Defiance. In victory, Magnanimity. In peace, Goodwill." The inscription was not accepted.
Winston Churchill, *My Early Life* (1930). Churchill would later use this epigram as the "moral" for his *The Second World War*.

Those who can win a war well can rarely make a good peace and those who could make a good peace would never have won the war.
Winston Churchill, *My Early Life* (1930).

What they could do with round here is a good war. What else can you expect with peace running wild all over the place? You know what the trouble with peace is? No organization.
Bertolt Brecht, *Mother Courage*, Act I (1939).

When you're at war you think about a better life; when you're at peace you think about a more comfortable one.
Thornton Wilder, *The Skin of Our Teeth*, Act III (1942).

The international community is a world in which war is an instrument of national policy and the national domain is the military base from which the state fights and prepares for war during the temporary armistice called peace.
Nicholas Spykman, *America's Strategy in World Politics* (1942).

Since wars begin in the minds of men, it is in the minds of men that the defenses of peace must be constructed.
United Nations Educational, Scientific, and Cultural Organization (UNESCO) Constitution (1945).

The statistics of suicide show that, for non-combatants at least, life is more interesting in war than in peace.
William R. Inge, *The End of an Age* (1948).

I don't believe in peace at any price—no honest man does. But I don't believe that because peace is difficult that war is inevitable.
President Harry S. Truman, speech in Elkhart, Indiana, October 26, 1948.

Youth is the first victim of war; the first fruit of peace. It takes twenty years or more of peace to make a man; it takes only twenty seconds of war to destroy him.
Baudouin I of Belgium, address to joint session of U.S. Congress, May 12, 1959.

An inglorious peace is better than a dishonorable war.
Mark Twain quoted in Bernard DeVoto, ed., *Letters from the Earth* (1962).

The mere absence of war is not peace.
John F. Kennedy, State of the Union Address, January 14, 1963.

We must be constantly prepared for the worst and constantly acting for the best— strong enough to win a war and wise enough to prevent one.
President Lyndon B. Johnson, State of the Union Address, January 8, 1964.

Thirty years ago . . . I coined the maxim "If you want peace, understand war". . . . The necessary amplification of the maxim is now "If you wish for peace, understand war—particularly the guerrilla and subversive forms of war."
B. H. Liddell Hart, *Strategy*, 2nd ed. (1967).

Peace is a continuation of war by other means.
General Vo Nguyen Giap, quoted in *Newsweek* (February 5, 1973).

A Russian saying has it that Russia will never start a war, but will wage peace so vigorously that no stone will be left standing upon another.
James Sherr, *Soviet Power* (1987).

war and politics
War is nothing but a continuation of political intercourse, with a mixture of other means.
Karl von Clausewitz, *On War* (1832). This, Clausewitz' most famous sentence, is often stated (translated) as: "War is the continuation of politics by other means."

A political scheme that cannot be carried out except by soldiers will not be a permanent one.
George Bernard Shaw, *John Bull's Other Island*, Preface (1904).

A great soldier might be a baby politician.
Henry Adams, *The Education of Henry Adams* (1907).

The commander in his operations has to keep military victory as the goal before his eyes. But what statesmanship does with his victories or defeats is not his province. It is that of the statesman.
Field Marshal Helmuth von Moltke quoted in Paul von Hindenburg, *Out of My Life* (1920).

The determination of the final goal of a war, the decisive objective, falls evidently to the political side of national life, which alone can tell us why war is made at all and why the nation takes up the sword after laying down the pen.
Marshal Ferdinand Foch, *Precepts and Judgments* (1920).

War is not the continuation of policy. It is the breakdown of policy.
General Hans von Seeckt, *Thoughts of a Soldier* (1929).

Politics is war without bloodshed while war is politics with bloodshed.
Mao Tse-tung, *On a Prolonged War* (1938).

The politician, who has to persuade and confute, must keep an open and flexible mind, accustomed to criticism and argument; the mind of the soldier, who commands and obeys without question, is apt to be fixed, drilled, and attached to definite rules.

That each should understand the other better is essential for the conduct of modern war.
Field Marshal Archibald Wavell, speaking in 1939, quoted in *Time* (June 28, 1943).

War, like politics, is a series of compromises.
B. H. Liddell Hart, *Thoughts on War* (1944).

I am the first to admit that a war is waged in pursuance of political aims, and if the Combined Chiefs of Staff should decide that the Allied effort to take Berlin outweighs purely military considerations in the theater, I would cheerfully readjust my plans and my thinking so as to carry out such an operation.
General Dwight D. Eisenhower quoted in Alfred D. Chandler, Jr., ed., *The Papers of Dwight David Eisenhower: The War Years*, IV (1970).

The pre-requisite for a policy of limited war is to reintroduce the political element into our concept of warfare and to discard the notion that policy ends when war begins or that war can have goals distinct from those of national policy.
Henry A. Kissinger, *Nuclear Weapons and Foreign Policy* (1957).

Lenin . . . especially admired Clausewitz's insistence that war and politics were not separate antithetical activities, but simply alternative methods pressed into the service of a single policy. Whether one or the other was chosen at any junction in inter-state relations was determined by what the ends required and by no other consideration.
G. R. Urban, *Detente* (1976).

In determining the essence of war, Marxism-Leninism uses as its point of departure the position that war is not an aim in itself, but only a tool of politics. The acceptance of war as a tool of politics also determines the interrelation of military strategy and politics, which is based on the principle of the full dependence of the former on the latter.
Marshal V. D. Sokolovsky, former Chief of the Soviet General Staff, quoted in Christy Campbell, *Weapons of War* (1983).

war as sport

As flies to wanton boys are we to th' gods—
They kill us for their sport.
William Shakespeare, *King Lear*, Act IV (1605).

But playing at war, that's what's vile; and playing at magnanimity and all the rest of it. That magnanimity and sensibility is like the magnanimity and sensibility of the lady who turns sick at the sight of a slaughtered calf —she is so kindhearted she can't see blood—but eats fricasseed veal with a very good appetite. They talk of the laws of warfare, of chivalry, of flags of truce, and humanity to the wounded, and so on. That's all rubbish.
Leo Tolstoy, *War and Peace* (1865–69).

The sand of the desert is sodden red,
Red with the wreck of a square that broke;
The gatling's jammed and the colonel dead,
And the regiment blind with the dust and smoke.
The river of death has brimmed its banks
And England's far and honour a name.
But the voice of a schoolboy rallies the ranks;
'Play up!, play up! and play the game!'
Henry John Newbolt, "Vitai Lampada," in *The Island Race* (1898).

One of our men flew over the Lille aerodrome [on April 1, 1915] and dropped a football. All the Germans rushed for cover, imagining that a bomb was coming down, but when, after many enormous rebounds, the ball at length came to rest, they approached it cautiously, and on it they read:
"April Fool! *Gott Strafe England*!"
Captain P. A. Thompson, *Lions Led by Donkeys* (1927).

Upon the fields of friendly strife
Are sown the seeds
That, upon other fields, on other days
Will bear the fruits of victory.
General Douglas MacArthur, inscription over the entrance to the gymnasium at West Point written while MacArthur was Superintendent (1919–22); reprinted in his *Reminiscences* (1964).

War is the only sport that is genuinely amusing. And it is the only sport that has any intelligible use.
H. L. Mencken, *Prejudices*, V (1926).

For when the One Great Scorer comes to mark against your name, He writes—not that you won or lost—but how you played the game.
Grantland Rice, "Alumnus Football," *Only the Brave and Other Poems* (1941).

A fighter pilot . . . in the Battle of Britain . . . found (those are his own words) "Success in the game is the great incentive to subdue fear. Once you've shot down two or three the effect is terrific and you'll go on till you're killed. It's love of the sport rather than sense of duty that makes you go on without minding how much you are shot up."
Air Commodore Symonds quoted in Lord Moran, *The Anatomy of Courage* (1945).

Our military forces are one team—in the game to win regardless of who carries the ball. This is no time for "fancy Dans" who won't hit the line with all they have on every play, unless they can call the signals. Each player on this team—whether he shines in the spotlight of the backfield or eats dirt in the line—must be an all-American.
General Omar Bradley, testimony to the House Armed Services Committee, October 19, 1949.

The race is not always to the swift nor the battle to the strong—but that's the way to bet it.
Damon Runyon, *Runyon on Broadway* (1950).

Serious sport has nothing to do with fair play. It is bound up with hatred, jealousy, boastfulness, disregard of all rules, and sadistic pleasure in witnessing violence: in other words, it is war minus the shooting.
George Orwell, *Shooting an Elephant* (1950).

Peter: We are two down, and the ball's in the enemy court. War is a psychological thing, Perkins, rather like a game of football. And you know how in a game of football ten men often play better than eleven—?
Jon: Yes, sir.
Peter: Perkins, we are asking you to be that one man. I want you to lay down your life, Perkins. We need a futile gesture at this stage. It will raise the whole tone of the war.
Allan Bennett and others, *Beyond the Fringe* (1963).

He spoke with homicidal eloquence, keeping the game alive with genial and well-judged jokes. Man, it seemed, had been created to jab the life out of the Germans. To hear the Major talk one might have thought that he did it himself every day before breakfast. His final words were: "Remember that every Boche you kill is a point scored to our side."

Siegfried Sassoon quoted in B. Gardner, *The Big Push* (1968).

Officials in both foreign and economic policy areas have too eagerly embraced the "game plan" image of the sports world. They now constantly project their "economic game plan" or "Vietnam game plan" even though the phrase carries overtones of fun and frivolity that don't quite suit the serious business of ending the war in Southeast Asia or restoring economic vigor at home.

Alan Otten, *The Wall Street Journal*, December 23, 1970.

One way of showing the sporting spirit was to kick a football toward the enemy lines while attacking. This feat was first performed by the 1st Battalion of the 18th London Regiment at Loos in 1915. It soon achieved the status of a conventional act of bravado. . . . The most famous football episode was Captain W. P. Nevill's achievement at the Somme attack. Captain Nevill, a company commander in the 8th East Surreys, bought four footballs, one for each platoon, during his last London leave before the attack. He offered a prize to the platoon which, at the jump-off, first kicked its football up to the German front line.

Paul Fussell, *The Great War and Modern Memory* (1975). While Nevill was killed during the attack, the balls were kicked as a signal to advance.

The real trouble with the Yanks is that they are completely ignorant as to the rules of the game we are playing with the Germans. You play so much better when you know the rules.

Field Marshal B. L. Montgomery quoted in David Irving, *The War Between the Generals* (1981).

war colleges

What was taught in the military schools was no longer the art of defending strong places, but that of surrendering them honorably after certain conventional formalities.

French Revolutionary Lazare Carnot, speaking of 18th-century Europe, quoted in Bernard Brodie and Fawn Brodie, *From Crossbow to H-Bomb* (1972).

Correct theories, founded upon right principles, sustained by actual events of wars, and added to accurate military history, will form a true school of instruction for generals. If these means do not produce great men, they will at least produce generals of sufficient skill to take rank next after the natural masters of the art of war.

General Antoine Henri Jomini, *Summary of the Art of War* (1838).

One criticism I have of all the schools where they tried to pound into my head some military erudition, is that I was never given a hint of what a headache could come out of a quarter of a million prisoners of war, when transportation facilities are clogged and evacuation from the theater can be at the rate of only about thirty thousand a month.

General Dwight D. Eisenhower, May 25, 1943 letter to General George C. Marshall, reprinted in Joseph Patrick Hobbs, *Dear General* (1971).

We get officers here who have spent their careers looking through gunsights or periscopes or binoculars. We want to expand the size of their horizons and to show them that they alone are not going to win the war.

Admiral James E. Service, U.S. Naval War College, quoted in *The New York Times* (November 25, 1984).

If we are serious about military reform, we had better understand that its effects will be temporary at best, *unless* we change the manner in which our officers, particularly at the highest levels, think about their profession and about how they should prepare to fight a war. If we are to have successful, lasting reform of our military establishment, it must begin at the war colleges.
Williamson Murray, "Grading the War Colleges," *National Interest* (Winter 1986–87).

A perception exists that our intermediate and senior colleges are "gentlemen's courses." . . . This perception is not without basis.
General Russell E. Dougherty, speaking for a reviewing board of retired generals and admirals, *The New York Times* (September 20, 1988).

The Army War College was built to send the best and the brightest over to think and reflect. I would say over the years that concept was eroded. We are now at a point where people are not sent over to think, but to be fire-hosed with specific subject matter to a point where they don't have any time to do any thinking.
John H. Johns, professor at the Industrial College of the Armed Forces, *The Chronicle of Higher Education* (March 15, 1989).

war correspondents
I have made arrangements for the correspondents to take the field . . . and I have suggested to them that they should wear a white uniform to indicate the purity of their character.
General Irvin McDowell, speaking during the American Civil War, quoted in William Howard Russell, *My Diary North and South* (1863).

"All the danger of war and one-half per cent the glory": such is our motto, and that is the reason why we [war correspondents] expect large salaries.
Winston Churchill, *Ian Hamilton's March* (1900).

[Richard Harding Davis] was one of those magnetic types, often otherwise second-rate, who establish patterns of living for others of their kind, and the notion of the novelist as war-correspondent which prevailed so long in American writing began in the early nineties undoubtably with him.
Van Wyck Brooks, *The Confident Years: 1885–1915* (1952).

The average war correspondent . . . insensibly acquired cheerfulness in the face of vicarious torment and danger. In his work it came out at times in a certain jauntiness of tone that roused the fighting troops to fury against the writer. Through his despatches there ran a brash implication that the regimental officers and men enjoyed nothing better than "going over the top"; that a battle was just a rough jovial picnic, that a fight never went on long enough for the men, that their only fear was lest the war should end this side of the Rhine.
C. E. Montague, *Disenchantment* (1922).

The way to attend a war, for any right-thinking American correspondent, was to watch Richard Harding Davis and try to approximate his distinguished style. You needed almost as many wardrobe changes as a touring matinee idol, since it was necessary to be properly dressed for a legation garden party or scrambling up hills to catch a panoramic view of battle, which you then described in Olympian prose.
Richard O'Connor, *Jack London* (1964).

Early in life I had noticed that no event is ever correctly reported in a newspaper, but in Spain [during the Civil War of 1936–39], for the first time, I saw newspaper

reports which did not bear any relation to the facts, not even the relationship which is implied in an ordinary lie.
George Orwell, *Looking Back on the Spanish War* (1945).

[On D-Day] correspondents on Juno [Beach] had no communications until Ronald Clark of United Press came ashore with two baskets of carrier pigeons. The correspondents quickly wrote brief stories, placed them in the plastic capsules attached to the pigeons' legs and released the birds. Unfortunately the pigeons were so overloaded that most of them fell back to earth. Some, however, circled overhead for a few moments—and then headed toward the German lines. Charles Lynch of Reuter's stood on the beach, waved his fist at the pigeons and roared, "Traitors! Damned traitors!" Four pigeons ... "proved loyal." They actually got to the Ministry of Information in London within a few hours.
Cornelius Ryan, *The Longest Day* (1959).

[At Arnheim during World War II] I thought the wheels of the glider were for landing. Imagine my surprise when we skidded along the ground and the wheels came up through the floor. I got another shock. Our helmets, which we all swore were hooked, came flying off on impact and seemed more dangerous than the incoming shells. After landing, I grabbed the first helmet I saw, my trusty musette bag with the Olivetti typewriter inside and began crawling toward the canal which was the rendezvous point. When I looked back, I found a half dozen guys crawling after me. It seems that I had grabbed the wrong helmet. The one I wore had two neat stripes down the back indicating that I was a lieutenant.
Walter Cronkite quoted in Cornelius Ryan, *A Bridge Too Far* (1974).

Upon meeting General George Patton during the Second World War [John] McCloy had asked the celebrated military hero if he had ever read the leather-bound volumes of Clausewitz and Jomini that were conspicuously displayed in his command tent. "Hell, no," Patton had answered. "But it impresses the hell out of the war correspondents."
Gregg Herken, *Counsels of War* (1987).

[Edward R. Murrow] began, "This is London." The phrase would become synonymous with the man, imitated endlessly, usually poorly. The mistake was to assume a pause: "This ... is London." Murrow made no pause, but accentuated the first word and understated the last two, which, spoken in his darkly arresting delivery, gave the simple phrase its surprising power and drama: "THIS is London."
Joseph E. Persico, *Edward R. Murrow* (1988).

A civilian journalist by the name of David Duncan was sent up to me. He was taking pictures for *Life*, and he was to go along with me. . . . the last thing I needed was to be responsible for a civilian. I laid it out for him point-blank: "I don't have time to mollycoddle you! I don't have blankets for you at night. I don't have rations for your meals. If you wanna stay, don't get in my way. Hang around the background. And let me tell you one final thing. If you're gonna get hit, get killed. I don't have men to carry you back to an aid station. If you get killed, I don't have to worry about you."
Captain Francis "Ike" Fenton, Jr. quoted in Donald Knox, *The Korean War: Pusan to Chosin* (1985).

It is impossible to realize how much of Ernest Hemingway still lives in the hearts of men until you spend time with the professional war correspondents. Most of the Americans are stuck in the Hemingway bag and they tend to romanticize war, just as he did. Which is not surprising: unlike fighting in the war itself, unlike big-game hunt-

ing, working as a war correspondent is almost the only classic male endeavor left that provides physical danger and personal risk without public disapproval and the awful truth that for correspondents, war is not hell. It is fun.
Nora Ephron, "The War Followers," *New York Magazine* (November 12, 1973).

It soon became clear that Slam [S. L. A. Marshall], whose job it was to teach [military history techniques to] these men being flown all over South Vietnam at the Army's expense, couldn't have been less interested in them or whether they learned the technique at all. Not just in the first one, but in all four schools, the Military History Detachment officers sat on the sidelines and watched while Slam . . . conducted the actual interviews. Slam never placed them in charge or asked them any questions—in truth, he simply ignored them. Meanwhile, every evening Slam counted the longhand pages of notes he'd taken that day as post people would count money. He'd glance through the pages, noting all the soldiers' names, which he'd taken down during the interviews perhaps even more assiduously than the action— "Every name is worth ten books at the cash register," he'd declare.
David H. Hackworth, *About Face* (1989). Hackworth concluded that Marshall was "less a military analyst than a military ambulance chaser, more a voyeur than a warrior, the Louella Parsons of the U.S. Army."

war crimes
War is the greatest of all crimes; and yet there is no aggressor who does not color his crime with the pretext of justice.
Voltaire, *The Ignorant Philosopher* (1767).

On a beautiful [Virginia] estate a pregnant women was found murdered in her bed through several bayonet stabs; the barbarians [the British] had opened both of her breasts and written above her bed canopy, "Thou shalt never give birth to a rebel." In another room, was just as horrible a sight: five cut-off heads arranged on a cupboard in place of plaster-cast-figures which lay broken to pieces on the floor. Dumb animals were no less spared. The pastures were in many places covered with dead horses, oxen, and cows.
Karl Gustav Tornquist, a Swedish naval officer serving with the French during the 1780s, *Naval Campaigns of Count de Grasse* (1942).

If execution of an order given in line of duty violates a statute of the penal code, the superior giving the order is alone responsible. However, the subordinate obeying the order is liable to punishment as an accomplice if . . . he knew that the order involved an act the commission of which constituted a civil or military crime or offense.
Article 47 of the German Military Penal Code of 1872 quoted in Telford Taylor, *Nuremberg and Vietnam* (1971). Taylor, an American prosecutor at Nuremberg after World War II, states that this article "remained in effect throughout the war, and was reaffirmed in principle by no less a person than Dr. Joseph Goebbels."

There is a hoary convention that holds that morality ends at the threshold of affairs of state, not to speak of war. It is expressed in many well-spoken aphorisms or quotations, like the remark of Talleyrand on Napoleon's execution of the Duc d'Enghien: "It was worse than a crime, it was a blunder!" Thus wit establishes immunity, and the man who spent a million lives to make himself and his family royal has gone down in history as a genius who committed no crimes, only a few costly blunders.
Bernard Brodie, *War and Politics* (1973).

When you look at the startling ruins of Nuremberg, you are looking at a result of the war. When you look at the prisoners on view in the courthouse, you are looking at 22 of the causes.
Janet Flanner, on the post-World War II Nuremberg trials, *Janet Flanner's World* (1979).

An aggressive war is the great crime against everything good in the world. A defensive war, which must necessarily turn to aggressive at the earliest moment, is the necessary great counter-crime. But never think that war, no matter how necessary, nor how justified, is not a crime. Ask the infantry and ask the dead.
Ernest Hemingway, introduction to *Treasury of the Free World* (1946).

Today it is not considered a war crime or atrocity to kill 1,000 civilians with a bomb or napalm, although it is still considered such a crime or atrocity to kill one civilian with a pistol.... Rules of conduct during armed conflict have been discarded and nations throughout the world, instead of policing their own conduct, have played the game, "Your war crime is bigger than mine."
Representative Don Edwards, *The Washington Post* (February 21, 1970).

We are just as responsible as the Germans were in World War II. We're doing all the horrible things the Nazis, the Fascists and the Communists did. The only difference is we do it in the name of liberating people, democratizing them, freeing them. It's ghastly hypocrisy.
Ernest Gruening, speaking of Vietnam, *The Washington Post* (February 8, 1971).

Only the winners get away with their lies, as only the winners decide what were the war crimes.
Garry Wills, *The New York Times* (July 10, 1975).

One U-boat commander, Heinz Eck, claimed that he was merely following his orders when he machine-gunned in their open boats the crew of a freighter he sank on 13 March 1944. He also destroyed the boats in the hope that no trace would ever be found of his victims. Unfortunately for him three survivors eluded his machine-gunner and they were later picked up by a destroyer. Heinz Eck and his machine-gunner were, in their turn, among the survivors when their U-boat was sunk. They were both court-martialled, sentenced to death and executed by the British.
The other U-boat survivors in this case were treated as prisoners of war.
Richard Hough, *The Longest Battle* (1986).

There have been many newspaper and magazine accounts of what has become known as the "MGR"—Mere Gook Rule. In Vietnam, "MGR" was a short-hand explanation for a battlefield crime that was investigated but not brought to trial or for a case that the Army prosecuted, but which resulted in an acquittal. Thus, the planners of the My Lai 4 assault could reason that anyone in the hamlet must be a Viet Cong or Viet Cong sympathizer and, therefore—by applying the "MGR"—the area could be shelled and bombed at will.
Seymour M. Hersh, *Cover-Up* (1972).

war games
Thus war became essentially a regular game in which time and change shuffled the cards; but in its significance, it was only diplomacy somewhat intensified, a more forceful way of negotiating, in which battles and sieges were the diplomatic notes.
Karl von Clausewitz, *On War* (1832).

War is a game where you win every time, save one.
René Quinton, *Soldier's Testament* (1930).

The enemy of our games [before World War II] was always Japan—and the courses were so thorough that after the start of WWII—nothing that happened in the Pacific was strange or unexpected. Each student was required to plan logistic support for an advance across the Pacific—and we were well prepared for the fantastic logistic efforts required to support the operations of the war.
Admiral Chester W. Nimitz, writing in 1965, quoted in Thomas B. Buell, "Admiral Raymond A. Spruance and the Naval War College," *Naval War College Review* (March 1971).

An umpire [in a war game] decided that a bridge had been destroyed by an enemy attack and flagged it accordingly. From then on, it was not to be used by men or vehicles. Shortly, a corporal brought his squad up to the bridge, looked at the flag, and hesitated for a moment; then resolutely marched his men across it. The umpire yelled at him:
"Hey, don't you see that that bridge is destroyed?"
The Corporal answered, "Of course I can see it's destroyed. Can't you see we're swimming?"
President Dwight D. Eisenhower, *At Ease* (1967).

What are we to make of a civilization . . . which has not been able to talk about the prospect of killing almost everybody, except in prudential and game-theoretic terms?
J. Robert Oppenheimer quoted in N. P. Davis, *Lawrence and Oppenheimer* (1968).

According to Air Force Chief of Staff General Charles Gabriel, in recent years it's been the civilians in the military high command who've been the most hawkish.
"I think you'll find today in all the war games we run, that the military are by far the more cautious of any of the players," he said. "The civilians are more aggressive than the military when it comes to playing a scenario involving escalation."
James Coates and Michael Kilian, *Heavy Losses* (1985).

war guilt
The Allied and Associated Governments affirm and Germany accepts the responsibility of Germany and her allies for causing all the loss and damage to which the Allied and Associated Governments and their nationals have been subjected as a consequence of the war imposed upon them by the aggression of Germany and her allies.
Treaty of Versailles (1919), Article 231.

The War was premeditated by the Central Powers together with their Allies, Turkey and Bulgaria, and was the result of acts deliberately committed in order to make it unavoidable. Germany, in agreement with Austria-Hungary, deliberately worked to defeat all the many conciliatory proposals made by the Entente Powers.
The finding of the "Commission on the Responsibility of the Authors of the War," chaired by U.S. Secretary of State Robert Lansing. Article 231 of the Treaty of Versailles, the "war-guilt clause," was based on this. Reprinted in Sidney Bradshaw Fay, *The Origins of the World War* (1932).

A thousand years will pass and the guilt of Germany will not be erased.
Hans Frank, German Governor General of Poland during World War II, quoted in William L. Shirer, *The Rise and Fall of the Third Reich* (1959).

war office
The British soldier can stand up to anything except the British War Office.
George Bernard Shaw, *The Devils' Disciple* (1901).

[Prior to World War I, Herbert] Asquith, when Chancellor, told me that he had had before him a proposal for the construction of an underground passage from the War Office to the Horse Guards with cellars where papers might be sorted and work car-

ried on in case of aerial attack, upon which [Sir George] Murray had minuted: "This may be safely turned down. No sane enemy, acquainted with our institutions, would destroy the War Office."
Sir Austin Chamberlain, *Down the Years* (1935).

[The war office kept three sets of figures,] one to mislead the public, another to mislead the Cabinet, and the third to mislead itself."
British Prime Minister (at the beginning of World War I) Herbert Asquith quoted in Alistair Horne, *The Price of Glory* (1962).

war plans

In war nothing can be gained except by calculation. Whatever has not been profoundly meditated in all its details is totally ineffectual.
Napoleon I, writing in 1806, quoted in J. C. Herold, *The Mind of Napoleon* (1955).

I am accustomed to think out three or four months in advance what I should do, and I base my calculations on the worst [situation].
Napoleon I quoted in J. F. C. Fuller, *The Conduct of War* (1961).

War plans cover every aspect of a war, and weave them all into a single operation that must have a single, ultimate objective in which all particular aims are reconciled. No one starts a war—or rather, no one in his senses ought to do so—without first being clear in his mind what he intends to achieve by that war and how he intends to conduct it. The former is its political purpose; the latter its operational objective.
Karl von Clausewitz, *On War* (1832).

War on paper and war on the field are as different as darkness from light, fire from water, or heaven from earth.
W. C. Falkner, *Little Brick Church* (1882).

In any military scheme that comes before you, let your first questions to yourself be: Is this consistent with the requirement of concentration?
Alfred Thayer Mahan, *Naval Strategy* (1911).

The primary consideration in making a plan should be to find the "line of least expectation"—by the enemy— rather than to take the one which seems most suited to the attacker's own desires.
B. H. Liddell Hart, *Thoughts on War* (1944).

Modern battles are fought by platoon leaders. The carefully prepared plans of higher commanders can do no more than project you to the line of departure at the proper time and place, in proper formation, and start you off in the right direction.
General George C. Marshall, *Selected Speeches and Statements* (1945).

A good plan violently executed *now* is better than a perfect plan next week.
General George S. Patton, Jr., *War as I Knew It* (1947).

No plan of operations reaches with any certainty beyond the first encounter with the enemy's main force.
Field Marshal Helmuth von Moltke quoted in Alfred Vagts, *A History of Militarism*, rev. ed. (1959).

Gentlemen, you don't have a war plan. You have a war spasm.
Bernard Brodie, in response to the 1950 nuclear war plans of the Strategic Air Command, quoted in Norman Moss, *Men Who Play God* (1968).

Any damned fool can write a plan. It's the execution that gets you all screwed up.
General James F. Hollingsworth quoted in Harry G. Summers, Jr., *On Strategy* (1982).

[Bernard] Brodie . . . had written a short, internally circulated memorandum on the analogies between war plans and sex—the no-cities/withhold plan that he had conceived was likened to withdrawal before ejaculation, while the SAC war plan was like going all the way.

With this in mind, [Herman] Kahn told the assembled officers at SAC, "Gentlemen, you don't have a war plan, you have a war orgasm."
Fred Kaplan, *The Wizards of Armageddon* (1983).

Planning in the Pentagon often consists of reworking countless documents each year, inserting a few well-phrased items reflecting the current wisdom, changing "happy" to "glad," securing numerous "chops" (approvals) from superiors, and "crashing" to get the final product on the street in the allotted time frame. A premium is placed on accomplishing the task rather than innovative thinking.
Lieutenant Colonel Tyrus W. Cobb quoted in James Coates and Michael Kilian, *Heavy Losses* (1985).

war powers
The President shall be Commander in Chief of the Army and Navy of the United States, and of the Militia of the several States, when called into the actual service of the United States. . . .
Constitution of the United States, Article II, Section 2 (1787).

The most important conclusion from all this, in my mind, is the failure of that provision in the Constitution of the United States, that the power of declaring war, is given exclusively to Congress. It is now established as an irreversible precedent that the President of the United States has but to declare that war exists, with any Nation upon Earth, by the act of that Nation's Government, and the war is essentially declared. . . .

It is not difficult to foresee what its ultimate issue will be to the people of Mexico, but what it will be to the People of the United States, is beyond my foresight, and I turn my eyes away from it.
Former President John Quincy Adams, December 26, 1847 letter to Albert Gallatin, quoted in Samuel Flagg Bemis, *John Quincy Adams and the Union* (1956).

Allow the President to invade a neighboring nation whenever *he* shall deem it necessary to repel an invasion . . . and you allow him to make war at pleasure. . . . If today he should choose to say he thinks it necessary to invade Canada, to prevent the British from invading us, how could you stop him? You may say to him, "I see no probability of the British invading us"; but he will say to you, "Be silent: I see it, if you don't."
Abraham Lincoln, speaking at the time of the 1848 Mexican War, quoted in Bernard Brodie, *War and Politics* (1973).

In the present war . . . the Fuehrer must have all the rights postulated by him which serve to further or achieve victory. Therefore—without being bound by existing legal regulations—in his capacity as Leader of the nation—the Fuehrer must be in a position to force with all means at his disposal every German, if necessary, whether he be common soldier or officer, low or high official or judge, leading or subordinate official of the party, worker or employer—to fulfill his duties. In case of violation of these duties, the Fuehrer is entitled after conscientious examination, regardless of so-called well-deserved rights, to mete out due punishment and to remove the offender from his post, rank and position without introducing prescribed procedures.
Adolf Hitler's formal war powers as passed by the Reichstag [the German legislature] on April 26, 1942. According to William L. Shirer, *The Rise and Fall of the Third Reich* (1959), this act legalized his "absolute power of life and death over every German and simply suspended any laws which might stand in the way of this." Shirer concludes that "not even in

medieval times nor further back in the barbarous tribal days had any German arrogated such tyrannical power."

There is going to be no involvement of America in war unless it is the result of the constitutional process that is placed upon Congress to declare it.
President Dwight D. Eisenhower, news conference, March 10, 1954.

I could not help being amazed at the way in which this great decision was being made. With no submission to Congress, whose duty it is to declare war, the members of the executive branch . . . agreed to enter the Korean War.
General Douglas A. MacArthur, *Reminiscences* (1965).

The great tragedy of the Johnson Administration was its subversion of the Constitutional warmaking responsibility of the Congress by false information and deception. The President and his aides misrepresented the facts about an alleged unprovoked attack upon our naval forces in the Gulf of Tonkin on August 4, 1964. The fault of the Congress, including this speaker, was in believing the President of the United States, in having too much confidence in a man and in neglecting to insist upon the full exercise of the Constitutional power of the Congress.
Senator J. William Fulbright, *The Washington Post* (April 17, 1971).

War Powers Resolution
The President in every possible instance shall consult with Congress before introducing United States Armed Forces into hostilities or into situations where imminent involvement in hostilities is clearly indicated by the circumstances, and after such introduction shall consult regularly with the Congress until United States Armed Forces are no longer engaged in hostilities or have been removed from such situations.
The War Powers Resolution of 1973, Public Law 93-148.

[Some members of Congress have gone] to court alleging that the deployment of U. S. forces in the Persian Gulf constitutes a violation of the War Powers Act. What kind of wacky world is this where the President is taken to court every time he moves our troops around?
Vice President George Bush, *The New York Times* (August 26, 1987).

The Act has been a failure. It has not prevented Presidents from pursuing risky military adventures before enlisting Congressional support. It has not facilitated unity between the Legislative and Executive branches.
Senator Alan Cranston, *Los Angeles Times* (October 26, 1987).

war prayers
Truly I think he that prays and preaches best will fight best.
Oliver Cromwell, letter to Colonel Francis Hacker, December 25, 1650, reprinted in Maurice Ashley, ed., *Cromwell* (1969).

Eternal Father! strong to save,
Whose arm hath bound the restless wave,
Who bidd'st the mighty ocean deep
Its own appointed limits keep;
O, hear us when we cry to Thee
For those in peril on the sea!
William Whiting, *The Navy Hymn* (1860).

I know that the Lord is always on the side of the right. But it is my constant anxiety and prayer that I and this nation should be on the Lord's side.

President Abraham Lincoln's reply to the question of whether or not the Lord was on our side during the Civil War, quoted in Francis B. Carpenter, *Six Months at the White House with Abraham Lincoln* (1867).

O Lord our God, help us to tear their soldiers to bloody shreds with our shells; help us to cover their smiling fields with the pale forms of their patriot dead; help us to drown the thunder of the guns with the shrieks of their wounded, writhing in pain; help us to lay waste their humble homes with a hurricane of fire; help us to wring the hearts of their unoffending widows with unavailing grief; help us to turn them out roofless with their little children to wander unfriended the wastes of their desolated land in rags and hunger and thirst, sports of the sun flames of summer and the icy winds of winter, broken in spirit, worn with travail, imploring Thee for the refuge of the grave and denied it— For our sakes who adore Thee, Lord, blast their hopes, blight their lives, protract their bitter pilgrimage, make heavy their steps, water their way with tears, stain the white snow with the blood of their wounded feet! We ask it in the spirit of love. . . .

Mark Twain, "The War Prayer," written in 1904 but first published in 1916, quoted in Alex Ayres, *The Wit and Wisdom of Mark Twain* (1987).

Even the churches, bound by Christian teaching to condemn war in general, were able to approve this particular war [World War I], because "civilization is at issue." The fact that the Kaiser had told his people to "go to church and kneel before God and pray for his help for our gallant army" caused no concern. Clearly, God would be able to discern the essential difference between Christian Englishmen and Christian Germans.

Phillip Knightley, *The First Casualty* (1975).

[In December 1944, General George] Patton had ordered his chaplain to publish a prayer for good weather for his . . . attack. "See if we can't get God to work on our side."

"Sir," replied Chaplain O'Neill, "it's going to take a pretty thick rug for that kind of praying."

"I don't care if it takes a flying carpet."

"Yes, sir," replied O'Neill reluctantly. "But it usually isn't customary among men of my profession to pray for clear weather to kill fellow men."

"Chaplain, are you teaching me theology or are you the chaplain of the Third Army? I want a prayer."

John Toland, *Battle: The Story of the Bulge* (1959). The "weather prayer" was written and distributed to the troops. It read in part: "Almighty and merciful Father, we humbly beseech Thee of Thy great goodness, to restrain these immoderate rains with which we have had to contend. Grant us fair weather for battle."

The attack killed Igor Mikhovich, an army conscript from the coal city of Donetsk, in the southern Ukraine. Standing beside the twisted wreckage of the truck's cab, which had been thrown to the side of the snow-flanked highway, the Soviet television reporter, Mikhail Leshchinsky, appeared to be struggling with his emotions. "God willing, this will be the last Soviet death in this country in this war," he said.

John F. Burns, "Soviets Are Glum About Kabul's Future," *The New York Times* (February 10, 1989).

war room

Gentlemen, this is outrageous. You can't fight in here. This is the War Room.
Peter Sellers as the President of the United States, stopping a fight between his military advisors in *Dr. Strangelove* (1964), directed by Stanley Kubrick; screenplay by Stanley Kubrick and others from the novel *Red Alert* by Peter George.

Deep in the Pentagon behind heavy oak doors is a super secret room. . . . Shifts of officers from all four branches of the military maintain a round-the-clock vigil in this two-story chamber. A red telephone provides a direct link to the White House. Lifting a beige phone instantly establishes contact with any U.S. military commander anywhere in the world. One wall is covered with huge computer-fed display screens which flash the readiness of all American forces. A touch of a button will provide an item-by-item inventory of strategic weapons "on target." This is the War Room—the National Military Command Center; nerve center for the most potent military force in the world—control room for the modern automated war.
Robert C. Aldridge, *First Strike!* (1983).

wars of national liberation

Can conditions in other countries come to a point where the people exhaust their patience and rise up with arms in hand? They can. What attitude do Marxists have toward such uprisings? The most favorable. These uprisings must not be identified with wars among states, with local wars, because in these uprisings the people are fighting to exercise their right to self-determination and for their social and independent national development; these are uprisings against rotten reactionary regimes and against colonialists. Communists fully and unreservedly support such just wars and march in the van of the peoples fighting wars of liberation.
Soviet Premier Nikita Khrushchev, speech of January 6, 1961, reprinted in Walter Lefeber, ed., *The Dynamics of World Power*, II (1973).

We shall have to deal with the problems of "wars of liberation." These wars are often not wars at all. In these conflicts, the force of world Communism operates in the twilight zone between political subversions and quasi-military action. Their military tactics are those of the sniper, the ambush, and the raid. Their political tactics are terror, extortion, and assassination.
Robert S. McNamara, Secretary of Defense, speech of February 17, 1962, quoted in Paul Kecskemeti, *Insurgency as a Strategic Problem* (1967).

There is another type of warfare—new in its intensity, ancient in its origin—war by guerrillas, subversives, insurgents, assassins; war by ambush instead of by combat, by infiltration instead of aggression, seeking victory by eroding and exhausting the enemy instead of engaging him. It is a form of warfare uniquely adapted to what have been strangely called "wars of liberation," to undermine the efforts of new and poor countries to maintain the freedom that they have finally achieved. It preys on unrest and ethnic conflicts.
President John F. Kennedy, speech at Annapolis, June 6, 1962.

In today's world, with the enemies of freedom talking about "wars of national liberation," the old distinction between "civil war" and "international war" has already lost much of its meaning.
President Lyndon B. Johnson, speech at Baylor University, May 28, 1965.

The war is described as an exemplary war, a war, that is, which will prove to the Communists once and for all that so-called "wars of national liberation" cannot succeed. In fact, we are not proving that. What, indeed, are we proving in Vietnam except that, even with an army of half a million men and expenditures which approach $30

billion a year, we cannot win a civil war for a regime which is incapable of inspiring the patriotism of its own people?
Senator J. William Fulbright, testimony before the U.S. Senate Committee on Foreign Relations, March 11, 1968.

We are against doctrines which justify the export of revolution and counterrevolution.
Mikhail Gorbachev, speaking in Havana, *The New York Times* (April 5, 1989).

Waterloo

I tell you Wellington is a bad general, the English are bad soldiers; we will settle the matter by lunch time.
Napoleon I, speaking to his generals on the morning of the Battle of Waterloo, June 18, 1815, quoted in Robert M. Johnston, *The Corsican* (1910).

The history of the battle is not unlike the history of a ball! Some individuals may recollect all the little events of which the great result is the battle lost or won; but no individual can recollect the order in which, or the exact moment at which, they occurred, which makes all the difference as to their value or importance.
Duke of Wellington, quoted in John Keegan, *The Face of Battle* (1976).

The battle of Waterloo was won on the playing fields of Eton.
Traditionally attributed to the Duke of Wellington, but according to Elizabeth Longford, *Wellington: The Years of the Sword* (1969), he "probably never said anything or thought anything of the kind."

Waterloo is a battle of the first rank won by a captain of the second.
Victor Hugo, *Les Misérables* (1862).

An English army led by an Irish general: that might be a match for a French army led by an Italian general.
George Bernard Shaw, *The Man of Destiny* (1897).

Probably the Battle of Waterloo *was* won on the playing-fields of Eton, but the opening battles of all subsequent wars have been lost there.
George Orwell, *The Lion and the Unicorn* (1941).

It has been a damned serious business—Blucher and I have lost 30,000 men. It has been a damned nice thing—the nearest run thing you ever saw in your life. . . . By God! I don't think it would have done if I had not been there.
Duke of Wellington quoted in Thomas Creevey, *The Creevey Papers* (1934).

The gruesomeness of the aftermath was proportioned to the grandeur of the rest of the occasion. Thousands of wounded lay for days dying all over the field, some struggling to bandage themselves while coachloads of sightseers who had driven down from Brussels ate basket lunches and surveyed the scene as if it were already a battle canvas. By night looters, including a number of women, went among the fallen, stealing their valuables and killing those of the still living who protested too loudly.
Charles Fair, *From the Jaws of Victory* (1971).

weapons

Wisdom is better than weapons of war.
The Bible, Ecclesiastes 9:18.

The means of destruction are approaching perfection with frightful rapidity.
General Antoine Henri Jomini, *Summary of the Art of War* (1838).

I tell you that in the arts of life man invents nothing; but in the arts of death he outdoes Nature herself, and produces by chemistry and machinery all the slaughter of plague, pestilence and famine. . . . In the arts of peace, man is a bungler. . . . His heart is in his weapons.
George Bernard Shaw, *Man and Superman* (1903).

In ancient warfare, the spear and the shield were used, the spear to attack and destroy the enemy, and the shield to defend and preserve oneself. To the present day, all weapons are still an extension of the spear and the shield. The bomber, the machine-gun, the long-range gun and poison gas are developments of the spear, while the air-raid shelter, the steel helmet, the concrete fortification and the gas mask are developments of the shield. The tank is a new weapon combining the functions of both spear and shield.
Mao Tse-tung, *On a Prolonged War* (1938).

When wars are fought with tanks and planes, defeat or victory is decided on the assembly line. We see the relationship between technology and military power, but we have only begun to recognize that technology is more than the fabrication of new weapons. It also includes the way in which we organize our society to produce those weapons, for on that organization may depend the volume of our output, the speed of our production.
I. F. Stone, "The Shake-up We Need," *The Nation* (December 22, 1941).

No new weapon can be introduced without changing conditions, and every change in conditions will demand a modification in the application of the principles of war.
J. F. C. Fuller, *Armoured Warfare* (1943).

Ages in which the dominant weapon is expensive or difficult to make will tend to be ages of despotism, whereas when the dominant weapon is cheap and simple, the common people have a chance. Thus, for example, tanks, battleships and bombing planes are inherently tyrannical weapons, while rifles, muskets, long-bows, and hand-grenades are inherently democratic weapons. A complex weapon makes the strong stronger, while a simple weapon— so long as there is no answer to it—gives claws to the weak.
George Orwell, *Tribune* (October 19, 1945).

It is good policy to choose that weapon whose anti-weapon imposes the greatest possible strain on the production facilities and military efforts of the opponent.
Oskar Morgenstern, *The Question of National Defense* (1959).

To paraphrase Will Rogers, I think this [the Reagan] Administration has never seen a weapons system that it didn't like.
Representative Les Aspin quoted in R. Brownstein and N. Easton, *Reagan's Ruling Class* (1983).

Military commanders over the ages have noted that soldiers often tend to lose equipment they don't like. There also have been concerns about equipment such as certain laser designation and fire-control systems, which require an operator to stand at a spot where the laser beam could travel a straight line to designate a target such as a tank, a spot at which the soldier could find himself exposed to hostile fire. However, this equipment has yet to be tested in a real war.
Jeff Hecht, *Beam Weapons* (1984).

In the third world, we are selling 20th-century weapons to people who have the emotions of the 19th century.
Dominique Moisi, Deputy Director of the French Institute of International Relations, *The New York Times* (December 27, 1988).

Weapons, though they are sometimes described as lethal, never ever serve to kill. Instead all they do is give their owners . . . "antipersonnel capability". . . . Rather than destroy enemy weapons, which after all consist of nice gadgets basically similar to our own, modern military technology "engages" targets, and "services," "neutralizes," or "suppresses" them. If a particularly vivid description is needed, it "defeats" them and "takes them out," the latter term being a direct derivation from children's games such as tag or hide-and-seek.
Martin van Creveld, *Technology and War* (1989).

Man became man, in part, because he held a weapon in his hand.
Robert L. O'Connell, *Of Arms and Men* (1989).

West Point

I give it as my fixed opinion that but for our graduated cadets the war between the United States and Mexico might, and probably would, have lasted some four or five years, with, in its first half, more defeats than victories falling to our share, whereas in two campaigns we conquered a great country . . . without the loss of a single battle or skirmish.
General Winfield Scott, speaking before the Civil War, quoted in Russell F. Weigley, *History of the United States Army*, enlarged ed. (1984).

When he reported to Chief of Staff [Peyton] March, [General Douglas] MacArthur was promptly told that he was to assume the superintendency at West Point in June [1919]. Caught by surprise, he objected: "I am not an educator. I am a field soldier. Besides there are so many of my old professors there. I can't do it." His protest was abruptly dismissed by March's retort: "Yes . . . you can do it."
D. Clayton James, *The Years of MacArthur*, I (1970). According to William Manchester in *American Caesar* (1978), one of the reasons MacArthur did "do it" was that the appointment as superintendent carried with it the rank of brigadier general in the regular army; otherwise MacArthur "would revert to his prewar rank of major."

Based on my own past experience, I felt that the English Department had always been the weakest in the academic structure [at West Point]. I suspected that the trenchant views of Jefferson Davis on the subject expressed on leaving the post of Secretary of War [in 1857] were still valid: "It has long been the subject of remark that the scholars in the exact sciences, were barely mediocre in polite literature. Their official reports frequently exhibit poverty of style."
General Maxwell D. Taylor, talking of West Point right after World War II when he was Superintendent, *Swords and Plowshares* (1972).

The Long Gray Line has never failed us. Were you to do so, a million ghosts in olive drab, in brown khaki, in blue and gray, would rise from their white crosses thundering those magic words—Duty-Honor-Country.
This does not mean that you are war mongers. On the contrary, the soldier, above all other people, prays for peace, for he must suffer and bear the deepest wounds and scars of war. . . .
In my dreams I hear again the crash of guns, the rattle of musketry, the strange mournful mutter of the battlefield. But in the evening of my memory, always I come

back to West Point. Always there echoes and re-echoes in my ears—Duty-Honor-Country.

Today marks my final roll call with you. But I want you to know that when I cross the river my last conscious thoughts will be of the Corps—and the Corps—and the Corps.

General Douglas MacArthur, speech at West Point, May 12, 1962, reprinted in his *Reminiscences* (1964).

The sentiment of West Point lays over the land like a blanket. There is a plaque on a rock near the football stadium, a quotation attributed to George Catlett Marshall, *I have a secret and dangerous mission. Send me a West Point football player.*

Ward Just, *Military Men* (1970).

To be a West Pointer and to have chosen the Army as a career means to have committed oneself to doing all the things necessary to becoming a general.

Bernard Brodie, *War and Politics* (1973).

The purpose of West Point is to train combat officers, and women are not physically able to lead in combat. Maybe you could find one woman in 10,000 who could lead in combat, but she would be a freak and we're not running the military academy for freaks. . . . The pendulum has gone too far. They're asking women to do impossible things. I don't believe women can carry a pack, live in a foxhole, or go a week without taking a bath.

General William C. Westmoreland, *The Christian Science Monitor* (June 7, 1976).

The most famous moment in Whistler's West Point career occurred during his chemistry examination. Asked to discuss silicon, he supposedly asserted, "Silicon is a gas," causing his interrogator to end the questioning by saying, "That will do, Mr. Whistler." The episode was concluded years later when Whistler [who left West Point to become a famous painter] declared, "If silicon had been a gas, I might have become a general."

Gordon Fleming, *The Young Whistler* (1978).

Most accounts of West Point fall into two categories: straight-out histories, and novels. . . . The histories have tended to glamorize, to romanticize the atmosphere and to dwell on the spectacular accomplishments of those graduates whose names have become household words to the American public. Dwelling on these superstars . . . has caused most histories to neglect the role the Academy has played in developing its vital "other" graduates, the men who have commanded regiments, divisions, air wings. And if the histories have been wanting, the novels have been worse, sensational and utterly foreign to the truth.

John Eisenhower, introduction to *Cradle of Valor* by Dale O. Smith (1988).

Whiz Kids

In common with many other military men, active and retired, I am profoundly apprehensive of the pipe-smoking, tree-full-of-owls type of so-called professional "defense intellectuals" who have been brought into this nation's capitol. I don't believe a lot of these often over-confident, sometimes arrogant young professors, mathematicians and other theorists have sufficient worldliness or motivation to stand up to the kind of enemy we face.

General Thomas D. White, "Strategy and the Defense Intellectuals," *The Saturday Evening Post* (May 4, 1963).

[Secretary of Defense Robert] McNamara sponsored a group of young intellectu-als. . . . These were the "Whiz Kids," . . . so-called because of their self-assured disre-spect for tradition as they ranged happily among the sacred cows of the Pentagon. The group included Alain C. Enthoven, . . . an economist who earlier, at RAND, had spe-cialized in strategy and strategic weapons.

. . . one often told Pentagon story concerns an occasion when he visited U.S. Air Force Headquarters in Germany. He was met by an assortment of generals, with decades of accumulated experience and yards of ribbons. Enthoven, fresh-faced and youthful, listened with growing impatience as the number one general outlined plans for briefing their visitor. Finally Enthoven interrupted. "General," he said, "I don't think you understand. I didn't come for a briefing. I came to tell you what we have decided."
Henry L. Trewhitt, *McNamara* (1971).

General Curtis LeMay. . . absolutely despised the Whiz Kids. He was horrified when Harold Brown [later to be Secretary of Defense under President Carter], McNamara's thirty-four-year-old R&D director, tried to tell him which bomber the Air Force should really want. "Why, that son of a bitch was in junior high school while I was out bombing Japan!" LeMay said.
Fred Kaplan, *The Wizards of Armageddon* (1983).

will

At the battle of Borodino Napoleon did not fire at any one, nor kill any one. All that was done by his soldiers. Therefore it was not he who killed those men. The soldiers of the French army went out to slay their fellow-men at Borodino, not owing to Napo-leon's commands, but through their own desire to do so. The manner in which these men slaughtered one another did not depend on Napoleon's will, but proceeded inde-pendently of him, from the wills of the hundreds of thousands of men who took part in the affair. It only seemed to Napoleon that all this was due to his will.
Leo Tolstoy, *War and Peace* (1865–69).

It is not enough to order discipline. The officer must have the will to enforce it, and its vigorous enforcement must instill subordination in the soldiers. It must make them fear it more than they fear the enemy's blows.
Ardant du Picq, *Battle Studies* (1868).

A general has much to bear and needs strong nerves. The civilian is too inclined to think that war is only like the working out of an arithmetical problem with given numbers. It is anything but that. On both sides it is a case of wrestling with powerful, interwoven physical and psychological forces, a struggle which inferiority in numbers makes all the more difficult. It means working with men of varying force of character and with their own views. The only quality that is known and constant is the will of the leader.
General Erich Ludendorff, *My War Memories* (1920).

The resources of men in wartime are inexhaustible. Fatigue is a defect of the will.
René Quinton, *Soldier's Testament* (1930).

War is conflict; fighting is an elemental exposition of the age-old efforts to survive. It is the cold glitter of the attacker's eye, not the point of the questing bayonet, that breaks the line. It is the fierce determination of the driver to close with the enemy, not the mechanical perfection of the tank, that conquers the trench. It is the cataclysmic

ecstasy of conflict in the flier, not the perfection of his machine gun, which drops the enemy in flaming ruin. Yet volumes are devoted to armament; pages to inspiration.
Major George S. Patton, Jr., "Success in War," [1931] *Infantry Journal Reader*, ed. J. I. Greene (1943).

You need infantry still to win battles, and impregnable positions are only as impregnable as the will of those who hold them.
Ernest Hemingway, "Hemingway Reports Spain," *The New Republic* (January 12, 1938).

The strongest will is of little use if it is inside a dead body.
B. H. Liddell Hart, *Why Don't We Learn From History?* (1943).

The aim of a nation in war is . . . to subdue the enemy's will to resist, with the least possible human and economic loss to itself.
B. H. Liddell Hart, *Thoughts on War* (1944).

It is fatal to enter any war without the will to win it.
General Douglas MacArthur, keynote address at the 1952 Republican National Convention in Chicago, *The New York Times* (July 8, 1952).

The will to conquer is the first condition of victory. [*Victoire, c'est la Volonte!*]
Marshal Ferdinand Foch quoted in Barbara W. Tuchman, *The Guns of August* (1962).

Will was what [General] Stilwell had, the absolute, unbreakable, unbendable determination to fulfill the mission no matter what the obstacles, the antagonists, or the frustrations. When the road that he fought to cut through Burma [in World War II] at last reached China, after his recall, a message from his successor recognized that the first convoy to make the overland passage, though Stilwell wasn't there to see it, was the product of "your indomitable will."
Barbara W. Tuchman, "Generalship," *Parameters* (Spring 1972).

We have the power to destroy his [North Vietnamese] war-making capacity. The only question is whether we have the *will* to use that power. What distinguishes me from [President] Johnson is that I have the *will* in spades.
President Richard M. Nixon, *RN: Memoirs* (1978).

The failure to invoke the national will was one of the major strategic failures of the Vietnam War. It produced a strategic vulnerability that our enemy was able to exploit.
Harry G. Summers, Jr., *On Strategy* (1982).

winning

I had rather die than be whipped.
Confederate General James E. B. "Jeb" Stuart, statement after being mortally wounded at Yellow Tavern, Virginia, on May 12, 1864, quoted in Douglas S. Freeman, *Lee's Lieutenants*, III (1951).

Napoleon had no liking for an unsuccessful general because he knew the part success plays in winning the allegiance of men. Moreover when men have achieved something their spirit bounds up. The secret of success in war is success.
Lord Moran, *The Anatomy of Courage* (1945).

Winning isn't everything, it's the only thing.
Red Sanders, Vanderbilt University football coach, speaking in 1948, quoted in Leo Green, *Sportswit* (1984). This is often attributed to football coach Vince Lombardi. In *Vince Lombardi on Football*, ed. George L. Flynn (1973), Lombardi says, "I have been quoted as saying, 'Winning is the only thing.' That's a little out of context. What I said is that 'Winning is not everything—but making the effort to win is.' "

When a free man dies, he loses the pleasure of life; a slave loses pain. Death is the only freedom a slave knows. That's why he's not afraid of it. That's why we'll win.
Kirk Douglas, *Spartacus* (1960), directed by Stanley Kubrick; screenplay by Dalton Trumbo, from the novel by Howard Fast.

We won the battle of Normandy, [but] considering the high price in American lives, we lost.
Martin Blumenson, *Breakout and Pursuit* (1961).

[Air Force] General [Thomas S.] Power finally agreed to hear [William] Kaufmann's counterforce briefing. It took place at SAC Headquarters in Omaha on December 12, 1960. Not two minutes into the lecture, Power interrupted with a long, angry tirade against everything that Kaufmann was saying.
"Why do you want us to restrain ourselves?" Power bellowed. "Restraint! Why are you so concerned with saving *their* lives? The whole idea is to *kill* the bastards!" After several minutes of this, he finally said, "Look. At the end of the war, if there are two Americans and one Russian, we win!"
Kaufmann—his patience exhausted—snapped back, "Well, you'd better make sure that they're a man and a woman."
Fred Kaplan, *The Wizards of Armageddon* (1983). In a related remark, Senator Richard Russell said in the Senate during an October 2, 1968 debate on antiballistic missiles that "if we have to start over again with another Adam and Eve, then I want them to be Americans and not Russians."

A countervailing strategy is a strategy that denies the other side any possibility that it could win—but it doesn't say that our side would win.
Harold Brown quoted in Gregg Herken, *Counsels of War* (1987).

women in the military

The law now says women can't go into combat. The American people are not ready for it, nor am I. But I have authorized a woman to be an explosives ordnance disposal officer; she'll defuse bombs. And of the top four Marines at the engineer's school at Camp Lejeune, three were women. I fully expect a woman to take my place one day.
General Louis H. Wilson, Commandant, U.S. Marine Corps, *People* (September 13, 1976).

If the Equal Rights Amendment were approved, say, and women were permitted to serve in combat units, then the U.S. Navy would certainly move quickly to abide by the law of the land. Every sailor on ship isn't engaged in pushing projectiles around. We still have yeomen and pay clerks and computer programmers and electronic repairmen and the kinds of jobs that women can perform splendidly. The transition would have to be carefully planned. Any time you have boys-girls it's a little difficult; but the problems, I guess, are no different than what's happening in college dormitories.
Admiral James L. Holloway III, Chief of Naval Operations, *The New York Times* (May 1, 1977).

I do not doubt the Army has women who can complete a combat course, endure three days or three weeks under field conditions, and shoot as straight as any man. But in my whole lifetime, I have never known 10 women who I thought could endure three months under actual combat conditions in an Army unit. I think we should continue to have a legal bar against women in combat units—not because they are women but because the average woman is simply not physically, mentally or emotionally qualified to perform well in combat situations for extended periods.
General Elizabeth P. Hoisington, Former Director, Woman's Army Corps, *Los Angeles Herald Examiner* (February 12, 1978).

There is no question but that women could do a lot of things in the military. So could men in wheelchairs. But you couldn't expect the services to want a whole company of people in wheelchairs.
General Lewis B. Hershey, quoted in Patricia M. Murphy, "What's a Nice Girl Like You Doing in a Place Like This," *Air University Review* (September–October 1978).

The men in the Corps called them [Women Marines] "BAMs," for "broad-assed Marines," and they called the men "HAMs," for "hairy-assed Marines."
William Manchester, *Goodbye, Darkness* (1980).

Barring women from combat has resulted in complex and arbitrary restrictions that limit our military flexibility. At the present time, each branch of the military has elaborate determinations for which specific assignments have high combat probability. These designations often change depending on the world situation.... Women soldiers make up roughly 10 per cent of our armed forces and are well integrated throughout. To keep tabs on all of them and try to restrict them from forward battle positions would not only be difficult, it would limit our flexibility.... The fact is that we cannot afford to encumber our military commanders with combat restrictions that affect a large fraction of their troops. We must open up our combat billets to all qualified soldiers.
Senator William Proxmire, *The Washington Post* (March 25, 1986).

I think women are too valuable to be in combat.
Caspar W. Weinberger, U.S. Secretary of Defense, *U.S. News and World Report* (May 19, 1986).

Major Cannon R. Page of the 1st Army Corps sat in his office contemplating the new decision to allow young women to serve in uniform— Wacs in the army, and in the navy Waves. "What in hell are we supposed to do with them?" he complained. "Young girls away from home the first time and thrown in here with all these horny enlisted men? Does the army want to send a girl home to her mother with the clap? Or pregnant? It's going to be a goddamned mess!"
For the most part, it wasn't.
David Brinkley, *Washington Goes to War* (1988).

World War I

If there is ever another war in Europe, it will come out of some damned silly thing in the Balkans.
Otto von Bismarck, remark recalled by German diplomat Albert Ballin in 1914, quoted in Winston Churchill, *The World Crisis* (1928).

The lamps are going out all over Europe; we shall not see them lit again in our lifetime.
Sir Edward Grey, on the eve of war, August 3, 1914, quoted in Barbara W. Tuchman, *The Guns of August* (1962).

We were quite ready to fight anybody ... and would equally readily have fought the French. Our motto was, "We'll do it. What is it?"
General Sir Tom Bridges, at the beginning of World War I, *Alarms and Excursions* (1938).

When you march into France ... let the last man on the right brush the Channel with his sleeve.
Field Marshal Alfred von Schlieffen, on the plan to conquer France, quoted in Herbert Rosinski, *The German Army* (1939).

We are about to engage in a battle on which the fate of our country depends and it is important to remind all ranks that the moment has passed for looking to the rear; all our efforts must be directed to attacking and driving back the enemy. Troops that can advance no farther, must, at any price, hold on to the ground they have conquered and die at the spot rather than give way. Under the circumstances which face us, no act of weakness can be tolerated.
French Marshal Joseph Joffre, proclamation to his troops before the 1914 Battle of the Marne, quoted in *The Memoirs of Marshal Joffre* (1932).

On 5 June the *Hampshire*, with [Lord] Kitchener [Minister of War] on board, stuck a mine within two hours of leaving Scapa Flow. Kitchener and most of the crew were drowned. So perished the only British military idol of the First World War. The next morning [Lord] Northcliffe burst into his sister's drawing-room with the words: "Providence is on the side of the British Empire after all."
A. J. P. Taylor, *English History 1914–1945* (1965). According to Sir Arthur Conan Doyle, Kitchener "had flashes of genius but was usually stupid."

This, the greatest of all wars, is not just another war—it is the last war!
H. G. Wells, *The War That Will End War* (1914).

Our invasion of Belgium is contrary to international law but the wrong—I speak openly—that we are committing we will make good as soon as our military goal is reached.
Theobold von Bethmann-Hollweg, German Chancellor, speaking to the Reichstag on August 4, 1914, quoted in *The New York Times* (August 5, 1914).

You will be home before the leaves have fallen from the trees.
Kaiser William II, to his troops departing for France in August 1914, quoted in Evelyn Blucher, *An English Wife in Berlin* (1920).

I discovered to my amazement that average men and women were delighted at the prospect of war. I had fondly imagined what most pacifists contended, that wars were forced upon a reluctant population by despotic and Machiavellian governments.
Bertrand Russell, *Autobiography* (1967).

He kept us out of war!
Martin H. Glynn, Governor of New York, speech at the 1916 Democratic National Convention in St. Louis in praise of President Woodrow Wilson's policy of neutrality in World War I, *The New York Times* (June 15, 1916). This became the campaign slogan that helped Wilson win election to a second four-year term—when he would lead the United States into the war.

In Flanders fields the poppies blow
Between the crosses, row on row.
John McRae, *In Flanders Fields* (1917).

The last war, during the years of 1915, 1916, 1917 was the most colossal, murderous, mismanaged butchery that has ever taken place on earth. Any writer who said otherwise lied. So the writers either wrote propaganda, shut up, or fought.
Ernest Hemingway, *Men at War* (1942).

There was H. W. Garrod of Merton [College, Oxford University] who early in the 1914 war was handed a white feather by a young woman in a London street with the remark, "I am surprised that you are not fighting to defend civilization." Garrod answered smartly, "Madam, I *am* the civilization that they are fighting to defend."
Dacre Balsdon, *Oxford Now and Then* (1970).

We intend to begin unrestricted submarine warfare on the first of February. We shall endeavor in spite of this to keep the United States neutral. In the event of this not succeeding, we make Mexico a proposal of alliance on the following basis: make war together, make peace together, generous financial support, and an understanding on our part that Mexico is to reconquer the lost territory in Texas, New Mexico, and Arizona. The settlement in detail is left to you.

Arthur Zimmermann, German Foreign Minister, telegram of January 16, 1917 to Count Johann von Bernstorff, the German Ambassador in Washington. It was intercepted and deciphered by British Naval Intelligence and became a major factor in America's entry into World War I. Reprinted in Barbara W. Tuchman, *The Zimmermann Telegram* (1958).

America has joined forces with the Allied Powers, and what we have of blood and treasure are yours. Therefore it is with loving pride we drape the colors in tribute of respect to this citizen of your great republic. And here and now in the presence of the illustrious dead we pledge our hearts and our honor in carrying this war to a successful issue. Lafayette, we are here.

Colonel Charles E. Stanton, speech at the tomb of the French-born American Revolutionary War General Marquis de Lafayette, July 4, 1917. It is often erroneously reported that General Pershing made the statement "Lafayette, we are here" when he first disembarked in France. According to Richard Goldhurst, *Pipe Clay and Drill* (1977), when "Stanton included the phrase 'Lafayette, nous voila' for delivery at Lafayette's tomb, Pershing struck it out as 'uncharacteristic.' On reflection, however, he told Stanton to deliver it himself at the ceremonies."

Over there, over there, send the word, send
    the word over there!
That the Yanks are coming, the Yanks are
    coming,
The drums rum-tumming ev'rywhere:
So prepare, say a pray'r,
Send the word, send the word to beware!
We'll be over, we're coming over,
And we won't come back till it's over, over
    there.

George M. Cohan, "Over There" (1917).

To think that George [the King of England] and Nicky [the Tsar of Russia] should have played me false! If my grandmother [Queen Victoria] had been alive she would never have allowed it.

Kaiser William II, on the outbreak of World War I, quoted in Evelyn Blucher, *An English Wife in Berlin* (1920).

You are ordered abroad as a soldier of the King to help our French comrades against the invasion of a common enemy.... Remember that the honor of the British Army depends on your individual conduct. It will be your duty not only to set an example of discipline and perfect steadiness under fire but also to maintain the most friendly relations with those whom you are helping in this struggle. In this new experience you may find temptations both in wine and women. You must entirely resist both temptations, and, while treating all women with perfect courtesy, you should avoid any intimacy. Fear God. Honor the King.

Field Marshal Horatio Kitchener, message to be kept by every British soldier in his pay-book, quoted in Sir George Arthur, *Life of Lord Kitchener* (1920).

In military operations against the Imperial German Government, you are directed to cooperate with the forces of the other countries employed against that enemy; but in so doing the underlying idea must be kept in view that the forces of the United States are a separate and distinct component of the combined forces, the identity of which must be preserved.

Newton D. Baker, Secretary of War, secret orders to General John J. Pershing, May 26, 1917, quoted in John J. Pershing, *My Experiences in the World War*, I (1931).

America should have minded her own business and stayed out of the World War. If you hadn't entered the war the Allies would have made peace with Germany in the Spring of 1917. Had we made peace then there would have been no collapse in Russia followed by Communism, no breakdown in Italy followed by Fascism, and Germany would not have signed the Versailles Treaty, which has enthroned Nazism in Germany. If America had stayed out of the war, all these "isms" wouldn't to-day be sweeping the continent of Europe and breaking down parliamentary government, and if England had made peace early in 1917, it would have saved over one million British, French, American, and other lives.

Winston Churchill, speaking in 1936 to William Griffin of the *New York Enquirer*, quoted in J. F. C. Fuller, *A Military History of the Western World*, III (1956). Churchill admitted to the interview but denied these words in *The New York Times* (October 22, 1942).

The real weakness of Allied strategy was that it never existed. Instead of one great war with a united front, there were at least six separate and distinct wars with a separate, distinct and independent strategy for each. There was some pretence at timing the desperate blows with a rough approach to simultaneity. . . . There was no real unity of conception, co-ordination of effort or pooling of resources in such a way as to deal the enemy the hardest knocks at his weakest point.

David Lloyd George, *The War Memoirs*, IV (1937).

It will be a national war which will not be settled by a decisive battle but by a long wearisome struggle with a country that will not be overcome until its whole national force is broken, and a war which will utterly exhaust our own people, even if we are victorious.

General Helmuth von Moltke, predicting the nature of the next war to the Kaiser in 1906, quoted in Barbara W. Tuchman, *The Guns of August* (1962).

In memory's eye I could see those staggering columns of the First World War, bending under soggy packs, on many a weary march from dripping dusk to drizzling dawn, slogging ankle deep through the mire of shell-shocked roads, to form grimly for the attack, blue-lipped, covered with sludge and mud, chilled by the wind and rain, driving home to their objective, and, for many, to the judgment seat of God. I do not know the dignity of their birth but I do know the glory of their death.

General Douglas MacArthur, speech at West Point, May 12, 1962, reprinted in his *Reminiscences* (1964).

The First World War was a war of no tactics, no strategy, no mind. Just slaughter.

Paul Fussell, *The Great War and Modern Memory* (1975).

War, at least modern war, as waged on the Western Front, is horrible and ghastly beyond all imagination of the civilian. Nevertheless it has an awe-inspiring grandeur of its own and it ennobles and brings out the highest in a man's character such as no other thing could. Could one but remove the horrible suffering and mutilation it would be the finest purifier of nations ever known. Even as it is, it is the finest forge of character and manliness ever invented, when taken in small doses. The unfortunate thing is, that this war has become an over-dose.

B. H. Liddell Hart, unpublished manuscript written in 1916, quoted in Brian Bond, *Liddell Hart* (1977).

The standards for the American Army . . . will be those of West Point. The rigid attention, upright bearing, attention to detail, uncomplaining obedience to instructions required of the cadet will be required of every officer and soldier of our armies in France.
General of the Armies John J. Pershing quoted in Frank E. Vandiver, *Black Jack*, II (1977).

If there was one thing the Americans became deathly sick of it was constantly hearing of the debt they owed France and, particularly, Lafayette. The famous remark, "Lafayette, we are here" never really cut much ice with the Doughboys. One of them summed up the feeling of the whole AEF when he was told his outfit was moving back in after surviving the slaughter at Soissons.
"O. K.," he groaned, "we've paid off that old fart, Lafayette. What Frog son-of-a-bitch do we owe now?"
Henry Berry, *Make the Kaiser Dance* (1978).

Nuclear weapons may have had something like a crystal ball effect. Imagine what would have happened if the statesmen who led the world into this century's first great conflagration in 1914 had possessed a crystal ball showing them the world of 1918. The leaders of 1914 expected a short, sharp war, followed by business as usual. One suspects that if the German Kaiser, the Russian Tsar and Austrian Emperor had seen a picture of 1918—with their thrones vacant, their empires destroyed—they would have drawn back from the brink of war that summer.
Joseph S. Nye, Jr., *Nuclear Ethics* (1986).

Looking at the Versailles treaty of 1919, Marshal Foch declared: "This is not peace. This is an armistice for twenty years."
Paul Seabury and Angelo Codevilla, *War* (1989).

World War II

It seems unfortunately true that the epidemic of world lawlessness is spreading. When an epidemic of physical disease starts to spread, the community . . . joins in a quarantine of the patients in order to protect the health of the community against the spread of the disease.
President Franklin D. Roosevelt, speech in Chicago, October 5, 1937. This call for a quarantine of aggressors fell on deaf international ears. According to James Chace and Caleb Carr, *America Invulnerable* (1988), "at the time of the Quarantine Speech . . . he was trying to urge the nations of the world to find new ways of controlling aggression and at the same time to get a reading of American public opinion on the subject. It was that reading, when it came, that caused him to back away from forceful action. Though many American citizens shared Roosevelt's shock at the behavior of Japan, Germany and Italy and liked the overall tone of his speech, few were ready to support programs that might lead to war. Roosevelt would later remark of this period that 'It's a terrible thing to look over your shoulder when you are trying to lead—and to find no one there.' "

How horrible, fantastic, incredible, it is that we should be digging trenches and trying on gas-masks here because of a quarrel in a faraway country between people of whom we know nothing.
Neville Chamberlain, Prime Minister of Great Britain, radio broadcast on September 27, 1938, quoted in Keith Feiling, *The Life of Neville Chamberlain* (1946).

This is a sad day for all of us, and to none sadder than to me. Everything that I have worked for, everything that I have hoped for, everything that I have believed in during my public life has cracked into ruins.
Neville Chamberlain, Prime Minister of Great Britain, speech in the House of Commons after the start of the war with Germany, quoted in *Time* (September 11, 1939).

And while I am talking to you mothers and fathers, I give you one more assurance. I have said this before, but I say it again and again and again: Your boys are not going to be sent into any foreign wars.

President Franklin D. Roosevelt, campaigning speech, Boston, October 30, 1940. According to Samuel Irving Rosenman in *Working With Roosevelt* (1952), "Every time the President had made this statement before Boston—and every time thereafter—he added to it the words he himself had so carefully added to the foreign policy plank: 'Except in the case of attack.' I suggested that he add the same words this time but he suddenly got stubborn about it—I could not understand why. 'It's not necessary,' he said. 'If we're attacked it's no longer a foreign war.'"

On the morning of December 11 the Government of Germany, pursuing its course of world conquest, declared war against the United States. The long-known and the long-expected has thus taken place. The forces endeavoring to enslave the entire world now are moving toward this hemisphere. . . . Italy has declared war against the United States. I therefore request the Congress to recognize a state of war between the United States and Germany, and between the United States and Italy.

President Franklin D. Roosevelt, message to Congress, December 11, 1941.

I don't see great danger coming from America even if she should enter the war.

Adolf Hitler's 1941 assessment of the military potential of the United States, quoted in William L. Shirer, *The Rise and Fall of the Third Reich* (1959). According to Shirer, "the Fuehrer [was] too ignorant, Goering too arrogant and Ribbentrop too stupid to comprehend the potential military strength of the United States—a blunder which had been made in Germany during the First World War by Wilhelm II, Hindenburg and Ludendorff."

I deem it highly important that we should shake hands with the Russians as far to the east as possible.

Winston Churchill, to General Dwight D. Eisenhower on April 2, 1944, *The Second World War: Triumph and Tragedy* (1953).

The war against the Japanese and other diseases of the jungle will be pressed forward.

Winston Churchill, speech in the House of Commons, September 28, 1944.

The refusal of the British and Russian peoples to accept what appeared to be inevitable defeat was the great factor in the salvage of our civilization.

General George C. Marshall, *Biennial Report of the Chief of Staff of the U.S. Army* (September 1, 1945).

One day President Roosevelt told me that he was asking publicly for suggestions about what the war should be called. I said at once, "the Unnecessary War."

Winston Churchill, *The Second World War: The Gathering Storm* (1948).

Future generations may discuss the Second World War as "just another war." Those who experienced it know that it was a war justified in its aims and successful in accomplishing them. Despite all the killing and destruction that accompanied it, the Second World War was a good war.

A. J. P. Taylor, *The Second World War* (1975).

While the rest of the world came out bruised and scarred and nearly destroyed, we came out with the most unbelievable machinery, tools, manpower, money. The war was fun for America.

Paul Edwards, quoted in Studs Terkel, *The Good War* (1984).

World War II, Europe

A phrase has spread from civilians to soldiers and back again: "This is a phoney war."

Pertinax, *The Gravediggers of France* (1942). The "phoney war" lasted from the fall of Poland at the end of September 1939 to the spring of 1940, when Germany started its Blitzkrieg in the West. According to William L. Shirer, *The Rise and Fall of the Third Reich* (1959), "the German man in the street was beginning to call it the 'sit-down war'—Sitzkrieg." The British called it the "bore war."

If we see that Germany is winning the war we ought to help Russia, and if Russia is winning we ought to help Germany, and in that way let them kill as many as possible, although I don't want to see Hitler victorious under any circumstances. Neither of them thinks anything of their "pledged word."

Senator Harry S. Truman, *The New York Times* (June 24, 1941).

They're overpaid, overfed, oversexed and over here.

Description of American forces in Britain during World War II, usually attributed to British entertainer Tommy Trinder.

That he was the first to cross the Rhine was an enormous feather in his cap, not simply because he was the first but also because Montgomery, his archfoil, was supposed to have been....

Patton was not going to let his triumph pass without some gesture to memorialize it. He had beaten Monty by one day, and in one of the great moments of World War II he symbolized his personal victory....

General George S. Patton unzipped his fly and pissed into the Rhine river!!

Now, this is no mere legend circulated through Third Army ranks and exaggerated or distorted from one telling to the next. No, it is very much a matter of historical record. I might add that Patton was photographed during this grand gesture, and I have a photostat of that shot.... Of course, the newspapers failed to pick up on this moment, which was only to be expected. I mean, it's not exactly like raising the flag on Iwo Jima.

So our historic slice into the heartland of the enemy was accompanied by—forgive me—a tinkle of brass.

Nat Frankel and Larry Smith, *Patton's Best* (1978). According to Captain Harry C. Butcher, *My Three Years With Eisenhower* (1946), "Patton's colorful and profane phrases made his daily situation reports too florid. Consequently, the War Department had instructed General Patton to write his reports in less colorful and more official language. Patton complied. His first report was a model of such military literature, but below his signature was a postscript: 'I peed in the Rhine today.' "

I hope that in the final settlement of the war, you insist that the Germans retain Lorraine because I can imagine no greater burden than to be the owner of this nasty country where it rains everyday and where the whole wealth of the people consists in assorted manure piles.

General George S. Patton, Jr., letter to Secretary of War Henry L. Stimson, quoted in Martin Blumenson, ed., *The Patton Papers*, II (1974).

It is said, and with some truth, that while the Germans fight for world domination and the English for the defense of England, the Americans fight for souvenirs. This may not be the final end for our dogfaces, but it helps.

John Steinbeck, *Once There Was A War* (1958).

The Third Army set out to traverse the American battlefields of the First World War.... A story circulating among the staffs had a general telling a regimental com-

mander: "Colonel, we had better bypass that next city: I made some pretty tall promises to a girl back there in 1918."
Russell F. Weigley, *Eisenhower's Lieutenants* (1981).

Discussing the fate of the German fleet with Truman and Churchill [at the Potsdam Conference of July 1945], Stalin proposed they split it three ways, a suggestion which elicited an impassioned speech from the prime minister, who proposed that these were engines of destruction that should be sent to the bottom of the sea. After the peroration Stalin observed laconically, "Let us divide them anyway, and if Mr. Churchill wishes he can sink his share."
Alex de Jong, *Stalin* (1986).

The mission of this Allied Force was fulfilled at 3 A.M., local time, May 7, 1945.
General Dwight D. Eisenhower, telegram to the Combined Chiefs of Staff, at the end of World War II, Europe.

Our strategy . . . was developed according to the manuals and fought along the lines for which we trained in our military schools. I don't think we learned anything new—anything that should have changed the course of our strategy in the campaign during which we crushed the German Army.
General Wade H. Haislip, *The New York Times* (December 27, 1971).

Arnhem
The object is to lay a carpet of airborne troops down over which our ground forces can pass.
General Frederick "Boy" Browning explaining Operation Market-Garden in 1944. He was later asked, "whether the 'carpet' was to consist of live airborne troops or dead ones." Quoted in Cornelius Ryan, *A Bridge Too Far* (1974).

On the narrow corridor that would carry the armored drive, there were five major bridges to take. They had to be seized intact by airborne assault. It was the fifth [for Operation Market-Garden], the crucial bridge over the Lower Rhine at a place called Arnhem, sixty-four miles behind the German lines, that worried Lieutenant General Frederick Browning, Deputy Commander, First Allied Airborne Army [on September 10, 1944]. Pointing to the Arnhem bridge on the map he asked, "How long will it take the armor to reach us?" Field Marshal Montgomery replied briskly, "Two days." Still looking at the map, Browning said, "We can hold it for four." Then he added, "But, sir, I think we might be going a bridge too far."
General Roy E. Urquhart, *Arnhem* (1958).

Although Montgomery asserted that it had been 90 percent successful, his statement was merely a consoling figure of speech. All objectives save Arnhem had been won, but without Arnhem the rest were as nothing. In return for so much courage and sacrifice, the Allies had won a 50-mile salient—leading nowhere.
John C. Warren, *Airborne Operations in World War II, European Theater* (1956).

In my prejudiced view, if the operation had been properly backed from its inception, and given the aircraft, ground forces, and administrative resources necessary for the job—it would have succeeded in spite of my mistakes, or the adverse weather, or the presence of the 2nd DD Panzer Corps in the Arnhem area. I remain MARKET-GARDEN'S unrepentant advocate.
Field Marshal Sir Bernard Montgomery, *Memoirs* (1958).

Axis Agreement
Germany, Italy and Japan undertake to assist one another with all political, economic and military means when one of the three contracting powers is attacked by a power at present not involved in the European war or the Chinese-Japanese conflict.
The Axis pact of September 27, 1940, quoted in *Time* (October 7, 1940).

The soft under-belly of the Axis.
Winston Churchill, speech in the House of Commons, referring to southern Europe, November 11, 1942. Walter Isaacson and Evan Thomas write in *The Wise Men* (1986), "[Stalin] seemed to accept Churchill's plan for a probe into the Nazis' 'soft underbelly' on the Mediterranean as an alternative to an immediate cross-Channel invasion. 'The Prime Minister drew a picture of a crocodile and pointed out that it was as well to strike the belly as the snout,' [Averell] Harriman reported to Roosevelt."

The first crack in the Axis has come.
President Franklin D. Roosevelt, address to the nation, July 28, 1943. The "crack" refers to the invasion of Sicily.

Battle of Britain
Now that we're thoroughly frightened, we'll be all right. Until the British are frightened, they never do anything but play cricket, football, hopscotch and tennis.
George Bernard Shaw, *Time* (June 3, 1940).

What General Weygand called the Battle of France is over. I expect that the Battle of Britain is about to begin. Upon this battle depends the survival of Christian civilization. Upon it depends our own British life, and the long continuity of our institutions and our Empire. The whole fury and might of the enemy must very soon be turned on us. Hitler knows that he will have to break us in this island or lose the war. If we can stand up to him, all Europe may be free and the life of the world may move forward into broad, sunlit uplands. But if we fail, then the whole world, including all that we have known and cared for, will sink into the abyss of a new Dark Age, made more sinister, and perhaps more protracted, by the lights of perverted science. Let us therefore brace ourselves to our duties, and so bear ourselves that, if the British Empire and its Commonwealth last for a thousand years, men will say, "This was their finest hour."
Winston Churchill, speech in the House of Commons, June 18, 1940.

As sure as God made little apples, we are going to get a lot of more bombing. It's the noise that frightens. Don't be frightened. Be angry. It's a good cure.
Sir Hugh Elles, Britain's civil defense chief, *Time* (July 1, 1940).

The US ambassador in London—Joseph Kennedy, the father of the man who became President—had little faith in Britain's ability to survive, and he didn't mind who knew it. As early as 1 July [1940] the British Prime Minister had written in his diary, "Saw Joe Kennedy who says everyone in the USA thinks we shall be beaten before the end of the month." Now there was only a week of it left. The British Foreign Office heard that Kennedy had summoned neutral journalists to a press conference in order to tell them that Hitler would be in London by 15 August. Such behavior infuriated Foreign Office officials—one wrote "He is the biggest Fifth Columnist in the country"—but there was little they could do about him.
Len Deighton, *Fighter* (1978).

Hitler may feel that he cannot bring off a successful invasion and may seek to gain new, easy but sterile conquests in Africa and Asia. Were it not for this little island under a great leader, he would accomplish his desires. We may fail. But supposing we do not fail? That was their finest hour. I have always loved England. But now I am in

love with England. What a people! What a chance! The whole of Europe humiliated except us. And the chance that we shall by our stubbornness give victory to the world.
Harold Nicolson, letter of July 31, 1940, *Diaries and Letters of Harold Nicolson*, II (1967).

Never in the field of human conflict was so much owed by so many to so few.
Winston Churchill, speech in the House of Commons, praising Royal Air Force pilots, August 20, 1940.

Here in London, which Herr Hitler says he will reduce to ashes and which his aeroplanes are now bombarding, our people are bearing up unflinchingly. Our Air Force has more than held its own. We are waiting for the long promised invasion. So are the fishes.
Winston Churchill, BBC broadcast to the people of France, October 21, 1940.

The best immediate defense of the United States is the success of Great Britain defending itself.
President Franklin D. Roosevelt, press conference, December 17, 1940.

The futility of it all was depressing at times. . . . It was a simple cockney who reduced the whole thing to the ultimate in absurdity for me one night. "It's a crazy war, guv'nor," he said, "I don't see why Jerry doesn't bomb Berlin and let the RAF take care of London. We'd both save petrol and we'd be none the worse."
Raymond Daniell, *Civilians Must Fight* (1941).

"How does our bombing compare with London's?" the doorman [in Liverpool] inquired. . . . "Is London's bombing worse than ours?" By this time, we knew enough never to tell any Englishman that his town had been outbombed anywhere; so we evaded the question with a question: "You've had a lot of raiding, haven't you?" With pride, he replied: "Had a hundred and forty-five—Jerry started on us a month before he started banging London."
Ben Robertson, *I Saw England* (1941).

I have often wondered what would have happened if two hundred thousand German storm troops had actually established themselves ashore. The massacre would have been on both sides grim and great. . . . They would have used terror, and we were prepared to go all lengths. I intended to use the slogan, "You can always take one with you."
Winston Churchill, *The Second World War: Their Finest Hour* (1949).

Whether or not 1940 was anyone else's finest hour, it was certainly Churchill's.
George Orwell, *New Leader* (May 14, 1949).

I'm standing on a rooftop looking out over London. At the moment everything is quiet. For reasons of national as well as personal security, I'm unable to tell you the exact location from which I'm speaking. Off to my left, far away in the distance, I can see just that faint red angry snap of antiaircraft bursts against the steel-blue sky. But the guns are so far away that it's impossible to hear them from this location.
    About five minutes ago the guns in the immediate vicinity were working. I can look across just at a building not far away and see something that looks like a flash of white paint down the side, and I know from daylight observation that about a quarter of that building has disappeared, hit by a bomb the other night. I think probably in a minute we shall have the sound of guns in the immediate vicinity. The lights are swinging over in this general direction now. You'll hear two explosions. There they are!

That was the explosion overhead, not the guns themselves. I should think in a few minutes there may be a bit of shrapnel around here. . . .
Edward R. Murrow, radio broadcast from London during the Blitz, quoted in Alexander Kendrick, *Prime Time* (1969); and Joseph E. Persico, *Edward R. Murrow* (1988).

A straightforward defensive battle can never end in an instantly recognized victory; the Battle of Britain came to be seen as a triumph only later. For the moment, invasion had been merely postponed, while night bombers were ranging unhindered over Britain. Fighter Command's reputation tarnished somewhat and [Air Marshal] Dowding—who had never been publicized as the commander—was finally and quietly relieved of command.
Gavin Lyall, "Air Chief Marshal Lord Dowding," *The War Lords*, ed. Sir Michael Carver (1976).

Why should I be disturbed by some wretched little barbarian in a machine? This thing has no surprises for me. I foresaw it long ago.
H.G. Wells' attitude toward the Blitz, quoted in David C. Smith, *H. G. Wells* (1986).

London is less celebrated for its beauty, though there are those who prefer it because, among other reasons, it never occurred to Londoners—and certainly not to Churchill—that England's capital should be surrendered rather than be submitted to the ravages of battle. The British were prepared to sacrifice London house by house, to be destroyed rather than dishonored. The French loved honor, but loved Paris more, as they would demonstrate.
William Manchester, *The Last Lion*, II (1988).

Battle of France

[In 1939] the Army High Command, spurred on by Hitler to mount an offensive, was intending to use, once again, the so-called "Schlieffen Plan" of 1914. It is true that this had the advantage of simplicity, though hardly the charm of novelty. Thoughts therefore soon turned to alternative solutions.
General Heinz Guderian, *Panzer Leader* (1952).

Winston Churchill himself, who had taken over as Prime Minister on the first day of battle . . . was awakened at half past seven on the morning of May 15 by a telephone call from Premier Paul Reynaud in Paris, who told him in an excited voice, "We have been defeated! We are beaten!" Churchill refused to believe it. The great French Army vanquished in a week? It was impossible. "I did not comprehend," he wrote later, "the violence of the revolution effected since the last war by the incursion of a mass of fast-moving armor."
William L. Shirer, *The Rise and Fall of the Third Reich* (1959).

I know that a declaration of war does not lie within your hands alone. But I have to tell you that . . . if you cannot give France in the coming days a positive assurance that the United States will come into the struggle within a short space of time . . . you will then see France go under like a drowning man after having thrown a last look toward the land of liberty from which she was expecting salvation.
Paul Reynaud, Premier of France, June 14, 1940, formal appeal to President Franklin D. Roosevelt, quoted in William L. Shirer, *The Collapse of the Third Republic* (1969).

This war has not been decided by the Battle of France. This war is a world war. All our mistakes, all our delays, all our suffering, do not alter the fact that there is in the universe all the means needed to crush our enemies one day.
General Charles de Gaulle, BBC broadcast of June 18, 1940. According to William L. Shirer, *The Collapse of the Third Republic* (1969), "Not one single French military or political figure

of any consequence, even in London, offered to join the defiant general. He was utterly alone."

Battle of the Atlantic

Our American merchant ships must be protected by our American Navy. It can never be doubted that the goods will be delivered by this nation, whose Navy believes in the tradition of "Damn the torpedoes; full speed ahead!"
President Franklin D. Roosevelt, speech in Washington, D.C., October 27, 1941.

No attempt of any kind must be made at rescuing the crews of ships sunk. This prohibition applies to the picking up of men in the water and putting them in lifeboats, righting capsized lifeboats. . . . Be harsh, bearing in mind that the enemy take no regard of women and children in his bombing attack on German cities.
Admiral Karl Doenitz, 1942 order to U-boat commanders, quoted in Richard Hough, *The Longest Battle* (1986).

We got word that a [merchant] ship had been sunk during the night. I was on the signal tower when we reached the spot, just as dawn was lighting the scene. We saw hundreds of bodies in the water and lifeboats full of men swirled about us. It took me awhile to figure out why we did not stop to pick any of them up—they were frozen to death at the oars of their lifeboats. I saw the sea dotted with bobbing heads in life jackets. I started counting but realized there were hundreds so I gave up.
Robert Weikart, a merchant seaman, quoted in *Time* (March 8, 1943).

When war was declared, first against Great Britain, later against the United States, we in the German Navy saw ourselves as David being sent out to do battle with Goliath. At one point, when there were only 11 U-boats operational in the Atlantic against the enormous battle fleets of our enemies, it took a sort of cheeky gallows humor to put about the "positive" side of things: "Ah well, all the more tonnage to be sunk."
Peter Cremer, *U-Boat Commander* (1984).

Battle of the Bulge

All Hitler wants me to do is to cross a river, capture Brussels, and then go on and take Antwerp! And all this in the worst time of the year through the Ardennes where the snow is waist deep and there isn't room to deploy four tanks abreast let alone armored divisions! Where it doesn't get light until eight and it's dark again at four and with re-formed divisions made up chiefly of kids and sick old men—and at Christmas!
General Sepp Dietrich, complaining in 1944 of his assigned duties as head of the Sixth Panzer Army, quoted in Peter Elstob, *Hitler's Last Offensive* (1971).

Nuts!
This is the best-known single-word statement of World War II, spoken by Brigadier-General Anthony McAuliffe on December 22, 1944, in response to the demand of the Germans that he surrender his surrounded troops at Bastogne. There has been much speculation that McAuliffe really used another four-letter word much in use during World War II, but all historical accounts support the accuracy of "Nuts!" See John Toland, *Battle: The Story of the Bulge* (1959); Russell Weigley, *Eisenhower's Lieutenants* (1981); Charles B. MacDonald, *A Time for Trumpets* (1985).

The Americans have engaged 30 or 40 men for every one we have engaged and they have lost 60 to 80 men for every one of us. [It was] the greatest American battle of the war and will, I believe, be regarded as an ever famous American victory.
Winston Churchill, speech in the House of Commons, January 18, 1945.

As they left, Eisenhower was muttering. "Every time I get a new star," he said, "I get attacked." He had been promoted before the Kasserine Pass too.

"And every time you get attacked," replied Patton with a twinkle, "I pull you out."
David Irving, *The War Between the Generals* (1981).

"The present situation," he [General Eisenhower] said, "is to be regarded as one of
opportunity for us and not of disaster. There will be only cheerful faces at this conference table." To which [General] Patton responded: "Hell, let's have the guts to let the
sons of bitches go all the way to Paris. Then we'll really cut 'em up and chew 'em up."
Charles B. MacDonald, *A Time for Trumpets* (1985).

Blitzkrieg

We had seen a perfect specimen of the modern Blitzkrieg: the close interaction on
the battlefield of army and air force; the violent bombardment of all communications
and of any town that seemed an attractive target; the arming of an active Fifth Column; the free use of spies and parachutists; and above all, the irresistible forward
thrust of great masses of armor.
Winston Churchill, *The Second World War: The Gathering Storm* (1948).

When the theory had been originally developed, in Britain, its action had been
depicted in terms of the play of "lightning." From now on, aptly but ironically, it came
into worldwide currency under the title of "Blitzkrieg"—the German rendering.
B. H. Liddell Hart, *Memoirs*, II (1965).

Militarily, the Nazi forces had operated with awesome efficiency [in 1940]. The
coordination between air and ground, tanks and motorized infantry, exceeded anything we had ever dreamed of in the U.S. Army. We were amazed, shocked, dumbfounded, shaking our heads in disbelief. Here was modern open warfare—war of
maneuver—brought to the ultimate.
Omar Bradley and Clay Blair, *A General's Life* (1983).

Armored divisions would take the line of least resistance much as water flows down
a slope. Fanning out into the enemy's rear, their aim would be less to overcome enemy
resistance than to isolate and cut off segments of his forces. Victory in a campaign was
usually due less to heavy casualties on the defeated side than to confusion, disorganiza-
tion, and sheer panic. To paraphrase a famous dictum of Napoleon's, lightening war
was made with the tanks' tracks, not their guns.
Martin van Creveld, *Technology and War* (1989).

concentration camps

The things I saw beggar description. . . . I made a visit deliberately in order to be in a
position to give *first-hand* evidence of these things if ever, in the future, there develops
a tendency to charge these allegations merely to "propaganda."
General Dwight D. Eisenhower, letter to General George C. Marshall on visiting a German
concentration camp, April 15, 1945, quoted in Stephen D. Ambrose, *Eisenhower*, I (1983).

There were two rows of bodies stacked up like cordwood. They were thin and very
white. Some of the bodies were terribly bruised, though there seemed to be little flesh
to bruise. Some had been shot through the head, but they bled but little. All except two
were naked. I tried to count them as best I could and arrived at the conclusion that all
that was mortal of more than five hundred men and boys lay there in two neat
piles. . . .
I pray you to believe what I have said about Buchenwald. I have reported what I saw
and heard, but only part of it. For most of it I have no words.
Edward R. Murrow's radio broadcast on the liberation of Buchenwald (April 1945), quoted
in Alexander Kendrick, *Prime Time* (1969).

The banality of evil.
Hannah Arendt, *Eichmann in Jerusalem* (1963). This phrase drew great criticism. Barbara W. Tuchman wrote in *The New York Review of Books* (May 29, 1966) that "Eichmann was an extraordinary, not an ordinary man, whose record is hardly one of the 'banality' of evil. For the author of that ineffable phrase—as applied to the murder of six million—to have been so taken in by Eichmann's version of himself as just a routine civil servant obeying orders is one of the puzzles of modern journalism. From a presumed historian it is inexplicable."

One could smell the Wobelein Concentration Camp before seeing it. And seeing it was more than a human being could stand. Even after three years of war it brought tears to my eyes. Living skeletons were scattered about, the dead distinguishable from the living only by the blue-black color of their skin compared to the somewhat greenish skin, taut over the bony frames of the living.
General James M. Gavin, *On To Berlin* (1978).

D-Day
Believe me, Lang, the first twenty-four hours of the invasion will be decisive . . . the fate of Germany depends on the outcome . . . for the Allies, as well as Germany, it will be the longest day.
Field Marshal Erwin Rommel to an aide, April 22, 1944, quoted in Cornelius Ryan, *The Longest Day* (1959).

It's no exaggeration to say that all Amsterdam, all Holland, yes the whole west coast of Europe, right down to Spain, talks about the invasion day and night, debates about it, and makes bets on it and—hopes. . . .
The best part of the invasion is that I have the feeling that friends are approaching. We have been oppressed by those terrible Germans for so long, they have had their knives so at our throats, that the thought of friends and delivery fills me with confidence!
The Diary of Anne Frank (1953).

If things look black on the beaches, hold on! Do your best to move forward. There will be no turning back. More troops and equipment will follow you. There will be no surrender unless you are wounded and out of ammunition.
General Omar Bradley, in his last address to Colonel Red Reeder's Twelfth Infantry Regiment before the Normandy invasion, quoted in Edwin P. Hoyt, *The GI's War* (1988).

Our landings in the Cherbourg-Havre area have failed to gain a satisfactory foothold and I have withdrawn the troops. My decision to attack at this time and place was based upon the best information available. The troops, the air, and the Navy did all that bravery and devotion to duty could do. If any blame or fault attaches to the attempt it is mine alone.
General Dwight D. Eisenhower's June 5, 1944 prepared statement to be released to the press if the D-Day invasion failed, reprinted in Captain Harry C. Butcher, *My Three Years With Eisenhower* (1946).

You are about to embark upon the Great Crusade toward which we have striven these many months. The eyes of the world are upon you. The hopes and prayers of liberty-loving people everywhere march with you. In company with our brave allies you will bring about the destruction of the German war machine, the elimination of Nazi tyranny over the oppressed peoples of Europe, and security for ourselves in a free world.
Your task will not be an easy one. Your enemy is well trained, well equipped and battle-hardened. He will fight savagely. But the free men of the world are marching together to Victory.

Good Luck! And let us beseech the blessing of Almighty God upon this great and noble undertaking.
General Dwight D. Eisenhower, message to Allied forces just prior to D-Day, June 6, 1944.

The history of warfare does not know any such undertaking so broad in conception, so grandiose in scale, and so masterly in execution.
Joseph Stalin's words of tribute on the D-Day landing, quoted in *Newsweek* (June 26, 1944).

So far as I know, we entered France without anybody making a historic remark about it. Last time, you know, it was "Lafayette, we are here." The nearest I heard to a historic remark was made by an ack-ack gunner, sitting on a mound of earth about two weeks after D-day, reading the *Stars and Stripes* from London. All of a sudden he said, "Say, where's this Normandy beachhead it talks about in here?"
I looked at him closely and saw that he was serious, so I said, "Why, you're sitting on it."
And he said, "Well, I'll be damned. I never knowed that."
Ernie Pyle, *Brave Men* (1944).

Colonel Charles D. Canham . . ., a bloody handkerchief tied around a wrist wound, moved through the dead, the dying and the shocked, waving groups of men forward. "They're murdering us here!" he said. "Let's move inland and get murdered!"
Cornelius Ryan, *The Longest Day* (1959).

Many men who had spent hours worrying about their chances of survival now [on D-Day] couldn't wait to reach the beaches. The boat trip was proving more terrible than their worst fear of the Germans. Seasickness had struck . . . like a plague, especially in the rolling landing craft. Each man had been supplied with antiseasickness pills, plus an article of equipment which was listed in the loading sheets with typical Army thoroughness as "Bag, vomit, one."
Cornelius Ryan, *The Longest Day* (1959).

Too many people knew about Overlord already—the time and place. By mid-May [1944] no fewer than 549 officers assigned to SHAEF headquarters alone would have the vital information. Some men could not keep the secret. On April 18, General Edwin Sibert, Bradley's G-2—intelligence officer—was eating in the public dining room at Claridge's when Major General Henry Miller, of the Ninth Air Force, began arguing with a Red Cross woman and, "obviously intoxicated," according to Sibert, named the target date for Overlord three times, in a voice loud enough to be heard even by the waiters. Sibert sent a handwritten report to Bradley. . . . Miller . . . was busted to lieutenant colonel and sent home in disgrace.
David Irving, *The War Between Generals* (1981).

D-Day was one of the greatest political blunders of all time. If Great Britain and the United States had uttered a single word publicly of encouragement to the conspirators [against Hitler] then Montgomery and Eisenhower would have walked ashore, and Rommel would have been there to salute them. . . . In their blind hatred of Germany they failed to see the greater enemy beyond the horizon—Russia. Only fools could have failed to perceive that the real enemy was Russia and that one day the western powers would need a strong and democratic Germany to act as a counterweight to Bolshevism.
Charles V.P. von Luttichau quoted in Anthony Cave Brown, *Bodyguard of Lies* (1975). Brown comments that "Von Luttichau was both right and wrong. Certainly the course of history would have been altered if the Allies had been able to walk ashore on D-Day. But to hold the Allies solely responsible for the phenomenon of Hitler, and his continuation in

power even to the moment of his suicide in a ravaged Berlin, is to absolve the conspirators . . . and the German people themselves, of their share of the responsibility."

Dieppe

The raid was a reconnaissance in force, having a vital part of our agreed offensive policy.
Official British description of the Dieppe raid, *Time* (August 31, 1942).

The most interesting bit of fact I have picked up, and I think my source reliable, is that the Canadians have spoken up vigorously for an early second front at official military discussions of the problem here. This may help to explain why Dieppe was so predominantly a Canadian affair. It looks as though the British said, "Well, if you're so anxious for a second front, go and try one."
I. F. Stone, "Capital Thoughts on a Second Front," *The Nation* (October 3, 1942).

To the end of his life, "Dieppe" was engraved upon Mountbatten's heart, and the name would always raise an instant defensive response, almost as if he were protesting too much.
Richard Hough, *Mountbatten* (1981).

In fact the word "failure" cannot be applied in simple definition of the Dieppe raid. The lessons learned were of critical importance in the planning and execution of the invasion almost two years later, saving many times more lives than were lost in this operation. The most important was the realization that it would not be possible to attack and hold a port and use it for delivering supplies. The Allies would have to build their own ports.
Richard Hough, *The Longest Battle* (1986).

Dunkirk

Presume troops know they are fighting their way home to Blighty. Never was there such a spur to fighting.
Winston Churchill to Lord Gort at the beginning of the Dunkirk evacuation, quoted in Nicholas Harman, *Dunkirk* (1980). "Blighty" was a World War I term for *home*.

We must be very careful not to assign to this deliverance the attributes of a victory. Wars are not won by evacuations.
Winston Churchill, speech in the House of Commons, June 4, 1940.

The little ships, the unforgotten Homeric catalogue of *Mary Jane* and *Peggy IV*, of *Folkestone Belle, Boy Billy*, and *Ethel Maud*, of *Lady Haig* and *Skylark* . . . the little ships of England brought the Army home.
Philip Guedalla, *Mr. Churchill* (1942).

Winston Churchill, in his memoirs . . . assumes, quite correctly, that Hitler and above all Goering believed German air supremacy to be strong enough to prevent the evacuation of the British forces by sea. This belief was a mistake pregnant with consequence.
General Heinz Guderian, *Panzer Leader* (1952).

We've got the men away, but we've lost the luggage.
Winston Churchill's report to his cabinet on the Dunkirk evacuation, quoted in Hugh Dalton, *The Fateful Years* (1957).

This lack of sleep affected everyone, high and low, with one exception—General Montgomery. During the whole of the withdrawal he insisted on having meals at regu-

lar hours and never missed his normal night's sleep. Consequently when we arrived at Dunkirk he was fresh as when he started. And he was about the only one who was.
General Sir Brian Horrocks, *A Full Life* (1960).

"Al" Deere, the New Zealand ace . . . had experience of the army's bitterness. He was shot down . . . and crashlanded his Spitfire . . . on a beach fifteen miles from Dunkirk. Thumbing a lift and stealing a bicycle, he forged his way through the throng of refugees, and finally walked the last miles to the causeway. As he ran towards one of the evacuation destroyers, he was stoped by an angry army major.
"I am an RAF officer," said the bedraggled, roughly bandaged Deere. "I am trying to get back to my squadron which is operating over here."
"I don't give a damn who you are," shouted the major. "For all the good you chaps seem to be doing, you might as well stay on the ground." Deere escaped him and made his way to the wardroom of the destroyer, to be greeted by stony silence from a throng of army officers.
"Why so friendly?" asked Deere. "What have the RAF done?"
"That's just it . . . what have they done?"
Len Deighton, *Battle of Britain* (1980). According to William L. Shirer, *The Rise and Fall of the Third Reich* (1959), a goodly percentage of the Tommies on the beaches at Dunkirk were unaware of the extensive efforts of the RAF "since the air clashes were often above the clouds or some distance away. They knew only that they had been bombed and strafed all the way back from eastern Belgium to Dunkirk, and they felt their Air Force had let them down. When they reached the home ports some of them insulted men in the blue R.A.F. uniforms. Churchill was much aggrieved at this and went out of his way to put them right when he spoke in the House on June 4. The deliverance at Dunkirk, he said, 'was gained by the Air Force.' "

At Dunkirk . . . thousands of mines littered the shallow waters off the coast. Hitler was convinced that these would prevent any mass evacuation of British forces. German mines worked North Pole downward only . . . we magnetized our ships South Pole downward so that the ships repelled the mines. The Admiralty embarked on a massive program of reversing the magnetism of all the ships going to Dunkirk. The result was that not a single ship was lost to mines.
Peter Wright, *Spycatcher* (1987).

Holocaust

I herewith commission you to carry out all preparations with regard to . . . a total solution of the Jewish question in those territories of Europe which are under German influence. . . . I furthermore charge you to submit to me as soon as possible a draft showing the . . . measures already taken for the execution of the intended final solution of the Jewish question.
Hermann Goering's July 31, 1941 directive to Reinhard Heydrich, quoted in William L. Shirer, *The Rise and Fall of the Third Reich* (1959). According to Shirer, "Heydrich knew very well what Goering meant by the term [final solution] for he had used it himself nearly a year before at a secret meeting after the fall of Poland, in which he had outlined the first step in the final solution, which consisted of concentrating all the Jews in the ghettos of the large cities, where it would be easy to dispatch them to their final fate."

Those who were killed in the gas chambers by Hitler were the last Jews to die without defending themselves.
Golda Meir, Prime Minister of Israel, quoted in Israel and Mary Shenker, *As Good as Golda* (1970).

Granted that in warfare all parties may and usually do commit atrocities, it still remains true that the Germans pioneered in industrial methods of extermination. They were the first to build factories for that purpose, to deport the living *en masse* and process them, in certain installations, not merely into bones and ash but into usable by-products (soap, leather, reclaimed gold from teeth, etc.). Such methods certainly rate special mention if only because they contributed materially to the defeat and death of those who invented them.

Charles Fair, *From the Jaws of Victory* (1971).

There were many ways of not burdening one's conscience, of shunning responsibility, looking away, keeping mum. When the unspeakable truth of the Holocaust then became known at the end of the war, all too many of us claimed that they had not known anything about it or even suspected anything.

Richard von Weisacker, President of West Germany, speaking on the 40th anniversary of the end of World War II, *The New York Times* (May 12, 1985).

I do not bring forgiveness with me, nor forgetfulness. The only ones who can forgive are dead; the living have no right to forget.

Chaim Herzog, President of Israel, on visiting a concentration campsite in Germany, quoted in *The New York Times* (April 12, 1987).

lend-lease

Suppose my neighbor's home catches fire, and I have a length of garden hose four or five hundred feet away. If he can take my garden hose and connect it up with his hydrant, I may help him to put out his fire. Now, what do I do? I don't say to him before the operation, "Neighbor, my garden hose cost me $15, you have to pay me $15 for it." What is the transaction that goes on? I don't want $15—I want my garden hose back after the fire is over.

After the fire is put out, he puts the garden hose back, and if it is damaged beyond repair in putting out the fire, he (my neighbor) says, "All right, I will replace it."

Now, if I get a nice garden hose back, I am in pretty good shape.

President Franklin D. Roosevelt, in a press conference describing how lend-lease would theoretically work, December 17, 1940.

Give us the tools, and we will finish the job.

Winston Churchill, BBC broadcast, February 9, 1941.

The American Navy will provide protection as adequate as we can make it for ships of every flag carrying Lend-Aid supplies between the American Continent and the waters adjacent to Iceland. These ships are ordered to capture or destroy by every means at their disposal Axis-controlled submarines or surface raiders encountered in these waters. That is our answer to Mr. Hitler.

Secretary of the Navy Frank Knox, *Newsweek* (September 22, 1941).

In World War II we used a system called lend-lease, and I heard often in my headquarters people criticize this scheme.... I never could feel that way about it.... It took a rifle and a man to go out and advance the cause of the Allies against the enemies we had. If the U.S. could provide merely the rifle and get someone else to carry it in order to do the work that was necessary, I was perfectly content.

General Dwight D. Eisenhower, speech to members of Congress at the Library of Congress, February 1, 1951.

The American people have been so fooled as to the purpose and character of this bill that there remains no hope of adequately amending it. It is a war bill, and yet 95% of the people think it is only aid to Britain.

President Herbert Hoover, quoted in Richard Norton Smith, *An Uncommon Man* (1984).

Sicily

One chipper little man who had been shot full of shrapnel and machine-gun bullets was very chatty. I asked him what he thought of Sicily and he said, "The Germans were all right and the Eyties were all right but the mosquitoes were bloody awful!"
Noel Coward, *Middle East Diary* (1944).

[General George] Patton became nearly irrational in his determination to beat Monty to Messina. He stopped me on the road and exhorted: "I want to get to Messina just as fast as you can. I don't want you to waste time on these maneuvers, even if you've got to spend men to do it. I want to beat Monty into Messina." I was shocked. The orders sickened me. I ignored them. I continued to maneuver and refused to waste lives merely for the sake of winning a meaningless race.
General Omar N. Bradley (speaking) and Clay Blair, *A General's Life: An Autobiography* (1983).

Had it been left up to me, I would not have included Patton in Overlord. I did not look forward to having him in my command. He had shown in Sicily that he did not know how to run an army; his legendary reputation (now badly tarnished) was the product of an uncritical media buildup. But Ike insisted on Patton for his undeniable drive.
General Omar N. Bradley (speaking) and Clay Blair, *A General's Life: An Autobiography* (1983).

As far as General [Francis] de Guingand was concerned there was neither race nor rivalry from Montgomery's point of view—"no, none. It was all balls that, about who was going to get to Messina [in Sicily] first. We were *delighted* when we heard that Patton had got to Messina first"—and about the fictitious scene in the film *Patton*, de Guingand was even more acid: "Absolute cock, in the film: Monty marching at the head of the Highlanders—all balls!"
Nigel Hamilton, *Master of the Battlefield* (1983).

Tobruk

Tobruk was a pleasant coastal city sandwiched between the Mediterranean and the desert. It was also the only first-class natural harbor on the long Libyan coastline between Alexandria and Benghazi, and in a desert war where supplies were often difficult to come by (and living off the land was wholly impossible), the value of such a port could hardly be overestimated.
William K. Klingaman, *1941* (1988).

On the morning of June 21st [1942] Rommel was able to report that Tobruk was in his hands. Next day he learnt by wireless from Hitler's headquarters that he was a Field-Marshal, at forty-nine the youngest in the German Army. That evening he celebrated his promotion—on tinned pineapple and one small glass of whisky.... After dinner he wrote to his wife: "Hitler has made me a Field-Marshal. I would much rather he had given me one more division."
Desmond Young, *Rommel* (1950).

The commander of the army corps of which the New Zealand Division formed a part is reported to have wired, when the first contact was made: "Tobruk is relieved, but not half so much as I am!"
Russell Hill, "Tobruk Liberated," *They Were There*, ed. Curt Riess (1944).

Yalta

The leaders of the three great powers—the Soviet Union, the United States of America and Great Britain—have agreed that in two or three months after Germany

has surrendered and the war in Europe has terminated, the Soviet Union shall enter into the war against Japan on the side of the Allies.
> The Yalta Far Eastern Agreement of February 11, 1945, reprinted in Department of State, *Foreign Relations of the United States: The Conferences at Malta and Yalta* (1955).

I do not see any other way of realizing our hopes about world organization in five or six days. Even the Almighty took seven.
> Winston Churchill, on President Franklin D. Roosevelt's hopes to complete the Yalta Conference in five or six days, *The Second World War: Triumph and Tragedy* (1953).

What we were faced with at Yalta was how to make good our principles in territories that Stalin held. Stalin had the power to act, we had only the power to argue. . . . The West paid the political price for having failed to deter Hitler in the 1930s, for having failed to unite and to rearm against him.
> Walter Lippmann, writing in 1955, quoted in Ronald Steel, *Walter Lippman and the American Century* (1980).

World War II, Pacific

Every Japanese has been told it is his duty to die for the Emperor. It is your duty to see that he does.
> Instructions to U.S. Marines quoted in John W. Dower, *War Without Mercy* (1986).

If you are shot down, try and get picked up by the Japanese military as quickly as possible. The civilians will kill you outright.
> Advice to B-29 crews on bombing runs over Japan, quoted in Martin Caidin, *A Torch to the Enemy: The Fire Raid on Tokyo* (1960).

Our original plan called for 15,000 men to wipe out 9,000 Japs on New Georgia; by the time the island was secured, we had sent in more than 50,000. When I look back on [Operation] Elkton the smoke of charred reputations still makes me cough.
> Admiral William F. Halsey quoted in James H. Belote and William M. Belote, *Titans of the Sea* (1975).

Admiral [Chester] Nimitz made a speech, and he answered questions. Someone asked him whether he was going to continue bombing these Japanese islands in the Pacific or bypass them. Admiral Nimitz said that brought up a very difficult question as to whether it was better to bypass them or let them starve all at once by cutting off their supply, or let them live longer by reducing their number, in which case it would take him longer to get the island and use it. Jokingly he said that was the big problem: starve or bomb.
> Admiral Raymond D. Tarbuck quoted in D. Clayton James, *The Years of MacArthur*, II (1975).

Neither the British . . . nor the Americans really regarded the Japanese as human beings. Their fantastic bravery and spirit of self-sacrifice was seen merely as a dangerous form of insanity, and one killed them as one might exterminate a particularly intransigent pest.
> John Ellis, *The Sharp End: The Fighting Man in World War II* (1980).

The American submarine was the most decisive winning weapon of the Pacific campaign. No single class of warship did as much as the submarine to defeat the Japanese. . . . Yet the American people knew little about the work of the US submarine service at the time, and even today. . . their war-winning contribution is not widely appreciated.

There are three reasons for this. Firstly, by the very nature of the beast, its unexciting configuration, its secretive . . . almost underhand method of fighting does not make the submarine as immediately attractive a man o'war as, say, the mighty battleship. . . . Secondly, while Germany was being pilloried for its unrestricted warfare against merchantmen in the Atlantic, a similar campaign pursued with equal ruthlessness in the Pacific did not call for propaganda exploitation. Thirdly, the United States did not think it was in its interests to reveal its secrets and its successes to the enemy.
Richard Hough, *The Longest Battle* (1986).

Even after the passage of all these years it is very difficult for me to forgive the enemy who killed those young Americans or to forget the hatred and the ferocity that existed on both sides of the conflict. I have heard it said that men who go into battle against each other in their youth often become friends in their old age. This opportunity for reconciliation has never presented itself to me. Every Japanese of my own age whom I have met since the end of the war seems to have fought against the Chinese in China or the British in Malaya or the French in Indochina, never against the Americans in the islands of the Pacific. Remembering the scorched and blood-soaked islands where U.S. Marines and Japanese infantry engaged each other in combat, I am not surprised that this should be so.
Donald T. Regan, *For the Record* (1988).

Anyone who actually fought in the Pacific recalls the Japanese routinely firing on medics, killing the wounded (torturing them first, if possible), and cutting off the penises of the dead to stick in the corpses' mouths. The degree to which Americans register shock and extraordinary shame about the Hiroshima bomb correlates closely with the lack of information about the Pacific war.
Paul Fussell, *Thank God for the Atom Bomb* (1988).

Despite the best that has been done by everyone the war situation has developed not necessarily to Japan's advantage. Moreover, the enemy has begun to employ a new and most cruel bomb. We have resolved to pave the way for a grand peace for all the generations to come by enduring the unendurable and suffering the insufferable.
Emperor Hirohito's radio address to his nation at the close of the war, quoted in *Time* (August 27, 1945).

Cease firing, but if any enemy planes appear shoot them down in friendly fashion.
Admiral William F. Halsey's orders after the Japanese surrender was announced—necessitated by the fact that some Kamikaze pilots were still active, *Newsweek* (August 27, 1945). In Halsey's memoirs, he remembers his orders as "Investigate and shoot down all snoopers—not vindictively, but in a friendly sort of way." William F. Halsey and J. Bryan III, *Admiral Halsey's Story* (1947). Halsey states, "I was told later that one pilot had been overheard to ask, 'What do you mean, "not vindictively?"' And another answered, 'I guess they mean for us to use only three guns instead of six.'"

These proceedings are closed.
General Douglas MacArthur, final words on accepting Japan's surrender in Tokyo Bay aboard the USS *Missouri* on September 2, 1945, quoted in Alistair Cooke, *America* (1973).

Bataan
We're the battling bastards of Bataan:
No mama, no papa, no Uncle Sam,
No aunts, no uncles, no nephews, no nieces,
No rifles, no planes, or artillery pieces,

And nobody gives a damn.
Song of the U.S. soldiers during the 1942 defense of Bataan in the Philippines, quoted in *Time* (March 9, 1942); Louis Morton, *The Fall of the Philippines* (1953).

Dugout Doug MacArthur lies ashaking on the Rock
Safe from all the bombers and from any shock
Dugout Doug is eating of the best food on Bataan
And his troops go starving on.
Dugout Doug's not timid, he's just cautious, not afraid
He's protecting carefully the stars that Franklin made
Four-star generals are rare as good food on Bataan
And his troops go starving on.
Chorus:
Dugout Doug, come out from hiding
Dugout Doug, come out from hiding
Send to Franklin the glad tidings
That his troops go starving on!
Anonymously written song sung to the tune of "The Battle Hymn of the Republic" by General MacArthur's troops on Bataan in 1942, quoted in Ernest B. Miller, *Bataan Uncensored* (1949).

Bataan has fallen, but the spirit that made it stand—a beacon to all the liberty-loving people of the world—cannot fail!
Lieutenant Norman Reyes, radio report from Corregidor, April 9, 1942, quoted in Carlos P. Romulo, *I Saw the Fall of the Philippines* (1942).

Bataan is like a child in a family who dies. It lives in our hearts.
General Douglas MacArthur, comment on the first anniversary of the fall of Bataan, April 9, 1942, *The New York Times* (April 9, 1943).

No army has ever done so much with so little.
General Douglas MacArthur, comment on the fall of Bataan, *The New York Times* (April 11, 1942).

Most of the men on Bataan were probably too exhausted or disease-ridden to exhibit a strong reaction either way to MacArthur's leaving, but among some who responded negatively the feeling ran deep. . . . In one regiment on Bataan it became "standard practice" to say on the appropriate occasion, "I am going to the latrine, but I shall return."
D. Clayton James, *The Years of MacArthur*, II (1975).

Guadalcanal

And when he gets to Heaven,
To Saint Peter he will tell:
"One more Marine reporting, Sir—
I've served my time in Hell."
Marine grave inscription on Guadalcanal.

In the midst of the exciting run [during the 1942 naval battle over Guadalcanal], a dead calm Cdr William Cole [of the destroyer *Fletcher*] spoke through the louvered porthole between the bridge and the charthouse to let his exec, LCdr Joe Wylie, know how things were going. "You ought to see this. It looks like the Fourth of July out here." A few moments later, the captain added, "Aren't you glad our wives don't know where we are tonight?"
Eric Hammel, *Guadalcanal: Decision at Sea* (1988).

In our outfits we adopted the custom of dropping all ranks and titles. We used nicknames for the officers. All ranks used these nicknames for us. We did this because the Nips caught on to names of the officers and would yell or speak in the night. "This is Captain Joe Smith talking. A Company, withdraw to the next hill."
Colonel Merritt A. Edson quoted in K. Ayling, *Semper Fidelis* (1943).

Down the beach one of the Japs had jumped up and was running for the jungle. "There he goes!" was the shout. "Riddle the son of a bitch!" And riddled he was.
Richard Tregaskis, *Guadalcanal Diary* (1943).

Having sent General Patch to do a tailoring job in Guadalcanal, I am surprised and pleased at the speed with which he removed the enemy's pants to accomplish it.
Admiral William F. Halsey, *The New York Times* (February 11, 1943).

The cries in high-pitched English rent the darkness. "Blood for the Emperor! Marine you die!" A gutsy voice yelled back: "To hell with your goddamned Emperor! Blood for Franklin and Eleanor!"
John Costello, *The Pacific War* (1981).

Hiroshima

Sixteen hours ago an American airplane dropped one bomb on Hiroshima, an important Japanese Army base. The bomb has more power than 20,000 tons of T.N.T. It had more than two thousand times the blast power of the British "Grand Slam" which is the largest bomb ever yet used in the history of warfare.

The Japanese began the war from the air at Pearl Harbor. They have been repaid many fold. And the end is not yet. With this bomb we have now added a new and revolutionary increase in destruction to supplement the growing power of our armed forces. In their present form these bombs are now in production and even more powerful forms are in development.

It is an atomic bomb. It is a harnessing of the basic power of the universe. The force from which the sun draws its power has been loosed against those who brought war to the Far East.
Statement by the President of the United States (Harry S. Truman), White House Press Release on Hiroshima, August 6, 1945.

In Hiroshima, thirty days after the first atom bomb destroyed the city and shook the world, people are still dying, mysteriously and horribly, people who were uninjured in the cataclysm—from an unknown something which I can only describe as the atomic plague.
Wilfred Burchett, *Daily Express* (London) (September 5, 1945). This was the first report of radiation sickness.

A night-time atomic explosion high over Tokyo, in full sight of Emperor Hirohito and his Cabinet, would have been just as terrifying as Hiroshima. And it would have frightened the right people.
Edward Teller, *The Legacy of Hiroshima* (1962).

Concerning Hiroshima, [Harold] Agnew told a story about a pair of NATO officers, both World War II veterans, whom he had recently met in Europe. One of the two, an Englishman, had asked the other, a German, how he came by his wooden leg. "In the Battle of Britain," the German answered. Agnew said that the Englishman's reply reflected how he, Agnew, had always felt about the decision to drop the atomic bombs on Japan. "Good," the Englishman had said. "You bloody well deserved it."
Gregg Herken, *Counsels of War* (1987).

Hiroshima, which was not much of a city to begin with, sort of a Japanese Toledo, made the best of a horrid situation, and generated a respectable tourist trade from being flattened in an innovative manner. Nagasaki, at the wrong end of Japan and lacking an airport, just went back to work—nobody cares about who is second.
B. Bruce-Briggs, *The Shield of Faith* (1989).

Iwo Jima
Among the men who fought on Iwo Jima uncommon valor was a common virtue.
Admiral Chester W. Nimitz, March 16, 1945, quoted in E. B. Potter, *Nimitz* (1976).

Iwo Jima was the most savage and the most costly battle in the history of the Marine Corps.
General Holland Smith, USMC, quoted in Samuel Eliot Morison, *The Two-Ocean War* (1963).

The raising of that flag on Suribachi means there will be a Marine Corps for the next 500 years.
Secretary of the Navy James V. Forrestal quoted in Allan R. Millett, *Semper Fidelis* (1980).

Darkroom technicians knew immediately that the Suribachi photo was something very special. It didn't fit the pattern of a conventional news picture; the face of only one man was clearly visible, the rest were either hidden by hands and arms raising the flag, or their heads were turned.
But it was a masterpiece of instantaneous composition and lighting that captured the mood of the unfolding drama on Iwo Jima. Its stage-like setting and the powerful position of the men gave it the graven look of a posed statue; so much so, in fact, that cynics and critics of the Marine Corps later suggested the photo was staged. . . .
When the photo appeared on front pages of virtually every newspaper in the States, it became an instant symbol for millions on the homefront—an indelible portrait of patriotism and determination.
Bill D. Ross, *Iwo Jima* (1983).

kamikaze
With my death, I desire to make atonement to the souls of you who fell gallantly as human bullets.
Japanese Admiral Takejiro Onishi (in charge of kamikaze pilots towards the end of World War II), letter before he killed himself, *Time* (August 27, 1945).

Referring to the circumstances in which our pilots joined the suicide-squads, it is often asked: "Were they really volunteers, or acting on official orders?" I have no intention of glorifying this event, unique in the history of war, but as a witness who survived, I can affirm that our own wishes were in perfect accord with orders from the high command.
Ryuji Nagatsuka, *I Was a Kamikaze* (1972).

Very much like the Muslims of Iran in the 1970's and 1980's, Japanese serviceman were taught to believe that if they died in battle, especially if they died heroically, they would instantly become "gods," and join the guardian spirits of the nation.
Hachiro Hosokawa, Preface to Hatsuho Nacto, *Thunder Gods* (1989).

Midway
Sighted aircraft carrier. Am trailing same. Please notify next of kin.
Last message of an American search plane pilot in the Battle of Midway, quoted in *Newsweek* (June 7, 1943).

The Battle of Midway was the first decisive defeat suffered by the Japanese Navy in 350 years. Furthermore it put an end to the long period of Japanese offensive action, and restored the balance of naval power in the Pacific.
Admiral Ernest J. King, *Fleet Admiral King* (1952).

The attackers had got in unimpeded because our [Japanese] fighters, which had engaged the preceding wave of torpedo planes only a few moments earlier, had not yet had time to regain altitude. Consequently, it may be said that the American dive-bombers' success was made possible by the earlier martyrdom of their torpedo planes. Also, our carriers had no time to evade because clouds hid the enemy's approach until he dived down to the attack. We had been caught flatfooted in the most vulnerable condition possible—decks loaded with planes armed and fuelled for an attack.
Mitsuo Fuchida, *Midway* (1957).

Told by aides that the enemy was about to attack, Admiral Frank Jack Fletcher, bent over and studying charts, rejoined, "Well, I have my tin hat on. I can't do anything else now!"
James H. Belote and William M. Belote, *Titans of the Seas* (1975).

[After the Battle of Midway] the Chicago Tribune headlined: "NAVY HAD WORD OF JAPAN PLAN TO STRIKE AT SEA." The reporter Stanley Johnson had seen an after-action dispatch from which he was able to deduce the explosive revelation that victory had been made possible by a dramatic intelligence breakthrough. The story raised a storm behind the scenes, with [Admiral] King charging that it endangered the entire Pacific War. The panic blew over, however, when it appeared that Tokyo's intelligence staff apparently did not read American newspapers.
John Costello, *The Pacific War* (1981).

In human terms Midway had been a "cheap" battle for vanquished and victors alike. The Japanese had lost not more than 3000 dead, the Americans fewer than 1000—a total of fatalities lower than either Trafalgar or Jutland. The aeroplane, though deadly as a ship-killer in precision strikes, spared crews the terrible battering of repetitive gunnery salvoes in the flank-to-flank engagements of the battle line. This was not to mean that the great Pacific War would be a "cheap" campaign. As it swelled in intensity, and Japanese resistance to the American inexorable counter-offensive grew in desperation, crew losses would rise in horrifying number.
John Keegan, *The Price of Admiralty* (1988).

Pearl Harbor
There is a lot of talk around town to the effect that the Japanese, in case of a break with the United States, are planning to go all out in a surprise mass attack on Pearl Harbor. I rather guess that the boys in Hawaii are not precisely asleep.
U.S. Ambassador to Japan Joseph Grew's early 1941 report to Washington, quoted in Joseph C. Grew, *Turbulent Era* (1952).

The Germans have announced that they are going into winter quarters in front of Moscow. That means that Moscow is not going to fall this winter. That means that the Japanese cannot attack us in the Pacific without running the risk of a two-front war. The Japanese are too smart to run that risk.
Admiral Husband Kimmel on December 6, 1941, explaining why there would not be a war in the Pacific, quoted in Paul Stillwell, *Air Raid: Pearl Harbor* (1981).

The Japanese are presenting at 1 p.m. Eastern Standard Time today what amounts to an ultimatum. Also they are under orders to destroy their code machine immediately. Just what significance the hour set may have we do not know, but be on the alert accordingly.

General George C. Marshall, alert message sent on December 6, 1941, to warn Pacific commanders (it arrived in Pearl Harbor via Western Union during the Japanese attack), quoted in John Toland, *Infamy* (1982).

I am proud to report that the American people may feel fully confident in their Navy. In my opinion, the loyalty, morale and technical ability of the personnel are without superior. On any comparable basis, the United States Navy is second to none.

Secretary of the Navy Frank Knox, in his annual report on the Navy Department, released December 6, 1941, quoted in *The New York Times* (December 7, 1941).

I fear all we have done is to awaken a sleeping giant and fill him with a terrible resolve.

Attributed to Isoroku Yamamoto, the Japanese admiral who led the attack on Pearl Harbor.

[Admiral Chester W.] Nimitz arrived at Pearl Harbor in a Navy flying boat on Christmas morning, 1941. As a whaleboat carried him from his plane across the harbor to the dock, the Admiral could see a number of small craft moving about the harbor searching for the bodies of sailors. Corpses were still rising to the surface from the sunken battleships.

Disregarding Admiral King's idea that he ought to "rid Pearl Harbor of pessimists and defeatists," Nimitz brought to Hawaii only a flag secretary; he asked most of the old Pacific Fleet staff to serve under him. Some of the most able officers of the Navy were saved from professional oblivion in this way.

Ronald H. Spector, *Eagle Against the Sun* (1985).

Even now, when we know how meticulously and minutely (and, let us confess, brilliantly) the Japanese planned their attacks, we still find the Army Board of Inquiry talking nonsense about "the Oriental mind" and attributing the Pearl Harbor blitz to "the violent and uncivilized reasoning of the Japanese."

I. F. Stone, "Brass Hats Undaunted," *The Nation* (September 8, 1945).

The surprise attack on Pearl Harbor, far from being a "strategic necessity," as the Japanese claimed even after the war, was a strategic imbecility. One can search in vain for an operation more fatal to the aggressor.

Samuel E. Morison, *History of the U. S. Naval Operations in World War II*, III (1948).

Japanese naval officers in dress whites are frequent guests at [Pearl Harbor's] officers' mess [and] are very polite. . . . They always were. Except, of course, for that little interval there between 1941 and 1945.

William Manchester, *Goodbye Darkness* (1980).

At the sun-drenched pier at Pearl Harbor last month was an astonishing sight: the aircraft carrier USS Nimitz, with its sleek jet fighters lined up on deck; the nuclear-powered guided-missile cruiser USS Long Beach—and seven Japanese Navy destroyers flying the rising-sun flag. Each Japanese warship was decorated with garlands of flowers over its bow in welcome to the Hawaiian port, which Japan attacked on Dec. 7, 1941 to begin its war with the United States.

The arrival of the Japanese "Maritime Self-Defense Force" in Honolulu as part of extensive joint military exercises with the United States, Australia and Canada is one of many signs of change these days in East Asia and the Pacific.

Don Oberdorfer, "We Are Witnessing the Dawning of a New Pacific Age," *The Washington Post National Weekly* (August 8–14, 1988).

Pearl Harbor, European reactions

[On hearing of the Pearl Harbor attack] I could not conceal my relief and did not have to try to. I felt that whatever happened now, it was merely a question of time. Before, we had believed in the end but never seen the means, now both were clear.
Anthony Eden, *Memoirs: The Reckoning* (1965).

We cannot lose the war! Now we have a partner [Japan] who has not been defeated in three thousand years.
Hitler's reaction to the Pearl Harbor Attack, quoted in John Toland, *Adolf Hitler* (1976).

The war is over. Of course there are years of fighting ahead, but the Germans are beaten.
General Charles de Gaulle, on first hearing of the Pearl Harbor attack, quoted in Bernard Ledwidge, *De Gaulle* (1982).

wounded

Think also of the poor wounded. . . . Especially have a paternal care for your own and do not be inhuman to those of the enemy.
Frederick the Great, *Instructions for His Generals* (1747).

The history of a soldier's wound beguiles the pain of it.
Laurence Sterne, *Tristram Shandy* (1760).

Although Louis XIV did no actual fighting himself, he took the liveliest interest in all that happened to his armies, even to the personal welfare of the common soldiers. He issued orders that wounded men should receive the best of care. They might be needed again.
Will Cuppy, *The Decline and Fall of Practically Everybody* (1950).

It is nothing. For this we are soldiers!
Captain Guy V. Henry, remark after being seriously wounded by Indians in 1876, quoted in Fairfax Downey, *Indian Fighting Army* (1943). Henry recovered and eventually became a general.

The enlisted men were exceedingly accurate judges of the probable result which would ensue from any wound they saw. They had seen hundreds of soldiers wounded, and they had noticed that certain wounds always resulted fatally. They knew when they were fatally wounded, and after the shock of discovery had passed, they generally braced themselves and died in a manly manner. It was seldom that an American or Irish volunteer flunked in the presence of death.
Frank Wilkeson, *Recollections of a Private Soldier in the Army of the Potomac* (1887).

Safe with his wound, a citizen of life,
He hobbled blithely through the garden gate,
And thought: "Thank God they had to amputate!"
Siegfried Sassoon, *The One-Legged Man* (1918).

On the parados lay a wounded man of another battalion, shot, to judge by the blood on his clothes, through the loins or stomach. I went to him and he grunted, as if to say, "I am in horrible pain, you must do something for me; you must do something for me." I hate touching wounded men—moral cowardice, I suppose. One hurts them so much and there's so little to be done. I tried, without much success, to ease his equipment, and then thought of getting him into the trench. But it was crowded with men and there was no place to put him. So I left him. He grunted again angrily and looked at me with hatred as well as pain his eyes. It was horrible. It was as though he

cursed me for being alive and strong when he was in torture. I tried to forget him by taking a spade from one of the men and working fiercely on the parapet.
R. H. Tawney, on his experiences in World War I, quoted in Guy Chapman, ed., *Vain Glory* (1968).

It was the receipt of wounds, not the infliction of death, which demonstrated an officer's courage; that demonstration was reinforced by his refusal to leave his post even when wounded, or by his insistence on returning as soon as his wounds had been dressed; and it was by a punctiliousness in obeying orders which made wounds or death inevitable that an officer's honor was consummated.
John Keegan, *The Face of Battle* (1976).

I feel like a fugitive from th' law of averages.
The statement of an unwounded combat veteran depicted in a Bill Mauldin cartoon in *Up Front* (1944).

I caught a bullet through the chest. . . . I'll never forget the sequence of thoughts: "Oh shit I've been hit. I got it right in the gut. My girl, she's going to kill me." Then I said, "I don't got to worry about that, I'm going to die."
Then I was just on the ground looking up at the sky and I just felt a warm glow, very mellow, and I felt like a balloon that was deflating. I just felt, blubbbbbb, I was going down. Nothing I could do about it at all. "Okay," I said, "I don't got to worry about it, I'm going to die." And my last words were, "I don't believe it. On this shitty piece of ground, I'm going to die. I don't fucking believe it."
. . . .I woke up with tubes everywhere. But I was stunned, amazed, overwhelmed and ecstatic over the fact that I woke up at all.
The doctors came and said, "You're probably going to be paralyzed for the rest of your life." My reaction to that was, "So what?"
Bobby Muller quoted in Kim Willenson, *The Bad War: An Oral History of the Vietnam War* (1987).

Biographical Appendix

Abrams, Creighton Williams (1914–1974) U.S. Army General, commanded U.S. forces in Vietnam 1968–72.

Acheson, Dean G. (1893–1971) U.S. Secretary of State, 1949–53.

Acton, John E. (1834–1902) English Lord and historian.

Adams, Henry Brooks (1838–1918) U.S. historian.

Adams, John (1735–1826) U.S. President, 1797–1801.

Adams, John Quincy (1767–1848) U.S. President, 1825–29.

Addison, Joseph (1672–1719) British writer.

Adenauer, Konrad (1876–1967) Chancellor of West Germany, 1949–63.

Agnew, Spiro (b. 1918) U.S. Vice President, 1969–73.

Aiken, George D. (1892–1984) U.S. Senator from Vermont.

Alanbrooke [Alan Francis Brooke], 1st Viscount (1883–1963) British field marshal.

Alexander, Harold Rupert [Alexander of Tunis] (1891–1969) British field marshal.

Alexander the Great (356–323 B.C.) Macedonian conqueror.

Allen, Woody (b. 1935) U.S. filmmaker and writer.

Alsop, Joseph W., Jr. (b. 1910) U.S. journalist.

Andre, John (1750–1780) British army officer.

Andropov, Yuri (1914–1984) Soviet political leader.

Arbatov, Georgi A. (b. 1923) Soviet expert on United States.

Arends, Leslie C. (1895–1985) U.S. Representative from Illinois, 1935–75.

Arendt, Hannah (1906–1975) German-born U.S. political philosopher.

Aristotle (384–322 B.C.) Greek philosopher.

Armstrong, Hamilton Fish (1893–1973) U.S. journalist and editor of *Foreign Affairs*, 1928–72.

Arnold, Benedict (1741–1801) U.S. general turned traitor.

Arnold, Henry H. "Hap" (1886–1950) Commander of the U.S. Army Air Force during World War II.

Arnold, Matthew (1822–1888) British poet and essayist.

Aron, Raymond (1905–1983) French political writer.

Arthur, Chester Alan (1830–1886) U.S. President, 1881–85.

Asquith, Herbert Henry (1852–1928) British Prime Minister at the start of World War I.

Attila, King of the Huns (406–453) early Germanic invader of France and Italy.

Attlee, Clement R. (1883–1967) British Prime Minister, 1945–51.

Auchinleck, Claude John (1884–1981) British general.

Augustine, Saint (354–430) North African-born Christian philosopher.

Bacon, Francis (1561–1626) British philosopher.

Badoglio, Pietro (1871–1956) Italian general.

Baez, Joan (b. 1941) U.S. folksinger.

Bagheot, Walter (1826–1877) British historian.

Baldwin, Stanley (1867–1947) British Prime Minister, 1923–24; 1924–29; 1935–37.

Balfour, Arthur (1848–1930) British Prime Minister, 1902–05; Foreign Secretary, 1916–19.

Bancroft, George (1800–1891) U.S. historian and statesman.

Barrie, James M. (1860–1937) Scottish novelist and playwright.

Barth, John S. (b. 1930) U.S. novelist.

Baruch, Bernard Mannes (1870–1965) U.S. financier and statesman.

Beard, Charles Austin (1874–1948) U.S. historian.

Beatty, David (1871–1936) British admiral.

Beaufre, Andre (1902–1975) French general.

Beaverbrook, William M. (1879–1964) Canadian-born British publisher and political leader.

Beck, Ludwig (1880–1944) German general.

Bee, Bernard Elliott (1824–1861) Confederate army general.

Behan, Brendan (1923–1964) Irish playwright.

Belloc, Hilaire (1870–1953) French-born British poet and writer.

Benn, Tony (b. 1925) British politician.

Berhardi, Friedrich von (1849–1930) German general.

Berlin, Irving (1888–1989) Russian-born U.S. songwriter.

Berlin, Isaiah (b. 1909) British historian.

Bethmann-Hollweg, Theobald von (1856–1921) German statesman.

Bevan, Aneurin (1897–1960) British politician.

Bevin, Ernst (1881–1951) British foreign minister, 1945–51.

Bierce, Ambrose (1842–1914) U.S. writer.

Bismarck, Otto von (1815–1898) German chancellor.

Bligh, William (1754–1817) British admiral; captain of the *HMS Bounty* during the 1789 mutiny.

Blücher von Wahistatt, Gebhard Liberecht (1742–1819) German general who helped defeat Napoleon at Waterloo, 1815.

Bohlen, Charles E. (1904–1974) U.S. diplomat.

Bolt, Robert (b. 1924) British dramatist.

Boorstin, Daniel J. (b. 1914) U.S. historian.

Bradley, Omar Nelson (1893–1950) U.S. General of the Army.

Bragg, Braxton (1817–1876) Confederate general.

Brecht, Bertolt (1898–1956) German playwright.

Brezhnev, Leonid (1906–1982) head of the Communist Party of the Soviet Union, 1964–82.

Briand, Aristide (1862–1932) French Foreign Minister, 1925–32.

Brogan, Denis William (1900–1974) British political scientist.

Brooke, Rupert (1887–1915) British poet.

Bruce, David E. (1898–1977) U.S. diplomat.

Bryce, James (1838–1922) British historian and diplomat.

Brzezinski, Zbigniew (b. 1928) U.S. national security expert.

Buchwald, Art (b. 1925) U.S. journalist.

Buckley, William F., Jr. (b. 1925) U.S. writer.

Buckner, Simon Bolivar (1823–1914) Confederate general.

Bundy, McGeorge (b. 1919) U.S. national security analyst.

Burgoyne, John (1722–1792) British Army general; defeated at Saratoga, 1777.

Burke, Edmund (1729–1797) British statesman and orator.

Burnside, Ambrose Everett (1824–1881) U.S. Civil War general.

Bush, George Herbert Walker (b. 1924) U.S. President, 1988 to present.

Bush, Vannevar (1890–1974) U.S. engineer who mobilized scientists for World War II.

Butler, Benjamin Franklin (1818–1893) U.S. Army general and politician.

Byrd, Harry F. (1887–1966) U.S. Senator from Virginia, 1933–65.

Byron, Lord [George Gordon] (1788–1824) British romantic poet.

Caesar, Julius (102–44 B.C.) Roman general.

Calley, William L., Jr., (b. 1943) U.S. Army lieutenant.

Cambronne, Pierre de (1770–1842) French general.

Canaris, Wilhelm (1887–1945) German admiral.

Canning, George (1770–1827) British statesman.

Capone, Al (1899–1947) Italian-born U.S. gangster.

Carlson, Evans Fordyce (1896–1947) U.S. Marine Corps general.

Carlyle, Thomas (1795–1881) Scottish historian.

Carnot, Lazar (1753–1823) French general.

Carr, Edward Hallett (1892–1982) British political scientist.

Carroll, Lewis [Charles Dodgson] (1832–1898) British writer.

Carter, Jimmy [James Earl, Jr.] (b. 1924) U.S. President, 1977–81.

Carson, Edward Henry (1854–1935) British politician.

Castro, Fidel (b. 1926) Cuban communist dictator.

Catton, Bruce (1899–1978) U.S. historian.

Cavell, Edith (1865–1915) World War I English nurse executed by Germans.

Cervantes, Miguel de (1547–1616) Spanish novelist.

Chaffee, Adna (1842–1914) U.S. Army general.

Chamberlain, Neville (1869–1940) British Prime Minister, 1937–40.

Chennault, Claire Lee (1890–1958) leader of World War II "flying tigers."

Cherwell, Frederick Alexander Lindemann, Viscount (1886–1957) British physicist; science advisor to Winston Churchill during World War II.

Chesnut, Mary Boykin (1823–1886) Civil War diarist.

Chesterfield, 4th Earl of [Philip Dormer Stanhope] (1694–1773) British statesman.

Chesterton, Gilbert Keith (1874–1936) British novelist.

Churchill, John, 1st Duke of Marlborough (1650–1722) British general.

Churchill, Winston S. (1874–1965) British statesman and author; Prime Minister during most of World War II, 1940–45.

Cicero, Marcus Tullius (106–43 B.C.) Roman orator and statesman.

Cincinnatus, Lucius Quinctius (5th century B.C.) Roman general.

Clark, Mark Wayne (1896–1984) U.S. Army general.

Clausewitz, Karl Maria von (1780–1831) Prussian general and military theorist.

Clay, Lucius Dubignon (1897–1978) U.S. Army general.

Clemenceau, Georges (1841–1929) French Premier, 1906–09; 1917–20.

Cleveland, [Stephen] Grover (1837–1903) U.S. President 1885–89; 1893–97.

Clifford, Clark M. (b. 1906) U.S. Secretary of Defense, 1968–69.

Coffin, William Sloane, Jr. (b. 1924) U.S. clergyman.

Collingwood, Cuthbert (1740–1810) British admiral.

Colton, Caleb C. (1780?–1832) British clergyman.

Commager, Henry Steele (b. 1902) U.S. historian.

Commoner, Barry (b. 1917) U.S. ecologist.

Conquest, Robert (b. 1917) British political writer.

Conrad, Joseph (1857–1924) Polish-born British novelist.

Considine, Robert Bernard (1906–1975) U.S. journalist.

Cooke, [Alfred] Alistair (b. 1908) British-born U.S. journalist.

Coolidge, Calvin (1872–1933) U.S. President, 1923–29.

Cooper, James Fenimore (1789–1851) U.S. novelist.

Corneille, Pierre (1606–1684) French playwright.

Cornwallis, Charles (1738–1805) British general.

Coward, Noel (1899–1973) British actor and playwright.

Crane, Stephen (1871–1900) U.S. novelist and journalist.

Cromwell, Oliver (1599–1658) British general and statesman.

Cronkite, Walter (b. 1916) U.S. journalist.

Crook, George (1829–1890) U.S. Army general.

Culbertson, Ely (1893–1955) U.S. writer.

Cummings, William Thomas (1903–1944) U.S. Army chaplain on Bataan.

Cuppy, Will (1884–1949) U.S. writer.

Custer, George Armstrong (1839–1876) U.S. Army general.

Dana, Richard Henry (1787–1879) U.S. writer.

Daniels, Josephus (1862–1948) U.S. Secretary of the Navy, 1913–21.

Darlan, Jean Louise François (1881–1942) French admiral.

Davenant, Charles (1659–1714) British political writer.

Davis, Elmer (1890–1958) U.S. journalist.

Davis, Jefferson (1808–1889) President of Confederate States of America, 1861–65.

Davis, Richard Harding (1864–1916) U.S. journalist.

Dawes, Charles G. (1865–1951) U.S. statesman.

Dayan, Moshe (1915–1981) Israeli general.

Debs, Eugene Victor (1855–1926) U.S. socialist politician.

Decatur, Stephen (1779–1820) U.S. Navy officer.

De Gaulle, Charles (1890–1970) French general; President of France, 1959–69.

Dewey, George (1837–1917) U.S. Navy admiral.

Dewey, John (1859–1952) U.S. philosopher.

Diem, Ngo Dinh (1901–1963) Prime Minister of South Vietnam, 1954–63.

Disraeli, Benjamin (1804–1881) British politician and novelist.

Dobrynin, Anatoly F. (b. 1919) Soviet diplomat.

Doenitz, Karl (1891–1980) German admiral.

Donovan, William Joseph (1883–1959) head of OSS in World War II.

Doolittle, James Harold (b. 1896) U.S. Army Air Corps general who led the first air raid on Tokyo in 1942.

Douhet, Giulio (1869–1930) Italian general and theorist of air power.

Dowding, Hugh Caswall Tremenheere (1882–1970) British air marshal.

Dreyfus, Alfred (1859–1935) French army officer.

Dulles, Allen Welsh (1893–1969) U.S. intelligence expert, head of CIA 1953–61.

Dulles, John Foster (1888–1959) U.S. Secretary of State, 1953–59.

Du Picq, Ardant (1821–1870) French army officer.

Durant, William (1885–1981) U.S. historian.

Eban, Abba (b. 1915) Israeli diplomat.

Eccles, Marriner Stoddard (1890–1977) U.S. banker.

Eden, Anthony (1897–1977) British Prime Minister, 1955–57.

Ehrenberg, Ilya (1891–1967) Soviet journalist.

Eichmann, Adolf Otto (1906–1962) German Nazi war criminal executed by Israel.

Einstein, Albert (1879–1955) German-born U.S. physicist.

Eisenhower, Dwight David (1890–1969) U.S. General of the Army; President of the United States, 1953–61.

Eliot, Thomas Stearns (1888–1965) British poet.

Elizabeth I (1533–1603) Queen of England, 1558–1603.

Ellsberg, Daniel (b. 1931) Pentagon official who later "leaked" *The Pentagon Papers* in 1971.

Emerson, Ralph Waldo (1803–1882) U.S. philosopher and poet.

Engels, Friedrich (1820–1895) German philosopher of communism.

Erasmus, Desiderius (1466–1536) Dutch philosopher.

Falkenhayn, Erich von (1861–1922) German general.

Farragut, David Glasgow (1801–1870) U.S. Navy admiral.

Feiffer, Jules (b. 1929) U.S. cartoonist.

Fermi, Enrico (1901–1954) Italian-born U.S. physicist.

Fisher, John (1841–1920) British admiral.

Foch, Ferdinand (1851–1929) French army marshal.

Fonda, Jane (b. 1937) U.S. film actress.

Foot, Michael (b. 1913) British political leader.

Ford, Gerald Rudolph (b. 1913) U.S. President, 1974–77.

Forrest, Nathan Bedford (1821–1877) Confederate general.

Forrestal, James Vincent (1892–1949) first U.S. Secretary of Defense, 1947–49.

Fortescue, John William (1859–1933) British historian.

Fowles, John (b. 1926) British novelist.

Frank, Anne (1929–1945) German-born Dutch Jewish diarist.

Franklin, Benjamin (1706–1790) U.S. statesman and inventor.

Frederick II (Frederick the Great) (1712–1786) Prussian king.

Freeman, Douglas Southall (1886–1953) U.S. historian.

French, John (1852–1925) British general.

Freud, Sigmund (1856–1939) Austrian psychiatrist.

Friedman, Milton (b. 1912) U.S. economist.

Fuchs, Klaus (b. 1911) German-born U.S. physicist who gave A-bomb secrets to Soviet Union.

Fulbright, James William (b. 1905) U.S. Senator from Arkansas, 1944–74.

Fuller, John Frederick Charles (1878–1966) British general and military writer.

Fuller, Richard Buckminster (1895–1983) U.S. engineer and architect.

Galbraith, John Kenneth (b. 1908) Canadian-born U.S. economist.

Gamelin, Maurice (1872–1958) French general.

Gandhi, Indira (1917–1984) Indian Prime Minister, 1966–77; 1980–84.

Gandhi, Mohandas K. (1869–1948) nationalist leader of India.

Garibaldi, Giuseppe (1807–1882) Italian military leader.

Gavin, James Maurice (1907–1990) U.S. Army general.

Gehlen, Reinhard (1902–1979) German intelligence expert.

Genghis Khan (1162–1227) Mongol conqueror.

George III (1738–1820) King of England during American Revolution.

George V (1865–1936) King of England during World War I.

George VI (1895–1952) King of England during World War II.

Giap, Vo Nguyen (b. 1912) North Vietnamese general.

Gibbon, Edward (1737–1794) British historian.

Giraud, Henri (1879–1949) French general.

Giraudoux, Jean (1882–1944) French writer.

Gladstone, William Ewart (1809–1898) British statesman.

Goddard, Robert Hutchings (1882–1945) U.S. rocket scientist.

Goebbels, (Paul) Joseph (1897–1945) German Nazi leader.

Goering, Hermann (1893–1946) German Nazi leader.

Goethe, Johann Wolfgang von der (1843–1916) German writer.

Goldman, Eric [Frederick] (b. 1915) U.S. historian.

Goldsmith, Oliver (1728–1774) British playwright.

Goldwater, Barry Morris (b. 1909) U.S. politician.

Goldwyn, Samuel (1882–1974) Polish-born U.S. film producer.

Goltz, Colmar von der (1843–1916) German field marshal.

Gompers, Samuel (1850–1924) U.S. labor leader.

Gooch, George Peabody (1873–1968) British historian.

Gorbachev, Mikhail (b. 1931) Soviet political leader.

Gordon, Charles George (1833–1885) British general.

Grahame, Kenneth (1859–1932) British author.

Grant, Ulysses Simpson (1822–1885) U.S. general; President, 1869–77.

Graves, Robert (1895–1985) British poet and novelist.

Grechko, Andrei (1903–1976) Soviet army marshal.

Greeley, Horace (1811–1872) U.S. editor.

Greene, Graham (b. 1904) British novelist.

Gregory, Dick (b. 1932) U.S. comedian and social activist.

Grew, Joseph Clark (1880–1965) U.S. diplomat.

Grey, Edward (1862–1933) British foreign secretary, 1905–16.

Gromyko, Andrei (1909–1989) Soviet diplomat.

Grotius, Hugo (1583–1645) Dutch "father" of international law.

Groves, Leslie Richard (1896–1970) U.S. Army general.

Gruber, Edmund L. (1879–1941) U.S. Army officer.

Gruening, Ernest Henry (1887–1974) U.S. Senator from Alaska, 1959–68.

Guderian, Heinz Wilhelm (1888–1954) German general.

Guedalla, Philip (1889–1944) British writer.

Gunther, John (1901–1970) U.S. journalist.

Haig, Alexander Meigs, Jr. (b. 1914) U.S. Army general; Chief of White House Staff, 1973–74.

Haig, Douglas, 1st Earl Haig of Bemersyde (1861–1928) British field marshal.

Halberstam, David (b. 1934) U.S. writer.

Haldeman, Robert (b. 1926) President Nixon's chief of staff, 1969–73.

Hale, Edward Everett (1822–1909) U.S. clergyman and author.

Hale, Nathan (1755–1776) American Revolutionary hero.

Halifax, Edward (1881–1959) British diplomat.

Halleck, Henry Wager (1815–1872) U.S. Army general.

Halsey, William Frederick, Jr., (1882–1959) U.S. Navy admiral.

Hamilton, Alexander (1755–1804) American political leader.

Hamilton, Ian (1853–1947) British general.

Hannibal (247–183 B.C.) Carthaginian general.

Hardy, Thomas (1840–1928) British novelist.

Harington, John (1561–1612) British courtier.

Harkins, Paul D. (b. 1904) U.S. Army general.

Harriman, William Averell (1891–1986) U.S. diplomat.

Hawkins, Sir John (1532–1595) British explorer.

Hearst, William Randolph (1863–1951) U.S. publisher.

Heisenberg, Werner (1901–1976) German physicist.

Heller, Joseph (b. 1923) U.S. novelist.

Hellman, Lillian (1905–1984) U.S. playwright.

Helms, Richard M. (b. 1913) U.S. intelligence expert; head of CIA, 1966–73.

Hemingway, Ernest (1899–1961) U.S. novelist.

Henry, Patrick (1736–1799) American Revolutionary leader.

Hersey, John (b. 1914) U.S. novelist.

Hershey, Lewis Blaine (1893–1977) U.S. Army general, Director of Selective Service System, 1941–70.

Hesse, Hermann (1877–1962) German novelist.

Hindenburg, Paul von (1847–1934) German field marshal.

Hitler, Adolf (1889–1945) German Nazi dictator, 1933–45.

Hobbes, Thomas (1588–1679) British political philosopher.

Hochhuth, Rolf (b. 1931) German playwright.

Ho Chi Minh (1890–1969) President of North Vietnam, 1954–69.

Hoffer, Eric (b. 1902) U.S. philosopher.

Hoffman, Max (1869–1927) German general.

Hofstadter, Richard (1916–1970) U.S. historian.

Holmes, Oliver Wendell, Jr., (1841–1935) Associate Justice of U.S. Supreme Court, 1902–32.

Hood, John Bell (1831–1879) Confederate Army general.

Hook, Sidney (1902–1989) U.S. philosopher.

Hooker, Joseph (1814–1879) Union Army general.

Hoover, Herbert Clark (1874–1964) U.S. President, 1929–33.

Hope, Bob (b. 1903) British-born U.S. comedian.

Hopkins, Harry Lloyd (1890–1946) U.S. World War II lend-lease administrator.

Horace (65–8 B.C.) Roman poet.

Howe, Julia Ward (1819–1910) U.S. writer.

Hubbard, Elbert (1856–1915) U.S. writer.

Hughes, Charles Evans (1862–1948) U.S. Secretary of State, 1921–25; Chief Justice of United States, 1930–41.

Hugo, Victor (1802–1885) French novelist.

Hull, Cordell (1871–1955) U.S. Secretary of State, 1933–44.

Humphrey, Hubert Horatio (1911–1978) U.S. Vice President, 1965–69; Senator from Minnesota, 1949–65, 1971–78.

Hutchins, Robert M. (1899–1977) U.S. educator and author.

Huxley, Aldous (1894–1963) British writer.

Ibarruri, Delores (1895–1989) Spanish communist leader.

Ickes, Harold L. (1874–1952) U.S. Secretary of the Interior, 1933–46.

Inge, William R. (1860–1954) British prelate.

Irving, Washington (1783–1859) U.S. writer.

Jackson, Andrew (1767–1845) U.S. President, 1829–37.

Jackson, Henry M. "Scoop" (1912–1983) U.S. Senator from Washington State, 1953–83.

Jackson, Thomas Jonathan "Stonewall" (1824–1863) Confederate Army general.

James, William (1842–1910) U.S. philosopher.

Janowitz, Morris (b. 1919) U.S. sociologist.

Jefferson, Thomas (1743–1826) U.S. President, 1801–09.

Jellicoe, John (1859–1935) British admiral.

Jervis, John, Earl of St. Vincent (1735–1823) British admiral.

Jodl, Alfred (1890–1946) German Army general hanged for war crimes.

Joffre, Joseph Jacques Cesaire (1852–1931) French Army marshal.

Johnson, Hiram Warren (1866–1945) U.S. Senator from California, 1917–45.

Johnson, Lyndon Baines (1908–1973) U.S. President, 1963–69.

Johnson, Samuel (1709–1784) British lexicographer.

Johnson, U. Alexis (b. 1908) U.S. diplomat.

Johnston, Joseph Eggleston (1807–1891) Confederate Army general.

Jomini, Antoine Henry (1779–1869) French general and military theorist.

Jones, James (1921–1977) U.S. novelist.

Jones, John Paul (1747–1792) American Revolutionary naval hero.

Kahn, Herman (1922–1983) U.S. national security analyst.

Kant, Immanuel (1724–1804) German philosopher.

Keegan, John (b. 1934) British military analyst.

Keitel, Wilhelm (1882–1946) German army field marshal hanged for war crimes.

Kellogg, Frank Billings (1956–1987) U.S. Secretary of State, 1925–29.

Kennan, George Frost (b. 1904) U.S. diplomat and historian.

Kennedy, Edward Moore (b. 1932) U.S. Senator from Massachusetts, 1963 to present.

Kennedy, John Fitzgerald (1917–1963) U.S. President, 1961–63.

Kennedy, Joseph Patrick (1888–1969) U.S. businessman and diplomat.

Kennedy, Robert Francis (1925–1968) U.S. Attorney General, 1961–64; Senator from New York, 1964–68.

Kenney, George Churchill (1889–1974) U.S. Air Force general.

Kesselring, Albert (1885–1960) German air force field marshal.

Key, Ellen (1849–1926) Swedish writer.

Key, Francis Scott (1779–1843) U.S. lawyer and poet.

Khrushchev, Nikita (1894–1971) Soviet Premier, 1958–64.

Kimmel, Husband Edward (1882–1968) U.S. Navy admiral.

King, Ernest Joseph (1878–1956) U.S. Navy admiral.

King, Martin Luther, Jr. (1929–1968) U.S. clergyman and civil rights leader.

Kinkaid, Thomas Cassin (1888–1972) U.S. Navy admiral.

Kipling, Rudyard (1865–1936) British writer.

Kirkpatrick, Jeane Jordan (b. 1926) U.S. diplomat and writer.

Kissinger, Henry Alfred (b. 1923) U.S. Secretary of State, 1973–77.

Kitchener, Horatio Herbert, 1st Earl Kitchener of Khartoum (1850–1916) British army field marshal.

Kluck, Alexander von (1846–1934) German army general.

Knox, Philander Chase (1853–1921) U.S. Secretary of State, 1909–13.

Koestler, Arthur (1905–1983) Hungarian-born British writer.

Kosygin, Alexei (1904–1980) Soviet Premier, 1964–80.

Krueger, Walter (1881–1967) U.S. Army general.

Kutuzov, Prince Mikhail (1745–1813) Russian army field marshal.

Ky, Nguyen Cao (b. 1930) Premier of South Vietnam, 1965–67; Vice President, 1967–71.

Lafayette, Marie Joseph Paul, Marquis de (1757–1834) French general; American Revolutionary hero.

La Rochefoucauld, François de (1613–1680) French writer.

Laski, Harold Joseph (1893–1950) British political economist.

Lasswell, Harold Dwight (1902–1978) U.S. political scientist.

Lattre de Tassigny, Jean de (1889–1952) French general.

Lawrence, James (1781–1813) U.S. Navy captain.

Lawrence, Thomas Edward ("of Arabia") (1888–1935) British soldier and author.

Le Carré, John (b. 1931) British novelist.

Leahy, William Daniel (1875–1959) U.S. Navy admiral.

Lean, David (b. 1908) British film director.

Lee, Charles (1731–1782) American Revolutionary general.

Lee, Henry "Light-Horse Harry" (1756–1818) American Revolutionary cavalry officer.

Lee, Robert Edward (1807-1870) Confederate Army general.

LeMay, Curtis Emerson (b. 1906) U.S. Air Force general.

Lemnitzer, Lyman (b. 1899) U.S. Army general.

Lenin, Vladimir Ilich (1870–1924) Soviet communist leader.

Leonidas I (early 5th century B.C.) King of Sparta, 490–480 B.C.

Liddell Hart, Basil Henry (1895–1970) British military writer.

Lincoln, Abraham (1809–1865) U.S. President, 1861–65.

Lindsay, John V. (b. 1921) U.S. politician and former mayor of New York City.

Lippmann, Walter (1889–1974) U.S. journalist and author.

Lloyd George, David (1863–1945) British Prime Minister, 1916–22.

Lodge, Henry Cabot, Jr. (1902–1985) U.S. politician and diplomat.

Lombardi, Vincent Thomas (1913–1970) U.S. football coach.

Longfellow, Henry Wadsworth (1807–1882) U.S. poet.

Longstreet, James (1821–1904) Confederate Army general.

Lorenz, Konrad (b. 1903) Austrian zoologist.

Lovelace, Richard (1619–1658) British poet.

Lowell, James Russell (1819–1891) U.S. diplomat and writer.

Lowell, Robert (1917–1977) U.S. poet.

Luce, Clare Boothe (1903–1987) U.S. writer and politician.

Ludendorff, Erich Friedrich Wilhelm (1865–1937) German army general.

MacArthur, Arthur (1845–1912) U.S. Army general.

MacArthur, Douglas (1880–1964) U.S. General of the Army.

Macaulay, Lord Thomas Babington (1809–1859) British statesman and historian.

Machiavelli, Niccolò (1469–1527) Italian author and statesman.

MacKinder, Halford John (1861–1947) British political geographer.

Macmillan, Harold (1894–1986) British Prime Minister, 1957–63.

Madison, James (1751–1836) U.S. President, 1809–17.

Mahan, Alfred Thayer (1840–1914) U.S. Navy admiral and naval theorist.

Mahan, Dennis Hart (1802–1888) U.S. military writer.

Mailer, Norman (b. 1923) U.S. novelist.

Malcolm X [Little] (1925–1965) U.S. black leader.

Mao Tse-tung [Zedong] (1893–1976) Chinese communist leader.

Marcos, Ferdinand (1917–1989) Filipino dictator.

Marshall, George Catlett (1880–1959) U.S. General of the Army; U.S. Secretary of State, 1947–49.

Marshall, Samuel L. A. (1900–1977) U.S. military journalist.

Marx, Karl (1818–1883) German philosopher of communism.

Maugham, William Somerset (1874–1965) British writer.

Mauldin, Bill (b. 1921) U.S. cartoonist and author.

McAuliffe, Anthony Clement (1898–1975) U.S. Army general.

McCarthy, Eugene J. (b. 1916) U.S. Senator from Minnesota, 1959–71.

McCarthy, Joseph R. (1908–1957) U.S. Senator from Wisconsin, 1947–57.

McClellan, George Brinton (1826–1885) U.S. Army general.

McCloy, John Jay (b. 1895) U.S. Assistant Secretary of War, 1941–45.

McGovern, George Stanley (b. 1922) U.S. Senator from South Dakota, 1963–81.

McKinley, William (1843–1901) U.S. President, 1897–1901.

McLuhan, Marshall (1911–1981) Canadian sociologist.

McNamara, Robert Strange (b. 1916) U.S. Secretary of Defense, 1961–68.

Meade, George Gordon (1815–1872) U.S. Army general.

Meany, George (1894–1980) U.S. labor leader.

Medina-Sidonia, 7th Duque de (1550?–1619?) Spanish admiral.

Meir, Golda (1898–1978) Israeli Prime Minister, 1969–74.

Mencken, Henry Louis (1880–1956) U.S. editor and author.

Menon, V. K. Krishna (1897–1974) Indian diplomat.

Miller, Jonathan (b. 1934) British writer and director.

Miller, Merle (1919–1986) U.S. journalist and writer.

Mills, C. Wright (1916–1962) U.S. sociologist.

Milne, Alan Alexander (1882–1956) British writer.

Milton, John (1608–1674) British poet.

Mitchell, Margaret (1909–1949) U.S. novelist.

Mitchell, William (1879–1936) U.S. Army Air Corps general.

Mitscher, Marc Andrew (1887–1947) U.S. Navy admiral.

Mollenhoff, Clark (b. 1921) U.S. journalist.

Moltke, Helmuth Johannes Ludwig, Graf von (1848–1916) German army general.

Moltke, Helmuth Karl Bernard, Graf von (1800–1891) Prussian field marshal.

Mondale, Walter Frederick (b. 1928) U.S. Vice President, 1977–81.

Monroe, James (1758–1831) U.S. President, 1817–25.

Montaigne, Michel de (1533–1592) French writer.

Montcalm, Louis Joseph de, Marquis de Saint-Veran (1712–1759) French army general.

Montesquieu, Charles de (1689–1755) French philosopher.

Montgomery, Bernard Law, 1st Viscount of Alamein (1887–1976) British Army field marshal.

Moorehead, Alan M. (b. 1910) Australian historian.

Moorer, Thomas Hinman (b. 1912) U.S. Navy admiral.

Morgenthau, Hans J. (1904–1980) German-born U.S. political scientist.

Morgenthau, Henry, Jr. (1891–1967) U.S. Secretary of the Treasury, 1934–45.

Morison, Samuel Eliot (1887–1976) U.S. historian.

Morse, Wayne Lyman (1900–1974) U.S. Senator from Oregon, 1945–69.

Mosby, John Singleton (1833–1916) Confederate officer.

Mosley, Oswald (1896–1980) British Fascist politician.

Moynihan, Daniel Patrick (b. 1927) U.S. diplomat; Senator from New York, 1977 to present.

Murphy, Audie (1924–1971) U.S. film actor; most-decorated soldier of World War II.

Murphy, Robert (1894–1978) U.S. diplomat.

Murrow, Edward Roscoe (1908–1965) U.S. journalist.

Mussolini, Benito (1883–1945) Italian dictator.

Nagumo, Chuichi (1887–1944) Japanese admiral.

Napoleon I (1769–1821) French general and emperor.

Nehru, Jawaharlal (1889–1964) Indian statesman.

Nelson, Viscount Horatio (1758–1805) British admiral.

Nevins, Allan (1890–1971) U.S. historian.

Ney, Michel, Duc d'elchingen, Prince de la Moskowa (1769–1815) French Army marshal.

Nicolson, Harold (1886–1968) British diplomat.

Niemoeller, Martin (1892–1984) German theologian.

Nietzsche, Friedrich William (1844–1900) German philosopher.

Nightingale, Florence (1820–1910) British nurse.

Nimitz, Chester William (1885–1966) U.S. admiral.

Nitze, Paul Henry (b. 1907) U.S. national security expert.

Niven, David (1910–1983) British actor.

Nixon, Richard Milhouse (b. 1913) U.S. President, 1969–74.

Norstad, Lauris (b. 1907) U.S. Army general.

Novak, Robert David (b. 1931) U.S. journalist.

Nunn, Sam (b. 1938) U.S. Senator from Georgia.

Oppenheimer, Julius Robert (1904–1967) U.S. physicist.

Orwell, George [Eric Blair] (1903–1950) British writer.

Page, Walter Hines (1855–1918) U.S. diplomat.

Pahlevi, Muhammad Reza (1919–1980) Shah of Iran, 1941–79.

Paine, Thomas (1737–1809) U.S. Revolutionary writer.

Palme, Olof (1927–1986) Swedish political leader.

Palmerston, Henry John Temple, Viscount (1784–1865) British statesman.

Pareto, Vilfredo (1848–1923) Italian sociologist.

Parker, John (1729–1775) American Revolutionary leader.

Pascal, Blaise (1623–1662) French philosopher.

Patton, George Smith, Jr. (1885–1945) U.S. Army general.

Pauling, Linus Carl (b. 1901) U.S. chemist and peace activist.

Paulus, Friedrich (1890–1957) German field marshal.

Pearson, Drew (1897–1969) U.S. journalist.

Pérez de Cuéllar, Javier (b. 1920) Peruvian diplomat; UN Secretary General, 1982 to present.

Perkins, Frances (1880–1965) U.S. Secretary of Labor, 1933–45.

Perry, Oliver Hazard (1785–1819) U.S. Navy captain.

Pershing, John Joseph (1860–1948) U.S. General of the Armies.

Petain, Henri Philippe Omer (1856–1951) French army marshal.

Picasso, Pablo (1881–1973) Spanish artist.

Pickett, George Edward (1825–1875) Confederate army general.

Pitt, William (1759–1806) British Prime Minister, 1783–1801.

Pitt, William, Earl of Chatham (1708–1778) British statesman.

Plato (427?–347 B.C.) Greek philosopher.

Plutarch (1st century B.C.) Greek biographer.

Podhoretz, Norman (b. 1930) U.S. editor and writer.

Polybius (2nd century B.C.) Greek historian.

Pope, Alexander (1688–1744) British poet.

Pope, John (1822–1892) U.S. Army general.

Porter, Cole (1891–1964) U.S. composer and lyricist.

Porter, David (1780–1843) U.S. Navy officer.

Porter, David Dixon (1813–1891) U.S. Navy admiral.

Prescott, William (1726–1775) American Revolutionary officer.

Pritchett, Victor Sawdon (b. 1900) British writer.

Pulaski, Count Casimir (1747–1779) Polish cavalry general; American Revolutionary War General.

Puller, Lewis Burwell (1898–1971) U.S. Marine Corps general.

Putnam, Israel (1718–1790) American Revolutionary War general.

Pyle, Ernie (1900–1945) U.S. journalist and war correspondent.

Qaddafi, Muammar (b. 1942) Libyan dictator.

Quinton, René (1866–1925) French writer.

Rabi, Isidor (b. 1898) U.S. physicist.

Rabin, Yitzhak (b. 1922) Israeli general and political leader.

Radford, Arthur William (1896–1973) U.S. Navy admiral.

Raeder, Erich (1876–1960) German admiral.

Raglan, Fitzroy James Henry Somerset, 1st Baron Raglan (1788–1855) British army field marshal.

Raleigh, Sir Walter (1522–1618) British statesman, explorer, and historian.

Ramsey, Sir Bertram Home (1883–1945) British admiral.

Rankin, Jeannette (1880–1973) U.S. Representative from Montana, 1917–19; 1941–43.

Reagan, Ronald Wilson (b. 1911) U.S. President, 1981–1989.

Reed, John (1887–1920) U.S. journalist.

Remarque, Erich Maria (1898–1970) German novelist.

Reston, James "Scotty" (b. 1909) U.S. journalist.

Revere, Paul (1735–1818) American patriot and silversmith.

Reynaud, Paul (1878–1966) French Premier in 1940.

Reynolds, Quentin (1902–1965) U.S. journalist.

Ribbentrop, Joachim von (1893–1946) German foreign minister (1938–45) hanged as a war criminal.

Rice, Grantland (1880–1954) U.S. journalist.

Richthofen, Manfred Freiherr von (1892–1918) World War I German aviator.

Rickenbacker, Edward Bernon (1890–1973) U.S. aviator.

Rickover, Hyman George (1900–1986) U.S. Navy admiral.

Ridgway, Matthew Bunker (b. 1895) U.S. Army general.

Ritter, Gerhard (1888–1967) German historian.

Roberts, Chalmers M. (b. 1910) U.S. journalist.

Rogers, Will (1879–1935) U.S. humorist.

Rokossovski, Konstantin Konstanti-novich (1896–1968) Soviet army marshal.

Rommel, Erwin Johannes Eugin (1891–1944) German field marshal.

Romney, George (b. 1907) Governor of Michigan, 1963–1969.

Roosevelt, Eleanor (1884–1962) wife of President Franklin D. Roosevelt.

Roosevelt, Franklin Delano (1882–1945) U.S. President, 1933–45.

Roosevelt, Theodore (1858–1919) U.S. President, 1901–09.

Root, Elihu (1845–1937) U.S. Secretary of War, 1899–1904; U.S. Secretary of State, 1905–09.

Rosecrans, William Starke (1819–1898) U.S. Army general.

Rosten, Leo (b. 1908) U.S. writer.

Rostow, Walt Whitman (b. 1916) U.S. economist and national security expert.

Rousseau, Jean Jacques (1712–1778) French philosopher.

Rubin, Jerry (b. 1938) antiwar activist and writer.

Rundstedt, Karl Rudolf von (1875–1953) German field marshal.

Rusk, Dean (b. 1909) U.S. Secretary of State, 1961–69.

Russell, Bertrand (1872–1970) British philosopher and mathematician.

Russell, John (1792–1878) British politician.

Russell, Richard (1897–1971) U.S. Senator from Georgia, 1933–71.

Russell, William Howard (1820–1907) British war correspondent.

Sagan, Carl Edward (b. 1934) U.S. astronomer.

Saint-Exupéry, Antoine de (1900–1944) French aviator and writer.

Sakharov, Andrei (1921–1989) Soviet physicist.

Salinger, Pierre E. (b. 1925) U.S. journalist.

Salisbury, Harrison Evans (b. 1908) U.S. journalist.

Salisbury, Robert A. T. Gascoyne-Cecil, Marquess of (1830–1903) British political leader.

Sandburg, Carl (1878–1967) U.S. poet and biographer.

Santayana, George (1863–1952) U.S. philosopher.

Sassoon, Siegfried (1886–1967) British poet.

Savile, George, Marquis of Halifax (1633–1695) British statesman.

Saxe, Maurice de (1696–1750) French marshal.

Schiller, Johann Christoph Friedrich von (1759–1805) German writer.

Schlafly, Phyllis (b. 1924) U.S. conservative political activist.

Schlesinger, Arthur Meier, Jr. (b. 1917) U.S. historian.

Schlesinger, James R. (b. 1929) Director of CIA, 1973; U.S. Secretary of Defense, 1973–75.

Schlieffen, Alfred, Graf von (1833–1913) German field marshal.

Schmidt, Helmut Henrich (b. 1918) West German chancellor, 1974–82.

Scipio Africanus, Publius Cornelius (237–183 B.C.) Roman general.

Scott, Walter (1771–1832) Scottish novelist and poet.

Scott, Winfield (1786–1866) U.S. general.

Seaborg, Glenn Theodore (b. 1912) U.S. nuclear chemist.

Seeckt, Hans von (1866–1936) German general.

Seeger, Alan (1888–1916) U.S. poet.

Shaftesbury, Lord Anthony Ashley Cooper, 7th Earl (1801–1885) British statesman.

Shakespeare, William (1564–1616) English poet and dramatist.

Shanker, Albert (b. 1928) U.S. labor leader.

Sharon, Ariel (b. 1928) Israeli general and political leader.

Shaw, George Bernard (1856–1950) Irish playwright.

Sheridan, Philip Henry (1831–1888) Union Army general.

Sherman, William Tecumseh (1820–1891) Union Army general.

Sherwood, Robert Emmet (1896–1955) U.S. writer.

Shirer, William Lawrence (b. 1904) U.S. journalist and historian.

Shoup, David Monroe (b. 1904) U.S. Marine Corps general.

Shultz, George Pratt (b. 1920) U.S. Secretary of State, 1982–89.

Shute, Nevil (1899–1960) British novelist.

Sihanouk, Prince Norodom (b. 1922) Cambodian political leader.

Sikorski, Wladyslaw (1881–1943) Polish general.

Sims, William Sowden (1858–1936) U.S. Navy admiral.

Slessor, John (b. 1887) British air marshal.

Slim, William Joseph, 1st Viscount Slim (1891–1970) British field marshal.

Smith, Adam (1723–1790) Scottish economist.

Smith, Holland McTyeire (1882–1967) U.S. Marine Corps general.

Smith, Walter Bedell (1895–1961) U.S. Army general.

Smuts, Jan Christiaan (1870–1950) British field marshal.

Snow, C. P. (1905–1980) British novelist.

Snow, Edgar Parks (1905–1972) U.S. journalist.

Sontag, Susan (b. 1933) U.S. writer.

Sorensen, Theodore C. (b. 1928) U.S. lawyer; President Kennedy's chief speech writer.

Southey, Robert (1774–1843) British poet and historian.

Spaatz, Carl (1891–1974) U.S. Air Force general.

Speer, Albert (1905–1981) German Nazi official convicted of war crimes.

Spock, Benjamin (b. 1903) U.S. physician, author.

Spruance, Raymond Ames (1886–1969) U.S. Navy admiral.

Spykman, Nicholas John (1893–1943) U.S. political geographer.

Stalin, Joseph (1879–1953) Soviet dictator.

Stallings, Laurence (1894–1968) U.S. novelist and playwright.

Stark, John (1728–1822) American Revolutionary War general.

Stein, Gertrude (1874–1946) U.S. writer.

Steinbeck, John (1902–1968) U.S. writer.

Stendhal [Henri Beyle] (1783–1842) French novelist.

Sterne, Laurence (1713–1842) British novelist.

Steuben, Baron Friedrich William Augustus (1730–1794) German-born American Revolutionary War general.

Stevenson, Adlai Ewing (1900–1965) U.S. politician.

Stilwell, Joseph Warren (1883–1946) U.S. General.

Stimson, Henry Lewis (1867–1950) U.S. Secretary of War, 1911–13; 1940–45.

Stoppard, Tom (b. 1937) British playwright.

Story, Joseph (1779–1845) U.S. jurist.

Strachey, Lytton (1880–1932) British biographer.

Stuart, James Ewell Brown "Jeb" (1833–1864) Confederate cavalry commander.

Sulzberger, Arthur Hays (1891–1968) U.S. publisher.

Sun Tzu (400–320 B.C.) Chinese philosopher.

Swift, Jonathan (1667–1745) British writer.

Swope, Herbert Bayard (1882–1958) U.S. journalist.

Sylvester, Arthur (b. 1901) Pentagon press officer, 1961–67.

Szilard, Leo (1898–1964) Hungarian-born U.S. physicist.

Szulc, Tad (b. 1926) U.S. journalist.

Tacitus (1st century B.C.) Roman historian.

Taft, Robert Alphonso (1889–1953) U.S. Senator from Ohio, 1939–53.

Taft, William Howard (1857–1930) U.S. President, 1909–19.

Taylor, Alan John Percivale (b. 1906) British historian.

Taylor, Maxwell Davenport (1901–1987) U.S. general, diplomat.

Taylor, Telford (b. 1908) U.S. lawyer.

Taylor, Zachary (1784–1850) U.S. Army general; President, 1849–50.

Tedder, Arthur William, 1st Baron Tedder (1890–1967) British air marshal.

Teller, Edward (b. 1908) Hungarian-born U.S. physicist.

Tennyson, Alfred Lord (1809–1892) British poet.

Terkel, Studs (b. 1912) U.S. journalist.

Thackeray, William M. (1811–1863) British novelist.

Thant, U (1909–1974) Burmese Diplomat; UN Secretary General, 1961–71.

Thatcher, Margaret (b. 1925) British Prime Minister, 1979 to present.

Thieu, Nguyen van (b. 1923) South Vietnamese President, 1967–75.

Thomas, Lowell (1892–1981) U.S. journalist.

Thoreau, Henry David (1817–1862) U.S. naturalist and writer.

Timoshenko, Semyon Konstantinovich (1895–1970) Soviet Army marshal.

Tocqueville, Alexis de (1805–1859) French writer.

Togo, Count Heihachiro (1846–1934) Japanese admiral.

Tojo, Hideki (1884–1948) Japanese military and political leader hung for war crimes.

Tolstoy, Leo (1828–1910) Russian novelist.

Torrington, Arthur Herbert (1647–1716) British admiral.

Toynbee, Arnold J. (1889–1975) British historian.

Treitschke, Heinrich von (1834–1896) German historian.

Trenchard, Hugh Montague, 1st Viscount Trenchard (1873–1956) British air marshal.

Trevor-Roper, Hugh Redwald (b. 1914) British historian.

Trotsky, Leon (1879–1940) Russian communist leader.

Truman, Harry S. (1884–1972) U.S. President, 1945–53.

Tuchman, Barbara W. (1912–1989) U.S. historian.

Turenne, Henri de la Tour d'auvergne, Vicomte de (1611–1675) French Army marshal.

Turing, Alan (1912–1954) British mathematician.

Turner, Stansfield (b. 1923) U.S. Navy admiral.

Twain, Mark [Samuel Langhorne Clemens] (1835–1910) U.S. author.

Ulbricht, Walter (1893–1973) East German communist leader.

Upton, Emory (1839–1881) U.S. Army general.

Vance, Cyrus R. (b. 1917) U.S. Secretary of State, 1977–80.

Vandegrift, Alexander Archer (1887–1973) U.S. Marine Corps general.

Vandenberg, Arthur H. (1884–1951) U.S. Senator from Michigan, 1928–51.

Victoria I (1819–1901) Queen of England.

Vidal, Gore (b. 1925) U.S. novelist.

Vinci, Leonardo da (1452–1519) Italian artist and inventor.

Vinson, Carl (1883–1981) U.S. Representative from Georgia, 1914–65.

Voltaire [François-Marie Arouet] (1694–1788) French philosopher.

von Braun, Wernher (1912–1977) German Nazi rocket scientist turned U.S. rocket scientist.

Vonnegut, Kurt (b. 1922) U.S. novelist.

Voroshilov, Klement Y. (1881–1969) Soviet Army marshal.

Wainwright, Jonathan Mayhew (1883–1953) U.S. Army general.

Waldheim, Kurt (b. 1918) UN Secretary General, 1976–82; President of Austria.

Walker, Walton Harris (1899–1950) U.S. Army general.

Wallace, George C. (b. 1919) Governor of Alabama.

Wallace, Lewis (1827–1905) U.S. Army general and novelist.

Walpole, Robert (1676–1745) British statesman.

Ward, Artemus (1834–1867) U.S. humorist.

Washington, George (1732–1799) U.S. President, 1789–97.

Waugh, Evelyn (1903–1966) British novelist.

Wavell, Archibald Percival (1883–1950) British field marshal.

Webster, Daniel (1782–1852) U.S. statesman.

Welles, Orson (1915–1985) U.S. film actor, director, and writer.

Welles, Sumner (1892–1961) U.S. diplomat.

Wellington, Arthur Wellesley, 1st Duke of (1769–1852) British general who defeated Napoleon at Waterloo, 1815; British Prime Minister, 1928–30.

Wells, Herbert George (1866–1946) British author.

West, Rebecca (1892–1983) British writer.

Westmoreland, William Childs (b. 1914) U.S. Army general in command of all U.S. forces in Vietnam, 1964–68.

Weygand, Maxime (1867–1965) French general.

Wheeler, Earle Gilmore (1908–1975) U.S. Army general.

Wheeler, Joseph (1836–1906) U.S. and Confederate army general; served as U.S. Representative from Alabama 1881–99.

Whistler, James Abbott McNeill (1834–1903) U.S. artist.

White, Elwyn Brooks (1899–1985) U.S. author and essayist.

White, Thomas Dresser (1901–1966) U.S. Air Force general.

Whitman, Walt (1819–1892) U.S. poet.

Whittier, John Greenleaf (1807–1892) U.S. poet.

Wilde, Oscar (1854–1900) Irish poet and dramatist.

Wilder, Thornton (1897–1975) U.S. novelist and playwright.

Will, George F. (b. 1941) U.S. political columnist.

William II (1848–1941) German Kaiser during World War I.

Willkie, Wendell L. (1892–1944) U.S. politician.

Wilson, Charles Erwin (1890–1961) U.S. Secretary of Defense, 1953–57.

Wilson, Harold (b. 1916) British Prime Minister, 1964–70; 1974–76.

Wilson, Thomas Woodrow (1856–1924) U.S. President, 1913–21.

Wingate, Orde C. (1903–1944) British Army general.

Wolfe, James (1727–1759) British general.

Wolfe, Tom (b. 1931) U.S. novelist.

Wolseley, Garnet Joseph (1833–1913) British field marshal.

Wood, Leonard (1860–1927) U.S. Army general.

Wouk, Herman (b. 1915) U.S. novelist.

Wright, Quincy (1890–1970) U.S. political scientist.

Xenophon (431–350 B.C.) Greek historian.

Yamamoto, Isoroku (1884–1943) Japanese admiral who led attack on Pearl Harbor in 1941.

Yeager, Charles E. (b. 1923) U.S. test pilot, first to break sound barrier, 1947.

York, Alvin Cullum (1887–1964) U.S. World War I hero.

Zhou Enlai [Chou En-Lai] (1898–1976) Chinese statesman.

Zhukov, Georgi K. (1896–1974) Soviet Army marshal.

Zumwalt, Elmo Russel, Jr. (b. 1920) U.S. Navy admiral.

Index